The English Workshop
A Programmed Approach

Fifth Edition

Keith Slocum

Professor of English
Montclair State University
Upper Montclair, New Jersey

McGraw-Hill Irwin

Boston   Burr Ridge, IL   Dubuque, IA   Madison, WI   New York   San Francisco   St. Louis
Bangkok   Bogotá   Caracas   Kuala Lumpur   Lisbon   London   Madrid   Mexico City
Milan   Montreal   New Delhi   Santiago   Seoul   Singapore   Sydney   Taipei   Toronto

 **McGraw-Hill**
Irwin

THE ENGLISH WORKSHOP: A PROGRAMMED APPROACH

Some ancillaries, including electronic and print components, may not be available to
customers outside the United States.

This book is printed on acid-free paper.

   3 4 5 6 7 8 9 QPD/QPD 0 9 8 7 6

ISBN-13: 978-0-07-293590-5
ISBN-10: 0-07-293590-1

Cover Illustration: Ralph Mercer/Solus Images
Photo Credits: Corbis p. 403; John Madere/Corbis Stock Market p.3; Digital Stock
Corporation p. 61; Fisher/Thatcher/Stone p. 513; John Riley/Stone p. 275, 341;
Anna Lundgren/Super Stock p. 161; Wendy's International, Inc. p. 453

Library of Congress Cataloging-in-Publication Data
Slocum, Keith 1945—
    The English Workshop: A Programmed Approach/Keith Slocum.—
    5th ed.
    p. cm
    Includes index.
    ISBN 0-07-826287-9
    1. English language-The English Workshop—Programmed instruction.
I. Title.
PE1115.S587   1993
808'.066651—dc20   92-39653
                    CI

TABLE OF CONTENTS

Inside Your Book

This book was designed for you to help you learn. It contains 8 units divided into 20 chapters, and 6 appendices. This structure, together with special self-learning features, will help you learn and develop fluency with written and spoken English grammar.

Understanding Unit Concepts

The chapters are organized into **units** that cover eight major concepts of English grammar and communication. The **unit title** sets the stage for the chapter content.

Two-page unit openers help you understand the value of learning the concepts in the book.

Profile in Success details the role that good English grammar and communication skills have played in the career of a successful professional.

The **unit photograph** presents a visual of successful professionals at work.

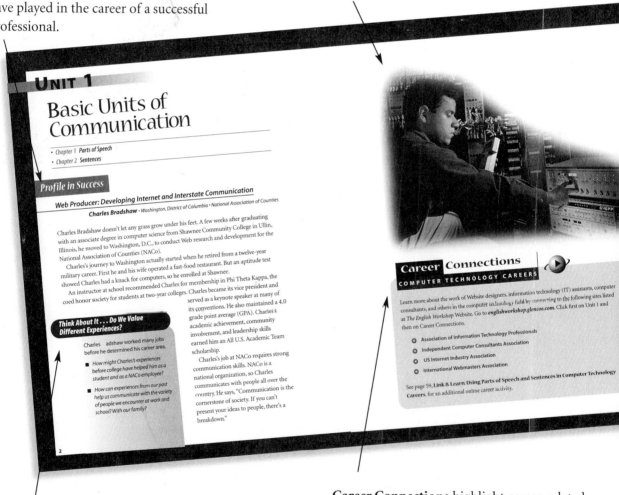

Think About It . . . builds on the Profile in Success and sets up a critical discussion of the connections between basic English skills and career and personal happiness.

Career Connections highlight career-related Websites that you can access at *The English Workshop* Website. You will learn more about featured unit career areas at those sites.

Previewing Chapter Concepts

1. The **Chapter Preview** outlines the chapter and its learning features.

2. **Objectives** alert you to the major concepts in each chapter. Turn the objectives into questions. Then, as you work with the chapter, look for the answers to the questions.

3. A **Study Plan** provides ways to study important concepts you will learn in each chapter. Review the Study Plan at the start of each chapter and return to it after you finish the chapter. Use it as you study and prepare for tests.

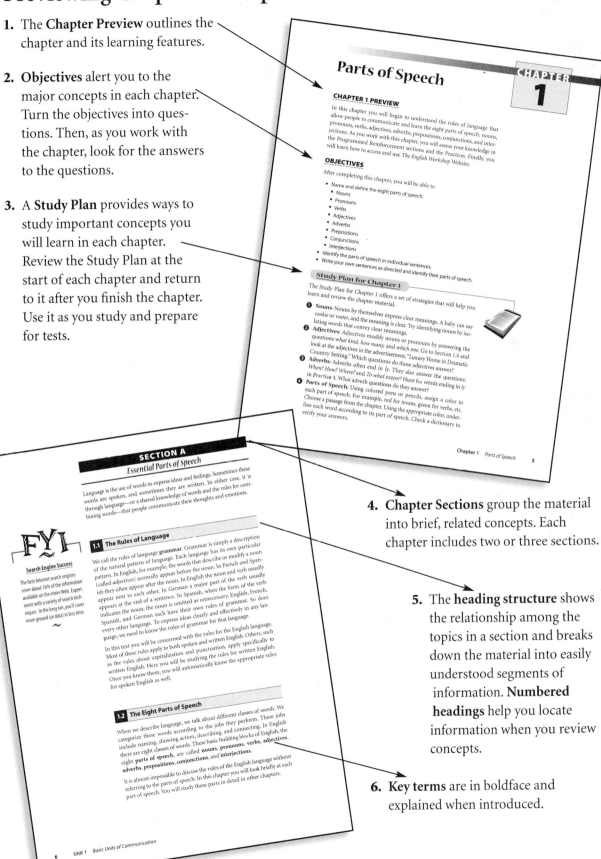

4. **Chapter Sections** group the material into brief, related concepts. Each chapter includes two or three sections.

5. The **heading structure** shows the relationship among the topics in a section and breaks down the material into easily understood segments of information. **Numbered headings** help you locate information when you review concepts.

6. **Key terms** are in boldface and explained when introduced.

Developing Chapter Concepts

Colorful in-text examples, graphics, and special features enhance and strengthen your learning about basic grammar and communication skills.

Programmed Reinforcement ends each section. This learning tool guides you on a self-assessment and review of the section material. It poses questions and provides answers so that you may recognize what you know and what you need to review.

A **Coverage Key** correlates each **Statement** to the chapter part it reviews. If you miss a question, the Coverage Key allows you easy access to information you will want to review.

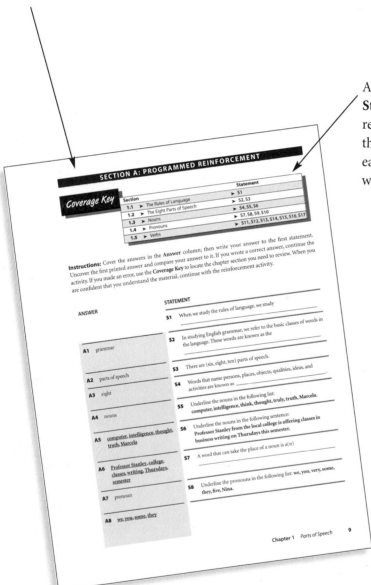

SECTION A: PROGRAMMED REINFORCEMENT

Coverage Key

Section		Statement
1.1	➤ The Rules of Language	➤ S1
1.2	➤ The Eight Parts of Speech	➤ S2, S3
1.3	➤ Nouns	➤ S4, S5, S6
1.4	➤ Pronouns	➤ S7, S8, S9, S10
1.5	➤ Verbs	➤ S11, S12, S13, S14, S15, S16, S17

Instructions: Cover the answers in the **Answer** column; then write your answer to the first statement. Uncover the first printed answer and compare your answer to it. If you wrote a correct answer, continue the activity. If you made an error, use the **Coverage Key** to locate the chapter section you need to review. When you are confident that you understand the material, continue with the reinforcement activity.

ANSWER	STATEMENT
	S1 When we study the rules of language, we study
A1 grammar	**S2** In studying English grammar, we refer to the basic classes of words in the language. These words are known as the
A2 parts of speech	**S3** There are (six, eight, ten) parts of speech.
A3 eight	**S4** Words that name persons, places, objects, qualities, ideas, and activities are known as
A4 nouns	**S5** Underline the nouns in the following list: computer, intelligence, think, thought, truly, truth, Marcela.
A5 computer, intelligence, thought, truth, Marcela	**S6** Underline the nouns in the following sentence: Professor Stanley from the local college is offering classes in business writing on Thursdays this semester.
A6 Professor Stanley, college, classes, writing, Thursdays, semester	**S7** A word that can take the place of a noun is a(n)
A7 pronoun	**S8** Underline the pronouns in the following list: we, you, very, some, they, five, Nina.
A8 we, you, some, they	

Chapter 1   *Parts of Speech*   9

Special tips in the margin reinforce chapter concepts and provide useful insights.

Grammar Tips point out useful ways to consider the chapter material, restate concepts in a brief review, or offer mnemonic devices.

Punctuation Tips focus on rules of punctuation.

Grammar Tip

Nouns Name

Remember the function of *nouns* (*na*ming) begins with the same letter as the word itself (*nouns*).

Punctuation Tip

No Comma Needed

In the examples on the left, no comma is required between the subject and the verb in the correct sentences.

Style Tips emphasize stylistic rules.

Amounts of Checks

Capitalize only the first letter of the first word spelled out on checks.

The **Job Talk** feature defines contemporary workplace jargon.

Netiquette

The term *netiquette*, a blend of *–net* (*Internet*) and *etiquette* (manners), is the code of acceptable conduct for using the Internet or e-mail. If you violate this code, expect a *flame*, an angry Internet response.

The **Looking Ahead** feature signals that you will study related concepts in future chapters.

LOOKING AHEAD

Adjective Placement
You will learn more about adjective placement in Chapter 10.

Success Tips are brief suggestions to increase your successes in school and at work while boosting your self-confidence.

CORRECTING OTHERS As you improve your English skills, avoid correcting your coworkers or supervisors in front of others. Not everyone will view your corrections as a friendly attempt to help.

Search Engine Success

The best Internet search engines cover about 16% of the information available on the entire Web. Experiment with a variety of search techniques. In the long run, you'll cover more ground (or data) in less time.

Indefinite Pronouns
Section 4.10, on page 114, includes a list of common indefinite pronouns.

The **FYI** feature shares interesting facts about the unit career area.

Flashbacks refer to related material that has been covered in previous sections.

Reviewing and Applying Concepts

A **Chapter Summary** sums up the major points of the chapter.

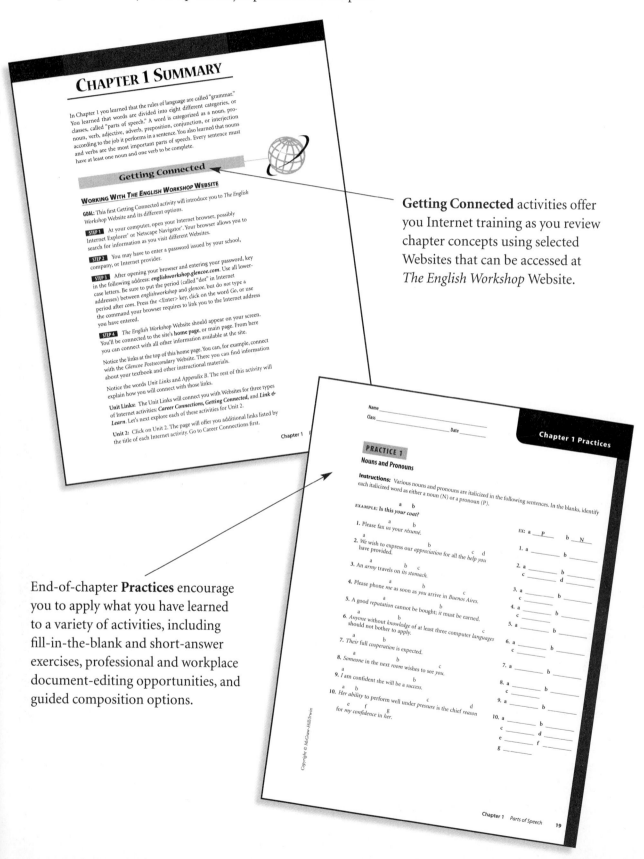

CHAPTER 1 SUMMARY

In Chapter 1 you learned that the rules of language are called "grammar." You learned that words are divided into eight different categories, or classes, called "parts of speech." A word is categorized as a noun, pronoun, verb, adjective, adverb, preposition, conjunction, or interjection according to the job it performs in a sentence. You also learned that nouns and verbs are the most important parts of speech. Every sentence must have at least one noun and one verb to be complete.

Getting Connected

WORKING WITH THE ENGLISH WORKSHOP WEBSITE

GOAL: This first Getting Connected activity will introduce you to *The English Workshop* Website and its different options.

STEP 1 At your computer, open your Internet browser, possibly Internet Explorer® or Netscape Navigator®. Your browser allows you to search for information as you visit different Websites.

STEP 2 You may have to enter a password issued by your school, company, or Internet provider.

STEP 3 After opening your browser and entering your password, key in the following address: *englishworkshop.glencoe.com.* Use all lowercase letters. Be sure to put the period (called "dot" in Internet addresses) between *englishworkshop* and *glencoe,* but do *not* type a period after *com.* Press the <Enter> key, click on the word *Go,* or use the command your browser requires to link you to the Internet address you have entered.

STEP 4 *The English Workshop* Website should appear on your screen. You'll be connected to the site's **home page,** or main page. From here you can connect with all other information available at the site.

Notice the links at the top of this home page. You can, for example, connect with the *Glencoe Postsecondary* Website. There you can find information about your textbook and other instructional materials.

Notice the words *Unit Links* and *Appendix B.* The rest of this activity will explain how you will connect with those links.

Unit Links: The Unit Links will connect you with Websites for three types of Internet activities: *Career Connections, Getting Connected,* and *Link & Learn.* Let's next explore each of these activities for Unit 2.

Unit 2: Click on Unit 2. The page will offer you additional links listed by the title of each Internet activity. Go to Career Connections first.

Chapter 1

Getting Connected activities offer you Internet training as you review chapter concepts using selected Websites that can be accessed at *The English Workshop* Website.

End-of-chapter **Practices** encourage you to apply what you have learned to a variety of activities, including fill-in-the-blank and short-answer exercises, professional and workplace document-editing opportunities, and guided composition options.

Name _____
Class _____
_____ Date _____

Chapter 1 Practices

PRACTICE 1
Nouns and Pronouns

Instructions: Various nouns and pronouns are italicized in the following sentences. In the blanks, identify each italicized word as either a noun (N) or a pronoun (P).

EXAMPLE: Is *this your* coat?

1. Please fax *us your* résumé.

2. *We* wish to express *our appreciation* for all the *help you* have provided.

3. An *army* travels on *its stomach.*

4. Please phone *me* as soon as *you* arrive in *Buenos Aires.*

5. A good *reputation* cannot be bought; *it* must be earned.

6. *Anyone* without *knowledge* of at least three computer *languages* should not bother to apply.

7. *Their* full *cooperation* is expected.

8. *Someone* in the next *room* wishes to see *you.*

9. *I* am confident *she* will be a *success.*

10. *Her ability* to perform well under *pressure* is the chief *reason* for *my confidence* in *her.*

EX: a __P__   b __N__

1. a _____ b _____

2. a _____ b _____
   c _____ d _____

3. a _____ b _____
   c _____

4. a _____ b _____
   c _____

5. a _____ b _____

6. a _____ b _____
   c _____

7. a _____ b _____

8. a _____ b _____
   c _____

9. a _____ b _____

10. a _____ b _____
    c _____ d _____
    e _____ f _____
    g _____

Copyright © McGraw-Hill/Irwin

Chapter 1   *Parts of Speech*   19

REVIEW: UNIT 1

Name _____ Date _____

Class _____

Basic Units of
Communication

Unit 1—Composition Review

Instructions: This Composition Review deals with the concepts you have studied so far.
First, read the time sheet below so that you are familiar with it. Then answer the questions
that appear beneath it and on the next page. Finally, read the Writing Situation on the next
page, and assume the role of the assigned writer. Develop a paragraph based on information
from the time sheet.

Time sheet   FEDERAL
                                         WORK-STUDY

NEW
STATE
UNIVERSITY

DEPARTMENT _Computer Lab_
NAME _Celeste Simone_
ADDRESS _754 Floyd Street, Apt. 4 - E_
Fort Worth, TX 71632   FROM _4/14_   TO _4/27_   20 - -
BI-WEEKLY PAYROLL

	MONTH/DAY	AM ARRIVED	AM LEFT	PM ARRIVED	PM LEFT	HOURS
SAT/SUN					1	3
MON	4/17	10			1	3
TUES	4/18	10			2	3
WED	4/19	11		1	4	5
THURS	4/20					
FRI						2
SAT/SUN		9	11		1	3
MON	4/23	10			1	3
TUES	4/24	10			1	2
WED	4/25	11		1	4	3
THURS	4/26					25
FRI	4/27					
TOTAL						

DATE _4/27/ - -_
DATE _4/27/ - -_

EMPLOYEE _Celeste Simone_
SUPERVISOR _Arlene Brighton_

QUESTIONS:
1. What days did Celeste Simone NOT work? _____
_____

Copyright © McGraw-Hill/Irwin

Unit 1   Basic Units of Communi...

Unit Reviews encourage you to apply
what you have learned to composition
or editing activities.

Link & Learn

**USING PARTS OF SPEECH AND SENTENCES IN COMPUTER
TECHNOLOGY CAREERS**

GOAL: Reinforce what you learned in Unit 1 about the parts of speech and
the sentence while using the Internet to explore various computer technology Websites.

STEP 1: Go to *englishworkshop.glencoe.com*, the address for *The
English Workshop* Website. Click first on Unit 1; then click on Link &
Learn to access a list of computer technology sites you may use in this
activity. Select one of the sites, and click on it.

STEP 2: Skim the different topics available at the home page of the
Website you selected. Find a topic that interests you. Maybe you'd like
to learn about a professional organization or a particular career. Click
on the link of the topic you select.

STEP 3: Read the online material. Make a printout of at least one page.

STEP 4: Using the printout, do the following:

   a. Look for one sentence that includes *at least five* of the eight parts
   of speech. You may find a sentence with all eight parts of speech;
   however, such sentences are rare. Underline or highlight the sentence you select, and label the parts of speech.

   b. In reviewing the printout, did you find any interjections? If you
   did, explain on the back of the printout why you think they were
   used. If you found no interjections, explain why you think none
   were used.

   c. Circle and label the complete subjects and complete predicates of
   five other sentences in the document. Underline the simple subject once and the verb twice.

   d. Look for one example of each of the four different types of sentences: statement, question, command, and exclamation. Label
   each type of sentence as you find it. If you can't find a particular
   kind of sentence, such as an exclamation, explain on the back of
   your printout why you think it was not used in the document you
   selected for this activity.

STEP 5: Write your name on the front of the printout, and turn it in
to your instructor.

Unit 1   *Basic Units of Communication*   **59**

Link & Learn offers an additional
Internet activity that combines
exploration of career Websites
with exercises that reinforce the
Unit concepts.

Working With
the Appendices

Six informative appendices provide you with
information about proofreading marks; spelling
rules and computer spelling and grammar checkers; print and online resources; abbreviations;
and commonly confused words. Activities are
also included. *Appendix B: Print and Online
References* lists directions to an online dictionary
and thesaurus.

Basic Units of Communication

Profile in Success

Web Producer: Developing Internet and Interstate Communication

Charles Bradshaw · Washington, District of Columbia · National Association of Counties

Charles Bradshaw doesn't let any grass grow under his feet. A few weeks after graduating with an associate degree in computer science from Shawnee Community College in Ullin, Illinois, he moved to Washington, D.C., to conduct Web research and development for the National Association of Counties (NACo).

Charles's journey to Washington actually started when he retired from a twelve-year military career. First he and his wife operated a fast-food restaurant. But an aptitude test showed Charles had a knack for computers, so he enrolled at Shawnee.

An instructor at school recommended Charles for membership in Phi Theta Kappa, the coed honor society for students at two-year colleges. Charles became its vice president and served as a keynote speaker at many of its conventions. He also maintained a 4.0 grade point average (GPA). Charles's academic achievement, community involvement, and leadership skills earned him an All U.S. Academic Team scholarship.

Charles's job at NACo requires strong communication skills. NACo is a national organization, so Charles communicates with people all over the country. He says, "Communication is the cornerstone of society. If you can't present your ideas to people, there's a breakdown."

Think About It . . . Do We Value Different Experiences?

Charles Bradshaw worked many jobs before he determined his career area.

- How might Charles's experiences before college have helped him as a student and as a NACo employee?

- How can experiences from our past help us communicate with the variety of people we encounter at work and school? With our family?

Career Connections

COMPUTER TECHNOLOGY CAREERS

Learn more about the work of Website designers, information technology (IT) assistants, computer consultants, and others in the computer technology field by connecting to the following sites listed at *The English Workshop* Website. Go to ***englishworkshop.glencoe.com***. Click first on Unit 1 and then on Career Connections.

- **Association of Information Technology Professionals**
- **Independent Computer Consultants Association**
- **US Internet Industry Association**
- **International Webmasters Association**

See page 59, **Link & Learn: Using Parts of Speech and Sentences in Computer Technology Careers**, for an additional online career activity.

Parts of Speech

CHAPTER 1 PREVIEW

In this chapter you will begin to understand the rules of language that allow people to communicate and learn the eight parts of speech: nouns, pronouns, verbs, adjectives, adverbs, prepositions, conjunctions, and interjections. As you work with this chapter, you will assess your knowledge in the Programmed Reinforcement sections and the Practices. Finally, you will learn how to access and use *The English Workshop* Website.

OBJECTIVES

After completing this chapter, you will be able to

- Name and define the eight parts of speech:
  - Nouns
  - Pronouns
  - Verbs
  - Adjectives
  - Adverbs
  - Prepositions
  - Conjunctions
  - Interjections
- Identify the parts of speech in individual sentences.
- Write your own sentences as directed and identify their parts of speech.

Study Plan for Chapter 1

The Study Plan for Chapter 1 offers a set of strategies that will help you learn and review the chapter material.

❶ **Nouns**: Nouns by themselves express clear meanings. A baby can say *cookie* or *water*, and the meaning is clear. Try identifying nouns by isolating words that convey clear meanings.

❷ **Adjectives**: Adjectives modify nouns or pronouns by answering the questions *what kind, how many,* and *which one*. Go to Section 1.6 and look at the adjectives in the advertisement, "Luxury Home in Dramatic Country Setting." Which questions do those adjectives answer?

❸ **Adverbs**: Adverbs often end in *ly*. They also answer the questions: *When? How? Where?* and *To what extent?* Hunt for words ending in *ly* in Practice 4. What adverb questions do they answer?

❹ **Parts of Speech**: Using colored pens or pencils, assign a color to each part of speech. For example, red for nouns, green for verbs, etc. Choose a passage from the chapter. Using the appropriate color, underline each word according to its part of speech. Check a dictionary to verify your answers.

Language is the use of words to express ideas and feelings. Sometimes these words are spoken, and sometimes they are written. In either case, it is through language—or a shared knowledge of words and the rules for combining words—that people communicate their thoughts and emotions.

Search Engine Success

The best Internet search engines cover about 16% of the information available on the entire Web. Experiment with a variety of search techniques. In the long run, you'll cover more ground (or data) in less time.

1.1 The Rules of Language

We call the rules of language **grammar**. Grammar is simply a description of the natural pattern of language. Each language has its own particular pattern. In English, for example, the words that describe or modify a noun (called *adjectives*) normally appear before the noun. In French and Spanish they often appear after the noun. In English the noun and verb usually appear next to each other. In German a major part of the verb usually appears at the end of a sentence. In Spanish, when the form of the verb indicates the noun, the noun is omitted as unnecessary. English, French, Spanish, and German each have their own rules of grammar. So does every other language. To express ideas clearly and effectively in any language, we need to know the rules of grammar for that language.

In this text you will be concerned with the rules for the English language. Most of these rules apply to both spoken and written English. Others, such as the rules about capitalization and punctuation, apply specifically to written English. Here you will be studying the rules for written English. Once you know them, you will automatically know the appropriate rules for spoken English as well.

1.2 The Eight Parts of Speech

When we describe language, we talk about different classes of words. We categorize these words according to the jobs they perform. These jobs include naming, showing action, describing, and connecting. In English there are eight classes of words. These basic building blocks of English, the eight **parts of speech**, are called **nouns**, **pronouns**, **verbs**, **adjectives**, **adverbs**, **prepositions**, **conjunctions**, and **interjections**.

It is almost impossible to discuss the rules of the English language without referring to the parts of speech. In this chapter you will look briefly at each part of speech. You will study these parts in detail in other chapters.

1.3 Nouns

A **noun** *names* something—a person, place, object, quality, idea, or activity.

person—Maria, architect, child
place—New Delhi, outside, office
object—minivan, building, computer

quality—honesty, sincerity, courage
idea—beauty, truth, love
activity—listening, speaking, writing

Nouns are one of the two most important classes of words in the English language (the other is verbs). Sentences revolve around nouns because nouns can be both the subjects and the objects of verbs.

The following employment ad contains many kinds of nouns. All of them have been italicized. Notice that they are all *names* of something. Some of the words may look like nouns, but they have not been italicized because they are not being used as nouns.

Grammar Tip

Nouns Name

Remember the function of *nouns* (naming) begins with the same letter as the word itself (*nouns*).

---

4 — CLASSIFIED / FRIDAY, OCTOBER 19, 20-- / DAILY NEWSPAPER

Systems Development & Systems Analysis
Rosement Cosmetics, fast becoming a significant *force* in the cosmetics/fragrance *industries*, seeks *individuals* to further advance our automation *efforts*. If you recognize the *advantages* of working in a small *shop environment* and are able to develop strong working *relationships* with user *departments* and key management *staff*, contact us immediately! Excellent verbal communication *skills* are imperative for all *positions*.

1.4 Pronouns

A **pronoun** is a noun substitute. It provides both efficiency and variety of expression. Look at the next sentence, which includes no pronouns.

Victoria said **Victoria** needed the laptop computer **Victoria's** mother had given **Victoria** if **Victoria** was going to complete **Victoria's** accounting assignment on time.

Now look at the same sentence written with pronouns:

Victoria said *she* needed the laptop computer *her* mother had given *her* if *she* was going to complete *her* accounting assignment on time.

Grammar Tip

Pro + Noun

The prefix *pro* has several meanings, including "taking the place of." *Pronoun* literally means "taking the place of (a) noun."

Netiquette

The term *netiquette*, a blend of *–net* (*Internet*) and *etiquette* (manners), is the code of acceptable conduct for using the Internet or e-mail. If you violate this code, expect a *flame*, an angry Internet response.

The noun to which a pronoun refers—the noun for which it stands—is its **antecedent**. It is important that the antecedent be clear to the reader. Review the list of common pronouns in the table below.

Common Pronouns			
I	me	my	some
you	him	your	none
he	her	his	anyone
she	us	its	somebody
it	them	our	nobody
we		their	anybody
they			everybody

1.5   Verbs

As you saw earlier, the verb is one of the two most important parts of speech. A verb can be either a word or a group of words. Usually the verb tells you what the subject does. This kind of verb is called an **action verb**. Words such as *run, write, argue, teach, build,* and *talk* are action verbs.

Often a verb joins, or links, the subject to words that describe it. This kind of verb is called a **state-of-being verb**, or a **linking verb**. Some common linking verbs include *am, are, is, was, were, has been,* and *will be*. When linking verbs are used in combination with various forms of action verbs, they function as **helping verbs**.

Every sentence must have at least one verb and one noun. Verbs and nouns are the two most important parts of speech because they are the only parts of speech required in all sentences. You need to be able to recognize verbs to see whether a sentence is complete and whether a statement is really a sentence.

Look at the examples. Notice how the verbs are used to make statements, ask questions, or give commands.

Grammar Tip

Three Types of Verbs

Verbs may show action, link subjects to descriptive words, or help other verbs.

Statements

I *quit*.
Deena *will be leaving* soon.
Anan *commutes* to school.

The entire staff *should have been told*.
Ms. Murcoa *reprimanded* Tom.
The network *is* down.

Questions

Who *is* it?

What *do* you *think*?

Commands

Send this memo to our suppliers.
Tell me about the interview.

Just *do* it.
Take a deep breath and *relax*.

Coverage Key

Section		Statement
1.1 ➤	The Rules of Language	➤ S1
1.2 ➤	The Eight Parts of Speech	➤ S2, S3
1.3 ➤	Nouns	➤ S4, S5, S6
1.4 ➤	Pronouns	➤ S7, S8, S9, S10
1.5 ➤	Verbs	➤ S11, S12, S13, S14, S15, S16, S17

Instructions: Cover the answers in the **Answer** column; then write your answer to the first statement. Uncover the first printed answer and compare your answer to it. If you wrote a correct answer, continue the activity. If you made an error, use the **Coverage Key** to locate the chapter section you need to review. When you are confident that you understand the material, continue with the reinforcement activity.

ANSWER

STATEMENT

S1 When we study the rules of language, we study

A1 grammar

S2 In studying English grammar, we refer to the basic classes of words in the language. These words are known as the

A2 parts of speech

S3 There are (six, eight, ten) parts of speech.

A3 eight

S4 Words that name persons, places, objects, qualities, ideas, and activities are known as _____.

A4 nouns

S5 Underline the nouns in the following list:
computer, intelligence, think, thought, truly, truth, Marcela.

A5 computer, intelligence, thought, truth, Marcela

S6 Underline the nouns in the following sentence:
Professor Stanley from the local college is offering classes in business writing on Thursdays this semester.

A6 Professor Stanley, college, classes, writing, Thursdays, semester

S7 A word that can take the place of a noun is a(n)

A7 pronoun

S8 Underline the pronouns in the following list: **we, you, very, some, they, five, Nina.**

A8 we, you, some, they

S9 The noun to which a pronoun refers is known as its _____

_____

A9 antecedent

S10 Underline the pronouns in the following sentences. Draw a line to their antecedents.
  a. Gary told me that his brother was applying to law school.
  b. Madeleine asked her supervisor for his advice.
  c. I heard Consuelo say that her new computer has its own DVD player.

A10 a. Gary told <u>me</u> that <u>his</u> brother was applying to law school.
  b. Madeleine asked <u>her</u> supervisor for <u>his</u> advice.
  c. <u>I</u> heard Consuelo say that <u>her</u> new computer has <u>its</u> own DVD player.

S11 A verb is a word that shows (a) action, (b) state of being, or (c) either action or state of being.

A11 c

S12 Underline the action verbs in the following list:
are, write, enter, entrance, composition, click, learns, will be.

A12 <u>write</u>, <u>enter</u>, <u>click</u>, <u>learns</u>

S13 Another name for a state-of-being verb is a(n)

_____ verb.

A13 linking

S14 Underline the linking verbs in the following list:
was, would have been, thought, am, teach.

A14 <u>was</u>, <u>would have been</u>, <u>am</u>

S15 To be a sentence, a statement (must have, need not have) at least one verb. A sentence (may, may not) have more than one verb.

A15 must have, may

S16 Which of the following statements do not contain verbs?
  a. The digital camera market
  b. The market is expanding
  c. The market in digital cameras
  d. The market has expanded

A16 a, c

S17 Underline the verbs in the following sentences:
  a. The text of the speech can be found on our home page.
  b. Belinda showed Greg the Web site she had been developing.
  c. Will you send me a copy of your report when you have finished it?
  d. Explain to me why you are late.

A17 a. <u>can be found</u>
  b. <u>showed</u>, <u>had been developing</u>
  c. <u>Will send</u>, <u>have finished</u>
  d. <u>Explain</u>, <u>are</u>

So far you have looked at the two most important parts of speech—nouns and verbs. You have also looked at pronouns, or noun substitutes. These three parts of speech form the core of a sentence. In this section you will briefly examine how the remaining parts of speech—adjectives, adverbs, prepositions, and conjunctions—add more information to a sentence.

1.6 Adjectives

Adjectives are words that *modify*—describe—nouns or pronouns. They answer questions such as *what kind, how many*, and *which one*. Which of the following adjectives describe your boss: *tall, short, young, old, successful, sullen, incompetent, energetic, demanding, inefficient, unreasonable*, or *fair*?

Adjectives usually precede the nouns and pronouns they modify, but they also may follow these words, especially when they are used with linking verbs. In the following real estate ad, all adjectives have been italicized. Some of the italicized words may look to you like other parts of speech, but they have been italicized because they are being used as adjectives in this passage. Notice that the words *a, an*, and *the* have been italicized. As you will learn, these words form a special group of adjectives known as **articles.**

LOOKING AHEAD

Adjective Placement
You will learn more about adjective placement in Chapter 10.

●

8 — CLASSIFIED / FRIDAY, OCTOBER 19, 20-- / DAILY NEWSPAPER

> ***Luxury** Home in **Dramatic Country** Setting*
> *This stunning* fieldstone and *cedar* contemporary home is dramatically situated on *three wooded* acres overlooking *the beautiful* Jacksonburg River in *desirable* Woodland Township. Enhanced by *terraced* landscaping, *this outstanding* home affords *four generous* bedrooms, *three marble* bathrooms, *an 18′×16′* artist's studio, *an enormous stone* fireplace in *a breathtaking* living room with *cathedral* ceiling, and *a heated 38′×20′* in-ground pool. *A peaceful* retreat with *direct* access to *New Jersey corporate* centers allows you *superb contemporary* living.

CORRECTING OTHERS As you improve your English skills, avoid correcting your coworkers or supervisors in front of others. Not everyone will view your corrections as a friendly attempt to help.

1.7 Adverbs

Adverbs modify verbs, adjectives, and other adverbs. They answer such questions as *when, how, where,* and *to what extent.* Adverbs may either precede or follow the verbs they modify, but adverbs usually precede the adjectives and adverbs they modify.

Adverbs That Modify Verbs

Mr. Forte spoke rapidly (*how*) and loudly (*how*).
He left early (*when*) and quickly (*how*) walked to his car.
I put the report there (*where*).

Grammar Tip

Words Ending in *ly*

Eight of the adverbs used in the sentence examples end in *ly*; six do not. Most adverbs end in *ly*, but not all do. Remember the adverbs in the sentence examples that do **not** end in *ly*.

Adverbs That Modify Adjectives

Megan is extremely (*to what extent*) conscientious.
The cost is surprisingly (*to what extent*) low.
Needlessly (*how*) complicated instructions annoy me.

Adverbs That Modify Adverbs

He performs his duties exceptionally (*how*) well.
She arrived too (*how*) late.
The applicant responded somewhat (*to what extent*) nervously.

1.8 Prepositions

Prepositions show the relationship between a noun or noun equivalent—the **object** of the preposition—and another word in the sentence. The preposition and its object, along with any modifier, form a **prepositional phrase**. These phrases usually function as adjectives or adverbs. Common prepositions include *at, by, for, from, in, of, to,* and *with.*

Examples of Prepositional Phrases

Key: m = modifiers, op = object of the preposition, p = preposition

Grammar Tip

Prepositional Phrases

Prepositions should not appear by themselves in a sentence. Prepositions will always be followed by a noun or pronoun acting as an object.

prepositional phrase	prepositional phrase
p m op	p m m op
at the office	*in* the foreseeable future
p m m op	p m op
for a few days	*to* the bank

We will discuss prepositions in detail in Chapter 12. For now, you need to be able to recognize prepositional phrases as modifiers and to distinguish them from sentence subjects.

1.9 Conjunctions

Conjunctions connect words or groups of words. The most common conjunctions—including *and, but, or,* and *nor*—are called **coordinating conjunctions**. They act as connectors between equal, or coordinate, parts of sentences. Other conjunctions such as *since, because, if, although, unless,* and *before* are known as **subordinating conjunctions**. These connectors show a dependency of one sentence part on another.

In each of the following sentences, the conjunction is placed between the two sentence parts it connects.

> Ms. Shurley *and* Mr. Gross were promoted.
> They were both promoted after their first assignment, *but* I was not.
> I must get a promotion *or* I will look for another job.
> I feel disappointed *because* I was not promoted.
> I intend to look for another job *if* I am not promoted.

Some conjunctions may be placed at the beginning of a sentence rather than between the sentence parts. For example, you could rewrite the last two examples this way:

> *Because* I was not promoted, I feel disappointed.
> *If* I am not promoted, I intend to look for another job.

1.10 Interjections

An **interjection** is a word used to show strong feelings or sudden emotions. An exclamation point or a comma usually follows an interjection. Because interjections do not contribute to the basic meaning of a sentence, they are seldom used in workplace documents. Look at these examples:

> *Ouch!* That hurts!
> *Oh,* I don't believe that will happen.

1.11 Parts of Speech Review

You have now looked at each of the eight parts of speech. Every sentence must contain at least two of them, the noun and the verb. Most sentences contain more. Here is one that contains all eight:

```
IN PN      N    PREP   N    V   ADV  ADJ  CON    ADJ
```
Yes, your knowledge of grammar will be very useful and rewarding.

Coverage Key

Section		Statement
1.6 ➤ Adjectives		➤ S18, S19, S20, S21, S22
1.7 ➤ Adverbs		➤ S18, S19, S23, S24, S25, S26, S27
1.8 ➤ Prepositions		➤ S28, S29, S30, S31, S32
1.9 ➤ Conjunctions		➤ S33, S34, S35, S36 S37, S38
1.10 ➤ Interjections		➤ S39, S40, S41

Instructions: Cover the answers in the **Answer** column; then write your answer to the first statement. Uncover the first printed answer and compare your answer to it. If you wrote a correct answer, continue the activity. If you made an error, use the **Coverage Key** to locate the chapter section you need to review. When you are confident that you understand the material, continue with the reinforcement activity.

ANSWER

STATEMENT

S18 The two parts of speech that describe or modify other words are called _____ and _____.

A18 adjectives, adverbs

S19 a. _____ modify nouns and pronouns.
b. _____ modify verbs, adjectives, and adverbs.

A19 a. Adjectives
b. Adverbs

S20 Underline the adjectives in the following list:
seven, efficient, the, truly, being, Saul, me, a, happy.

A20 <u>seven</u>, <u>efficient</u>, <u>the</u>, <u>a</u>, <u>happy</u>

S21 Underline the adjectives in the following sentences. Draw a line to the words they modify.
a. **The manager gave me a big raise.**
b. **The new supervisor is a skilled communicator.**
c. **Janvi is intelligent and articulate.**
d. **The five cardboard boxes contain new office stationery.**

A21 a. The manager gave me <u>a big</u> raise.
b. The <u>new</u> supervisor is <u>a skilled</u> communicator.
c. Janvi is <u>intelligent</u> and <u>articulate</u>.
d. The <u>five cardboard</u> boxes contain <u>new office</u> stationery.

A22 adjectives

A23 adverbs

A24 verbs, adjectives, adverbs

A25 *ly*

A26 <u>very</u>, <u>sincerely</u>, <u>rarely</u>, <u>there</u>, <u>often</u>

A27 a. She arrived <u>early</u>.
b. Juan speaks <u>slowly</u> and <u>distinctly</u>.
c. We are <u>very</u> dissatisfied with your service.
d. She arrived <u>unexpectedly early</u>.

A28 prepositions

A29 prepositional phrase

A30 adjectives, adverbs

A31 <u>of</u>, <u>with</u>, <u>from</u>, <u>to</u>

S22 Words that answer questions such as *what kind, how many,* and *which one* are _____ .

S23 Words that answer questions such as *when, where, how,* and *to what extent* are _____ .

S24 Adverbs modify _____ , _____ and _____ .

S25 Most adverbs end in _____ .

S26 Underline the adverbs in the following list:
blue, very, sincerely, writing, rarely, there, often.

S27 Underline the adverbs in the following sentences. Draw a line to the words they modify.
a. **She arrived early.**
b. **Juan speaks slowly and distinctly.**
c. **We are very dissatisfied with your service.**
d. **She arrived unexpectedly early.**

S28 Words that join noun or pronoun objects to other words in the sentence are called

_____ .

S29 The preposition and its object, plus any words that modify that object, are known collectively as a(n) _____ .

S30 Prepositional phrases usually act as either of two parts of speech:
_____ or _____ .

S31 Underline the prepositions in the following list:
none, of, with, very, extra, from, to, because.

S32 Underline the prepositions once and their objects twice in the following sentences.
   a. The package is on the chair near the door.
   b. All of the orders must be filled before noon.
   c. In a few days I will be flying to Dallas to meet with your representatives at corporate headquarters.

A32
   a. The package is <u>on</u> the <u>chair</u> <u>near</u> the <u>door</u>.
   b. All <u>of</u> the <u>orders</u> must be filled <u>before</u> <u>noon</u>.
   c. <u>In</u> a few <u>days</u> I will be flying <u>to</u> <u>Dallas</u> to meet <u>with</u> your <u>representatives</u> <u>at</u> corporate <u>headquarters</u>.

S33 Conjunctions are
   a. modifiers,
   b. connectors,
   c. action words,
   d. name words.

A33 b

S34 There are two kinds of conjunctions, coordinating, and subordinating. Coordinating conjunctions connect (equal, unequal) parts of sentences.

A34 equal

S35 The words *and, but, or,* and *nor* are (coordinating, subordinating) conjunctions.

A35 coordinating

S36 Conjunctions that show a dependency of one sentence part on another are called _____ conjunctions.

A36 subordinating

S37 Which of the following are not subordinating conjunctions?
although, because, but, if, or, since

A37 but, or

S38 Underline the conjunctions in each of the following:
   a. Ray and Pepe are eager to accept her offer, but I have reservations.
   b. We have made many improvements in our procedures since you and Liz were last here.
   c. Because we have not received payment for more than three months, we will be forced to seek legal action unless you settle your account within seven days.

A38
   a. <u>and</u>, <u>but</u>
   b. <u>since</u>, <u>and</u>
   c. <u>Because</u>, <u>unless</u>

S39 A word that shows strong feelings or sudden emotions is a(n) _____ .

A39 interjection

S40 An interjection is usually followed by (a) a period, (b) a colon, or (c) an exclamation point.

A40 c

S41 Interjections (are, are not) often used in workplace documents because they (do, do not) contribute greatly to the basic meaning of a sentence.

A41 are not, do not

CHAPTER 1 SUMMARY

In Chapter 1 you learned that the rules of language are called "grammar." You learned that words are divided into eight different categories, or classes, called "parts of speech." A word is categorized as a noun, pronoun, verb, adjective, adverb, preposition, conjunction, or interjection according to the job it performs in a sentence. You also learned that nouns and verbs are the most important parts of speech. Every sentence must have at least one noun and one verb to be complete.

Getting Connected

WORKING WITH *THE ENGLISH WORKSHOP* WEBSITE

GOAL: This first Getting Connected activity will introduce you to *The English Workshop* Website and its different options.

STEP 1   At your computer, open your Internet browser, possibly Internet Explorer® or Netscape Navigator®. Your browser allows you to search for information as you visit different Websites.

STEP 2   You may have to enter a password issued by your school, company, or Internet provider.

STEP 3   After opening your browser and entering your password, key in the following address: ***englishworkshop.glencoe.com***. Use all lowercase letters. Be sure to put the period (called "dot" in Internet addresses) between *englishworkshop* and *glencoe*, but do *not* type a period after *com*. Press the <Enter> key, click on the word *Go*, or use the command your browser requires to link you to the Internet address you have entered.

STEP 4   *The English Workshop* Website should appear on your screen. You'll be connected to the site's **home page**, or main page. From here you can connect with all other information available at the site.

Notice the links at the top of this home page. You can, for example, connect with the *Glencoe Postsecondary* Website. There you can find information about your textbook and other instructional materials.

Notice the words *Unit Links* and *Appendix B*. The rest of this activity will explain how you will connect with those links.

Unit Links: The Unit Links will connect you with Websites for three types of Internet activities: ***Career Connections, Getting Connected,*** and ***Link & Learn.*** Let's next explore each of these activities for Unit 2.

Unit 2: Click on Unit 2. The page will offer you additional links listed by the title of each Internet activity. Go to Career Connections first.

- **Career Connections:** Click on the Career Connections link for Unit 2. You'll see a list of Website addresses and an overview for each. Click on one of the addresses. You'll find yourself at a professional Website devoted to one or more careers in the law field, the career area highlighted in Unit 2. The additional eight Career Connections will link to career areas spotlighted in each of the eight other units.

  Return to the Unit 2 page by clicking on "Back to Glencoe Online," located in the upper right-hand corner, or by clicking on the "Back" button, located at the top left corner of your browser window.

- **Getting Connected:** Click next on the Getting Connected link for Unit 2. These sites are divided into chapters, specifically Chapters 3, 4, and 5—the chapters in Unit 2. Each chapter includes a Getting Connected that will help you review the chapter material. Under Chapter 3 you'll find a list of Internet addresses with an overview of each. In future Getting Connected activities, you will choose one or more of the listed sites as you follow instructions printed in the book. Turn to page 45 to preview a Getting Connected activity. When you finish your preview, go back to the Unit 2 page.

- **Link & Learn:** At the Unit 2 page, click on the Link & Learn link to see the Internet addresses for that Unit 2 activity. With future Link & Learn activities, you'll select one or more listed Websites as you follow instructions printed in the book. To preview a Link & Learn, turn to page 59. You may also visit one of the Unit 2 Link & Learn sites now. When you have completed previewing the Link & Learn sites, return to *The English Workshop* home page by clicking "Home" on the left.

Appendix B: At the home page of the Website, click on the Appendix B link. There you'll find online references that complement *Appendix B: Print and Online References*. To learn about online references, visit one or more of those sites, and read the material in Appendix B.

STEP 5 If you've done all the work to this point, you've successfully reviewed *The English Workshop* Website. Now exit from the Website following the steps your Internet browser requires. In general, you can go to the <File> menu; then click and drag your cursor to <Close>.

Name _____

Class _____ Date _____

PRACTICE 1

Nouns and Pronouns

Instructions: Various nouns and pronouns are italicized in the following sentences. In the blanks, identify each italicized word as either a noun (N) or a pronoun (P).

        a   b

EXAMPLE: **Is this *your coat*?**

EX: a ___P___   b ___N___

         a   b

1. Please fax *us* your *résumé*.

1. a ___P___   b ___N___

    a   b   c d

2. *We* wish to express our *appreciation* for all the *help you* have provided.

2. a ___P___   b ___N___
   c ___N___   d ___P___

       a   b   c

3. An *army* travels on *its stomach*.

3. a ___N___   b ___P___
   c ___N___

         a   b   c

4. Please phone *me* as soon as *you* arrive in *Buenos Aires*.

4. a ___P___   b ___P___
   c ___N___

         a   b

5. A good *reputation* cannot be bought; *it* must be earned.

5. a ___N___   b ___P___

    a   b   c

6. *Anyone* without *knowledge* of at least three computer *languages* should not bother to apply.

6. a ___P___   b ___N___
   c ___N___

    a   b

7. *Their* full *cooperation* is expected.

7. a ___P___   b ___N___

      a   b   c

8. *Someone* in the next *room* wishes to see *you*.

8. a ___P___   b ___N___
   c ___P___

    a   b

9. *I* am confident she will be a *success*.

9. a ___P___   b ___N___

    a b   c   d

10. *Her ability* to perform well under *pressure* is the chief *reason*

       e   f   g

   for *my confidence* in *her*.

10. a ___P___   b ___N___
   c ___N___   d ___N___
   e ___P___   f ___N___
   g ___P___

PRACTICE 2

Action and Linking Verbs

Instructions: Place a check in the blanks to indicate whether the italicized words are action or linking verbs.

	ACTION	LINKING
EXAMPLE: I *received* a raise last week.	**EX:** ✓	_____
1. I *am* pleased to meet you.	1. _____	✓
2. The mayor and council *are* now in closed session.	2. _____	✓
3. Our company *manufactures* digital processing equipment.	3. ✓	_____
4. This *was* his final demand.	4. _____	✓
5. He *demanded* absolute loyalty.	5. ✓	_____
6. The union *has negotiated* a new contract.	6. ✓	✓
7. My parents *were* in town for a visit last week.	7. _____	✓
8. They *visited* the store.	8. ✓	_____
9. The shop *will be closed* tomorrow.	9. ✓	✓
10. *Close* the door.	10. ✓	_____

PRACTICE 3

Verbs

Instructions: Underline the verbs in the following sentences.

EXAMPLE: Karl <u>wrote</u> his paper Tuesday morning and <u>e-mailed</u> it that afternoon.

1. Amir <u>left</u> work <u>early</u> today.

2. Close the door and sit down.

3. Their offer features free Internet access.

4. They offer free Internet access.

5. Take your time; consider your options; then act decisively.

6. The mayor and council will be meeting in closed session.

7. We need efficiency more than we need economy.

8. Several dozen applicants have already responded to our advertisement, which appeared in Tuesday's paper.

9. Supporting documentation is included in the appendix.

10. Supporting documentation has been appended.

Name _____

Class _____ Date _____

PRACTICE 4

Adjectives and Adverbs

Nouns → Pronouns → *ly*
verbs *adj*

Instructions: In the blanks, identify each of the italicized words as an adjective (ADJ) or an adverb (ADV).

       a   b

EXAMPLE: The *squeaky* wheel *usually* gets the grease.   EX: a __ADJ__ b __ADV__

1. The *effective* speaker pronounces words *clearly*.   1. a __ADJ__ b __ADV__

2. We need a *knowledgeable* and *articulate* spokesperson to present our position *effectively*.   2. a __ADJ__ b __ADJ__ c __ADV__

3. The assistant manager is *primarily* responsible for that.   3. a __ADV__

4. The assistant manager's *primary* responsibility is to see that.   4. a __ADJ__

5. Mr. Rosario *slowly* and *painstakingly* made all the *necessary* adjustments to the equipment.   5. a __ADV__ b __ADV__ c __ADJ__

6. His *slow*, *painstaking* method proved successful.   6. a __ADJ__ b __ADJ__

7. *Intelligent* and *enthusiastic* employees are *certainly* an asset to any organization.   7. a __ADJ__ b __ADJ__ c __ADV__

8. Employees who behave *intelligently* and *enthusiastically* are *certain* to be an asset to any organization.   8. a __ADV__ b __ADV__ c __ADJ__

9. Without an *immediate* change in our advertising, we are *sure* to lose a *large* portion of the market.   9. a __ADJ__ b __ADJ__ c __ADJ__

10. We must change our *advertising* appeal *immediately* or we will *surely* lose a *large* portion of the market.   10. a __ADJ__ b __ADV__ c __ADV__ d __ADJ__

Chapter 1 Practices

Name _____

Class _____ Date _____

PRACTICE 5

Conjunctions and Prepositional Phrases

Instructions: In each sentence, underline the conjunction once and the prepositional phrase twice.

EXAMPLE: Mimi <u>and</u> Erik are studying <u>for an accounting exam</u>.

1. Much of their stock is damaged and outdated.
2. Bob or Rudolpho will represent us at the conference.
3. Mr. Lewis came to the meeting, but Ms. Liebowitz did not attend.
4. I must consult with my attorney before I make any commitments.
5. Although I am not satisfied with the agreement, I am happy it has been completed.
6. We will bargain in good faith if you will.
7. Since Jill Robinson resigned last week, we have been without a regional representative.
8. If you want my advice, get out of the stock market.
9. Mail a check for the balance before you forget.
10. Today your check was returned by the bank because your account is overdrawn.

PRACTICE 6

Parts of Speech

Instructions: Complete each sentence below. In the blanks at the right, identify the part of speech used. Use all eight parts of speech.

EXAMPLE: The <u>check</u> is in the mail.   EX. _____noun_____

1. The _____mail_____ room is locked.   1. ____adj____
2. Marie's colleagues took _____her_____ to lunch yesterday.   2. ____pronoun____
3. Mr. Cosco _____and_____ Mr. Pine will be arriving shortly.   3. ____con____
4. _____Wow_____! I've been promoted.   4. ____interjun____
5. I'll meet you _____in_____ the lobby.   5. ____preposition____
6. Online trading is a _____rapidly_____ expanding field.   6. ____adv____
7. Please _____send_____ me the information.   7. ____Verb____
8. Your order _____is_____ processed.   8. ____linking verb____
9. Both _____men_____ were unavailable for comment.   9. ____Noun____
10. Luis is taking an evening course in _____history_____.   10. ____Noun____

22   Chapter 1   *Parts of Speech*

Name _____

Class _____ Date _____

PRACTICE 7

Parts of Speech

Instructions: For each word in the sentences below, identify its part of speech. Write your answers in the blanks.

       a   b   c   d   e   f   g   h

EXAMPLE: Laptop computers are becoming smaller and more powerful.

a. _____adjective_____   b. _____noun_____   c. _____verb_____   d. _____verb_____

e. _____adjective_____   f. ___conjunction___   g. _____adverb_____   h. ___adjective___

    a   b   c   d   e   f   g   h   i   j k   l   m   n

1. Joan quickly wrote and signed the memorandum before she left for an important appointment.

    a   b   c   d   e   f   g   h   i   j   k   l   m   n   o

2. Yes, Mr. Sen, the rush order for additional software was shipped directly to your offices yesterday.

     a   b   c   d   e   f   g   h   i   j   k   l   m

3. Although Maria and the accountant returned from the conference early yesterday afternoon, they

     n   o   p

arrived too late.

1. a _____
   b _____
   c _____
   d _____
   e _____
   f _____
   g _____
   h _____
   i _____
   j _____
   k _____
   l _____
   m_____
   n _____

2. a _____
   b _____
   c _____
   d _____
   e _____
   f _____
   g _____
   h _____
   i _____
   j _____
   k _____
   l _____
   m_____
   n _____
   o _____

3. a _____
   b _____
   c _____
   d _____
   e _____
   f _____
   g _____
   h _____
   i _____
   j _____
   k _____
   l _____
   m_____
   n _____
   o _____
   p _____

PRACTICE 8

Composition: Working With Parts of Speech

Instructions: Write complete sentences in which you use each of the words below as a noun, an adjective, and a verb.

EXAMPLE: **TYPING**

    (a)   **(noun)** I took a course in typing in high school. _____

    (b)   **(adjective)** I bought a ream of typing paper. _____

    (c)   **(verb)** I will be typing my term paper this weekend. _____

1. **FILE**

    (a)   (noun) _____

    (b)   (adjective) _____

    (c)   (verb) _____

2. **WASTE**

    (a)   (noun) _____

    (b)   (adjective) _____

    (c)   (verb) _____

3. **WORK**

    (a)   (noun) _____

    (b)   (adjective) _____

    (c)   (verb) _____

4. **WRITING**

    (a)   (noun) _____

    (b)   (adjective) _____

    (c)   (verb) _____

5. **SUPPLY**

    (a)   (noun) _____

    (b)   (adjective) _____

    (c)   (verb) _____

Sentences

CHAPTER 2 PREVIEW

Chapter 1 introduced the parts of speech. The next eleven chapters will discuss each in detail. In this chapter you will examine how parts of speech combine to form a complete sentence. In addition to understanding the four basic kinds of sentences, you will learn how to correct common sentence errors. As you work with this chapter, you will continue to assess your knowledge in the Programmed Reinforcement sections and the Practices. Finally, you will use Internet search tools to locate information about subjects and predicates.

OBJECTIVES

After completing this chapter, you will be able to

- Define a complete sentence.
- Recognize the subject and the verb in a sentence.
- Identify the four basic kinds of sentences:
  - Statements
  - Questions
  - Commands
  - Exclamations
- Turn various types of sentence fragments into complete sentences.
- Combine dependent and independent clauses into complex sentences.
- Construct compound sentences with coordinating conjunctions.
- Correct run-on sentences.

Study Plan for Chapter 2

The Study Plan for Chapter 2 offers a set of strategies that will help you learn and review the chapter material.

1. **Sentence Patterns**: Statements usually follow a subject+verb pattern. Questions follow a verb+subject or helping verb+subject+main verb pattern. For commands the pattern is always subject+verb, but the subject—*you*—is often understood and not written.
2. **Fragments**: To determine if a group of words is a fragment or a sentence, place the clause *It is true that . . .* in front of the group of words. Read the combination aloud. If the combination sounds sensible to you, it's probably a complete sentence.
3. **Subject Question**: Find the predicate of a sentence; then find the subject by asking *who* or *what* in front of the predicate.
4. **Participles as Fragments**: Check word groups with any word ending in *ing*. This word may be a participle you mistook for a verb.

SECTION A
Complete Sentences

The sentence, not the word, is the basic unit of communication in the English language. The sentence alone can express a complete thought. Because it is such a fundamental unit, you will begin your study of English grammar by learning how to recognize a complete sentence, break it down into its essential parts, and identify its four basic types.

2.1 A Complete Sentence or Thought

A **sentence** is a group of words that expresses a complete thought. Every sentence must contain two essential parts:

1. A **subject**, which tells about whom or what you are talking.
2. A **predicate** which tells something about the subject—what the subject is or does, or what is being done to the subject.

Every subject consists of a noun or noun equivalent, and every predicate consists of some form of the verb. In other words, every sentence must contain a noun and a verb. You cannot express a complete thought without them.

A Complete Sentence With Subject and Verb Only

Researchers disagree.

This sentence expresses a complete thought, answering:

1. Who or what are we talking about? *Researchers* (the subject)
2. What does the subject do? *disagree* (the predicate)

A Complete Sentence With Adjectives Added

These three leading political researchers disagree.

Although adjectives have been added, they do not change the subject. The subject is still *researchers* and the predicate is still *disagree*.

A Complete Sentence With Adjectives and Prepositional Phrases Added

These three leading political researchers disagree very strongly sometimes about the accuracy of exit polling.

The word group above is a complete sentence. *These three leading political* describes *researchers. Very strongly sometimes about the accuracy of exit polling* describes *disagree.* The subject and predicate remain the same.

Subjects and Predicates: Complete and Simple

The subject and all words that describe it are called the **complete subject**. The particular word about which something is said is the **simple subject** or **subject**. The predicate and all words that describe it are called the **complete predicate**. We call the particular word or words that tell us what the subject is or does the **simple predicate**. The simple predicate is the verb.

complete subject

simple
subject

These three leading political *researchers*

complete predicate

simple
predicate
disagree very strongly sometimes about the accuracy of exit polling.

2.2 Subjects and Verbs

You can identify the subject and the verb of a sentence by asking yourself questions about who or what is doing the action and what is being done.

Identifying Subjects and Action Verbs in Simple Sentences

With a simple sentence that follows the common English sentence order of subject before verb, it is usually easy to identify the subject and then the verb, especially if the sentence has an action verb. Two questions you may use to find the subject and action verb are:

Subject Question: Who or what is the doer of the action? The word or words that answer this question will be the subject.

Verb Question: What does the subject do? Or, what is being done to the subject? The word or words that answer these questions will be the verb.

When locating a subject and a verb, disregard all other words that merely describe a subject or a predicate.

Grammar Tip

Subjects and Verbs
Finding subjects and verbs is as easy as 1 & 2.
1. Verb first
2. Subject second

Sentence 1: **Aaron reads his textbook carefully.**
Subject Question: Who or what is the doer of the action? **Answer:** *Aaron*
Verb Question: What does the subject (*Aaron*) do? **Answer:** *reads*

Sentence 2: **The pleasant and helpful salesperson refunded the customer's money.**
Subject Question: Who or what is the doer of the action?
Answer: *salesperson*
Verb Question: What did the subject (*salesperson*) do?
Answer: *refunded*

Identifying Subjects and Linking Verbs in Simple Sentences

As you will recall from Chapter 1, verbs may identify the action that the subject in a sentence is doing, reflect the state-of-being of the subject, or serve as linking verbs. *Are* and *is* are common linking verbs. To find the subjects and verbs in sentences with linking verbs, try (1) locating the verb and (2) using these questions:

Verb Question: What is the linking verb in the sentence?
Subject Question: Who or what _____?
(Fill in the blank with the verb)

Sentence 3: The credit slips for returned merchandise are under the cash drawer in the register.
Verb Question: What is the linking verb in the sentence? **Answer:** *are*
Subject Question: What *are*? **Answer:** *slips*

Identifying Subjects and Verbs in Complicated Sentences

When sentences are more complicated, it is often easier to identify the verb first and then to locate the subject using the verb. Questions you may use to find the verb and subject in complicated sentences are:

Verb Question: What word indicates action in the sentence? What is the linking verb in the sentence?
Subject Question: Who or what _____?
(Fill in the blank with the verb)

Sentence 4: Between two wet and angry elderly women sat a small, giggling boy with an empty water pistol.
Verb Question: What word indicates action? **Answer:** *sat*
Subject Question: Who *sat*? **Answer:** *boy*

Sentence 5: At the top of the résumé is the applicant's name.
Verb Question: What is the linking verb in the sentence? **Answer:** *is*
Subject Question: Who or what *is*? **Answer:** *name*

Sentence 6: There are two federal agents here to see you.
Verb Question: What is the linking verb? **Answer:** *are*
Subject Question: Who *are*? **Answer:** *agents*

Identifying Subjects, Helping Verbs, and Main Verbs

In Chapter 1 you learned that a linking verb used in combination with other verbs becomes a *helping verb*. The helping verb and the main verb should be read as a unit. This unit is considered the verb in the sentence.

Sentence 7: The floor was refinished last month.
Verb Question: What words indicate action in the sentence?
Answer: *was refinished*
Subject Question: What *was refinished*? **Answer:** *floor*

Grammar Tip

There **Sentences**

In sentences beginning with *there*, the subject usually comes after the verb. The verb is usually a state-of-being, or linking, verb.

Sentence 8: Your return will be credited to your account.
Verb Question: What words indicate action in the sentence?
Answer: *will be credited*
Subject Question: What *will be credited*? **Answer:** *return*

Sentence 9: Your purse could have been stolen while you were
away from your desk.
Verb Question: What words indicate action in the sentence?
Answer: *could have been stolen*
Subject Question: What *could have been stolen*? **Answer:** *purse*

The helping verb may be separated from the main verb, especially in a question. Notice that the helping verb and the main verb are separated by the pronoun *you* in the next two sentences.

Sentence 10: Can you install the new software by Wednesday?
Verb Question: What words indicate action in the sentence?
Answer: *can install*
Subject Question: Who *can install*? **Answer:** *you*

Sentence 11: Do you know the cost of the new textbook?
Verb Question: What words indicate action in the sentence?
Answer: *do know*
Subject Question: Who *do*(es) *know*? **Answer:** *you*

Identifying Linking and Action Verb Phrases

When the final verb in the verb phrase is a linking verb, the entire phrase is linking.

Sentence 12: The dot-com stocks should have been valuable.
Verb Question: What is the linking verb phrase in the sentence?
Answer: *should have been*
Subject Question: What *should have been*? **Answer:** *dot-com stocks*

If the final verb is an action verb, then the verb phrase is an action verb.

Sentence 13: The dot-com stocks should have been sold.
Verb Question: What phrase indicates action in the sentence?
Answer: *should have been sold*
Subject Question: What *should have been sold*? **Answer:** *dot-com stocks*

Learn to recognize the frequently used helping verbs in the list below. These words will help you form both action and linking verb phrases.

Grammar Tip

Verb Units

One or more words may appear between the helping verb and main verb, but the verb unit of helping verb + main verb still offers one undivided meaning.

am	is	are	was	were	been
have	has	had			
will					
would	could	should			
can	must				
do	does	did			

Identifying Compound Subjects and Verbs

When the subject is composed of two or more items, as in the next example, it is called a **compound subject**.

> **Sentence 14: November and December are our peak sales months.**
> **Verb Question:** What is the linking verb? **Answer:** *are*
> **Subject Question:** What *are*? **Answer:** *November* and *December*

The verbs in the next two sentences consist of more than one action. Each of the next sentences has a **compound verb**—a verb that indicates more than one action.

> **Sentence 15: Sales last year rose in May and fell in June.**
> **Verb Question:** What words indicate actions in the sentence?
> **Answer:** *rose* and *fell*
> **Subject Question:** What *rose* and *fell*? **Answer:** *Sales*

> **Sentence 16: Your order is being processed and will be shipped within 48 hours.**
> **Verb Question:** What words indicate actions in the sentence?
> **Answer:** *is being processed* and *will be shipped*
> **Subject Question:** What is *being processed* and *will be shipped*?
> **Answer:** *order*

Identifying Understood Subjects in Commands

In some sentences the verb may not appear to have a subject. For example, what is the subject in the next sentence?

> **Sentence 17: Please sit down.**

Use the verb and subject questions to determine the subject of this sentence.

> **Verb Question:** What word indicates action in Sentence 17? **Answer:** *sit*
> **Subject Question:** Who or what should *sit*? **Answer:** The person being told to sit, or *you* (understood)

Sentence 17 is a type of sentence called a **command**. The subject of most commands is *understood* to be the person being addressed in the command—the person who is being told to do something. In English, that understood person is designated as *you* (understood).

> **Sentence 18: Sit down and be quiet!**
> **Verb Questions:** What actions are indicated in the sentence?
> **Answer:** *sit*
> What linking verb is in the sentence? **Answer:** *be*
> **Subject Question:** Who should *sit* and *be*? **Answer:** *you* (understood)

As you have seen, the words in a sentence perform different tasks. You put these words into classes according to the jobs they do and call these classes the eight parts of speech.

Sentences also perform different tasks and can be classified according to the jobs they do. In English, there are four basic kinds of sentences that perform different tasks. The four kinds of sentences are **statements**, **questions**, **commands**, and **exclamations**.

Statement

A **statement** makes an assertion and ends with a period.

> Sales last year rose in May and fell in June.
> The computer network is down.

Question

A **question** ends with a question mark.

> Can you install the new software by Wednesday?
> What accessories are available with this model?

Command

A **command** ends with a period. A strong command ends with an exclamation point. Remember that the subject in a command is always understood to be *you*, even though *you* may not be stated.

> Please examine your new checks carefully.
> Stand still!

In spoken language, the speaker's voice tells you whether a command is strong. In writing, the exclamation point serves this purpose.

Exclamation

Stand still! illustrates the fourth kind of sentence, the **exclamation**, which expresses strong feeling or sudden emotion. Exclamations are followed by exclamation points. Because the subject or the verb (or both the subject and the verb) is usually implied, exclamations may not appear to be complete sentences. They are used sparingly in workplace documents and school assignments. The following examples include the understood parts in parentheses.

> [That's] Fantastic!
> What an incredible coincidence [this is]!
> [There's a] Fire!

Kludge

The noun *kludge* is computer talk for a complex, often messy solution to a computer programming problem. As a slang term, it signifies the opposite of a clean, elegant solution.

SECTION A: PROGRAMMED REINFORCEMENT

Coverage Key

Section		Statement
2.1	➤ A Complete Sentence or Thought	➤ S1, S2, S3, S5, S6, S24
2.2	➤ Subjects and Verbs	➤ S4, S7, S8, S9, S10, S11, S12, S13, S14, S15, S16, S17
2.3	➤ Four Basic Kinds of Sentences	➤ S18, S19, S20, S21, S22, S23

Instructions: Cover the answers in the **Answer** column; then write your answer to the first statement. Uncover the first printed answer and compare your answer to it. If you wrote a correct answer, continue the activity. If you made an error, use the **Coverage Key** to locate the chapter section you need to review. When you are confident that you understand the material, continue with the reinforcement activity.

ANSWER

STATEMENT

S1   A sentence is a group of words that expresses a complete
_____.

A1   thought

S2   To express a complete thought, every sentence must include (a) someone or something to talk about, (b) something to say about that person or thing, or (c) both a and b.

A2   c

S3   The _____ of a sentence tells us about whom or what you are talking.

A3   subject

S4   The subject of a sentence is the _____ of the action.

A4   doer

S5   The _____ of a sentence tells us what the subject is or does. Another name for the simple predicate is the _____.

A5   predicate, verb

S6   Because every sentence must contain a subject and a verb, every sentence must have _____ essential parts.

A6   two

S7   **The President sat at the head of the table.** In this sentence the subject is _____, which answers the question _____. The verb is _____ _____, which answers the question _____.

A7   **President,** *who,* **sat,** *did what*

S8 **The new brochures are very colorful.** In this sentence the subject is _____, which answers the question _____ _____. The verb is _____, which answers the question _____.

A8 brochures, *what*, **are**, *are what*

S9 **The orientation meeting for new employees was held on Tuesday morning after the breakfast.** The subject is _____, which answers the question _____. The verb is _____, which answers the question _____.

A9 meeting, *what*, **was held**, *what was done to the subject*

S10 **Mr. Zirin, in my opinion, can hold the audience's attention better than anyone else on the staff.** The subject is _____. The verb is _____.

A10 **Mr. Zirin, can hold**

S11 In the preceding sentence *can* is called a(n) _____.

A11 helping verb

S12 Underline the words that can serve as helping verbs: **could, will, walk, has, write, have, does, talk, do.**

A12 <u>could</u>, <u>will</u>, <u>has</u>, <u>have</u>, <u>does</u>, <u>do</u>

S13 State-of-being verbs such as *am, are, is, was, were, be, been* (can, cannot) also serve as helping verbs.

A13 can

S14 Identify the subject and verb in each of the following sentences.
  a. **Sometime next week the position of information technologies director will be offered to Ms. Olafson.**
  b. **As the new director, Ms. Olafson will be extremely busy.**
  c. **When will Ms. Olafson assume her new position?**

A14 a. Subject—**position**, verb—**will be offered**; b. Subject—**Ms. Olafson**, verb—**will be**; c. Subject—**Ms. Olafson**, verb—**will assume**

S15 **Oats and wheat are basic commodities on the market.** The subject in this sentence is _____ and _____. A subject that has two parts is called a(n) _____ subject.

A15 Oats, wheat, compound

S16 **The value of my investment rose in the first quarter last year and then dropped the next two quarters.** In this sentence the verb is _____ and _____. This is called a(n) _____ verb because it is composed of more than _____ part.

A16 rose, dropped, compound, one

S17 **Irma and Jamal finished scanning the photographs and went to lunch.** The subject is _____ and _____; the verb is _____ and _____. Both the subject and verb are _____.

A17 **Irma, Jamal, finished, went, compounds**

S18 There are four basic kinds of sentences: statements,

_____, _____, and

_____.

A18 questions, commands, exclamations

S19 **E-mail me the figures as soon as you have them.** This sentence is a (command, question). The subject in this sentence is not expressed; it is _____.

A19 command, understood

S20 **Make a backup copy of important files.** The understood subject is

_____.

A20 you

S21 **Where am I?** This sentence is a(n) _____.
It ends with a(n) _____.

A21 question, question mark

S22 **Patent law is a highly specialized field.** This sentence is a(n)
_____. It ends with a(n) _____.

A22 statement, period

S23 **That's incredible!** This sentence is a(n) _____. It ends
with a(n) _____.

A23 exclamation, exclamation point

S24 Let us review. A sentence is a group of words that contains a(n)
_____ and a(n) _____ and
expresses a(n) _____

A24 subject, verb, complete thought

SECTION B
Incomplete Sentences

In the first section, you focused on what makes a group of words a sentence and looked at the four basic kinds of sentences. Now you will examine expressions that are not complete thoughts or sentences. You will develop strategies for identifying sentence fragments and converting them into simple or complex sentences that express a complete thought.

2.4 Sentence Fragments

In the preceding pages you learned what makes a group of words a complete sentence. Now you are going to examine various types of expressions that are not complete sentences.

Carmela.

Is this a sentence? Obviously not. It names a subject, *Carmela*, but it does not tell what the subject does. It is not a sentence because it contains no verb and does not express a complete thought. It is a **sentence fragment**.

My colleague Carmela.

Is this a sentence? Again, the answer is no. The subject is described, but you are still not told what it does. You still have no verb and no complete thought. Remember, a sentence must have both a subject and a verb and also must express a complete thought. Now look at these expressions:

My colleague Carmela. Received a community service award.

Is either of these parts a complete sentence?

1. My colleague Carmela.
2. Received a community service award.

No. Part 1 contains a subject but no verb. Part 2 contains a verb but no subject. Alone, each part is merely a fragment of a sentence.

However, turning sentence fragments like Parts 1 and 2 above into a complete sentence is simple:

My colleague Carmela received a community service award.

TIME BUDGET If you're juggling multiple commitments—such as family, school, and work—budget time at the start of each week for each responsibility. But remain flexible: allow yourself to adjust this budget on a daily basis.

The sentence now includes a subject and a verb and expresses a complete thought. Here are more examples of fragments and complete sentences.

<u>FRAGMENTS:</u>	Our book, the latest, most authoritative work on the subject. Has just been published.
<u>COMPLETE SENTENCE:</u>	Our book, the latest, most authoritative work on the subject, has just been published.
<u>FRAGMENTS:</u>	The interest rate that we are offering you. Is the lowest you can get anywhere.
<u>COMPLETE SENTENCE:</u>	The interest rate that we are offering you is the lowest you can get anywhere.
<u>FRAGMENTS:</u>	Pat was promoted to the position of regional manager. And was given a salary increase.
<u>COMPLETE SENTENCE:</u>	Pat was promoted to the position of regional manager and was given a salary increase.

The last example contains a compound verb, *was promoted* and *was given*, and a single subject, *Pat*. When the second half of the compound verb is written alone, the result is a fragment because it has no subject.

Grammar Tip

Complete Thought?

To be a sentence, an expression must contain a subject and a verb and express a complete thought. If an expression does not express a complete thought, it is not a sentence.

It is true that ...

2.5 | More Sentence Fragments

The preceding fragments were easily corrected because they could be joined together to form complete sentences that include a subject and a verb and express a complete thought.

Phrases as Fragments

Sometimes fragments lacking a subject or verb cannot be so easily corrected. These are fragments involving phrases. A **phrase** is a group of related words without a subject or verb. Look at this example:

<u>WRONG</u>   Her book, the latest, most authoritative work on the subject. Now in stock.

Her book, the latest, most authoritative work on the subject contains a subject but no verb. The phrase *now in stock* doesn't contain a subject or a verb. Simply joining these two fragments will not be enough because there will still be no verb. You need to supply one. You could correct these fragments in several ways:

<u>RIGHT:</u>   ✔ Her book, the latest, most authoritative work on the subject, *is* now in stock.

<u>RIGHT:</u>   ✔ Now in stock, her book *is* the latest, most authoritative work on the subject.

<u>RIGHT:</u>   ✔ Her book, now in stock, *is* the latest, most authoritative work on the subject.

Now look at this example:

WRONG: An innovative course. Designed to improve your computer skills.

An innovative course contains a subject but no verb. The phrase *Designed to improve your communication skills* doesn't contain a subject or a helping verb. More words are needed to make these fragments complete sentences:

RIGHT: ✔ An innovative course has been designed to improve your computer skills.

RIGHT: ✔ An innovative course is now being offered. It is designed to improve your computer skills.

RIGHT: ✔ E-Communications is an innovative course. It is designed to improve your computer skills.

RIGHT: ✔ E-Communications, an innovative course, is designed to improve your computer skills.

RIGHT: ✔ E-Communications is an innovative course designed to improve your computer skills.

Although fragments that have no predicate are frequently used in advertising, you should avoid using them in standard workplace correspondence. Make sure that your sentences have both a subject and a verb and that they express a complete thought.

Participles as Fragments

Another type of sentence fragment that you should be careful to avoid seems to have both a subject and a verb. When you examine it closely, you see that it doesn't contain a verb and doesn't express a complete thought.

Jill, running at full speed.

Let's test this example to see if it is a sentence.

1. Who? *Jill* (the subject)
2. Doing what? *Running* (the apparent verb)
3. Complete thought? No! It leaves us with the question: Jill, running at full speed, *did what?*

This sentence fragment may be completed as follows:

Jill, running at full speed, fell.

Now you have a complete sentence.

```
        complete subject
┌──────────────────────────┬─────┐
│ simple                   │     │
│ subject                  │ verb│
└──────────────────────────┴─────┘
Jill, running at full speed, fell.
```

In this example, the phrase *running at full speed* serves as an adjective modifying *Jill. Running* is called a **participle**.

Participles like *running* can appear by themselves or in phrases in other parts of a sentence. Whatever their position, do not let them fool you into thinking that they are verbs.

<u>Wrong:</u>   Failing to give his employer any notice. Zack suddenly quit his job to work for another company.

<u>Right:</u>   ✔ Failing to give his employer any notice, Zack suddenly quit his job to work for another company.

<u>Wrong:</u>   His body trembling with anger. Mr. Fuentes told Ralph to leave immediately.

<u>Right:</u>   ✔ His body trembling with anger, Mr. Fuentes told Ralph to leave immediately.

LOOKING AHEAD

Participles
You'll examine the formation and use of participles in more detail in Chapter 9.

●

Grammar Tip

Picturing Clause Types

Visualize the relationship between independent and dependent clauses: the independent clause stands alone while the dependent clause hangs on to the independent one.

INDEPENDENT
E
P
E
N
D
E
N
T

Clauses as Fragments

The final type of sentence fragment involves a clause. A <u>**clause** is a group of related words</u> that contains both a subject and a verb. However, a clause does not always express a complete thought. Look at this example:

> Since the ad appeared.

This is not a complete sentence. Although *Since the ad appeared* contains a subject, *ad*, and a verb, *appeared*, the word *Since* limits your thought and leaves you up in the air. You want to know what happened *since the ad appeared*. You must add something to complete the thought. For example, you might say, *Since the ad appeared, sales have increased.*

dependent clause   independent clause
Since the **ad** appeared, **sales** have increased.

Independent Clauses. In the previous sentence, there are two distinct parts, each containing a subject and a verb. *Since the ad appeared* and *sales have increased* are clauses, but there is a difference between them. *Sales have increased* expresses a complete thought; it could stand alone as a sentence. For this reason it is called an **independent clause**. A sentence made up of one independent clause is a **simple sentence**.

Dependent Clauses. In contrast, *Since the ad appeared* cannot stand by itself as a sentence. The word *Since* makes it *dependent* on the rest of the sentence. For this reason it is called a **dependent clause**. It depends on the independent clause, *sales have increased*, to complete it.

There are many words like *since* that make a thought *dependent* on a main thought. Some other examples appear below. In each case the clause beginning with the italicized word or words is the dependent clause. The remaining clause is the independent clause.

> Although Kerry's interview went well, another candidate was hired.
> We kept trying *until* it was too late.
> There is a monthly service fee *if* you fail to maintain a minimum balance.

2.6 Complex Sentences

In Chapter 1 you learned that words and word phrases such as *since, although, as soon as, because,* and *until* are subordinating conjunctions. They begin dependent clauses. Sentences like the ones listed above, which are composed of a dependent clause linked to an independent clause, are called **complex sentences**. You will examine complex sentences further in Chapter 13. The important thing to remember is never to write a dependent clause by itself as though it were a complete sentence. You must connect a dependent clause with an independent clause to form a complete sentence.

WRONG: Though their computer is excellent. Their software is inferior.
RIGHT: ✔ Though their computer is excellent, their software is inferior.

WRONG: We won it. Because our bid was low.
RIGHT: ✔ We won it because our bid was low.

Clauses beginning with *that* or *which* also form sentence fragments when they stand alone. *That* and *which* clauses should be connected with the independent clauses with which they are associated.

WRONG: I have an old computer. Which I use rarely.
RIGHT: ✔ I have an old computer, which I use rarely.

WRONG: Lieutenant Fredricks told everyone in the office a long joke. That no one thought was funny.
RIGHT: ✔ Lieutenant Fredricks told everyone in the office a long joke that no one thought was funny.

SECTION B: PROGRAMMED REINFORCEMENT

Coverage Key

Section		Statement
2.4	➤ Sentence Fragments	➤ S25, S28, S29
2.5	➤ More Sentence Fragments	➤ S26, S27, S29, S30, S31, S32, S33, S34, S35, S36, S37, S38, S39, S40, S41, S42
2.6	➤ Complex Sentences	➤ S43, S44, S45, S46

Instructions: Cover the answers in the **Answer** column; then write your answer to the first statement. Uncover the first printed answer and compare your answer to it. If you wrote a correct answer, continue the activity. If you made an error, use the **Coverage Key** to locate the chapter section you need to review. When you are confident that you understand the material, continue with the reinforcement activity.

ANSWER

STATEMENT

S25 A group of words that does not express a complete thought is a(n) _____ fragment _____.

A25 fragment

S26 A phrase is a(n) _____ _____.

A26 group of related words without a subject or a verb

S27 **The efficient assistant.** This fragment is a phrase that needs (a subject, a verb) to make it a complete sentence.

A27 a verb

S28 **Made copies.** This is another fragment. What is needed to make it a sentence? (a subject, a verb)

A28 a subject

S29 **The efficient assistant. Made copies.** Write these two sentence fragments as one complete sentence. _The efficient assistant made copies_

A29 **The efficient assistant made copies.**

S30 What three elements of every sentence appear in **The efficient assistant made three copies?** (a) _subject_, (b) _verb_, (c) _complete thought_

A30 subject, verb, complete thought

S31 **Chee, feeling he had no hope.** This (is, is not) a complete sentence.

A31 is not

S32 In the **S31** example, **feeling** is not a verb but a(n)_____. The part of speech needed to make the thought expressed in **S31** a complete sentence is a(n)_____.

A32 participle, verb

A33 is

A34 verb, verb

A35 independent, can

A36 dependent, cannot

A37 express a complete thought

A38 is not

A39 dependent, independent

A40 sentence

A41 dependent, does not

A42 independent, does

A43 dependent, independent
complex

A44 independent, <u>while you were at
lunch</u> (dependent clause), <u>Ray
phoned</u> (independent clause)

A45 Although sales increased, net
profits are unchanged.

A46 b.

S33 **Chee, feeling he had no hope, resigned.** This (<u>is</u>, is not) a
complete sentence.

S34 A clause must contain a subject and a(n) _____verb_____.
The words **our offices** are not a clause; they contain no
_____verb_____.

S35 A clause that expresses a complete thought is a(n) _independent_
clause. An independent clause (<u>can</u>, cannot) stand alone.

S36 A clause that does not express a complete thought is a(n)
_____dependent_____ clause. It (can, <u>cannot</u>) stand alone.

S37 **Because I felt sick.** This is a fragment. It has a subject **I** and a verb
felt. It does not _express a complete thought_ .

S38 **I stayed home from school.** This (is, is not) a fragment.

S39 **Because I felt sick** is a(n) _____ clause, and **I
stayed home** is a(n) _____ clause.

S40 **Because I felt sick, I stayed home.** This is a (fragment, sentence).

S41 **When Yumi receives the data.** This is a(n) _____
clause because it (does, does not) express a complete thought.

S42 **She will fix the report.** This is a(n) _____
clause because it (does, does not) express a complete thought.

S43 **When Yumi receives the data, she will fix the report.**
This sentence contains a(n) _____ clause and
a(n) _____ clause. It is called a(n) _____
sentence.

S44 **Ray phoned while you were gone.** This sentence contains a
dependent clause and a(n) _____ clause. Underline
the dependent clause once and underline the independent
clause twice.

S45 Write the following correctly: **Although sales increased. Net profits
are unchanged.**
_____
_____

S46 Which of the following is correct?
a. I was late for work. Because there was an accident.
b. I was late for work because there was an accident.

In this section, you will learn how complete sentences can be combined to create compound sentences and how to avoid writing run-on sentences.

2.7 Compound Sentences

You will now learn how complete sentences can be combined to create longer sentences. Some methods are acceptable. Others are not.

Look at these two sentences:

> I would like to go to the dinner.   I will be out of town.

You may combine these two sentences into one thought:

> I would like to go to the dinner, *but* I will be out of town.

Grammar Tip

Seven CCs

English includes seven coordinating conjunctions, or CCs. They include:

> *and*
> *but*
> *or*
> *nor*
> *for*
> *so*
> *yet*

This combined sentence is better than the two sentences because it expresses the relationship between Sentences 1 and 2 more accurately.

In the example above, the two sentences were combined by using a comma and the word *but*. The word *but*, as you know, is a **coordinating conjunction**. So are *and, or, nor, for, so,* and *yet*. A sentence made up of two independent clauses joined by a coordinating conjunction is a **compound sentence**.

> Profits this year were high, *and* next year's will be even higher.
> You may pay in advance, *or* we will bill you at the time of delivery.
> I do not seek your support, *nor* will I accept it.
> Ms. Smock received the largest bonus, *for* she worked the hardest.
> Ms. Smock worked the hardest, *so* she received the largest bonus.
> Mr. Howell made little effort, *yet* he too received a large bonus.

Join two sentences—or *two independent clauses*—by using both a comma and a coordinating conjunction to express the relationship between the sentences.

The comma may be omitted when two short independent clauses are joined by *and* or *or*.

Another way to join two statements is to use the semicolon. Use this mark of punctuation only when the two thoughts are very closely related.

> Thank you for your advice; it was most helpful.

LOOKING AHEAD

You will examine coordinating conjunctions and other conjunctions in more detail in Chapter 13.

●

Either coordinating conjunctions or semicolons are grammatically correct ways to join two sentences to express the relationship between them. However, the sentence-combining methods you will study next are incorrect because they create errors known as run-on sentences.

2.8 Run-On Sentences

A **run-on sentence** is a sentence error that occurs when two separate sentences are written as one. There are two types of run-on sentences.

1. Two sentences are joined only by a comma, without a conjunction.

WRONG: I would like to go to the retirement dinner, I will be out of town.

WRONG: Thank you for your advice, it was most helpful.

This joining of two or more independent clauses with only a comma is known as a **comma fault**, or a **comma splice**. This common error can be easily corrected in one of several ways:

- Make two independent clauses two separate sentences.
- Join two independent clauses with a comma and a conjunction.
- If sense permits, join the two independent clauses with a semicolon.

2. A run-on sentence can happen when two statements are joined with no mark of punctuation at all.

WRONG: I would like to attend the conference I will be out of town.

WRONG: Thank you for your advice it was most helpful.

This error, known as a **fused sentence**, can be corrected in the same way as the comma fault.

WRONG: Here are the items we look forward to serving you again.

WRONG: Here are the items, we look forward to serving you again.

RIGHT: ✔Here are the items. We look forward to serving you again.

RIGHT: ✔Here are the items; we look forward to serving you again.

WRONG: We are new our clocks are unmatched in quality.

WRONG: We are new, our clocks are unmatched in quality.

RIGHT: ✔We are new. Our clocks are unmatched in quality.

BETTER: ✔We are new, but our clocks are unmatched in quality.

New Languages

Although fluency in traditional computer languages remains useful, a knowledge of newer, object-oriented programming languages and tools like C++, Visual Basic, and Java is gaining the lead in importance.

Coverage Key

Section		Statement
2.7	➤ Compound Sentences	➤ S47, S50, S53, S54
2.8	➤ Run-on Sentences	➤ S48, S49, S50, S51, S52, S54

Instructions: Cover the answers in the **Answer** column; then write your answer to the first statement. Uncover the first printed answer and compare your answer to it. If you wrote a correct answer, continue the activity. If you made an error, use the **Coverage Key** to locate the chapter section you need to review. When you are confident that you understand the material, continue with the reinforcement activity.

ANSWER

STATEMENT

S47 You may use which of the following methods to combine sentences?
- a. Use a comma and coordinating conjunction
- b. Use a comma only
- c. Use a semicolon
- d. Use a semicolon and a coordinating conjunction

A47 a, c

S48 Writing two separate sentences as one sentence is a common error called a(n) _____ sentence.

A48 run-on

S49 There are two kinds of run-on sentences. Two sentences joined by a comma are called a(n) _____.
Two sentences joined without any mark of punctuation are called a(n) _____.

A49 comma fault (or comma splice), fused sentence

S50 Use the conjunction *but* to correct the following run-on sentence: **Here is your test booklet do not open it now.**

A50 Here is your test booklet, but do not open it now.

S51 Correct the following run-on sentence by using a period and starting a new sentence: **We must change our window display the new spring merchandise has just arrived.**

A51 We must change our window display. The new spring merchandise has just arrived.

S52 It (is, is not) permissible to separate two complete sentences by a comma alone.

A52 is not

S53 When two sentences are closely related, they may be joined to make one sentence with the mark of punctuation called a _____.

A53 semicolon

S54 Where would you insert the semicolon in this run-on sentence? **Save your receipt you will need it for tax purposes.**

A54 Save your receipt; you will need it for tax purposes.

CHAPTER 2 SUMMARY

In this chapter you learned that a sentence has a subject and a predicate and expresses a complete thought. You also discovered that there are four basic kinds of sentences: statements, questions, commands, and exclamations. You examined various incomplete sentences, or sentence fragments, and learned how to turn them into complete sentences. Finally, you developed strategies for correcting two types of run-on sentences.

Getting Connected

USING INTERNET SEARCH TOOLS

GOAL: How do you find information you need on the Internet? Several Internet search tools are available free of charge to help you find what you're looking for. Search tools locate information on the Internet by using **keywords,** or **search words**, provided by the user (that's you). The Internet search tool combs through huge amounts of information stored on the Internet, looking for the keywords you provide. When it finds information that matches the words in your search, it delivers a list of results to your computer. You can then choose the results that seem most relevant to your needs.

In this activity, you'll practice using Internet search tools while locating information about subjects and predicates.

STEP 1 Go to *englishworkshop.glencoe.com*, the address for *The English Workshop* Website, and click on Unit 1. Next click on Getting Connected for Unit 1, and then click on Chapter 2. At the Chapter 2 Getting Connected option, you'll see a list of Websites that include Internet search tools. Begin the activity by selecting one of the search-tool links and clicking on it.

STEP 2 Scan the opening page of the Website, and locate the Search function. In the Search function, enter the key words "subjects and predicates." For this activity, include the quotation marks. Click on the Search button or press <Enter> on the keyboard.

STEP 3 The results of your search will appear as a list of Websites that contain information about subjects and predicates. Select one that interests you and click on it. When the page appears, explore the information presented. Not all of the results will provide the kind of information you want. If that happens, return to the list of search results and select another Website to visit.

STEP 4　　Now that you have some idea of how to use an Internet search tool, practice by using different search tools and comparing the results of your search. Different search tools will provide different results because, among other reasons, each tool searches for information in a slightly different way. To begin, return to *The English Workshop* Website.

STEP 5　　From the list of search-tool links, select three to use for this activity. On a sheet of paper, write the names of the tools you select in the left margin, spacing each one a third of the page down. Title the page *Search Tool Results.*

STEP 6　　Select a topic for your search. You may use the following suggestions for search words or come up with your own: "subjects and predicates," "sentence fragments," "compound-complex sentences." Write down the search words you select.

STEP 7　　Conduct your search using each of the tools you selected, and note the following items on the *Results* sheet:

　　a. How many results did the search return? Write the number beside the name of each search tool on the *Results* sheet.

　　b. Now assess the value of the results. A search may list a large number of hits, but the search will be valuable only if you find information you can use. For each search tool, visit two to four of the Websites listed in the search result and evaluate the information at each site. Do you find the information helpful, somewhat helpful, or confusing? On the *Results* sheet, record the number of sites you visited and your assessment of each one.

　　c. Finally, explain in a few sentences which tool you liked best. Consider these criteria: Was the tool easy to use? Was it fast? How many results did it return? Did it return many or few relevant sites? Would you use that search again?

STEP 8　　Write your name on the *Results* sheet and turn it in to your instructor.

Tip　　There are many ways to use Internet search tools. To learn more about using them, look for buttons labeled "Search Assistance" or "Advanced Search" at the search tool sites.

Name _____

Class _____ Date _____

PRACTICE 1

Four Basic Kinds of Sentences

Instructions: Identify the sentence type: *S*—Statement, *C*—Command, *Q*—Question, or *E*—Exclamation.

EXAMPLE: **The title of this book is *The English Workshop*.**   EX. _____S_____

1. Here is your order.   1. _____S_____

2. Please give it to me.   2. _____C_____

3. Where is your order?   3. _____Q_____

4. Here it is!   4. _____E_____

5. We wish to speak with either Ms. Frye or Ms. Yu.   5. _____S_____

6. May we speak with either Ms. Frye or Ms. Yu?   6. _____Q_____

7. Where did you put the overhead transparencies for this afternoon's meeting?   7. _____Q_____

8. The overhead transparencies for this afternoon's meeting are missing.   8. _____S_____

9. What a break!   9. _____E_____

10. Tell me where the transparencies are.   10. _____C_____

11. Please read, initial, and return the report by noon tomorrow.   11. _____C_____

12. Will you be able to read and return the report by noon tomorrow?   12. _____Q_____

13. Put in stop-loss orders on these stocks.   13. _____C_____

14. Have you put in stop-loss orders on these stocks?   14. _____Q_____

15. The investment counselor will arrive and complete her presentation early.   15. _____S_____

16. When will the investment counselor arrive?   16. _____Q_____

17. Look out!   17. _____C/E_____

18. I told you to look out.   18. _____S_____

19. Near them sat the two partners of the firm.   19. _____S_____

20. Aren't those the two partners of the firm sitting near them?   20. _____Q_____

21. Just off the main road is a narrow driveway leading to the back entrance.   21. _____S_____

22. Save your receipt.   22. _____C_____

23. Why should I save my receipt?   23. _____Q_____

24. You will need your receipt for tax purposes.   24. _____S_____

25. #*$%* taxes!!!   25. _____E_____

Name _____

Class _____ Date _____

PRACTICE 2

Subjects and Verbs

Instructions: In each of the following sentences, underline the subject once and the verb twice. Ask yourself: (1) Who or what? *(the subject)* and (2) Does what or is what? *(the verb)*. Ignore all other words.

EXAMPLE: **The new <u>supervisor</u> <u>outlined</u> his plan clearly and succinctly.**

1. I like this book.

2. This book has been purchased by nearly 200,000 readers.

3. Did you enjoy it?

4. Where should I put the overhead transparencies for this afternoon's meeting?

5. Ms. Lopez, after some hesitation, has approved the request.

6. Mr. Gomez and Ms. Crowell are in Stockholm this week.

7. Neither Mr. Black nor Mr. Alvarado has submitted his expense form for this month.

8. We wish to speak with either Ms. Richards or Ms. Yu.

9. Neither of them is here.

10. Orders for durable goods rose in October and rose again in November.

11. Please read, initial, and return the report by noon tomorrow.

12. Have the contracts been signed and mailed?

13. Have you signed and mailed the contracts?

14. An increase in consumer recognition of our product's name is the object of our promotional campaign.

15. The investment counselor will arrive and complete her presentation early.

16. Give it to me this minute!

17. Waiting at the airport were the accountant and the attorney.

18. Near them sat the two partners of the firm.

19. Needed more than economy is efficiency.

20. Just off the main road is a narrow driveway leading to the back entrance.

PRACTICE 3

Sentence Fragments

Instructions: Some of the expressions below are complete thoughts. In the blanks, write *C* next to the expressions that are complete sentences. Write *F* next to the expressions that are sentence fragments.

EXAMPLE: **In spite of orders to the contrary.**   EX. _____ **F** _____

1. Confirming a report in Thursday's business section of the paper.   1._____

2. Due to a lack of experience and maturity.   2._____

3. We agree.   3._____

4. W. O. Roberts, the most noted authority on aerodynamics in recent years.   4._____

5. Where are we going?   5._____

6. The admissions office will process your application as soon as it arrives.   6._____

7. When the order arrives and is processed by the receiving department. 7._____

8. Nearing the attainment of the production goals set at our last meeting.   8._____

9. Nearly everyone present, including President Chen and her aides.   9._____

10. Nearly everyone was present, including President Chen and her aides.   10._____

11. There is no time for further discussion.   11._____

12. In spite of his long record of service and his promise to make full restitution,   12._____
    he was fired.

13. Forgetting all the instructions the supervisor had given in the morning.   13._____

14. All the instructions the supervisor had given in the morning were forgotten.   14._____

15. Reviewing all the résumés that had been submitted in response to the   15._____
    announcement of an opening and selecting those candidates who would be
    contacted for an interview.

16. After reviewing all the résumés that had been submitted in response to the   16._____
    announcement of an opening, she selected those candidates who would be
    contacted for an interview.

17. Although we were certain she was a fine leader and were willing to follow her.   17._____

18. We were certain she was a fine leader and were willing to follow her.   18._____

19. Certain she was a fine leader and willing to follow her.   19._____

20. Certain that she was a fine leader, we were willing to follow her.   20._____

PRACTICE 4

Sentence Fragments and Complete Sentences

Instructions: Below are some of the expressions from Practice 3. For each complete sentence, underline the subject with one line and the verb with two lines. Turn each fragment into a complete sentence. Then underline the subject with one line and the verb with two lines.

EXAMPLE: **In spite of orders to the contrary, <u>Joyce</u> <u>sneaked</u> out of the house and <u>went</u> to the movies.**

1. Due to a lack of experience and maturity. _____

   _____

2. We agree. _____

3. Where are we going? _____

4. When the order arrives and is processed by the receiving department. _____

   _____

5. Nearly everyone present, including President Chen and her aides. _____

   _____

6. Nearly everyone was present, including President Chen and her aides. _____

   _____

7. Forgetting all the instructions the supervisor had given in the morning. _____

   _____

8. All the instructions the supervisor had given in the morning were forgotten. _____

   _____

9. Reviewing all the résumés that had been submitted in response to the announcement of an opening and selecting those candidates who would be contacted for an interview. _____

   _____

   _____

10. After reviewing all the résumés that had been submitted in response to the announcement of an opening, she selected those candidates who would be contacted for an interview. _____

    _____

    _____

Name _____

Class _____ Date _____

PRACTICE 5

Dependent and Independent Clauses

Instructions: A clause is a group of words with a subject and a verb. A *dependent* clause is one that cannot stand alone as a sentence. An *independent* clause is one that can stand alone as a sentence. In each sentence below, a group of words is italicized. In the blank to the right, write *D* if the italicized group of words is a dependent clause; write *I* if it is an independent clause; or, write *N* if it is not a clause.

EXAMPLE: **I was unable to complete the assignment *because there was a power failure* last night.**   EX. _____D_____

1. I prefer the computer *with the larger display screen.*   1._____

2. He led the sales force *because of his ambition.*   2._____

3. *Because she was ambitious,* she soon impressed her employers.   3._____

4. *We can offer this guarantee* because of our high quality control.   4._____

5. *Our high quality control makes it possible* for us to offer this guarantee.   5._____

6. *Watching the action on the floor of the stock exchange* is an exciting experience.   6._____

7. *Although we have worked hard,* we have yet to show a profit.   7._____

8. We have yet to show a profit *despite our hard work.*   8._____

9. *She is an excellent broker* because of her thorough knowledge of the market.   9._____

10. She is an excellent broker *because she knows the market thoroughly.*   10._____

11. *When a course is canceled,* students must rearrange their schedules.   11._____

12. A *canceled course* means that students have to rearrange their schedules.   12._____

13. A course *that has been canceled* can seriously disrupt students' schedules.   13._____

14. *Because we have years of experience,* we can satisfy all your printing requirements.   14._____

15. *Because of our years of experience,* we can satisfy all your printing requirements.   15._____

16. We will notify you *as soon as the verdict is announced.*   16._____

17. *She would be an excellent spokesperson for our company* because she is personable and articulate.   17._____

18. *When shopping for a home,* you should take into account the value of other homes in the area.   18._____

19. When shopping for a home, *take into account the value of other homes in the area.*   19._____

20. *When you are shopping for a home,* consider carefully the value of other homes in the area.   20._____

Name _____

Class _____ Date _____

PRACTICE 6

Simple and Complex Sentences

Instructions: A simple sentence is a sentence made up of one independent clause. A complex sentence is a sentence made up of an independent clause and a dependent clause. In the blank to the right of each example, write *S* if the sentence is a *simple* sentence; write *X* if it is a *complex* sentence; write *F* if it is a sentence *fragment*.

EXAMPLE: **Please call me as soon as your plane lands.**　　　　EX. _____X_____

1. We will expect your decision within ten days.　　　　1._____

2. You will not be billed until you have received the entire order.　　　　2._____

3. If anything ever sounded as though it were unwise.　　　　3._____

4. Please try to arrive before ten o'clock to avoid any delay.　　　　4._____

5. You can avoid any delay if you arrive before ten o'clock.　　　　5._____

6. On the last Wednesday in April we will hold our meeting.　　　　6._____

7. Although I am aware that you have a prior engagement.　　　　7._____

8. Though you have a prior engagement, won't you try to attend?　　　　8._____

9. There are several good reasons for our unwillingness to participate.　　　　9._____

10. Although the owner reduced the asking price, the house remained unsold.　　　　10._____

11. The house remained unsold despite the lower asking price.　　　　11._____

12. Do you agree with the commission's report on unemployment?　　　　12._____

13. Because at present the available software is inadequate for our needs.　　　　13._____

14. Before the insurance company will pay the claim, its investigator must assess the damage.　　　　14._____

15. Before paying the claim, the insurance company wants its investigator to assess the damages.　　　　15._____

16. If he's staying, I'm leaving.　　　　16._____

17. In spite of her limited marketing experience, she was hired.　　　　17._____

18. She was hired even though she had limited marketing experience.　　　　18._____

19. In spite of the government's economic efforts, many consumers will face financial hardships.　　　　19._____

20. In spite of the economic efforts the government has made, consumers still face financial hardships.　　　　20._____

Name _____

Class _____ Date _____

Chapter 2 Practices

PRACTICE 7

Run-on Sentences

Instructions: Some of the following expressions are run-on sentences; others are correct sentences. Wherever there is an error in punctuation or capitalization, cross out the error and write your correction in the space above. If a sentence is entirely correct, write *C* in the blank.

EXAMPLE: _____ **I'm getting tired of. waiting. when will the doctor be available?**

1. _____ I was unable to finish marking your exams, I'll return them to you on Monday.

2. _____ Have your representative call to arrange a definite appointment.

3. _____ Have your representative call, a definite appointment should be made in advance.

4. _____ Perhaps later on we will be willing to do as your representative suggests, just now, though, we do not wish to change insurance carriers.

5. _____ At this time, however, we don't wish to change insurance carriers, we are sure you will understand.

6. _____ James Kuo, a man with considerable experience in office planning, will meet with you on March 4.

7. _____ James Kuo is a man with considerable experience in office planning, he will meet with you on March 4.

8. _____ Our brochure explains how tax-free municipal bonds offer the investor a significant tax savings.

9. _____ Tax-free municipal bonds offer the investor a significant tax savings, see our brochure for details.

10. _____ Thank you for your pledge it is through the contributions of viewers like you that we are able to continue to broadcast the fine programs that you have come to expect.

11. _____ Please tell us which items are in error we will rush you the correct items as soon as we have this information.

12. _____ Please take a few moments of your time to tell us of the improper shipment so that we will be in a position to rush you the correct items.

13. _____ Please take a few moments of your time to tell us the details of the improper shipment, once we have this information, we will be in a position to rush you the correct items.

14. _____ We are making our vacation plans for next summer, we are interested in your booklet describing New England.

15. _____ Please send us your booklet describing New England to assist us in making our vacation plans for next summer.

PRACTICE 8

Sentence Fragments and Run-on Sentences

Instructions: In the blank, write *C* for each complete sentence; write *F* for each sentence fragment; write *R* for run-on sentences.

EXAMPLE: **Leave your application with the receptionist we will contact you.**   EX. _____ R _____

1. Whenever the attorney consulted with her client.   1. _____

2. Stock prices fell in Europe the dollar ended mixed.   2. _____

3. Because of his initiative, and because he had the proper connections.   3. _____

4. What will happen next?   4. _____

5. Looking around, sizing up the situation, and considering all its ramifications.   5. _____

6. You will have to stay late tonight, this report must be completed.   6. _____

7. Though Ms. Blake is young, she is not immature.   7. _____

8. Stay late tonight, you will be paid overtime.   8. _____

9. Please review these documents they must be submitted by 4 p.m. today.   9. _____

10. So that these documents can be submitted by 4 p.m. today.   10. _____

11. Subject to your review, these documents must be submitted by 4 p.m. today.   11. _____

12. Examine the books for 30 days, return them if you aren't satisfied.   12. _____

13. Examine the books for 30 days, and return them if you aren't satisfied.   13. _____

14. You're fired!   14. _____

15. We followed the directions, but we were unable to assemble the display rack no matter how many different ways we arranged the pieces.   15. _____

16. Many are called few are chosen.   16. _____

17. While the person in the upper tax brackets who invests in municipal bonds can realize a significant tax advantage.   17. _____

18. Help!   18. _____

19. If we do not receive payment within five days, we will be forced to turn your account over to a collection agency.   19. _____

20. No holder of public office shall demand payment or contribution from another holder of a public office or position for the campaign purposes of any candidate or for the use of any political party.   20. _____

PRACTICE 9

Sentence Fragments and Run-on Sentences

Instructions: Manufacturers often include short messages with their products to promote goodwill between themselves and the consumer. The following promotional message is included with an electric razor. The message contains a number of sentence fragments and run-on sentences. Proofread the message below, crossing out all mistakes and writing in all necessary changes.

Congratulations you now own the finest shaving system in the world. That's why the Slick Electric Razor. Is the largest selling razor on the market today.

The Slick is a whole new experience in shaving satisfaction. The Slick has a rotating head. Which adjusts to the contour of your face. Its micrometer blades are self-cleaning. And self-sharpening. The Slick comes with nine different comfort settings to give you the optimum in shaving closeness and satisfaction. For incredibly close and comfortable shaves. Nothing beats a Slick. In addition, the Slick comes with a trimming edge for precise sideburns. And an attachment for beards and mustaches. Although you may have used another razor all your life. After you've used your Slick once, you'll never want to go back to your old razor again.

We're so confident that the Slick experience is unlike any other that we offer you this unconditional guarantee. Try the Slick for one month if you don't agree it's the best razor you've ever used. Return it for a full refund.

We know that once you've used the Slick, however, you'll wonder how you ever did without it. Because "Nothing beats a Slick."

PRACTICE 10

Composition: Converting Fragments Into Complete Sentences

Instructions: Phone messages are often written in phrases and fragments on preprinted forms. Rewrite the following message as a brief paragraph. Be sure to use complete sentences. Begin your paragraph with "While you were out, . . ."

While You Were Out

FOR ___Mr. Jacob Zimmerman___

DATE ___3/4/20--___   TIME ___1:00 p.m.___

M___s. Marla Oliveria___

OF ___Consolidated Services___

PHONE ___(703) 621-9000___   FAX ___(703) 621-9021___

MESSAGE ___Received contracts —___
___Has questions regarding___
___payment schedule — Must talk___
___with you before 4 p.m.___
_____

SIGNED ___Brian___

[X] TELEPHONED
[X] PLEASE CALL
[ ] RETURNED YOUR CALL
[ ] CAME TO SEE YOU
[ ] WILL CALL AGAIN
[ ] WANTS TO SEE YOU
[X] URGENT
[ ] WILL FAX MATERIALS

Mr. Zimmerman,

While you were out,

_____

_____

_____

_____

_____

Basic Units of Communication

Unit 1—Composition Review

Instructions: This Composition Review deals with the concepts you have studied so far. First, read the time sheet below so that you are familiar with it. Then answer the questions that appear beneath it and on the next page. Finally, read the Writing Situation on the next page, and assume the role of the assigned writer. Develop a paragraph based on information from the time sheet.

Time sheet

NEW STATE UNIVERSITY   **FEDERAL WORK-STUDY**

DEPARTMENT   _Computer Lab_
NAME   _Celeste Simone_
ADDRESS   _734 Floyd Street, Apt. 4 – E_
Fort Worth, TX 71632
BI-WEEKLY PAYROLL   FROM _4/14_   TO _4/27_   20 – –

	MONTH/DAY	AM ARRIVED	AM LEFT	PM ARRIVED	PM LEFT	HOURS
SAT/SUN						
MON						
TUES	4/17	10			1	3
WED	4/18	10			1	3
THURS	4/19	11			2	3
FRI	4/20			1	4	3
SAT/SUN						
MON	4/23	9	11			2
TUES	4/24	10			1	3
WED	4/25	10			1	3
THURS	4/26	11			1	2
FRI	4/27			1	4	3
TOTAL						25

EMPLOYEE _Celeste Simone_   DATE _4/27/ – –_
SUPERVISOR _Arlene Brighton_   DATE _4/27/ – –_

QUESTIONS:

1. What days did Celeste Simone NOT work? _____

_____

_____

continued from page 57

2. What days did Celeste work? _____

_____

_____

3. Who is Celeste's supervisor at work? _____

_____

_____

4. How many hours did Celeste work between April 17 and 27? _____

_____

_____

5. How can Celeste's supervisor be contacted if someone wishes to talk with her? _____

_____

_____

_____

_____

_____

_____

Writing Situation: Celeste is a full-time student at New State University, a part-time tutor at the campus computer lab, and a member of the university volleyball team. Linda Dun is the coach for the team. Each May Coach Dun asks university instructors and work supervisors to submit a brief report about the team members they teach or supervise.

Assume you are Celeste's supervisor at the computer lab. Write a brief, paragraph-long report using complete sentences. Explain (1) who you are and why you are writing the report to the coach (e.g., she asked you to do so); (2) the days Celeste worked between April 17 and 27 and the days she did not work; and (3) the total number of hours Celeste worked. You believe Celeste does an excellent job explaining concepts to new computer users, so write a sentence that praises her work. End the paragraph by explaining how you can be contacted if Coach Dun has additional questions.

Link & Learn

USING PARTS OF SPEECH AND SENTENCES IN COMPUTER TECHNOLOGY CAREERS

GOAL: Reinforce what you learned in Unit 1 about the parts of speech and the sentence while using the Internet to explore various computer technology Websites.

STEP 1: Go to *englishworkshop.glencoe.com*, the address for *The English Workshop* Website. Click first on Unit 1; then click on Link & Learn to access a list of computer technology sites you may use in this activity. Select one of the sites, and click on it.

STEP 2: Skim the different topics available at the home page of the Website you selected. Find a topic that interests you. Maybe you'd like to learn about a professional organization or a particular career. Click on the link of the topic you select.

STEP 3: Read the online material. Make a printout of at least one page.

STEP 4: Using the printout, do the following:

a. Look for one sentence that includes *at least five* of the eight parts of speech. You may find a sentence with all eight parts of speech; however, such sentences are rare. Underline or highlight the sentence you select, and label the parts of speech.

b. In reviewing the printout, did you find any interjections? If you did, explain on the back of the printout why you think they were used. If you found no interjections, explain why you think none were used.

c. Circle and label the complete subjects and complete predicates of five other sentences in the document. Underline the simple subject once and the verb twice.

d. Look for one example of each of the four different types of sentences: statement, question, command, and exclamation. Label each type of sentence as you find it. If you can't find a particular kind of sentence, such as an exclamation, explain on the back of your printout why you think it was not used in the document you selected for this activity.

STEP 5: Write your name on the front of the printout, and turn it in to your instructor.

Words That Name

Profile in Success

Paralegal: Developing Language Skills and Career Opportunities

Celia C. Elwell · *Oklahoma City, Oklahoma* · *Office of the Municipal Counselor*

In the early 1970s, when Celia Elwell graduated from high school in Ardmore, Oklahoma, she did not plan to co-write a textbook with a law professor, teach paralegal courses, publish articles, or serve as a paralegal to the Honorable Marian P. Opala, an Oklahoma supreme court justice.

After graduation Celia married and worked as a data entry clerk to support her husband while he pursued a degree in architecture. By 1982 she was juggling her work in front of a computer terminal with her work at home as a wife and mother. Then a lawyer offered her a job in his office. Law and the use of good English have been passions for Celia ever since.

Celia earned a Legal Assistant Certificate from the University of Oklahoma in a program that she attended on Saturdays. "I could still work a full week, take care of my family, and squeeze in time to study," she explains about her choice of programs. The school served Celia in another way. She has taught in the program for the past 15 years.

Reflecting on her career, Celia says, "I cannot overemphasize the importance of basic grammar in a professional setting. Clients know a law firm by our paperwork. Errors will lose a firm clients and respect. I have to use good grammar because my abilities reflect on the competency of my office."

Think About It... Have Times Changed?

Celia Elwell, who started her career thirty years ago, attributes much of her success to her efforts to learn proper English grammar.

- *How important is the knowledge of grammar to career success today?*

- *How important is it to personal success?*

- *What do you think helped Celia enjoy the opportunities and career success she has experienced?*

Career Connections

LAW CAREERS

Learn more about paralegals, legal assistants, court reporters, and other careers in the judicial field by connecting to the following sites listed on *The English Workshop* Website. Go to **englishworkshop.glencoe.com.** Click first on Unit 2 and then on Career Connections.

- National Federation of Paralegal Associations
- National Association of Legal Assistants
- National Court Reporters Association
- Justice Technology Information Network
- Officer.com

See page 159, **Link & Learn: Using Pronouns in Law Careers,** for an additional online career activity.

Nouns

CHAPTER 3 PREVIEW

In Chapter 2 you learned that a complete sentence must have a subject and a predicate. Because nouns serve as both subjects and objects of verbs, your study of the parts of speech will begin with nouns. In this chapter, you will continue to assess your knowledge in the Programmed Reinforcement sections and the Practices. Finally, you will use a Website to enhance your understanding of common and proper nouns.

OBJECTIVES

After completing this chapter, you will be able to

- Identify the different types and classes of nouns.
- Form the plurals of nouns with specific endings.
- Form the plurals of the following:
  - Old English nouns
  - Proper names
  - Foreign nouns
  - Compound nouns
  - Letters, numerals, signs, symbols, abbreviations, and individual words
  - Special nouns
- Form the possessives of both singular and plural nouns.
- Form possessives of nouns in special situations.

Study Plan for Chapter 3

The Study Plan for Chapter 3 offers a set of strategies that will help you learn and review the chapter material.

❶ **Spelling Practice**: Familiarity through repetition can be the key to mastering troublesome spelling words. Working with a study partner, try spelling the words aloud.

❷ **Plurals of Foreign Words**: Locate the plural forms of words that give you trouble. Write each correct singular form on one side of an index card and write the correct plural form on the other side. Study the cards until you've mastered them.

❸ **Possessive Nouns**: Circle every noun in your writing that ends in an *s* and verify that each shows ownership. If any do, an apostrophe should be before or after the *s*.

❹ **So Many Rules, So Little Time**: Become familiar with all the rules presented in this chapter; then focus on those that apply most directly to your needs. Learn them by heart. (Hint: your instructor or supervisor may help you determine what is most important for improving your writing skills.)

Plural Nouns

Writers sometimes have problems with the plural forms of nouns. In this section you will consider all types and classes of nouns. This will provide you with a good foundation for forming noun plurals.

3.1 Types and Classes of Nouns

In Chapter 1 you learned that nouns are used to name persons, places, objects, abstract qualities, ideas, and activities. Some examples are:

persons—child, associate, Mr. Harris, Sasha

places—lobby, courtroom, Chicago, college

objects—desk, chair, Internet, stationery

qualities—dependability, loyalty, initiative, reliability

ideas—beauty, truth, knowledge, happiness

activities—walking, e-mailing, supervising, thinking

Concrete and Abstract Nouns

Nouns are either concrete or abstract. **Concrete nouns** name specific things that can be experienced by one of the five senses—things that can be seen, felt, heard, tasted, or smelled. **Abstract nouns** name qualities and ideas. Most nouns are concrete. Because concrete nouns are more precise, specific, and forceful than abstract nouns, they are more effective in writing you do at work.

Common and Proper Nouns

LOOKING AHEAD

Capitalizing Proper Nouns
You'll discover the rules for capitalizing proper nouns in Chapter 20.

●

Nouns can be further divided into two classes: common nouns and proper nouns. A **common noun** names a general class of people, places, or objects. All nouns naming qualities, ideas, or activities are common nouns. A **proper noun** names a specific person, place, or object. Look at these paired examples:

COMMON NOUN	PROPER NOUN
woman	Heidi
country	Mexico
car	Mercedes-Benz

Notice that common nouns are *not* capitalized, but proper nouns are.

Singular and Plural Nouns

Nouns may be either singular or plural. Notice that the spelling of the singular and plural forms of each noun are different.

Singular	Plural	Singular	Plural
book	books	child	children
company	companies	alumnus	alumni

3.2 Spelling Rule for Most Plural Nouns

To form the plurals of *most* nouns, simply add *s*.

Singular	Plural	Singular	Plural
cartridge	cartridges	European	Europeans
desk	desks	receipt	receipts
idea	ideas	menu	menus

3.3 Nouns Ending in *s, ss, sh, x, z,* and *ch*

To form the plural of a noun that ends in *s, ss, sh, x, z,* or *ch*, add *es*.

Singular	Plural	Singular	Plural
box	boxes	glass	glasses
bus	buses	lunch	lunches
bush	bushes	waltz	waltzes

Grammar Tip

Exceptions to 3.3

1. quiz   quizzes
2. When *ch* has the sound of *k*, form the plural by adding *s*:
   epoch   epochs
   monarch monarchs
   stomach stomachs

3.4 Nouns Ending in *y*

The guidelines for forming plurals of nouns ending in *y* depend on whether the *y* follows a vowel or a consonant.

Nouns Ending in *y* Preceded by a Vowel

To form the plural of a noun that ends in *y* preceded by a vowel (*a, e, i, o, u*), simply add *s*.

Singular	Plural	Singular	Plural
alley	alleys	money	moneys or monies
alloy	alloys	survey	surveys
attorney	attorneys	valley	valleys

Nouns Ending in *y* Preceded by a Consonant

To form the plural of a noun that ends in *y* preceded by a consonant (any letter other than *a, e, i, o, u*), change the *y* to *i* and add *es*.

Singular	Plural	Singular	Plural
accessory	accessories	laboratory	laboratories
baby	babies	policy	policies
copy	copies	secretary	secretaries
country	countries	specialty	specialties

3.5 Nouns Ending in *o*

The guidelines for forming plurals of nouns ending in *o* depend on whether the *o* follows a vowel or a consonant.

Nouns Ending in *o* Preceded by a Vowel

To form the plural of a noun that ends in *o* preceded by a vowel, add *s*.

Singular	Plural	Singular	Plural
cameo	cameos	radio	radios
duo	duos	ratio	ratios
embryo	embryos	stereo	stereos
portfolio	portfolios	tattoo	tattoos

Nouns Ending in *o* Preceded by a Consonant

To form the plural of a noun ending in *o* preceded by a consonant, add either *s* or *es* depending on the word.

1. Some nouns in this category add *s*.

Singular	Plural	Singular	Plural
auto	autos	memo	memos
casino	casinos	photo	photos
ditto	dittos	tobacco	tobaccos
ego	egos	two	twos

2. Some nouns in this category add *es*.

Singular	Plural	Singular	Plural
echo	echoes	potato	potatoes
embargo	embargoes	tomato	tomatoes
hero	heroes	veto	vetoes

3. Some nouns in this category add either *s* or *es*. (The preferred form is listed first. You should use that form in workplace documents.)

Singular	Plural	Singular	Plural
cargo	cargoes, cargos	zero	zeros, zeroes
ghetto	ghettos, ghettoes	motto	mottoes, mottos
halo	halos, haloes	tuxedo	tuxedos, tuxedoes
memento	mementos, mementoes	volcano	volcanoes, volcanos

3.6 Nouns Ending in *f*, *fe*, or *ff*

Keep in mind the following two spelling rules when changing singular nouns that end in *f*, *fe, or ff* into plurals.

1. To form the plurals of most nouns in this category, add *s*.

Singular	Plural	Singular	Plural
belief	beliefs	plaintiff	plaintiffs
chef	chefs	proof	proofs
cliff	cliffs	handkerchief	handkerchiefs

2. To form the plurals of some common nouns in this category, change the *f* or *fe* to *v* and add *es*.

Singular	Plural	Singular	Plural
half	halves	self	selves
knife	knives	life	lives
thief	thieves	wolf	wolves

3.7 Old English Nouns

Certain Old English nouns have irregular plural forms. You should find these words very familiar.

Singular	Plural	Singular	Plural
child	children	man	men
foot	feet	mouse	mice
gentleman	gentlemen	ox	oxen
goose	geese	tooth	teeth
louse	lice	woman	women

Grammar Tip

Plural Musical Terms

Many musical terms ending in *o* add *s*:

alto	altos
banjo	banjos
concerto	concertos
piano	pianos
solo	solos
soprano	sopranos

Grammar Tip

Two Acceptable Spellings

A few nouns ending in *f* or *ff* have two acceptable spellings for their plural forms:

calf	calfs, calves
staff	staffs, staves
dwarf	dwarfs, dwarves
wharf	wharfs, wharves
scarf	scarfs, scarves

3.8 Proper Names

To form the plural of a proper name, add either *s* or *es*. Do not change the original spelling.

1. Most first names and surnames add *s* to form the plural.

Singular	Plural	Singular	Plural
Alberto	Alberto*s*	Slocum	the Slocum*s*
Marie	Marie*s*	Kelly	the Kelly*s*
Mary	Mary*s*	Wolf	the Wolf*s* (not: the Wolves)
Andy	Andy*s*	Feldman	the Feldman*s* (not: the Feldmen)
Dakota	Dakota*s*	Lightfoot	the Lightfoot*s* (not: the Lightfeet)

Grammar Tip

Avoid Awkward Pronunciations

Do not add the *es* ending if it makes the plural surname awkward to pronounce:

Hodges   the Hodg*es* (not: the Hodgeses)

McMasters   the McMasters (not: the McMasterses)

2. First names and surnames ending in *s*, *sh*, *x*, *z*, or *ch* add *es* to form the plural.

Singular	Plural	Singular	Plural
Thomas	Thomas*es*	Jones	Jones*es*
Josh	Josh*es*	Nash	the Nash*es*
Felix	Felix*es*	Bendix	the Bendix*es*
Inez	Inez*es*	Gomez	the Gomez*es*
Rich	Rich*es*	March	the March*es*

3.9 Foreign Nouns

A number of nouns in English are actually derived from words in a foreign language. These words usually take foreign endings, but many also have English plural endings. Although both the foreign plural and the English plural are considered acceptable, one form is usually preferred.

The following pages have lists of frequently used foreign nouns. Learn to recognize these words and their plural forms. For each word that has two plural forms, the preferred form—the one you should use—is marked with an asterisk (*). If you are uncertain of the meaning of some of these words, look them up in a dictionary.

Words Ending in *us*

Singular	English Plural	Foreign
alumnus (male)		alumn*i* (male)
apparatus	apparatus*es**	apparatus (no change)
cactus	cactus*es*	cact*i**
census	censu*ses*	
focus	focus*es**	foc*i*
fungus	fungu*ses*	fung*i**
nucleus	nucleu*ses*	nucle*i**
prospectus	prospectus*es*	
radius	radius*es*	rad*i*i**
status	status*es*	
stimulus		stimul*i*
syllabus	syllabus*es*	syllab*i**

Words Ending in *um*

Singular	English Plural	Foreign
addendum		addend*a*
auditorium	auditoriums*	auditori*a*
bacterium		bacteri*a*
curriculum	curriculums*	curricul*a*
datum	datum*s*	dat*a**
gymnasium	gymnasiums*	gymnasi*a*
honorarium	honorariums*	honorari*a*
maximum	maximums*	maxim*a*
memorandum	memorandums*	memorand*a*
minimum	minimums*	minim*a*
momentum	momentums*	moment*a*
podium	podiums*	podi*a*
referendum	referendums*	referend*a*
stadium	stadiums*	stadi*a*
symposium	symposiums*	symposi*a*
ultimatum	ultimatums*	ultimat*a*

Grammar Tip

The Plurals of *Medium*

Use the foreign plural *media* when referring to advertising and communication systems. In other cases, use the plural *mediums*.

Grammar Tip

Data/*Datum*

Most writers use *data* as both a singular and a plural noun. Many scientists and other researchers use *datum* as the singular form and *data* as the plural.

Words Ending in *a*

Singular	English Plural	Foreign
agenda	agenda*s*	
alumna (female)		alumn*ae*
antenna	antenna*s* (radios)	antenn*ae* (insects)
formula	formula*s**	formul*ae*
vertebra	vertebra*s*	vertebr*ae**

Words Ending in *on*

Singular	English Plural	Foreign
automaton	automaton*s**	automat*a*
criterion	criterions	criteri*a**
phenomenon	phenomenons	phenomen*a**

Words Ending in *x*

Singular	English Plural	Foreign
apex	apex*es**	apic*es*
appendix	appendix*es**	appendic*es*
index	index*es* (of books)	indic*es* (math symbols)
matrix	matrix*es*	matric*es**

Words Ending in *is*

Singular	English Plural	Foreign
analysis		analys*es*
axis		ax*es*
crisis		cris*es*
diagnosis		diagnos*es*
ellipsis		ellips*es*
emphasis		emphas*es*
hypothesis		hypothes*es*
parenthesis		parenthes*es*
prognosis		prognos*es*
synopsis		synops*es*
synthesis		synthes*es*
thesis		thes*es*

3.10 Compound Nouns

Compound nouns link two or more words to form one word.

1. When a compound noun is written as one solid word without hyphens, form the plural by making the last part plural.

Singular	Plural	Singular	Plural
birthday	birthdays	grandchild	grandchild*en*
businesswoman	businesswom*en*	letterhead	letterheads
bookshelf	bookshelves	printout	printouts
classmate	classmates	salesperson	salespersons
courthouse	courthouses	stockholder	stockholders

Exception: passerby   passer*s*by

This rule also applies to compounds ending in *ful*.

Singular	Plural	Singular	Plural
armful	armfuls	spoonful	spoonfuls
cupful	cupfuls	teaspoonful	teaspoonfuls

2. When a compound noun is written as two or three separate words or with one or two hyphens, make the principal word plural.

Singular	Plural	Singular	Plural
account payable	accounts payable	leave of absence	leaves of absence
attorney general	attorneys general	notary public	nota*ries* public
bill of lading	bills of lading	point of view	points of view
board of education	boards of education	runner-up	runners-up
editor in chief	editors in chief	sister-in-law	sisters-in-law

Note: Attorney generals and *notary publics* are also acceptable, but the plural forms listed above are preferred.

3. When a hyphenated compound noun does not contain a noun as one of its elements, make the last part plural.

Singular	Plural	Singular	Plural
follow-up	follow-ups	show-off	show-offs
has-been	has-beens	trade-in	trade-ins
know-it-all	know-it-alls	write-off	write-offs

Legal Research

Law offices rely on the Internet and software packages more and more to research legal literature stored in databases and on CD-ROMs. Paralegals must develop computer literacy to keep up with the fast-paced information age.

The plurals of letters, numerals, signs, symbols, abbreviations, and individual words are formed by adding *s*, *es*, or *'s*.

1. Add *s* to form the plural of capital letters (except *A*, *I*, *M*, and *U*), numerals, and most abbreviations.

Singular	Plural	Singular	Plural	Singular	Plural
9	9s	PTO	PTOs	bldg.	bldgs.
B	Bs	B.A.	B.A.s	no.	nos.
X	Xs	Ph.D.	Ph.D.s	vol.	vols.

Grammar Tip

Forming Plurals With *'s*

Use *'s* to form the plural only for the circumstances described in 3.11. Otherwise form the plural by adding *s* or *es* to a singular noun.

2. Add *s* or *es* to form the plural of individual words or terms, depending on the pronunciation.

Singular	Plural	Singular	Plural
yes	yeses	and	ands
no	noes	but	buts
if	ifs		

Some terms are generally pronounced as plurals.

ins and outs   pros and cons

ups and downs   haves and have-nots

whys and wherefores

3. Generally add *s* to form the plural of capital letters and words ending in capital letters. If the plural form is confusing—such as the plural form of *A*, or *As*—add the apostrophe for clarity. To form the plural of uncapitalized letters and abbreviations, add *'s*. To form the plural of symbols and lowercase abbreviations with internal periods, add *'s*.

Singular	Plural	Singular	Plural	Singular	Plural
R	Rs	q	q's	HMO	HMOs
A	A's	a	a's	*	*'s
I	I's	i	i's	#	#'s
M	M's	o	o's	c.o.d.	c.o.d.'s
U	U's	x	x's	d.b.a.	d.b.a.'s

Units of Measure	Singular and Plural Abbreviation	Units of Measure	Singular and Plural Abbreviation
foot or feet	ft	mile or miles	mi
gallon or gallons	gal	miles per gallon	mpg
gram or grams	g	miles per hour	mph
inch or inches	in	ounce or ounces	oz
pound or pounds	lb	quart or quarts	qt
liter or liters	L	revolutions per minute	rpm
meter or meters	m	yard or yards	yd

Punctuation Tip

Form the plurals of a few single-letter abbreviations by doubling the letter.

Units of Measure	Abbreviation	Units of Measure	Abbreviation
page 28	p. 28	page 245 and the following pages	pp. 245 ff.
pages 28 through 35	pp. 28–35	line 16	l. 16
pages 28, 32, and 35	pp. 28, 32, and 35	lines 16 through 19	ll. 16–19
page 245 and the following page	pp. 245 f.	note 4	n. 4
		notes 4 and 5	nn. 4–5

Mr., Ms., Mrs., and Miss

In most workplace documents it is always appropriate to use the traditional courtesy titles of *Mr.*, *Ms.*, *Mrs.*, and *Miss.* Unless a woman specifically requests to be addressed as *Miss* or *Mrs.*, use *Ms.*, which, like *Mr.* for men, makes no reference to marital status.

The plural of **Mr.** is *Messrs.* (from the French word *Messieurs*).
The plural of **Ms.** is *Mses.* or *Mss.* (used infrequently).
The plural of **Mrs.** is *Mmes.* (from the French word *Mesdames*).
The plural of **Miss** is *Misses* (no period follows).

These plural titles are typically used only in formal situations. In ordinary situations, the singular form is used and repeated with each name.

Mr. Del Rio and **Mr.** Chen   **Miss** Palana and **Miss** Taik

3.12 Special Nouns

1. Some nouns look plural but are singular in meaning. Use a singular verb when one of the following words is the subject of a sentence.

measles   summons   molasses   news

Example: Today's international **news** is very upsetting.

2. A number of nouns are always plural even though they refer to single things. Always use a plural verb when one of the following words is the subject of a sentence.

assets	earnings	pliers	scissors
auspices	glasses	premises	thanks
belongings	goods	proceeds	trousers
clothes	grounds	quarters	
credentials	odds	riches	
dues	pants	savings	

Example: The **proceeds** were donated to charity.

Grammar Tip

Pair of—Singular or Plural?

When the phrase *pair of* precedes a noun, the entire expression is singular. These pants *are* too tight. (pants = plural) This *pair of* pants *is* too tight. (pair = singular)

3. Some nouns are the same in the singular and the plural form. When one of these nouns is the subject, you must look at the meaning of the sentence to determine whether to use a singular or a plural verb.

corps	fish	Japanese	sheep
data	gross	means (method)	species
deer	head (of cattle)	moose	series
	headquarters		

Examples: One **means** of solving the parking problem is to build a garage.
Other **means** of solving the problem are being studied.

A special group of nouns that can be either singular or plural end in *ics*.

civics	genetics	phonetics	semantics
economics*	mathematics*	physics	statistics*
ethics*	politics*		

When used to refer to a body of knowledge or course of study, all these words take a singular verb. When used to refer to qualities or activities, the words followed by an asterisk (*) are considered plural and therefore take a plural verb.

Examples: **Mathematics** is my most difficult subject this semester.
The **mathematics** of his plan are simply not thought through.

Coverage Key

Section		Statement
3.1	➤ Types and Classes of Nouns	➤ S1, S2, S3, S4, S5, S6, S7, S8, S9
3.2	➤ Spelling Rule for Most Plural Nouns	➤ S10
3.3	➤ Nouns Ending in *s, ss, sh, x, z,* and *ch*	➤ S11
3.4	➤ Nouns Ending in *y*	➤ S12, S13
3.5	➤ Nouns Ending in *o*	➤ S14, S15, S16
3.6	➤ Nouns Ending in *f, ff,* or *fe*	➤ S17, S18
3.7	➤ Old English Nouns	➤ S19
3.8	➤ Proper Names	➤ S20
3.9	➤ Foreign Nouns	➤ S21
3.10	➤ Compound Nouns	➤ S22, S23, S24
3.11	➤ Letters, Numerals, Signs, Symbols, Abbreviations, and Individual Words	➤ S26, S27, S28, S29
3.12	➤ Special Nouns	➤ S25

Instructions: Cover the answers in the **Answer** column; then write your answer to the first statement. Uncover the first printed answer and compare your answer to it. If you wrote a correct answer, continue the activity. If you made an error, use the **Coverage Key** to locate the chapter section you need to review. When you are confident that you understand the material, continue with the reinforcement activity.

ANSWER	STATEMENT
	S1 Underline the correct answer. Nouns are (naming words, joining words, describing words).
A1 <u>naming words</u>	**S2** As naming words, nouns name persons, places, objects, qualities, ideas, or activities. The nouns *disk* and *computer* are _____. The nouns *apartment* and *Fort Worth* are _____. The nouns *honesty* and *loyalty* are _____.
A2 objects, places, qualities	**S3** All nouns are either concrete or abstract. _____ nouns name specific things that can be experienced by one of the five senses; _____ nouns name qualities and ideas.
A3 Concrete, abstract	**S4** Which of the following nouns are concrete? Which are abstract? **monitor, integrity, Lois Vuksta, music, coffee, beauty**
A4 concrete: **monitor, Lois Vuksta, music, coffee;** abstract: **integrity, beauty**	**S5** Nouns can also be divided into two classes—common nouns and proper nouns. A noun that names a general class of persons, places, or objects is a(n) _____.
A5 common noun	

S6 The word *employee* is a common noun that names a(n)

_____.

A6 person	**S7** In the sentence **Vera broke a window in her office**, underline the noun naming an object and underline twice the noun naming a place.
A7 <u>window</u>, <u>office</u>	**S8** A noun that names a specific person, place, or object is called a(n) _____. Proper nouns (always, sometimes, never) begin with capital letters. Underline the proper nouns in this sentence: **He was born in Boston near the Bunker Hill Memorial.**
A8 proper noun, always, <u>Boston</u>, <u>Bunker Hill Memorial</u>	**S9** Underline the proper nouns in this sentence: **The President addressed the Congress at the opening session on Thursday.**
A9 <u>President</u>, <u>Congress</u>, <u>Thursday</u>	**S10** Most nouns change from singular to plural simply by adding the letter _____. Write the plurals of **desk**, **plant**, **office**, and **bottle**. _____ _____ _____ _____
A10 *s*, desks, plants, offices, bottles	**S11** Most nouns that end in *s*, *ss*, *sh*, *x*, *z*, or *ch* form their plurals by adding _____. Write the plurals of **glass**, **fox**, **watch**, and **wish**. _____, _____, _____, _____
A11 *es*, glasses, foxes, watches, wishes	**S12** If a noun ends in *y* preceded by a vowel (*a, e, i, o, u*), form the plural by adding _____. Write the plurals of **attorney**, **delay**, **toy**, and **valley**. _____ _____ _____ _____
A12 *s*, attorneys, delays, toys, valleys	**S13** If a noun ends in *y* preceded by a consonant (any letter other than *a, e, i, o, u*), form the plural by _____ _____. Write the plurals of **copy**, **liability**, **university**, **study**, and **battery.** _____ _____ _____ _____ _____
A13 changing the *y* to *i* and adding *es*, copies, liabilities, universities, studies, batteries	**S14** If a noun ends in *o* preceded by a vowel, form the plural by adding _____. Write the plurals of **folio, embryo, cameo,** and **patio.** _____ _____ _____ _____
A14 *s*, folios, embryos, cameos, patios	**S15** Most nouns ending in *o* preceded by a consonant form their plurals by adding (*s, es,* either *s* or *es*) _____. Write the plurals of **potato, hero, ego, echo, zero,** and **veto.** _____ _____ _____ _____ _____ _____
A15 either *s* or *es*, potatoes, heroes, egos, echoes, zeros, vetoes	

S16 Some nouns that end in *o* preceded by a consonant form plurals by simply adding either *s* or *es*. There (are, are not) preferred ways to spell these words. Write the preferred plural of **cargo, zero, motto**.

_____ _____ _____

A16 are, **cargoes, zeros, mottoes**

S17 Most nouns that end in *f, fe,* or *ff* form their plurals by adding __. Write the plurals of these nouns correctly: **belief, chef, safe, cliff**.

_____ _____
_____ _____

A17 s, **beliefs, chefs, safes, cliffs**

S18 Some nouns that end in *f* or *fe* form their plurals by changing the *f* to _____ and _____. Write the plurals of these correctly: **knife, wife, thief, half**.

_____ _____
_____ _____

A18 *v*, adding *es*, **knives, wives, thieves, halves**

S19 The plurals of some Old English nouns are irregular. Write the plurals of the following words: **ox, tooth, child, mouse, foot**.

_____ _____ _____
_____ _____

A19 **oxen, teeth, children, mice, feet**

S20 Form the plural of proper names by adding either *s* or *es*. Write the plurals of the following proper nouns: **Ollhoff, Roberto, Mandy, Lynch.** _____ _____

_____ _____

A20 **Ollhoffs, Robertos, Mandys, Lynches**

S21 Some nouns have special foreign plural forms. How would you write these correctly: **phenomenon, alumnus, thesis, alumna, addendum**?

_____ _____
_____ _____

A21 **phenomena, alumni, theses, alumnae, addenda**

S22 Nouns made up of two or more separate words are called _____. If they are written as one word without a hyphen, the plural is formed by making the last part plural. How would you form the plurals of these words: **handful, stepchild, courthouse, spoonful, businessman**? _____ _____

_____ _____

A22 compound nouns, **handfuls, stepchildren, courthouses, spoonfuls, businessmen**

S23 If the compound noun is written with a hyphen or as two or three separate words, the principal or most important part is made plural: *brother-in-law—brothers-in-law*. Write the plurals of **sister-in-law, attorney general, editor in chief,** and **bill of lading**.

_____ _____
_____ _____

A23 **sisters-in-law, attorneys general, editors in chief, bills of lading**

S24 If the compound noun does not contain a noun as one of its elements, the plural is formed by making the last part plural. Write the plurals of the following: **write-off, no-show, cure-all, show-off**.

_____   _____

_____   _____

A24 write-offs, no-shows, cure-alls, show-offs

S25 Some nouns form their plurals either by undergoing an irregular change (*ox-oxen*) or by repeating the same form for both the singular and plural (*sheep-sheep*). Write the plurals of **deer, series, goose, gross, mouse,** and **tooth.** _____

_____   _____   _____

_____   _____   _____

A25 deer, series, geese, gross, mice, teeth

S26 The plurals of courtesy titles are used in formal situations. Write the plurals of the following: **Mr., Mrs., Ms., Miss.** _____

_____   _____   _____

A26 Messrs., Mmes., Mses. or Mss., Misses

S27 The plurals of letters, numerals, signs, symbols, abbreviations, and individual words are formed by adding
a. **s**
b. **es**
c. **'s**
d. **all of the above**
e. **none of the above**

A27 d.

S28 Use the 's to form the plural
a. **always**
b. never
c. **when necessary to prevent confusion**

A28 c.

S29 Write the following sentence correctly:
Dot the is, cross the ts, and erase the 8s.

A29 Dot the i's, cross the t's, and erase the 8s.

SECTION B
Possessive Nouns

Some writers have problems with the possessive forms of nouns and noun phrases. To make this easier, you will first examine when and where possessive nouns generally show up. You will learn how to apply a test to nouns to determine whether or not they should be possessives. You will discover that the trick to mastering possessive nouns is recognizing when and where apostrophes are required.

3.13 Guidelines for Forming Possessive Nouns

Possessive nouns are often used in the workplace. A possessive noun is one that shows ownership, authorship, brand, kind, origin, or measurement.

the company's inventory (ownership)	the teachers' convention (kind)
O'Neill's play (authorship)	the lamp's glow (origin)
Campbell's soup (brand)	two weeks' time (measurement)

Possessive nouns may be either singular or plural. The guidelines for forming both singular and plural possessive nouns should cause you little trouble.

3.14 Singular Nouns

1. Form the possessive of a singular noun by adding *'s*.

boss	boss's	Angelina	Angelina's
box	box's	Max	Max's
company	company's	Mr. Ross	Mr. Ross's
hero	hero's	Ms. Arnez	Ms. Arnez's

2. When the addition of *'s* to a singular noun makes pronunciation awkward, add only an apostrophe.

Moses	Moses' (Moses's: pronounced "Moseses"—too awkward)
Sophocles	Sophocles' (Sophocles's: pronounced "Sophocleses"—too awkward)
Achilles	Achilles' (Achilles' heel)
goodness	goodness' (for goodness' sake)

Grammar Tip

The Sounds of Possessives

To form the possessive of a singular noun ending in a *s* or *z* sound, pronounce the word aloud, listen to yourself, and write what you hear. Do you say "Charles *Dickens* house" or "Charles *Dickenses* house?" You should say "Charles *Dickens* house" and write "Charles *Dickens'* house." Do you say "*Dallas* football team" or "*Dallases* football team?" You should say "*Dallases* football team" and write "*Dallas's* football team."

3.15 Plural Nouns

Grammar Tip

Forming Plural Possessives

To avoid mistakes in forming the possessive case of plural nouns, always form the plural of the noun first. Then apply the appropriate rule to make that plural possessive.

1. Form the possessive of a regular plural noun (one ending in *s*) by adding only an apostrophe after the *s*.

Regular Plural Noun	Possessive	Regular Plural Noun	Possessive
bosses	bosses'	Maxes	Maxes'
boxes	boxes'	the Murpheys	the Murpheys'
companies	companies'	the Rosses	the Rosses'
heroes	heroes'	the Arnezes	the Arnezes'

2. Form the possessive of an irregular plural noun (one not ending in *s*) by adding *'s*.

Irregular Plural Noun	Possessive	Irregular Plural Noun	Possessive
alumni	alumni's	men	men's
children	children's	people	people's
geese	geese's	women	women's

3.16 A Test for Possessive Nouns

You can apply a test to help you determine whether a noun is possessive and therefore needs an apostrophe.

Background for the Test: Possessive nouns will always be followed by a stated or implied noun that names what the possessive noun owns. Think of that word as the "owned noun." Also, think of the apostrophe in a possessive noun as indicating that a phrase has been left out of the word group. The "missing" phrase is generally one beginning with *of, for,* or *belonging to.*

possible possessive   owned word

For example: Logans new briefcase is missing.

Is "Logans" a possessive noun that needs an apostrophe? Try the test.

Step 1: When you see a word you think may be a possessive, place the "owned noun" in front of it: *briefcase Logans*

Step 2: Place the word *of* between the owned noun and the noun you think may be possessive: *briefcase of Logans.*

Step 3: If the phrase makes sense, the noun you thought may be possessive is. Place an apostrophe or an apostrophe plus *s* at the end of the possessive noun: *Logan's new briefcase is missing.*

3.17 Possessives With Inanimate Objects

Most inanimate (nonliving) things should not be used in the possessive case.

> Avoid: The wall's color …
> Use: ✔ The color of the wall …

> Avoid: The building's architecture …
> Use: ✔ The architecture of the building …

Personified Possessives

When inanimate nouns are closely associated with people, however, the possessive form is acceptable.

the company's policy   the factory's location

Time and Measurement as Possessives

Many common expressions that refer to time and measurement also retain the possessive form.

a moment's hesitation	an hour's delay	eat to your heart's
a few moments' hesitation	four hours' delay	content
a minute's work	a week's salary	a month's wait
ten minutes' work	three weeks' salary	six months' wait
a dollar's worth	get your money's	a year's interest
a hair's breadth	worth	twenty years' interest

3.18 Guidelines for Forming Possessive Nouns in Special Situations

In writing, you will from time to time encounter situations that call for special techniques in forming possessives. The guidelines shown below will help you express those possessives correctly.

Joint Ownership

A problem arises when you want to show joint ownership. How would you write this phrase in possessive form?

The operetta by Gilbert and Sullivan …
Answer: Gilbert and Sullivan's operetta …

This refers to one operetta written by Gilbert and Sullivan.

To show joint ownership, write only the last name in possessive form.

Baker and Montero's firm …

This shows Baker and Montero own the firm jointly. Other examples are:

Ben and Jerry's ice cream ...
Rodgers and Hammerstein's musical ...

When you want to show *separate* ownership of distinct items, write the name of each owner in possessive form.

Baker's and Montero's firms are strong competitors.

This refers to two firms, one owned by Baker and the other by Montero.

New York's and Chicago's police forces are among the largest in the country.

This refers to the police force of each city separately.

Legalese

The noun *legalese* refers to the language of lawyers and paralegals. This includes foreign phrases like *quid pro quo*—Latin for "something for something," or "I'll give you this for that."

Abbreviations

To write the possessive form of an abbreviation, place *'s* after the final period or after the final letter if no periods are used. For a plural abbreviation, place an apostrophe after the *s* but not before it.

CBS's ratings   The Wainright Co.'s staff
three M.D.s' offices   John D. Rockefeller Jr.'s fortune
AOL's policy   both MBAs' credentials

Compound Nouns

When forming the possessive of compound nouns, add an apostrophe or *'s* to the final element in the compound according to the basic guidelines for forming possessives.

Singular	Singular Possessive
eyewitness	eyewitness's
has-been	has-been's
grandchild	grandchild's
notary public	notary public's
brother-in-law	brother-in-law's

Plural	Plural Possessive
eyewitnesses	eyewitnesses'
has-beens	has-beens'
grandchildren	grandchildren's
notaries public	notaries public's
brothers-in-law	brothers-in-law's

With plural possessive forms such as *brothers-in-law's* or *notaries public's* you may need to revise the sentence to avoid awkward constructions.

AWKWARD: He obtained two notaries public's seals.
BETTER: ✔ He obtained the seals of two notaries public.

AWKWARD: Tashi envied his two brothers-in-law's homes.
BETTER: ✔ Tashi envied the homes of his two brothers-in-law.

Noun Phrases

Sometimes the expression to be made possessive consists of more than one word. In these cases, think of the whole phrase as one expression and put the possessive on the last word of it.

Catherine the Great's reign was long.
Someone else's proposal was accepted.

When the possessive of a noun phrase is awkward, rephrase it.

<u>AWKWARD:</u>	The man just entering the elevator's sister manages our computer networks.
<u>BETTER:</u>	✔ The sister of the man just entering the elevator manages our computer networks.

Also rephrase sentences to avoid attaching a possessive to an *of* phrase or to another possessive.

<u>AWKWARD:</u>	A neighbor of mine's car was stolen.
<u>BETTER:</u>	✔ The car of a neighbor of mine was stolen.

<u>AWKWARD:</u>	One of my friends' son was elected to the council.
<u>BETTER:</u>	✔ The son of one of my friends was elected to the council.

<u>AWKWARD:</u>	Read the substitute teacher's students' evaluations.
<u>BETTER:</u>	✔ Read the students' evaluations of the substitute teacher.

Names of Organizations

Many organizational names and titles contain nouns that could be considered either possessive or descriptive. If these words are possessive, they require an apostrophe. If they are descriptive, they do not. Always follow the form that appears on the official letterhead or the official listing of the organization.

Ladies' Home Journal	Actors' Equity Association
Macy's	*Cliffs Notes*
McDonald's	Lands' End clothing
Reader's Digest	Manufacturers Trust Company
Men's Health	Underwriters Laboratories Inc.

Nouns in Apposition

Sometimes two nouns that refer to the same thing are used together, the second noun making the first clearer. For example,

Ms. Ramos, my assistant, is ill.

These two nouns are said to be in **apposition;** that is, the second identifies the first. The second noun is known as the **appositive.** When these nouns are used in the possessive case, make only the appositive possessive.

Ms. Ramos, my assistant's computer will be upgraded next week.
That is Mr. DePietro, my supervisor's car.

The comma that normally follows the appositive is omitted after the possessive ending. If such wording seems awkward, rephrase the sentence.

The computer of my assistant, Ms. Ramos, will be upgraded next week.
That car belongs to Mr. DePietro, my supervisor.

Possessive Nouns That Modify Unexpressed Nouns

Sometimes the possessive noun is not followed by the noun it modifies, either because that noun has been left out or because it appears elsewhere in the sentence. In either case, the possessive noun should still appear in the possessive form.

We went to Saleh's [home] after work.
That briefcase is Sharon's.
This year's sales have already surpassed last year's.

NETWORKING Meet, or "network" with people in a variety of positions. Someday any one of them may offer good advice or open a door to new opportunities and future employers.

Coverage Key

Section		Statement
3.13 ➤	Guidelines for Forming Possessive Nouns	➤ S30
3.14 ➤	Singular Nouns	➤ S31
3.15 ➤	Plural Nouns	➤ S32
3.16 ➤	A Test for Possessive Nouns	➤ S41
3.17 ➤	Possessives With Inanimate Objects	➤ S40
3.18 ➤	Guidelines for Forming Possessive Nouns in Special Situations	➤ S33, S34, S35, S36, S37, S38, S39, S42

Instructions: Cover the answers in the **Answer** column; then write your answer to the first statement. Uncover the first printed answer and compare your answer to it. If you wrote a correct answer, continue the activity. If you made an error, use the **Coverage Key** to locate the chapter section you need to review. When you are confident that you understand the material, continue with the reinforcement activity.

ANSWER	STATEMENT
	S30 When a noun shows ownership, authorship, brand, kind, origin, or measurement, a(n) _____ is added to it.
A30 apostrophe	**S31** To form the possessive of a singular noun, add _____ unless it makes pronunciation difficult, in which case add _____ _____. Write the possessive forms of the following phrases: a. **the room of the boy** _____ b. **the offices of the company** _____ c. **the desk of the boss** _____ d. **the heel of Achilles** _____ e. **the job of my sister-in-law** _____
A31 's, an apostrophe only, a. **boy's room** b. **company's offices** c. **boss's desk** d. **Achilles' heel** e. **sister-in-law's job**	**S32** To form the possessive of a plural noun that ends in *s*, add _____. To form the possessive of a plural noun that does not end in *s*, add _____. Write the possessive form of the following phrases: a. **the field hockey team of the women** _____ b. **the pay of two weeks** _____ c. **the accounts of the eyewitnesses** _____ d. **the home of the Bycheks** _____ e. **the choice of the people** _____
A32 an apostrophe, 's, a. **the women's field hockey team** b. **two weeks' pay** c. **eyewitnesses' accounts** d. **the Bycheks' home** e. **the people's choice**	

S33 To show joint ownership by two or more people, write (only the first name, only the last name, both names) as a possessive. Write the possessive form of the following phrases to show joint ownership:
The plays of Kaufman and Hart _____
The musicals of Lerner and Loewe _____

A33 only the last name, **Kaufman and Hart's plays, Lerner and Loewe's musicals**

S34 Write the possessive forms of the following abbreviations:
YMHA, SEC, U.S.A., three Ph.D.s. _____ _____
_____ _____

A34 YMHA's, SEC's, U.S.A.'s, three Ph.D. s'

S35 To show possession, the apostrophe is placed (before, after) the last word in a compound noun. Place a possessive in this sentence:
The salesperson of the year record is outstanding.

A35 after, **The salesperson of the year's record is outstanding.**

S36 Rewrite the sentence in **S35** without possessives.
_____

A36 The record of the salesperson of the year is outstanding.

S37 When two nouns in apposition are used in the possessive case, (a) only the first noun is made possessive, (b) only the second noun is made possessive, (c) both nouns are made possessive.

A37 b. only the second noun is made possessive

S38 Place an apostrophe or 's where needed:
a. **Dr. Mona Furness, the pediatrician bill arrived today.**
b. **That is Dr. Li, my professor office.**

A38 a. **Dr. Mona Furness, the pediatrician's bill arrived today.**
b. **That is Dr. Li, my professor's office.**

S39 Rewrite the sentences in **A38** without possessives.
_____
_____ .

A39 a. **The bill from the pediatrician, Dr. Mona Furness, arrived today.**
b. **That is the office of my professor, Dr. Li.**

S40 Some authorities think it is awkward to write a possessive for an inanimate object. Change the examples from the possessive form:
the table's dimensions _____
the greasepaint's smell _____

A40 the dimensions of the table, the smell of the greasepaint

S41 Place apostrophes in any words that should show possession in this sentence: **The union agreement covers mens stores and ladies stores under Huangs presidency.**

A41 men's, ladies', Huang's

S42 Rewrite the following sentence, using possessives:
The novels of Dickens, the operettas of Gilbert and Sullivan, the poetry of Wordsworth, and the plays of G.B.S. are all part of the literary heritage of Britain.

_____
_____

A42 Dickens' novels, Gilbert and Sullivan's operettas, Wordsworth's poetry, and G.B.S.'s plays are all part of Britain's literary heritage.

CHAPTER 3 SUMMARY

In this chapter you focused on the various types and classes of nouns. You learned how to form the plural and possessive forms of nouns, including concrete, abstract, common, and proper nouns. You studied the rules for correctly spelling plural nouns with different word endings and different language origins. You also learned how to spell compound nouns and other types of nouns. Finally, you examined the guidelines for forming both singular and plural possessive nouns and discovered how to deal with possessives in special situations, such as joint ownership.

Getting Connected

VISTING A WEBSITE FAQ LIST

GOAL: One of the remarkable characteristics of the English language is its flexibility. The language is dynamic, or ever-changing, so it can accommodate new words that come out of new technologies, global events, and social changes. The English language, in other words, has kept up with the times. The Internet, for example, has given the language many new terms, including *Internet, online, Cyber schools, netiquette,* and *dot-com.* Another new term the Internet has given us is *FAQ,* an abbreviation that means *Frequently Asked Questions.* Many Websites provide an FAQ list where users may find answers to common questions about the content or operation of the Website.

In this activity, you'll go online to an FAQ list at a Website, and you'll use the content of the FAQ list to enhance your understanding of the different types and classes of nouns.

STEP 1 Begin this activity by preparing a noun chart on a separate sheet of paper. Your chart will have two columns and six rows. Label the columns with the noun classes: *Common* and *Proper;* label the rows with the noun types: *Persons, Places, Objects, Qualities, Ideas,* and *Activities.* For this activity, you will complete this chart according to the instructions that begin at Step 4. Your chart should look something like the one below.

Noun Chart

	Common	Proper
Persons	_____	_____
Places	_____	_____
Objects	_____	_____
Qualities	_____	_____
Ideas	_____	_____
Activities	_____	_____

STEP 2   Go to *englishworkshop.glencoe.com,* the address for *The English Workshop* Website, and click on Unit 2. Next click on Getting Connected, and then click on Chapter 3. At the Chapter 3 Getting Connected option, you'll see a list of Websites that include FAQ lists.

STEP 3   The sites cover a wide range of topics, including the Internet Public Library, the Library of Congress, the Environmental Protection Agency (EPA), a seismology laboratory, and the Peace Corps. Select one site that interests you, and click on that link.

STEP 4   Write the site you selected on your Noun Chart sheet.

STEP 5   Make a printout of at least one page of the FAQ list you selected. Working from the printout will help you complete this activity.

STEP 6   As you read over several of the questions and answers on the printout, search for nouns to complete the Noun Chart you created in Step 1. Look for common and proper nouns to complete each row when possible. The suggestions below will help you complete the chart:

a. Circle or highlight the nouns on the printout before you transfer them to the chart. Doing so will prevent you from "losing" the words you want to list.

b. Find two common and two proper nouns for each type of noun.

c. Look for general naming words that identify groups of people for the *Common* column in the row labeled *Persons.* For example, you might find a noun such as *scientists* to place in the *Common* column.

d. Hunt for specific naming words spelled with a capital letter—such as the name of a country, city, or person—to place in the *Proper* column. Initials used to identify an organization, a company, or a government agency, such as the *EPA,* could also be placed in this column.

e. Don't look for abstract nouns to enter into the *Proper* column. We listed *n/a* in the *Proper* column for abstract nouns because they name ideas that don't exist in a physical form.

STEP 7   Proofread the chart when you have completed it. Write your name on your chart and on the printout you used to create it. Turn in both items to your instructor.

Name _____

Class _____ Date _____

PRACTICE 1

Plural Nouns

Instructions: Write the plural form of each of these nouns in the blank.

EXAMPLE: letter _____*letters*_____

1. invoice _____*s*_____
2. business _____*es*_____
3. tax _____*es*_____
4. embargo _____*es*_____
5. menu _____*s*_____
6. virus _____*es*_____
7. plaintiff _____*s*_____
8. proof _____*s*_____
9. woman _____*women*_____
10. bookkeeper _____*s*_____
11. waltz _____*es*_____
12. grandchild _____*ren*_____
13. radio _____*s*_____
14. quiz _____*zes*_____
15. copy _____*ies*_____
16. delay _____*ies s*_____
17. chief _____*s*_____
18. glitch _____*es*_____
19. facility _____*ies*_____
20. veto _____*es*_____
21. wife _____*wives*_____
22. handkerchief _____*s*_____
23. journey _____*s*_____
24. company _____*ies*_____
25. self _____*ves*_____

26. memorandum _____*s*_____
27. basis _____*bases*_____
28. x _____*s*_____
29. crisis _____*crises*_____
30. census _____*es*_____
31. criterion _____*s*_____
32. soliloquy _____*s*_____
33. Hernandez _____*the es*_____
34. stimulus _____*i*_____
35. 1040 _____*s*_____
36. L _____*s*_____
37. rpm _____*s*_____
38. bureau _____*es*_____
39. A _____*s*_____
40. scissors _____*es*_____
41. medium _____*s*_____
42. colloquy _____*s*_____
43. C.P.A. _____*s*_____
44. Jones _____*Joneses*_____
45. Bendix _____*the es*_____
46. formula _____*s*_____
48. Ms. _____*Miss*_____
47. two-by-four _____*s*_____
49. certificate of deposit _____*s*_____
50. Hastings _____*The*_____

Name _____

Class _____ Date _____

PRACTICE 2

Singular and Plural Forms

Instructions: Some of the words listed below are singular, some are plural, and others may be either singular or plural. Put a check mark in the appropriate column to show whether the word is singular or plural, and write the opposite form in the other column. If the word takes the same form in both the singular and the plural, place a check mark in both columns.

	SINGULAR	PLURAL
EXAMPLE: exercise	EX. ✓	exercises
1. spoonful	1. _____	_____
2. analyses	2. _____	_____
3. criterion	3. _____	_____
4. alumnus	4. _____	_____
5. datum	5. _____	_____
6. status	6. _____	_____
7. mother-in-law	7. _____	_____
8. species	8. _____	_____
9. sheep	9. _____	_____
10. syllabi	10 _____	_____
11. appendix	11. _____	_____
12. agenda	12. _____	_____
13. indices	13. _____	_____
14. means	14. _____	_____
15. politics	15. _____	_____

PRACTICE 3

Plural Nouns

Instructions: These paragraphs contain many plural nouns that are spelled incorrectly. Cross out each misspelled noun and write the correct form above it.

ALPSUNDBERG OUTLOOK

                ies   *ys*   *s*

Industrys of all sorts have flourished in the central vallies of the Alpsundberg Mountaines.

                                  es   *es*   *s*

Each year, huge quantities of tomatos, potatoes, and radishs are shipped from the valleys to marketes

                                                     s

across the country. The area is also famous for its fine tobaccoes, which are bought by all the large

                      ies

cigar companys.

                                                                                              ies   *ies*

In addition to these agricultural products, the region has fine facilitys for steel foundrys and

                                                    s   *ies*

for the manufacture of computer componentses and accessorys.

                                                                 s

Analysises of the datas from the latest reports and surveyses confirm that the industries of

                                                    ys

this region should continue to flourish for year's to come.

PRACTICE 4

Singular and Plural Nouns

Instructions: Choose the appropriate verb in each of the sentences. If the subject is singular, use a singular verb. If the subject is plural, use a plural verb. Each pair lists the singular verb first.

EXAMPLE: **Corporate headquarters (is, are) located on Route 72 in Schaumberg.**   EX. _____is_____

1. My belongings (is, are) in my locker.   1. _____

2. The bases for my contention (is, are) beyond dispute.   2. _____

3. (Was, Were) the memoranda left on my desk?   3. _____

4. The alumni (is, are) fully behind the dean.   4. _____

5. What new formulae (was, were) presented by her?   5. _____

6. Parentheses (presents, present) occasional punctuation problems.   6. _____

7. An editor realizes that plot synopses (is, are) important.   7. _____

8. The fathers-in-law (has, have) met for the first time.   8. _____

9. The crisis in her illness (is, are) past.   9. _____

10. The World Series (is, are) on television this evening.   10. _____

11. The crises (has, have) been averted.   11. _____

12. The latest phenomenon in the electronics industry (seems, seem) to involve fiber optics.   12. _____

13. Many handfuls of rice (was, were) thrown at the bride and groom.   13. _____

14. Proper ethics (was, were) the subject of his monthly magazine column.   14. _____

15. What (is, are) the most important criteria in evaluating a résumé?   15. _____

16. Statistics (is, are) my most difficult course this semester.   16. _____

17. The statistics (suggests, suggest) that the demand for healthful convenience foods is increasing.   17. _____

18. Her politics (is, are) much more conservative than her mother's.   18. _____

19. There's an old saying that politics (makes, make) strange bedfellows.   19. _____

20. The economics of his proposal (has, have) not been adequately thought through.   20. _____

Name _____

Class _____ Date _____

PRACTICE 5

Possessive Nouns

Instructions: Below are 20 possessive phrases. Rewrite them in the correct possessive form by eliminating the *of* phrase.

EXAMPLE: **the office of the principal**

1. the books of the student
2. the clothes of the babies
3. the clothes of the baby
4. the ties of the men
5. the ties of the man
6. the wool of the sheep
7. the approval of the boss
8. the statement of the vice presidents
9. the finances of the firm
10. the children of my sister-in-law
11. the policy of FAO Schwarz
12. the piano music of Brahms
13. the editorials of *The New York Times*
14. the association of the teachers
15. the response of Eduardo, my colleague
16. the views of the M.B.A.s
17. the office equipment manufactured by IBM
18. the answer given by Shantay Davis
19. the work done by the volunteers
20. the mistakes made by our employees

EX. ____the principal's office____

1. ____the student's books____
2. ____the babies clothes____
3. ____the baby's clothes____
4. _____
5. _____
6. _____
7. _____
8. _____
9. _____
10. _____
11. _____
12. _____
13. _____
14. _____
15. _____
16. _____
17. _____
18. _____
19. _____
20. _____

Name _____

Class _____ Date _____

PRACTICE 6

Possessive Nouns

Instructions: Each of the following sentences contains one or more possessive nouns from which the apostrophe or 's has been omitted. In the blank, rewrite these possessive nouns correctly.

EXAMPLE: **Phil lost his keycard for the mens room.**   EX. _____men's_____

1. Robertas trouble is that she takes nobodys advice.   1. _____

2. Yesterdays techniques cannot succeed in todays market.   2. _____

3. You have one weeks time to accept or reject this companys offer.   3. _____

4. At last Tuesdays public meeting, the board of directors announced plans for a major expansion.   4. _____

5. The new sales managers plan was discussed at the boards last meeting.   5. _____

6. Mr. Paul, the chairpersons report included details on the proposed employees cafeteria.   6. _____

7. The camp directors view was that drastic changes had to be made in Keenans plan.   7. _____

8. At the meeting it was agreed that new couches should be installed in the womens lounge by years end.   8. _____

9. My sister-in-laws son left college after two years study.   9. _____

10. Frederick the Wises policies are comparable to the fiscal policies of the Farmers National Alliance.   10. _____

11. The account executives convention dealt with the new organizations policies.   11. _____

12. Gomezs and Warners temporary agencies have been rivals for years.   12. _____

13. A committee to support the U.S.s policy in Europe sent a flood of telegrams to Senator Aristophanes office.   13. _____

14. The A.A.A.s vehicle policy is under the I.C.C.s direction.   14. _____

15. Both embassies are only a stones throw from the university.   15. _____

16. We asked Charles opinion, but he refused to discuss Smiths plan.   16. _____

17. Chan and Yehs consulting agency is one of the citys finest firms.   17. _____

18. Rahman and Jones policies are in complete agreement with the district attorneys suggested code of conduct.   18. _____

19. Browns and Whites stores compete in the babies wear line.   19. _____

20. Sanchez and Ruizs store handles a complete line of mens items.   20. _____

PRACTICE 7

Plural and Possessive Nouns

Instructions: Fill in the form of the noun called for in each column—singular possessive, plural, or plural possessive.

SINGULAR	SINGULAR POSSESSIVE	PLURAL	PLURAL POSSESSIVE
EXAMPLE: employee	employee's	employees	employees'
1. book	book's	bookes	'
2. child			
3. tax			
4. Smith & Smith			
5. life			
6. ratio			
7. body			
8. criterion			
9. attorney			
10. businesswoman			
11. radio			
12. memorandum			
13. secretary-treasurer			
14. hero			
15. stockholder			
16. roof			
17. journey			
18. letterhead			
19. committee			
20. county			
21. boss			
22. medium			
23. party			
24. ox			
25. attorney general			

PRACTICE 8

Nouns

Instructions: The following letter contains a number of errors in the use of noun plurals and possessives. Whenever you locate an error, cross it out and write the correct form above it.

SuperSales Company

843 North Highway 29 • Milwaukee, WI 53217

June 3, 20--

Ms. Judy Sunayama
SalesTemps Associates
1049 Kellog Street
Green Bay, WI 54303

Dear Ms. Sunayama:

Thank you for your letter of May 10 asking about the wayes in which we pay our representative's. We are flattered a successful businesswomen would seek advice about our operations.

Each of our salespeoples works on an individual contract, so there are different basises on which each is paid. Our sales representatives' themselves have requested that we keep this information confidential. We would be violating our employee's confidence if we were to divulge the termes of these contractes. We feel that business ethics are involved. Accordingly, it is against our companies policy to give out this information. We are certain you understand our reason's for this position.

May we recommend instead Larry Moses's new book, "Establishing a Sale's Organization." It offers practical suggestion's to solve problemes that arise when launching a new business. You should find its analysises of the various problem's causes and effects useful. Mr. Moses has included the datas (compiled by Ph.D.'s) on which he bases his conclusions. His findings demonstrate, for example, that a businesses' net proceeds is not a meaningful criteria on which to base merit raises. We have found Mr. Moses's study very helpful and think that you will, too.

Please accept our sincere best wish's on your latest venture.

Sincerely,

Gregg Banks, Director of Human Resources

PRACTICE 9

Composition: Using Plural Nouns

Instructions: Compose complete sentences using the plural form of each noun in parentheses.

EXAMPLE: **(tooth)** <u>I have an appointment to have my teeth cleaned.</u> _____

1. (beneficiary) _____

_____

_____

2. (trade-in) _____

_____

_____

3. (half) _____

_____

_____

4. (up and down) _____

_____

_____

5. (datum) _____

_____

_____

Name _____

Class _____ Date _____

PRACTICE 10

Composition: Using Possessive Nouns

Instructions: Compose complete sentences using the possessive form of each noun in parentheses.

EXAMPLE: **(women)** **The women's track team won first place at the conference meet.**

1. (business) _____

_____

_____

2. (politicians)_____

_____

_____

3. (editor in chief)_____

_____

_____

4. (the O'Malleys) _____

_____

_____

5. (two CEOs) _____

_____

_____

Pronouns

CHAPTER 4 PREVIEW

In Chapter 3 you focused on the noun. Now you will study the pronoun, which substitutes for the noun. You will study pronoun usage and learn the cases and types of personal pronouns. As you work with this chapter, you will continue to assess your comprehension with the Programmed Reinforcement sections and the Practices. Finally, you will visit a Website to review English pronouns.

OBJECTIVES

After completing this chapter, you will be able to

- Identify the correct forms of personal pronouns.
- Use correctly the three cases of personal pronouns:
  - The subjective case
  - The possessive case
  - The objective case
- Identify pronouns in terms of person, number, and gender.
- Use compound personal pronouns correctly.
- Recognize other types of pronouns:
  - Demonstrative pronouns
  - Interrogative pronouns
  - Indefinite pronouns
  - Relative pronouns
  - Reciprocal pronouns

Study Plan for Chapter 4

The Study Plan for Chapter 4 offers a set of strategies that will help you learn and review the chapter material.

❶ **Personal Pronouns**: Make a chart with three columns: *Subject, Object,* and *Possessive,* then list the pronouns that go in each column.

❷ **Troublesome Pronouns**: Create flash cards for troublesome pronouns such as *its, whose, that, which,* and *who.* Write the type of pronoun each is and a correct example.

❸ **Written Pronouns**: Use a letter, a memo, or an ad to practice identifying pronouns. Underline each pronoun and identify its form.

❹ **Spoken Pronouns**: Listen carefully to the use of pronouns. Someone may incorrectly say, "*Me* and my wife went shopping." Train yourself to hear such errors.

SECTION A
Pronoun Basics

You will begin your study of pronouns by learning their purpose and basic classifications. This section will summarize the subjective, objective, and possessive pronoun cases. It will also cover compound personal and reflexive pronouns. You will continue with possessives and again examine when and where an apostrophe is necessary.

4.1 The Purpose of Pronouns

In Chapter 1 you learned that pronouns take the place of nouns. Compare the following pairs of sentences:

WITHOUT PRONOUNS	WITH PRONOUNS
1. The **Kona Bottling Company** announced that the **Kona Bottling Company** intends to change the focus of the **Kona Bottling Company's** advertising campaign to increase the sale of **Kona Bottling Company's** products.	1. The **Kona Bottling Company** announced that *it* intends to change the focus of *its* advertising campaign to increase the sale of *its* products.
2. **Ramona** returned to **Ramona's** home to change into **Ramona's** evening clothes because **Ramona** was to be the featured speaker at a banquet given by **Ramona's** company to honor **Ramona**.	2. **Ramona** returned to *her* home to change into *her* evening clothes because *she* was to be the featured speaker at a banquet given by *her* company to honor *her*.

The above sentences show how pronouns (1) reduce sentence length, (2) provide variety, and (3) eliminate awkwardness. This chapter will show you how to use pronouns correctly and effectively.

4.2 Personal Pronouns

The most common pronouns are known as **personal pronouns.** These are used to refer to yourself and to other people. They indicate (1) the person speaking, (2) the person spoken to, or (3) the person or object spoken about. Personal pronouns take different forms depending on how they are used in a sentence. In the sample sentence above, two different pronouns are used as substitutes for Ramona: *she* and *her.*

Characteristics of Personal Pronouns

The following chart summarizes the characteristics of personal pronouns and identifies the correct forms. Refer to the chart as you read the definitions that follow it.

CASE	SUBJECTIVE		OBJECTIVE		POSSESSIVE	
Number	Singular	Plural	Singular	Plural	Singular	Plural
First Person (the one speaking)	I	we	me	us	my mine	our ours
Second Person (the one spoken to)	you	you	you	you	your yours	your yours
Third Person (the one spoken about)						
Masculine Gender	he	they	him	them	his	their theirs
Feminine Gender	she	they	her	them	her hers	their theirs
Neuter Gender	it	they	it	them	its	their theirs

Pronoun Cases

Case shows the relationship between a pronoun and the other words in the sentence. In English there are three cases, or forms:

1. The **subjective case** is used when the pronoun acts as the subject of a verb or as a subject complement.
2. The **objective case** is used when the pronoun serves as the object of a verb, a preposition, or an infinitive.
3. The **possessive** case is used when the pronoun shows possession or ownership.

The form of the pronoun in each case changes depending on person, number, and gender.

Pronoun Person

Person refers to who is speaking. Personal pronouns in the **first person** refer to the speaker. Personal pronouns in the **second person** refer to the person spoken to. Personal pronouns in the **third person** refer to the person or thing spoken about.

Pronoun Number

Number refers to how many persons are speaking or being spoken about. **Singular** pronouns indicate one person or thing; **plural** pronouns indicate more than one.

Pronoun Gender

Gender refers to the sex of the person or thing, which can be **masculine, feminine,** or **neuter.** Only pronouns in the third person show gender.

You have just studied how to form the possessive of nouns in Chapter 3, so let's begin with the possessive case of pronouns.

4.3	**The Possessive Case**

Like nouns in the possessive form, possessive pronouns are used to show ownership, authorship, brand, kind, or origin.

> **Maoko's** presentation skills are excellent.
> *Her* presentation skills are excellent.

> The **corporation's** profits have reached an all-time high.
> *Its* profits have reached an all-time high.

Possessive Forms

As the lists below indicate, most possessive pronouns have two possessive forms. Use *my, your, his, her, its, our,* or *their* when the possessive pronoun comes immediately before the noun it modifies. Use *mine, yours, his, hers, its, ours,* or *theirs* when the possessive form stands apart from the noun to which it refers.

POSSESSIVE PRONOUN BEFORE THE NOUN	POSSESSIVE PRONOUN APART FROM THE NOUN
This is *my* apartment.	This apartment is *mine*.
This is *your* training manual.	This training manual is *yours*.
That is *her* car.	That car is *hers*.
It will be *our* pleasure.	The pleasure will be *ours*.
It is *their* fault.	The fault is *theirs*.

No Apostrophes

Unlike possessive nouns, possessive pronouns have no apostrophes.

CORRECT POSSESSIVE PRONOUNS	INCORRECT POSSESSIVE PRONOUNS
This book is *yours*.	This book is *your's*.
That desk is *hers*.	That desk is *her's*.
The victory was *theirs*.	The victory was *their's*.
The card reached *its* destination.	The card reached *it's* destination.

Its/It's

Don't confuse the possessive pronoun *its* with the contraction for *it is* or *it has*. *Its* is a pronoun. *It's* is a contraction for the words *it is* or *it has*.

The company wanted to increase *its* sales.
(The company wanted to increase the **company's** sales.)

It's not going to be easy to increase sales.
(**It is** not going to be easy to increase sales.)

It's not been easy to increase sales.
(**It has** not been easy to increase sales.)

A Test for *Its/It's*

To determine whether to use *it's* or *its* in a sentence, substitute *it is* or *it has* for the form in question. If either *it is* or *it has* makes sense, use the contraction *it's*. If neither makes sense, use the possessive pronoun *its*.

Punctuation Tip

Possessive or Contraction

Remember, both *his* and *its* are possessive pronouns. Each has three letters. You would never put an apostrophe in *his*, so don't use one with the possessive pronoun *its*.

DECIDE: *Its* raining **or** *It's* raining?

SUBSTITUTE: *It is* raining.
That wording makes sense, so use: *It's* raining.

DECIDE: *Its* been raining all day **or** *It's* been raining all day?

SUBSTITUTE: *It has* been raining all day. That wording makes sense, so use: *It's* been raining all day.

DECIDE: The company postponed *its* picnic because of the rain **or** The company postponed *it's* picnic because of the rain?

SUBSTITUTE: The company postponed *it is* picnic because of the rain. The company postponed *it has* picnic because of the rain. Neither wording makes sense, so use: The company postponed *its* picnic because of the rain.

4.4 The Subjective Case

The **subjective case** is used when the pronoun acts as the subject of the verb.

SINGULAR

I want a raise.
You don't seem to understand.
He was fired.
She was promoted.

PLURAL

We should have asked for a transfer.
You met each other in Nepal.
They transferred to another division.
He and *she* are getting married.

Nouns in Apposition
Section 3.18, on page 83, looks at nouns in apposition and appositives.

■

Nouns and Pronouns in Apposition

When a noun and a pronoun refer to the same thing and are used together so that the noun identifies or clarifies the pronoun, they are *in apposition*. A pronoun and a noun may be used in apposition as the subject of the verb. For example,

> We *panelists* shared the platform.
> We *programmers* met for lunch.

Subject Complements

Subjective case pronouns also are used as subject complements. When a pronoun follows a linking verb and renames the subject, it is called a **subject complement** because it adds to, or *complements,* the information about the subject. Subject complements must be in the subjective case.

As you recall from Chapter 1, the most common linking verb, *to be,* appears in these forms:

> am   are   is   was   were

It also appears in all verb phrases ending in

> be   been   being

Look at these examples:

1. The **winner** *was* **I.**
2. The **person** responsible for the delay *is* **he.**
3. **Was it she** who raised this point?
4. The **people** who are being evasive *are* **they.**
5. The corporate **spies** *were thought to be* **she and I.**

Although it is grammatically correct to use the subjective case after linking verbs such as those listed above, the results may sometimes strike you as awkward or too formal. In such cases, rewrite the sentence and make the subject complement the pronoun. Compare the sentences above to the revised sentences below, which are grammatically correct yet sound less formal.

1. *I was* the *winner.*
2. *He is* the *person* responsible for the delay.
3. *Did she raise* this point?
4. *They* **(people)** *are being* evasive.
5. *She and I were thought to be* the corporate *spies.*

Appositive. The subjective case also is used when the pronoun acts as an appositive after a subject or subject complement.

> **Appositive after subject:** The *panelists,* Jean and *I,* shared the platform.
> **Appositive after subject complement:** The people who joined the panelists for lunch were the *programmers,* Austin and *I.*

EYE CONTACT Looking at someone shows interest in that person, and showing interest in a person is a step toward making a positive impression. In a job interview keep your eyes focused on your interviewer.

4.5 The Objective Case

The objective case of the pronoun is used when the pronoun acts as the object of a verb or a preposition. When the pronoun does the action, use the subjective form; when the pronoun is acted on, use the objective form.

Direct Objects

In the examples below, the pronouns *him, her,* and *me* act as **direct objects** of their respective verbs.

> **He** hit the ball. (subjective)
> The ball hit *him.* (objective)

> **She** congratulated the two men. (subjective)
> The two men thanked *her.* (objective)

> **I** was questioned about the new procedure. (subjective)
> They questioned *me* about the new procedure. (objective)

Grammar Tip

Object Review

Pronouns may serve as direct objects, indirect objects, objects of prepositions, and objects of infinitives.

Objects of Prepositions

In the following sentences, the pronouns are the **objects of prepositions**:

> Mr. Schwartz spoke with *her* about the bill.
> (*Her* is the object of the preposition *with.*)

> Ms. Gastner gave the order to *them.*
> (*Them* is the object of the preposition *to.*)

The last sentence could also be written this way:

> Ms. Gastner gave *them* the order.

Indirect Objects

In the sentence above, *them* is the indirect object of the verb *gave.* An **indirect object** comes before the direct object of the verb and tells to whom or for whom the action is done. For example,

> Mr. Patel sold *them* six cell phones.
> He sent *her* the bill.

In these sentences, *them* and *her* are indirect objects. Like all indirect objects, they can be restated by using the preposition *to:*

> Mr. Patel sold six cell telephones *to them.*
> He sent the bill *to her.*

Objective Case for Appositives

The objective case is used when the pronoun acts as an appositive after a direct object, an indirect object, or an object of a preposition.

I mailed the **representatives**, Luis and *him*, a check. (*Him* is in apposition with *representatives*, the indirect object of the verb *mailed*.)

I met with the **auditors**, Matt Seidel and *her*. (*Her* is in apposition with *auditors*, the object of the preposition *with*.)

Objects of Infinitives

LOOKING AHEAD

Infinitives
You'll learn more about infinitives in Chapter 9.

●

The objective case is also used for pronouns that serve as objects of infinitives. The **infinitive** is *to* plus the form of the verb listed in the dictionary.

I want *to hire her.*
I intend *to help him* with the inventory.
Mr. Stolarski wants *to transfer her and me* to corporate headquarters.

4.6 | A Strategy for Determining Pronoun Case

When a pronoun appears in combination with a noun or another pronoun, shorten the sentence by dropping the noun or other pronoun and the related conjunctions. Whatever case is correct in the shortened sentence will be correct in the completed sentence.

Paralegal Supply and Demand

As paralegals assume duties once performed by lawyers, they are expected to rank among the fastest growing occupations. However, stiff competition will continue as the number of graduates from paralegal programs increases.

SENTENCE 1: My son and (I, me) went to the ball game.

SHORTENED SENTENCE: *I* went to the ball game.

The subjective pronoun case *I* is used as the subject of the verb *went*.

COMPLETED SENTENCE: My son and *I* went to the ball game.

SENTENCE 2: The winners of the contest at the game were my daughter and (I, me).

SHORTENED SENTENCE: The winner of the contest was *I*. (Or, *I* was the winner.)

The subjective pronoun case *I* is used as the subject complement of *winner* after the linking verb *was*.

COMPLETED SENTENCE: The winners of the contest at the game were my daughter and *I*.

SENTENCE 3: My boss gave my daughter and (I, me) free passes to the game.

SHORTENED SENTENCE: My boss gave *me* free passes to the game.

The objective case *me* is used as the indirect object of the verb *gave*.

COMPLETED SENTENCE: My boss gave my daughter and *me* free passes to the game.

SENTENCE 4:   The storm drenched my daughter and (I, me).

SHORTENED SENTENCE: The storm drenched *me*.

The objective case *me* is used as the direct object of the verb *drenched*.

COMPLETED SENTENCE: The storm drenched my daughter and *me*.

4.7 Compound Personal Pronouns

Sometimes *self* or *selves* is added to some personal pronoun forms. The result is known as a **compound personal pronoun.**

myself	yourself	himself, herself, itself
ourselves	yourselves	themselves

Compound personal pronouns may be used as reflexive pronouns, or they may be used to add emphasis.

Reflexive Pronouns

When used as reflexives, compound pronouns indicate that the action described by the verb comes back to or is received by the doer. In other words, the subject of the verb is also the object of the verb.

Grammar Tip

~~Him~~   ~~Them~~
~~**Hisself**~~ and ~~**Theirselves**~~

The terms *hisself* and *theirselves* are nonstandard and are not used in formal English.

Subject   Object
I hurt *myself*.

I, the subject, refers to the same person as *myself*, the object.

Object
Give *yourself* a pat on the back.

Yourself, the object, refers to the same person as the subject, *you* understood.

Subject   Object
Members of Congress recently voted *themselves* a pay increase.

Members of Congress, the subject, refers to the same people as the object, *themselves*.

Emphatic or Intensive Use

Sometimes compound pronouns are used for added emphasis. The compound pronoun emphasizes the subject of the sentence:

I wrote this entire report myself.

President Ramirez herself attended the meeting.

You are going to have to clean up this entire mess yourself.

Salami Attack

A *salami attack* refers to a computer crime that is secretly committed over time in small (bite-sized) increments—or portions the size of salami slices.

Use compound pronouns only as reflexive pronouns or as emphatic words. Do not use compound pronouns as subjects or objects.

WRONG: Damon and *myself* are staying late tonight.
RIGHT: ✔ Damon and *I* are staying late tonight.
I is the correct pronoun to use in the sentence because *I* is part of the compound subject.

WRONG: He sent Teresa and *myself* the attachment.
RIGHT: ✔ He sent Teresa and *me* the attachment.
Me is the correct pronoun to use because *me* is the indirect object.

WRONG: Thousands like *yourself* have become regular listeners of our new morning program.
RIGHT: ✔ Thousands like *you* have become regular listeners of our new morning program.
You is the correct pronoun to use because *you* is the object of the preposition *like*.

Coverage Key

Section		Statement
4.1	➤ The Purpose of Pronouns	➤ S1
4.2	➤ Personal Pronouns	➤ S2, S3, S4, S6, S7
4.3	➤ The Possessive Case	➤ S5, S6, S7, S8
4.4	➤ The Subjective Case	➤ S9, S10, S11, S13, S17, S18, S19, S20, S21, S24, S25, S26
4.5	➤ The Objective Case	➤ S9, S10, S12, S13, S14, S15, S16, S20, S21, S22, S23, S25, S27
4.6	➤ A Strategy for Determining Pronoun Case	➤ S22, S23, S24, S26, S27
4.7	➤ Compound Personal Pronouns	➤ S28, S29, S30, S31, S32

Instructions: Cover the answers in the **Answer** column; then write your answer to the first statement. Uncover the first printed answer and compare your answer to it. If you wrote a correct answer, continue the activity. If you made an error, use the **Coverage Key** to locate the chapter section you need to review. When you are confident that you understand the material, continue with the reinforcement activity.

ANSWER

STATEMENT

S1   A pronoun takes the place of a _____.

A1   noun

S2   Pronouns may be in the first person, the second person, or the third person. *I* is the _____ person; *you* is the _____ person; *they* is the _____ person.

A2   first, second, third

S3   *I* is a pronoun that is in the first person singular. _____ is the first person plural pronoun.

A3   *We*

S4   The second person plural of the singular pronoun *you* is

_____.

A4   *you*

S5   *Company's* is the _____ form of the noun *company*.

A5   possessive

S6   Pronouns also have possessive forms. The first person singular is *my* or *mine*. *You* and *yours* are in the _____ person; _____ , _____ , and _____ are in the third person singular possessive.

A6   second, his, her, its

S7   Possessives of nouns must have an apostrophe or *'s*. This (is, is not) true of pronouns. Underline the correct possessive form: (a) **yours, your's**; (b) **ours, our's**; (c) **theirs, their's**.

A7   is not, (a) **yours**, (b) **ours**, (c) **theirs**

S8 *It's* is a contraction that means _____ or _____. The possessive pronoun is *its*. Underline the correct form: (a) **(It's, Its) time to punch the clock.** (b) **The company and (its, it's) affiliates are amalgamated.** (c) **(It's, Its) been a long time since I last saw you.**

A8 it is, it has,
       a. **It's**, b. **its**, c. **It's**

S9 In addition to the possessive, there are two other cases of pronouns: the _____ and the _____.

A9 subjective, objective

S10 When the pronoun does the action, use the _____ case; when the pronoun is acted on, use the _____ case.

A10 subjective, objective

S11 The pronouns *I, he, she, we,* and *they* are in the _____ _____ case.

A11 subjective

S12 The pronouns *me, him, her, us,* and *them* are in the _____ _____ case.

A12 objective

S13 She is in the _____ case. The objective case of *she* is _____.

A13 subjective, *her*

S14 Objective pronouns are used as objects of infinitives. They also are used as objects of _____ and as objects of _____.

A14 verbs, prepositions

S15 **Give the message to (he, him).** The correct pronoun is _____ _____. It is in the _____ case because it is the object of the _____ **to.**

A15 **him**, objective, preposition

S16 **Give (she, her) the message.** The correct pronoun is _____ _____. It is in the _____ case because it is the indirect object of the verb _____.

A16 **her**, objective, **give**

S17 The subjective pronoun is used in two situations—as the _____ _____ of a sentence or clause and after a(n) _____ verb.

A17 subject, linking

S18 **(I, Me) want to sign the petition.** The correct pronoun is _____ _____. It is in the _____ case because it is the _____ of the sentence.

A18 **I**, subjective, subject

S19 It was (they, them) who signed the petition. The correct pronoun is
_____. It is in the _____
case because it comes after the linking verb _____.

A19 they, subjective, **was**

S20 To be grammatically correct, you should not say *It is me* because *me* is
in the _____ case. You should say *It is I* because
the subjective case is needed after the _____ verb
_____.

A20 objective, linking, *is*

S21 Underline the correct form in each sentence. In the blank, write the
case. a. **I thought it was (she, her) who signed the petition.** _____
_____ b. **The petition was signed by (he, him)
and (I, me).** _____.

A21 a. <u>she</u>, subjective
b. <u>him</u>, <u>me</u>, objective

S22 Underline the words that may be left out in this sentence to
determine more easily which pronoun to use: **The donations were
accepted by Tara and (me, I).** Underline twice the correct pronoun.

A22 <u>Tara and</u>, <u>me</u>

S23 Underline the correct pronoun. **Our department was represented by
Josef and (she, her).** Give the case and reason.
Case: _____
Reason: _____

A23 <u>her</u>, objective case, object of
preposition **by**

S24 Underline the correct pronoun. **The newest employees are Aloka
and (me, I).** Give the case and reason.
Case: _____
Reason: _____

A24 <u>I</u>, subjective case, after linking
verb **are**

S25 Pronouns may be used in apposition to nouns in a sentence. When a
pronoun is used in apposition as a subject or is placed in apposition
to a subject or subject complement, it should be in the (subjective,
objective) case. When a pronoun is in apposition to a direct object, an
indirect object, or an object of a preposition, it should be in the
(subjective, objective) case.

A25 subjective, objective

S26 Underline the correct pronoun in each sentence. Give the case and
reason.
a. **(We, Us) administrative assistants are underpaid.**
Case: _____
Reason: _____
b. **The three supervisors, Marva, Hector, and (I, me), discussed
the problem yesterday.**
Case: _____
Reason: _____

A26 (a.) <u>We</u>, subjective case, used in
apposition as subject
(b.) <u>I</u>, subjective case, used in
apposition to subject

S27 Underline the correct pronoun in each sentence. Give the case and reason.

a. **I disagree with the other supervisors, Marva and (he, him), about what to do.**

Case: _____

Reason: _____

b. **I will see the other supervisors, Hector and (she, her), again today.**

Case: _____

Reason: _____

A27 (a.) **him**, objective case, in apposition to **supervisors** as the object of the preposition **with**

(b.) **her**, objective case, in apposition to **supervisors** as direct object of verb **will see**

S28 Sometimes *self* or *selves* is added to some forms of the personal pronoun to form _____ personal pronouns.

A28 compound

S29 Compound personal pronouns do two things. When they show that the subject of the verb is also its object, they are used as _____ _____ pronouns.

A29 reflexive

S30 Fill in the correct reflexive pronouns: a. **She made** _____ _____ **ill.** b. **He gave** _____ **a bonus.**

A30 a. **herself**
b. **himself**

S31 Sometimes compound personal pronouns are used to provide additional stress or emphasis. Which of the following sentences illustrate(s) this use?

a. **He himself will ship the packages.**
b. **He shipped the packages himself.**
c. **He shipped the packages to himself.**

A31 a., b.

S32 Compound personal pronouns should not be used when the sentence calls for a pronoun in the subjective or objective case. Which of the following sentences is/are correct?

a. **I want to congratulate yourself on a job well done.**
b. **Congratulate yourself on a job well done.**
c. **My boss and myself attended the conference.**
d. **I attended the conference myself.**

A32 b., d.

Other Types of Pronouns

In this section you will expand your knowledge of pronouns by examining demonstrative, interrogative, indefinite, relative, and reciprocal pronouns. The apostrophe plays no role here, except with the confused pair *whose/who's*.

4.8 Demonstrative Pronouns

Pronouns that are used to point out definite persons, places, or things are known as **demonstrative pronouns.** The two demonstrative pronouns are *this* and *that.* The plural of *this* is *these;* the plural of *that* is *those.*

Singular Demonstrative Pronouns
This is my desk.
That is your desk.

Plural Demonstrative Pronouns
These are my books.
Those are your books.

4.9 Interrogative Pronouns

The term *interrogative* means "questioning." **Interrogative pronouns** are pronouns that are used in asking questions. The interrogative pronouns are *who, whose, whom, which,* and *what.* Like other pronouns, they act as subjects and objects within their sentences.

Who is the new supervisor of your department?
Whose coat is this?
With *whom* do you wish to speak?
Which of these coats is yours?
What did you say?

What asks for general information concerning a person, thing, statement, and so forth. *Which* identifies the person or thing being referred to.

What is your opinion?
What can we do?
Which car is yours?
Which applicants do you wish to interview?

LOOKING AHEAD

Demonstrative Pronouns
You'll explore the use of demonstrative pronouns in Chapter 10.

●

LOOKING AHEAD

Who/Whom
You will learn how to choose between who *and* whom *in the next chapter.*

●

Who's/Whose?

Whose and *who's* are sometimes confused with each other. Like the apostrophe in *it's,* the apostrophe in *who's* indicates the contraction of two words, *who + is* or *who + has.*

> *Who's* going to the luncheon? (*Who is* going to the luncheon?)
> *Who's* made the greatest improvement this semester? (*Who has* made the greatest improvement this semester?)

Whose, without the apostrophe, is the *possessive pronoun.* Possessive pronouns do not have apostrophes (*yours, his, hers, its, ours, theirs*).

> *Whose* turn is it to walk the dog?
> I don't know *whose* pen I have.

Grammar Tip

Who's/Whose?

Substitute *who is* or *who has* whenever you need to determine whether to use *who's* or *whose.* If either *who is* or *who has* makes sense in your sentence, use the contraction *who's.* If neither makes sense, use the possessive pronoun *whose.*

LOOKING AHEAD

Indefinite Pronouns as Antecedents
When you read about antecedents in the next chapter, you'll learn more about the indefinite pronouns listed here.

●

4.10 Indefinite Pronouns

A large number of pronouns do not refer to particular persons, places, or things. For this reason they are known as **indefinite pronouns**. Here are the most common ones:

all	either	nothing
another	everybody	one
any	everyone	one another
anybody	everything	ones
anyone	few	other
anything	many	others
both	neither	several
each	nobody	some
each one	none	someone
each other	no one	something

4.11 Relative Pronouns

In Chapter 2 you learned the definition of a *clause*—a group of words that has both a subject and a verb. There are two types of clauses: *independent clauses* can stand by themselves as sentences, *dependent,* or *subordinating clauses* cannot stand by themselves as separate sentences.

As you saw in Chapter 1, many words (e.g., *since, although, when, because*) can be used to subordinate one clause to another. The pronouns *who, whom, which,* and *that* also can relate one clause to another part of the sentence. These pronouns are called **relative pronouns** and the subordinating, or dependent, clauses they introduce are known as **relative clauses.** Look at the following examples. The bold words relate the italicized parts to the rest of the sentence.

Who, Whom, Which, and *That*

When should you use *who, whom, which,* or *that?*

Who or *whom* always refers to a person.

> She is the woman **who** *will be our next president.*
> The woman **to whom** *you were speaking* will be our next president.

Which always refers to an animal or inanimate object, never to a person.

> The book, **which** *was one of my favorites,* never made the best-seller list.
> Economics is the subject **that** *I like best.*

That also refers to animals and inanimate objects. It may refer to people when they are spoken of as a class or type. Individual people are always referred to as *who* or *whom.*

> Mr. Olenik captured the dog **that** *was menacing the children.*
> Mr. Klein is not the type of supervisor **that** *our department needs.*

Grammar Tip

Remembering Relative Pronouns

Remember: **Who** and **whom** always refer to people. **Which** refers only to inanimate objects or animals. **That** is used for people when spoken of as a type or class, But **who** and **whom** are used for individual people.

4.12 Reciprocal Pronouns

Reciprocal pronouns indicate a mutual relationship between people or things. The two reciprocal pronouns are *each other* and *one another.*

Each other refers only to two persons or things. *One another* always refers to three or more persons or things.

> The two visitors knew *each other.*
> The three visitors knew *one another.*

SECTION B: PROGRAMMED REINFORCEMENT

Coverage Key

Section		Statement
4.8	➤ Demonstrative Pronouns	➤ S33
4.9	➤ Interrogative Pronouns	➤ S34, S35, S36
4.10	➤ Indefinite Pronouns	➤ S37
4.11	➤ Relative Pronouns	➤ S38, S39
4.12	➤ Reciprocal Pronouns	➤ S40

Instructions: Cover the answers in the **Answer** column; then write your answer to the first statement. Uncover the first printed answer and compare your answer to it. If you wrote a correct answer, continue the activity. If you made an error, use the **Coverage Key** to locate the chapter section you need to review. When you are confident that you understand the material, continue with the reinforcement activity.

ANSWER	STATEMENT
	S33 *This* and *that* are called *demonstrative pronouns*. The plural of *this* is _____; the plural of *that* is _____.
A33 *these, those*	**S34** The pronouns *who, whose, whom, which,* and *what* are interrogative pronouns. They are used to _____.
A34 ask questions	**S35** You will never confuse *who's* and *whose* if you remember that *who's* is a contraction of the words _____.
A35 *who is* or *who has*	**S36** Underline the correct words: **Tell me (whose, who's) dictation this is, and I'll tell you (whose, who's) responsible for the confusion.**
A36 whose, who's	**S37** Underline the indefinite pronouns in the following list: **both, each, whose, either, few, mine, nobody, your, one, several, what.**
A37 both, each, either, few, nobody, one, several	**S38** Underline the relative pronoun in the following sentence and underline twice the word it relates to. a. **Here is the elevator that needs to be repaired.** b. **I spoke with the person who repaired the copier.**
A38 a. that, elevator b. who, person	**S39** *Who* is a relative pronoun that refers to a person. _____ and _____ are relative pronouns that refer to things.
A39 *Which, that*	**S40** *Each other* and *one another* are known as reciprocal pronouns. *Each other* refers to _____ people or things; *one another* refers to _____ or more.
A40 two, three	

CHAPTER 4 SUMMARY

In this chapter you learned the correct forms and uses of various types of pronouns. You discovered that the most common pronouns are personal pronouns, which have three cases: the subjective, the objective, and the possessive. You learned how to identify pronouns in terms of person, number, and gender, and how and when to use compound personal pronouns. Finally, you learned to recognize and use demonstrative, interrogative, indefinite, relative, and reciprocal pronouns.

Getting Connected

FINDING PRONOUNS AT YOUR FINGERTIPS

GOAL: The Internet puts the world at your fingertips—virtually speaking at least. The Internet never closes, which makes it an ideal resource for gathering information for school reports, work projects, or your own personal enrichment. Suppose you want to find out who invented the windshield wiper (Mary Anderson, in 1903), where the expression "the real McCoy" comes from (the name of the man who invented a lubricator for steam engines), or who invented the microwave oven (Percy Spencer). With access to the Internet, that kind of information is just a few mouse clicks away.

In this activity, you'll go online to a Website containing information about inventors. You'll locate information about an inventor of your choice and use that information to demonstrate your understanding of the pronouns presented in this chapter.

STEP 1 Go to *englishworkshop.glencoe.com,* the address for *The English Workshop* Website, and click on Unit 2. Next click on Getting Connected, and then click on Chapter 4. At the Chapter 4 Getting Connected option, you'll see a list of Websites that include information about inventors. Begin this activity by selecting one of the sites and clicking on it.

STEP 2 The general information featured at the Websites listed for this activity will be of the same nature, but it will probably be organized differently at each site. Determine how the information about inventors is organized at the Website you selected. Is it organized by categories of inventors (for example, African American inventors, European inventors, or female inventors)? by the names of inventors (for example, Mary Anderson, Elijah McCoy, or Percy Spencer)? or by types of inventions (for example, windshield wiper, engine lubricant, or microwave oven)?

STEP 3 Select the category or index that will lead you to an inventor you would like to learn more about. Once you find the information, read it.

STEP 4   You will need a printout of the material about the inventor to complete this activity. Make a printout of at least one page.

STEP 5   Use the printout to search for at least five types of pronouns listed in **a.** through **g.** below. Circle or highlight each pronoun as you come to it. In the margin of the printout, identify the type of pronoun each is and, when needed, its function (for example, *Subjective pronoun that is a subject* or *Subjective pronoun that is a subject complement*).

a. Subjective pronoun functioning as the subject of a verb, a subject complement after a linking verb, or an appositive.
b. Objective pronoun functioning as a direct object, an indirect object, or the object of a preposition.
c. Compound personal pronoun used reflexively or emphatically.
d. Demonstrative pronoun—*this, that, these,* or *those*—located at the beginning of a sentence and followed by a form of the verb *to be.*
e. Interrogative pronoun. (Be careful not to confuse *whose* for *who's.*)
f. Indefinite pronoun.
g. Reciprocal pronoun.

STEP 6   Conduct a special search for relative pronouns that introduce relative clauses. When you find a relative pronoun, circle it and underline the relative clause it introduces. If you cannot locate a relative pronoun and a relative clause in the material you selected, create one based on the information you've learned about the inventor. For example, a biographical entry about Percy Spencer, the inventor of the microwave oven, includes the fact that he never graduated from grammar school. That information can be used to create a sentence about Spencer using a relative clause:

> *Percy Spencer,* **who never graduated from grammar school,** *invented the microwave oven.*

STEP 7   After you've completed this activity, write your name on the front of your printout, and turn it in to your instructor.

PRACTICE 1

Personal Pronouns

Instructions: Fill in the missing pronouns in the following chart.

CASE	SUBJECTIVE		OBJECTIVE		POSSESSIVE	
NUMBER	**SINGULAR**	**PLURAL**	**SINGULAR**	**PLURAL**	**SINGULAR**	**PLURAL**
First Person (the one speaking)	I	_we_	_me_	_us_	my / _mine_	_our_ / ours
Second Person (the one spoken to)	_you_	_you_	you	_you_	your / _yours_	_yours_ / _yours_
Third Person (the one spoken about)						
Masculine Gender	_he_	they	_him_	_them_	_his_	_their_ / _theirs_
Feminine Gender	_she_	____	_her_	____	_her_ / _hers_	their / _theirs_
Neuter Gender	_it_	____	_it_	____	_its_	their / _theirs_

PRACTICE 2

Possessive Pronouns

Instructions: In the blank, write the correct pronoun.

EXAMPLE: **The next move is (yours, your's).** — EX. __**yours**__

1. Virtue is (its, it's) own reward. — 1. _it's_
2. The package on top is (ours, our's). — 2. _our's_
3. The next car the attendant brings should be (my, mine). — 3. _mine_
4. (His, His's) was the most impressive presentation of the afternoon. — 4. _His_
5. Sincerely (yours, your's). — 5. _yours_
6. I'm certain the contract will be (theirs, there's). — 6. _theirs_
7. That should be (my, mine) car now. — 7. _my_
8. This report of (hers, her's) analyzes (there, their) marketing strategy. — 8. _hers_
9. (Its, It's) not clear whether the fruit is (yours, your's) or (theirs, their's). — 9. _It's_
10. Tell me (whose, who's) analysis is more accurate, mine or (hers, her's). — 10. _____

PRACTICE 3

Possessive Nouns and Pronouns

Instructions: This e-mail message gives you practice in the proper use of possessive nouns and pronouns. Wherever a possessive noun or pronoun is spelled wrong, cross it out and write the correct form above it.

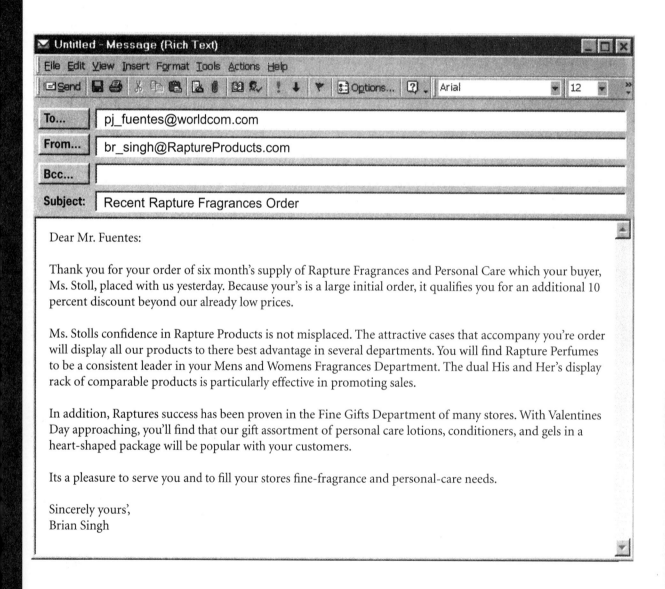

Dear Mr. Fuentes:

Thank you for your order of six month's supply of Rapture Fragrances and Personal Care which your buyer, Ms. Stoll, placed with us yesterday. Because your's is a large initial order, it qualifies you for an additional 10 percent discount beyond our already low prices.

Ms. Stolls confidence in Rapture Products is not misplaced. The attractive cases that accompany you're order will display all our products to there best advantage in several departments. You will find Rapture Perfumes to be a consistent leader in your Mens and Womens Fragrances Department. The dual His and Her's display rack of comparable products is particularly effective in promoting sales.

In addition, Raptures success has been proven in the Fine Gifts Department of many stores. With Valentines Day approaching, you'll find that our gift assortment of personal care lotions, conditioners, and gels in a heart-shaped package will be popular with your customers.

Its a pleasure to serve you and to fill your stores fine-fragrance and personal-care needs.

Sincerely yours',
Brian Singh

[handwritten notes in margin: "help? ⟶ p.1060", "action verb objective pro.", "to be verb subjective pro."]

PRACTICE 4

Subjective and Objective Case Pronouns

Instructions: In the blank, write the correct pronoun.

EXAMPLE: **(She, Her)** takes the subway to work.   EX. _____ **She** _____

1. (He, Him) was not allowed to leave.   1. ____ He ____

2. It is (I, me).   2. ____ I ____

3. She wanted to hire (he, him) for the job.   3. ____ She ____

4. Contrary to our advice, (they, them) bought the stock.   4. ____ they ____

5. Luis and (I, me) submitted separate requests.   5. ____ I ____

6. Initially (she, her) was uncertain of her duties.   6. ____ she ____

7. The message was sent by (she, her).   7. ____ her ____

8. I thought it was (they, them).   8. ____ they ____

9. Permit (I, me) to raise an objection.   9. ____ me ____

10. Could it have been (we, us) who were responsible?   10. ____ we ____

11. Mr. Hainski walked by (they, them) without recognizing (they, them)   11. ____ them ____

12. The one to be promoted should have been (he, him).   12. ____ he ____

13. Only Alana and (I, me) were on duty then.   13. ____ I ____

14. Congratulations are due to (he, him).   14. ____ him ____

15. The last person to leave was (she, her).   15. _____

16. The two people, (he, him) and Ms. Ortiz, are new.   16. _____

17. I have given Mr. Shin and (she, her) my answer.   17. _____

18. The accountants, Mr. Abrahams and (she, her), calculated the costs.   18. ____ She ____

19. Alfredo was as much upset by Mr. Marquand's recommendations as (I, me) was.   19. _____

20. Jean stood between (I, me) and the door.   20. _____

21. Separate requests were submitted by Luis and (I, me).   21. ____ me ____

22. If it were my decision, (I, me) would say that (we, us) should sue (they, them).   22. _____

23. If it was (he, him) who noticed the error, (he, him) should be rewarded.   23. _____

24. Promotions were given to Ms. Ortiz and (he, him).   24. _____

25. Ms. Ortiz and (he, him) were given promotions.   25. _____

Chapter 4 Practices

Class _____ Date _____

PRACTICE 5

Reflexive, Subjective and Objective Pronouns

Instructions: In the blank, write the correct pronoun.

EXAMPLE: **The members voted (themself, themselves) a pay increase.**   EX. ___themselves___

1. (You, Yourself) need time to think.   1._____

2. Give (you, yourself) time to think.   2._____

3. They would not allow (she, her) to leave.   3._____

4. Mr. Robinson (himself, hisself) will be there.   4._____

5. My spouse and (I, myself) want to thank you.   5._____

6. They assumed all responsibility (theirselves, themselves).   6._____

7. Selina stared at (he, him) as he entered the room.   7._____

8. Ouch! I just hurt (me, myself).   8._____

9. Ouch! You just hurt (me, myself).   9._____

10. The director told (we, us) that she had reached a decision.   10._____

11. Mr. Gustard and (I, myself) plan to attend.   11._____

12. Send the completed forms to Ms. Weng or (me, myself).   12._____

13. The idea came to (they, them) almost simultaneously.   13._____

14. He has no one to blame but (hisself, himself).   14._____

15. You will have to represent us (yourself, yourselve).   15._____

16. Mr. Marquand's recommendations upset Alfredo as much as they did (I, me).   16._____

17. The order (it's self, itself) was shipped Tuesday.   17._____

18. Ms. Bates promised to recommend (we, us) trainees for a bonus.   18._____

19. We want to get (ourselfs, ourselves) out of this difficulty.   19._____

20. Mr. McGuire spoke with their representatives, Mr. Ree and (she, her).   20._____

21. You should all congratulate (yourself, yourselves).   21._____

22. No one but Ming and (I, me) was on duty when the fire broke out.   22._____

23. Mail all inquiries to Mr. Carillo or (me, myself).   23._____

24. Everyone except Vardan and (I, me) seems to approve of the new system.   24._____

25. The records were examined by the accountants, Anya, Al, and (she, her).   25._____

PRACTICE 6

Other Types of Pronouns

Instructions: In the blank, write the correct pronoun.

EXAMPLE: **Professor Lauer is the kind of teacher (that, whom) all students deserve.**   EX. _____**that**_____

1. (Who's, Whose) car is this?   1._____

2. (Who's, Whose) going to represent us?   2._____

3. She and I are acquainted with (each other, one another).   3._____

4. (Which, What) is your name?   4._____

5. (Which, What) name tag is yours?   5._____

6. The champion and the challenger had great respect for (each other's, one another's) abilities.   6._____

7. (This, These) newspapers should be thrown away.   7._____

8. (That, Those) stack of newspapers should be thrown away.   8._____

9. You are the kind of court reporter (that, which) we need to attract.   9._____

10. (Whose, Who's) terminal needs to be repaired?   10._____

11. (Whose, Who's) repairing the terminal?   11._____

12. Where does (these, those, this) stack of files belong?   12._____

13. This is the judge (which, whom) I told you about.   13._____

14. The committee members spoke with (one another, each other) until it was time to convene.   14._____

15. (What, Which) are your views on this matter?   15._____

16. (What, Which) of these three positions best represents your views on this matter?   16._____

17. A dog (who, that) does not require much exercise would be an appropriate pet for him.   17._____

18. (Whose, What, Which) briefcase is this, his or hers?   18._____

19. Ms. DeStephano spent the weekend comparing the four proposals with (one another, each other).   19._____

20. He is the person (that, whom) I recommend.   20._____

Name _____

Class _____ Date _____

PRACTICE 7

Composition: Using Pronouns

Instructions: Supply an appropriate pronoun where shown by the parentheses. Then turn these sentence starters into complete sentences.

EXAMPLE: **Please give (** me **)** __a hand with this carton._____

1. My assistant and (   ) _____

2. The two trainees, Donna and (   ) _____

3. Was it (   ) _____

4. Lanny gave the clients, Ms. Cooper and (   ) _____

5. Shirin sent (   ) _____

6. Just between you and (   ) _____

7. Ask either (   ) or (   ) _____

8. Except for Gino and (   ), _____

9. It was (   ) _____

10. An experienced person like (   ) _____

11. Do (   ) _____

12. This report of (   ) _____

13. If (   ) _____

14. It is (   ) opinion that _____

15. (   ) student _____

The Use of Pronouns

CHAPTER 5 PREVIEW

In Chapter 4 you looked at the different types and cases of pronouns. In this chapter you will select the correct pronoun in various situations. You will also learn about agreement between pronouns and their antecedents and about principles of pronoun usage. As you work with this chapter, you will assess your knowledge in the Programmed Reinforcement sections and the Practices. Finally, you will access the navigation options of a newspaper Website to find material that will help you review pronoun usage.

OBJECTIVES

After completing this chapter, you will be able to

- Identify the antecedent of a pronoun.
- Make pronouns agree with their antecedents in number and gender.
- Solve common pronoun usage problems.
- Use correctly *who* (or *whoever*) and *whom* (or *whomever*).
- Determine whether to use *we* or *us* directly before a noun.
- Determine whether to use the subjective or objective case after *than* or *as*.
- Use the correct pronoun after a preposition.
- Differentiate between the one-word and two-word versions of words such as *everyone, anyone,* and *someone.*
- Avoid using redundant pronouns.

Study Plan for Chapter 5

The Study Plan for Chapter 5 offers a set of strategies that will help you learn and review the chapter material.

❶ **Pronoun and Antecedent Agreement**: Underline the pronouns in a newspaper article, and then locate the antecedent for each pronoun you underlined. Compare each pronoun with its antecedent to see if it agrees in number and gender.

❷ **Spoken Errors**: Pay attention to your speech and the speech of others. Try to avoid common gender pronouns in speech and in writing. Learn to recognize others' errors so that you will not repeat them.

❸ **Explanatory Phrases**: Make a list of the explanatory phrases that mislead readers into using the wrong pronouns in sentences. Memorize the list and see if you can find examples of those phrases in reading material at school or work. Use the list with Practice 4.

❹ ***Who/Whom* Strategies**: Write a summary of each substitution strategy from Section 5.9 on a separate index card. Include on each card at least one complete example of the strategy. Use the cards to help you with Practice 5.

In this section you will learn how pronouns and antecedents agree in number and gender. You will also study strategies for solving various pronoun usage problems.

5.1 Pronouns and Antecedents

When a pronoun is used in place of a noun, the noun that it replaces is called the **antecedent** of that pronoun. *Cede* means "to go" and *ante* means "before." An antecedent goes *before* the pronoun.

Walter Kosaburo says ***he*** is tired.

Judith Leverenz was unable to complete ***her*** assignment.

Our salespeople believe ***they*** cannot meet the quota.

Because a pronoun renames, or stands in place of, its antecedent, it should be as similar to the antecedent as possible. This means that the pronoun should agree with its antecedent in both number and gender. In the sentences above, for example, *Walter Kosaburo* calls for the masculine singular pronoun *he*, *Judith Leverenz* calls for the feminine singular pronoun *her*, and *salespeople* requires the plural pronoun *they*.

In the earlier sentences the antecedent and the correct pronoun were obvious. Sometimes, however, determining the antecedent and the correct pronoun can be a little more complicated. The following guidelines will help you make the right choices.

5.2 Two Antecedents With *And*

Always use a plural pronoun to represent two or more antecedents connected by *and*.

Jack and *Jill* are on ***their*** way up the hill.

Ms. Barrios and *Mr. O'Leary* deserve whatever awards ***they*** receive.

Ms. Barrios and *Mr. O'Leary* deserve whatever awards are presented to ***them***.

Ms. Barrios and *Mr. O'Leary* deserve ***their*** awards.

Pro Bono

The American Bar Association (ABA) reports that most paralegals offer *pro bono*, or unpaid, assistance in the area of family law. The adjective *pro bono* comes from Latin, meaning "for the public good."

Now look at this sentence:

> The secretary and treasurer submitted (his, her, their) reports.

Any of these pronouns could be correct. If the offices of secretary and treasurer are held by only one person, *his* or *her* is correct. If the two offices are held by two different persons, then *their* is correct. However, if two people hold the two offices, the sentence should be rewritten:

> The **secretary** and the **treasurer** submitted **their** reports.

The second *the* clearly tells the reader that *two* officers are involved.

5.3 Two Antecedents With *Or/Nor*

When two antecedents are connected by *or* or *nor*, use a singular pronoun if both antecedents are singular. Use a plural pronoun if both antecedents are plural.

> **Either Ms. Pulaski** or **Ms. Velez** will get **her** wish.

> **Neither** the **Rudmans** nor the **Changs** have paid **their** dues.

When *or* or *nor* joins a singular noun with a plural noun, the pronoun should agree in number with the closer antecedent. To avoid awkward sentences in such constructions, always place the plural antecedent last.

Flashback

Indefinite Pronouns
Section 4.10, on page 114,
includes a list of common
indefinite pronouns.

■

AWKWARD	BETTER
Neither the employees nor the owner knew what *she* was doing.	Neither the owner nor the employees knew what *they* were doing.

5.4 Indefinite Pronouns as Antecedents

In Chapter 4 you looked at a list of indefinite pronouns, or pronouns that do not refer to particular persons, places, or things. Now you will learn how to work with indefinite pronouns when they act as antecedents for other pronouns.

Singular Indefinite Pronouns

Some indefinite pronouns are always singular. They include:

anybody	everybody	many a(n)
anyone	somebody	nobody
each	someone	no one

(handwritten annotations:) Everyone, something, either / everything, one, neither / every, anything, nothing / another, anyone / None, some / singular or plural

When any one of these pronouns is used as an antecedent, it requires a singular pronoun.

The sergeant asked the women for a volunteer, but *no one* raised *her* hand.

Nobody was eager to risk *his* or *her* life.

Many a man has placed *his* confidence in our product.

We have selected *each* of the women on the basis of what *she* will contribute to the company.

Grammar Tip

Pronoun Number and Prepositional Phrases

When determining the number of a pronoun, ignore prepositional phrases that follow antecedents.

Prepositional Phrases Between Pronouns and Antecedents. Prepositional phrases should be ignored in determining the correct pronoun to use with an antecedent. The prepositional phrase *of the women* in the last sentence does not change the requirement that the singular pronoun *she* be used with the singular antecedent *each*. In the sentences below each prepositional phrase ends in a plural noun, but the pronoun choice is based on the antecedent.

Each of our competitors has reduced *its* inventory.

At the Girl Scout banquet last night, *each* of the fathers received a special award from *his* daughter.

Plural Indefinite Pronouns

Some indefinite pronouns are always plural. They include:

both	many	others
few	several	(All) *singular or plural*

LOOKING AHEAD

Indefinite Pronouns
In Chapter 8 you'll learn how to make verbs agree with indefinite pronouns.

●

When any one of these pronouns is used as an antecedent, it requires a plural pronoun.

Several of the men raised *their* hands; *others* had *their* hands raised for *them*.

Few were eager to risk *their* lives.

Many women have placed *their* confidence in our product.

Both women were selected on the basis of what *they* will contribute to the company.

5.5 The Problem With Common Gender Pronouns

Most problems in choosing pronouns involve number, but sometimes you may have difficulty determining which gender to use.
Which pronoun should you use in the following sentence?

Everyone in the class did (his, her, their) homework.

Everyone in the class did their homework is incorrect because *everyone* is singular. But is *everyone* masculine or feminine? It could be either. In the past most writers solved the problem of how to refer to an antecedent of indefinite sex by using a masculine pronoun, which they considered the **common gender pronoun**. Sentences that referred to both females and males and sentences that included singular indefinite pronouns were automatically written with male pronouns. Look at the following sentences written with common gender pronouns:

Everyone in the class did ***his*** homework.

Not a ***person*** left ***his*** seat before the final curtain.

Someone left ***his*** headlights on.

Strategies for Avoiding Common Gender Pronouns

Today most writers recognize that it is insensitive to arbitrarily use the masculine pronoun to refer to both men and women and that common gender pronouns are inherently sexist. Thus, the sensitive writer avoids common gender pronouns. Here are some strategies for avoiding the common gender pronoun.

<u>Common Gender:</u> *Everyone* in the class did ***his*** homework.

<u>Strategy 1:</u>   Make both the antecedent and the pronoun plural.

All the students in the class did ***their*** homework.

<u>Strategy 2:</u>   Substitute the definite article *the* for the pronoun.

Everyone in the class did *the* homework.

<u>Strategy 3:</u>   Use both masculine and feminine singular pronouns that agree with the singular *everyone*.

Everyone in the class did ***his*** or ***her*** homework.

Strategy 3 is frequently used for individual sentences, but it can become awkward if used repeatedly in longer passages.

Grammar Tip

Everyone and Their Don't Mix

Do not use the plural pronoun *their* with the singular antecedent *everyone*.

You may use any of these strategies to avoid using common gender pronouns. Remember, however, that it is always grammatically incorrect to use a plural pronoun with a singular antecedent.

WRONG:

Everyone in the class did ***their*** homework.

Feminine Pronouns Only? If the context of a sentence clearly indicates that the pronoun refers to a *feminine* antecedent, use a *feminine* pronoun.

Neither of the waitresses does ***her*** job well.

Each parolee from the Women's House of Detention must meet with ***her*** parole officer once a week.

Male and Female Gender. If the sentence contains both a masculine and a feminine antecedent, then use both the masculine and feminine pronouns.

Each man and woman in the audience enthusiastically showed ***his*** or ***her*** approval.

The ***host*** or ***hostess*** should always personally greet ***his*** or ***her*** guests.

If the resulting sentence is awkward, rewrite it.

All the men and women in the audience enthusiastically showed ***their*** approval.
or
Members of the audience enthusiastically showed ***their*** approval.
or
Enthusiastic approval was shown by *every* man and woman in the audience.

The host or hostess should personally greet guests.
or
Guests should be personally greeted by the host or hostess.

5.6 Explanatory Phrases

When determining the correct pronoun to use in a sentence, ignore explanatory phrases that fall between the pronoun and its antecedent. Explanatory phrases include *as well as, in addition to, and not, together with, accompanied by, rather than,* and *so forth.*

WRONG:

John, as well as other members of the department, has volunteered *their* services.

RIGHT:

✔ *John,* as well as other members of the department, has volunteered **his** services.

WRONG:

Ms. Yeh, rather than Mr. Basha, will give us *their* opinion of the proposal by Friday.

RIGHT:

✔ *Ms. Yeh,* rather than Mr. Basha, will give us **her** opinion of the proposal by Friday.

WRONG:

Warren, in addition to his sisters, has voiced *their* support for our plan.

RIGHT:

✔ *Warren,* in addition to his sisters, has voiced **his** support for our plan.

5.7 Collective Antecedents

Collective nouns such as *committee, jury, faculty, class, crowd,* and *army* may be either singular or plural depending on their meaning in a sentence. Each of these words refers to a group of people. When you are referring to that group as a single unit, use a singular pronoun.

The **committee** held **its** meeting.

The **class** had **its** picture taken.

When you refer to the individuals that make up the group, however, use a plural pronoun.

The **committee** were called at **their** homes one at a time.

The **jury** brought in **their** split verdict.

If such sentences seem awkward, rewrite them with plural nouns.

The **committee members** were called at **their** homes one at a time.

The **members of the jury** brought in **their** split verdict.

Company names are generally thought of as collective nouns, and as such are usually considered singular.

Whitney's is having **its** biggest automotive department sale ever.

Anderson Consulting offers summer seminars in writing to **its** staff accountants.

Because a company is made up of individuals, a writer could be referring to those individuals when he or she uses a company's name.

I called **Shoe World** to find out if **they** were accepting applications.

In this sentence a singular pronoun sounds awkward, so the plural *they* is preferable. Usually, however, company names are considered singular and require singular verbs and pronouns for grammatical correctness.

Shoe World is having **its** biggest storewide sale in years.

Ben & Jerry's Homemade, Inc., sells **its** chunky and smooth ice cream in Japan, France, Israel, England, and other countries.

FSCreations produces CD-ROMS for textbook publishers and others; **it** always delivers the products on time.

The **Oregon Association of Minority Entrepreneurs (OAME)** serves **its** members and the citizens of Oregon well.

The College of William and Mary stores antique documents in **its** special collections section.

Professional Certification

A paralegal is not required to become a CLA, or Certified Legal Assistant. But certification from a professional society, such as the National Association of Legal Assistants, can offer advantages in a competitive labor market.

5.8 Ambiguous Reference

When using pronouns in your writing, be sure that the meaning of each one is clearly understood. Learn ways to avoid unclear pronoun usage.

Ambiguous Pronoun Reference

Look at this sentence:

Rico called Fred when he was in Seattle.

Who was in Seattle, Rico or Fred? You cannot tell from this sentence because the pronoun reference is ambiguous. Here's how the sentence could be improved:

When **Rico** was in Seattle, **he** called Fred.

Here are two other examples of ambiguous personal pronoun reference.

AMBIGUOUS: I listened to Jan's plan and Frieda's argument against it
                and decided I agreed with *her*.

CLEAR: ✔ I listened to Jan's plan and Frieda's argument against it
                and decided I agreed with Jan.

AMBIGUOUS: We closed the sale and completed the shipment. *It* was
                a large one.

CLEAR: ✔ We closed the sale, which was a large one, and com-
                pleted the shipment.

Be sure that pronouns are correct in number and gender. Also be sure that
the antecedent to which each pronoun refers is clear.

Absent Pronoun Reference

In the first sentence of the last pair above, the pronoun *it* is ambiguous
because *it* can refer to either *sale* or *shipment*. Sometimes *it* can be ambiguous because of the absence of the word to which *it* refers. For example,

My sister takes piano lessons, but I'm not interested in *it*.

In this sentence, there is no singular noun to which *it* refers. The sentence
should be reworded to avoid this ambiguity.

My sister takes piano lessons, but I'm not interested in learning *how to play*.

Ambiguous Relative Pronouns

Relative pronouns can also be used ambiguously. Look at this sentence:

Mr. Okada refused to reconsider his decision, which upset me.

Were you upset by Mr. Okada's decision? Or were you upset by his refusal
to reconsider it? Rewrite the sentence to make your meaning clear.

I was upset by Mr. Okada's refusal to reconsider his decision.

SECTION A: PROGRAMMED REINFORCEMENT

Coverage Key

Section		Statement
5.1	➤ Pronouns and Antecedents	➤ S1, S2, S3, S4, S5
5.2	➤ Two Antecedents With *And*	➤ S6
5.3	➤ Two Antecedents With *Or/Nor*	➤ S7, S8, S9
5.4	➤ Indefinite Pronouns as Antecedents	➤ S10, S11, S12
5.5	➤ The Problem With Common Gender Pronouns	➤ S13, S14
5.6	➤ Explanatory Phrases	➤ S15
5.7	➤ Collective Antecedents	➤ S16, S17
5.8	➤ Ambiguous Reference	➤ S18, S19

Instructions: Cover the answers in the **Answer** column; then write your answer to the first statement. Uncover the first printed answer and compare your answer to it. If you wrote a correct answer, continue the activity. If you made an error, use the **Coverage Key** to locate the chapter section you need to review. When you are confident that you understand the material, continue with the reinforcement activity.

ANSWER

STATEMENT

S1 The word that a pronoun refers to is called the _____ of that pronoun.

A1 antecedent

S2 If the antecedent that a pronoun relates to is singular, the pronoun must be _____. If the antecedent is plural, the pronoun must be _____.

A2 singular, plural

S3 **All employees must do (his, their) best.** In the previous sentence, **employees** is the antecedent of the pronoun. **Employees** is (singular, plural). The pronoun that agrees with **employees** is **(his, their)**.

A3 plural, **their**

S4 **Every boy must do (his, their) best.** In the previous sentence, the antecedent to the pronoun is _____, which is (singular, plural). Therefore the correct pronoun is _____.

A4 **boy, singular, his**

S5 A pronoun and its antecedent must agree not only in number—singular or plural—but also in gender—masculine or feminine. Underline the correct pronoun in the next sentence. **Every girl must do (his, her, their) best.**

A5 <u>her</u>

S6 If the antecedent consists of two nouns connected by *and*, the pronoun must be _____ in number. Underline the correct pronoun in the following sentence: **The Merit Company and the Vitality Company will make (his, its, their) decision known later today.**

A6 plural, <u>their</u>

S7 When two antecedents are connected by *or* or *nor*, the pronoun will agree in number with the antecedent that is (closer to, farther from) the verb phrase.

A7 closer to

S8 In the next sentence, underline the closer antecedent once and the correct pronoun twice. **Neither the mother nor the daughters will accept (her, their) share of the reward.**

A8 <u>daughters,</u> <u>their</u>

S9 **Either the parents or the girl will give her statement to the press tomorrow.** Rewrite the previous sentence to make it less awkward.

_____

_____ .

A9 Either the girl or her parents will give their statement to the press tomorrow.

S10 This is a partial list of indefinite pronouns: *anybody, anyone, each, everybody, everyone, nobody, no one, somebody, someone.* When used as an antecedent, each of these expressions calls for a (singular, plural) pronoun.

A10 singular

S11 Underline the correct pronoun in the following sentences.
a. **Nobody wants to waste (her, their) money.**
b. **Did anyone here lose (his, their) keys?**

A11 a. <u>her</u>
b. <u>his</u>

S12 A phrase—a group of words—that comes between the singular antecedent and the pronoun does not alter the fact that the pronoun is singular. For the next sentence, do both (a) and (b). **Each of the Web programmers has (her, their) duties cut out for (her, them).**
a. Underline the group of words after the antecedent that you should ignore in determining the number of the pronoun.
b. Underline the correct pronouns.

A12 a. <u>of the Web programmers</u>
b. <u>her</u>, <u>her</u>

S13 In the past most writers used a (masculine, feminine) pronoun as a common gender pronoun to refer to an antecedent of indefinite sex. Today the sensitive writer (uses, does not use) common gender pronouns.

A13 masculine, does not use

S14 Show two ways you would revise the following sentence to eliminate the common gender pronoun:

Everyone in the office gave his donation to United Charities.

1. _____

   _____

2. _____

   _____

A14 Four possibilities:
1. **Everyone in the office gave his or her donation to United Charities.**
2. **Everyone in the office gave a donation to United Charities.**
3. **Everyone in the office donated to United Charities.**
4. **All the people in the office gave their donations to United Charities.**

S15 Phrases such as *together with, accompanied by, in addition to,* and *as well as* do not make a singular word plural. Underline the correct pronoun: **Vera, as well as her staff, did (her, their) best to avert a strike.**

A15 <u>her</u>

S16 Words such as *committee, jury, crowd,* and *army* are usually singular but may be plural if referring to the individuals in a group. Underline the correct pronouns in the following sentences:

a. **The committee will make (its, their) recommendations public tomorrow.**

b. **The committee argued about (its, their) conflicting views.**

A16 <u>its</u>, <u>their</u>

S17 Because company names are thought of as collective nouns, normally they are considered (singular, plural). Underline the pronoun that correctly completes the next sentence.

Levy Brothers lost most of (its, their) inventory in a fire.

A17 singular, <u>its</u>

S18 It is important to avoid the use of pronouns that are not clearly understood. In the next sentence, which pronoun is not clear?

Amanda accidentally banged her watch on the glass coffee table and broke it.

A18 it

S19 Rewrite the ambiguous sentence in **S18** to make it clear.

_____

_____

_____

_____

_____

_____

_____

_____

_____

_____

A19 **Amanda broke her watch when she accidentally banged it on the glass coffee table.**
or
Amanda broke the glass coffee table when she accidentally banged her watch on it.

SECTION B
Proper Use of Pronouns

In this section you will study the use of *who/whom*, *whoever/whomever*, *us/we*, and *than/as*. You will learn how to avoid problems with pronouns that follow prepositions and how to use pronouns that can be written as one or two words.

5.9 *Who/Whom*

Which word is correct in the following sentence?

(Who, Whom) did you say you wanted to see?

After you complete this section, you will be able to make the correct choice for the sentence above and for others sentences that use *who* or *whom*.

Whom is the *objective* case of the pronoun *who*. You use *whom* as

- The *object* of a verb.
- The *object* of a preposition.

Who is the *subjective* case. You use *who*

- As the *subject* of a sentence or a clause.
- After a *linking* verb.

Substitution Strategies: *Who* or *Whom*?

Whenever you must choose between *who* and *whom*, try a variety of substitution strategies.

Substitute. Substitute *he* or *him*, or *she* or *her*. If *he* or *she* fits, *who* is correct. If *him* or *her* fits, the objective case—*whom*—is correct.

1. **(Who, Whom) is it?**
   Substitute *He* or *Him*: *He* is it? Not: *Him* is it?
   The subjective pronoun *he* fits the sentence, so you should use the subjective pronoun *who*.
   The correct version is: *Who* is it? (the subjective case)

2. **You were referring to (who, whom)?**
   Use *she* or *her*: You were referring to *her*? Not: You were referring to *she*?
   The objective pronoun *her* fits the sentence, so you should use the objective pronoun *whom*.
   The correct version is: You were referring to *whom*? (the objective case)

Rearrange and Substitute. To use the substitution technique in some sentences, you will rearrange the wording so that *he* or *him*, or *she* or *her*, makes sense. When you have figured out which substitute pronoun makes sense in the sentence, use the corresponding version of *who* or *whom*.

Grammar Tip

Who/Whom

Substitute *he* or *she* for *who* (because each of those pronouns is *subjective*) and *him* or *her* for *whom* (because each of those pronouns is *objective*).

1. (Who, Whom) do you want?

Substitute *he* or *him*. Rearrange the sentence so that *he* or *him* is at the end of the question and makes sense:

Do you want *him*? Not: Do you want *he*?

The objective pronoun *him* fits the rearranged sentence, so you should use the objective pronoun *whom* in the original sentence.

The correct version is: *Whom* do you want?

Divide and Substitute. For sentences that include relative clauses, break the sentence into its clauses and test the appropriate clause separately.

1. He is a person (who, whom) is respected by all.

In this sentence *who* or *whom* is part of a relative clause; it joins the second clause to the first clause. In sentences like this one, break the sentence into its separate clauses.

Clause 1: He is a person. Clause 2: (Who, Whom) is respected by all.

Substitute *he* or *him* in the appropriate clause:

He is respected by all. Not: *Him* is respected by all.

The subjective pronoun *he* fits the appropriate clause, so you should use the subjective pronoun *who* in the original sentence.

The correct version is: *He* is a person *who* is respected by all.

2. She is a person (who, whom) we all respect.

In this sentence *who* or *whom* is part of a relative clause; it joins the second clause to the first clause. Break the sentence into its clauses.

Clause 1: She is a person. Clause 2: We all respect (who, whom).

Substitute *she* or *her* in the appropriate clause:

We all respect *her*. Not: We all respect *she*.

The objective pronoun *her* fits the appropriate clause, so you should use the objective pronoun *whom* in the original sentence.

The correct version is: She is a person *whom* we all respect.

Decide and Rearrange. In some sentences, figuring out how to rearrange the clauses so that *she* or *her,* or *he* or *him,* makes sense will be a challenge. Review the examples below.

1. He is a person (who, whom) I am positive can be trusted.

Do not let the phrase *I am positive* fool you. This sentence can be separated and rearranged to read:

I am positive he is a person (who, whom) can be trusted.

Substitute *he* or *him* for *who* or *whom:*

He can be trusted. Not: *Him* can be trusted.

The subjective pronoun *he* fits the rearranged clauses, so you should use the subjective pronoun *who* in the original sentence.

The correct version is: He is a person *who* I am positive can be trusted.

2. (Who, Whom) did you say was at the door?

Rearrange this sentence to read:
Did you say (who, whom) was at the door?
Substitute *he* or *him* for *who* or *whom*:
He was at the door. Not: *Him* was at the door.
The subjective pronoun *he* fits the rearranged sentence, so you should use the subjective pronoun *who* in the original sentence.
The correct version is: *Who* did you say was at the door?

Strategic Application: *Who* or *Whom*?

Let's return to the original problem sentence that began this section:

(Who, Whom) did you say you wanted to see?

Now use the appropriate substitution strategy to determine the correct choice of pronoun. Compare your answer with the strategy shown below.

Rearrange the clauses so that *she* or *he* will make sense in the sentence:
Did you say you wanted to see (who, whom)? or You did say you wanted to see (who, whom).
Substitute *he* or *him*:
Did you say you wanted to see *him*? or You did say you wanted to see *him*.
Not: Did you say you wanted to see *he*? or You did say you wanted to see *he*.
The objective pronoun *him* fits the rearranged sentence, so you should use the objective pronoun *whom* in the original sentence.
The correct version is: *Whom* did you say you wanted to see?

Grammar Tip

Objective Pronouns

If you use *he* or *him* as your substitute pronouns, remember that both objective pronouns, *him* and *whom,* end in an *m*.

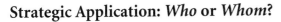

5.10	*Whoever/Whomever*

Whoever is the *subjective* case. You use *whoever*

- As the *subject* of a sentence or a clause.
- After a *linking* verb.

Whomever is the *objective* case. You use *whomever* as

- The *object* of a verb.
- The *object* of a preposition.

Substitution Strategies: *Whoever/Whomever*

You can determine whether to use *whoever* or *whomever* in a sentence by using substitution strategies that are similar to the substitution strategies you used for *who* or *whom*.

Substitute. Substitute *he* or *him,* or *she* or *her.* If *he* or *she* fits, *whoever* is correct. If *him* or *her* fits, *whomever* is correct.

(Whoever, Whomever) answers the phone should be pleasant.

Use *she* or *her*: *She* answers the phone. Not: *Her* answers the phone.

The subjective pronoun *she* fits the sentence, so you should use the subjective pronoun *whoever*.

The correct version is: *Whoever* answers the phone should be pleasant.

Ignore and Substitute. When *whoever* or *whomever* does not begin a sentence, ignore all words in the sentence before *whoever* or *whomever,* and substitute *he* or *him.*

He always accepts help from (whoever, whomever) will give it.

Ignore all words before *whoever* or *whomever* in the sentence, and substitute *he* or *him.*

He will give it. Not: *Him* will give it.

The subjective pronoun *he* fits the sentence that is left after you ignore the words before *whoever* or *whomever,* so you should use the subjective pronoun *whoever* in the original sentence.

The correct version is: He always accepts help from *whoever* will give it.

Ignore, Complete, and Substitute. In some sentences that do not begin with *whoever* or *whomever,* you will need to add a pronoun so that you can work with a complete thought.

1. **Give the prize to (whoever, whomever) you please.**

   Ignore all words in the sentence before *whoever* or *whomever.*

   You will be left with the words "You please."

   Add *she* or *her* to the end of those words so that you can work with a complete thought: You please *her.*

   The objective pronoun *her* fits the sentence that is left after you ignore all words before *whoever* or *whomever* and add a pronoun to the end of those words.

   The correct version is: Give the prize to *whomever* you please.

2. **Give the prize to (whoever, whomever) deserves it.**

   Ignore all words in the sentence before *whoever* or *whomever.*

   You will be left with the words *deserves it.* Add *he* or *him* to the beginning of those words so that you can work with a complete thought:

   He deserves it.

   The subjective pronoun *he* fits the sentence that is left after you ignore all words before *whoever* or *whomever* and add a pronoun to the beginning of those words.

   The correct version is: Give the prize to *whoever* deserves it.

Us is the *objective* case of the pronoun *we*. *We* is the *subjective* case.

Noun-Dropping Strategies: *We/Us*

Many people have trouble determining whether to use *us* or *we* directly before a noun. You can use strategies to help you solve that pronoun usage problem, just as you learned to use substitution strategies to help you determine when to use *who* or *whom* and *whoever* or *whomever*.

Drop the Noun. An easy way to determine whether *we* or *us* is the correct pronoun to use before a noun is to drop, temporarily, the noun and complete the sentence with your choice of pronoun, either *we* or *us*.

Grammar Tip

We/Us

If you aren't sure which pronoun to use in sentences such as those to the left, simplify the sentence by temporarily dropping the noun. The answer should then be obvious.

1. **(We, Us) designers have interesting work.**
   Temporarily drop from the sentence *designers*—the noun that appears after the pronouns—and you will have:
   We have interesting work.
   Here is the correct version with the dropped noun back in place:
   We designers have interesting work.

2. **The award was presented to (we, us) paralegals.**
   Temporarily drop from the sentence *paralegals*—the noun that appears after the pronouns—and you will have:
   The award was presented to *us*.
   Here is the correct version with the dropped noun back in place:
   The award was presented to *us* paralegals.

3. **Kyle asked (we, us) interns to be present.**
   Temporarily drop from the sentence *interns*—the noun that appears after the pronouns—and you will have:
   Kyle asked *us* to be present.
   Here is the correct version with the dropped noun back in place:
   Kyle asked *us* interns to be present.

Grammar Tip

We/Us In Speech

More people probably confuse the use of *we* or *us* when speaking than when writing. Learn to use the *We/Us* Substitution Strategies in your head.

People also have difficulty determining which pronoun case—the subjective or the objective—to use after *than* or *as*. Another substitution strategy will help you know which pronoun case to use.

Complete the Meaning. If you aren't sure which pronoun to use after *than* or *as*, temporarily add a word to complete the meaning of the sentence. Then use the pronoun that fits the new sentence.

1. **She is better at surfing the Internet than (I, me).**

    Complete the meaning of the sentence by temporarily adding a verb, and use the pronoun that fits the new sentence:

    She is better at surfing the Internet than *I am*.

    Not: She is better at surfing the Internet than *me am*.

    The subjective pronoun *I* fits the sentence created when *am* is added to complete the meaning of the original sentence, so you should use the subjective pronoun *I* in the original sentence.

    The correct version is: She is better at surfing the Internet than *I*.

2. **He would rather work with Janos than (I, me).**

    Complete the meaning of the sentence by temporarily adding a preposition, and use the pronoun that fits the new sentence:

    He would rather work with Janos than *with me*.

    Not: He would rather work with Janos than *with I*.

    The objective pronoun *me* fits the sentence created when *with* is added to complete the meaning of the original sentence, so you should use the objective pronoun *me* in the original sentence.

    The correct version is: He would rather work with Janos than *me*.

In some sentences either the subjective case or the objective case may be correct. Which pronoun you choose will depend on what you mean. For example,

3. **Kevin upsets his mother more than (I, me).**

    Complete the meaning of the sentence by adding a clause that indicates what you mean, and use the pronoun that fits the new sentence:

    Choice A: Kevin upsets his mother more than *I upset her*.

    Choice B: Kevin upsets his mother more than *he upsets me*.

    If you mean **Choice A**, the original sentence would need the subjective pronoun. You would use:

    Kevin upsets his mother more than *I*.

    If you mean **Choice B**, the original sentence would need the objective pronoun. You would use:

    Kevin upsets his mother more than *me*.

Grammar Tip

Always An Object—

When a pronoun is the object of the preposition, it should *always* be in the objective case, no matter where it appears in the sentence.

5.13 Pronouns After Prepositions

When a preposition appears near the beginning of a sentence, you might be tempted to use the subjective case of the pronoun connected to the preposition. For example,

<u>WRONG:</u>   Between you and *I*, this stock is presently undervalued.

<u>RIGHT:</u>   ✔ Between you and *me*, this stock is presently undervalued.

Several other prepositions, including *but, by, like, for,* and *except,* are often used in constructions that might tempt you to use the subjective case. Like all prepositions, they require the objective case of the pronoun.

WRONG: No one except you and *he* seems to be able to do the job.
RIGHT: ✔ No one except you and *him* seems to be able to do the job.

WRONG: Successful CEOs like Mr. Yang and *she* deserve big salaries.
RIGHT: ✔ Successful CEOs like Mr. Yang and *her* deserve big salaries.

Grammar Tip

One or Two Words?

anyone+ **of phrase** = any one
everyone + **of phrase** = every one
someone+ **of phrase** = some one

Use a similar technique to distinguish between *nobody* and *no body,* and between *somebody* and *some body.*

5.14 No One/Any One/Anyone

No one is always written as two words. Sometimes people become confused about whether to write *anyone, someone,* or *everyone* as one word or two. A good rule to follow is to write these words as two words when they are followed by an *of* phrase and to write these words as one word at other times.

Everyone was present.
Every one **of** the salespeople was present.

Someone in your group needs to take charge.
Could *some one* **of** his rank have ordered the officers to cease fire?

5.15 Redundant Pronouns

Look at this sentence:

Mr. Kowalski, he will attend the banquet.

Remember that a pronoun takes the place of a noun. In the sentence above, the noun that *he* would replace, *Mr. Kowalski,* is already present. The *he* merely repeats the information. The *he* is a *redundant* pronoun. The sentence should read: Mr. Kowalski will attend the banquet.
Here are other examples.

WRONG: Ms. Roberts and Mr. Zarrillo, they will be here shortly.
RIGHT: ✔ Ms. Roberts and Mr. Zarrillo will be here shortly.
RIGHT: ✔ They will be here shortly.

WRONG: Our firm, it is celebrating its tenth anniversary.
RIGHT: ✔ Our firm is celebrating its tenth anniversary.
RIGHT: ✔ It is celebrating its tenth anniversary.

In each wrong sentence above, the subject already has been stated; it should not be restated through the use of an unnecessary pronoun.

Punctuation Tip

No Comma Needed

In the examples on the left, no comma is required between the subject and the verb in the correct sentences.

Coverage Key

Section	Statement
5.9 ➤ Who/Whom	➤ S20, S21, S22, S23, S24, S25, S26, S42
5.10 ➤ Whoever/Whomever	➤ S27, S28, S29
5.11 ➤ We/Us	➤ S30, S31, S41
5.12 ➤ Than/As	➤ S32, S33, S34, S41
5.13 ➤ Pronouns After Prepositions	➤ S35, S43
5.14 ➤ No One/Any One/Anyone	➤ S36, S37, S44
5.15 ➤ Redundant Pronouns	➤ S38
1.4 ➤ Pronouns (Chapter 1) and 4.2 Personal Pronouns (Chapter 4)	➤ S39
4.3 ➤ The Possessive Case (Chapter 4)	➤ S40

Instructions: Cover the answers in the **Answer** column; then write your answer to the first statement. Uncover the first printed answer and compare your answer to it. If you wrote a correct answer, continue the activity. If you made an error, use the **Coverage Key** to locate the chapter section you need to review. When you are confident that you understand the material, continue with the reinforcement activity.

ANSWER

STATEMENT

S20 The pronouns *who* and *whom* sometimes cause trouble. *Who* is in the _____ case, whereas *whom* is in the _____ case.

A20 subjective, objective

S21 Because *who* is in the subjective case, it may be used in only two situations: as the _____ of a sentence or clause, or after a(n) _____ verb.

A21 subject, linking

S22 In the next sentence, underline the correct pronoun and list the case and reason the pronoun is that case.
(Who, Whom) in your opinion will receive the promotion?
Case: _____
Reason: _____

A22 <u>Who</u>, subjective; subject of the sentence

S23 In the next sentence, underline the correct pronoun and list the case and reason the pronoun is that case.
I wonder to (who, whom) we should award the contract.
Case: _____
Reason: _____

A23 <u>whom</u>, objective, object of the preposition **to**

S24 Underline the correct pronoun in the next sentence.
He is the man (who, whom) I believe damaged the copier.

A24 <u>who</u>

	S25 Underline the correct pronoun in the next sentence. **Tell me (who, whom) you think is the mechanic to (who, whom) we should give the bonus.**
A25 <u>who</u>, <u>whom</u>	**S26** Underline the correct pronoun in the next sentence. **She is the writer (whom, who) I am positive is the one (whom, who) we should select as editor.**
A26 <u>who</u>, <u>whom</u>	**S27** *Whoever* and *whomever* are used like *who* and *whom*. That means that *whoever* is in the _____ case and *whomever* is in the _____ case.
A27 subjective, objective	**S28** When choosing between *whoever* and *whomever*, disregard all words that come (before, after) either pronoun. In the following sentence, underline the words that you should disregard and choose the correct pronoun. **I will choose (whoever, whomever) I prefer.**
A28 before, Ignore **I will choose**, **whomever**	**S29** In the next sentence, underline the words you should disregard and choose the correct pronoun. **I will choose (whoever, whomever) is the better candidate.**
A29 Ignore **I will choose**, whoever	**S30** **(We, Us) seniors may register for employment interviews this semester.** You quickly know the correct pronoun form in the previous sentence is _____ if you omit the word _____ .
A30 We, seniors	**S31** In the next sentence, choose the correct pronoun and underline the word you may omit to double-check your choice. **Judge Liu gave the merit award to (we, us) paralegals.**
A31 us, omit <u>paralegals</u>	**S32** To determine which case of pronoun should follow the conjunction *as* or *than*, you can often add a simple verb after the pronoun in question. What verb would you use in the following sentence? **She organizes as well as (me, I).** _____ Choose the correct pronoun in the previous sentence.
A32 **do** or **organize**, I	**S33** Underline the correct pronoun in the next sentence. **Benito is more ambitious than (her, she).** The _____ case is correct because the pronoun is the _____ of the understood verb _____ .
A33 <u>she</u>, subjective, subject, is (than she is)	**S34** Underline the correct pronoun in the next sentence. **He would rather work for Ms. Stein than (me, I).** The _____ case is correct because the pronoun is the _____ of the understood preposition _____ .
A34 <u>me</u>, objective, object, for (than for me)	

S35 *Between* is a preposition. Underline the correct pronouns in the next sentence.

The team leader divided the work between (her, she) and (me, I).

The _____ case is correct because the pronouns are

the _____ of the preposition _____.

A35 her, me, objective, objects, **between**

S36 Pronouns such as *anyone*, *someone*, and *everyone* may be written as one word or two words. They are written as (one, two) word(s) when a phrase beginning with *of* follows. Underline the correct word or words in the next sentence. **(Everyone, Every one) of the disks was defective.**

A36 two, Every one

S37 Underline the correct words in the next sentence. **(Everyone, Every one) on the staff may go, but (noone, no one) has gone yet.**

A37 Everyone, no one

S38 A *redundant pronoun* is an unnecessary pronoun because it repeats the subject of the sentence. Which pronouns should be omitted in the following sentences?

a. **Our company, it makes kitchen cabinets.**

b. **My brother, he owns his own business.**

c. **I will phone the personnel director myself.**

A38 a. it
    b. he
    c. none

S39 **Review:** A pronoun takes the place of a _____; each pronoun is singular or _____ and is in the first, second, or _____ person.

A39 noun, plural, third

S40 Underline the correct answers in the following review sentence. **(It's, Its) clear that (ours, our's) is the software (who, that) is superior.**

A40 It's, ours, that

S41 Underline the correct pronouns in the following review sentence. **Our government expects all its citizens to do (his, their) best because neither the President nor the members of Congress (is, are) able to do (his, their) work alone.**

A41 their, are, their

S42 Underline the correct pronouns in the following review sentence. **It is (we, us) (who, whom) are more deserving than (he, him).**

A42 we, who, he

S43 Underline the correct pronouns in the following review sentence. **Between you and (I, me) I don't care (who, whom) is promoted or (who, whom) they select.**

A43 me, who, whom

S44 Underline the correct words in the following review sentence. **(Anyone, Any one) of the supervisors but (he, him) works well under pressure.**

A44 Any one, him

CHAPTER 5 SUMMARY

In this chapter you learned that pronouns allow writers to communicate without repeating noun forms. You discovered that pronouns and their antecedents must agree in number and gender and that sensitive writers use pronouns of indefinite gender. You examined strategies for correctly distinguishing between subjective and objective pronouns such as *who* and *whom* and between one-word and two-word versions of pronoun pairs such as *everyone* and *every one*.

Getting Connected

USING WEBSITE OPTIONS

GOAL: Visitors to Websites often say they cannot find what they need because the sites have too much information. To overcome information overload, learn to read and use the options and links offered on a Website. In this activity you will use the options on a newspaper Website to look for an article that will help you review pronoun usage.

STEP 1 Go to *englishworkshop.glencoe.com,* the address for *The English Workshop* Website, and click on Unit 2. Next click on Getting Connected, and then click on Chapter 5. At the Getting Connected option, you will see a list of newspaper Website links. These links will connect you to three types of sites:

(1) national newspapers, such as *USA Today*
(2) nationally known newspapers, such as *The New York Times*
(3) newspaper Websites that should help you access newspapers for your local area.

Select a newspaper you would like to use for this activity and click on that link.

STEP 2 All Websites allow users to access information in different ways. Once you are at the site of your choice, read the different options available. Use the options to link to an article on a major current event that interests you.

STEP 3 Obtain a printout of the article. You may need to copy the text into a word-processing document or download the material.

STEP 4 As you read the article, circle or highlight each pronoun you find. After you have marked each pronoun, return to the article and locate each pronoun's antecedent.

(continued on next page)

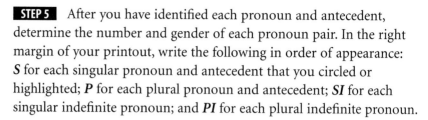

STEP 5   After you have identified each pronoun and antecedent, determine the number and gender of each pronoun pair. In the right margin of your printout, write the following in order of appearance: *S* for each singular pronoun and antecedent that you circled or highlighted; *P* for each plural pronoun and antecedent; *SI* for each singular indefinite pronoun; and *PI* for each plural indefinite pronoun.

STEP 6   In the article look for examples of the following. In the margins identify each as indicated:

a. Explanatory phrases that fall between the pronoun and antecedent (see Section 5.6): Write *EP* for each explanatory phrase.
b. Collective antecedents (See Section 5.7): Write *CA* for each collective antecedent.
c. *Who/Whom:* Write *W* for who and *WM* for whom.
d. *Whoever/Whomever:* Write *WH* for *whoever* and *WHM* for *whomever*.
e. *Anyone/Any one:* Write *A* for *anyone* and *AO* for *any one*.
f. *Everyone/Every one:* Write *E* for *everyone* and *EO* for *every one*.
g. *Someone/Some one:* Write *S* for *someone* and *SO* for *some one*.

STEP 7   Count the number of times *who* and *whoever* appear in the article and the number of times *whom* and *whomever* appear. Note these numbers on the back of your printout. Did the subjective form *(who/whoever)* or the objective form *(whom/whomever)* appear more often?

Even if you found no examples of either pronoun, identify which case of the pronoun you think newspaper writers use more often and why.

STEP 8   In the article look for examples of how writers deal with the common gender pronoun issue. If a writer uses the common gender pronoun, underline or highlight each instance. If she or he avoids the common gender pronoun and uses other pronouns, underline or highlight each instance. On the back of your printout, explain why you believe some writers avoid the common gender pronoun or why you believe some writers use the common gender pronoun.

STEP 9   Write your name on the front of your printout, and give the material to your instructor.

Tip   Some newspaper sites offer links to information about the region or city the newspaper covers. If you access a newspaper in a small town, you should also be able to read about local history, government news, and other information.

PRACTICE 1

Pronouns—Antecedents and Number

Instructions: In the column marked *Pronoun*, write the pronoun. In the column marked *Antecedent*, write the antecedent. In the column marked *Number*, write *S* if the antecedent is singular and *P* if the antecedent is plural.

	PRONOUN	ANTECEDENT	NUMBER
EXAMPLE: Mrs. Louette had her house appraised.	EX. ___her___	___Mrs. Louette___	___S___
1. Mr. Perez is proud of his daughter.	1. _his_	_Mr. Perez_	_S_
2. The Blairstown Ambulance Corps knows it can count on continued community support.	2. _____	_____	_S_
3. The boys' bicycles lay on their sides.	3. _____	_____	_P_
4. Ms. Deloria can protect the firm if she acts quickly.	4. _____	_____	_S_
5. The company stands behind its products.	5. _____	_____	_S_
6. Somebody forgot her briefcase.	6. _____	_____	_S_
7. Each of the saleswomen has had her office refurnished.	7. _____	_____	_S_
8. The new equipment is worth every cent spent on it.	8. _____	_____	_S_
9. All employees must protect their computer files.	9. _____	_____	_P_
10. The jury withdrew to consider its verdict.	10. _____	_____	_S_
11. Neither the desk nor the table looks its age.	11. _____	_____	_S_
12. Mr. Clemente, in addition to the entire staff, will offer his resignation.	12. _____	_____	_S_
13. Neither Ms. Kinney nor the boys have invested their money wisely.	13. _____	_____	_P_
14. Mr. Wu and Ms. Berman are on their way to the meeting.	14. _____	_____	_P_
15. Mr. Wu, as well as Ms. Berman, is on his way to the meeting.	15. _____	_____	_S_

Name _____

Class _____ Date _____

PRACTICE 2

Nonsexist Pronouns

Instructions: Rewrite the following sentences to eliminate the common gender pronouns.

EXAMPLE: **No one had his assignment finished. <u>No one had the assignment finished.</u>**

1. Somebody forgot his briefcase. _____

   _____

2. Each member of our sales staff must do his share. _____

   _____

3. Each of the department heads has had his office refurbished. _____

   _____

4. If somebody does an outstanding job, he should be rewarded for his efforts. _____

   _____

5. Is a person still forced to retire when he reaches age 65? _____

   _____

6. Many a person is promoted to a position he does not deserve. _____

   _____

7. A new car owner must have his car serviced regularly to keep his warranty in effect. _____

   _____

   _____

8. Laws against discrimination in hiring based on age protect a person if he is between 40 and 70 years old.

   _____

   _____

9. Every applicant will have his résumé reviewed by each committee member. _____

   _____

   _____

10. If a person knows how to communicate effectively, he will go far in the workplace. _____

    _____

    _____

PRACTICE 3

Ambiguous Pronoun Reference

Instructions: Rewrite each sentence to eliminate an ambiguous pronoun reference.

EXAMPLE: **Joe told Bill that he should break for lunch. <u>Joe told Bill to break for lunch.</u>**

1. I read in the financial section that World Business Products intends to purchase a controlling interest in International Conglomerate and that the value of its stock had almost doubled. _____

   _____

   _____

2. Now that Mr. O'Rourke has assumed many of Mr. Park's responsibilities, he has been much happier. _____

   _____

3. The cleaners washed, waxed, and polished both the main floor and the second floor. They were very dirty.

   _____

4. Ms. Aybar dropped a vase on her foot and broke it. *Ms. Aybar dropped the vase one*

   her foot and broke her foot.

5. Mildred told Kendra that she had lost weight. *Mildred lost weight and*

   told kendra

6. Mr. Lam spoke sharply to Joe, telling him that unless his job performance quickly improved, he would be very unhappy. _____

   _____

7. The three supervisors told their staffs that they would receive the director's recommendations the following morning. _____

   _____

8. Jesse took the stool off the counter and climbed onto it. _____

   _____

9. My aunt is a carpenter, but I'm not interested in it. _____

   _____

10. The toddler of a friend of mine likes to watch reruns of *I Love Lucy,* which my friend finds very amusing.

    _____

    _____

PRACTICE 4

Pronoun and Antecedent Agreement

Instructions: This Practice involves the agreement of a pronoun with its antecedent. In the spaces provided, write the proper pronouns.

EXAMPLE: **Each of the factories is operating at (its, their) peak capacity.**

EX. _____its_____

1. Every woman in that class has become successful in (his, her, his or her, their) chosen field.

1. _____

2. The crisis will soon be over, but (its, their) effect will last for years.

2. _____

3. Neither Ms. Chapman nor her associates had been in (his, her, his or her, their) office.

3. _____

4. No one in class raised (his, her, his or her, their) hand.

4. _____

5. All the members received (his, her, his or her, their) invitations.

5. _____

6. Each of the books had been autographed on (its, their) inside cover.

6. _____

7. Neither Maria nor Madeline had been able to meet (his, her, his or her, their) sales quota.

7. _____

8. None of the women will make (his, her, his or her, their) views public.

8. _____

9. Smith and Desai Landscaping has grown until (it, they) is the largest business in (its, it's, their) field.

9. _____

10. If somebody does an outstanding job, (he, she, he or she, they) should be rewarded for (his, her, his or her, their) efforts.

10. _____

11. The memoranda have been filed in (its, their) proper place.

11. _____

12. Acme Lumber, in addition to Zenith Lumber, is reducing (its, their) inventory.

12. _____

Name _____

Class _____ Date _____

PRACTICE 5

Who/Whom and Whoever/Whomever

Instructions: This Practice asks you to choose between *who* and *whom* and between *whoever* and *whomever*. In the space provided, write the correct word.

EXAMPLE: (Who, Whom) is next?   EX. _____ **Who** _____

1. (Who, Whom) is calling?   1. _____

2. (Who, Whom) should I say is calling?   2. _____

3. We have chosen a woman (who, whom) you all know. 3. _____

4. We have chosen a woman (who, whom) is known by all. 4. _____

5. He likes (whoever, whomever) likes him.   5. _____

6. He likes (whoever, whomever) he meets.   6. _____

7. I know a person (who, whom) I think can do the job. 7. _____

8. Elena is a person (who, whom) I think can be counted on 8. _____
   to get the job done.

9. (Who, Whom) were you speaking of?   9. _____

10. (Whoever, Whomever) gets there first should begin setting up. 10. _____

11. One man (who, whom) was nominated refused to accept. 11. _____

12. Choose (whoever, whomever) you think is the best qualified. 12. _____

13. Have you decided (who, whom) you want for this position? 13. _____

14. The sales rep (who, whom) I expected was detained. 14. _____

15. (Who, Whom) do you think stole the money?   15. _____

16. (Who, Whom) do you suspect of having stolen the money? 16. _____

17. Which is the boy (who, whom) you suspect of having 17. _____
    stolen the money?

18. Was it Patricia (who, whom) you were expecting? 18. _____

19. Of all the people (who, whom) I know, he is the 19. _____
    one (who, whom) can most be relied on.

20. He is a person (who, whom) I feel confident we 20. _____
    can rely on.

PRACTICE 6

Proper Use of Pronouns

Instructions: Cross out each incorrect pronoun in the following sentences, and write the correct pronoun above each one. There may be more than one error in a sentence.

EXAMPLE: Abe Cordasco and ~~her~~ *she* have more seniority than ~~me~~ *I*.

1. Everyone of the drivers except she has been affected by the downsizing.

2. Us three, Jan, Jaime, and me, were transferred.

3. There's would be a most difficult task for any one.

4. The order directed we maintenance personnel to start work fifteen minutes earlier.

5. Every one at the party wishes they could play the piano like he.

6. Between you and I, no one is sure that her job is safe.

7. Ms. Torres is just as good a motivator as him.

8. Karl and Julie, they are not so efficient as us.

9. Us salespeople must plan this campaign of our's carefully.

10. There new positions require some one with extensive experience in biotechnology.

11. She would rather work with Lutfi than he or me.

12. No one except Ms. Dorjee and he was able to attend.

13. Mr. Zaroff from the main office, he will bring the copies of the contracts for they to sign.

14. No body can say it was us technicians whom were to blame.

15. Is Jace taller than she or yourself?

PRACTICE 7

Pronoun Errors

Instructions: The letter below includes many errors. Cross out each incorrect word and write the correction above it. Pay particular attention to the use of possessive pronouns and to the agreement of pronouns with their antecedents.

DEPARTMENT OF LEGAL ASSISTANCE EDUCATION
Dell Business Building, Suite 53   Clifton Community College   Ashton, North Carolina 28901-6574

December 7, 20--

Mr. Marco Glenn, Ph.D., President
Legal Educators of America
2546 Avenue of the Americas
New York, NY 10172

Dear Dr. Glenn:

I'm writing to explain that us members of the Department of Legal Assistance Education at Clifton College enjoyed the annual convention of the Legal Educators of America. Because ours' is a new department, each of our instructors felt it their personal obligation to attend and learn all they could. Professor Aziz and Professor Moore, who I believe you met during the convention, they sends their special thanks and appreciation.

Them two women and myself enjoyed the speech given by Ms. Valdez and Mr. Nash. Their's is an unusual combination of talents, and them complement one another. I noticed that during there presentation every member of the audience was attentive. I don't believe any one wanted to miss a word. Its rare to meet people whom are so well informed.

Your planning committee should congratulate itself. The many publishers' exhibits were excellent, and the sessions were very informative. All the moderators, especially Dr. Chen, gave her presentations very well. We believe noone could have done a better job than her. Talent such as her's is rare.

Thank you again for an excellent conference.

Sincerely,

Joel Barra, J.D.

PRACTICE 8

Composition: Using Pronouns

Instructions: Write complete sentences that include the phrases in parentheses as antecedents of pronouns.

EXAMPLE: **(both Mel and Ida)** <u>I asked both Mel and Ida for their advice.</u>

1. (either Anne or Louisa) _____

_____

2. (neither Miss Zee nor her assistants) _____

_____

3. (few) _____

_____

4. (each of our clients) _____

_____

5. (many a product) _____

_____

6. (several people) _____

_____

7. (Levy Brothers Department Store) _____

_____

8. (every one) _____

_____

9. (anyone) _____

_____

10. (everyone) _____

_____

11. (any one) _____

_____

12. (nobody) _____

_____

13. (committee) _____

_____

14. (whoever) _____

_____

15. (whomever) _____

_____

Words That Name

Unit 2—Editing Review

Instructions: Use the concepts you have studied so far to help you locate errors in the paragraphs below. Cross out each error you find and write the correction in the space above it.

Paralegal Studys Program

The paralegal profession continues to be one of the fastest growing professiones in the country. According to statistics provided by the United State's Department of Labor. This datum supports the fact that enrolling in Valley State Universities' Paralegal Program will provide yourselve with the training for an excellent career in the field of law.

Today paralegals—sometimes referred to as legal assistantes or legal analystses—work under the supervision of attornies in a variety of area's. Ranging from real estate, litigation, and family law. To patent, trademark, and estate practice. When some one becomes a paralegal, he assumes a key role in providing efficient and economical service to the public and the legal community. Paralegals cannot give legal advice, make court appearances, or set legal feeses. Only the attorney hisself or herself can do that. But paralegals carry out many other taskes performed by an attorney. Including writing legal brieves and memorandi, as well as analysises and synopsises of judicial opiniones. Paralegals are not limited to law offices and corporationes the judiciary and the public sector also provide career opportunitys. A paralegals career is limited only by their imagination.

(Editing Review continued on page 158)

(Editing Review continued from page 157)

The curricula in the Paralegal Study's Program includes a wide range of valuable

The curricula in the Paralegal Study's Program includes a wide range of valuable

courses. Including "Conflict and It's Resolution." This is a course that is required of

every one whose in the program. The foci of this class is on how to resolve conflict.

Through mediation and negotiation. When two people they disagree with one

another, you'll learn the techniques for how to resolve it. Issues of culture, gender,

race, and age in resolving conflictes between people whom are in disagreement and

the criterions to consider. Will also be presented in that course.

The paralegal profession offers the opportunity for intellectual challenge,

professional growth, financial security. And service to others. You can be a part of the

Valley State University Legal Studys vast alumnus's network by becoming part of the

Universitys' nationally recognized quality Paralegal Program.

Link & Learn

USING PRONOUNS IN LAW CAREERS

GOAL: Reinforce what you learned about nouns and pronouns in Unit 2 by using the Internet to explore the use of nouns and pronouns in Websites about justice careers.

STEP 1 Go to ***englishworkshop.glencoe.com,*** the address for *The English Workshop* Website, and click on Unit 2 Link & Learn to access a list of professional law Websites you may use in this activity.

STEP 2 Skim through several pages of materials at your chosen site. Find a page that includes common nouns and *at least five* pronouns. Print the page you select and circle five common nouns. Then underline at least five pronouns on the printout and draw a line from each pronoun to its antecedent. Attach the printout to this page.

STEP 3 How do the writers of the Website deal with the common gender pronoun? Choose all strategies below that apply to what you see on the site you selected, and circle passages on the page that prove your point.

   a. The plural pronoun *they, them,* or *their* is used to avoid the common gender pronoun.
   b. *He/she, his/hers,* or *him/her* is used to avoid the common gender pronoun.
   c. *He or she, his or hers,* or *him or her* is used to avoid the common gender pronoun.
   d. The definite article *the* is substituted for a pronoun.
   e. Pronouns are not used.
   f. *He, him,* or *his* is used to refer to both genders.

STEP 4 On the back of the Website printout, explain why you think the writers chose these pronouns.

STEP 5 Also on the back of the printout, state whether you believe the writers selected an appropriate strategy for dealing with common gender pronouns. Explain why you think the strategy is appropriate or inappropriate.

STEP 6 Finally, write your name on the front of the printout, and turn it in to your instructor.

Words That Show Action

Profile in Success

Automotive Technician: Mastering Car Parts and the English Language

Paulo Rizzo · *Cape Girardeau, Missouri* · *Wieser Honda*

How do you get from Rio de Janeiro, Brazil, to Cape Girardeau, Missouri? For Paulo Rizzo, who was born in Rio, the route began at basketball camp in Orlando, Florida, when he was 17. Deciding to play high school basketball in the United States, he moved to Sikeston, Missouri. State regulations, however, prohibited his playing for the local school team. Instead, he graduated and began studying industrial technology at a community college.

After a year Paulo decided to change his major to automotive technology and switch schools. He loved cars, but he didn't know the language well enough to talk about them in English.

"I had a lot to learn," says Paulo. "I couldn't communicate with everybody because I didn't know the English words for all the car parts. I'd go home at night and use the Internet to look up more information about vehicles and the names of the parts."

The time Paulo spent learning English has paid off. He graduated with an associate degree in automotive technology and now works as a mechanic for Wieser Honda. "We have a variety of customers," Paulo says. "I have to be able to communicate with everybody—to help them understand what's wrong with their autos and how we can fix them."

Think About It . . . How Can Success Be Measured?

Paulo first planned a career in basketball. When that plan was disrupted, he focused on industrial technology. Then he switched directions again.

- *Does success depend on accomplishing a single goal or one's first goals?*

- *How has Paulo been successful?*

- *How important are communication skills to Paulo's career success?*

Career Connections
AUTOMOTIVE CAREERS

Learn more about the work of master automotive technicians, service advisors, parts specialists, and others in the automotive field by connecting to the following sites listed at *The English Workshop* Website. Go to ***englishworkshop.glencoe.com***. Click first on Unit 3 and then on Career Connections.

- Automotive Service Association
- Automotive Service Excellence
- Car Care Council
- United States Council for Automobile Research Consortia and Tech Teams (USCAR)
- National Highway Traffic Safety Administration

See page 273, **Link & Learn: Using Verbs in Automotive Careers**, for an additional online career activity.

Verbs

CHAPTER 6 PREVIEW

In Chapter 2 you saw that a sentence requires a subject and a predicate. Having learned about the subject in the last three chapters, you will now focus on the heart of the predicate—the verb. In this chapter you will examine the simple and the perfect verb tenses. As you work with this chapter, you will continue to assess your knowledge in the Programmed Reinforcement sections and the Practices. Finally, you will sign up for a free e-mail account and enhance your understanding of the various verb tenses.

OBJECTIVES

After completing this chapter, you will be able to

- Distinguish between action verbs and linking verbs.
- Form and use the three simple verb tenses:
  - The present tense
  - The past tense
  - The future tense
- Form and use the three perfect verb tenses:
  - The present perfect tense
  - The past perfect tense
  - The future perfect tense

Study Plan for Chapter 6

The Study Plan for Chapter 6 offers a set of strategies that will help you learn and review the chapter material.

1 **Linking Verbs and Action Verbs**: Pretend you are a sixth-grade teacher preparing a lesson on linking and action verbs. Create a chart for the classroom with sample sentences illustrating how these two verb types are used. Include the verbs that can be used as linking verbs in some cases and as action verbs in others.

2 **Verb Tenses**: Review the three simple verb tenses and the three perfect verb tenses. Examine something you have written recently—a letter for work, a school paper, or some other document. Find the verbs. Which tenses did you use?

3 **Verb Tense Timeline**: With a partner, review the verb tense timeline in Section 6.11. Write sample sentences for each of the six verb tenses. Select verbs from the Practice sentences at the end of the chapter.

4 **Tense Tests**: In Sections 6.9 and 6.10, you will find two tests for determining when to use specific verb tenses. Use those tests as you answer Practices 3 and 4 at the end of the chapter.

The verb makes a direct statement about the subject. Much of the power and effectiveness in writing stems from the careful selection of verbs. Look at the following sentences. Notice how your attitude toward Mr. Rubio depends on the verb used to describe how he entered his office.

Mr. Rubio *went* into his office.
Mr. Rubio *strode* into his office.
Mr. Rubio *slunk* into his office.
Mr. Rubio *retreated* into his office.
Mr. Rubio *stomped* into his office.
Mr. Rubio *scurried* into his office.

6.1   Linking Verbs and Subject Complements

Most verbs express action. *Run, write, yell, sleep, think,* and thousands of other verbs are **action verbs.** However, some verbs express a condition or a state of being. **State-of-being verbs** are also called **linking verbs.** They join or link the subject of a sentence to nouns and pronouns that rename the subject or to adjectives that describe the subject. The words that rename or describe the subject are **subject complements**—they complete the meaning of the subject.

Grammar Tip

Subject Complements

A complement "fills up or completes" something. A subject complement fills up or completes the meaning of the subject in a sentence. But a compliment is a remark of admiration.

NOUN COMPLEMENT: **Jan** is the new department *manager.*

Manager is a noun complement. It completes the sentence by renaming the subject, *Jan.*

PRONOUN COMPLEMENT: The **person** who caused the trouble was *he.*

He is a pronoun complement. It completes the sentence by renaming the subject, *person.*

ADJECTIVE COMPLEMENT: **Griselda** will be very *happy.*

Happy is an adjective complement. It completes the sentence by modifying, or describing, the subject, *Griselda.*

LOOKING AHEAD

To Be *Verb Chart*
A chart listing all the forms of the verb to be *appears in Chapter 7.*

●

Types of Linking Verbs

The sample sentences above use forms of *to be,* the most frequently used linking verb. Its forms are *am, are, is, was, were, be, being,* and *been.*

Other linking verbs include *feel, seem, appear, taste, sound, look, smell, grow,* and *become.* Each of these could be replaced by the verb *is* or *was.*

LINKING VERBS	IS OR WAS REPLACEMENT
1. Joe *looks* sick.	1. Joe *is* sick.
2. She *appeared* nervous.	2. She *was* nervous.
3. He *felt* helpless.	3. He *was* helpless.
4. The proposal *seems* practical.	4. The proposal *is* practical.
5. The soy milk *tasted* sweet.	5. The soy milk *is* sweet.
6. The singer *sounded* off-key.	6. The singer *was* off-key.
7. The leaves *smell* damp.	7. The leaves *are* damp.
8. The crowd *grew* restless.	8. The crowd *was* restless.
9. The rich copper grating *became* tarnished.	9. The rich copper grating *was* tarnished.

Sense Verbs

Each of the five common linking verbs describes a sense experience: *feel, taste, sound, look,* and *smell*.

Linking or Action Verbs?

Some linking verbs can serve as action verbs, depending on their use in a sentence. Compare the use of *to taste* in the next sentences:

> This soup *tastes* salty.
> The cook *tasted* the soup to see if it was properly seasoned.

In the first sentence, *tastes* is a linking verb; it links the quality of saltiness to the subject *soup*. The word *was* could replace the word *tastes*. In the second sentence, *tasted* is an action verb; it names the action of the cook, who samples the soup. The word *was* could not replace the word *tasted* in this sentence. Review the additional examples presented below.

LINKING VERBS	ACTION VERBS
Candy *tastes* **(is)** sweet.	*Taste* the candy.
Velvet *feels* **(is)** soft.	The dressmaker *feels* the cloth.
Buttermilk *smells* **(is)** sour.	We *smelled* the flowers by the door.
The instructor *appears* **(is)** tired.	The instructor *appeared* in the doorway.

New Auto Skills

Linking Verb Review

All forms of the verb *to be* (*am, are, is, was, were, be, being,* and *been*), whether used alone or combined with another verb, are linking verbs. Verbs such as *become, seem, appear, prove, grow, remain, feel, taste, sound, look,* and *smell* can be either linking verbs or action verbs. When they can be replaced by a form of *to be*, they are linking verbs. When they cannot be replaced by a form of *to be*, they are action verbs.

There are more computers in today's car than in the first space capsule. Ten to fifteen computers control everything from the engine to the radio. In school, acquire hands-on experience with computers as well as cars.

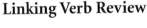

6.2 | **The Simple Tenses**

Verbs do more than express action or a state of being. They also express time. Verbs change their form depending on the time of the event they depict. The different forms a verb can take are called the **tenses** of the verb.

Grammar Tip

Third Person Singular

The third person singular (*he, she*) form of the verb always ends in *s* or *es*.
He *works*.   She *goes*.   It *is*.

You probably know and correctly use the three simple verb tenses: the **present** tense, the **past** tense, and the **future** tense. You would never say *I will go to the bank yesterday:* you know that when you refer to an action that occurred yesterday, you must use the past tense of the verb *to go*. You would correctly say, *I went to the bank yesterday.*

Let's review the simple tenses next.

6.3 The Present Tense

Present tense verbs may be used in four ways.

1. The present tense is used to express an action or state of being that is happening at the present time.

> I *am* satisfied.
> He *is* in the service area.
> Your argument *makes* sense to me.
> Kobe *shoots* and *scores*.

2. The present tense is used to describe action that is customary or habitual.

> I *exercise* every morning.
> Kathleen *walks* twice a day.
> We *buy* our eggs locally.
> I *take* my car to Shelby's Garage.

3. The present tense is used to express general truths or opinions.

> I *live* 90 miles from Iowa.
> The earth *revolves* around the sun.
> The Tarheels *play* their best at home.
> Soccer *is* a better game than chess.

4. The present tense is sometimes used to express future action.

> Stephen *graduates* from the eighth grade next Friday.
> The Titans *play* the Rams this Saturday.

When present tense verbs express future action, a clue always indicates that the event is happening now, not later. In the sentences above, *next Friday,* and *this Saturday* broadcast that the events in the sentences will occur later.

6.4 The Past Tense

The past tense is used to refer to a definite past event or action.

> He *e-mailed* it earlier.
> April *changed* the oil this morning.
> I *went* to the movies yesterday.
> She *received* a degree last year.

Most verbs form the past tense by adding *d* or *ed* to the end of the verb, such as *e-mailed* and *received* above. Other words form the past tense in different ways. The past tense of *to go*, for example, is *went*.

6.5 Do, Does, Did

In questions, the words *do*, *does*, and *did* are used only in the simple present and past tenses.

> *Do* you *see* her every day?
> *Does* he *sell* insurance?
> *Did* you *go* to the movies yesterday?
> *Did* she *receive* her degree last year?

In the sentences above, *do*, *does*, and *did* assist the main verb. They are acting as **helping verbs,** or **auxiliaries**. The auxiliary verbs *do*, *does*, and *did* can also be used in making statements. For example,

> You *do see* her every day.
> He *does sell* insurance.
> We *did go* to the movies.
> She *did receive* her degree.

The sentences above illustrate the *emphatic* form of the verb, which is used to give greater emphasis to the action expressed by the verb.

Negation

Do, *does*, and *did* are also used to express negation.

> He *does not sell* insurance.
> We *did not go* to the movies.
> You *do not see* her every day.
> She *did not earn* a degree.

LOOKING AHEAD

More on Helping Verbs
Helping verbs are used before the main verb to build a verb phrase. You will read more about other helping verbs later in this chapter in Section B: Perfect Tenses.

6.6 The Future Tense

The future tense is used to indicate that an event will take place or a condition will exist at a future time. Form the future tense by placing *will* or *shall* before the main form of the verb.

I *will go* with you tomorrow.
You *will see* her every day.

Angel *will rotate* the tires later.
She *will receive* her degree eventually.

Shall/Will

At one time there were precise distinctions regarding when to use *shall* and when to use *will*. Most writers no longer observe these distinctions. They use *will* for all persons and all kinds of expressions. The use of *shall* is limited to the following situations:

Questions asking for permission are frequently begun with *shall*.

Shall I call home?

Shall I send in Karen?

In legal documents, *shall* is used to express obligation.

The undersigned shall pay the sum of Eight Hundred Dollars ($800).

Should/Would

The distinctions once applied to *should* (past tense of *shall*) and *would* (past tense of *will*) are no longer observed. Use *should* to express (1) obligation, (2) possibility, or (3) probability. In all other situations, use *would*.

OBLIGATION: I *should* finish grading these exams before going to bed.
POSSIBILITY: *Should* school be closed, the test will be rescheduled.
PROBABILITY: Unless something unexpected happens, I *should* have your exams for you by next class meeting.

Coverage Key

Section		Statement
6.1	➤ Linking Verbs and Subject Complements	➤ **S1, S2, S3, S4, S5, S6**
6.2	➤ The Simple Tenses	➤ **S7, S8**
6.3	➤ The Present Tense	➤ **S9, S10**
6.4	➤ The Past Tense	➤ **S11**
6.5	➤ *Do, Does, Did*	➤ **S12, S13**
6.6	➤ The Future Tense	➤ **S14, S15, S16, S17**

Instructions: Cover the answers in the **Answer** column; then write your answer to the first statement. Uncover the first printed answer and compare your answer to it. If you wrote a correct answer, continue the activity. If you made an error, use the **Coverage Key** to locate the chapter section you need to review. When you are confident that you understand the material, continue with the reinforcement activity.

ANSWER

STATEMENT

S1 A verb is a word that generally expresses (a) action, (b) the name of a place, (c) a description.

A1 a

S2 There are two types of verbs: action verbs and _____ verbs.

A2 linking

S3 A linking verb such as *seems* expresses a state of being, not an action. It may be replaced by the verb _____.

A3 *is*

S4 Verbs relating to the senses may often be either linking or action verbs, depending on the way they're used. In which sentence does the verb express action?
a. **The boy tasted the frosting.**
b. **The frosting tasted sweet.**

A4 a.

S5 In the blank at the end of each sentence, write whether *looked* is used as an action verb or a linking verb.
a. **Mr. Enix looked nervous.** _____
b. **Mr. Enix looked nervously at his watch.** _____

A5 a. linking verb
b. action verb

S6 In the following group of verbs, two are always action verbs; the others are usually linking verbs. Underline the two words that are always action verbs: **appear, become, seem, write, feel, speak.**

A6 <u>write</u>, <u>speak</u>

S7 The tense of a verb is related to (a) person, (b) degree, (c) time.

A7 c

S8 There are three simple verb tenses: the _____, the _____, and the _____.

A8 present, past, future

S9 Use the _____ tense to express customary or habitual action. Complete the sentence with the present tense form of the verb *to park:* **I always _____ my car in the same parking space.**

A9 present, **park**

S10 The present tense is used to express action or state of being that (a) is customary or habitual, (b) indicates general truths, (c) is happening at the present, (d) all of the above.

A10 d

S11 To form the past tense of most verbs add _____ or _____ at the end of the verb.

A11 d, ed

S12 When you want to ask a question in the past or present tense, you need to use one of three helping verbs: _____, _____, and _____.

A12 *do, does, did*

S13 When *do, does,* and *did* are used as helping verbs in a statement, this is known as the _____ form of the verb.

A13 emphatic

S14 At one time there were a number of rules regarding the use of *shall* and *will* in forming the future tense. Most writers today (do, do not) observe these rules. They form the future tense by placing _____ before the verb.

A14 do not, *will*

S15 Current practice is to use *shall* rather than *will* in which of the following situations? (a) in questions asking for permission, (b) in legal documents to express obligation, (c) in statements to express great emotion.

A15 a, b

S16 In choosing between *should* and *would,* you generally use _____ _____ to express obligation, possibility, or probability; otherwise, you use _____.

A16 *should, would*

S17 Use either *should* or *would* to complete each of the following sentences:
   a. **She _____ like to see your résumé.**
   b. **I _____ place my résumé online.**
   c. **You _____ give your résumé to all the companies on this list.**

A17 a. **would,** b. **should,** c. **should**

SECTION B
Perfect Tenses

In this section you will add the present, past, and future perfect tenses to your list of verb tenses. These will sharpen your skills as a writer.

6.7 Three Perfect Tenses

The **perfect tenses** refer to an action completed or *perfected* at the time of the statement. The three perfect tenses are the **present perfect,** the **past perfect,** and the **future perfect.** Each is used to describe an action completed before an action in the corresponding simple tense.

Each perfect tense requires a form of the verb *to have* plus a form of the main verb called the **past participle.** *Wanted* is the past participle of the verb *to want,* and *brought* is the past participle of the verb *to bring.*

PRESENT PERFECT: has or have wanted, has or have brought
PAST PERFECT: had wanted, had brought
FUTURE PERFECT: will have wanted, will have brought

6.8 The Present Perfect Tense

The **present perfect tense** refers to an action started in the past but continuing into the present. The present perfect tense combines the verb *has* or *have* with the past participle of the main verb. If the subject is in the third person singular, use *has.* In all other cases, use *have.* For example,

She *has filed* only one report so far.

This sentence means that she has filed a report; the phrase *so far* indicates she will probably file more reports.

I *have shopped* online many times.

Have shopped indicates that I expect to shop online again. If I don't plan to do so, I would say *I shopped online many times.* The simple past tense *shopped* shows that the action is completed once and for all. The present perfect indicates that the action (shopping) started in the past and continues.

Tahir and Jane's bickering *has gone* on for weeks.

Has gone indicates that the bickering is still happening. If the bickering had stopped, then you would say *Tahir and Jane's bickering went on for weeks.*

Grammar Tip

The Perfect Tenses
Use the perfect tense to describe an action completed before an action in the corresponding simple tense.

Grammar Tip

The Present Perfect
Use the present perfect to refer to an action that was started in the past but continues into the present.

Grammar Tip

Simple Past or Present Perfect Tense?

As you have seen, the decision to use the simple past or the present perfect depends on the precise meaning you wish to convey.

Action Verb: Ms. Liang (came, has come) to see us many times.

Which is right, *came* or *has come*? The answer depends on what we mean. If Ms. Liang still comes to see us, then use the present perfect, *has come*: *Ms. Liang has come to see us many times.* If Ms. Liang will not be visiting again, use *came* to indicate that the action began and ended in the past: *Ms. Liang came to see us many times.*

Linking verb: Our offices (were, have been) there for years.

If the offices remain in the same place, use the present perfect, *have been: Our offices have been on the same corner for years.* If the offices have been moved elsewhere, use the past tense to indicate that the state of the offices being on the corner began and ended in the past: *Our offices were there for years.*

Action Just Completed

The present perfect tense is also used to indicate that an action started in the past has just been completed.

> I *have finished* reading the report.   Eureka! I *have found* it.
> Ty and Jane's bickering *has* finally *stopped.*   Her plane *has* just *landed.*

Present Tense Error: Avoid the common error of substituting the present tense for the present perfect tense.

> <u>Wrong:</u>   I am here three months.
> <u>Right:</u>   ✔ I have been here for three months.

6.9 The Past Perfect Tense

Form the **past perfect tense** by combining the auxiliary verb *had* with the past participle of the main verb. This tense indicates an action that was completed before another past action. For example,

> I arrived after she *had left.*
> She *had left* before I arrived.
> I *had stopped* payment on the check by the time he reached the bank.

The past perfect tense also indicates an action that was completed before a past time. For example,

> It *had stopped* raining by noon.
> The mechanic *had finished* the repairs by then.

CHAPTER 6 SUMMARY

In this chapter you learned that most verbs express action and are called *action verbs.* Other verbs express a state of being and are called *linking verbs.* Because verbs tell us *when* something happens, there are three simple verb tenses—present, past, and future—and three perfect tenses—present perfect, past perfect, and future perfect. You learned when to use the perfect tenses instead of the simple tenses. You also discovered how to use the helping verb *to have* with the perfect tenses.

Getting Connected

SETTING UP A FREE E-MAIL ACCOUNT

GOAL: Americans send more than 6 trillion **e-mail,** or electronic-mail messages each year. Though e-mail has not completely replaced **snail mail** (a letter mailed in a stamped envelope), it has changed the way individuals throughout the world work, play, shop, and communicate.

The next four Getting Connected activities will introduce you to the ways of e-mail while you practice the material covered in each chapter. You will set up a free e-mail account, send an e-mail message, open an e-mail message, and finally, add a word-processing document to a message.

In this Getting Connected you'll register for a free e-mail account and use the experience to demonstrate your understanding of verb tenses, linking verbs, and actions verbs.

STEP 1 Go to *englishworkshop.glencoe.com,* the address for *The English Workshop* Website, and click on Unit 3. Next click on Getting Connected, and then click on Chapter 6. At the Chapter 6 Getting Connected option, you'll see a list of Websites that offer free e-mail.

STEP 2 Choose the e-mail with which you want to establish your free account, and click on the appropriate link. You'll go to the registration page for the free e-mail.

STEP 3 Follow the instructions for completing the registration form. You'll be asked to provide two important items:

a. **User name:** The user name is the first part of an e-mail address. It's how the provider identifies you. A user name may be a combination of letters and numbers. For example, someone named *Luis Sabbas* may use *lsabbas* as his user name. Or he might combine his name and ZIP Code for the user name: *luis10019.*

In an e-mail address, the user name appears first and is followed by the **domain name,** sometimes called the **host.** *Hotmail.com, excite.com, lycos.com,* and *yahoo.com* are all domain names. The user name and domain name are separated by the @ (or *at*) symbol. Mr. Sabbas's e-mail address might be: *lsabbas@yahoo.com.*

b. Password: A password is a code word that protects your e-mail account from being abused by others. Each time you access your e-mail account, you'll be asked to provide your password.

Select a password you'll remember, such as a favorite relative's birthday, the name of your goldfish, or a word from a favorite song. Write down your password, but don't share it with others.

STEP 4 When you register for free e-mail, you may be invited to receive information on various topics. Unless you're certain you want the information, decline the invitation; otherwise, you might find your mailbox cluttered with unwanted e-mail.

STEP 5 The e-mail provider may request that you read an electronic document about the rules and regulations for using the free account. You must indicate your agreement to abide by these regulations before you can use the account.

STEP 6 Once you are registered you'll be ready to learn how to send and receive e-mail, which will be explained in The Getting Connected Activities for Chapters 7 and 8.

STEP 7 Referring to "The Verb Tense Timeline," in Section 6.11 on page 174, write six sentences about registering for a free e-mail account. Write a sentence to illustrate each of the verb tenses on the chart. Your sentences could describe some of the steps you followed and how you plan to use the e-mail account. For example, the following sentence illustrates the present perfect tense: *I have just completed the registration process for a free e-mail account at* _____. Identify each verb tense and label each verb as *action* or *linking.*

STEP 8 When you've completed your sentences, close your e-mail account. Do *not* delete any message you may have received from the e-mail provider.

STEP 9 Write your name at the top of your work and turn it in to your instructor.

Name _____

Class _____ Date _____

PRACTICE 1

Action and Linking Verbs

Instructions: Underline the verb in each sentence below. Then write *A* in the blank if the verb is an action verb or *L* if the verb is a linking verb.

can be replaced then it is linking

EXAMPLE: **The student <u>seemed</u> calm after the exam.**

ACTION OR LINKING

EX. _____ L _____

1. He felt nervous before the meeting.

2. The book appeared after a three-day search.

3. My office appears smaller with the new desk.

4. Sales grew rapidly during this quarter.

5. The room grew quiet at the sound of the gavel.

6. May I taste the punch before the guests arrive?

7 The sentry looks still but alert.

8. We looked for the book for three days.

9. Did you feel the coarse texture of the fabric?

10. She sampled all the desserts.

11. This job becomes tedious very quickly.

12 The stew smells delicious.

13 I can smell the fumes from here.

14. Did you taste those pies?

15. Do they taste overly tart to you?

16. I don't feel well.

17. Pedro appears certain of a promotion.

18. The advertisement appeared in yesterday's paper.

19. The situation looks promising.

20. Sometimes looks are deceiving.

1. _____ L _____
2. _____ A _____
3. _____ L _____
4. _____ A _____
5. _____ L _____
6. _____ A _____
7. _____ L _____
8. _____ A _____
9. _____ A _____
10. _____ L _____
11. _____ L _____
12. _____ A _____
13. _____ L _____
14. _____ A _____
15. _____ A/L _____
16. _____ L _____
17. _____ L _____
18. _____ A _____
19. _____ L _____
20. _____ A _____

Sophos → okay, need to study a little more
progressing, roommates confirm peace
Divorce, Sunday - Single afterward
mother sickly but rest of the five okay - visit often
life → lonely, single, upset.

Name _____

Class _____ Date _____

PRACTICE 2

The Present Perfect or Simple Past Tense

Instructions: Some of the following sentences call for a verb in the present perfect tense. Others require one in the simple past tense. In the blank, write the correct verb for each sentence.

EXAMPLE: **Since you left the sales floor, there (be) very little activity.**　　EX. ___**has been**___

1. During the past four months our division (generate) nearly $1 million in sales.　　1.___has___

2. We (be) here for the past hour.　　2.___have___

3. He (miss) class three times last week.　　3.___missed___

4. The present governor (be) in office for seven years.　　4._____

5. The former governor (be) in office for one term.　　5._____

6. Because he was unemployed, he (default) on his loan.　　6._____

7. During the time I have been here, the clerk (accomplish) nothing.　　7._____

8. The clerk (accomplish) nothing the entire time I was there.　　8._____

9. Profits (drop) sharply since the remodeling of the mall began.　　9._____

10. The network (be) down most of yesterday afternoon.　　10._____

11. The network (be) down for nearly an hour so far.　　11._____

12. I (be) in this office since 9 a.m.　　12._____

13. He (serve) the company for nearly 20 years now.　　13._____

14. She (travel) to St. Louis last week.　　14._____

15. I (substitute) for this company since graduating.　　15._____

16. While I was ill, no one (answer) my e-mail.　　16._____

17. He (serve) the company for 20 years before his retirement.　　17._____

18. I (substitute) for this company until last July.　　18._____

19. My candidate (maintain) the lead from the outset.　　19._____

20. The surprise candidate (maintain) the lead in the polls until last week.　　20._____

has or have waited

add d or ed

PRACTICE 3

The Past Perfect or Simple Past Tense

Instructions: In the blank, write the correct past perfect or simple perfect verb tense for each sentence.

EXAMPLE: **The mail (arrive) before we opened the office.**   EX. _____**had arrived**_____

1. The mechanic (complete) eight oil changes by noon.   1. _____

2. As the bell rang, I (finish) answering the final question.   2. _____

3. By the time the bell rang, I (finish) the final question.   3. _____

4. We (ship) the order before we received your notice.   4. _____

5. We (help) him distribute leaflets last week.   5. _____

6. Your officers (be) helpful throughout yesterday's meeting.   6. _____

7. The inspector knew the crowd (be) dispersed before she arrived.   7. _____

8. We smelled smoke as soon as we (open) the door.   8. _____

9. By 10 a.m. I (contact) every member of the committee.   9. _____

10. This morning I (contact) every committee member.   10. _____

Name _____

Class _____ Date _____

PRACTICE 4

The Future Perfect or Simple Future Tense

Instructions: In the blank, write the correct future perfect or simple future verb tense for each sentence.

EXAMPLE: **By the time this reaches you, we (finalize) our plans.**   EX. _____**will have finalized**_____

1. I (escort) you to lunch after the conference.

2. By noon Wednesday we (close) the deal.

3. We (close) the deal on Wednesday.

4. We (implement) these changes by the time you return.

5. I (contact) you from the airport tomorrow.

6. When you arrive we (complete) the initial work.

7. When will Ms. Hodge (reach) the motel?

8. She (reach) the motel later this evening.

9. Certainly she (reach) the motel by 10 p.m.

10. She (finish) her report by then.

1. _____will_____

2. _____will have closed_____

3. _____will_____

4. _____will have /ed_____

5. _____will_____

6. _____will have /ed_____

7. _____

8. _____will_____

9. _____will have /ed_____

10. _____will have /ed_____

PRACTICE 5

Verb Tenses

Instructions: The following letter contains many intentional errors in verb tenses. Cross out all errors and write the necessary corrections in the space above each error.

Clarkson ◆ Company

February 27, 20--

Ms. Marian Akeo
2650 Alta Vista Street
Casper, WY 82601

Dear Ms. Akeo:

During the last four years you had sent us an order regularly every other week. You always express your complete satisfaction with our products'. That was why we are puzzled now. Our records indicated that we have not received an order from you in nearly two months. Had something happened? Possibly something has developed of which we are unaware.

If we have made a mistake in filling an order, please tell us. We at Clarkson Company valued our customers and will try to keep our customers satisfied. A satisfied customer was the foundation of our company. We did not feel satisfied until you were.

If there will be a problem, please tell us. If not, will you please review the list of our merchandise, which I have enclosed. In addition, you noticed that we instituted a new billing procedure that I think you would have liked. It is more convenient for you than our previous one. I also wanted to bring to your attention the current price reductions: there is a 15 percent reduction in the deluxe line and a 20 percent reduction in the standard lines. These reductions were explained fully on the enclosed list.

These new prices and procedures will have illustrated our continuing efforts to satisfy our customers. Why not take advantage of them by placing an order today? We have hoped to hear from you soon.

Very truly yours,

Thomas Blue Eagle, Accounts Manager

2729 N. PLACITA NUEVA ◆ TUCSON, AZ 85741

Name _____

Class _____ Date _____

PRACTICE 6

Verb Tenses

Instructions: In the blank, write the tense of each italicized verb.

EXAMPLE: **Wareman's** *employs* **nearly 200 people.**   EX. _____ <u>Simple Present</u>

1. She *does expect* to receive a reply soon.   1. _____

2. Akiko *met* with her accountant yesterday.   2. _____

3. Sheila *has worked* at Wareman's since 1975.   3. _____

4. Victor *had made* the motion and Maki *had*   4. _____
   seconded it before Parnell could voice an objection.   _____

5. By April our companies *will have merged* with   5. _____
   Xerxes Corporation.

6. You *do understand* my position, don't you?   6. _____

7. Unless we are able to reach an agreement by Friday, contractual   7. _____
   requirements *will force* us to submit the dispute to binding
   arbitration.

8. My car *depreciated* in value nearly 30 percent   8. _____
   during the first 12 months.

9. The department assistants *had assembled*   9. _____
   the class handouts by noon.

10. By the time Claudia *has edited* these chapters,   10. _____
    Keith *will have written* another one.   _____

11. By the end of my freshman year, I *had earned* 36 hours of credit.   11. _____

12. By the end of my freshman year, I *will have*   12. _____
    earned 36 hours of credit.

13. John and Isabel *studied* music for 15 years.   13. _____

14. John and Isabel *have studied* music for 15 years.   14. _____

15. Charmaine *had run* the fastest time of the day   15. _____
    until Paula finished her qualifying run.

16. I *was* worried about the condition of the transmission.   16. _____

17. I *am* worried about the condition of the transmission.   17. _____

18. By the time he completes the project, Jeremiah   18. _____
    will have been at sea for more than 13 months.

19. When I know the experiment is finished, I *will dismiss* the class.   19. _____

20. The employee we honor today *had* a distinguished career.   20. _____

Name _____

Class _____ Date _____

PRACTICE 7

Composition: Using the Simple Tenses

Instructions: Write complete sentences containing the verb forms specified in the parentheses.

EXAMPLE: **(first person simple past tense of *to go*)**
        I went to the park yesterday evening.

1. (first person simple future tense of *to pay*)

_____

_____

2. (third person simple past tense of *to be*)

_____

_____

3. (third person emphatic past tense of *to buy*)

_____

_____

4. (third person present tense of *to sell*)

_____

_____

5. (second person emphatic present tense of *to work*)

_____

_____

Name _____

Class _____ Date _____

PRACTICE 8

Composition: Correcting Verb Tenses

Instructions: The verb tenses in the following sentences contain errors. Correct each error. Then, in one or more complete sentences, explain as specifically as you can the reasons for the corrections you made.

has lived
EXAMPLE: **Ms. Fiore ~~lives~~ in this apartment since September.**

The present perfect tense, not the simple present, is used to show action that was started in the past but continues into the present.

1. We had solved our cash flow problem last year.

_____

_____

2. The board members agreed on this plan of action before they adjourned for lunch.

_____

_____

3. Lois's chronic absenteeism will have caused her to be fired.

_____

_____

4. Maya will complete her analysis by the end of the week.

_____

_____

5. Right now, Edgar planned to major in business education.

_____

_____

More Verbs

CHAPTER

7

CHAPTER 7 PREVIEW

In this chapter you will focus on the six tenses of the progressive verb form. You will learn to distinguish between transitive and intransitive verbs and to form the principal parts of regular and irregular verbs. You will continue to assess your comprehension in the Programmed Reinforcement sections and the Practices. Finally, you will compose and send an e-mail message using your e-mail account.

OBJECTIVES

After completing this chapter, you will be able to

- Form the progressive form of the verb for all six tenses:
  - Present progressive
  - Past progressive
  - Future progressive
  - Present perfect progressive
  - Past perfect progressive
  - Future perfect progressive
- Determine when to use the simple verb tense and when to use the progressive form.
- Identify and use correctly the principal parts of regular and irregular verbs.
- Form verb phrases using helping verbs with present and past participles.
- Distinguish between a transitive verb and an intransitive verb.
- Use correct forms of confusing verb pairs *lay/lie, set/sit,* and *raise/rise.*

Study Plan for Chapter 7

The Study Plan for Chapter 7 offers a set of strategies that will help you learn and review the chapter material.

❶ Past Participle Forms: Cover the columns for the Past Participle forms in the irregular verb charts. Read aloud the present form of a verb. Then, determine its participle form and say that aloud.

❷ Transitive Verb *Lay*: When *lay* is used to mean "place," it requires a direct object—the thing being placed or laid.

❸ Transitive Verb *Set*: Like *lay,* the verb *set* can also mean "place." It too requires a direct object—the thing being placed or *set.*

❹ Transitive Verb *Raise*: A good dictionary will probably list many definitions for the verb *raise.* Whatever definition you use, *raise* always needs a direct object—the thing that has been raised.

SECTION A
Progressive Forms and Principal Verb Parts

In this section you will discover when and where to use the progressive instead of the simple present. After looking at regular verb families, you will examine in detail how the principal parts of irregular verbs change (or do not change) in spelling as their tenses shift. Mastering the irregular verb families will be a matter of practice and memorization. Paying attention to patterns among verb families will make this process easier.

7.1 The Progressive Form

The **progressive form** is used to show that the action described is continuing or unfinished at the time indicated by one of the six tenses. Look at these sentences:

> The mechanic *is working* on your truck right *now*.

This sentence is in the **present progressive.** The action is in progress at the present time. The mechanic is working now. The work is unfinished.

> Finn *was studying* when Jace called.

This sentence is in the **past progressive.** Finn's studying was in progress when it was interrupted by Jace. His studying was unfinished.

Notice that each of the principal verbs—*working* and *studying*—ends in *ing*. This form of the verb is called the **present participle.** Also notice that each verb is preceded by a form of the verb *to be*.

To indicate that an action is, was, or will be unfinished, use the progressive form of the verb. The progressive is formed by using the appropriate form of the verb *to be* with the *ing* form of the principal verb (the present participle).

Progressive Forms of *To Call*

Here are the progressive forms of the verb *to call* for the six tenses, using the third person singular.

Present progressive:	Troy is calling all our clients.
Past progressive:	He was calling all our clients.
Future progressive:	He will be calling all our clients.
Present perfect progressive:	He has been calling all our clients.
Past perfect progressive:	He had been calling all our clients.
Future perfect progressive:	He will have been calling all our clients.

Grammar Tip

The Progressive Equation

Form of *to be* + *ing* form of verb = progressive form

are + *learning* = present progressive form

was + *learning* = past progressive form

Simple Tense or Progressive Form?

Occasionally you will have to decide whether to use the simple tense or the progressive form. Ask yourself whether the action is or was finished. If the action is finished, use the simple tense. If the action was interrupted or is unfinished, use the progressive form.

SENTENCE 1: **I (read, was reading) my e-mail when the fire alarm sounded.**

ASK: Was the action finished?

ANSWER: No. It was interrupted by the fire alarm and unfinished.

THEREFORE: Use the past progressive form: I *was reading* my e-mail when the fire alarm sounded.

SENTENCE 2: **She (develops, is developing) the film at this very moment.**

ASK: Is the action finished?

ANSWER: No. She is still developing the film, so the action is unfinished.

THEREFORE: Use the present progressive form: She *is developing* the film at this very moment.

SENTENCE 3: **We (reviewed, were reviewing) for the exam every evening last week.**

ASK: Was the action finished?

ANSWER: Yes. The review was completed by the end of the week. No action was interrupted.

THEREFORE: Use the simple past tense: We *reviewed* for the exam every evening last week.

SENTENCE 4: **They (worked, were working) feverishly until dawn.**

ASK: Was the action finished?

ANSWER: Yes. This example is tricky. The dawn did not interrupt the work. Instead, the dawn marked the moment when the work stopped.

THEREFORE: Use the simple past tense because you know the work ended. It was not interrupted: They *worked* feverishly until dawn. But use the past progressive form to indicate action that was interrupted and not finished: They *were working* feverishly when time ran out.

SENTENCE 5: **I (listened, was listening) to the radio when the accident happened.**

ASK: Was the action completed?

ANSWER: No. It was interrupted by the accident and unfinished.

THEREFORE: Use the past progressive form: I *was listening* to the radio when the accident happened.

Lights-Out Factory

The *lights-out factory* is a high-tech ideal for the (near?) future. Entirely automated, it houses no humans and therefore requires no lights for human eyes to monitor its operations.

SENTENCE 6: **We (will eat, will be eating) dessert by the time Josephine reaches the restaurant.**

ASK: Will the action be finished?

ANSWER: No. The individuals will still be eating dessert when Josephine reaches the restaurant.

THEREFORE: Use the future progressive form: We *will be eating* dessert by the time Josephine reaches the restaurant.

7.2 The Principal Parts of the Verb

The **principal parts of the verb** are the (1) present, (2) past, and (3) perfect, or the (1) present, (2) past, and (3) past participle. By knowing these principal parts, you can form all simple and perfect tenses.

In Section 6.11 in Chapter 6, the verb *to work* was used in a chart outlining the six tenses. Did you notice that all six tenses were formed by using either *work* or *worked* plus a helping verb? The simple present and past, of course, require no helping verb. The word *work* is a regular verb that follows a common pattern when it changes tenses.

Grammar Tip

Past Tense = Past Participle

The past tense of regular verbs is identical in form to the past participle.

7.3 Regular Verbs

Like the verb *to work,* most verbs are **regular verbs.** They form the past tense by adding *d* or *ed* to the present tense, and they form the present perfect tense by placing the word *has* or *have* before the past tense. The following are examples of regular verbs:

REGULAR VERBS

Present	Past	Present Perfect
receive	received	has or have received
like	liked	has or have liked
allow	allowed	has or have allowed
call	called	has or have called

Verbs Ending in y. For regular verbs ending in a consonant plus *y*, change the *y* to *i* and add *ed* to form the past tense.

REGULAR VERBS ENDING IN Y

Present	Past	Present Perfect
cry	cried	has or have cried
comply	complied	has or have complied

Verbs Ending in a Vowel and a Consonant. For regular verbs ending in a vowel and consonant (except *w*, *x*, or *y*) with the accent on the final syllable, double the final consonant before adding *ed*.

REGULAR VERBS ENDING IN A VOWEL AND A CONSONANT

Present	Past	Present Perfect
permit	permitted	has or have permitted
occur	occurred	has or have occurred
ship	shipped	has or have shipped

You already know the principal parts of most regular verbs and can form all six tenses of regular verbs as the chart below indicates.

PRINCIPAL PARTS OF THE REGULAR VERB *TO RECEIVE*

Present Tense	Singular	Plural
First person:	I receive	we receive
Second person:	you receive	you receive
Third person:	he, she, it receives	they receive

Past Tense		
First person:	I received	we received
Second person:	you received	you received
Third person:	he, she, it received	they received

Future Tense		
First person:	I will receive	we will receive
Second person:	you will receive	you will receive
Third person:	he, she, it will receive	they will receive

Present Perfect Tense		
First person:	I have received	we have received
Second person:	you have received	you have received
Third person:	he, she, it has received	they have received

Past Perfect Tense		
First person:	I had received	we had received
Second person:	you had received	you had received
Third person:	he, she, it had received	they had received

Future Perfect Tense		
First person:	I will have received	we will have received
Second person:	you will have received	you will have received
Third person:	he, she, it will have received	they will have received

Grammar Tip

Nonstandard Contraction

Ain't is a nonstandard contraction of *am not.* Some people also use it to mean *are not, is not, has not,* or *have not. Ain't* is generally not acceptable in writing or speaking.

Some verbs do not form their past and perfect tenses in the regular manner. These verbs are called **irregular verbs.**

Irregular *To Be* and *To Have* Verbs

The two most common irregular verbs—*to be* and *to have*—are used to form the perfect and the progressive tenses. The principal parts of *to have* are *have, has,* and *had.* The verb *to be*—the most important verb in the English language—is also the most irregular. The following chart details this important verb in all six tenses.

PRINCIPAL PARTS OF THE IRREGULAR VERB *TO BE*

Present Tense	**Singular**	**Plural**
First person:	I am	we are
Second person:	you are	you are
Third person:	he, she, it is	they are

Past Tense		
First person:	I was	we were
Second person:	you were	you were
Third person:	he, she, it was	they were

Future Tense		
First person:	I will be	we will be
Second person:	you will be	you will be
Third person:	he, she, it will be	they will be

Present Perfect Tense		
First person:	I have been	we have been
Second person:	you have been	you have been
Third person:	he, she, it has been	they have been

Past Perfect Tense		
First person:	I had been	we had been
Second person:	you had been	you had been
Third person:	he, she, it had been	they had been

Future Perfect Tense		
First person:	I will have been	we will have been
Second person:	you will have been	you will have been
Third person:	he, she, it will have been	they will have been

Other Irregular Verbs

Fortunately, the other irregular verbs are not as irregular as *to be* and *to have*. Most follow one of several basic patterns and thus can be grouped. For instance, there are obvious similarities among the following forms:

Present	Past	Past Participle
drink	drank	drunk
sink	sank	sunk
shrink	shrank	shrunk

Irregular Verb Families

The following lists group words according to the patterns they follow when changing tenses. Study these word families and their patterns by reading them *aloud* so that you can *hear* the similarities. *Hearing* these sound patterns is the quickest, surest way to master the principal parts.

No helping verb has been provided with the past participle because the helping verb will change with the tense and the speaker. In the case of *drunk*, for example, the present perfect tense would be *has drunk* (third person singular) or *have drunk* (all other persons), the past perfect would be *had drunk*, and the future perfect would be *will have drunk*.

Irregular Verb Family 1: *-ought* and *-aught*

Present	Past	Past Participle
think	thought	thought
bring	brought	brought
buy	bought	bought
fight	fought	fought
seek	sought	sought
teach	taught	taught

Irregular Verb Family 2: *-an/-un, -am/-um, -ang/-ung,* and *-ank/-unk*

Present	Past	Past Participle
begin	began	begun
run	ran	run
swim	swam	swum
ring	rang	rung
sing	sang	sung
spring	sprang	sprung
sink	sank	sunk
shrink	shrank	shrunk
drink	drank	drunk

Grammar Tip

Checking Principal Verb Parts

If a verb is irregular, the dictionary will list the principal parts. If no principal parts are listed, the verb is regular and its past tense and past participle are formed by adding *d* or *ed*.

Irregular Verb Family 3: *-ew/-own, -ew/-awn, -ore/-orn, and -owed/-own*

Present	Past	Past Participle
blow	blew	blown
grow	grew	grown
know	knew	known
throw	threw	thrown
fly	flew	flown
draw	drew	drawn
withdraw	withdrew	withdrawn
wear	wore	worn
swear	swore	sworn
show	showed	shown

Irregular Verb Family 4: *-t/-t*

Present	Past	Past Participle
leave	left	left
build	built	built
deal	dealt	dealt
feel	felt	felt
bend	bent	bent
lend	lent	lent
send	sent	sent
spend	spent	spent
mean	meant	meant
keep	kept	kept
sleep	slept	slept
sweep	swept	swept
weep	wept	wept
lose	lost	lost

Irregular Verb Family 5: Vowels That Do Not Change With Endings *-en* and *-ten*

Present	Past	Past Participle
awake	awoke	awoken or awakened
break	broke	broken
speak	spoke	spoken
steal	stole	stolen
choose	chose	chosen
freeze	froze	frozen
forget	forgot	forgotten

SELF-TALK Start paying attention to your self-talk. It may be having a negative effect on your attitude at work or in school. Try replacing this negative inner voice with an uplifting one.

Irregular Verb Family 6: Vowels That Change With Endings
-EN, -DEN, AND -TEN

Present	Past	Past Participle
take	took	taken
mistake	mistook	mistaken
shake	shook	shaken
fall	fell	fallen
arise	arose	arisen
eat	ate	eaten
drive	drove	driven
strive	strove	striven
give	gave	given
forbid	forbade	forbidden
hide	hid	hidden
write	wrote	written
typewrite	typewrote	typewritten
underwrite	underwrote	underwritten
bite	bit	bitten

The verbs in the group below are irregular because they do not change at all. They are the same in the present, past, and perfect tenses.

Irregular Verb Family 7: Verbs That Do Not Change

Present	Past	Past Participle
bid	bid	bid
burst	burst	burst
bet	bet	bet
cost	cost	cost
cut	cut	cut
forecast	forecast	forecast
hurt	hurt	hurt
let	let	let
put	put	put
quit	quit	quit
read	read	read
spread	spread	spread
thrust	thrust	thrust

Note: Although the past and past participle forms of *read* are spelled the same, they are pronounced differently.

The verbs in the final group below do not belong to any of the above families and illustrate a variety of patterns. Say the words aloud until they sound familiar.

High-Tech Manuals

Employers look for strong communication and analytical skills in automotive service technician trainees. Technical manuals demand good reading skills—not just mechanical talent.

Present	Past	Past Participle
come	came	come
become	became	become
bleed	bled	bled
lead	led	led
flee	fled	fled
meet	met	met
bind	bound	bound
stand	stood	stood
win	won	won
hold	held	held
stick	stuck	stuck
strike	struck	struck
string	strung	strung
have	had	had
say	said	said
make	made	made
do	did	done
go	went	gone
see	saw	seen

Grammar Tip

Frequently Used Helping Verbs	
am	do
are	does
is	did
was	
were	may
been	might
	must
has	
have	will
had	would
	should
can	
could	

7.5 Helping Verbs

Never use the present and past participles alone. They must always be used with one or more helping verbs in a verb phrase.

Most helping verbs can be used with other helping verbs (*did have, could have*), with the combined form *have been* (*may have been, must have been*), or with the present participle *being* (*am being, was being*).

I *should have stayed* home.   You *might have been* injured.
You *should have been* more careful.   You *were being* foolish.

7.6 Past Participle Mistakes

If you know the principal parts of the verb and remember that participles cannot be used alone, you will never make the common mistake of substituting the past participle of an irregular verb for the simple past tense.

WRONG	RIGHT
(Misused Past Participle)	**(Simple Past)**
1. I *seen* your picture.	**1.** I *saw* your picture.
2. She *begun* to feel ill today.	**2.** She *began* to feel ill today.
3. Quasimodo *rung* the bell.	**3.** Quasimodo *rang* the bell.

Coverage Key

Section			Statement
7.1	➤	The Progressive Form	➤ **S1, S2, S3, S4**
7.2	➤	The Principal Parts of the Verb	➤ **S5**
7.3	➤	Regular Verbs	➤ **S7, S8, S9**
7.4	➤	Irregular Verbs	➤ **S6, S9, S10, S11, S12, S13, S14, S15, S16, S18**
7.5	➤	Helping Verbs	➤ **S18**
7.6	➤	Past Participle Mistakes	➤ **S17**

Instructions: Cover the answers in the **Answer** column; then write your answer to the first statement. Uncover the first printed answer and compare your answer to it. If you wrote a correct answer, continue the activity. If you made an error, use the **Coverage Key** to locate the chapter section you need to review. When you are confident that you understand the material, continue with the reinforcement activity.

ANSWER

STATEMENT

S1 The progressive form of the verb ends in _____.
It is known as the _____.

A1 **ing**, present participle

S2 In the sentence **I am reading now,** the progressive form of the verb means that the action is (finished, still in progress).

A2 still in progress

S3 Choose the correct sentence:
   a. **I was scanning a document when the computer froze up.**
   b. **I scanned the document when the computer froze up.**

A3 a.

S4 a. Ilya (come) up the stairs right now. Write the correct form of the verb **come:** _____
   b. **We (work) on the transmission all day.** Write the correct form of the verb **work:** _____
   c. **When the power failed, we (watch) television.** Write the correct form of the verb **watch:** _____

A4 a. **is coming** (present progressive),
   b. **worked** (simple past),
   c. **were watching** (past progressive)

S5 The present, the past, and the perfect (past participle) tenses of the verb are known as its _____.

A5 principal parts

S6 Verbs may form their past and perfect tenses in a regular or a(n) _____ manner.

A6 irregular

S7 The verb **to walk** is an example of a(n) _____ verb. Its principal parts are present: _____; past: _____; and past participle: _____.

A7 regular; **walk, walked, walked**

S8 In a regular verb, the past tense and the _____ are identical.

A8 past participle

S9 Which of the following are regular verbs? **call, try, bring, teach, talk**

A9 **call, try, talk**

S10 The verb **drink** is a(n) _____ verb. Write the principal parts of the verb **drink**; present: _____; past: _____; and past participle: _____.

A10 irregular; **drink, drank, drunk**

S11 **I gave the list to the clerk who had begun the inventory.** The tense of **gave** is _____; the tense of **had begun** is _____.

A11 past, past perfect

S12 Fill in the appropriate forms of the verbs:

Present tense	Past tense	Past participle
tear	_____	_____
_____	_____	flown

A12 tore, torn;
fly, flew

S13 Fill in the appropriate forms of the verbs:

Present tense	Past tense	Past participle
spring	_____	_____
_____	shrank	_____

A13 sprang, sprung;
shrink, shrunk

S14 Write the correct verbs in these sentences:
a. **I asked you because I (think) you knew.** _____
b. **She (quit) the team last week.** _____

A14 a. **thought**
b. **quit**

S15 Write the correct verbs in these sentences:
a. **I have (swim) twice a week this month.** _____
b. **The well has (go) dry.** _____
c. **He (see) that movie last week.** _____

A15 a. **swum**
b. **gone**
c. **saw**

S16 Write the correct verbs in these sentences:
a. **He has (choose) a few samples.** _____
b. **The pipe (burst) in the factory.** _____

A16 a. **chosen**
b. **burst**

S17 The past participle of an irregular verb (may, may not) be used as a substitute for the simple tense.

A17 may not

S18 Which of the following sentences is/are correct?
a. **She done very well.**   c. **He came to my home yesterday.**
b. **She did very well.**   d. **He come to my house yesterday.**

A18 b., c.

Moving beyond verb tenses, you will now learn how to classify verbs as either transitive or intransitive. This next section will illustrate the value of knowing the difference between these two verb types.

7.7 Transitive and Intransitive Verbs

A sentence must have a noun or pronoun as its subject and a verb as its predicate. You can combine a noun and a verb and still not have a meaningful sentence. For example,

The student mailed.

This expression contains the noun *student* and the verb *mailed*. Is it a sentence? No. It does not express a complete meaning. It lacks an explanation of what was mailed. This expression needs an object of the verb *mailed*—a word that will tell us what was mailed. For example,

The student mailed the package.

The noun *package* is the object of the verb *mailed* because it tells us what was mailed.

Transitive Verbs

A verb that needs an object to make sense is called a **transitive verb** because the action *transfers* to the object.

Milos put the letter on the table.

The verb *put* is transitive; the object of the transitive verb *put* is *letter*. The transitive verb requires an object to complete a meaningful statement.

Intransitive Verbs

Many verbs do not require objects to complete the meaning of a sentence. For example,

Ms. Cagnon spoke.   The plaster shook.   The group met.

Each of the verbs above completes the sentence without an object. None of these verbs requires an object. They are intransitive. A verb that does not take an object is called an **intransitive verb.**

Grammar Tip

Dictionary Help

Your dictionary will tell you whether a verb is transitive, intransitive, or both.

Transitive or Intransitive?

Some verbs can be either transitive or intransitive depending on their use in a sentence. In the previous examples, *spoke, shook,* and *met* are all *intransitive* because they do not take objects. However, these verbs and certain others can also be used as transitive verbs.

VERBS THAT CAN BE EITHER INTRANSITIVE OR TRANSITIVE

Intransitive
1. Ms. Cagnon spoke.
2. The group met.
3. The plaster shook.

Transitive
1. Ms. Cagnon spoke French fluently.
2. Mr. Rettig met Mr. Auch.
3. The two opponents shook hands after the match.

The sentences with transitive verbs all take objects.

Once you are familiar with the difference between transitive and intransitive verbs, you will be better able to decide on the proper verb needed when using such frequently confused verbs as *lie/ lay, sit/set,* and *rise/raise.*

Grammar Tip

Lay/Lie

Lay is *transitive;* it **always** needs an object to complete its meaning.
Lie is *intransitive;* it **never** needs an object to complete its meaning.

7.8 Lay/Lie

The two words *lay* and *lie* are probably confused more often than any other pair of words in the English language. Yet they have very different meanings and are different types of verbs.

- *To lay* means *to place. To lay* is *transitive* because it needs an object.
- *To lie* means *to recline. To lie* is *intransitive* because it does not need an object.

Memorize the forms of *lay* and *lie.*

PRINCIPAL FORMS OF *LAY* AND *LIE*

	Present	Past	Past Participle	Present Participle
Transitive	lay	laid	laid	laying
Intransitive	lie	lay	lain	lying

Review how the verbs are used differently in the sentences below.

SAMPLE SENTENCES OF *LAY* AND *LIE*

Transitive—Lay
1. I lay the book on the table.
2. I laid the book on the table.
3. I was laying the book on the table when he entered.
4. I have laid the book on the table as you requested.

Intransitive—Lie
1. I lie on the grass.
2. I am lying on the grass.
3. I lay on the grass yesterday.
4. I have lain on the grass every afternoon this week.

Notice that each sentence with a form of *lay* has an object. However, no sentences with any form of *lie* have objects.

Lay/Lie Test

You can test whether you need a form of *lay* or a form of *lie* in a sentence. Determine whether you need a transitive verb—because the sentence needs an object of the verb—or an intransitive verb—because the sentence needs no object. Use the object-finding question *what* or *whom* after the verb.

SENTENCE 1: **Please (lay, lie) the book on the table.**
Ask *what* after the verb: (*Lay, Lie*) what?
Answer: *the book.*
The sentence needs an object, so the transitive verb *lay* is needed.

SENTENCE 2: **Sugar, our cat, often (lays, lies) on the front steps.**
Ask *what* after the verb: (*Lays, Lies*) what?
No answer to the object-finding question makes sense given the sentence, so the intransitive verb *lies* is needed.

SENTENCE 3: **The workers (lay, laid) the carpeting yesterday.**
Ask *what* after the verb: (*Lay, Laid*) what?
Answer: *the carpeting.*
The sentence needs an object, so the transitive verb *laid* is needed.

SENTENCE 4: **I (lay, laid) in bed all day yesterday.**
Ask *what* after the verb: Has (*laid, lay*) what?
No answer to the object-finding question makes sense given the sentence, so the intransitive verb *lay* is needed.

SENTENCE 5: **They have (lain, laid) their cards on the table.**
Ask *what* after the verb: Have (*lain, laid*) what?
Answer: *their cards.*
The sentence needs an object, so the transitive verb *laid* is needed.

SENTENCE 6: **Zeb has (lain, laid) in a hospital bed for more than a month.**
Ask *what* after the verb: Has (*lain, laid*) what?
No answer to the object-finding question makes sense given the sentence, so the intransitive verb *lain* is needed.

SENTENCE 7: **The books have (laid, lain) on the shelves for years.**
Ask *what* after the verb: Have (*laid, lain*) what? No answer to the object-finding question makes sense given the sentence, so the intransitive verb *lain* is needed.

SENTENCE 8: **The books are still (laying, lying) there.**
By now you should be able to use the object-finding question to determine which verb, transitive or intransitive, is needed.

If you understand the difference between *lay* and *lie,* you should easily master the distinctions between *set* and *sit* and between *raise* and *rise.*

7.9 Set/Sit

- *To set* means *to place. To set* is *transitive.*
- *To sit* means *to be seated. To sit* is *intransitive.*

Memorize the forms of *set* and *sit.*

Grammar Tip

Set/Sit

Set is *transitive;* it **always** needs an object to complete its meaning.
Sit is *intransitive;* it **never** needs an object to complete its meaning.

PRINCIPAL FORMS OF *SET* AND *SIT*

	Present	Past	Past Participle	Present Participle
Transitive	set	set	set	setting
Intransitive	sit	sat	sat	sitting

Review how the two verbs are used differently in the sentences below.

SAMPLE SENTENCES OF *SET* AND *SIT*

Transitive—*Set*
1. He *sets* the planter in the window.
2. He is *setting* the planter in the window.
3. He *set* the planter in the window yesterday.
4. He *has set* the planter in the window as requested.

Intransitive—*Sit*
1. The director *sits* at the head of the table.
2. The director *is sitting* at the head of the table.
3. The director *sat* at the head of the table yesterday.
4. The director *has sat* at the head of the table at every meeting.

Set/Sit Test

Set is transitive and always needs an object to complete its meaning by telling what was set. *Sit* never takes an object to complete its meaning; it is intransitive. Test whether you need the transitive verb *set* or the intransitive verb *sit* by using the object-finding question.

SENTENCE 1: **Melissa can (set, sit) in front of the computer for hours.**
Ask *what* after the verb: Can (*set, sit*) what?
No answer to the object-finding question makes sense given the sentence, so the intransitive verb *sit* is used.

SENTENCE 2: **She has been (setting, sitting) for hours.**
Ask *what* after the verb: Has been (*setting, sitting*) what?
No answer to the object-finding question makes sense given the sentence, so the intransitive verb *sitting* is used.

SENTENCE 3: **She is careful not to (set, sit) her drink near the keyboard.**
Ask *what* after the verb: (*Set, Sit*) what?
Answer: *her drink.*
The sentence needs an object, so the transitive verb *set* is needed.

The verb *to set* has several meanings other than *to place.* For example,

The sun *sets* in the west.
It takes about one day for the cement *to set.*

Do not use *sit* in these situations.

7.10 *Raise/Rise*

- *To raise* means *to lift. To raise* is *transitive.*
- *To rise* means *to get up. To rise* is *intransitive.*

Memorize the forms of *raise* and *rise.*

PRINCIPAL FORMS OF RAISE AND RISE

	Present	Past	Past Participle	Present Participle
Transitive	raise	raised	raised	raising
Intransitive	rise	rose	risen	rising

Review how the two verbs are used differently in the sentences that follow on the next page.

Grammar Tip

Rise/Raise

Raise is transitive; it **always** needs an object to complete its meaning.
Rise is intransitive; it **never** needs an object to complete its meaning.

Transitive—*Raise*	Intransitive—*Rise*
1. I *raise* the flag each morning.	**1.** I *rise* early every morning.
2. I *raised* the flag at dawn this morning.	**2.** I *rose* early yesterday.
3. I have *raised* the flag every morning.	**3.** I *have risen* early every morning this week.
4. I *have been raising* the flag every morning this summer.	**4.** I *have been rising* early every morning this week.

Raise/Rise Test

Grammar Tip

Visual Clue for Intransitives

Lⓘe
Sⓘt ——— ⓘntransitive
Rⓘse

Raise is transitive and always needs an object to complete its meaning. It requires a word to tell us what was raised. Because *rise* never takes an object to complete its meaning, it is intransitive. Again, use the object-finding question *what* to help determine whether you need the transitive verb *raise* or the intransitive verb *rise*.

SENTENCE 1: **After he fell, he (raised, rose) himself off the floor.**
Ask *whom* after the verb: (*Raised, Rose*) whom?
Answer: *himself.*
The sentence needs an object, so the transitive verb *raised* is needed.

SENTENCE 2: **The hot-air balloon (raised, rose) from the ground.**
Ask *what* after the verb: (*Raised, Rose*) what?
No answer to the object-finding question makes sense given the sentence, so the intransitive verb *rose* is used.

SENTENCE 3: **The balloon was (raising, rising) rapidly when the pilot made an error.**
Ask *what* after the verb: Was (*raising, rising*) what?
No answer to the object-finding question makes sense given the sentence, so the intransitive verb *rising* is used.

7.11 Summary of Transitive and Intransitive Verbs

The three verbs—*lay, set,* and *raise*—are transitive and require objects to complete their meaning. Whenever there is no answer to the question *what* after a form of one of those verbs, that verb is intransitive and must be a form of the verbs *lie, sit,* or *rise.*

Coverage Key

Section		Statement
7.7	➤ Transitive and Intransitive Verbs	➤ **S19, S21, S22, S23**
7.8	➤ Lay/Lie	➤ **S20, S24, S25, S26**
7.9	➤ Set/Sit	➤ **S27, S28**
7.10	➤ Raise/Rise	➤ **S29**

Instructions: Cover the answers in the **Answer** column; then write your answer to the first statement. Uncover the first printed answer and compare your answer to it. If you wrote a correct answer, continue the activity. If you made an error, use the **Coverage Key** to locate the chapter section you need to review. When you are confident that you understand the material, continue with the reinforcement activity.

ANSWER

STATEMENT

S19 **The officer approved the loan. Loan** is the recipient of the action. It is the _____ of the verb _____.

A19 object, **approved**

S20 To find the object of a verb, ask yourself *what* or _____ after the verb.

A20 *whom*

S21 Underline two objects of verbs in this sentence. **She complimented her assistant and gave him a bonus.**

A21 <u>assistant</u>, <u>bonus</u>

S22 A verb that takes an object is called a *transitive* verb. A verb that does not need an object is called a(n) _____ verb.

A22 intransitive

S23 Underline the transitive verbs in these sentences:
a. **He put the mail on the desk.**
b. **Lay the envelope on the desk.**

A23 a. <u>put</u>; b. <u>Lay</u>

S24 **To lie** means *to recline;* **to lay** means *to place.* What are the three parts of the verb **to lie?** What are the three parts of the verb **to lay?**

A24 lie; lay; lain; lay; laid; laid

S25 Underline the verb that is intransitive: **to lie** or **to lay.**

A25 <u>to lie</u>

S26 Underline the correct forms:
   a. I need (to lie, to lay) down on the couch.
   b. He has (laid, lain) in front of the television all afternoon.
   c. She (lay, laid) the mail on the table and walked out.
   d. I'm going to (lie, lay) down the law.

A26 a. <u>to lie,</u>
   b. <u>lain,</u>
   c. <u>laid</u>
   d. <u>lay</u>

S27 **Set** is a transitive verb; it (needs, does not need) an object to complete its meaning. Underline the object of *set:* **Please set the table for two.**

A27 needs, <u>table</u>

S28 **Sit** is intransitive; it (needs, does not need) an object to complete its meaning. Which is correct? **Michelle can (sit, set) in front of the computer for hours.**

A28 does not need, **sit**

S29 **Raise** is transitive; it always takes an object. Which is correct? **Ms. Lotito has just (rise, raised) an interesting point.**

A29 raised

CHAPTER 7 SUMMARY

In this chapter you learned that the progressive form of a verb ends in *ing* and that progressive verbs are used when an action is continuing or unfinished. You found that verbs have three principal parts, and you studied how to form those parts for regular and irregular verbs. You also discovered that the present and past participles are used in verb phrases with one or more helping verbs, and you picked up a method for identifying transitive and intransitive verbs. Finally, you learned the principal forms of three pairs of confusing verbs: *lay/lie, set/sit,* and *raise/rise.*

Getting Connected

SENDING AN E-MAIL MESSAGE

GOAL: In the Getting Connected for Chapter 6, you registered for a free e-mail account. This Getting Connected will help you learn to send e-mail messages from that account. Specifically, you will practice sending e-mail by creating, correcting, and sending to a classmate or friend a message discussing transitive and intransitive verbs.

STEP 1 Begin this activity by securing the e-mail address of one or more of your classmates or friends.

STEP 2 Go to *englishworkshop.glencoe.com,* the address for *The English Workshop* Website, and click on Unit 3. Next click on Getting Connected, and then click on Chapter 7. You'll see a list of Websites offering free e-mail, including the provider for your e-mail account. Begin the activity by selecting your e-mail provider.

STEP 3 Log on to your account by entering your user name and the password you selected previously.

STEP 4 When you have accessed the account, you might see that you have mail. Do *not* delete any mail from your mailbox yet. You may need it for the Getting Connected in Chapter 8.

Locate the options for reading e-mail or composing new mail. Click on the Compose option. You should see a screen that includes a blank message form. The format of the blank message form may vary among the different e-mail providers, but usually the blank form contains four major elements:

a. An address line, usually marked *To:,* where you place the e-mail address of the recipient.
b. A line marked *Cc:* or *CC:,* where you place the e-mail address of a person to whom you wish to send a copy of the message.

c. A line marked *Subject,* where you enter a few words stating the subject of the message.

d. A blank area, where you write the message.

STEP 5   Locate the address (*To:*) line and enter the e-mail address of the recipient. Be sure to enter a complete e-mail address that includes the user name and the domain name (for example, *username@domain.com*).

STEP 6   Locate the *Subject* line and enter two or three words that describe the subject of your message. Do not use all capital letters. For this activity, enter the words *Transitive and Intransitive Verbs.*

STEP 7   Perhaps you would like to send a copy of this message to your instructor, another classmate, a friend, or a relative. Enter that person's complete e-mail address on the *Cc:* line.

STEP 8   Enter the body of your message in the blank message space. Although e-mail tends to be less formal than other written communication, consider following a traditional letter format, especially if your e-mail is for work or school. Therefore, you could begin your message with a greeting. For example,

Hi, _____,

Here is some information about transitive and intransitive verbs I wanted to share with you.

For this activity, write a message that explains the difference between transitive and intransitive verbs, including example sentences for each.

STEP 9   If your e-mail account includes a spellchecker, use it. Then proofread your message and make any necessary corrections. Sign the message by entering your name (not your user name) on a separate line at the end of the message.

STEP 10   Click the Send button when you're ready to send the message.

STEP 11   Close out of your e-mail account.

PRACTICE 1

Progressive Form or Simple Past Tense?

Instructions: In the blank, write the correct progressive or simple past tense form of the verb for each sentence.

EXAMPLE: **Bill (cross) against the light when he fell.**   EX. _____ **was crossing** _____

1. Mr. Chay (develop) the pictures now.   1. _____

2. Lee Johnson (complete) the application right now.   2. _____

3. We (send) the new price list last month.   3. _____

4. Ms. Rey (see) Mr. Highwater in his office at this very minute. 4. _____

5. Last Christmas we (sell) hundreds of home video games. 5. _____

6. Now we (experience) the effects of last month's cutbacks. 6. _____

7. While we (talk), the phone rang.   7. _____

8. I (speak) with Ms. Ramos when we were disconnected. 8. _____

9. Weren't you (visit) the home office when the fire broke out? 9. _____

10. She (try) to complete the assignment before she leaves today. 10. _____

PRACTICE 2

Regular Verbs

Instructions: In the blank, fill in the correct form of the verb for each sentence.

EXAMPLE: Ms. Allen (work) here since 1965.   EX. __has worked__

1. Ms. Perez (hurry) to the airport when she was called to the telephone.   1. _____

2. We (describe) this process in detail in the next issue.   2. _____

3. We (accumulate) too large an inventory last year.   3. _____

4. By this time last year we (accumulate) a large inventory.   4. _____

5. Was he (allow) to examine your records with no witnesses present?   5. _____

6. Why was he (examine) your records with no witnesses present?   6. _____

7. So far, 12 people (respond) to our questionnaire.   7. _____

8. By this time next week we (close) on the house.   8. _____

9. Petra (study) for the accounting exam until midnight.   9. _____

10. Petra (study) for the accounting exam when the power went out.   10. _____

PRACTICE 3

Irregular Verbs

Instructions: In the blank, write the correct form of the verb shown in each sentence.

EXAMPLE: **I (have) my brakes fixed recently.**

EX. _____ *had* _____

1. He had (arise) by the time I called.

    1. _____

2. I (awake) before dawn this morning.

    2. _____

3. The dog had (bite) the pet store owner.

    3. _____

4. The tire had (blow) out.

    4. _____

5. All sales records have been (break).

    5. _____

6. I have (come) to offer my condolences.

    6. _____

7. Isaac had (do) no wrong.

    7. _____

8. This show has (draw) a huge crowd.

    8. _____

9. He had (drink) too much.

    9. _____

10. We discovered that prices had (fall).

    10. _____

11. Their parents (forbid) their going.

    11. _____

12. Bjorn has (fly) millions of miles.

    12. _____

13. By morning the water had (freeze).

    13. _____

14. The situation has (get) out of control.

    14. _____

15. Ms. Moralez was (give) a raise.

    15. _____

16. Most of the staff had already (go) home.

    16. _____

17. It was (hide) under the stack of folders.

    17. _____

18. Have you (keep) all your receipts?

    18. _____

19. She has (lose) her opportunity.

    19. _____

20. Estelle has (lend) me the money.

    20. _____

21. Chia (mean) what he said.

    21. _____

22. Miguel had (meet) most of them before.

    22. _____

23. I had (mistake) you for him.

    23. _____

24. Your account is (overdraw).

    24. _____

Continued on next page

Practice 3 (continued)

25. The profit (shrink) drastically.

25. _____

26. They have (seek) the answer in vain.

26. _____

27. The building (shake) under the force of the earthquake.

27. _____

28. The profits (shrink) drastically last week.

28. _____

29. We (spend) several hours last night discussing the problem.

29. _____

30. The coil (spring) from its covering.

30. _____

31. They have (build) a factory on the river.

31. _____

32. Jake's trousers (burst) at the seams.

32. _____

33. By noon it had already (cost) me two weeks' salary.

33. _____

34. The container was (cut) across the top.

34. _____

35. The problems were (deal) with as they (arise).

35. _____

36. Has Jonathan (show) you how to operate the machine?

36. _____

37. Kiri has (sing) this opera many times.

37. _____

38. The ship had (sink) to the bottom.

38. _____

39. I (sleep) until noon yesterday.

39. _____

40. Had she (speak) to you about it?

40. _____

41. Our company has always (stand) for the finest quality.

41. _____

42. The two pieces had (stick) together.

42. _____

43. Catastrophe (strike) the city.

43. _____

44. All year long Sarah (strive) for the top.

44. _____

45. The jury was (swear) to secrecy.

45. _____

46. Malcolm (sweep) out the garage.

46. _____

47. You have (take) too much.

47. _____

48. I would have (teach) the course differently.

48. _____

49. Has she (tear) up those papers?

49. _____

50. I had (think) he was much taller.

50. _____

51. Mr. de Vargas has (throw) his support to Mr. Magome.

51. _____

52. I have (tell) you how I feel about this.

52. _____

53. Sol's aunt (undertake) his obligations last week.

53. _____

54. The company has (underwrite) all his debts.

54. _____

55. Yesterday I (wear) my blue suit.

55. _____

PRACTICE 4

Irregular Verbs

Instructions: On each line is printed the present tense of an irregular verb. Write the past tense and the present perfect tense of each verb.

PRESENT	PAST	PRESENT PERFECT
EXAMPLE: **I have**	I _____ **had** _____	I _____ **have** _____
1. I am	I _____	I _____
2. It bursts	It _____	It _____
3. They cost	They _____	They _____
4. You deal	You _____	You _____
5. We drive	We _____	We _____
6. You eat	You _____	You _____
7. I forbid	I _____	I _____
8. She knows	She _____	She _____
9. I lead	I _____	I _____
10. You mistake	You _____	You _____
11. We pay	We _____	We _____
12. He reads	He _____	He _____
13. You show	You _____	You _____
14. I shrink	I _____	I _____
15. We sing	We _____	We _____
16. You speak	You _____	You _____
17. I spend	I _____	I _____
18. They stand	They _____	They _____
19. We take	We _____	We _____
20. She teaches	She _____	She _____
21. We tear	We _____	We _____
22. You throw	You _____	You _____
23. I write	I _____	I _____
24. He wears	He _____	He _____
25. I withdraw	I _____	I _____

PRACTICE 5

Confusing Pairs of Verbs

Instructions: This practice involves the proper use of *lay/lie, set/sit* and *raise/rise*. From the words in parentheses, choose the correct verb and write the correct form in the blank.

EXAMPLE: **The blame was (lay, lie) at her doorstep.**   EX. _____ **Laid** _____

1. The journal has (lay, lie) on the shelf for years.   1. _____

2. The auditor (lay, lie) the ledger on the desk.   2. _____

3. Please (lay, lie) down.   3. _____

4. Jesse is always (lay, lie) the blame on someone else.   4. _____

5. They say they will (lay, lie) the carpet tomorrow.   5. _____

6. Ms. Pai (lay, lie) the foundations for a solid business.   6. _____

7. Are those folders still (lay, lie) there?   7. _____

8. He has (set, sit) in the same spot for hours.   8. _____

9. Have they (set, sit) long enough to be rested?   9. _____

10. The value of this stock has (raise, rise) almost 30 points.   10. _____

11. Last week he (raise, rise) an objection to nearly every motion. 11. _____

12. (Set, Sit) down in that chair.   12. _____

13. Please (raise, rise) your hand if you agree.   13. _____

14. We must try to (raise, rise) above such petty bickering.   14. _____

15. I must have dropped my checkbook when I (set, sit) down.   15. _____

16. I must have dropped my checkbook when I (set, sit)
    the briefcase down.   16. _____

17. The oil companies have (raise, rise) the price of gasoline in
    recent months.   17. _____

18. The price of gasoline has (raise, rise) in recent months.   18. _____

19. In recent months gasoline prices have continued to (raise, rise). 19. _____

20. Gas prices (raise, rise) last month.   20. _____

PRACTICE 6

More Verbs

Instructions: Assume that the following excerpt is to be placed on a Website about employment searches. Review and correct the excerpt, crossing out each error and making the necessary changes in the space above it.

What To Expect At The Job Interview

The interviewer will be evaluating you from the moment you step through the door until sometime after you leave. Thus it will be very important to have made a good first impression. Be sure to dress appropriately. If you are a man, you should have been wearing a coat and tie. If you were a woman, you should have worn a dress or suit. be on time. Strove to arrive early if you could have. If for some reason you are delayed, call to have notified the interviewer and explain why. Arriving late will be making you feel nervous. It will also be giving the interviewer the impression that you are unreliable.

After you have came in, meeted the interviewer, and shaked hands, set down in the chair the interviewer will be indicating. While you were talking, don't be playing with objects like a pen or pencil you may have brung with you. An interviewer will be interpreting such obvious nervousness as an inability to perform well under pressure on the job itself. Above all, don't be fiddling with objects on the interviewer's desk. Let them lay there.

The interviewer will ask you about your past and present work experience. Don't evaluate your jobs. Just be describing them as accurately and as fully as you could. Don't say, "My last job isn't much. I was just waiting on tables, and the duties that I perform now aren't very demanding either." No matter how insignificant you thought a job was, the interviewer will be seeing it as demonstrating your initiative, ability to work with others, and sense of responsibility.

Name _____

Class _____ Date _____

PRACTICE 7

Composition: Using Verb Tenses

Instructions: Identify the tense of each of the following verbs or verb phrases, then use each in a complete sentence.

EXAMPLE: saw   simple past   I saw your daughter on television last night. _____

1. has been _____ _____

2. sought _____ _____

3. tore _____ _____

4. have become _____ _____

5. will have cost _____ _____

6. had lain _____ _____

7. had been sitting _____ _____

8. rose _____ _____

9. will be raising _____ _____

10. will be laying _____ _____

PRACTICE 8

Composition: Using Verb Tenses

Instructions: Write complete sentences using each of the following verbs in the tense indicated in parentheses.

EXAMPLE: **listen (present progressive)** _____ **I am listening to the radio.** _____

1. apply (future progressive) _____

2. give (simple past) _____

3. begin (past perfect) _____

4. grow (present perfect) _____

5. speak (future perfect) _____

6. invest (simple present) _____

7. mean (simple future) _____

8. set (past progressive) _____

9. raise (past perfect progressive) _____

10. lie (future perfect progressive) _____

Subject and Verb Agreement

CHAPTER 8 PREVIEW

In this chapter you will learn that subjects and verbs must be in agreement. You will learn how to determine whether a subject is singular or plural and how to deal with compound subjects, indefinite pronouns, phrases, and—above all—meaning. You will continue to assess your knowledge in the Programmed Reinforcement sections and the Practices. Finally, you will go online to retrieve and open an e-mail message.

OBJECTIVES

After completing this chapter, you will be able to

- Define what is meant by the agreement of subject and verb.
- Determine whether to use a singular or a plural verb with a compound subject involving *and, either/or,* or *neither/nor.*
- Identify singular and plural indefinite pronouns.
- Ignore prepositional phrases and explanatory phrases when determining the correct verb form.
- Determine whether a word is singular or plural by looking at its meaning rather than its form.
- Solve problem situations involving words that can be singular or plural.
- Solve other problem situations involving inverted sentences, linking verbs, and clauses with relative pronouns.

Study Plan for Chapter 8

The Study Plan for Chapter 8 offers a set of strategies that will help you learn and review the chapter material.

❶ Subject and Predicate Agreement: Correct identification of the subject is key to making sure the predicate (verb) and subject agree. Ask yourself the question, *Who or what is the doer of the action?* The answer will tell you the subject of the sentence.

❷ Pronoun Flash cards: Make flash cards to help you master the correct usage of singular, plural, and indefinite pronouns.

❸ Prepositional Phrase Cover-up: When locating the subject of a sentence that includes a prepositional phrase, cover the phrase to avoid confusing the object of the preposition as the subject of the sentence.

❹ Relative Pronoun Agreement: Determine the verb form that agrees with the subject of a relative clause by verifying the word to which the relative pronoun relates.

In this section you will learn what it means for a subject to be in proper grammatical relationship, or "agreement," with a verb. The agreement guidelines offered here will describe how to match singular subjects with singular verbs and plural subjects with plural verbs. These guidelines will include the more tricky indefinite pronouns.

8.1 Basics of Subject and Verb Agreement

For a sentence to be grammatically correct, its verb must agree with its subject in number. This means that if the subject is singular, you use a singular verb. If the subject is plural, you use a plural verb.

For example, in the sentence *The kitchen is on the first floor,* the singular noun *kitchen* requires the singular verb *is.* In the sentence *The bedrooms are on the second floor,* the plural noun *bedrooms* requires the plural verb *are.* The sentences below provide examples of subject and verb agreement:

Singular Subject and Singular Verb	Ms. Lang lives next door.
Plural Subject and Plural Verb	The Langs live next door.
Singular Subject and Singular Verb	She is planning to move.
Plural Subject and Plural Verb	They are planning to move.

Most of the time when you form sentences, you probably make subjects and verbs agree without consciously thinking about it. For example, complete the following sentence with a form of the verb *to be:*

My car (*is, are*) for sale.

If you grew up speaking English, you probably selected *is:*

My car *is* for sale.

Now complete the following sentence with a form of the verb *to be:*

Ten previously owned cars (*is, are*) for sale at the *Getacar.com* Website.

Again, if you have had extensive opportunities to hear and speak English, you probably quickly offered:

Ten previously owned cars *are* for sale at the *Getacar.com* Website.

Sometimes the relationship between the subject, or subjects, and the verb, or verbs, is easy to determine. At other times, only close examination reveals the number of the subject and, therefore, the necessary form of the verb. Now that you understand the basics of subject and verb agreement, we can review the guidelines for more complicated sentence structures.

8.2 Compound Subjects

A **compound subject** consists of two or more subjects joined by a conjunction. These subjects may be all singular, all plural, or a combination of singular and plural. The resulting compound subject may also be either singular or plural, as you will see in the following situations.

And

When two or more parts of a compound subject are linked by *and*, the subject is plural and a plural verb is required. Usually this is obvious.

> Alberto *and* Portia *are* going to be married next month.
> The Acme Company *and* the Omega Corporation *are* merging.
> Good mechanics *and* good repair technicians *are* always in demand.

However, sometimes the word *and* links a subject that is actually singular.

Compound Subjects That Refer to Single Nouns or Pronouns. When a compound subject refers to a single person or thing, the subject is singular and it requires a singular verb.

> This poet *and* scholar *devotes* herself totally to each class she teaches.

Although *poet* and *scholar* are linked by *and*, both refer to the pronoun, *she.*

Sometimes only the verb conveys whether a writer is using a singular or plural compound subject.

> The secretary and treasurer *is* here.

In the sentence above, the singular verb *is* indicates that one person serves as both the secretary and treasurer.

> *The* secretary and *the* treasurer *are* here.

In the previous example, the plural verb *are* indicates that a different person holds each office. The use of *the* before each subject noun shows that the compound subject concerns two people—the secretary and the treasurer.

Two Items as One Unit. If two items are so closely identified that they are considered one unit, use a singular verb.

Certification

Certification through the National Automotive Technicians Education Foundation (NATEF) is voluntary for technician programs. Its stamp of approval lets you know that a program meets standards for instructional facilities, equipment, staff, and curriculum.

Bacon and eggs is a standard breakfast in their house.
Bread and butter is Tyler's favorite snack.

But: *Bacon* and *eggs are* on my shopping list. *Bread* and *butter are,* too.

The meaning of the sentence determines whether the items act as one unit.

8.3   *Either/Or* and *Neither/Nor*

When two or more parts of a compound subject are connected by *or* or *nor,* the verb should agree in number with the part of the subject closest to the verb.

When all parts of the compound subject are the same number, agreement is easily achieved, as the examples below indicate.

Either Ms. Soong *or* Mr. Shapiro *has* the application.
Both parts of the compound subject are singular.

Neither the chairs *nor* the tables *have arrived.*
Both parts of the compound subject are plural.

When part of the compound subject is singular and another is plural, the part closer to the verb determines the number of the verb.

Either Mr. Sawyer *or* his assistants *have* evaluated the engine problems.
Because *assistants,* a plural part of the compound subject, is closer to the verb, use the plural verb *have.*

Either the assistants *or* Mr. Sawyer *has* evaluated the engine problems.
Because *Mr. Sawyer,* a singular part of the compound subject, is closer to the verb, use the singular verb *has.*

The last sentence example above is grammatically correct, but it sounds awkward. To avoid such awkwardness, place the plural part of a compound subject closer to the verb. Although each of the last two sentence examples above is correct, the first one is preferred because it sounds better.

8.4   Singular Indefinite Pronouns

Chapter 4 lists a number of *indefinite* pronouns—that is, pronouns that do not refer to particular persons, places, or things. Many of these pronouns are singular. You will find them listed on the next page. When any one of these pronouns is the subject of a sentence, use a *singular* verb.

anyone	everyone	someone	no one	one
anybody	everybody	somebody	nobody	each
anything	everything	something	nothing	either
				neither

SAMPLE SENTENCES WITH SINGULAR INDEFINITE PRONOUNS

1. Anyone *is* eligible to apply for the position.
2. Anything *goes.*
3. Everybody here *plans* to attend.
4. Someone *is going* to suffer for this.
5. Nobody *does* it better.
6. One of our aircraft *is* missing.
7. Each of the officers in the firm *holds* a graduate degree.
8. Neither of her mistakes *was* significant.

When the singular pronouns listed above are used as adjectives to modify the subject, the subject is also considered singular, even though it may have more than one part.

1. *One* airplane *is* missing.
2. *Each* person here *is* concerned.
3. *Either* technician *is* able to help you.
4. *Neither* mistake *was* significant.

Every and *Many a*

The words *every* and *many a* are not pronouns, but they function in a similar manner. When *every* or *many a* modifies a subject, the subject is considered singular.

Every man and woman who purchases a ticket *has* a chance of winning.
Many a satisfied customer *has passed* through these doors.

8.5 Plural Indefinite Pronouns

The following indefinite pronouns are always plural. When they are used as subjects or as adjectives modifying subjects, a plural verb is required.

both	few	many	others	several

1. Both women *deserve* the prize, but only one *will receive* it.
2. Many *are called,* but few *are chosen.*
3. Several people *are* unable to attend; the others *are* all *coming.*

8.6 Prepositional Phrases

The subject of a sentence is *never* part of a prepositional phrase. When determining the subject of a sentence, ignore any prepositional phrases. The following sentences illustrate this principle.

SAMPLE SENTENCES WITH PREPOSITIONAL PHRASES

1. *No one* at headquarters *is* capable of doing a better job.
2. *Each* of the officers in the firm *holds* a graduate degree.
3. *Either* of her assistants *is* able to help you.
4. *Neither* of her mistakes *was* significant.
5. The *invoice* for the last three shipments *has been lost.*
6. The *message* from your representative *has been received.*
7. The *range* of applications *is* extensive.
8. The *officers* in the firm *hold* graduate degrees.
9. The *invoices* for the last shipment *have been lost.*
10. The *messages* from your representative *have been received.*

Grammar Tip

Common Prepositions

Some of the most common prepositions are *of, in, with, for, at, by, from,* and *to.*

8.7 Explanatory and Additional Phrases

When determining whether to use a singular or a plural verb, always ignore phrases beginning with expressions such as the following:

along with	and not	in addition to
accompanied by	besides	including
as well as	except	rather than

These and similar expressions give supplementary, incidental information that could be omitted. They do not affect whether the subject is singular or plural.

The new bumper, *as well as the new door handle,* has been received.
My employer, *in addition to her associates,* was pleased.
Mr. Schmidt, *together with his assistant,* is scheduled to arrive at noon.
No one, *not even Mayor Fabend's own family members,* knows her plans.

8.8 Titles

The titles of articles, books, CD-ROMs, magazines, musical compositions, and the like are often plural in form. Nevertheless, because they name one thing, they are considered singular and take a singular verb.

1. "Notes on New Cars" appears in *Highway Happenings*.
2. *Classic Automobiles* is an illustrated history of fine cars.
3. *Songs for a Rainy Afternoon* features classic reggae compositions.
4. *Highway Happenings* is a magazine about trends in automobile design.
5. "The Three Little Pigs" is a favorite children's story.

8.9 Meaning

In determining whether a subject is singular or plural, look at the meaning of the word rather than at its form. For example, although the word *news* ends in *s*, it is singular in meaning and needs a singular verb.

> No news *is* good news.
> Today's economic news *is* encouraging.

Singular Nouns That End in *s*

The names of some school subjects and some diseases that end in *s* are also singular in meaning: *civics, economics, electronics, linguistics, physics, politics, mathematics, measles,* and *mumps.*

> Economics *is* a required subject, but linguistics *is* not.
> Mumps *is* a dangerous illness if not treated properly.
> Measles *is* a mild disease.

Plural Nouns That Refer to Singular Things

A number of nouns such as *dues, earnings,* and *winnings* are always plural, even though each refers to a single thing.

> Union dues *are collected* every month.
> Winnings from state lotteries *are subject* to income tax.
> My extra earnings from fixing cars on the weekends *pay* my rent.

Nouns That Can Be Either Singular or Plural

Nouns such as *series* and *means* can be either singular or plural, depending on how they are used in a sentence.

> One possible means of solving the problem *has* already *been tried.*
> All possible means *are going* to be investigated.
> A series of editorials in the *Times criticizes* the mayor's conduct.
> The series of editorials in the *Times, News,* and *Record* all *criticize* the mayor.

News *in Chapter 3*
You first learned in Section 3.12, on page 74, that news *is singular.*

■

More on Special Nouns
See page 74 in Section 3.12 for a more extensive list of nouns that are always singular, always plural, or either singular or plural.

■

Coverage Key

Section		Statement
8.1	➤ Basics of Subject and Verb Agreement	➤ S1, S2, S3
8.2	➤ Compound Subjects	➤ S4, S5
8.3	➤ *Either/Or* and *Neither/Nor*	➤ S6, S7, S8
8.4	➤ Singular Indefinite Pronouns	➤ S9, S10, S13
8.5	➤ Plural Indefinite Pronouns	➤ S11, S12, S13
8.6	➤ Prepositional Phrases	➤ S14
8.7	➤ Explanatory and Additional Phrases	➤ S15, S16
8.8	➤ Titles	➤ S17
8.9	➤ Meaning	➤ S18, S19

Instructions: Cover the answers in the **Answer** column; then write your answer to the first statement. Uncover the first printed answer and compare your answer to it. If you wrote a correct answer, continue the activity. If you made an error, use the **Coverage Key** to locate the chapter section you need to review. When you are confident that you understand the material, continue with the reinforcement activity.

ANSWER	STATEMENT
	S1 If the subject of a sentence is singular, the verb must be _____. If the subject of a sentence is plural, the verb must be _____.
A1 singular, plural	**S2** **Ms. Bucci (is, are) leaving.** The subject, **Ms. Bucci,** is (singular, plural); the correct verb must be _____.
A2 singular, **is**	**S3** **Her aides (is, are) leaving.** The subject, **aides,** is (singular, plural); the verb must be _____.
A3 plural, **are**	**S4** Two subjects connected by **and** make the subject (singular, plural). Underline the verb: **Ms. Bucci and her aide (is, are) leaving.**
A4 plural, **are**	**S5** Choose the correct verbs: **Peanut butter and jelly (is, are) my favorite sandwich. The horse and buggy (was, were) once a popular mode of transportation.**
A5 is, was	**S6** When *or* or *nor* connect two subjects, the verb should agree with the subject that is _____ to it. **Neither the desk nor the chairs (seems, seem) right.** The subject closer to the verb is **chairs**; therefore, the correct verb is _____, which is (singular, plural).
A6 closer, **seem,** plural	

A7 has, singular

A8 Either the desk or the chairs have to be replaced.

A9 singular, singular

A10
a. is
b. has

A11 plural, plural

A12
a. are
b. seem

A13
a. knows   c. have
b. have   d. has

A14 never

A15 Mr. Hessein, is

A16 Ms. Eng, is (expected)

A17 singular, appears

A18 news, singular, is

A19 Linguistics, singular, is

S7 Either the chairs or the desk **(has, have) to be replaced.** The correct verb must be _____, which is also _____.

S8 Rewrite the example in **S7** to make it less awkward _____.

S9 *Each, everyone,* and *nobody* are all (singular, plural). When they are used as subjects, the verb must also be _____.

S10 Complete these sentences correctly:
a. **Everyone (is, are) allowed to leave early this afternoon.**
b. **Each of the posters (has, have) to be redone.**

S11 *Both, few, many, others,* and *several* are always (singular, plural). As subjects or as adjectives modifying subjects, the verbs must also be _____.

S12 Complete these sentences correctly:
a. **Few people (is, are) capable of handling so much responsibility.**
b. **Several in this office, however, (seems, seem) up to the task.**

S13 Complete these sentences correctly:
a. **Nobody (knows, know) the trouble I've seen.**
b. **Few (has, have) seen the trouble I have.**
c. **Many successful executives (has, have) spoken to us.**
d. **Many a successful executive (has, have) spoken to us.**

S14 The subject of a sentence is (never, always, occasionally) part of a prepositional phrase.

S15 Expressions such as *as well as, together with,* and *in addition to* do not change a singular subject into a plural subject. **Mr. Hessein, accompanied by his wife, (is, are) here.** The subject is _____. The correct verb is _____.

S16 **Ms. Eng, together with her assistants, (is, are) expected soon.** The subject is _____. The correct verb is _____.

S17 Titles of books and articles and the like are considered (singular, plural). Complete the following sentence: **"Hints from Hal" (appears, appear) in this week's newsletter.**

S18 **The news (is, are) good.** The subject, _____, is (singular, plural). The correct verb is _____.

S19 **Linguistics (is, are) my hardest subject.** The subject _____, is (singular, plural). The correct verb is _____.

You have already discovered that some nouns are versatile: they can be either singular or plural. In this section you will encounter other situations in which the same word, depending on its meaning, can be singular or plural when it is used as a subject.

8.10 Quantity

Grammar Tip

Number *Is* or *Are*?

When the word *number* is the subject of a sentence and is preceded by *the*, use a singular verb. When *number* is preceded by *a*, use a plural verb.

When an amount of money, a period of time, or another quantity is the subject and is considered a total amount, use a singular verb. When the subject is thought of as a number of individual units, use a plural verb.

Subject as Total Amount (Singular Verb)

1. Five hundred dollars *is* a reasonable amount.

2. Four months *is* a long time between letters.

3. The number of failures *is* low.

Subject as Individual Unit (Plural Verb)

1. Hundreds of dollars *have* already *been wasted* on this project.

2. Four months *have come* and *gone* since I last heard from you.

3. A number of people *have failed*.

8.11 Collective Nouns

A **collective noun** is a word that is singular in form but refers to a group of people or things. Here is a list of commonly used collective nouns:

audience	committee	council	group
board	company	department	jury
class	corporation	firm	mob

1. **A Group as a Unit.** When the group to which these nouns refer acts or is thought of as a unit, use a singular verb.

   The committee *is scheduled* to meet at one o'clock.
   The class *was discussing* a new repair technique.
   The jury *has rendered* its verdict.

2. **A Group as Individual Members.** When members of a group act or are thought of separately, use a plural verb.

   The committee *are* violently *debating* the merits of the system.
   The class *were arguing* with one another.
   The jury *are embroiled* in a major disagreement.

Although these three sentences are grammatically correct, they sound awkward. For this reason, it may be better to rewrite them as follows:

The *committee members* are violently debating the merits of the system.
The *students in class* were arguing with one another.
The men and women of the jury are embroiled in a major disagreement.

3. **Companies and Organizations.** The name of a company or organization should be viewed as a collective noun. Usually the name is treated as singular and takes a singular verb.

General Motors *is* one of America's best-known automobile manufacturers.
United Manufacturers of America *has opened* its main offices in Pittsburgh.

However, if you want to emphasize the individual people who make up the organization, use the plural verb.

United Manufacturers of America *have* always *satisfied* customers.

Grammar Tip

Organizational Agreement
Use a singular verb when you refer to an organization as *it* or *which.*
Use a plural verb when you refer to an organization as *they* or *who.*

8.12 *Some/None*

As you learned in Sections 8.4 and 8.5, some indefinite pronouns are always singular and others are always plural. The following indefinite pronouns can be singular or plural, depending on the noun to which they refer.

    all   any   more   none   some   most

When one of these pronouns refers to a quantity that is regarded as a whole, it is generally singular in meaning. When the pronoun refers to a number of people or things, it is plural in meaning.

These pronouns are usually followed by a prepositional phrase beginning with *of.* If the noun or pronoun in the prepositional phrase is singular, these pronouns are considered singular. If the noun or pronoun in the prepositional phrase is plural, these pronouns are considered plural.

SINGULAR

1. *Some of the firm's **capital*** is being earmarked for expansion.
2. Is *any of the **property*** flooded?
3. *All of this **area*** is zoned for commercial use.

PLURAL

1. *Some of the **employees*** have returned to work.
2. Are *any of the **workers*** still here?
3. *All of the **members*** are in favor of a strike.

Grammar Tip

8.13 Fractions and Percentages

Frequently a fraction or percentage is used as the subject of a sentence.

> *Three-fifths* of the people have arrived.
> *Sixty percent* of our quota has been met.

If a singular noun or pronoun follows the *of* phrase, use a singular verb. If a plural noun or pronoun follows, use a plural verb.

SINGULAR

1. *Fifty percent of the **farm*** is hers.
2. *One-quarter of the **order*** has been shipped.

PLURAL

1. *Half of the **farms*** are for sale.
2. *Twenty-five percent of the **orders*** have been shipped.

8.14 Subject and Verb Inversion

As you have seen, the normal sequence in a sentence is for the subject to come before the verb. However, in sentences that are in inverted sequence, the verb comes before the subject. When determining subject and verb agreement for inverted sentences, mentally rearrange the sentence into normal sequence to help identify the subject.

INVERTED SEQUENCE

1. Listed among those recommended for promotion (*was, were*) Dr. Rita Perez.

2. Enclosed (*is, are*) my deposit and registration form.

NORMAL SEQUENCE

1. Dr. Rita Perez *was* listed among those recommended for promotion. *Therefore:* Listed among those recommended for promotion *was* Dr. Rita Perez.

2. My deposit and registration form *are* enclosed. *Therefore:* Enclosed *are* my deposit and registration form.

Many inverted sentences begin with the adverbs *there* or *here*. Mentally rearrange these sentences to clarify the needed verb form.

INVERTED SEQUENCE

1. There (*is, are*) three new designs from which to choose.
2. Here (*is, are*) the brochures you requested.

NORMAL SEQUENCE

1. Three new designs from which to choose *are* there.
2. The brochures you requested *are* here.

8.15 Linking Verbs

A linking verb should agree with its subject—which comes before the verb, not with its complement—which comes after the verb.

Repeated absences *were* the reason for his being fired.

Were, a plural verb, agrees with *absences,* a plural subject.

The reason he was fired *was* his repeated absences.

Was, a singular verb, agrees with *reason,* a singular subject.

8.16 Clauses With Relative Pronouns

So far you have studied how a verb must agree with the subject of a sentence. A verb must also agree with the subject of a clause. A relative pronoun—*who, which,* or *that*—is often followed by a verb that must agree in number with the antecedent of the relative pronoun. Recognizing the real antecedent of the relative pronoun is not always easy. Try this sentence:

Eli is one of those people who (**is, are**) serious about exercise.

Does *who* relate to *one* or *people?* Notice that a statement is being made about a broad characteristic of *those people. Who,* therefore, relates to the plural word *people* and requires the plural verb *are.*

Eli is one of those people who *are* serious about exercise.

Now look at this sentence:

Eli is one of the applicants who (**is, are**) truly qualified.

Who is truly qualified, *Eli* or *the applicants?* A number of applicants are truly qualified; Eli is one of them. Therefore,

Eli is one of the applicants who *are* truly qualified.

Now look at this sentence:

Eli is the only one of the applicants who (**is, are**) truly qualified.

Here only Eli is truly qualified; the other applicants are not. Hence this sentence should read:

Eli is the only one of the applicants who *is* truly qualified.

When faced with such sentences, think through the meaning of the relative clauses carefully to determine the real antecedent.

Coverage Key

Section		Statement
8.10 ➤	Quantity	➤ S21, S22, S23, S24
8.11 ➤	Collective Nouns	➤ S25, S26, S27, S28
8.12 ➤	*Some/None*	➤ S29, S30, S31, S32, S33
8.13 ➤	Fractions and Percentages	➤ S34, S35
8.14 ➤	Subject and Verb Inversion	➤ S36
8.15 ➤	Linking Verbs	➤ S37
8.16 ➤	Clauses With Relative Pronouns	➤ S38

Instructions: Cover the answers in the **Answer** column; then write your answer to the first statement. Uncover the first printed answer and compare your answer to it. If you wrote a correct answer, continue the activity. If you made an error, use the **Coverage Key** to locate the chapter section you need to review. When you are confident that you understand the material, continue with the reinforcement activity.

ANSWER

STATEMENT

S21   Complete this sentence. **Ten dollars (was, were) the appropriate tip.**

A21 was

S22   Complete this sentence: **Ten wheel covers (was, were) missing.**

A22 were

S23   When the word *number* is the subject of a sentence and is preceded by *the*, use a (singular, plural) verb. **The number of bankruptcies (is, are) decreasing.**

A23 singular, **is**

S24   When the word *number* is preceded by *a*, use a (singular, plural) verb. **A number of checks (has, have) been mislaid.**

A24 plural, **have**

S25   The words that refer to a group—*committee, jury, class, crowd,* or *mob*—may be either singular or plural. When an entire group acts as a single unit, the verb is _____. When the group is thought of in terms of its individual members, the verb is _____.

A25 singular, plural

S26   Complete this sentence: **The board (is, are) ready to stop.**

A26 is

S27   Which verb correctly completes this sentence? **The faculty (is, are) arguing among themselves.** How would you rewrite it to make it sound less awkward? _____

A27 are, **The faculty members are arguing among themselves.**

S28 The name of a company is usually viewed as a collective noun and takes a singular verb. Which verb correctly completes this sentence? **Abrams, Kerr, and Phillips (is, are) a well-known firm.**

A28 is

S29 **Some** may be singular or plural. If the noun in the *of* phrase that follows **some** is singular, then **some** is (singular, plural). **Some of the work (is, are) very hard.** Choose the correct verb.

A29 singular, is

S30 If the noun in the *of* phrase that follows *some* is plural, then *some* is (singular, plural). **Some of the workers (is, are) dissatisfied.** Choose the correct verb.

A30 plural, **are**

S31 The words *any, all,* and *most* (may, may not) be singular or plural, depending on the words to which they refer. Complete the following:
  a. **Most of the offices (is, are) unoccupied.**
  b. **Most of the office space (is, are) still available.**
  c. **All the road (is, are) under repair.**

A31 may, a. **are**, b. **is**, c. **is**

S32 The word *none* may be singular or plural. Choose the correct verbs:
  a. **None of the food (is, are) edible.**
  b. **None of the cans of soda (is, are) cold enough.**

A32 a. **is**, b. **are**

S33 **None of the cans of soda are cold enough.** Rewrite this sentence to emphasize the idea that not a single can of soda is sufficiently cold.

_____
_____ .

A33 **Not one of the cans of soda is cold enough.**

S34 When fractions are used as subjects, if the phrase following the fraction has a singular noun, the verb is _____ ; if the phrase has a plural noun, the verb is

_____ .

A34 singular, plural

S35 Choose the correct verbs:
  a. One-third of the mechanics (have, has) arrived.
  b. Fifty percent of the stock (has, have) been ruined.

A35 a. **have**, b. **has**	**S36** **There were three speeches given.** Rewrite this sentence in subject-before-verb order.
	_____ Identify the subject and the verb.

A36 **Three speeches were given there.** subject: **speeches**; verb: **were given**

S37 A linking verb should agree with its (subject, complement). Which sentence(s) is/are correct?
  a. **The cause of his dismissal was his frequent absences.**
  b. **The cause of his dismissal were his frequent absences.**
  c. **His frequent absences was the cause of his dismissal.**
  d. **His frequent absences were the cause of his dismissal.**

A37 subject, a., d.

S38 **She is one of those people who (do, does) (her, their) best work under pressure.** Name the true antecedent of *who*. Choose the correct verb and the correct pronoun.

A38 **people, do, their**

CHAPTER 8 SUMMARY

In this chapter you learned that subjects and verbs in sentences must be in agreement; that is, a singular subject requires a singular verb, and a plural subject requires a plural verb. You were given several guidelines for establishing subject and verb agreement with compound subjects, singular and plural pronouns, indefinite pronouns, collective nouns, fractions and percentages, and other subjects. You discovered that the subject and verb of a relative clause also must be in agreement.

Getting Connected

READING AN E-MAIL MESSAGE

GOAL: Retrieving an e-mail message so that you can read it is a lot like going to your mailbox at home, taking out an envelope, and opening it. With an e-mail message, however, everything is done electronically. Messages are delivered electronically to your e-mail provider's site, where they are stored in your mailbox, called an **inbox.** To access your e-mail messages, you must log on to your e-mail provider's Website and access your inbox. Then you can open any messages waiting for you.

In this activity you'll open an e-mail message and use it to review what you have learned about subject and verb agreement. The e-mail message you'll open is the **Welcome Message** sent to you by the staff of the e-mail provider that you registered with when you set up your e-mail account in the Chapter 6 Getting Connected. E-mail providers send new users messages welcoming them to their company. Sometimes these messages include information about the use of the account.

STEP 1 Go to *englishworkshop.glencoe.com,* the address for *The English Workshop* Website, and click on Unit 3. Next click on Getting Connected for Unit 3, and then click on Chapter 8. At the Getting Connected option, you'll see a list of Websites offering free e-mail, including the provider for your e-mail account. Begin the activity by selecting your e-mail provider.

STEP 2 Since e-mail providers don't want to be clones of one another, they design their Websites to look different from one another. All the sites, however, do contain the same features more or less. Locate the link or button to access e-mail at your provider's Website, and click on it. (Look for a link or button titled "Check e-mail," "check mail," or a similar command.)

STEP 3 Log on or sign in to the e-mail program by entering your user name and password.

STEP 4   Locate the inbox where your e-mail is stored. Different sites will place the inbox in different locations, but the word *inbox* probably will appear somewhere. Click on the inbox.

STEP 5   A list of e-mail messages stored in your inbox will appear. At this point you will not see the actual messages, only general identifying information. That information can include the sender, the date, and the subject. The Welcome Message from the e-mail provider should be waiting for you. It should be easy to identify: it's probably the first message listed, and the company name of the e-mail provider should appear in the Sender column.

STEP 6   To open the provider's Welcome Message, you will probably need to click on the words in the Subject column. With some e-mail providers, you may have to click another column to open the message.

STEP 7   Read the Welcome Message, which, depending on the provider, may be brief or lengthy. You'll need a printout of the message to complete this activity, so print out at least one page of the message.

STEP 8   Using the printout, search the document for at *least five* of the subject-verb relationships listed below. Circle, underline, or highlight them on the printout as you find them. Be sure to highlight both the subject and the verb. In the margin, identify what you mark.

   a. Compound subject with a verb
   b. Compound subject using *either/or* or *neither/nor* with a verb
   c. Singular or plural indefinite pronoun as a subject word (*anyone, both, etc.*) with a verb
   d. Collective noun as a subject word with a verb
   e. Company name as a subject with a verb
   f. Inverted subject and verb
   g. Subject and verb of a clause with a relative pronoun

If you cannot find five of the relationships listed above, write *More Examples on Back.* Then flip the printout over and write original sentences showing some of the relationships above. Identify those relationships in your original sentences as you did for the sentences on the front of the printout. The sentences you identify on the front of your printout and those you identify on the back should demonstrate five of the relationships listed above.

STEP 9   Write your name on the page and turn it in to your instructor. Be sure to log off your e-mail account.

Name _____

Class _____ Date _____

PRACTICE 1

Subjects, Verbs, and Number

Instructions: In the column headed SUBJECT, write the subject of each sentence. In the column headed VERB, write the verb of each sentence. Then, in the column headed NUMBER, write *S* if the subject is singular or *P* if the subject is plural.

	SUBJECT	VERB	NUMBER
EXAMPLE: The number of bankruptcies this year was higher than last year. Ex.	number	was	S
1. Ms. Ortega, accompanied by her assistant, is coming to your office. 1.			
2. Gilbert's and Sullivan's are friendly competitors. 2.			
3. The designer and the engineer both seem competent. 3.			
4. A winner from among all the contestants will be chosen today and announced tomorrow. 4.			
5. Macaroni and cheese is a popular casserole dinner. 5.			
6. Either Mikki or her friends will be the best models for the new uniform. 6.			
7. Each of the applicants must complete a questionnaire. 7.			
8. Everybody in the sales force is asked to use the suggestion box. 8.			
9. Several people in the sales force have used the suggestion box. 9.			
10. The news of the sales losses is coming over the wire. 10.			

Name _____

Class _____ Date _____

PRACTICE 2

Subjects and Verbs

Instructions: Identify the subjects and verbs in the following e-mail message by underlining each subject once and each verb twice.

To: jpadler@autoworks.com

From: lhosaka@specialparts.com

Subject: Brake Cylinder Order

Hello, Mr. Adler:

In your recent e-mail message, you ordered five special brake cylinders for immediate delivery. Our production manager and our consulting engineer have informed me of some delays in retooling machines for your order.

We will rush this adjustment and put your order in quickly. The shipping department will, of course, inform you of the shipping date, and Ms. Jackson will visit you personally if necessary. Please understand our problems in retooling and accept our assurance of careful attention. Both Ms. Jackson and I look forward to serving you.

Yours,

Lawrence Hosaka, Customer Service Manager

PRACTICE 3

Subject and Verb Agreement

Instructions: In the blank, write the verb that agrees with the subject.

EXAMPLE: **"Death and Transfiguration" (is, are) a tone poem by Richard Strauss.**   EX. _____**is**_____

1. Each order (has, have) been received.   1._____

2. Several of the orders (has, have) been received.   2._____

3. Nobody among the trainees (seems, seem) capable of supervising   3._____
   such an important project.

4. *Advise and Consent* (is, are) the title of Drury's prize-winning political novel.   4._____

5. Many an employee (has, have) invested in company stock.   5._____

6. Neither of the setbacks (was, were) very costly.   6._____

7. Every boy and girl who toured the plant (was, were) given a souvenir.   7._____

8. Ms. Carr, together with her spouse, (is, are) conducting research.   8._____

9. Both Ms. Carr and her spouse (is, are) conducting research.   9._____

10. A series of changes in record-keeping procedures (is, are) expected soon.   10._____

11. News of the price decreases (was, were) announced to the buyers.   11._____

12. Each employee who completed the course (was, were)   12._____
    acknowledged in the staff newsletter.

13. Corned beef and cabbage (is, are) frequently served for dinner on   13._____
    St. Patrick's Day.

14. Her gambling losses (exceeds, exceed) her winnings.   14._____

15. The amount of her gambling losses (exceeds, exceed) that of her winnings.   15._____

16. Sixteen tons of coal (was, were) delivered to Ernie Ford.   16._____

17. The number of foreclosures (is, are) increasing.   17._____

18. An increased number of foreclosures (is, are) predicted for this quarter.   18._____

19. The worst part of the evening (was, were) the after-dinner speeches.   19._____

20. The after-dinner speeches (was, were) the worst part of the evening.   20._____

Name _____

Class _____ Date _____

PRACTICE 4

Subject and Verb Agreement

Instructions: Choose the correct verb. Indicate whether the verb is singular or plural by writing *S* if it is singular, *P* if it is plural.

	VERB	NUMBER
EXAMPLE: **Anybody who can pay the entrance fee (is, are) eligible to enter.**	EX. ___is___	___S___
1. Measles (is, are) a contagious disease.	1. _____	_____
2. Blue Cross and Blue Shield of New Jersey (is, are) my insurance carrier.	2. _____	_____
3. The committee (has, have) decided to issue their report next week.	3. _____	_____
4. The jury (was, were) asked by the judge to render its decision.	4. _____	_____
5. The faculty of the school (seems, seem) to be against new proposals.	5. _____	_____
6. Pearson, French, Hein, and Jackson (is, are) a leading publishing house.	6. _____	_____
7. Mathematics as well as economics (is, are) required.	7. _____	_____
8. The general public (is, are) convinced of the defendant's innocence.	8. _____	_____
9. The jury and the judge, as well as the general public, (is, are) convinced of the defendant's innocence.	9. _____	_____
10. The members of the ANTA Playhouse Company (is, are) planning a road trip.	10. _____	_____
11. A number of checks (was, were) returned marked "insufficient funds."	11. _____	_____
12. The number of area apartments available for rent (is, are) very small.	12. _____	_____
13. Most of the damage to the store and its contents (was, were) minor.	13. _____	_____
14. (Is, Are) all this area zoned residential?	14. _____	_____
15. Here (is, are) the series of articles you requested on improving productivity.	15. _____	_____

Name _____

Class _____ Date _____

PRACTICE 5

Subject and Verb Agreement

Instructions: Underline the subjects once and the verbs twice.

EXAMPLE: **If <u>you</u> or <u>someone</u> you know (<u>needs</u>, need) help, call our toll-free number.**

1. Among those with the highest sales totals (was, were) Jim Deloria.

2. There (was, were) three comments in the suggestion box.

3. The most effective part of the presentation (was, were) the closing slides.

4. The closing slides (was, were) the most effective part of the presentation.

5. None of the methods of transcription (is, are) beyond criticism.

6. Some of the company's investments (seems, seem) to have been affected by the market changes.

7. Some of the company's investment potential (seems, seem) to have been affected by the market changes.

8. Three-fifths of the crop (has, have) to be stored in silos.

9. Forty percent of the letters (has, have) to be corrected.

10. Half of the order (appears, appear) to be damaged.

11. The members of the jury (is, are) in complete disagreement.

12. (Has, Have) each of the orders been processed?

13. One million dollars (is, are) a great deal of money.

14. The number of books available for sale (is, are) low.

15. Thirty-six percent of our total product (is, are) shipped overseas.

16. None of the suppliers (has, have) called since our orders were sent.

17. These figures (is, are) very helpful.

18. This series of figures (is, are) much too confusing.

19. Any number of consequences (is, are) possible.

20. There (has, have) been a rash of recent accidents caused by careless cellular phone users.

Name _____

Class _____ Date _____

PRACTICE 6

Clauses With Relative Pronouns

Instructions: In the blank, write the correct verb(s) and/or pronoun.

EXAMPLE: **Ms. Gelb is one of those investors who (is, are) not afraid to take significant risks with (her, their) money.**

Ex. ___are, their___

1. Tyrone Kingsley is one person who (realizes, realize) the value of this investment.

1. _____

2. Tyrone Kingsley is one of the people who (realizes, realize) the value of this investment.

2. _____

3. Ms. Rosenfield is one of those executives who (is, are) unable to delegate responsibility.

3. _____

4. Anne Brady is the only member of the department who (knows, know) how to operate this machine properly.

4. _____

5. We are looking for one of those people who (is, are) not afraid to be aggressive.

5. _____

6. Ms. Garcia is the one person among our entire staff who (is, are) capable of making the project a success.

6. _____

7. Ethan is the only member of our department who (is, are) unafraid to voice an opinion.

7. _____

8. He is one of those people who (is, are) always complaining about (his, her, their) heavy responsibilities.

8. _____

9. She is different from any of those executives who (remains, remain) calm when (she, they) (is, are) harassed.

9. _____

10. Jill is one of those people who always (makes, make) (his, her, their) opinions known.

10. _____

PRACTICE 7

Subject and Verb Agreement

Instructions: The letter below contains a number of intentional errors in subject and verb agreement. Cross out each incorrect word and write your correction in the space above the word.

Modern Times

2643 Calumet Avenue, Chicago, IL 60506

April 12, 20--

Ms. M. L. Guevara
930 Chester Street
Little Rock, AR 72202

Dear Ms. Guevara:

Our records indicates your subscription to *Modern Times* have not yet been renewed. Since you have been a subscriber for years, we are wondering whether there is any reasons for the delay in your renewing. We hope not. Each of our previous letters express our appreciation of having you as a subscriber and explain our desire to have you remain on our subscription list.

The most important of our goals are your satisfaction. Your feedback are particularly welcome. If there are something we can do better, please let us know. Either a suggestion on how to improve our service or your general comments is always helpful. We believe *Modern Times* are the finest magazine in its field; your suggestions will help us keep it that way.

Whether drama, science, or politics are your area of interest, *Modern Times* have articles for you. Our new series of articles about history promise to be fascinating. We write for discerning readers. Surveys indicate that our subscribers is engineers, doctors, or lawyers. Many a reader have written to us praise. Ramon Garcia, one of several thousand people who is a charter subscriber, says his issues of *Modern Times* is an invaluable record of current culture.

We hope you will forward your renewal today to ensure that your name, in addition to the names of other discriminating readers, are included on our list of subscribers.

Sincerely yours,

Lester McMillan, Subscription Manager

PRACTICE 8

Composition: Making Subjects and Verbs Agree

Instructions: Complete the following sentence starters in a meaningful way. In sentences where a choice of verbs is offered, indicate which verb is being used by underlining it.

EXAMPLE: **The faculty (<u>has,</u> have) <u>voted by a majority of better than three to one to go on strike.</u>**

1. The committee (has, have) _____

   _____

2. None of the people who (has, have) _____

   _____

3. Not one of the proposals (was, were) _____

   _____

4. Many a business student (feel, feels) _____

   _____

5. Half of the audience (was, were) _____

   _____

6. The only one of the people who (has, have) _____

   _____

7. The percentage _____

   _____

8. The number _____

   _____

9. A number _____

   _____

10. Politics_____

   _____

Voice, Mood, and Verbals

CHAPTER 9 PREVIEW

In this chapter you will focus on voice and mood and the correct forms and uses of verbals. You will continue to work with the Programmed Reinforcement sections and the Practices. Finally, you will find out how to attach a document file to an e-mail message and send it.

OBJECTIVES

After completing this chapter, you will be able to

- Distinguish between the active voice and the passive voice.
- Convert passive voice sentences into active voice sentences.
- Recognize when it is appropriate to use the passive voice.
- Identify and use correctly the three moods in English:
  - The indicative mood
  - The imperative mood
  - The subjunctive mood
- Avoid awkward and inconsistent shifts in verb tense, mood, and voice.
- Construct and use infinitives and gerunds.
- Avoid and correct dangling verbal modifiers.
- Use parallel construction in composing sentences.

Study Plan for Chapter 9

The Study Plan for Chapter 9 offers a set of strategies that will help you learn and review the chapter material.

❶ **Active and Passive Voices**: Draw arrows from verbs to their objects in active sentences and from verbs to their subjects in passive ones.

❷ **Attachment Issues**: Dangling modifiers are sentence elements that fail to develop meaningful attachments to nouns or pronouns. In the sentence *Walking up the street, the house came into view,* the modifier is trying to attach itself to *house.* However, a *house* can't walk down the street, so both the attachment and the sentence fail.

❸ **Repairing Modifiers**: Fix dangling modifiers by rewriting sentences to involve the modifiers in meaningful attachments. Try instead, *Walking up the street, I saw the building come into view.*

❹ **Parallel Construction**: Proofread for parallel construction by looking for a series of items. Verify that the parts of the series all share the same construction.

SECTION A
Voice and Mood

You will conclude your study of verbs with a look at voice and mood, two of the most important properties of verbs. You will learn how to fine-tune your verb choices by following the guidelines for forming and using these properties correctly, and learn how to avoid inconsistencies that can occur as you write more and more complex sentences.

9.1 | Voice

One property verbs have is called **voice.** Voice indicates whether the subject of the sentence is *performing* or *receiving* the action described by the verb.

Active Voice

If the subject *does* the action, then the sentence is in the **active voice.**

> Maria *mailed* the package.   The manager *should have fired* him.
> Larry *is faxing* the letter.   Jan *will make* the arrangements.

Passive Voice

If the subject is *acted upon,* then the sentence is in the **passive voice.**

> The package *was mailed* by Maria.   He *should have been fired* by the
>   manager.
> The letter is *being faxed* by Larry.   The arrangements *will be made* by Jan.

With the passive voice, it is not necessary to include the doer of the action:

> The package *was mailed* yesterday.   The letter is *being faxed* now.
> He *should have been fired.*   The arrangements *will be made.*

The passive voice consists of a form of the helping verb *to be* followed by the past participle. If the verb does not consist of some form of *to be* plus the past participle, the sentence is not in the passive voice.

Use of the Passive Voice

You may have heard that you should *never* use the passive voice. This is not true. Sometimes the passive voice is the best choice. Writers use the passive voice to emphasize a point, show tact, and vary sentence patterns.

Emphasis. The passive voice is used to emphasize a point. For example: *Our firm was established in 1877.*

The establishment of the firm itself is important in this sentence, not the names of the people who established it. The writer selected the passive construction to emphasize the firm's establishment.

Writers often choose a passive construction when they want to de-emphasize the doer. For example: *Althea Jackson was presented with an award by the president.* Althea Jackson receives the greater emphasis by being made the subject of the passive sentence. To emphasize the giver of the award use the active voice. *The president presented Althea Jackson with an award.*

Tact. The passive voice also is used for reasons of *tact,* since it lets you avoid assigning responsibility to a doer of an action. Notice how the following passive sentences avoid naming the doer of the action.

PASSIVE	ACTIVE
1. Two errors *were made.*	1. The assistant *made* two errors.
2. Your notes *were checked.*	2. We *checked* your notes.
3. It *has not been received.*	3. You *failed* to send it.

In each of these pairs of examples, the passive voice construction, being more tactful, would ordinarily be preferred.

Variety. The passive voice is also used for sentence variety. Do not use both the active voice and the passive voice in the same sentence. Although the passive voice is useful, most writers and readers *prefer* the active voice because it is more forceful and less wordy.

Active vs. Passive

The following chart illustrates the differences between the active and passive forms of the verb *to write.*

TENSE	ACTIVE VOICE	PASSIVE VOICE
Present	*write* or *writes*	*am, are,* or *is written*
Present Progressive	*am, are,* or *is writing*	*am, are,* or *is being written*
Past	*wrote*	*was* or *were written*
Past Progressive	*was* or *were writing*	*was* or *were being written*
Future	*will write*	*will be written*
Future Progressive	*will be writing*	(no passive form)
Present Perfect	*have* or *has written*	*have* or *has been written*
Present Perfect Progressive	*have* or *has been writing*	(no passive form)
Past Perfect	*had written*	*had been written*
Past Perfect Progressive	*had been writing*	(no passive form)
Future Perfect	*will have written*	*will have been written*
Future Perfect Progressive	*will have been writing*	(no passive form)

Grammar Tip

Active vs. Passive

In the active voice, the subject does the action: *Sean tossed the ball.*

In the passive voice, the subject is acted upon: *The ball was tossed by Sean.*

The other property that verbs have is called **mood**, which refers to the manner in which the action of the state-of-being verb is expressed. There are three moods in English: indicative, imperative, and subjunctive.

Indicative Mood

The **indicative** mood is used to make statements and ask questions. It is the mood you have been examining in this chapter.

> I would like to apply for a position in your marketing division. (*statement*)
> We have no positions open right now. (*statement*)
> Do you expect any openings soon? (*question*)

Imperative Mood

The **imperative** mood is used to give a command, make a request, or give directions. It appears only in the present tense, second person—that is, those instances when the subject is understood to be *you*.

> Close the door. (*command*)
> Please pass the salt. (*request*)
> Turn right at the next intersection. (*directions*)

Subjunctive Mood

The **subjunctive** can be troublesome to many people. The subjunctive requires you to change the form of the verb.

The subjunctive is most frequently used in two situations:

1. To express a condition that is highly improbable or contrary to fact.
2. To express a wish.

Guidelines for Forming the Subjunctive

To form the subjunctive mood, do one of the following:

1. Substitute the word *be* for *am, are,* or *is.*
   If I may *be* so bold, let me offer you my assistance.
2. Substitute *were* for *was.*
   If it *were* my computer, I would install voice-recognition software.
3. Drop the *s* ending from the third person singular form of verbs in the present tense.
   It is vital that he *see* a doctor immediately.

Conditions Contrary to Fact. The following sentences are in the subjunctive mood because they express a situation that is known to be contrary to fact, or false.

If I *were* you, I would be more discreet.
(Because the speaker is not *you*, the statement is contrary to fact.)

If Ms. Edwards *were* here, your demands would be quickly met.
(Because Ms. Edwards is not here, the statement is contrary to fact.)

He behaves as if he *were* the only one affected by the announcement.
(Because he is not the only one affected, the statement is contrary to fact.)

Finally, look at this sentence:

If Roy was at the party, I didn't see him.

You cannot be certain that Roy was *not* at the party, so his presence is *not* contrary to fact. In this case, use the regular past tense, *was*. If you know for certain that Roy is not at the party, however, you should say, *If Roy were at this party, it would be really lively.*

Wishes. Use the subjunctive mood to express a wish. For example,

I wish I *were* king.	We wish we *were* able to help you.
I wish she *were* here now.	Oh, if only I *were* ten years younger.

That *Clauses*. The subjunctive mood is also used in *that* clauses following verbs expressing (1) desires, (2) recommendations, (3) demands, (4) suggestions, (5) resolutions, and (6) formal motions.

1. We desire that he *relinquish* all rights to the property. (*desire*)
2. Evelyn recommended they *be given* an exit interview. (*recommendation*)
3. Our instructor requires that we *submit* all papers through e-mail. (*demand*)
4. I suggest that Professor Chen *consider* these factors. (*suggestion*)
5. It is urgent that she *call* me as soon as she arrives. (*suggestion*)
6. Be it resolved that Edmund Armstrong *be awarded* the honorary degree of Doctor of Humane Letters. (*resolution*)
7. I move that the meeting *be adjourned*. (*formal motion*)

9.3 Inconsistent Shifts in Verb Tense

What's wrong with the verb forms in the following sentence?

George *came* into the office yesterday and *explains* about the delay.

The sentence is inconsistent in its use of tenses. It combines both the past tense (*came*) and the present tense (*explains*). Because this incident occurred yesterday, all of the verbs should be in the past tense: George *came* into the office yesterday and *explained* about the delay.

WRONG   I will be (*simple future*) in New York on Thursday, and she is going to be (*present progressive*) in Washington.

RIGHT ✔ I *will be* in New York on Thursday, and she *will be* in Washington. (*simple future*)

RIGHT ✔ I *am going* to be in New York on Thursday, and she is *going* to be in Washington. (*present progressive*)

Correct Tense Shifts

A sentence may combine several tenses, but it must do so logically:

I *was in* New York on Thursday, and *she will* be in Washington next Tuesday.
I *saw* her yesterday, *am seeing* her today, and *will see* her tomorrow.
I *thought* so then, *think* so now, and *will* always *think* so.
What *did* Ms. Worth *say* her first name *is*?
She *told* me her first name *is* Helen.

Grammar Tip

Is or Was?

Unless Ms. Worth changed her first name, the present tense *is Helen* is correct in the sentence to the right. Her name remains and is *Helen*.

9.4 **Inconsistent Shifts in Mood and Voice**

You should also be careful that the mood and voice of the verbs in a sentence are consistent. For example, the following sentence improperly combines the indicative and the subjunctive moods.

WRONG   If he *was* alive and I *were* richer, this shop would be a success.

RIGHT ✔ If I *were* richer and he *were* alive, this shop would be a success.

The following sentence also improperly combines the subjunctive and the indicative moods: *I wish that I were able to go to the prom and that she was going with me.* The sentence should be revised: *I wish I were able to go to the prom and that she were going with me.*

Similarly, avoid awkward shifts from active to passive voice in the same sentence: *Judy changed to the night shift, but the new shift was not liked by her.* This sentence should be revised to read: *Judy changed to the night shift, but she did not like the new shift.*

This sentence also makes an awkward shift: *It was decided by my manager that he would no longer tolerate late arrivals.* The revised sentence eliminates this shift. *My manager decided that he would no longer tolerate late arrivals.*

Be consistent and logical in your use of verbs, and avoid awkward and inconsistent shifts in tense, mood, and voice.

Coverage Key

Section		Statement
9.1	➤ Voice	➤ S1, S2, S3, S4, S5
9.2	➤ Mood	➤ S6, S7, S8, S9
9.3	➤ Inconsistent Shifts in Verb Tense	➤ S10
9.4	➤ Inconsistent Shifts in Mood and Voice	➤ S11

Instructions: Cover the answers in the **Answer** column; then write your answer to the first statement. Uncover the first printed answer and compare your answer to it. If you wrote a correct answer, continue the activity. If you made an error, use the **Coverage Key** to locate the chapter section you need to review. When you are confident that you understand the material, continue with the reinforcement activity.

ANSWER

STATEMENT

S1 *Voice* indicates whether the subject is the *doer* or *receiver* of the action described by the verb. If the subject *does* the action, the sentence is in the _____ voice. If the subject is acted upon, the sentence is in the _____.

A1 active, passive

S2 As a general principle, the _____ voice is preferred in writing you do at work.

A2 active

S3 Which of the following sentences is/are in the active voice?
   a. **Jack is phoning his wife now.**
   b. **Jack's wallet was stolen.**
   c. **Someone stole Jack's wallet.**
   d. **Jack said that his wallet had been stolen.**

A3 a., c., d.

S4 Sometimes, for purposes of tact or emphasis, the passive voice is preferable. Which sentence in each of the following pairs is more tactful?
   1. (a) **You failed to sign the check.**
      (b) **The check was not signed.**
   2. (a) **Several factual errors were made in the proposal.**
      (b) **You made several factual errors in your proposal.**

A4 1. (b), 2. (a)

S5 Which sentence places greater emphasis on Knox College?
   a. **Knox College was founded in 1837 in Galesburg, Illinois.**
   b. **Galesburg, Illinois, is the home of Knox College, which was founded in 1837.**

A5 a.

S6 There are three moods in English: the *indicative,* the *imperative,* and the *subjunctive.* Which mood is used in giving commands?

_____

A6 imperative

S7 Which mood is used to express a wish or a situation contrary to fact?

_____

A7 subjunctive

S8 Choose the correct verbs:
   a. **I wish I (was, were) younger.**
   b. **If he (was, were) still alive, things would be different.**
   c. **If she (was, were) here, I didn't see her.**
   d. **I'd consider quitting if I (was, were) you.**

A8
   a. **were**
   b. **were**
   c. **was**
   d. **were**

S9 What verb will correctly complete each of the following sentences?
   a. **I demand that everyone present _____ questioned.**
   b. **Karla moved that the proposal _____ approved as amended.**

A9
   a. **be**
   b. **be**

S10 Because verb tenses reflect logical relationships in time, they should not be used inconsistently. Rewrite the following sentences to make the verb tenses consistent.
   a. **Yesterday he comes into the office and resigned.**

   _____

   b. **I ordered the software upgrades last week, but the distributor had failed to send them.**

   _____
   _____

   c. **I will be leaving next month, but she stays.**

   _____

A10
   a. **Yesterday he came into the office and resigned.**
   b. **I ordered the software upgrades last week, but the distributor failed to send them.**
   c. **I will be leaving next month, but she will be staying.**

S11 The *mood* and *voice* of the verb in a sentence should also be consistent. Rephrase the following sentences:
   a. **Our problems would be more easily solved if I were richer or if he was still in charge.**

   _____
   _____

   b. **Judy changed the oil while the tires were rotated by Larry.**

   _____
   _____

A11
   a. **Our problems would be more easily solved if I were richer or if he were still in charge.**
   b. **Judy changed the oil while Larry rotated the tires.**

Verbals, Dangling Modifiers, and Parallel Construction

Up to now, you have been examining the various forms a verb can take when it is performing its most important function as the predicate of the sentence. Verbs can also assume other forms and act as other parts of speech. In this section you will discover how versatile the verb can be.

9.5 | Verbals

Review the following sentences:

1. Krystle decided *to run* in the park every morning before work.
2. Because *running* is an excellent form of exercise, Krystle felt that *running* would keep her physically fit.
3. *Running* through the park yesterday, Krystle sprained her ankle.

In the sentences above, the verb *to run* is used in several different forms, but never as the predicate of the sentence. Rather, it tells us what Krystle decided (Sentence 1); tells us what is an excellent form of exercise and what Krystle felt would keep her physically fit (Sentence 2); and helps to modify Krystle, who sprained her ankle (Sentence 3).

Each of the forms of *to run* illustrated in these sentences is a **verbal**—a verb form used as a noun, an adjective, or an adverb. The three kinds of verbals are **infinitives, gerunds,** and **participles.** Although verbals are taken from verbs and are like verbs in many ways, they cannot act as the predicate of a sentence. They can act only as nouns, adjectives, or adverbs.

9.6 | Infinitives

The **infinitive** almost always is preceded by the word *to.* The infinitive form is often used when referring to a verb: we usually say *to be, to have, to read,* and *to bring,* rather than *be, have, read,* and *bring.*

Infinitives as Nouns

The infinitive is used most often as a *noun,* both as the subject and as the object of a sentence.

> *To succeed* was Diego's sole desire. (*subject*)
> Diego wanted desperately *to succeed.* (*object*)

Infinitives as Adjectives or Adverbs

The infinitive can also be used to modify or describe other words in the sentence, in which case it acts as an adjective or an adverb.

Clothes *to suit* the occasion should be worn. (*adjective* modifying *clothes*)
He needed a permit *to build.* (*adjective* modifying *permit*)
I'd be glad *to help.* (*adverb* modifying the adjective *glad*)
She stayed late *to help.* (*adverb* modifying the verb *stayed*)

Infinitive Tenses

The infinitive can be expressed in both the present and perfect tenses. Take the infinitive *to see,* for instance:

To see China is exciting. (*present tense, active voice*)
To have seen China is to have fulfilled a dream. (*perfect tense, active voice*)
To be seen in China is chic. (*present tense, passive voice*)
To have been seen in China is remarkable. (*perfect tense, passive voice*)

Infinitives and Pronouns

Adjectives and Adverbs
You'll learn about adjectives and adverbs in Chapters 10 and 11.

The pronoun used after an infinitive is exactly the same as the pronoun used after any other verb. For example,

The director plans to recommend him and her for a promotion.

Him and *her* are objects of the infinitive *to recommend.*

Ms. Hill said she wanted to see me in her office.

Me is the object of the infinitive *to see.*

Infinitives, not *And*

Many people mistakenly use *and* in sentences such as these:

WRONG: You must try *and* make it.
WRONG: Try *and* be here on time.
WRONG: Check *and* see if the door is locked.

As you know, *and* is a coordinating conjunction; it joins two equal components. The sentences above do not call for a word to join two equal components; rather, they require objects of the verbs *try* (the infinitives *to make* and *to be*) and *check* (the infinitive *to see*).

RIGHT: ✔ You must try *to make* it.
RIGHT: ✔ Try *to be* here on time.
RIGHT: ✔ Check *to see* if the door is locked.

Similarly, *and* is mistakenly used in sentences such as these:

WRONG: Please be sure *and* call when you arrive.
WRONG: Before signing a contract, be sure *and* read the fine print.

Sure requires a modifying adverb: the infinitives *to call* and *to read.*

RIGHT: ✔ Please be sure *to call* when you arrive.
RIGHT: ✔ Before signing a contract, be sure *to read* the fine print.

9.7 Split Infinitives

You probably have heard of a **split infinitive.** A split infinitive simply means that a word or words have been placed between *to* and the verb. At one time it was always considered a grammatical error to split an infinitive. This is no longer the case. In current usage it is not incorrect to split an infinitive, but split infinitives should be avoided when they result in awkward constructions. For example,

AWKWARD

1. I want *to next fall go* to England.
2. When it came to investments, he wanted *to, as the saying goes, have* his cake and *eat* it too.
3. I have *to sadly leave* you.
4. I intend *to frequently visit* you.
5. I would like *to, when gasoline prices go down, buy* a larger car.

BETTER ✔

1. I want *to go* to England next fall.
2. When it came to investments, as the saying goes, he wanted *to have* his cake and *eat* it too.
3. Sadly, I have *to leave* you.
4. I intend *to visit* you frequently.
5. When gasoline prices go down, I would like *to buy* a larger car.

SUCCESSFUL FAILURE When you face a stressful situation, avoid becoming paralyzed by a fear of failure. Assure yourself that failure has been a stepping-stone to success for many.

Debatable Split Infinitives. The next two sentences have split infinitives, but they are not awkward like the preceding examples, and some writers would find them acceptable.

To never be absent from class is a remarkable record.
I want you *to carefully consider* these two proposals for changing our shipping procedures.

Other writers would prefer that these sentences be revised as follows:

Never *to be* absent from class is a remarkable record.
I want you *to consider* carefully these two proposals for changing our shipping procedures.

Acceptable Split Infinitives. Sometimes, a split infinitive can appear to be the best choice to convey meaning. For example,

> *To deliberately falsify* your tax return can lead to serious consequences.

Both *Deliberately to falsify your tax return* and *To falsify deliberately your tax return* sound awkward.

> I have *to really study* for this exam or, I *really have to study* for this exam.

Both *I have really to study* and *I have to study really* sound awkward.

Grammar Tip

Gerund Definition

Gerunds are verb forms ending in *ing* that act as nouns.

9.8 Gerunds

The infinitive, as you have seen, can serve as a noun, adjective, or adverb. The **gerund,** however, is more limited. This verb form, which ends in *ing,* can act only as a *noun.* Look at these sentences:

> *Running* is excellent exercise.

Here the gerund *Running* is the subject of the sentence.

In this next sentence, *running* is the subject complement. The subject of the sentence is *exercise;* as the subject complement, *running* restates the subject.

> My favorite exercise is *running.*

In the following sentence, *running* acts as the object of the verb *enjoyed.*

> Krystle enjoyed *running* in the park.

Flashback

More Subject Complements
For more information on subject complements, see Section 4.4 on page 104.

■

With few exceptions, the use of gerunds should pose no problems for you. Two exceptions are the use of nouns or pronouns to modify gerunds, and the placement of gerunds within a sentence.

Nouns and Pronouns That Modify Gerunds

Which is correct?

> *(Jacob's, Jacob)* resigning from the committee came as a surprise.
> We did not learn about *(his, him)* leaving the company until yesterday.

The possessive pronoun *his* and the possessive noun *Jacob's* are correct. Nouns or pronouns that modify gerunds must be in the possessive case.

> WRONG: *Jacob* resigning from the committee came as a surprise.
> RIGHT: ✔ *Jacob's* resigning from the committee came as a surprise.

The use of the possessive pronoun before the gerund may not seem as intuitive to you as the use of the possessive noun since you must use the objective pronoun in a sentence similar to the one requiring a possessive:

We did not learn about *him*.

But the above sentence does not have a gerund phrase. Because the gerund phrase *leaving the company until yesterday* completes the sentence example above, you must use the possessive pronoun *his*.

Grammar Tip

Possessive Case Needed
A noun or pronoun used to modify a gerund must be in the possessive case.

9.9 Participles

The third verbal, the **participle,** functions as an adjective that describes or modifies a noun. The participle can take different forms; it can appear as a single word, or it can be part of a phrase—**a participial phrase.**

The Present Participle

The most common form adds *ing* to make the **present participle.**

Running, Krystle tripped.
The person *standing* by the door wishes to speak with Lars.

In the first sentence, the participle *Running* modifies Krystle by describing Krystle when she tripped. In the second, the participial phrase *standing by the door* identifies the person who wishes to speak with Lars.

The Past Participle

The second form, the **past participle,** is usually formed by adding *ed.* As you know, the past participle of regular verbs is also formed by adding *ed.*

Angered, the union members threatened to strike.
The arbiter *called* into the negotiations attempted to help the two sides reach a settlement.

In the first sentence, *Angered* describes the union members and acts as an adjective; in the second, *called into the negotiations* describes the arbiter and also acts as an adjective.

Irregular Past Participles. Irregular verbs, as you know, form their past participles in various other ways. These, too, can serve as adjectives.

"Found Manuscript" is the title of a song by Emaline Green.
The painting, *bought* for only a few hundred dollars, was later discovered to be a valuable masterpiece.
The roadside was littered with debris *thrown* from the passing cars.

Grammar Tip

Present Participle
The present participle shows that the action it expresses is occurring at the same time as the action expressed by the main verb.

In the first sentence above, *Found* describes the *manuscript;* in the second, *bought for only a few hundred dollars* describes the painting; and in the third, *thrown from the passing cars* describes the debris.

The Perfect Participle

The third form used as an adjective is the **perfect participle.** It is formed by adding *having* to the past participle, whether it is a regular or irregular verb: *having called, having drunk, having seen, having completed.*

> *Having said* what he wanted to say, Fred left the room.
> The secretary, *having read* the minutes of the previous meeting, sat down.
> The missing child *having been found,* the search was ended.

In the first sentence, *Having said what he wanted to say* describes Fred; in the second, *having read the minutes of the previous meeting* describes the secretary; in the third, *having been found* describes the child.

Grammar Tip

Past Participle and Perfect Participle

Both of these participle forms show that the action described occurs before the action that is expressed by the main verb.

9.10 Dangling Verbal Modifiers

As you have seen, verbals frequently are used in phrases that describe other words in a sentence. Each of these phrases must be used correctly and placed properly in the sentence so that its relationship to other words in the sentence is absolutely clear. If the relationship of the phrase to the rest of the sentence is not clear, the result often is a **dangling modifier.** For example,

WRONG: *Walking* down the street, *the building* came into sight.

Obviously the building was not doing the walking, a person was. The sentence should be rewritten to make this point clear.

WRONG: *Walking down* the street, *the building* was seen by Carmen.

Although this sentence indicates who saw the building, it is still not correct because it still sounds as though the building is walking. This sentence also must be rewritten to clarify the relationship between *walking down the street* and the subject it modifies.

RIGHT: ✔ *Walking* down the street, *Carmen* saw the building.

Now it is clear that it was Carmen who was walking down the street. The revised sentence clarifies the relationship between the verbal phrase, *walking down the street,* and the noun it modifies, *Carmen.*

Verbal Phrase Placement

When a verbal phrase begins a sentence and modifies the subject of that sentence, the subject should immediately follow it.

WRONG: *Washing* the walls and *repainting* the woodwork, *the visitor* noticed the work crew.

Who was washing the walls and repainting the woodwork, and who noticed the work crew? The work crew was washing and repainting, not the visitor. You could rewrite the sentence so that the subject, *the work crew,* immediately follows the verbal phrase that begins the sentence.

RIGHT: ✔*Washing* the walls and *repainting* the woodwork, *the* work *crew* was noticed by the visitor.

However, the revised sentence sounds awkward. It is better to shift the verbal phrase so that it follows the noun it modifies:

BETTER: ✔The visitor noticed *the* work crew *washing* the walls and *repainting* the woodwork.

Other statements that are not so obviously humorous demand the same kind of logical relationship. For example,

DANGLING PARTICIPLE: *Skilled* in achieving compromise, *a strike* was averted by the arbiter.

RIGHT: ✔*Skilled* in achieving compromise, *the arbiter* averted a strike.

DANGLING PARTICIPLE: *Having climbed* for several hours to reach the summit, *the view* was inspiring to them.

RIGHT: ✔*Having climbed* for several hours to reach the summit, *they* found the view inspiring.

DANGLING GERUND: *By using* this new technique, *time* can be saved.

RIGHT: ✔*By using* this new technique, *you* can save time.

DANGLING GERUND: *On hearing* the weather forecast, *the class trip* should be postponed, the teacher decided.

RIGHT: ✔*On hearing* the weather forecast, *the teacher* decided to postpone the class trip.

DANGLING INFINITIVE: Unable to swim, a lifeguard rescued me.

RIGHT: ✔*Unable* to swim, *I* was rescued by a lifeguard.

Grammar Tip

Verbal Phrase Help

To verify that the correct noun follows a verbal phrase beginning a sentence, ask who or what is doing the action described in the verbal phrase.

DANGLING
INFINITIVE: *To determine* its value, *the book* will be appraised.
RIGHT: ✔*To determine* its value, *we* will have the book appraised.

It is also possible for a verbal modifier to dangle at the end of the sentence:

WRONG: Carmen saw the building walking down the street.

Again, it sounds as though the building is doing the walking rather than Carmen. The correct version of this sentence is still *Walking down the street, Carmen saw the building.*

Here is another example:

DANGLING
PARTICIPLE: *The student* was unable to respond to the teacher, *not having read the assignment.*
RIGHT: ✔*The student, not having read the assignment,* was unable to respond to the teacher.
RIGHT: ✔*Not having read the assignment, the student* was unable to respond to the teacher.

The sentence examples in this section illustrate that when using verbal phrases as modifiers, you must construct your sentences so that the relationship is clear between the verbal phrase and the word it describes.

When a verbal phrase begins a sentence, the next word should be the subject of the sentence. That word should answer the following question: *Who* or *what* is doing the action described in the verbal phrase?

Steel Collar Workers

As a spin-off of the blue collar and white collar worker, the steel collar worker represents a whole new workforce that requires no health benefits: the industrial robot.

9.11 Parallel Construction

Sentences that are **parallel** (or follow **parallel construction**) use the same structure for two or more parts. The following compound sentence demonstrates parallel construction:

Part 1   Part 2
Carlos wanted to leave, but Greta wanted to stay.

Both parts of the above sentence follow the same pattern.

Parallelism: Consistent Verb Tense

When you read earlier about avoiding shifts in verb tenses, in a sense you were learning about maintaining parallelism.

| | Part 1 | Part 2 | Part 3 |

Ms. Highwater *picked* up the receiver, *dialed* her broker, and *places* an order.

The sentence contains an inconsistent shift in tense. The verb in the third part is a present tense verb while the verbs in the other two parts are simple past tense verbs. The sentence should read:

| | Part 1 | Part 2 | Part 3 |

Ms. Highwater *picked* up the receiver, *dialed* her broker, and *placed* an order.

Verbals used in a series follow the same form throughout.

WRONG: The activities section on her résumé says she likes *swimming*, *boating*, and *to hike*.

This sentence presents two gerunds (*swimming* and *boating*) and one infinitive (*to hike*) as the objects of the verb *likes*. Use the same verb structure throughout. Either all gerunds (*She likes swimming, boating, and hiking*) or all infinitives (*She likes to swim, to boat, and to hike*) would be correct. Keep the types of verbals used in a series parallel.

Let's look at another example:

WRONG: *To read, to paint,* and *cooking* were his life's chief pleasures.
RIGHT: ✔ *To read, to paint,* and *to cook* were the chief pleasures in his life.
RIGHT: ✔ *Reading, painting,* and *cooking* were the chief pleasures in his life.

Computer Programming

To remain up to speed, welding machine operators need to increase their computer skills as they become more and more responsible for programming computer-controlled welding machines, which includes robots.

∼

Coverage Key

Section		Statement
9.5	➤ Verbals	➤ S12
9.6	➤ Infinitives	➤ S13, S14, S15, S16, S21
9.7	➤ Split Infinitives	➤ S17, S18, S19, S20
9.8	➤ Gerunds	➤ S23, S24, S25, S26, S27, S28
9.9	➤ Participles	➤ S22, S28, S29, S30, S31, S32
9.10	➤ Dangling Verbal Modifiers	➤ S33, S34, S35, S36, S37
9.11	➤ Parallel Construction	➤ S38, S39

Instructions: Cover the answers in the **Answer** column; then write your answer to the first statement. Uncover the first printed answer and compare your answer to it. If you wrote a correct answer, continue the activity. If you made an error, use the **Coverage Key** to locate the chapter section you need to review. When you are confident that you understand the material, continue with the reinforcement activity.

ANSWER

STATEMENT

S12 A verb form that is used as a noun, adjective, or adverb is called a(n) _____.

A12 verbal

S13 A verb preceded by the word *to* is a(n) _____.

A13 infinitive

S14 An infinitive may be used as a noun, adjective, or adverb. **To listen is important.** The infinitive **to listen** is used as a(n) (noun, adjective, adverb). It is the _____ of the verb **is.**

A14 noun, subject

S15 **I like to listen to music.** The infinitive **to listen** is used as a(n) (noun, adjective, adverb). It is the _____ of the verb **like.**

A15 noun, object

S16 An infinitive may also be followed by objects. Underline the objects of the infinitive in this sentence: **I plan to visit my friends and my relatives.**

A16 <u>friends, relatives</u>

S17 The term used to describe a situation in which one or more words come between *to* and the rest of the verb is a _____.

A17 split infinitive

S18 At one time split infinitives were considered grammatical errors and were avoided. In current usage, when should split infinitives be avoided?
  a. always
  b. never
  c. when they result in awkward constructions

A18 c

A19 when the semester is over, When the semester is over, I plan to go away for a week.

A20 clearly, I want to state clearly what I intend to do.

A21 a. to
b. and
c. to

A22 participle, waiting

A23 gerund

A24 writing, direct object

A25 listening, subject

A26 possessive

A27 a. his
b. Jean's

A28 gerund, present participle

A29 man

A30 a. Annoyed
b. Having completed

S19 Underline the words that split the infinitive in this sentence: **I plan to when the semester is over go away for a week.** Rewrite the sentence to eliminate the split infinitive. _____

S20 Underline the word that splits the infinitive in this sentence: **I want to clearly state what I intend to do.** Rewrite the sentence to eliminate the split infinitive. _____

S21 Sometimes people say *try and* when *try to* would be correct. Choose the correct word in the following sentences:
a. **Please try (and, to) see my side of things.**
b. **We may be forced to try (and, to) try again.**
c. **Try (and, to) stop me.**

S22 An *ing* form of a verb used as part of the progressive form is called a present _____. Underline the present participle in this sentence: **I am waiting for the next available bus.**

S23 A verb form ending in *ing* and used as a noun, as in the sentence **Hiking is healthful,** is called a(n) _____.

S24 Because a gerund is really a noun that is formed from a verb, it may be used as a subject or object in a sentence. In **He enjoyed writing to his interesting friends,** the gerund is _____ and it is used as a(n) _____.

S25 **Listening is an underdeveloped activity.** The gerund is _____ and it is used as a(n) _____.

S26 A noun or pronoun used to modify a gerund takes the _____ case.

S27 Complete these sentences:
a. **We were surprised at (him, his) leaving so soon.**
b. **(Jean, Jean's) quitting came as a complete shock.**

S28 **Filing is tedious work.** In this sentence **filing** is a(n) _____. **She was filing the letters.** In this sentence **filing** is a(n) _____.

S29 Underline the noun that **driving** modifies in this sentence: **Driving down the street, the man saw the holdup in progress.**

S30 Underline the participles in these sentences:
a. **Annoyed by the waiter's attitude, the customer called the restaurant manager.**
b. **Having completed her assignment, Rita decided to go.**

S31 The present participle is used to show an action occurring (before, at the same time as, after) the action expressed by the main verb in the sentence. The past participle and the perfect participle are used to express an action occurring (before, at the same time as, after) the action expressed by the main verb in the sentence.

A31 at the same time as, before

S32 Supply the proper form of the participle to complete the following sentences correctly:
   a. (**Peel**) **an onion, Marcia cut her finger.**_____
   b. (**Cut**) **her finger, Marcia put a bandage on it.**_____

A32 a. **Peeling**
   b. **Having cut**

S33 If the participle does not clearly relate to the noun that it modifies, it is called a *dangling participle.* Underline the dangling participle: **Walking along the street, the store came into sight.** Name the word that walking seems to modify:_____

A33 walking (dangling participle); **store**

S34 Is this a dangling participle construction? **Speaking softly because of a sore throat, the audience listened to the lecturer.** _____.

A34 Yes

S35 Is this a dangling participle construction? **Knowing the result, he quickly phoned his broker.** _____.

A35 No

S36 Rewrite the sentences in S33 and S34 to eliminate dangling participles.
   a. _____
   b. _____

A36 a. **Walking along the street, she saw the store.**
   b. **Speaking softly because of a sore throat, the lecturer addressed the audience.**

S37 Rewrite the following sentences to eliminate dangling modifiers.
   a. **Walking through the hall, the floor was slipped on by Rhonda**
   _____
   b. **To access the computer, your identification number should be entered first.**_____
   c. **While correcting the mistake, additional errors were discovered.**_____

A37 a. **Walking through the hall, Rhonda slipped on the floor.**
   b. **To access the computer, first enter your identification number.**
   c. **While correcting the mistake, we discovered additional errors.**

S38 Choose the word that destroys the parallelism of this sentence: **To swim, to hike, to play, and boating are enjoyable summer activities.** What word(s) would maintain parallelism in this sentence?
   _____

A38 boating, to boat

S39 Show two different ways to correct the lack of parallel structure: **Speaking, listening, and to take notes are student activities.**
   a. _____
   b. _____

A39 Speaking, listening, and taking notes... To speak, to listen, and to take notes...

CHAPTER 9 SUMMARY

In this chapter you learned how and when to construct the active voice and the passive voice. You discovered that a verb also expresses one of three "moods," or states of being: the indicative, the imperative, and the subjunctive. Besides being the predicate of a sentence, a verb can also function as a verbal noun or modifier when it is in the infinitive, gerund, or participle form. You also discovered how to avoid constructing sentences with dangling verbal modifiers and how to keep the parts of a sentence parallel.

Getting Connected

ATTACHING A DOCUMENT FILE TO AN E-MAIL MESSAGE

GOAL: For speed and convenience, nothing beats e-mail when you need to send documents such as letters, school papers, press releases, or reports. Your document will arrive across the street or across the country much faster than if it were sent by snail mail. Sending a document via e-mail involves a simple process known as **file attachment.** In this process, you retrieve a file from your computer's hard or floppy drive and electronically *attach* it to your e-mail message. When you send the e-mail message, the attachment goes with it.

In this activity, you'll practice attaching a document file to an e-mail message and sending it to yourself. You'll also reinforce what you have learned about verbs in this chapter.

STEP 1   First, create a short document based on the contents of Chapter 9. Do this by copying the following sentences into a document. Fill in the blanks with the correct missing words as you copy the sentences.

   a. *If the _____ does the action, the sentence is in the _____ voice.*

   b. *If the _____ is acted upon, the sentence is in the _____ voice.*

   c. *Most writers at work prefer the _____ voice because it is more forceful and more direct.*

   d. *The _____ and _____ of a verb in a sentence should be consistent.*

   e. *As a verbal, an infinitive is often used as a _____, both as _____ and _____.*

   f. *The verbal that ends with ing is called a _____ and is used as a _____.*

   g. *The verbal that functions as an adjective is called a _____.*

   h. *If a participle does not clearly relate to the noun it modifies, it is called a _____ _____.*

STEP 2 Use the spell checker in your word processor and proofread your document. Make corrections as needed and save the document, either to your computer's hard drive or to a floppy disk. Be sure you know where you've saved the document.

STEP 3 Go to ***englishworkshop.glencoe.com,*** the address for *The English Workshop* Website, and click on Unit 3. Next click on Getting Connected, and then click on Chapter 9. At the Chapter 9 Getting Connected option, you'll see a list of Websites offering free e-mail, including the provider for your e-mail account. Begin the activity by selecting your e-mail provider.

STEP 4 When you've accessed your e-mail account, click on the option that will allow you to compose a new e-mail message.

STEP 5 When the message page appears, fill in the *To:* line with your complete e-mail address. If you wish to send a copy of the message and the attachment to another person, enter that person's complete e-mail address on the *Cc:* line. On the *Subject:* line, key in the words *Voice, Mood, Verbals.*

STEP 6 In the blank message area, enter a brief message explaining the nature of the attachment. Generally, you want to let the receiver of your message know what is being sent and why you are sending it. A typical message might say, "Please review the attached document about Chapter 9, and respond with your comments." Enter a similar message or one of your own. Use the spell checker in your e-mail program and proofread your e-mail message.

STEP 7 Now you're ready to attach the document to the message. Do that by locating the option for attaching documents, or **files,** to the e-mail message. Look for a button labeled "Attachments," "Attach File," or something similar. Click the button, and follow the instructions for attaching the file. You'll need to know where you saved the file.

STEP 8 You may have to click on a Done button to complete the attachment process.

STEP 9 The original message screen should reappear. You should see the file listed in the Attachments line, which may be above or below the body of the message.

STEP 10 Finally, click the Send button to have your e-mail and file attachment electronically sent to its destination.

STEP 11 Return to your document. Key your name at the top of the page, print the document, and turn it in to your instructor. If you sent your instructor the e-mail message and attachment, skip this step.

Name _____

Class _____ Date _____

PRACTICE 1

Active and Passive Voices: Part A

Instructions: For each sentence, write the subject and the verb in the blanks. In the VOICE column, write *A* if the sentence is in the active voice or *P* if it is in the passive voice.

	SUBJECT	VERB	VOICE
EXAMPLE: The project was completed late.	EX. project	was completed	P
1. I am pleased to meet you.	_____	_____	_____
2. Our company began operations 20 years ago.	_____	_____	_____
3. Every employee was hoping for a bonus.	_____	_____	_____
4. Bonuses were given to every employee.	_____	_____	_____
5. Every employee received a bonus.	_____	_____	_____

Active and Passive Voices: Part B

Instructions: The following sentences are written in the passive voice. In the blank, rewrite each sentence in the active voice. Supply an appropriate subject as needed.

EXAMPLE : **The correct use of the subjunctive is presented in this chapter.**
This chapter presents the correct use of the subjunctive.

6. Your order was shipped yesterday. _____

_____

7. The annual conference was attended by Charles and Angela. _____

_____

8. The company was represented by Ms. O'Connor. _____

_____

9. Chester Martin's report should be studied carefully. _____

_____

10. Medical expenses for which you were reimbursed may not be deducted. _____

_____

PRACTICE 2

The Subjunctive or the Simple Past?

Instructions: In the blank, fill in the correct verb.

EXAMPLE : **I wish I (was, were) younger.**   EX. _____ were _____

1. Things were different when I (was, were) younger.   1. _____

2. If I (was, were) you, I would accept the invitation.   2. _____

3. She (was, were) not here Tuesday.   3. _____

4. (Was, Were) I you, I would do the same.   4. _____

5. I don't know if she (was, were) at the conference.   5. _____

6. If she (was, were) at the conference, I didn't see her.   6. _____

7. We require that each patron (present, presents) current identification.   7. _____

8. If I (was, were) the manager of this firm, I would change things.   8. _____

9. Since the fears proved unfounded, I (was, were) relieved.   9. _____

10. This is how I would act if I (was, were) in your place.   10. _____

11. I certainly wish it (was, were) cooler.   11. _____

12. I think that it (was, were) colder yesterday.   12. _____

13. If he (was, were) to be promoted, he would go far.   13. _____

14. If he (was, were) promoted, he kept it a secret.   14. _____

15. For security, the bookstore asks that each customer (leaves, leave) his or her books up front.   15. _____

16. I wish it (was, were) possible to start over.   16. _____

17. The dean recommended that only three of the eight professors (was, were, be) granted tenure.   17. _____

18. In line with the dean's recommendation, only three of the eight professors (was, were, be) granted tenure.   18. _____

19. I request that the board (grants, grant) my petition.   19. _____

20. If they (grants, grant) my petition, I will be glad.   20. _____

PRACTICE 3

Shifting Verbs and Dangling Modifiers: Part A

Instructions: If the sentence is correct, write *C* in the blank. If it is incorrect, cross out the error and use the space above the sentence to make the necessary change.

began
EXAMPLE: **Last week he interrupted and ~~begins~~ to complain.**

EX. _____

1. I have revised the chapters and Ms. Matsuda edited them.

1. _____

2. I wish you were younger or I was older.

2. _____

3. If Roberta was here, or if her mother were still alive, we would not have to face these difficulties.

3. _____

4. At 10 a.m. tomorrow, after she talks to Mr. Ramirez, she will meet the supervisor.

4. _____

5. I will supply the beverages for next week's meeting if you furnish the cups and napkins.

5. _____

Shifting Verbs and Dangling Modifiers: Part B

Instructions: In the blank, rewrite each sentence to correct a dangling verbal modifier and to show clearly the logical relationship between sentence parts. Supply an appropriate subject as needed.

EXAMPLE: **Running through the park, Krystle's ankle was sprained.**
Running through the park, Krystle sprained her ankle.

6. By using teleconferencing, meetings can be held by businesspeople who work in different cities.

_____

7. When shopping for an automobile, available standard and optional equipment must always be considered by the buyer. _____

_____

8. Written in Japanese, Ms. Arthur found the instructions useless. _____

_____

9. While entering the room, Mr. McCartney was seen leaving. _____

_____

10. Skilled in five computer languages, the program was quickly revised by Ms. Yen. _____

_____

Name _____

Class _____ Date _____

PRACTICE 4

Verbals

Instructions: If the sentence is correct, write *C* in the blank. If it is incorrect, cross out the error and use the space above the sentence to make the necessary changes. Be sure to correct any verbals that lack parallel structure and any ungrammatical forms of pronouns or nouns.

to
EXAMPLE: **Be sure ~~and~~ correct any errors you find.**   EX. _____

1. Mr. Voto says he wants to see you and I after work.   1. _____

2. Please try and find the missing files before tomorrow.   2. _____

3. The manager, studying the problem, found no solution.   3. _____

4. The manager studying of the problem brought no solution.   4. _____

5. Reading the paper at lunch, the news of the stock market upset us.   5. _____

6. Working at top speed, the audit was finished on time by the accountant.   6. _____

7. She wants to see Rafael and me and to carefully explain the new office   7. _____
   arrangements.

8. Knowing the answer, he raised his hand.   8. _____

9. To determine its feasibility, the program will be studied by experts.   9. _____

10. I was supposed to have gone to the conference last week.   10. _____

11. The ability to think logically, organizing clearly, and to communicate effectively   11. _____
    is characteristic of the successful executive.

12. Harper decided to admit his mistake and to ask for another chance to   12. _____
    redeem himself.

13. She wants to before the end of the week meet with us.   13. _____

14. To err is human; forgiving, divine.   14. _____

15. Listening to popular music no longer appeals to me as much as classical music.   15. _____

16. Mr. Sarwono asked Mari and I to join him.   16. _____

17. I intend to closely study all reports.   17. _____

18. What's your reaction to him winning the race?   18. _____

19. We started using the new scanner and to adapt it to our needs.   19. _____

20. They told her to try to be more punctual.   20. _____

PRACTICE 5

Verbs and Verbals

Instructions: The following letter contains a number of errors in the use of verbs and verbals. Whenever you locate an error, cross it out and write the correct form above it.

United Motors, Inc.
9505 Cheyenne St., Detroit, MI 48227

October 17, 20--

Ms. Hidalgo

3098 Gainsborough Dr.

Pasadena, CA 91107

Dear Ms. Hidalgo:

I have been very sorry you was unable to go to the auto show. If you was there, I know you would have enjoyed it. All major dealers were there to at various places around the track display their cars, trucks, and SUVs. The number of automotive products were the largest I ever seen. Jim, Judy, and I were having a great time. Judy is one of those people who wants to be aware of advances in automobiles, so she was particularly interested in the displays.

The best part of the show was the demonstration of the new Starfire 9000. A testdriver drive the car on the track to show we its capabilities. I, together with Judy and Jim, were certain you would be impressed by the performance, as was thousands of others who was there.

If you were to have attended, you would be seeing new automotive concepts. The Starfire 9000 was an all-new car. It had a new engine, streamlining, and controls.

Because of the special design features made possible by high-strength plastics, the Starfire 9000 accelerated from 0 to 60 miles per hour in under six seconds. I need not have told you how impressed everyone, including our friends and I, were. Maybe Jim and Judy will already tell you about it themselves.

Having demonstrated the car's excellent acceleration, the Starfire 9000 was then put through a series of maneuvers by the testdriver. In these tests the Starfire had demonstrated its ability to corner, veer sharply, and generally handling with ease.

According to the Starfire representatives, the company have spent millions on the car. While others were resting on their laurels, their engineers were stroving for more. The Starfire 9000 has been brung into being by devotion to a concept. It has sprang into being out of the minds of America's top automotive engineers. Just as the jet plane shrunk the highways of the air, so will the Starfire 9000 shrink the highways of the earth. With the Starfire 9000 the company have lain the groundwork for all new cars and have setted new standards for transportation. I don't know how much of the representatives comments is true. It is just by me that I want to drive Starfire. You must be sure and come to the next auto show to be seeing the Starfire and all the other cars and automotive products. If I was you, I would try and in the next few days make arrangements to be attending the next show, which will be holded in three weeks at Freeway Track and Arena. We all look forward to see you there.

Sincerely,

Josephine Ward

Promotions Coordinator

Words That Show Action

Unit 3—Editing Review

Instructions: Use the concepts you have studied so far to help you edit the paragraphs below. The paragraphs are from an article for a community newsletter written by the owner and operator of an automobile service garage. The article offers readers advice on how to change the oil in their cars. As you read through the paragraphs, use the information you have learned in the first three units to help you locate errors. Cross out each error you find, and write the correction in the space above it.

Do-It-Yourself Corner: Changing the Oil and Filter in Your Car

Having operated Bob's Auto Service now for five years, many of cars have been

serviced by me. A number of people has asked myself what the one thing is he can

do to prolong his car life. I tell them: Change your oil and filter regularly. That will

prolong the life of your engine more than anything you can be doing.

Now, of course, when you need your oil changed, I'd like you to have brung your

car to me. But changing the oil in your car. Is something you can do yourself. With

just a few basic tooles. In the next two pages I'll tell you how.

First, answers to some general questions.

There is two important safety precautions that must be remembered:

1. Never just rise your car on a jack and then try and work on it. The car could fall

   on you. If your car does not have enough ground clearance, it should be putted

   up on ramps before you lay under it.

2. The oil should not be changed by you when your engine is hot. You could burn

   yourselves on the hot metal as well as on the hot oil.

Now you will be ready to change your oil. And filter.

continued from page 271

1. Warm up the engine until it reaches operating temperature, then drove the car up on the ramps, shut off the engine, and set the parking brake.

2. Place a pan under the drain plug of the oil pan to catch the old oil.

3. Remove the oil cap to allow the oil to drain freely.

4. Removing the drain plug with a wrench and completely draining the oil.

5. While the oil is draining, you can remove the oil filter as well. If its hard to remove by hand, use an oil filter wrench.

6. Wipe the engine oil filter mounting surface with a clean rag.

7. Smear a little oil on the rubber gasket of the new filter. This helped create a tight seal between the mounting and the filter.

8. Screw in the oil filter until a slight resistance is felt by you, then hand tighten the filter an additional 2/3 turn.

9. The drain plug is reinstalled. Tighten this, but don't use excessive force.

10. Put in the new oil. Most cars will take between 4 and 5 quarts. Your owners' manual will tell you your cars capacity. Put the oil cap back on.

11. Now start your engine and check for leak's. If you see any sign of leakage around the drain plug or oil filter. These parts need to be retighten.

12. Back down off the ramps and run the engine until they reach operating temperature. Turn off the car and wait a few minutes for the oil to in the pan settle. Clean the dipstick and check the oil level. Adding more oil if necessary.

13. Finally, dispose of the used oil properly. Pour the old oil into one gallon plastic milk bottles and took it to a licensed oil recycling center, such as Bob's Auto Service and Repair. I'll dispose of it for you without charge.

If you change your oil and filter regularly and bring your car to me for other maintenance. You'll keep your car running for year's to come.

Link & Learn

USING VERBS IN AUTOMOTIVE CAREERS

GOAL: Reinforce what you learned in Unit 3 about verbs while exploring various Websites for automotive professionals.

STEP 1 Go to *englishworkshop.glencoe.com*, the address for *The English Workshop* Website. Click first on Unit 3; then click on Link & Learn to access a list of computer technology sites you may use in this activity. Select one of the sites, and click on it.

STEP 2 Skim the home page of the Website you selected, and locate an area that interests you. Click on that area and find material to work with during this activity. Print at least one full page of the material.

STEP 3 Reread what you printed and respond to the following:

a. Choose a paragraph from the selection you printed. Analyze its use of action and linking verbs. On the back of the printout, create a chart by writing the following labels near the left margin: *Sentences, Action Verbs, Linking Verbs, Helping Verbs*. Next list the number of sentences that appear in the paragraph that include action verbs, the number that include linking verbs, and the number that include helping verbs. Circle the verb type that appears most often.

b. Find an example of a sentence with a transitive verb. Underline the verb and draw an arrow to its object. Find an example of a sentence with an intransitive verb. Underline the verb.

c. Look for a sentence with a compound subject. Underline all parts of the subject once and underline the verb twice.

STEP 4 Write your name on the front of the printout, and turn it in to your instructor.

Words That Describe

Profile in Success

Hospital Nurse: Healing the Communication Gap

Christi Mansfield · *Baltimore, Maryland* · *Johns Hopkins Bayview Hospital*

Christi Mansfield confronts crises every day in her job as a nurse at Johns Hopkins Bayview Hospital in Baltimore, Maryland. Christi works in the high-risk labor and delivery room, where many of the patients are drug users or teens who have never visited a doctor.

Johns Hopkins is a teaching hospital. Some of the residents and medical students are still learning how to be sensitive to patients. Sometimes these students will unintentionally leave patients confused or upset, and Christi will need to calmly explain terms like *forceps* and *epidural* to scared teenagers in labor.

"I know if I wasn't there to help many of these moms, they'd be scared to death," says Christi, who is a single mother.

Now 29, Christi originally joined the army, hoping for medical training. All those slots were full, so she trained as a journalist. While stationed in Japan, she decided she wanted a medical career and left the army to attend Montgomery College in Tacoma Park, Maryland. There she served as vice president of the nurses' club and graduated with a 3.5 GPA.

"When it got tough, I got more determined," Christi recalls of her three years at Montgomery College. That's something she also keeps in mind for her future goal—a master's degree in women's health.

Think About It . . . Staying Cool Under Pressure

Christi Mansfield works in a stressful environment where emotions run high and there are frequent crises.

- *What factors contribute to the stressful atmosphere in which Christi works?*

- *How might such an atmosphere affect the communication between medical staff and patients?*

- *What communication skills are needed in a hospital environment?*

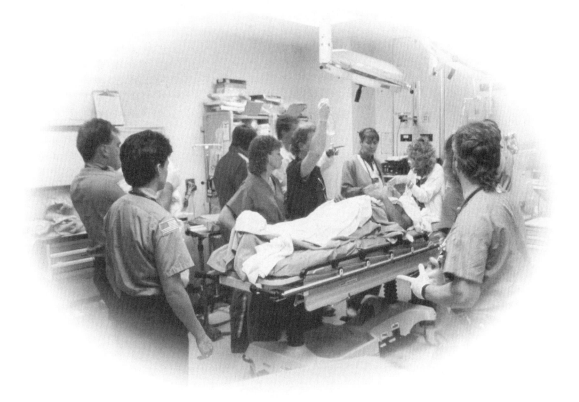

Career Connections

HEALTH CAREERS

Learn more about the work of practical nurses, registered nurses, surgical technicians, and others in the health field by connecting to the following sites at *The English Workshop* Website. Go to *englishworkshop.glencoe.com.* Click first on Unit 4 and then on Career Connections.

- American Association of Colleges of Nursing
- National League for Nursing
- NursingNet
- Advanced Medical Assistant of America
- National Organization for Associate Degree Nursing

See page 339, **Link & Learn: Using Adjectives and Adverbs in Health,** for an additional online career activity.

Adjectives

CHAPTER 10 PREVIEW

In this chapter you will learn to construct comparisons using the three forms, or degrees, of adjectives—positive, comparative, and superlative—and to avoid or solve common problems with adjectives. You will continue to assess your comprehension in the Programmed Reinforcement sections and in the Practices. Finally, you will learn to track news about the weather by going online.

OBJECTIVES

After completing this chapter, you will be able to

- Form the positive, comparative, and superlative degrees of adjectives.
- Use absolute adjectives in a comparison.
- Avoid double comparatives and superlatives.
- Recognize predicate adjectives.
- Use demonstrative pronouns as adjectives.
- Distinguish between confusing pairs such as *less/fewer* and *later/latter*.
- Construct a comparison within a group.
- Recognize when to capitalize proper adjectives.
- Determine whether or not to hyphenate compound adjectives.
- Solve problems involving misplaced modifiers.
- Determine how and when to use the definite and indefinite articles.

Study Plan for Chapter 10

The Study Plan for Chapter 10 offers a set of strategies that will help you learn and review the chapter material.

1. **Er and Est**: Use the *er* form of adjectives when comparing two things and the *est* form when comparing three or more things. Notice that *er* is two letters and *est* is three.

2. **Adjective Practice**: Cover the columns for the comparative and superlative forms of adjectives in the lists throughout the chapter. Read aloud the positive form of an adjective, and then say aloud the comparative and superlative forms.

3. **Absolute Adjectives**: When is an adjective absolute? Ask yourself, *Can something be more _____?* Fill in the blank with an adjective. If you answer *No*, the word is probably an absolute adjective—it expresses the quality to the highest degree. Try *dead, right,* and *complex.*

4. **Fewer/Less**: Is it *fewer* students or *less* students? Use *fewer* when you can count something, such as students. Use *less* when you have a quantity, such as a gob of mashed potatoes on your plate.

SECTION A
Forms of Adjectives

After reviewing how and when adjectives are used in general, you will examine how they are used in positive or negative comparisons. You will study the rules that apply to regular and irregular adjectives, and discover why some adjectives should never be involved in comparisons.

10.1 Adjective Review

An **adjective** is a word that describes or limits a noun or pronoun.

DESCRIPTIVE ADJECTIVES	LIMITING ADJECTIVES
a *boring* lecture	*one* check
clean laundry	*three* machines
helpful advice	*several* errors
incredible experience	*many* employees
lucky you	*much* excitement

Each of the adjectives above *modifies* the noun or pronoun that follows it. The adjectives modify or change the meaning of the nouns by offering descriptive or limiting information. Adjectives give life and color to language. The ability to use them skillfully is essential to effective writers.

Salespeople use adjectives in describing their products. A salesperson might tell a customer about the *new, improved* model that is *safe, nonpolluting, durable,* nearly *maintenance-free,* and clearly *superior* to its competing products while remaining quite *inexpensive.* Managers use adjectives when writing letters of recommendation. Was the employee *dependable, industrious, personable, articulate,* or *intelligent?* Or was the person *irresponsible, lazy, dull, inarticulate,* or *stupid?*

People who write advertising copy are often noted for their extravagant use of adjectives: The advertisement that proclaims a movie *Stunning! Remarkable! Extraordinary!* is one example. Here are two classified advertisements from the newspaper. Which position sounds more appealing? Which advertisement will draw the larger response? Why?

---

6 — CLASSIFIED / TUESDAY, NOVEMBER 12, 20--

NURSE – LPN/RN
F/T, for substance abuse center. Experience necessary. Excellent benefits. Fax resume to Director of Operations: 812-555-1234.

> **NURSE:**
> **CHEMICAL DEPENDENCY**
> An accredited intensive outpatient substance abuse treatment center offers challenging flex schedule for experienced detoxification program nurse. Candidate must be compassionate, competent, detail-oriented, and capable of working independently. Responsibilities include nursing assignments, patient and family counseling, and 24/7 on-call availability. If you are seeking employment in a dynamic, rapidly expanding organization, fax your resume to: Director of Operations, 812-555-6789.

The writer of the second advertisement has sought a positive reaction from the reader through a forceful use of adjectives.

10.2 Positive, Comparative, and Superlative Adjectives

There are three **forms,** or **degrees,** of the adjective: the simple or positive, the comparative, and the superlative.

Positive

The **positive** form describes a single item or a single group of items.

smart assistants   *fast* cars   *long* meeting

Comparative and Superlative

The other two forms of the adjective describe an item or group of items and allow you to compare one item with others. The **comparative** form of an adjective is used when you are comparing two things. To form the comparative of most simple adjectives, add *er.*

Sports cars are *faster* than stock cars.
We had a *longer* meeting this week than last week.

Grammar Tip

Grammar Tip

The **superlative** form of an adjective is used when you are comparing *three or more* things. To form the superlative of most simple adjectives, add *est*.

This is the *fastest* sports car in the world.
This is the *longest* meeting I've ever attended.

A long adjective such as *comfortable* would be too difficult to pronounce if *er* or *est* were added. Instead, form the comparative by placing *more* in front:

more comfortable   *more* difficult   *more* grateful   *more* durable

To form the superlative of long adjectives, you say:

most comfortable   *most* difficult   *most* grateful   *most* durable

Negative Comparisons

To indicate that one thing does not have as much of a particular quality as another, form the comparative by using *less* and the superlative by using *least*.

COMPARATIVE	SUPERLATIVE
1. This problem is *less difficult* than the previous one.	**1.** This is the *least difficult* of all the problems on the page.
2. She is *less athletic* than Alyce.	**2.** Dorothy is the *least athletic* of the three.

10.3 Rules for Forming the Comparative and Superlative

The general rules for when to add *er* or *est* and when to put *more* or *most* before an adjective are explained below.

Rule 1: One-Syllable Adjectives

If the positive form of the adjective is one syllable, add *er* or *est*.

short	shorter	shortest
long	longer	longest
sad	sadder	saddest

Rule 2: Adjectives That End in *y*

If the positive form is one or two syllables and ends in *y*, change the *y* to *i* and add *er* or *est*.

dry	drier	driest
lazy	lazier	laziest
lovely	lovelier	loveliest

Rule 3: Multisyllabic Adjectives

For other adjectives of two or more syllables, add *more* or *most*.

helpful	more helpful	most helpful
attractive	more attractive	most attractive
intelligent	more intelligent	most intelligent

Rule 4: Irregular Adjectives

A few adjectives are irregular and form their comparatives and superlatives in a different way. You are already familiar with most of them.

bad	worse	worst
good	better	best
little	less, lesser, littler	least, littlest
many, much	more	most
late	later	latest
late	latter	last
far	farther	farthest
far	further	furthest

10.4 Absolute Adjectives

The simple form of some adjectives, called **absolute adjectives,** expresses the adjective's quality to the highest degree. Therefore, these adjectives should not be used in comparisons. For example, because *unique* means *one of a kind,* nothing can be *more unique* or *most unique.*

Here is a list of some of these absolute adjectives.

alone	final	perpendicular	supreme
complete	full	right	true
correct	horizontal	round	unanimous
dead	instantaneous	single	unique
empty	parallel	square	vertical
endless	perfect	straight	wrong

Grammar Tip

Comparing Absolute Adjectives

If you must compare absolute adjectives, use the word *nearly.*
Avoid: This line is straighter than that one.
Use: This line is more *nearly* straight than that one.

Comparing Absolutes

In casual conversation absolute adjectives are often used in the comparative form. You might say that "Truer words were never spoken" or note that something is "deader than a doornail." Even the Preamble to the Constitution begins, "We, the People of the United States, in Order to form a more perfect Union . . . ," Such phrases are technically illogical.

TIME-SAVER If you've struggled with a problem but haven't come up with a solution, distance yourself from it. Shift to other work, take a walk, or even sleep on it. Time-out can save you time.

10.5 Double Comparatives and Superlatives

When using the comparative and the superlative forms of adjectives, avoid the following constructions:

WRONG: I am *more happier* than Sakamoto about our new assignment.
WRONG: This is the *most best* job I've ever had.
WRONG: This is the *bestest* job I've ever had.

Each of these sentences is incorrect because each contains a double comparison. In the first sentence, *happier* is already in the comparative degree; *more happier* is redundant and grammatically wrong. *Best* is itself a superlative; you can't be better than best. Therefore, both *most best* and *bestest* are incorrect. These double superlatives should also be avoided.

RIGHT: ✔ I am *happier* than Sakamoto about our new assignment.
RIGHT: ✔ This is the *best* job I've ever had.

10.6 Adjectives After Linking Verbs

In Chapter 6 you read about linking verbs—verbs that express a state of being rather than an action. Linking verbs include all forms of the verb *to be* and verbs like *feel, seem,* and *appear* when they are used in such a manner that they could be replaced by the verb *is.* For example,

Our assignment *is* difficult.   Our assignment *looks* difficult.

Predicate Adjectives

Normally an adjective directly precedes the noun it modifies. In the sentence *We have a difficult assignment,* the adjective *difficult* precedes the noun *assignment. Difficult* is also an adjective in the above sentence examples, but it appears after the noun *assignment.* An adjective that follows a linking verb and modifies the subject of the sentence is called a **predicate adjective.** Therefore, in the sentences above, *difficult* is a predicate adjective.

1. This day is *long.*   1. This day seems *long.*
2. His argument is *logical.*   2. His argument appears *logical.*

Both *long* and *logical* are predicate adjectives; *long* modifies *day,* and *logical* modifies *argument.* Remember that an adjective is still an adjective even if it is separated from its subject by a linking verb. You'll discover the significance of this fact in the next chapter, which addresses how to determine whether a sentence calls for an adjective or an adverb.

Coverage Key

Section		Statement
10.1	➤ Adjective Review	➤ **S1, S2, S3, S4, S5**
10.2	➤ Positive, Comparative, and Superlative Adjectives	➤ **S6, S7, S8, S9, S10**
10.3	➤ Rules for Forming the Comparative and Superlative	➤ **S11, S12, S13**
10.4	➤ Absolute Adjectives	➤ **S14**
10.5	➤ Double Comparatives and Superlatives	➤ **S15**
10.6	➤ Adjectives After Linking Verbs	➤ **S16**

Instructions: Cover the answers in the **Answer** column; then write your answer to the first statement. Uncover the first printed answer and compare your answer to it. If you wrote a correct answer, continue the activity. If you made an error, use the **Coverage Key** to locate the chapter section you need to review. When you are confident that you understand the material, continue with the reinforcement activity.

ANSWER

STATEMENT

S1 An adjective is a word that describes a(n)_____ or a(n) _____.

A1 noun; pronoun

S2 Choose the correct answer: Adjectives as a rule make sentences more (a) colorful, (b) brief, (c) grammatical.

A2 a

S3 Underline three adjectives in this sentence: **A red tie and green socks clash with conservative clothing.**

A3 <u>red, green, conservative</u>

S4 Underline three adjectives in this sentence: **The nervous applicant gave incomplete answers to the opening questions.**

A4 <u>nervous, incomplete, opening</u>

S5 **Ida coughed loudly, then resumed speaking.** *Loudly* is not an adjective because the word it modifies (*coughed*) is not a(n) _____; it is a(n)_____.

A5 noun; verb

S6 Adjectives may be used to compare one item with others. When you compare two things, you use the _____ form.

A6 comparative

S7 The comparative form of an adjective generally adds the letters _____ to the simple form.

A7 *er*

S8 Underline the simple adjective with one line and the comparative adjective with two lines: **The modernized factory is busier than it has been in years.**

A8 <u>modernized</u>, <u>busier</u>

S9 The superlative form of the adjective generally ends with the letters

_____.

A9 *est*

S10 Underline the two adjectives in the superlative form: **Ben is the strongest and fastest worker on the warehouse crew.**

A10 <u>strongest</u>, <u>fastest</u>

S11 Some adjectives of more than one syllable would sound awkward with the addition of *er* for the comparative form or *est* for the superlative form. The word *beautiful* is compared by having the word _____ precede it in the comparative form and the word _____ in the superlative form.

A11 *more; most*

S12 Underline any comparative forms and any superlative forms: **The longest runway today is too short for the larger, more powerful jets planned for the future.**

A12 comparatives—<u>larger</u>, <u>more powerful</u>; superlative—<u>longest</u>

S13 Write the comparative and superlative of the following simple adjectives: **lovely:** _____, _____
sympathetic: _____, _____
bad: _____, _____

A13 **lovelier, loveliest; more sympathetic, most sympathetic; worse, worst**

S14 Some adjectives such as *unique* and *perfect* are known as *absolute adjectives* because they express a quality to the highest degree. This means that logically they (can, cannot) be compared. Because *unique* means "one and only," underline the incorrect word in this sentence: **This is the most unique plan.**

A14 cannot, <u>most</u>

S15 In using adjectives it is considered (correct, incorrect) to use double comparatives or superlatives. Underline the incorrect words in these sentences:
 a. **My food processor is more bigger than hers.**
 b. **This is the most prettiest arrangement of flowers I've ever seen.**

A15 incorrect, a. <u>more</u>, b. <u>most</u>

S16 Underline the adjectives in these two sentences:
 a. **That is an interesting question.**
 b. **That question is interesting.**
In the second example, *interesting* is still an adjective because it modifies the noun _____ even though it is separated from its noun by a(n) _____ verb.

A16 a. <u>interesting</u>, b. <u>interesting</u>, **question**, linking

Uses of Adjectives

Adjective problems most commonly occur when two similar words are confused. In this section you will learn how to distinguish those pairs of adjectives that cause the most confusion for writers.

10.7 Demonstrative Pronouns

The **demonstrative pronouns** *this, that, these,* and *those* often act as adjectives. The plural of *this* is *these.* The plural of *that* is *those.* Be sure the adjective corresponds in number to the noun it modifies.

Grammar Tip

Near or Far?

The demonstrative pronouns *this* and *these* are used to indicate something nearby. *That* and *those* are used to indicate something farther away.

SINGULAR	PLURAL
1. *This* summary is excellent.	**1.** *These* summaries are excellent.
2. *That* office is ten miles away.	**2.** *Those* offices are ten miles away.

Adjectives With Tricky Nouns

Be careful with words such as *kind, sort,* and *type,* nouns that may sound plural but are actually singular. Write *this kind* or *that kind,* not *these kind* or *those kind.* The correct plural forms would be *these kinds* and *those kinds.*

SINGULAR	PLURAL
1. I prefer *this kind* of show.	**1.** I prefer *these kinds* of shows.
2. I don't like *that kind* of music.	**2.** I don't like *those kinds* of music.

Nonstandard Expressions

Avoid nonstandard expressions such as *this here* or *that there.*

WRONG	RIGHT
1. *This here* book is interesting.	**1.** *This* book is interesting.
2. *That there* sculpture is beautiful.	**2.** *That* sculpture is beautiful.
3. *These here* textbooks are heavy.	**3.** *These* textbooks are heavy.
4. *Those there* boxes are light.	**4.** *Those* boxes are light.

The Pronoun Them. The word *them* is a pronoun, not an adjective. Never use *them* to modify a noun or another pronoun.

These packages are mine. (Not: *Them* packages are mine.)
That kind is no good. (Not: *Them* kind is no good.)
Those kinds are no good. (Not: *Them* kinds are no good.)

Grammar Tip

Store Signs

Have you seen a sign in the supermarket marked "Ten items or less"? It should read "Ten items or fewer" or "Ten or fewer items."

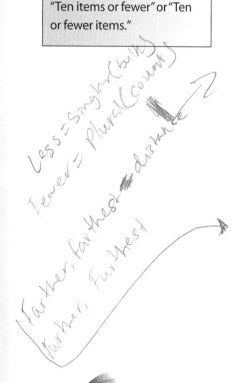

(handwritten notes in margin: Less = singular (bulk) / Fewer = Plural (count) / farther, farthest = distance / further, Furthest)

10.8 *Less/Fewer*

Most supermarkets have at least one checkout lane marked "Ten items or less." This widely used sign is grammatically incorrect. *Less* should be used to refer to abstract nouns and to items measured in bulk. *Fewer* should be used to refer to items that can be counted separately.

ABSTRACT NOUNS OR THOSE MEASURED IN BULK	NOUNS THAT CAN BE COUNTED SEPARATELY
1. This assignment took *less* time than I had anticipated.	**1.** I spent *fewer* hours on this project than I had expected.
2. We are using *less* electricity than last year.	**2.** We used far *fewer* kilowatts this month than last.

10.9 *Farther/Farthest* vs. *Further/Furthest*

Far and its related forms can be used as both adjectives and adverbs. The words *farther* and *farthest* should be used in reference to an actual physical distance. Use *further* and *furthest* in all other situations.

> Salt Lake City is *farther* west than Denver.
> You will travel *farther* on less gas when you drive our new minivan.
> Our offices are in the building *farthest* from the main entrance.

> This chapter requires *further* study.
> The defendant's story could not have been *further* from the truth.
> That was the *furthest* thing from my mind.

Grammar Tip

First/Last

If you are referring to more than two items, use *first* or *last* rather than *former* or *latter*. When using the word *first* or the word *last* to modify a number, always place it directly before the number: The *last* six people were refused admission.

10.10 *Later/Latter*

Later, the comparative form of *late*, refers to time. *Latter* means the second of two; it is usually used as the opposite of *former*, the first of two.

> I will be there *later* this evening.
> I'll schedule another appointment at some *later* date.
> Stern and Hines were both successful—the *former* through luck, the *latter* through hard work.
> Given the choice of two appointments, I'll take the *latter*.

Later can be used as both an adjective and an adverb. Since the decision about whether to use *later* or *latter* does not depend on what part of speech *later* is, both uses have been included here for ease of study.

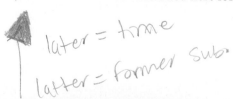

(handwritten notes: later = time / latter = former sub.)

Coverage Key

Section		Statement
10.7	➤ Demonstrative Pronouns	➤ **S17, S18, S19, S20, S21**
10.8	➤ Less/Fewer	➤ **S22, S23**
10.9	➤ Farther/Farthest vs. Further/Furthest	➤ **S24, S25, S26**
10.10	➤ Later/Latter	➤ **S27, S28, S29, S30, S31**

Instructions: Cover the answers in the **Answer** column; then write your answer to the first statement. Uncover the first printed answer and compare your answer to it. If you wrote a correct answer, continue the activity. If you made an error, use the **Coverage Key** to locate the chapter section you need to review. When you are confident that you understand the material, continue with the reinforcement activity.

ANSWER

STATEMENT

S17 The word *kind* or *type,* when preceded by *this* or *that,* is correct. When you use the plural *kinds* or *types,* you must change *this* to _____ and *that* to _____.

A17 *these, those*

S18 Underline the incorrect adjective in this sentence: **I like these kind of scissors.** The correct adjective is _____.

A18 these, this

S19 Underline the incorrect adjective in this sentence: **We no longer stock those type of cartridges.** The correct adjective is _____ _____.

A19 those, that

S20 This sentence contains a flagrant error in which a pronoun is used instead of an adjective. Underline the improper word: **Them cartridges are no longer in stock.** The proper word is _____ _____.

A20 Them, These or Those

S21 Rewrite this sentence correctly: **Them kind is obsolete.**

A21 That kind is obsolete. (or This kind is obsolete.)

S22 *Less* and *fewer* are adjectives that are sometimes confused. We say *less money* but *fewer checks.* We use *less* when items (are, are not) counted separately; we use *fewer* when items (are, are not) counted separately.

A22 are not, are

S23 Which is the correct sentence?
   a. **Fewer technicians are available now than before.**
   b. **Less nurses are unemployed today.**

A23 a.

S24 *Farther* and *further* are sometimes confused. The word that refers to an actual physical distance is _____.

A24 *farther*

S25 Underline the correct answer: **On the seventh hole Portia hit her drive the (farthest, furthest).**

A25 farthest

S26 Underline the correct answer:
I will tolerate no (farther, further) delays.

A26 further

S27 *Later* and *latter* are sometimes confused. The word that refers to time is _____. The word that refers to position is _____.

A27 *later, latter*

S28 Underline the correct answer:
I will see you (later, latter).

A28 later

S29 *Latter* means the second of two as opposed to _____, which means the first of two. Underline the correct answer: **The former answer is wrong; the (later, latter) is correct.**

A29 *former,* latter

S30 Underline the misplaced adjective: **The three last days have been very demanding.** Rewrite the sentence correctly._____

A30 last: The last three days have been very demanding.

S31 Underline the misplaced adjective: **The six first people who call the contest line will win concert tickets.** Rewrite the sentence correctly.

A31 first: The first six people who call the contest line will win concert tickets.

SECTION C
Comparisons in Groups, Compound Adjectives Misplaced Modifiers, and Articles

In this section you will build on your knowledge of adjectives by discovering how they are applied to comparisons within groups. After studying the guidelines for capitalizing proper adjectives and hyphenating compound adjectives, you will look at problems with modifiers and articles.

10.11 Group Identification

Review the following incorrect sentence:

WRONG: Isaiah is smarter than any person in his class.

What is wrong with this sentence? Isaiah is in his class, and he cannot be smarter than himself. Therefore, you must exclude Isaiah from the group by using *other* or *else*, or by using the superlative form.

RIGHT: ✔ Isaiah is smarter than any *other* person in his class.
RIGHT: ✔ I am smarter than anyone *else* in my class.
RIGHT: ✔ I am the *smartest* person in my class.

Here is another example:

WRONG: Milwaukee is larger than any city in Wisconsin.
RIGHT: ✔ Milwaukee is larger than any *other* city in Wisconsin.
RIGHT: ✔ Milwaukee is the *largest* city in Wisconsin.

Thus, the advertisement for a U.S. sporting goods manufacturer that says "We make more tennis balls than any company in America" is grammatically incorrect. It should state, "We make more tennis balls than any other company in America."

10.12 Capitalization of Proper Adjectives

Proper adjectives are adjectives derived from proper nouns—the names of specific people, places, or things.

Rule 1: Derived Proper Nouns—Connections Intact

Capitalize proper adjectives just as you capitalize the proper nouns from which they come.

American technology	Keynesian economics
Asiatic culture	Machiavellian principles
French dressing	Victorian architecture

Rule 2: Derived Proper Nouns—Connections Lost

Do not capitalize adjectives that are no longer associated with the original proper nouns.

china closet	morocco binding
diesel engine	oriental rug
french fries	pasteurized milk
jersey wool	venetian blinds

Whenever you are in doubt about whether an adjective should be capitalized, consult a current print or online dictionary.

10.13 Compound Adjectives

The word *compound* means the uniting of two or more elements. You have already studied compound nouns, compound predicates and compound sentences. Now you will examine the **compound adjective.**

Like compound nouns, compound adjectives are made up of two or more words that function as a unit. Sometimes, like compound nouns, they are written as one word:

commonsense	handpicked
easygoing	handwritten
halfhearted	homemade
timesaving	

Sometimes, like other compound nouns, they are hyphenated:

clear-cut	tax-exempt
first-rate	time-consuming
half-baked	time-tested
high-ranking	

A good current dictionary will list these and other such compound adjectives to help you determine which are which. However, not all compound adjectives will be listed in your dictionary.

For example, would you write *up to date* or *up-to-date?* Would you use *above average* or *above-average?* The correct answer depends on where these words appear in the sentence.

Style Tip

Name Games

Don't capitalize a proper adjective that is no longer exclusively associated with the person or country from which it originally derived its name.

Punctuation Tip

When to Hyphenate Compound Adjectives

In most cases:

Compound-Adjective Noun

vs.

Noun Compound Adjective

Hyphenating General Compound Adjectives

Compound adjectives are generally hyphenated when they come immediately *before* the noun they describe; they are normally *not* hyphenated when they come *after* the noun. Look at these examples:

<u>HYPHENATED</u>

1. Please provide us with *up-to-date* enrollment figures.
2. Juan received *above-average* grades in all of his courses.
3. Ms. Renko's *off-the-record* remarks were very interesting.

<u>NOT HYPHENATED</u>

1. Please provide us with enrollment figures that are *up to date.*
2. Juan's grades in all of his courses were *above average.*
3. Ms. Renko's most interesting remarks were *off the record.*

A number of common compound adjectives do not require hyphens when they appear before a noun. You will find a sample list of these adjectives under Rule 4 on the next page. In most cases, however, use hyphens in compound adjectives that appear *before* a noun.

For compound adjectives that appear *after* a noun, the general rule is to not use a hyphen. But there are exceptions, depending on how the sentence is phrased. Most exceptions to the general rules are beyond the scope of this discussion; they are fully explained in comprehensive style manuals such as *The Gregg Reference Manual.* Follow the general rules listed below about using or not using hyphens with compound adjectives.

The Health Industry Boom

Of the 30 occupations predicted to grow the fastest, 12 are in health services. People are living longer, and Baby Boomers are now contributing to the booming population of senior citizens.

Rule 1: Units of Measure

Compound adjectives are often formed by joining a numeral with words of measure such as *inch, foot, mile, pound, month,* and *quart.* The basic rule on hyphenating or not hyphenating compound adjectives still pertains:

an eight-foot ceiling	a ceiling eight feet high
a five-mile walk	a walk of five miles
a four-year period	a period of four years
a 30-year mortgage	a mortgage of 30 years

number f (-) word

In the hyphenated adjectives preceding the noun, the unit of measure is always singular: a three-liter jar, *not* a three-liters jar.

Rule 2: Compound Adjectives That Are *Always* Hyphenated

A few compound adjectives are always hyphenated regardless of their position in a sentence.

- *Right-handed and left-handed:*

Mr. Golen is *right-handed.*
Propane tank valves are fitted with *left-handed* threads.

double-spaced
single-spaced

LOOKING AHEAD

Proper Nouns

In Chapter 20 you will learn more about how to capitalize proper nouns.

• Compound adjectives formed with *self:*

Mikel is a *self-made* man.
This truth is *self-evident.*

• Numerical adjectives from *twenty-one* through *ninety-nine:*

The Todds celebrated their *twenty-fifth* anniversary last week.
This flight was their one hundred and *twenty-ninth.*

Rule 3: Hyphenated Compound Adjectives in a Series

In a series of compound adjectives, be sure to retain the hyphen even though all of the adjectives are not fully expressed.

The biology class included *two-, three-,* and *four-hour* laboratories.
One-, three-, and *six-acre* parcels of land were available.

Rule 4: Compound Adjectives That Are *Not* Hyphenated

Some common compound adjectives are not hyphenated before a noun. For example,

charge account customer	money market funds	real estate agent
high school graduation	post office box	social security tax
income tax return	public relations gimmick	

Punctuation Tip

Dictionary Use

If you are unsure whether a hyphen is required, consult a print or online dictionary.

Rule 5: *Well-* vs. *Well*

Although *well* is technically an adverb in most situations, compounds such as *well-known, well-handled,* and *well-read* are considered adjectives. They follow the basic rule on hyphenating or not hyphenating adjectives.

Our *well-known* label is easily recognized.
Our label is *well known.*

Rule 6: Adverbs Ending in *ly*

Do not extend the principle of hyphenating compound adjectives to other types of compound modifiers. When a compound modifier contains an adverb ending in *ly,* it should *not* be hyphenated in any position.

A *frequently misspelled* word is **maintenance.**
The word **maintenance** is *frequently misspelled.*

10.14 Misplaced Modifiers

As you saw in Chapter 9, a participial phrase may be used to modify a noun. If it is not used properly, however, a dangling participle may result.

WRONG: *Serving lunch,* a customer's foot tripped the waitress.
RIGHT: ✔ *Serving lunch,* the waitress tripped over a customer's foot.

Similarly, an adjective phrase may be used to modify a noun. For example, in the sentence *The desk with the steel legs is sturdy,* the adjective phrase *with the steel legs* describes the noun *desk.*

You should always place an adjective phrase as close as possible to the word it modifies. Failure to do so can result in strange sentences like these:

WRONG: They delivered the piano to the woman *with mahogany legs.*
RIGHT: ✔ They delivered the piano *with mahogany legs* to the woman.

WRONG: We have a new razor for men *with special vibrating blades.*
RIGHT: ✔ We have a new razor *with special vibrating blades* for men.
BETTER: ✔ We have a new men's razor *with special vibrating blades.*

Sentence Revision

Although the problem of a misplaced adjective phrase can often be corrected simply by shifting the phrase closer to the noun it modifies, you may have to revise the sentence.

WRONG: With his arms full of packages, Joe's ankle was sprained when he tripped over a step because he was unable to see.
RIGHT: ✔ Unable to see with his arms full of packages, Joe tripped over a step and sprained his ankle.

10.15 Articles

In grammar, the three adjectives *a, an,* and *the* have a special name—**articles.** The word *the* is called a **definite article.** The words *a* and *an* are called **indefinite articles.**

Definite and Indefinite Articles

When you say *The book is on the desk,* you are pointing out a particular book on a particular desk. When you say *A book is on the desk,* you are not referring to any specific book; you are simply indicating that some type of book is on the desk.

You should never have any trouble using the definite article. Which indefinite article to use is all determined by ease of pronunciation.

Use *a* before all *consonant sounds,* including sounded *h,* long *u,* and *o* with the sound of *w* (as in *one*).

a day	a hotel	a unit	a one-day event
a week	a house	a university	a once-in-a-lifetime opportunity

Use *an* before silent *h* and all *vowel sounds* except long *u.*

an apple	an honor	an ulcer
an event	an hour	an understanding
an incident	an heir	an ulterior motive
an orange		

The *sound* determines whether to use *a* or *an,* not the spelling. Do not assume that all words beginning with a vowel require *an.* Words beginning with a consonant that are pronounced with a vowel sound require *an,* not *a.*

a euphemism	an M.B.A. degree
(long *u,* or *yoo*)	(the *M* is pronounced *em*)
a European vacation	an FDA ruling
(long *u*)	(the *F* is pronounced *eff*)
a ewe	an R-rated movie
(long *u*)	(the *R* is pronounced *are*)
a unicycle	an X-ray
(long *u*)	(the *X* is pronounced *ex*)

Article Repetition

Occasionally, you will need to determine whether to repeat the article in a series of things. For example,

The red and (the) white sweat suits are on sale.

Should you repeat *the?* Your choice depends on what you mean. If each sweat suit is part white and part red, then omit the second *the: The red and white sweat suits are on sale.* For the sake of clarity, you might use hyphens to clarify your meaning: *The red-and-white sweat suits are on sale.*

However, if there are two types of sweat suits—one all white and the other all red—add the second *the: The red and the white sweat suits are on sale*

The president and *the* chairperson arrived. (Two people arrived.)
The president and chairperson arrived. (One person holding both positions arrived.)
The steel and *the* plastic storage boxes are in place. (Some boxes are steel; some are plastic.)
The steel-and-plastic storage boxes are in place. (Storage boxes of part steel and part plastic are in place.)

Coverage Key

Section		Statement
10.1	➤ Adjective Review	➤ **S49**
10.2	➤ Positive, Comparative, and Superlative Adjectives	➤ **S49**
10.11	➤ Group Identification	➤ **S32**
10.12	➤ Capitalization of Proper Adjectives	➤ **S33, S34, S35**
10.13	➤ Compound Adjectives	➤ **S36, S37, S38, S39, S40, S41, S42**
10.14	➤ Misplaced Modifiers	➤ **S43, S44**
10.15	➤ Articles	➤ **S45, S46, S47, S48**

Instructions: Cover the answers in the **Answer** column; then write your answer to the first statement. Uncover the first printed answer and compare your answer to it. If you wrote a correct answer, continue the activity. If you made an error, use the **Coverage Key** to locate the chapter section you need to review. When you are confident that you understand the material, continue with the reinforcement activity.

ANSWER	STATEMENT
	S32 In the sentence **He is more personable than any executive I have met,** what word has been incorrectly omitted before the word **executive?** Answer: _____
A32 other	**S33** Proper adjectives are derived from proper names. When they are associated with the original proper name, they are (capitalized, not capitalized).
A33 capitalized	**S34** Correct the capitalization of proper adjectives in this sentence: **The american soccer team wore Jersey wool sweaters.**
A34 American, jersey	**S35** Do the same with this sentence: **The victorian age was marked by ornateness like Oriental designs tooled on Moroccan leather.**
A35 Victorian, oriental, moroccan	**S36** A compound adjective like *well made* or *high level* is usually hyphenated when it comes (before, after) the noun modified.
A36 before	**S37** Underline the compound adjective in this sentence: **Your account is up to date.** It (is, is not) hyphenated because it comes (before, after) the noun.
A37 <u>up to date,</u> is not, after	**S38** Underline the compound adjective in this sentence: **She has an up-to-date showroom.** It is hyphenated because it comes _____ the noun.
A38 <u>up-to-date,</u> before	

S39 A numerical compound adjective from *twenty-first* to *ninety-ninth* is (always, sometimes, never) hyphenated when spelled out. Choose the correct answer: **This anniversary is the (thirty third, thirty-third).**

A39 always, **thirty-third**

S40 Compound adjectives involving the word *self*—for example, *self-evident*—(are, are not) hyphenated.

A40 are

S41 Here are compound adjectives combining a numeral with words such as *inch, mile,* or *foot.* Insert hyphens where necessary: **eight inch ruler, three mile run, box of four pounds, four pound box.**

A41 **eight-inch ruler, three-mile run, four-pound box**

S42 In a series of compound adjectives preceding a noun, hyphens should be retained even though all the adjectives are not completely expressed. Indicate where hyphens should be placed in the following sentence: **In her certification program Cyrene had two, three, and four hour classes.**

A42 two-, three-, and four-hour classes

S43 A group of words describing a noun is called an adjective phrase. Such a phrase should be placed next to the noun it describes. Underline the group of words that is misplaced: **The filing cabinet belongs to the purchasing department with the scratched top.** Underline with 2 lines the word this phrase should follow.

A43 <u>with the scratched top</u> should follow <u>cabinet</u>

S44 Do the same in this sentence: **I gave the report to the assistant with the corrections.**

A44 <u>with the corrections</u> should follow <u>report</u>

S45 The article *an* rather than *a* is used in **an antique** because *antique* begins with a(n) _____ sound.

A45 vowel

S46 You should write **an understatement** because the *u* has a(n) _____ sound. You write **a union** because here the *u* has a(n) _____ sound.

A46 vowel, long u

S47 Insert *a* or *an:* _____ **unique problem;** _____ **usual offer;** _____ **unusual offer;** _____ **error;** _____ **honest mistake**

A47 **a unique; a usual; an unusual; an error; an honest**

S48 The article *the* repeated in the sentence **The secretary and the treasurer spoke** means that (one, two) people are involved. How many people are involved in this sentence? **The secretary and treasurer spoke.** _____

A48 two, one

S49 To review, an adjective modifies a(n) _____. It may be compared by changing the simple form to the _____ form when comparing two; to the _____ form when comparing more than _____.

A49 noun or pronoun, comparative; superlative, two

CHAPTER 10 SUMMARY

In this chapter you learned that adjectives are words that describe or limit (modify) a noun or pronoun. You studied the three degrees of adjectives, how to form them, and how to use them correctly. You also learned how to use absolute adjectives, predicate adjectives, and proper adjectives. You now know when to use hyphens in compound adjectives, and how to use definite and indefinite articles correctly. You also discovered how to avoid common mistakes when using demonstrative pronouns and how to choose correctly from confusing pairs of words such as *less/fewer* and *farther/further*.

Getting Connected

TRACKING NEWS ABOUT THE WEATHER ONLINE

GOAL: Perhaps you've heard that severe thunderstorms and winds are affecting a large area of the Midwest or another region of the country where you're planning to travel or where many of your friends and relatives live. What can you do to learn more about the situation? You could watch television and wait for a weather update. You could also visit the Website of a national weather-reporting service or national news organization to find current details about the weather conditions that concern you.

In this activity you'll learn how to read weather Websites that are frequently updated. You'll go online to a weather-related Website, read a news article about the weather, and use the article to demonstrate your understanding of adjectives.

STEP 1 Go to *englishworkshop.glencoe.com*, the address for *The English Workshop* Website, and click on Unit 4. Next click on Getting Connected, and then click on Chapter 10. At the Chapter 10 Getting Connected option, you'll see a list of Websites that provide information about the weather. Select a weather link and click on it.

STEP 2 Look over the page that appears on the Website you've selected. At a weather-reporting site such as *weather.com,* you'll probably see a headline and a summary of a major weather-related news story. It's likely you'll also see headlines for other stories about the weather. At a news-reporting site such as *cnn.com,* the weather is only part of the content offered. If you decide to work with a news-reporting Website, you'll need to look for a menu of the different sections and click on the one related to weather.

STEP 3 At the site you've chosen, select a weather-related news story that interests you, and follow the links to locate the full story. Read over the full news story about the weather. As you read, note the type of adjectives used in the story, paying special attention to comparisons, capitalized proper adjectives, and compound adjectives.

STEP 4 Make a printout of the story you've selected.

STEP 5 Working from the printout, read the weather news story again and locate *at least seven* of the types of adjectives or specific adjectives listed below. Highlight or circle each type of adjective you find, and label each accordingly (for example, *post adj* for a positive adjective, *comp adj* for a comparative adjective, and *super adj* for superlative). You don't need to label the specific adjectives (e.g., *farther, less*). To check your answers and reinforce your understanding, draw an arrow from the adjective to the word in the sentence it modifies.

> **a.** positive (or simple) form of an adjective
> **b.** comparative form of an adjective
> **c.** superlative form of an adjective
> **d.** absolute adjective
> **e.** demonstrative adjective
> **f.** proper adjective
> **g.** hyphenated compound adjective
> **h.** *farther/further*
> **i.** *less/ fewer*
> **j.** *later/latter*
> **k.** *first/last*
> **l.** adjective after a linking verb

STEP 6 For each adjective you locate, indicate in the margin whether the adjective is descriptive or limiting. Use *D* for each descriptive adjective and *L* for each limiting one.

STEP 7 Write your name at the top of your printout from the Website, and turn it in to your instructor.

 Tip Are you interested in finding out about the weather in your area? Scan the Website you visited to see if that option is available. Look for a place to enter the name of your city or your ZIP Code, or search for a drop-down menu of cities and countries.

PRACTICE 1

Adjectives

Instructions: Underline with one line the adjectives in each of the following sentences. Then underline with two lines the word each adjective modifies.

EXAMPLE: **He missed the last bus.**

1. Althea marked the papers with a red pen.

2. He prepared a light supper.

3. The colored lights were dimmed.

4. Where is my wool hat?

5. This is a first-class operation.

6. Our latest records show a deficit.

7. We sent an order for surgical supplies.

8. Liam slowly walked to his first class.

9. Your application is incomplete.

10. Here is our new catalog.

11. Send me your final approval.

12. It was a very efficient system.

13. Forgive my late report.

14. The table has a smooth finish.

15. Luigi and Adela went horseback riding.

16. It's a very smooth-riding car.

17. This is an easy problem.

18. This problem is easy.

19. I am hungry.

20. Mr. McPhee looks puzzled.

Name _____

Class _____ Date _____

PRACTICE 2

Adjectives

Instructions: In the blank provided, write the proper form of the adjective in parentheses.

EXAMPLE: **Of the two employees, Gina is (conscientious).**   EX. **more conscientious**

1. Though our Raleigh plant is large, the Durham plant is (large).   1. ~~more~~ larger

2. Although Mr. Pulaski and Ms. Jones are intelligent, Mr. Roberto is the (wise).   2. most wises

3. The left sleeve is (long) than the right.   3. longer

4. Reza believes New York City is the (exciting) of the two cities.   4. more exciti

5. Reza believes New York City is the (exciting) city in the world.   5. most exitin

6. She is the (lazy) person in the whole office.   6. laziest

7. Which of this pair has the (bright) colors?   7. brighter

8. Of all our forty-three offices, the (new) is in Los Angeles.   8. most newes

9. Test this one, then that one, and choose the (good).   9. better

10. Which of the designs is the (pretty)?   10. prettiest

11. Which of these two posts is (vertical)? more   11. verticaler

12. Of all these boxes, which one is (square)?   12. square

13. Which city has a (dry) climate, Phoenix or Dallas?   13. drier

14. I don't think anyone is (dedicated) than she is.   14. most

15. She is the (dedicated) nurse on the floor.   15. most

16. She is certainly (dedicated) than Ralph.   16. more

17. Ours is the (dedicated) nursing staff you will find.   17. most

18. You will not find a (dedicated) staff than ours.   18. more

19. Peter is the (irresponsible) person I've ever met.   19. most

20. I know of no one (irresponsible) than he.   20. more

PRACTICE 3

Part A: *This, That, These, Those*

Instructions: In the blank provided, write the proper adjective.

EXAMPLE: **Mr. Battista always wears (this, these) style of trousers.**   EX. ____this____

1. Do you like (that, those) kind of music?   1. _____

2. (This, Those) forms of investment are government insured.   2. _____

3. (That, Those) make of car sells very well.   3. _____

4. Would you call (this, these) models the best for our purposes?   4. _____

5. (That, Those) kind of investment can be very risky.   5. _____

6. (This, These) type of fabric is very durable.   6. _____

7. (This, These) shoes are too casual for business attire.   7. _____

8. Where do you buy (this, these) type of shoes?   8. _____

9. I don't associate with (that, those) kind of people.   9. _____

10. I don't associate with (that, those) people.   10. _____

Part B: *Less* and *Fewer*

Instructions: In the blank provided, write the correct word.

EXAMPLE: **I have (less, fewer) energy than I used to have.**   EX. ____less____

1. They delivered (less, fewer) wood than we had ordered.   1. _____

2. They delivered (less, fewer) cords of wood than we had ordered.   2. _____

3. This laptop computer weighs (less, fewer) than five pounds.   3. _____

4. (Less, Fewer) than ten people applied for the position.   4. _____

5. We can do the same amount of work with (less, fewer) assistants.   5. _____

6. Their firm has sent (less, fewer) orders than anticipated.   6. _____

7. There is (less, fewer) unemployment than anticipated.   7. _____

8. There were (less, fewer) than ten applicants for the job.   8. _____

9. This air conditioner uses (less, fewer) electricity than any other model.   9. _____

10. This air conditioner uses (less, fewer) kilowatts of electricity than other models.   10. _____

Name _____

Class _____ Date _____

PRACTICE 4

Farther/Further and *Later/Latter*

Instructions: In the blank provided, fill in the proper word.

EXAMPLE: I'd like to make an appointment for (later, latter) this afternoon.   EX. ____later____

1. Enjoy yourself. It's (later, latter) than you think.   1. _____

2. Our hotel suite is (farther, further) from the elevator than yours is.   2. _____

3. Lee sat in the chair (farthest, furthest) from the interviewer.   3. _____

4. The former speaker introduced the guest; the (later, latter) spoke at length.   4. _____

5. The two senators spoke. The former said, "I will discuss this issue with you again (later, latter) this evening."   5. _____

6. We must complete this project without (farther, further) delay.   6. _____

7. The car is in the (farthest, furthest) parking lot.   7. _____

8. The (later, latter) we meet tonight, the less time we will have.   8. _____

9. The (later, latter) part of the address contained some important points.   9. _____

10. With (farther, further) analysis we are certain to find the solution.   10. _____

11. Professor Crowell always urged his students to push their thinking (farther, further).   11. _____

12. I will go to the (farthest, furthest) place in the world for you.   12. _____

13. (Further, Farther) than that, I cannot continue compromising with you.   13. _____

14. The (later, latter) portion of the report recommended specific changes.   14. _____

15. Resigning is the (farthest, furthest) thing from my mind.   15. _____

16. Margery prefers the earlier episodes of *Seinfeld* to the (later, latter).   16. _____

17. There is no time for (farther, further) discussion.   17. _____

18. Plant the flowers no (later, latter) than May.   18. _____

19. We'll have (farther, further) details on this topic (later, latter) in tonight's broadcast.   19. _____

20. We'll explore this topic (farther, further) at a (later, latter) point in the semester.   20. _____

PRACTICE 5

Capitalization and Hyphenation

Instructions: In the blank provided, fill in the proper word.

EXAMPLE: A (**first-rate**, first rate) mechanic is difficult to find.
EX. ____**first-rate**____

1. The (Victorian, victorian) age began in the 1830s.
1. _____

2. A (Persian, persian) rug may be very valuable.
2. _____

3. Many significant writing tasks for (entry-level, entry level) workers are collaborative.
3. _____

4. Bernard was a (well-intentioned, well intentioned) nurse who made mistakes.
4. _____

5. The fact that Twyla cannot perform the work is (self-evident, self evident).
5. _____

6. The owners put up a (last-ditch, last ditch) effort to avoid bankruptcy.
6. ___last-ditch___

7. The latest branch opening was our (twenty-first, twenty first).
7. _____

8. In this office we need workers who are (well-disciplined, well disciplined).
8. _____

9. She wore a (hand-knitted, hand knitted) sweater made from real (Jersey, jersey) wool.
9. _____

10. Do you know when the (Alaskan, alaskan) pipeline was completed?
10. _____

11. We do not accept (third-party, third party) checks.
11. _____

12. The (Japanese, japanese) imports have captured a large share of the automobile market.
12. _____

13. Listen to WIMP for (up to the minute, up-to-the-minute) news.
13. _____

14. The housing development contained both (three and four bedroom, three- and four-bedroom) homes.
14. _____

15. Leon's prophecy of failure was largely (self fulfilling, self-fulfilling).
15. _____

16. This is our (forty second, forty-second) year in business.
16. _____

17. The (Native American, native american) artisans created (well-made, well made) tools.
17. _____

18. The United States has a large number of (first- and second-generation, first and second generation) immigrants fluent in both their native tongues and English.
18. _____

19. I admire Alfredo's (never say die, never-say-die) attitude.
19. _____

20. She has the (selfsame, self-same) attitude toward achieving success as he does.
20. _____

Name _____

Class _____ Date _____

PRACTICE 6

Part A: Indefinite Articles

Instructions: In the blanks provided, write the correct article, either *a* or *an*.

EXAMPLE: __A__ man wearing __an__ unusual jacket left __a__ package.

1. ___A___ humorist is ___a___ human being with ___an___ peculiar sense of humor.

2. ___An___ understanding of all operations in our plant is ___a___ necessity for ___a___ supervisor.

3. ___An___ hour before dawn is ___an___ inhuman hour for ___a___ human being to be awakened.

4. ___A___ union leader should be ___an___ honest person, for to lead ___a___ union is ___an___ undertaking of great responsibility.

5. After ___an___ one-hour wait I had ___an___ X-ray taken at ___a___ hospital that accepts payment from ___an___ HMO plan.

Part B: Indefinite Articles

Instructions: In some of the following sentences, the article has been incorrectly repeated or left out. Make any necessary corrections. Write *C* in front of any sentence that is correct.

EXAMPLE: _C_ Tyrone has both a new and a used garden tractor for sale.

___C___ 1. Mildred wore a blue and a gold sweater to the game.

___C___ 2. The secretary and the vice president met at noon.

___C___ 3. Carlos was elected to be both the vice president and the secretary.

___C___ 4. The car has a blue and a white finish.

_____ 5. We have in stock two models, a chromium and an aluminum one.

_____ 6. Mildred was undecided whether to wear a blue or a gold sweater to the game.

_____ 7. Tractorama has both a new and a used garden tractors for sale.

___C___ 8. An old and a dirty pair of trousers hung on the wall of the mud room.

___C___ 9. The chromium and the aluminum models are both out of stock.

_____ 10. We have an opening for an RN or an LPN.

PRACTICE 7

Adjectives

Instructions: The letter below contains many errors. Cross out each error and make the necessary change in the space above it. Underline any changes you make.

Video Mart
4347 Sixth Ave.
Portland, ME 04102

June 26, 20--

Ms. Arnez
198 Falmouth St.
Portland, ME 04102

Dear Ms. Arnez:

This letter is to confirm the details of our recentest phone conversation and our desire to obtain your services as a marketing consultant.

As I told you, Video Mart's metropolitan area sale on video cassettes and DVDs has proved to be our bestest ever. The sale is excitinger and spectacularer than any sale in our history.

During the two first weeks we sold no less than 6,000 cassettes and DVDs in each of our local two stores. In fact, the South Street store has sold the greatest number of cassettes even though the store is furthest from the heart of town. This is a extremely unusual situation, most unique in the history of them two stores.

While we couldn't be more happy with the success of the South Street store, we are puzzled about the relative drop in sales experienced by our central store, which annually receives our first, second, or third place award in the eastern region for most sales. Because you are a well known and highly-respected marketing analyst, we are seeking your expert advice.

Name _____

Class _____ Date _____

We would like you to visit our Sixth Avenue store on Monday. You can't miss it, walking down Sixth Avenue toward Elm. Ms. Johnson, our store manager, and her assistant, Mr. Kahn, know you are coming. The first will provide you with any information you require regarding the operation of the store.

Please determine the reasons why this store has least sales than the South Street store. Also, please give us a honest opinion of Ms. Johnson's effectiveness as manager.

It is our intention to expand our stores and increase our market share farther by offering for rent or sale TVs, VCRs, DVD players, camcorders—all the most finest state of the art video equipment. Since we want to use the Sixth Avenue store as the central store for this new-product line, we need to know why the Sixth Avenue store's sales are down.

With your assistance we hope the central store will regain its status as the top store in the area and one of the more better Video Mart outlets in the East.

Sincerely,

Claude Jago, General Manager

PRACTICE 8

Composition: Using Adjectives

A. Writing Want Ads

The beginning of this chapter presented a pair of classified advertisements for a position in the medical field. As you saw, the more appealing position was described in detail using effective adjectives.

Write a classified advertisement similar to the more appealing one. First, choose a job with which you are familiar. You could choose your present job, a previous one, or one that you would like to have. In your ad be sure to use effective adjectives to attract qualified people to apply for the position.

_____

_____

_____

_____

_____

_____

_____

_____

_____

_____

_____

_____

_____

_____

_____

_____

PRACTICE 9

Composition: Using Adjectives

B. Writing "Position Wanted" Ads

Sometimes people place their own ads in the classified section of the newspaper under the general heading "Positions Wanted." For example:

---

2 — CLASSIFIED / Friday, April 2, 20-- / DAILY NEWSPAPER

POSITIONS WANTED

**ADMINISTRATIVE ASSISTANT/
SECRETARY**

Diplomatic, energetic individual with college education, ten-years' administrative assistant experience, and good computer and telephone skills desires challenging position as administrative assistant to over-burdened theatrical executive. Excellent references. Call (973) 555-2468.

Write your own ad for the "Positions Wanted" section. What kind of position are you seeking? What are your qualifications and attributes? Write a forceful ad using effective adjectives to make the reader want to contact you.

_____

_____

_____

_____

_____

_____

Adverbs

CHAPTER 11 PREVIEW

In this chapter you will study how adverbs modify verbs, adjectives, and other adverbs. You will learn how to convert adjectives into adverbs, examine strategies for solving common adverb problems, and pick up tips about hyphenation. As you work with this chapter, you will assess your knowledge in the Programmed Reinforcement sections and the Practices. Finally, while learning about online movie reviews, you will reinforce your understanding of adverbs.

OBJECTIVES

After completing this chapter, you will be able to

- Form adverbs from adjectives.
- Determine whether to use an adjective or an adverb after a verb.
- Solve problems involving confusing pairs of adjectives and adverbs.
- Form the comparative and superlative degrees of adverbs.
- Avoid double negatives.
- Determine where to place the word *only* in a sentence for absolute clarity.
- Determine when to hyphenate compound modifiers with adverbs.
- Avoid using unnecessary adverbs.
- Avoid confusing compound expressions with similar adverbs.

Study Plan for Chapter 11

Study Plan

The Study Plan for Chapter 11 offers a set of strategies that will help you learn and review the chapter material.

❶ **Adverb Questions**: Adverbs answer *how, when, where,* or *to what degree.* Use these questions to help you identify the adverbs. For example, *Mr. Forte spoke softly.* Ask yourself, *How* did Mr. Forte speak? The answer is *softly,* the adverb in the sentence.

❷ **Verbs—Adverbs or Adjectives?** Use adverbs to modify action verbs. Adjectives will follow linking verbs as predicate adjectives (think of these as "verb adjectives.")

❸ **Confusing Pairs**: Make a set of flash cards for *bad/badly, good/well, most/almost, real/really,* and *sure/surely.* Write one word on one side of each card; on the reverse side, identify the word as either an adverb or an adjective and write a sentence example.

❹ **No-No Negatives**: Proofread for no-no, or double, negatives by underlining each negative in a sentence. Count to ensure that you do not accidentally have two negatives that cancel out each other.

SECTION A
Adverbs and Adjectives

In this section you will make a transition from adjectives to adverbs. Now that you have a full sense of how adjectives function, you will examine the rules for converting them into adverbs.

11.1 Adverb Review

Adverbs are more versatile modifiers than are adjectives. Not only do adverbs modify verbs, they also modify adjectives and other adverbs.

> The production team worked **swiftly.** (The adverb **swiftly** modifies the verb *worked.*)
>
> Broadway is an **exceptionally** wide street. (The adverb **exceptionally** modifies the adjective *wide.*)
>
> The accountant spoke **too** rapidly. (The adverb ***too*** modifies the adverb rapidly.)

Adverb Questions

An **adverb** is a word that modifies a verb, an adjective, or another adverb by indicating *how, when, where,* or t*o what degree* (*how much, how often, how large, how small, how long,* and so on).

> The book was **carefully** edited. *How* was it edited? **Carefully.**
>
> The order was shipped **promptly.** *When* was it shipped? **Promptly.**
>
> The officials came **here.** *Where* did they come? **Here.**
>
> They were **very** pleased. *How much* were they pleased? **Very.**
>
> They are **seldom** satisfied. *How often* are they satisfied? **Seldom.**

11.2 Rules for Forming Adverbs

Many adverbs are formed from another part of speech—usually from an adjective. The following rules can help you form adverbs correctly.

Rule 1: Most Adjectives

In general, adverbs are formed merely by adding *ly* to the adjective.

ADJECTIVE	ADVERB	ADJECTIVE	ADVERB
slow	slowly	familiar	familiarly
efficient	efficiently	sole	solely

Job Talk

Electronic Cadaver

An *electronic cadaver* is a hi-tech substitute for the real thing. As a computer program, it offers a clean, humane way to dissect a virtual (or computer-simulated) body.

In spelling, remember that in most cases the *ly* adverb ending is simply attached to the existing word. Adjectives that end with *e* or *al* fall into the same category—just attach the *ly*.

separate + ly = separately   accidental + ly = accidentally
scarce + ly = scarcely   cordial + ly = cordially
authoritative + ly = authoritatively   official + ly = officially

Rule 2: Adjectives Ending in *y*

When the adjective ends in *y*, form the adverb by changing the *y* to *i* and adding *ly*.

ADJECTIVE	ADVERB	ADJECTIVE	ADVERB
busy	busily	satisfactory	satisfactorily
happy	happily	temporary	temporarily

Rule 3: Adjectives Ending in *able* or *ible*

When the adjective ends in *able* or *ible*, form the adverb by dropping the final *e* and adding *y*.

ADJECTIVE	ADVERB	ADJECTIVE	ADVERB
noticeable	noticeably	forcible	forcibly
considerable	considerably	horrible	horribly

Rule 4: Adjectives That Change Spelling

Some adjectives change spelling when they are formed into adverbs.

ADJECTIVE	ADVERB	ADJECTIVE	ADVERB
due	duly	whole	wholly
true	truly		

Adverbs That Do Not End in *ly*

There are also many adverbs that do not end in *ly* and are not formed from adjectives. Here is a partial list:

again	here	now	since	too
almost	how	often	so	very
far	much	quite	soon	well
fast	near	rather	then	when
hard	never	seldom	there	where

Coverage Key

Section		Statement
11.1	➤ Adverb Review	➤ S1, S2, S3, S4, S5
11.2	➤ Rules for Forming Adverbs	➤ S6, S7, S8, S9, S10, S11, S12 S13, S14

Instructions: Cover the answers in the **Answer** column; then write your answer to the first statement. Uncover the first printed answer and compare your answer to it. If you wrote a correct answer, continue the activity. If you made an error, use the **Coverage Key** to locate the chapter section you need to review. When you are confident that you understand the material, continue with the reinforcement activity.

ANSWER

A1 verbs, adjectives, adverbs

A2 **reacted**, verb

A3 **careless**, adjective

A4 **carelessly**, adverb

A5 e.

A6 *ly*

A7 adverb, adjective

A8 minutly, purposly; minutely, purposely

STATEMENT

S1 Adjectives modify (describe) nouns; adverbs modify _____, _____, or _____.

S2 **The patient reacted slowly.** The adverb **slowly** modifies the word _____, which is a(n) _____.

S3 **That was a very careless mistake.** The adverb **very** modifies the word _____, which is a(n) _____.

S4 **He filed the documents quite carelessly. Quite** is an adverb that modifies the word _____, which is a(n) _____.

S5 An adverb usually answers which of the following? (a) how, (b) when, (c) where, (d) to what degree, (e) all of the above.

S6 Most adverbs are formed by adding _____ to adjectives.

S7 **Eagerly** is a(n) _____ derived from the _____ **eager.**

S8 Underline the two misspelled adverbs: **separately, accidentally, minutly, purposly.** Write them correctly: _____ and _____.

S9 When an adjective ends in *y*, to form the adverb you change the *y* to _____ and add _____ as in *busy-busily, happy-happily.*

A9 *i, ly*

S10 Change the following adjectives into adverbs: **easy, lazy, satisfactory.**_____

_____

_____.

A10 easily, lazily, satisfactorily

S11 To form the adverb from an adjective ending in *able* or *ible*, as in *noticeable*, drop the _____ and add

_____.

A11 *e, y*

S12 Change the following adjectives into adverbs: **forcible, peaceable, changeable.** _____

_____

_____.

A12 forcibly, peaceably, changeably

S13 Some adjectives become adverbs through other spelling changes. Write the adverbs for **due, true, whole.** _____

_____

_____.

A13 duly, truly, wholly

S14 Some familiar adverbs do not end in *ly.* Underline the adverbs in this list: **blue, lucky, never, quiet, quite, soon, very.**

A14 <u>never, quite, soon, very</u>

Writers often have to decide whether to use an adverb or an adjective. This section will demonstrate how to make that choice with confidence.

Grammar Tip

Adverbs With Action and Linking Verbs

Adverbs **add** details to action **verbs.**

Adjectives can be the final link in a chain:

> *Subject+Linking Verb+Adjective*

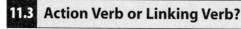

11.3   Action Verb or Linking Verb?

Determining whether to use an adverb or an adjective is simple: Use an adverb to modify an action verb. Use an adjective after a linking verb.

The fire burned fiercely.
Burned is an *action* verb; therefore, use the adverb *fiercely.*

The material was sent promptly.
Sent is an *action* verb; therefore, use the adverb *promptly.*

The manager shouted excitedly.
Shouted is an *action* verb; therefore, use the adverb *excitedly.*

Predicate Adjective or Adverb?

Complete this sentence: *The manager is (excited, excitedly).*

Did you have any trouble deciding to use *excited,* the adjective, instead of *excitedly,* the adverb? In the sentence above, *excited* is a predicate adjective. Remember, a predicate adjective follows a linking verb and modifies the subject of the sentence. The adjective *excited* follows the linking verb and describes the subject *manager.*

The same is true in this sentence: *The manager looks excited.* You know that *looks* in this sentence is a linking verb. Therefore, the adjective *excited* should be used because it follows the linking verb *looks* and describes the subject, *manager.*

Consider this sentence: *He looked (excited, excitedly) for the missing wallet.* Could *looked* be replaced by a form of the verb *to be,* such as *was?* No. Therefore, *looked* is an *action* verb and requires the adverb *excitedly: He looked excitedly for the missing wallet.*

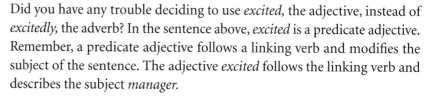

In Chapter 6, you learned that linking verbs can be replaced by a form of the verb to be.

Bad/Badly

Should you use *bad* or *badly* in the following sentence? *The situation looks (bad, badly).* The verb *looks,* as used here, is a linking verb; therefore, you use the adjective *bad: The situation looks bad.*

Here is a similar sentence: *The package of chicken smells (bad, badly).* In this sentence *smells* is a linking verb; therefore, you use the adjective *bad: The package of chicken smells bad.*

Good/Well

Now look at this sentence: *Dinner tasted (good, well). Good* is an adjective. *Well* is usually an adverb. Because *tasted* is a linking verb, you use the adjective *good: Dinner tasted good.* Note again that *tasted* could be replaced by the *to be* verb *was: Dinner was good.*

Look at the next sentence: *He performed (good, well).* The verb *performed* is an action verb; therefore, you use the adverb *well: He performed well.*

The only exception to this rule occurs when *well* is used as an adjective meaning *healthy.* In such a case, because *well* is an adjective, it can be used after a linking verb: *He is well (healthy). He feels well (healthy). He looks well (healthy).* But remember: *The bread smells good. He works well. She spoke good English. She spoke English well.*

11.4 Confusing Pairs

In addition to *good/well* and *bad/badly,* there are a few other pairs of words that are often misused. Usually a problem occurs because the adjective is used instead of the adverb.

Grammar Tip

Most/Almost

To decide whether to use *most* or *almost,* substitute the word *nearly.* If *nearly* fits, use *almost;* if it doesn't, use *most.*

1. **Most/Almost.** *Most* can be an adjective, a noun, or an adverb. As an adjective or a noun, it means *the majority.*

   Most students take a course in composition during their first semester.

   As an adverb, *most* means *to the greatest degree.*

   Mr. and Mrs. Colabella are two of our *most* loyal customers.

   In contrast, the word *almost* is an adverb meaning *nearly.*

   The tickets are *almost* sold out.

   Be careful not to use *most* when you mean *almost.*

   WRONG: Most all the apartments have been rented.
   RIGHT: ✔ Almost all the apartments have been rented.
   RIGHT: ✔ *Most* of the apartments have been rented.

Grammar Tip

Real/Very

To decide between *real* and *very,* replace them with *genuine* and *extremely.* If *genuine* fits, use *real.* If *extremely* fits, use *very.*

2. **Real/Really/Very.** *Real* is an adjective that means *genuine. Very* is an adverb that means *extremely.* When faced with a choice of *real* or *very,* substitute *genuine* or *extremely.* If *genuine* fits, *real* is correct. If *extremely* fits, *very* is correct.

   Which is correct in the sentence below?

   I am (*real, very*) pleased.

Since you would say I am *extremely* pleased (**not:** I am *genuine* pleased), use *very*: I am *very* pleased (**not:** I am *real* pleased).

RIGHT: ✔ It gives me real (*genuine*) pleasure to introduce the next speaker.

RIGHT: ✔ We are very (*extremely*) pleased with the outcome.

RIGHT: ✔ It was a real (*genuine*) diamond.

RIGHT: ✔ A diamond is very (*extremely*) hard.

Really, meaning truly or genuinely, is also an adverb. *Really* and *very* are often used interchangeably.

I am *very* (extremely) interested in this position.
I am *really* (truly) interested in this position.

If you know when to use *real* or *very*, you know when to use *real* or *really*.

3. **Sure/Surely.** *Sure* is an adjective meaning *confident* or *certain*. *Surely* is an adverb meaning *certainly* or *undoubtedly*.

Michael is quite *sure* of himself.   He *surely* did an outstanding job.
Raise your hand if you're *sure*.   *Surely*, I'd be glad to help.

Don't use *sure* as an adverb; use *surely* or *very*.

WRONG: I was *sure glad* I had brought my umbrella.
RIGHT: ✔ I was *surely glad* I had brought my umbrella.
RIGHT: ✔ I was *very glad* I had brought my umbrella.

Coverage Key

Section		Statement
11.3	➤ Action Verb or Linking Verb?	➤ S15, S16, S17, S18, S19, S20, S21
11.4	➤ Confusing Pairs	➤ S22, S23, S24, S25, S26, S27, S28

Instructions: Cover the answers in the **Answer** column; then write your answer to the first statement. Uncover the first printed answer and compare your answer to it. If you wrote a correct answer, continue the activity. If you made an error, use the **Coverage Key** to locate the chapter section you need to review. When you are confident that you understand the material, continue with the reinforcement activity.

ANSWER

STATEMENT

S15 In deciding whether to use an adjective or an adverb after a verb, you should remember that an adverb modifies a(n) _____ verb while an adjective comes after a(n) _____ verb.

A15 action, linking

S16 A linking verb shows a state of being, not an action. It may be replaced by the verb _____.

A16 *is* (or *to be*)

S17 She writes (**good, well**). You use the adverb _____ because **writes** is a(n) (action, linking) verb.

A17 **well,** action

S18 After the argument, they both felt (**bad, badly**). You use the adjective _____ because **felt** is a(n) (action, linking) verb.

A18 **bad,** linking

S19 This machine is slow. You use the _____ slow because **is** is a(n) _____ verb. **This machine runs slowly.** You use the _____ slowly because **runs** is a(n) _____ verb.

A19 adjective, linking, adverb, action

S20 Choose the correct form:
  a. **The flowers smell (sweet, sweetly).**
  b. **The coffee tastes (bitter, bitterly).**
  c. **She feels (healthy, healthily).**

A20 a. **sweet,** b. **bitter,** c. **healthy**

S21 *Well* is usually an adverb, as in **He plays well.** In **He feels well,** the word **well** is a(n) _____ meaning _____.

A21 adjective, healthy

S22 (**Almost, Most**) everyone was present. The correct word is _____, meaning *nearly.*

A22 **Almost**

S23 Which is correct?

    a. (**Almost, Most**) **all the order was returned.**

    b. (**Almost, Most**) **of the order was returned.**

A23 a. **Almost,** b. **Most**

S24 *Real* and *very* are sometimes confused. _____ is an adjective meaning *genuine;* _____ is an adverb meaning *extremely.*

A24 *Real, very*

S25 **I am (real, very) happy to receive this award.** The correct word, _____, is an _____ modifying **happy,** which is a(n) _____.

A25 **very,** adverb, adjective

S26 *Really* is an _____ meaning *truly* or *genuinely.* **We are (real, really) sorry we are unable to help.** The correct word, _____, is an _____ modifying **sorry,** which is a(n) _____.

A26 adverb, **really,** adverb, adjective

S27 *Sure* means *certain; surely* means *certainly.* **I am (sure, surely) glad that prices have leveled off.** The correct word, _____, is an _____ that modifies **glad,** which is an _____.

A27 **surely,** adverb, adjective

S28 Which is correct?

    a. (**Sure, Surely**) **I'll lend you the money.**

    b. **I'll be (sure, surely) to lend you the money.**

A28 a. **Surely,** b. **sure**

So far you have learned how to form adverbs and how to determine whether a sentence calls for an adjective or an adverb. Now you will discover how to use adverbs correctly in various situations.

11.5 Comparison of Adverbs

Adverbs may be compared, just like adjectives. One- or two-syllable words add *er* or *est:*

soon	sooner	soonest
early	earlier	earliest

Except:

often	more often	most often

Adverbs that are long usually are formed by using *more* and *most:*

carefully	more carefully	most carefully
sincerely	more sincerely	most sincerely

Comparative and Superlative Adverbs

As with adjectives, you can form the comparative and superlative forms of adverbs by using *less* and *least:*

often	less often	least often
efficiently	less efficiently	least efficiently

Remember to use the comparative form when comparing two; use the superlative when comparing three or more.

I arrived *earlier* than he did.
Of all the team members, I arrived *earliest.*

Any of Them: Consider the next sentence. *I arrived earlier than any of them.* Why is the comparative used when *them* indicates that there are at least two others? *Earlier* is used because it compares the speaker with *any of them.* As you know from Chapter 5, *any* is singular—it means *any one.*

A few adverbs are compared irregularly. Some of these words appeared in the last chapter under the list of irregular adjectives. Such words are used both as adjectives and as adverbs.

Positive	Comparative	Superlative
far	farther	farthest
far	further	furthest
badly	worse	worst
well	better	best
little	less	least
much	more	most

Adverbs Without Comparative or Superlative Degrees

Like absolute adjectives, some adverbs cannot be compared. The following adverbs do not have a comparative or superlative degree.

back	never	so	very
before	no	then	whenever
by	not	there	yes
ever	now	thus	
here	past	too	

As with adjectives, be careful to avoid double comparatives and double superlatives when comparing adverbs.

Wrong: We can fill your order *more sooner* than they can.
Right: ✔ We can fill your order *sooner* than they can.

Wrong: We can fill your order the *most soonest* of all your suppliers.
Right: ✔ We can fill your order the *soonest* of all your suppliers.

Another double construction that is grammatically incorrect is the **double negative.** Here is a common example:

Wrong: They *don't* know *nothing.*

This sentence contains two negative words, *don't* and *nothing.* Each of these negatives cancels the other. Eliminating or replacing either of the negative words in the sentence above results in a correct sentence.

RIGHT:	✔ They know *nothing*.
RIGHT:	✔ They *don't* know *anything*.

WRONG:	It *wasn't nothing*.
RIGHT:	✔ It *was nothing*.
RIGHT:	✔ It *wasn't anything*.

Other Negatives

Some words that do not look like negatives really are—words such as *scarcely, hardly, never, neither,* and *but.* These words are negative in themselves. Never add the word *not* to them.

Say: We can *scarcely* see you in this fog. (Not: We *can't scarcely* see you in this fog.)

Say: We could *hardly* have decided otherwise. (Not: We *couldn't hardly* have decided otherwise.)

Say: It could *never* happen here. (Not: It *couldn't never* happen here.)

Say: It was *neither* of them. (Not: It *wasn't neither* of them.)

Say: I understand all *but* one of them. (Not: I *don't* understand all *but* one of them.)

Double Negatives as Deliberate Positives

It is possible to use two negatives deliberately to express a positive thought:

Alan is *not unaware* of the consequences of his decision.

This statement means that Alan is aware of the consequences of his decision. Another example is:

It was *not nothing*.

This statement really means that it was something. As the two sentences illustrate, a writer can choose to use a double negative to create a particular effect. *It was not nothing* is more forceful than *It was something*. Usually, however, a writer uses a negative just to express a negative thought. In such a situation, one negative is enough.

11.8 Placement of *Only*

The word *only* can be used as both an adjective and an adverb. Its position in a sentence can dramatically change the meaning of the sentence.

The four sentences on the next page show how you can completely change the meaning by merely moving the word *only.*

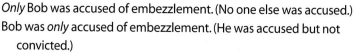

Only Bob was accused of embezzlement. (No one else was accused.)

Bob was *only* accused of embezzlement. (He was accused but not convicted.)

Bob was accused of *only* embezzlement. (Embezzlement is not a serious offense.)

Bob was accused of embezzlement *only*. (He was not accused of anything else.)

Health & IT Progress

Information technology, or IT, is critical to the healthcare industry. Hand-held computers now record vital patient data, which is then sent directly to a main database—minimizing errors, saving paper, and perhaps saving lives.

To help ensure that the meaning of your sentence is absolutely clear, always place the word *only* as close as possible to the word it modifies.

WRONG: I *only* paid $8.50.
RIGHT: ✔ I paid *only* $8.50.

WRONG: I *only* filed my application a day late.
RIGHT: ✔ I filed my application *only* a day late.

11.9   Compound Modifiers With Adverbs

In Chapter 10 you learned that compound adjectives are generally hyphenated when they come immediately before the noun they describe; they usually are not hyphenated when they come after the noun.

Compound Adverbs With *ly* Form

When a compound modifier contains an adverb in the *ly* form, it does not need to be hyphenated in any position because the position of the *ly* adverb already tells you that the adverb is modifying the next word.

A *privately* owned corporation is exempt from certain regulations.
Corporations that are *privately* owned are exempt from certain regulations.

The *overly* eager trainee upset the tray.
The trainee, who was *overly* eager, upset the tray.

Other Compound Adverbs

For purposes of clarity, however, compound modifiers with adverbs lacking *ly* are governed by the same rule as compound adjectives.

The *fast*-talking salesperson pressured him into buying the more expensive model.
The medicine provides *long*-lasting relief.
This medicine provides relief that is *long* lasting.

11.10 Unnecessary Adverbs

Sometimes the adverbial meaning of *how*, *when*, *where*, or *how much* is expressed in other words in the sentence. In that case, do not use an adverb unnecessarily. In the following sentences, each word in parentheses is redundant and therefore unnecessary.

> Recopy this page (over).
> I will repeat the question (again).
> Freyda has returned (back) from Europe.
> They must cooperate (together) in order to succeed.
> Erase this (out).
> We must seek (out) a solution.
> I will follow (after) you in my car.

11.11 Compound Words Confused With Adverbs

Some compound expressions, usually those beginning with *all*, resemble adverbs. People sometimes confuse these expressions with the adverbs themselves. If you examine these expressions, however, you will see that the meanings are quite different. Make sure you distinguish between these compound expressions and the adverbs they resemble.

- **all together** (meaning *many combined*)
  altogether (meaning *completely*)
  The applications are *all together* on the table in the conference room.
  I'm not *altogether* certain that I know what you mean.

- **all ways** (meaning *every manner*)
  always (meaning *forever*)
  He tried *all ways* possible to make the patient comfortable.
  He *always* tried to make every patient he treated as comfortable as
     possible.

- **all ready** (meaning *completely prepared*)
  already (meaning *previously*)
  The copies of the report were *all ready* for her signature.
  She has *already* signed the copies of the report.

- **some time** (meaning *a period of time*)
  sometime (meaning at some *unspecified time*)
  It took me *some time* to prepare the documents for her signature.
  The documents will be ready for her signature *sometime* tomorrow.

Coverage Key

Section		Statement
11.5	➤ Comparison of Adverbs	➤ **S29**
11.6	➤ Irregular Adverbs	➤ **S29, S30**
11.7	➤ Double Negatives	➤ **S31, S32, S33, S34**
11.8	➤ Placement of *Only*	➤ **S35**
11.9	➤ Compound Modifiers With Adverbs	➤ **S36, S37**
11.10	➤ Unnecessary Adverbs	➤ **S38, S39**
11.11	➤ Compound Words Confused With Adverbs	➤ **S40, S41, S42, S43, S44, S45, S46, S47**

Instructions: Cover the answers in the **Answer** column; then write your answer to the first statement. Uncover the first printed answer and compare your answer to it. If you wrote a correct answer, continue the activity. If you made an error, use the **Coverage Key** to locate the chapter section you need to review. When you are confident that you understand the material, continue with the reinforcement activity.

ANSWER

STATEMENT

S29 Write the comparative and superlative degrees for these adverbs:
soon _____
quietly _____
well _____

A29 sooner, soonest; more quietly, most quietly; better, best

S30 Write the correct form: **This copier performs the** (superlative of **badly**) **of all three.** _____.

A30 worst

S31 Underline the two negative words in this sentence: **She didn't fill out none of the forms correctly.** This sentence illustrates the error called the _____.

A31 didn't, none; double negative

S32 Rewrite this double-negative sentence correctly: **The salesperson wasn't able to see none of the buyers.**
_____.

A32 The salesperson wasn't able (or was unable) to see any of the buyers. Or, The salesperson was able to see none of the buyers.

S33 **We aren't never going to go.** The double negative in this sentence can be corrected by changing the word _____ to _____, or the contraction _____ to _____.

A33 never to ever or aren't to are

S34 A writer may use two negatives to convey a positive thought or express a particular effect. Rewrite the next sentence using a deliberate double negative. **We are moved by the tragic circumstances that led to the crime.**

_____

_____

_____

A34 We are not unmoved by the tragic circumstances that led to the crime.

S35 Which word does *only* refer to in the following sentences?
a. Only Luis worked on Saturday._____.
b. Luis only worked on Saturday. _____.
c. Luis worked only on Saturday. _____.

A35 a. Luis, b. worked, c. Saturday

S36 When a compound modifier contains an adverb in the *ly* form, the modifier is (a) always, (b) sometimes, (c) never hyphenated. Compound modifiers with adverbs lacking *ly* are usually hyphenated when they come (before, after) the word they modify.

A36 c, before

S37 Which of the following compound modifiers should be hyphenated?
a. She was very well prepared for the interview.
b. A truly inspired speech highlighted the conference.
c. I need a fast acting medication for my headache.

A37 c. fast-acting

S38 Unnecessary adverbs should be eliminated. Underline the words that should be omitted:
a. He returned the bills back to me.
b. Please repeat the instructions again.
c. Recopy the page over.
d. Erase this mistake out.

A38 a. back   b. again
      c. over   d. out

S39 Underline the words that should be omitted:
a. Please empty out your locker before the end of the day.
b. We entered into the conference room for the meeting.
c. I reread the chapter over to be sure I understood it.
d. The nations cooperated together to resolve the shortage of water.

A39 a. out   b. into
      c. over   d. together

S40 *Altogether* and *all together* are sometimes confused. _____ means *many combined*; _____ means *completely*.

A40 *All together, altogether*

S41 Which words are correct? **The members of the staff worked (altogether, all together) until they were (altogether, all together) satisfied.**

A41 **all together, altogether**

S42 *All ways* and *always* are sometimes confused. _____ means *at all times* or *forever*; _____ means *every possible means*.

A42 *always, all ways*

S43 Which choices are correct? **(All ways, Always) try to excel in (all ways, always).**

A43 **Always, all ways**

S44 *All ready* and *already* are sometimes confused. _____ means *by this time*; _____ means *prepared*.

A44 *Already, all ready*

S45 **The workers were (all ready, already) finished by noon, and they were (all ready, already) for lunch.**

A45 **already, all ready**

S46 *Some time* and *sometime* occasionally are confused. _____ means *a period of time*; _____ means *at some unspecified time*.

A46 *Some time, sometime*

S47 Which choices are correct? **Please set aside (some time, sometime) for a meeting (some time, sometime) tomorrow.**

A47 **some time, sometime**

CHAPTER 11 SUMMARY

In this chapter you learned how to form adverbs from adjectives. You also discovered how to distinguish between adverbs and adjectives, such as *bad/badly* and *good/well*, and between confusing pairs or threesomes, such as *most/almost*, *real/really/very*, and *sure/surely*. You learned how to form the comparative and superlative forms of adverbs, how to place adverbs correctly in a sentence, how to deal with double negatives, and how to use compound adverbs correctly in various situations.

Getting Connected

IDENTIFYING ADVERBS IN ONLINE MOVIE REVIEWS

GOAL: The Internet represents many things to many people. That's good news for movie lovers looking for information about celebrities, film history, Hollywood memorabilia, and the latest movie reviews. Even if you're not a big moviegoer, there may be a time when you'll need to turn to the resources of the Internet for information about a movie. Let's say, for example, that your boss is making plans to entertain a client who loves movies, and she or he asks you to locate and print a review of a movie that recently opened. You can do that by visiting an online movie review Website. Some movie review Websites are devoted exclusively to movie reviews; other sites offer reviews derived from local and national news organizations.

In this activity you'll use a movie review you discover at a Website to reinforce your understanding of adverbs.

STEP 1   Go to *englishworkshop.glencoe.com,* the address for *The English Workshop* Website, and click on Unit 4. Next click on Getting Connected, and then click on Chapter 11. At the Chapter 11 Getting Connected option, you'll see a list of Websites containing movie reviews.

STEP 2   Select one of the movie review Websites to visit, and click on that link. You may visit more than one Website during this activity.

STEP 3   Scan the home page of the Website you've selected. The information at different Websites will be presented differently, but you should be able to locate a list of movie reviews. If the list appears immediately, look for a link labeled "Current Reviews," "In Theaters," or "Archives" to help you locate the list of movie reviews. Once you've located a list, scroll down it and click on a movie review that interests you.

STEP 4   As you read the review, notice the use of adverbs to modify action verbs, adjectives, or other adverbs. Has the review writer used many adverbs? only a few? hardly any? What might be the reasons for the frequency or scarcity of adverbs? Do you notice any mistakes in the use of *real, really,* or *very?*

STEP 5   At this point, if the review you selected does not contain many adverbs, you should select another one with more adverbs.

STEP 6   Make a printout of the review you've selected.

STEP 7   Working from the printout, reread the review and locate *at least seven* of the items listed below. Highlight or circle each adverb type, and label it. For example, write *how much* for an adverb telling *how much,* *comp.* for an adverb used in a comparison, or *mod. adj.* for an adverb modifying an adjective. You don't need to label the specific adjectives. To check your answers and reinforce your understanding, draw an arrow from the adverb to the action verb, adjective, or other adverb in the sentence it modifies.

> **a.** adverb telling *how much* or *how often*
> **b.** adverb telling *when*
> **c.** adverb telling *where*
> **d.** adverb telling *to what degree*
> **e.** adverb used in a comparison
> **f.** adverb modifying an adjective
> **g.** adverb modifying another adverb
> **h.** absolute adverbs
> **i.** *bad/badly*
> **j.** *real/really/very*
> **k.** *most/almost*
> **l.** *sure/surely*
> **m.**adverb *only* correctly placed in a sentence
> **n.** redundant adverbs (e.g., *She repeated the question again.*)

STEP 8   If the movie review uses any adverbs incorrectly, highlight or circle them. In the margin or on the back of your printout, briefly explain what the error is and how it should be corrected.

STEP 9   Write your name at the top of your printout, and turn it in to your instructor.

PRACTICE 1

Adverbs: Part A

Instructions: Underline the adverb in each of the following sentences. Then, using two lines, underline the verb, adjective, or adverb it modifies.

EXAMPLE: Mr. Forte spoke softly.

1. We walked quietly to the hospital.
2. Quickly, he leaped into his car.
3. The matter is entirely finished.
4. We strongly urge you to accept this offer.
5. Proofread carefully all statistical entries.
6. They came home very late.
7. Your money will be cheerfully refunded.
8. Our new heart monitor is functioning perfectly.
9. She travels to Memphis on business often.
10. I feel rather tired.

PRACTICE 2

Adverbs: Part B

Instructions: Each of the following sentences contains at least two adverbs. Underline all the adverbs in each sentence. Then, draw an arrow from each adverb to the word it modifies.

EXAMPLE: Mr. Forte speaks softly and carries an extremely big stick.

1. Our services are often imitated, seldom duplicated.
2. I'm very glad this really boring movie is finally over.
3. We are extremely grateful to receive so generous a contribution.
4. The copier, which was just recently repaired, is broken again.
5. If I am not mistaken, it will take us nearly an hour to walk there.
6. This deal is almost too good to be true.
7. When will I see you again?
8. The visiting nurse came here much later than expected.
9. I never expected to see you again so soon.
10. How much farther is it?

PRACTICE 3

Adjectives and Adverbs

Instructions: In the blank next to each of the adjectives below, write the equivalent adverb.

EXAMPLE: careful __carefully__

1. real _____
2. sole _____
3. busy _____
4. primary _____
5. credible _____
6. extreme _____
7. whole _____
8. true _____
9. accidental _____
10. substantial _____

11. easy _____
12. extraordinary _____
13. principal _____
14. considerable _____
15. willful _____
16. crafty _____
17. noticeable _____
18. annual _____
19. bad _____
20. good _____

PRACTICE 4

Review: Action and Linking Verbs

Instructions: Underline the verb in each of the following sentences. Then, in the blank provided, write *A* if the verb is used as an action verb and *L* if it is used as a linking verb.

EXAMPLE: **This proposition <u>is</u> a once-in-a-lifetime opportunity.**   EX. __L__

1. Mr. Maki looks taller than his brother.   1. _____
2. He looked at me with real anger in his eyes.   2. _____
3. By this time tomorrow she will be green with envy.   3. _____
4. This bread smells very fresh.   4. _____
5. Smell the aroma of this freshly baked bread.   5. _____
6. She knows the case history of her patients.   6. _____
7. The two systems seem quite comparable.   7. _____
8. Mario lay down on his bed after dinner.   8. _____
9. The attorney rested her case.   9. _____
10. The attorney rested after the long trial.   10. _____

PRACTICE 5

Adverbs or Adjectives?

Instructions: For each sentence below, write the proper form of the word in parentheses in the blank provided.

EXAMPLE: **Mr. Schnell does everything very (slow).**   EX. ___*slowly*___

1. He was (careful) when he tasted the mixture.   1. _____

2. He tasted the mixture (careful).   2. _____

3. Return the merchandise as (quick) as possible.   3. _____

4. Felice is very (content).   4. _____

5. The situation seems (bad).   5. _____

6. I am (extreme) tired from my long journey.   6. _____

7. The plant grew more and more (quick).   7. _____

8. We are (certain) you will be comfortable.   8. _____

9. You are (certain) to be comfortable.   9. _____

10. You will (certain) be comfortable.   10. _____

11. We (certain) hope you are comfortable.   11. _____

12. We feel he has been (extraordinary) competent at his task.   12. _____

13. He has displayed (extraordinary) competence at his task.   13. _____

14. Our situation has grown (bad).   14. _____

15. We can accomplish our goals (easy).   15. _____

16. He behaved (indignant) when he was denied credit.   16. _____

17. Mr. Dumont became (angry) and threatened his employees (loud).   17. _____

18. Ordinarily, the bell tolls (soft), but today it sounds (loud).   18. _____

19. He became (indignant) because he was denied credit. 19. _____

20. He feels (indignant) because he was denied credit.   20. _____

Name _____

Class _____ Date _____

PRACTICE 6

Troublesome Adverb/Adjective Choices

Instructions: In the blank provided, write the appropriate word from the choice provided.

EXAMPLE: **The job was done quite (good, well).**   EX. _____**well**_____

1. You did the job very (good, well).   1. _____

2. You did a very (good, well) job.   2. _____

3. It gives us (real, really) satisfaction.   3. _____

4. (Sure, Surely) you will want to consult your attorney.   4. _____

5. We have (real, really) valid reasons for our position.   5. _____

6. We (sure, surely) hope you feel better soon.   6. _____

7. Though he was sick, he is now completely (good, well).   7. _____

8. (Most, Almost) of the time we work quite hard.   8. _____

9. Dana was (real, really) pleased to meet them.   9. _____

10. We are (sure, surely) grateful for your continued support.   10. _____

11. These are (most, almost) all the supplies that are left.   11. _____

12. Were the (real, really) situation known, there might be a scandal.   12. _____

13. The proposition sounds (good, well) to me.   13. _____

14. We feel confident you will do (good, well) in your new position.   14. _____

15. That is the only (sure, surely) way to deal with this problem.   15. _____

16. (Most, Almost) every department was finished with the inventory by noon.   16. _____

17. (Most, Almost) departments were finished with the inventory by noon.   17. _____

18. Are you (real, really) sure of your facts?   18. _____

19. She is (sure, surely) of her skills.   19. _____

20. (Most, Almost) anyone who dresses (well, good) can look (well, good).   20. _____

PRACTICE 7

Adverbs and Double Negatives

Instructions: Rewrite the following hastily written memo, correcting all double negative expressions and incorrect adverbs.

TO:	Joe
FROM:	Alison
DATE:	March 8, 20--
SUBJECT:	Update on Temple Laboratories

Jim Marshall hasn't scarcely visited us more than a few times (two or three at the mostest) in the past few months. I hope we haven't done nothing to offend him. After all, we haven't hardly started in our association with Temple Laboratories, and we certainly don't want to do nothing that would jeopardize our relationship.

Look into this situation more farther and report your findings to me.

PRACTICE 8

Only

Instructions: *Only* is correctly placed in one of the following sentences. Write *C* after this sentence. In each of the remaining sentences, *only* is improperly placed. Indicate the proper placement of the word.

EXAMPLE: **I only met her once.**   EX. _____

1. The director only read the first letter.   1. _____

2. Joel and Ang were allowed to leave; only Bill was forced to stay.   2. _____

3. Our computer consultants only answer software questions.   3. _____

4. Tomás only promotes the most aggressive employees.   4. _____

5. We're an insurance company that doesn't only insure good drivers.   5. _____

only — before noun
wo — or adverbs ending with ly

PRACTICE 9

Compound or Single-Word Modifiers

Instructions: In the blank provided, write the correct form of the word in parentheses.

EXAMPLE: **She proposed (much needed, much-needed) reforms.**   EX. __much-needed__

1. Lorraine is an (exceedingly capable, exceedingly-capable) nurse practitioner.   1._____

2. The three children were (well behaved, well-behaved).   2._____

3. He is (all together, altogether) biased in his views.   3._____

4. In (all ways, always) this edition seems superior.   4._____

5. Many students have (all ready, already) taken some college courses.   5._____

6. You may go when you are (all ready, already).   6._____

7. (All together, Altogether) I counted 33 people.   7._____

8. The new business failed (all together, altogether).   8._____

9. (Strategically located, Strategically-located) display cases should be placed in each store.   9._____

10. Display cases in each store should be (strategically located, strategically-located).   10._____

11. Jean is (all ways, always) a model employee.   11._____

12. Our country is facing (increasingly difficult, increasingly-difficult) problems.   12._____

13. This is the (best tasting, best-tasting) coffee I've ever had.   13._____

14. I will meet with you (some time, sometime) tomorrow afternoon.   14._____

15. I have (some time, sometime) free tomorrow afternoon.   15._____

16. No one disputes your (exceptionally high, exceptionally-high) standards.   16._____

17. The election campaign was (well designed, well-designed).   17._____

18. This decision will have (far-reaching, far reaching) consequences.   18._____

19. The consequences of this decision will be (far reaching, far-reaching).   19._____

20. I think the truck drivers are (all ready, already) to end their strike.   20._____

Name _____

Class _____ Date _____

PRACTICE 10

Adverbs

Instructions: The following letter contains many errors. Cross out each error and make the necessary change in the space above it.

MEDICO SUPPLIES, INC.
739 Puritan Way
Boston, MA 02189-3614

April 30, 20--

Mr. Henry Billings
498 Market Street
Allentown, PA 18103

Dear Henry:

I enjoyed seeing you at the Northeast Regional meeting in Ohio. You looked real good, despite your fast paced travel schedule. I hope your trip was all together relaxing.

Our company is growing very quick. Our district's sales of surgical supplies last year are a fraction of our anticipated sales this year. We have surpassed last-year's totals only in the first quarter. Due to our highly-successful marketing strategy, our situation is growing more better every day. I am all together certain that, if we cooperate together, the goals we set can be easily-accomplished.

However, I feel badly about the competition in the South. If one looks close at sales figures there, one will see the rate of increase isn't hardly a third of what we had project.

Of course, our office in the West has done good. They are real quick rising up to the top. I wish our other offices followed advice as complete and thoroughly as they do.

My schedule looks well for our meeting in Texas next month. Let's spend sometime at lunch so that you can give me your assessment of the sales situation in the South.

Sincerely,

Jana Abramson

Name _____

Class _____ Date _____

PRACTICE 11

Composition: Using Adjectives and Adverbs

Instructions: If the underlined word in the sentences below is an adjective, rewrite the sentence using the adverb form of the word; if the underlined word is an adverb, rewrite the sentence using the adjective form of the word. Be sure that each sentence is grammatically correct and conveys the same basic meaning as the original sentence.

EXAMPLE: **This is a very <u>poorly</u> designed workstation.**
<u>The design of this workstation is very poor.</u>

1. This Website has been <u>cleverly</u> designed. _____

_____

_____

2. The river flowed <u>rapidly</u>. _____

_____

_____

3. Thank you for your <u>prompt</u> payment. _____

_____

4. Thank you for sending the information so <u>promptly</u>. _____

_____

_____

5. You must give this matter your <u>immediate</u> attention. _____

_____

_____

6. Please answer all questions <u>completely</u>. _____

_____

_____

7. Ms. Diamond is <u>easily</u> influenced. _____

_____

_____

8. He was not <u>seriously</u> injured in the accident. _____

_____

_____

9. She is a <u>good</u> writer. _____

_____

Words That Describe

Unit Four—Editing

Instructions: Use the concepts you have studied so far to help you locate errors in the following passage from a nursing textbook that addresses the ethical problem of euthanasia. Cross out each error you find, and write the correction in the space above it.

PART FIVE: PATIENT'S WHOM WANT TO DIE

Whom should decide whether to give or withhold treatment that could save some one's life? In the following two situations, each patient has made a decision about how their life should end. How should you be responding?

CASE ONE: NO LIVING WILL

You are a nurse at the Grove Center. Mrs. Schiller has been a patient there for near six years. At the age of 87, you consider her one of your favorite patients. "Annie," as you call her, is all ways bright, alert, and acting cheerfully. She plays the piano. And accompanies Mr. Miller, who fancies hisself a singer. She suffers from a heart condition. But her pacemaker keeps her heart beating regular, her blood thinner is working proper, and she is one of the most well adjusted residents.

Mrs. Schiller has invested wise, and money pay her expenses. But she knows this money won't last forever. She believes her assets is something that should go to her heirs. A living will has not been made by her, but she has sayed, "When its my time, I am wanting you to let me went natural." She feels she had lived a full life, her children are all growed her money should go to them, and her husband, whom died most ten years ago, is waiting for she to join him.

(Continued on next page)

continued from page 337

While making your rounds, Mrs. Schiller is found by you slumped over in her chair. Her pulse was weak and irregular. Her color is pale. She is breathing shallow.

What should you do?

CASE TWO: HELP ME DIE PLEASE?

A new nurse on the surgical floor of a hospital, you work the night shift. You find this rotation particular disturbing because many of your patients have terminal cancer. You wish yourself could do some thing about the suffering you see.

One patient is Jim Lopez, a 49 year old mechanic who has spended the lastest five days in your unit. He has lung cancer, the result of a two pack a day habit. He is in constantly pain and has trouble breathing. He was tolded his condition will no longer respond to treatment and he has, at mostest, six monthes.

At 3 a.m. Mr. Lopez pushes his call button. When you went into his room, he tells you that his pain is real bad. While you set with him, he tells you where things stood: His medical insurance is about to run out. Him and his wife have growed apart over the past few years since he become ill. Now that he is no longer able to work, she is working to help support the family, which includes three childs. She is also struggling to care for his mother in law. Whose in poorly health.

Suddenly he says, "I want to die. Please help me. I only have a few months to live. My term insurance is due. I can't pay it. If I die now, my wife and kids will get the money, and my pain will stop." He lays there staring at you.

What should you have done?

Them storys are fictional. Still, you may have to face these kind of situations when you work with patients whom are dying.

Link & Learn

Using Adjectives and Adverbs in Health Careers

GOAL: Reinforce what you learned about adjectives and adverbs in Unit 4 while going online for information about nursing and health careers.

STEP 1 Go to *englishworkshop.glencoe.com*, the address for *The English Workshop* Website. Click first on Unit 4; then click on Link & Learn to access a list of nursing and health career related sites you may use in this activity. Select one of the sites, and click on it.

STEP 2 Skim the home page of the Website you selected, and review the materials that interest you. Find an article or passage that contains *at least ten* adjectives and adverbs. Make a printout of the article or passage.

STEP 3 In the article or passage, underline each adjective and circle each adverb. On the back of your printout, write a sentence indicating which of these two parts of speech appears more often.

STEP 4 Reread your printout (or locate other passages on the Website) and find *at least two* examples of *five* of the following:

    a. *ly* adverbs (See Section 11.2, Rule 1.)
    b. adjectives that end in *y* (not *ly*) (See Section 11.2, Rule 2.)
    c. adjectives that end in *able* or *ible* (See Section 11.2, Rule 3.)
    d. adverbs that do not end in *ly* (See Section 11.2, Rule 4.)
    e. predicate adjectives (See Section 11.3.)
    f. comparative adverbs (See Section 11.5.)
    g. superlative adverbs (See Section 11.5.)
    h. compound adverbs (See Section 11.9.)

STEP 5 Do you find examples of *bad/badly, less/fewer, first/last,* or *farther/further*? On the back of the printout, note any instances of these adverbs, and explain why they are used correctly or incorrectly in the passages you selected.

STEP 6 Write your name on the front of the printout, and turn it in to your instructor.

Words That Perform Other Jobs

Profile in Success

Accountants and Business Managers: Communicating About Numbers

Lisa Diane Morse · *Chandler, Arizona* · *Bashas'*

"I was tired of getting entry-level jobs," says Lisa Diane Morse of Chandler, Arizona. So, at the age of 35, she enrolled in an accounting class at Chandler-Gilbert Community College. She recalls, "I didn't think I could do the work at first. I'd been away from school for so long."

She passed. Not only that, Lisa earned an associate degree in business, graduating with a 4.0 GPA. To do it, she had to juggle the demands of school and a full-time accounting job. Still, she found time to serve as a chapter vice-president of Phi Theta Kappa. The mother of a two-year-old, Lisa also volunteered for a charity that helps abused children. She jokes that she averaged only three hours of sleep a night. The lack of sleep paid off when she was named to the All-USA Academic Team, a national scholarship competition that rewards academic achievement as well as leadership and community service. As a result, Lisa's tuition at the University of Arizona, where she plans to complete a bachelor's degree, is already paid.

Now a junior accountant with Bashas', a supermarket chain, Lisa emphasizes the importance of communication skills. She says, "Being an accountant is not just number-crunching. Once you analyze all the data, you have to be able to explain it to non-accountants in verbal form and written form."

Think About It . . . Are Good Grades Everything?

Often Lisa Diane Morse has to explain technical information to individuals who do not have an accounting or business background.

- *How does a common background help individuals communicate?*

- *What strategies might individuals use when communicating technical information, such as mathematical data, to others who do not have the same technical expertise?*

Career Connections

BUSINESS MANAGEMENT CAREERS

Learn more about the work of auditor analysts, technology managers, small business managers, and others in the business management field by connecting to the following sites listed at *The English Workshop* Website. Go to *englishworkshop.glencoe.com*. Click first on Unit 5 and then on Career Connections.

- American Management Association
- National Business Association
- National Small Business Network
- American Society of Women Accountants
- National Society of Accountants
- Phi Beta Lambda (Future Business Leaders of America)

See page 401, **Link & Learn: Using Other Parts of Speech in Business Careers**, for an additional online career activity.

Prepositions

CHAPTER 12 PREVIEW

In this chapter you will focus on prepositions and learn to choose correctly among frequently confused words. As you study the differences between formal and informal communication, you will discover which prepositions are considered appropriate or necessary in written English. You will assess your knowledge in the Programmed Reinforcement sections and the Practices. Finally, you will enhance your understanding of prepositions by visiting a Website about the history of the Internet.

OBJECTIVES

After completing this chapter, you will be able to

- Identify prepositional phrases.
- Recognize common one-word prepositions and compound prepositions.
- Choose correctly among commonly confused words, such as:
  - *among/between*
  - *in/into*
  - *beside/besides*
  - *like/as*
  - *around/about*
- Avoid inappropriate colloquial expressions.
- Recognize when prepositions are necessary or unnecessary.
- Determine when it is appropriate to end a sentence with a preposition.
- Choose the right preposition after particular words.

Study Plan for Chapter 12

The Study Plan for Chapter 12 offers a set of strategies that will help you learn and review the chapter material.

❶ **Preposition Lists**: Break the list of prepositions in Section 12.3 into mini-lists of five to ten prepositions. Review one mini-list at a time.

❷ **Preposition Test**: Fill in the blank for this sentence: *The cat hid _____ the bed.* Any word you can put in the blank that makes sense is a preposition. For example, *The cat hid (below/by/near) the bed.* A few prepositions, such as *concerning* and *like* and *since* will not pass this test.

❸ *In/Into*: To indicate a location, use the word *in.* To show something moves from the outside to the inside, use *into.* For example, *Place the plums **into** the bowl **in** the kitchen.*

❹ **Misuse of *Of***: *I should **of** studied* "sounds" right because native speakers of English often slide words together. However, in written form, *I should of* is a big mistake. The correct form is *I should **have** studied.* Do not write *of* when you mean *have.*

In this section you will return to prepositions. After studying lists of common one-word and compound prepositions, you will focus again on problems that writers often encounter with confusing pairs.

12.1 The Preposition

Words such as *of, at, in, on,* and *between* are prepositions. A **preposition** connects a noun or pronoun with the body of the sentence. It shows the relationship between that noun or pronoun and another word in the sentence. The noun or pronoun connected by the preposition is the **object** of that preposition.

> **of Ohio**—*Ohio* is the *object* of the preposition *of*
> **at the time**—*time* is the *object* of the preposition *at*
> **in the room**—*room* is the *object* of the preposition *in*
> **on the way**—*way* is the *object* of the preposition *on*
> **between you and me**—*you* and *me* are the *objects* of the preposition *between*

Personal Pronouns
Review the chart on personal pronouns in Section 4.2, on page 101.

∎

Remember that nouns do not change form from the subjective case to the objective case, but pronouns do. In the last example above, the correct form is *between you and* **me,** not *between you and* **I.**

12.2 The Prepositional Phrase

A phrase introduced by a preposition is called a **prepositional phrase.**

> I went to the office.

In this sentence, *to the office* is a prepositional phrase. *To* is the preposition; *office* is the object of the preposition. *To* shows the relationship between *went* and *office.*

> I went to the newly decorated office.

The prepositional phrase is *to the newly decorated office.* The preposition is *to;* its object is still *office* despite the descriptive words *newly decorated.*

> The folders are on the desk.

In this sentence the preposition *on* shows the relationship between *desk,* which is the object of the preposition, and *folders.* A number of prepositions may be used to show the relationship between *folders* and desk. Each preposition would express a different relationship.

The folders are *in the desk.*   The folders are *under the desk.*
The folders are *behind the desk.*   The folders are *near the desk.*

12.3 Common One-Word Prepositions

Because prepositions express different relationships, you must select the correct preposition to convey your exact meaning. Here is a list of the most common prepositions. You don't need to memorize the list; instead, learn to recognize these words as prepositions.

about	below	during	off	toward
above	beneath	except	on	under
across	beside	for	over	underneath
after	besides	from	regarding	until
against	between	in	respecting	up
along	beyond	inside	since	upon
around	but	into	through	with
at	by	like	throughout	within
before	concerning	near	till	without
behind	down	of	to	

12.4 Compound Prepositions

In addition to one-word prepositions, a number of familiar word groups are used as though the whole group were one preposition. Learn to recognize these word groups, known as **compound prepositions:**

apart from	contrary to	in place of	on account of
as for	devoid of	in reference to	to the extent of
as regards	from beyond	in regard to	with respect to
as to	from out	in spite of	
by way of	in addition to	instead of	

12.5 Confusing Pairs of Prepositions

Most errors in the use of prepositions involve using one preposition instead of another, omitting necessary prepositions, or including unnecessary ones. Sometimes people confuse two similar prepositions, mistakenly using one when the other is required. This section will show you how to make correct choices with five commonly confused pairs.

Among/Between

Between is correct only when there are *two* people or things involved. *Among* is correct when there are *three or more*. Look at this sentence: *There is a difference of opinion (among/between) you and me*. The sentence should read *There is a difference of opinion between you and me* because there are only *two* people involved—*you* and *me*. The sentences below use *among* and *between* correctly.

> The estate was divided evenly *among* all the heirs.
> The estate was divided evenly *between* the two heirs.
> *Between* you and me, we have nothing to fear.
> The judges had to select one story from *among* a number of excellent entries.
> The final choice was *between* my story and Robin's.

In/Into

What is the difference between the next two sentences?

> Maureen is in the room.   Maureen went into the room.

In means "within." *Into* means "from the outside to within." In other words, *in* expresses location; it does not imply action or movement. By contrast, *into* expresses an action of moving from one place (outside) to another place (inside).

> The application forms are *in* the bottom drawer.
> She reached *into* the bottom drawer to get the application forms.

The words *in* and *into* in the same sentence may change the meaning completely.

> The boxer ran *in* the ring. (Was he afraid?)
> The boxer ran *into* the ring. (Was he eager?)

Beside/Besides

To avoid confusing *beside* and *besides*, remember that *beside* means "by the side of."

> Along came a spider and sat down *beside* her. (at her side).

Besides with an *s* has a completely different meaning: "in addition to."

WRONG: The spider sat down *besides* Ms. Muffet.
RIGHT: ✔ The temporary service sent an assistant and two other accountants *besides* him. (*in addition to him*)

Grammar Tip

Location or Action?

IN=location, no movement
INTO=action, movement

RIGHT: ✔ They worked *beside* her in a joint effort to finish the project.
(*at her side*)

RIGHT: ✔ No one will be there *besides* us. (*in addition to us*)

Like/As

The two words *like* and *as* cause many people a great deal of trouble. The usual error is to use *like*, a preposition, as a conjunction. The correct choice is *as*.

WRONG: My new job is not working out *like* I had hoped it would.
RIGHT: ✔ My new job is not working out *as* I had hoped it would.

Sometimes, however, people are so worried about using *like* improperly that they use *as* where *like* is really the correct word.

WRONG: He performed his duties just *as* a professional.

Successful writing demands that you correctly distinguish between *like* and *as*. Fortunately, knowing how and when to use *like* or *as* isn't difficult.

Like. *Like* is a preposition meaning *similar to* or *in a similar manner to*.

RIGHT: ✔ Saul looks *like* his father.
RIGHT: ✔ *Like* his father, Saul always arrived early.
RIGHT: ✔ She handled the bulldozer *like* an expert.
RIGHT: ✔ Your attaché case looks just *like* mine.

Use the preposition *like* with a noun or pronoun in the objective case that is not followed by a verb. In general, when you use *like*, you are comparing nouns. *Like* is never a conjunction.

As. When you need a conjunction to express similarity, the correct word is *as* (or *as if* or *as though*). For example,

RIGHT: ✔ "*As* Maine goes, so goes the nation" is an old political proverb.
RIGHT: ✔ He doesn't complain *as* he once did.
RIGHT: ✔ She worked *as if* there were no tomorrow.
RIGHT: ✔ They behaved *as though* they had something to hide.

Thus, *as* is usually used with an adverbial clause. When you want to compare verbs, use *as*. But, in elliptical constructions that leave out the verb, you may use *like*.

RIGHT: ✔ Estelle took to skiing *like* a duck to water.

However, if the verb is present, use *as*.

RIGHT: ✔ Estelle took to skiing *as* a duck *takes* to water.

Grammar Tip

Beside + s
Besides means "in addition to." It's the word *beside* "in addition to" an *s*.

Grammar Tip

Although *as* serves mostly as a conjunction, it is occasionally used as a preposition. In these cases it means *in the role* or *capacity of.*

Chuck works *as* a horse on weekends.

If Chuck works very hard, he works *like a horse.* (If he is paid to dress up in a horse costume, he works *as a horse.*)

Around/About

Do not use *around* (meaning "circular") for *about* (meaning "approximately").

WRONG: I should be home *around* an hour from now.

RIGHT: ✔ I should be home *about* an hour from now. (*approximately an hour from now*)

Conversely, do not use *about* when you mean *around.*

WRONG: Lena paced *about* the room.

RIGHT: ✔ Lena paced *around* the room. (*Lena paced in circles*)

Coverage Key

Section		Statement
12.1	➤ The Preposition	➤ S1, S2
12.2	➤ The Prepositional Phrase	➤ S3
12.3	➤ Common One-Word Prepositions	➤ S4
12.4	➤ Compound Prepositions	➤ S5
12.5	➤ Confusing Pairs of Prepositions	➤ S6, S7, S8, S9, S10, S11, S12, S13, S14, S15

Instructions: Cover the answers in the **Answer** column; then write your answer to the first statement. Uncover the first printed answer and compare your answer to it. If you wrote a correct answer, continue the activity. If you made an error, use the **Coverage Key** to locate the chapter section you need to review. When you are confident that you understand the material, continue with the reinforcement activity.

ANSWER

STATEMENT

S1 A preposition (connects, does not connect) a noun or pronoun with the body of the sentence. It (shows, does not show) the relationship that exists between that noun or pronoun and another word in the sentence.

A1 connects, shows

S2 The word that the preposition connects to the body of the sentence is called the _____ of that preposition.

A2 object

S3 In the phrase ... **in the room, in** is a(n) _____ and **room** is the _____ of **in**.

A3 preposition, object

S4 Here is a list of prepositions with one adverb and one adjective inserted: **to, with, for, until, certainly, besides, during, smart, against.** The adverb is _____ and the adjective is _____ .

A4 certainly, smart

S5 Groups of two or three words sometimes act as prepositions. Underline two such phrases in this sentence: **In regard to the order, the duplicate was used in place of the original.**

A5 <u>In regard to, in place of</u>

S6 *Between* is a preposition that is used when (two, three or more) people or things are involved. *Among* is a preposition that is used when (two, three or more) people or things are involved.

A6 two, three or more

A7 a. among
b. between

A8 c.

A9 a. into
b. in

A10 *beside, besides*

A11 Besides, beside

A12 *like*

A13 a. like
b. as
c. like
d. as
e. As

A14 *about, around*

A15 a. about
b. around

S7 Choose the correct word:
a. **This year's profits were divided equally (between, among) the eight partners.**
b. **Just (among, between) you and me, this project is almost certain to fail.**

S8 **He walked (in, into) the room.** Which is correct? (a) **in,** (b) **into,** or (c) both may be correct.

S9 Choose the correct words:
a. **She got off the bus and went (in, into) the bank.**
b. **She was (in, into) the bank when the robbery occurred.**

S10 *Besides* and *beside* can be easily differentiated if you remember that _____ means *by the side of* and _____ means *in addition to.*

S11 Choose the correct words. **(Besides, Beside) all other seating arrangements, the treasurer must sit (besides, beside) the president.**

S12 Which of these two words is never a conjunction: *like* or *as?*_____

S13 Choose the correct words in the following sentences.
a. **Denee looks just (like, as) her mother.**
b. **Denee works (like, as) a retail clerk after school.**
c. **Although she is only a trainee, Denee handles herself (like, as) a professional.**
d. **She performs (like, as) I knew she would.**
e. **(As, Like) I was saying, Denee is an exceptional employee.**

S14 The prepositions *around* and *about* should not be used interchangeably. The word that means *approximately* is (*around, about*); the word that means *circular* is (*around, about*).

S15 Choose the word that correctly completes this sentence:
a. **He should return in (about, around) 20 minutes.**
b. **Four laps (about, around) the track is the equivalent of one mile.**

SECTION B
Misuse of Prepositions

In this section you will continue to study confusing pairs (threesomes, and even foursomes). You will sharpen your knowledge of how, when, and where to use prepositions correctly. You will also discover how important it is to evaluate whether a writing situation is formal or informal.

12.6 More Confusing Words

This section will show you how to make correct choices with an additional six groupings of commonly confused words.

From/Than/With

When one thing is unlike something else, then it is *different from* something else, not *different than* something else. For example,

> This may differ *from* what you had thought.
> My approach to this problem is different *from* yours.
> Approach this problem differently *from* the way you did the previous one.

However, when *differ* is used as a verb meaning "disagree," it calls for the preposition *with:*

> We differ *with* your conclusion.

Grammar Tip

Different From

The *f* of *different* must be followed by the *f* of *from*.

di**ff**erent ─┐ ┌─ **f**rom

Over/To/At/During

Over means "above" or "in excess of." Do not use *over* when you mean *to, at,* or *during.*

> Come *to* my house tonight. (Not: Come *over* my house.)
> Let's meet *at* my home. (Not: Let's meet *over* my home.)
> We held the meeting *during* the weekend. (Not: We held the meeting *over* the weekend.)

To/At

In the lesson on verbs, you learned that the word *to* functions as part of the infinitive: *to walk, to study,* and so on. Now consider *to* as a preposition: *to the office* or *to new heights.* However, do not use *to* for *at. At* indicates location, whereas *to* indicates motion.

> Shelly was *at* a party last night. (Not: Shelly was *to* a party last night.)
> I was *at* her graduation. (Not: I was *to* her graduation. But: I went *to* her graduation.)

Infinitives
To review the use of to *in infinitives, go back to Section 9.6 on page 251.*

■

To/Too/Two

Do not use the adverb *too,* meaning "also" or "excessively," or the adjective *two,* meaning "the numeral 2," for the preposition *to.* For example,

> There are *too* many entrants *to* give out only *two* prizes.
> *Too* much has been said *to* the public about the *two* experimental drugs.

Off/Off Of/From

Do not use the word *of* after the word *off.*

> WRONG: The alarm clock fell *off* of the nightstand.
> RIGHT: ✔ The alarm clock fell *off* the nightstand.

Do not use *off of* when you mean *from.*

> WRONG: She used it to buy my old car *off of* me.
> RIGHT: ✔ She used it to buy my old car *from* me.

Of/Have

Do not use *of* when you mean *have.* When you speak quickly, the helping verb *have* sounds like the preposition *of.* Don't be misled. The word *of* never directly follows the word *might, must, could, should,* or *would.*

> SAY: ✔ I might *have* gone. (Not: I might of gone.)
> SAY: ✔ I would *have* been there by now. (Not: I would of been there by now.)
> SAY: ✔ I should *have* known better. (Not: I should of known better.)

12.7 Colloquial Expressions

Many expressions used in casual conversation and informal writing are not considered appropriate for more formal situations. Such informal conversational expressions are considered **colloquial.** These expressions are not substandard, but the careful writer avoids using them in formal correspondence. Here are examples of colloquial expressions.

Outside Of/Except

Do not use the colloquial expression *outside of* when you mean *except.*

> COLLOQUIAL: Everyone was present *outside of* Peter.
> PREFERRED: ✔ Everyone was present *except* Peter.

352   Unit 5   *Words That Perform Other Jobs*

Inside Of/Within

Inside of properly refers to place. When referring to time, avoid the colloquial *inside of* in favor of the more proper *within*.

COLLOQUIAL: Ms. Nguyen will receive her money *inside of* a week.
PREFERRED: ✔ Ms. Nguyen will receive her money *within* a week.

In Back Of/Behind

Use *behind* instead of the more colloquial *in back of.*

COLLOQUIAL: The Albertsons sat *in back of* us at the concert.
PREFERRED: ✔ The Albertsons sat *behind* us at the concert.

Occupational Outlooks

Every industry employs general managers, but the wholesale, retail, and service industries employ more than six out of ten of the persons employed in this job category. Research the employment conditions of a specific career in the U.S. Department of Labor's *Occupational Outlook Handbooks.*

12.8 Unnecessary Prepositions

Avoid prepositions that clutter your sentence without adding content.

SAY: ✔ Where are you going? (Not: Where are you going *to*?)
SAY: ✔ Where is your car? (Not: Where is your car *at*?)
SAY: ✔ I cannot help feeling worried. (Not: I cannot help *from* feeling worried.)
SAY: ✔ I want you to see this. (Not: I want *for* you to see this.)
SAY: ✔ Until yesterday, I was not optimistic. (Not: *Up* until yesterday, I was not optimistic.)
SAY: ✔ In two weeks it will be over. (Not: In two weeks it will be over *with*.)

12.9 Necessary Prepositions

Be careful not to omit prepositions that are necessary. Do not forget the word *of* in combinations such as *type of* and *style of.*

What *type of* work do you do? (Not: What type work do you do?)
Tell him what *style of* car we want. (Not: Tell him what style car we want.)

The word *of* must also be used in *all of* and *both of* constructions when *all* or *both* is followed by a pronoun. It is not needed when *all* or *both* is followed by a noun, however.

WRONG: *Both* them must be renegotiated.
RIGHT: ✔ *All* the contracts must be renegotiated.
RIGHT: ✔ *All of* them must be renegotiated.
RIGHT: ✔ *Both* contracts must be renegotiated.
RIGHT: ✔ *Both of* them must be renegotiated.

Grammar Tip

Pronoun Number and Prepositional Phrases

Do not omit the preposition *from* after the verb *to graduate.*

WRONG: I graduated high school two years ago.
RIGHT: ✔ I graduated *from* high school two years ago.

12.10 Sentences Ending With a Preposition

At one time, language authorities were opposed to ending any sentence with a preposition; many writers still follow this practice in formal writing.

AWKWARD: Omar is the person whom I went to the meeting *with*.
BETTER: ✔ Omar is the person *with* whom I went to the meeting.
BETTER YET: ✔ I went to the meeting *with* Omar.

AWKWARD: Whom are you giving the check *to*?
BETTER: ✔ *To* whom are you giving the check?

Many successful writers, however, no longer follow this practice so rigidly. Although they may revise some sentences to eliminate awkward final prepositions, they may not revise all sentences that end with a preposition. For example, many writers would find this sentence acceptable:

I don't know which organization he is a member *of.*

Others would prefer the following: *I don't know of which organization he is a member.* Similarly, many writers would find this sentence acceptable: *I don't know which organization she belongs to.* Others would prefer to rephrase it: *I don't know to which organization she belongs.*

What should you do? Whenever possible, construct sentences that do not end with a preposition; but if a sentence ends more naturally with a preposition than without, leave it as is. Being too rigid in correcting a perceived breach of the rules can result in an awkward sentence. For example, *What did I come in here for?* is preferable to *For what did I come in here?*

Short questions and statements often end naturally with prepositions:

I don't know what you're talking *about.*
What do you have to worry *about?*
What is this made *of?*
What is this good *for?*

In each of the above cases, revising the sentence would result in constructions that most people would consider awkward:

I don't know *about* what you are talking.
About what do you have to worry?
Of what is this made?
For what is this good?

Remember what Sir Winston Churchill reportedly said when told that he should not end a sentence with a preposition: "That is the sort of English up with which I will not put."

Skunk Works

In a corporation, the *skunk works* is a small, often isolated department whose function is to generate new ideas. The expression comes from the comic strip *Li'l Abner* by Al Capp.

SECTION B: PROGRAMMED REINFORCEMENT

Coverage Key

Section		Statement
12.6	➤ More Confusing Words	➤ S16, S17, S18, S19, S20, S21, S22, S23
12.7	➤ Colloquial Expressions	➤ S24
12.8	➤ Unnecessary Prepositions	➤ S25, S26
12.9	➤ Necessary Prepositions	➤ S27, S28
12.10	➤ Sentences Ending With a Preposition	➤ S29

Instructions: Cover the answers in the **Answer** column; then write your answer to the first statement. Uncover the first printed answer and compare your answer to it. If you wrote a correct answer, continue the activity. If you made an error, use the **Coverage Key** to locate the chapter section you need to review. When you are confident that you understand the material, continue with the reinforcement activity.

ANSWER	STATEMENT
	S16 The preposition that should follow the word *different* is (*from, than*). Choose the correct answers: a. **Credit cards are different (from, than) debit cards.** b. **Credit cards differ (from, than) debit cards.** c. **The bank treats credit cards differently (from, than) debit cards.**
A16 *from* a. **from** b. **from** c. **from**	**S17** *Over* is a preposition meaning "above" or "in excess of." It (can, cannot) also be used to mean *to, at,* or *during.*
A17 cannot	**S18** Choose the correct answers: a. **Come (over, to) my house this evening.** b. **I worked on my tax return (over, during) the weekend.** c. **I was (to, at) the library all day yesterday.**
A18 a. **to** b. **during** c. **at**	**S19** The words *to, too,* and *two* are frequently confused. The word that means "excessively" or "also" is _____ while _____ means "one plus one" and _____ indicates direction.
A19 *too, two, to*	**S20** Choose the correct forms: **I am (to, two, too) busy (to, two too) compare the reports submitted by the (to, two, too) agencies.**
A20 too, to, two	

A21 of

A22 off of, from

A23 have

A24
 a. except
 b. within
 c. behind

A25 <u>for</u>, <u>at</u>

A26 <u>to</u>, <u>up</u>

A27 of

A28 d

A29 a. To whom did you wish to
  speak?
 b. Mr. Cupo is the person with
  whom I had the interview.
  (Or: I had the interview with
  Mr. Cupo.)

S21 Underline the preposition that should be eliminated: **Please take that calendar off of the desk and put it into the wastebasket.**

S22 In the sentence **He borrowed money off of the cashier,** the prepositions incorrectly used are _____; the correct preposition is _____.

S23 **I should of stayed in bed.** The preposition **of** is incorrectly substituted for the verb _____.

S24 Choose the prepositions a careful writer would prefer in the following sentences:
 a. **Everyone (outside of, except) Marjorie and Phil was there.**
 b. **I expect to have a firm offer (inside of, within) a week.**
 c. **The company holds season tickets (in back of, behind) home plate.**

S25 Unnecessary prepositions should be eliminated. Underline two that should be eliminated in this sentence: **I want for you to tell me where you will be at this evening.**

S26 Underline the unnecessary prepositions in this sentence: **Where are you going to, and up until when will you stay?**

S27 Other prepositions should not be omitted. What necessary preposition is omitted in this sentence? **What type _____ appliance would make a suitable gift?**

S28 Which of the following sentences is grammatically incorrect?
 a. **Both of the computers need repair.**
 b. **Both computers need repair.**
 c. **All of the student nurses are present.**
 d. **All them are present.**

S29 Sentences should not end awkwardly with a preposition. Revise the following sentences to eliminate such awkwardness.
 a. **Whom did you wish to speak to?** _____
 b. **Mr. Cupo is the person I had the interview with.** _____

SECTION C
Use of Particular Prepositions

Certain words call for one preposition to express their intended meanings clearly. In other cases several prepositions may be used with a particular word to convey different but acceptable meanings. This section offers a list of words and the prepositions they require to denote specific meanings.

Grammar Tip

Prepositional Combos

Acceptable combinations of prepositions and certain words have developed over time.

12.11 Particular Prepositions

This chart indicates how prepositions can convey the meaning you desire.

Words + Particular Prepositions	Sentence Examples
abide by (a decision)	We will *abide by* your decision.
accompanied by (a person)	Jo was *accompanied by Tim*.
accompanied with (an object)	The proposal was *accompanied with* a detailed cost analysis.
acquainted with (familiar with)	Are you *acquainted with* the ENC?
adapted from (taken and modified from)	These new plans were *adapted from* an earlier set.
adapted to (adjusted to)	These plans can be *adapted to* fit your needs.
agree to (terms)	We *agreed to* the terms.
agree upon (a plan)	They *agreed upon* a plan of action.
agree with (an opinion)	I *agree with* what you're saying.
agree with (a person)	I *agree with* you.
allude to (refer indirectly to)	She *alluded to* problems.
angry at (an occurrence or object)	I am *angry at* Tara's refusal.
angry with (a person)	I am *angry with* Tara for that joke .
annoyed by (something)	She was *annoyed by* the poster.
annoyed with (a person)	Ms. Engle was *annoyed with* her.
argue for (something)	They *argued for* a radical change.
argue with (a person)	They men *argued with* each other.
compare to (suggest a similarity)	Work may be *compared to* a community.
compare with (examine for specific similarities)	*Compare* this washing machine *with* any of its competitors.
compensate for (make up for)	We must *compensate for* lost time.
comply with (conform to)	We must *comply with* a new set of regulations.
concur in (an opinion)	I *concur in* the majority opinion.
concur with (a person or thing)	In this matter I *concur with* Jake.
consistent with (compatible with)	Is this *consistent with* our policy?
convenient for (a purpose)	This location is *convenient for* a variety of reasons.

MONEY TACTICS Some claim that the secret to financial security is pretending to have only 80% of your income to spend. Translate your financial worries into financial planning: develop annual and monthly budgets, and determine your boundaries and allowances ahead of time.

convenient to (a location)	The new site is *convenient to* public transportation.
correspond by (by means of)	They *corresponded by* telegram.
correspond to (is equivalent to)	This machine *corresponds to* our current model.
correspond with (write a letter to)	She *corresponds with* friends.
deal in (a kind of business)	My broker *deals in* municipal bonds and securities.
deal with (people)	My broker does not know how to *deal with* troublesome clients.
deal with (subjects)	He declined to *deal with* the topic of acid rain.
differ about (something)	We *differ about* means but not about ends.
differ from (a thing)	Yarn colors will *differ from* one dye lot to another.
differ with (an opinion)	Bob *differs with* my view.
disappointed at (or *in* a thing)	I'm *disappointed at* the poor level of service.
disappointed with (a person)	You will never be *disappointed with* her.
encroach on (or *upon*; intrude gradually)	Be careful not to *encroach on* another salesperson's territory.
equivalent to (equal to)	Her responsibilities are roughly *equivalent to* mine.
identical with (uniform with, equal to)	This year's model is *identical with* last year's.
independent of (not *from*)	I reached my decision *independent of* yours.
indicative of (not *to*; demonstrates)	This report is *indicative of* the high quality of her work.
indifferent to (uncaring about)	Craig seems *indifferent to* the needs of others.
inquire about (interrogate, question)	Mr. Bikoff is going to *inquire about* office space in that building.
inquire after (one's health)	They *inquired after* her health.
inquire of (ask a person)	Feel free to *inquire of* our representative if the need arises.
interfere in (something)	Don't *interfere in* something that doesn't concern you.
interfere with (a person)	Don't *interfere with* me.
liable for (responsible for)	You will be *liable for* damages.
liable to (susceptible to)	During the winter months we are more *liable to* colds and flu.
live at (a certain address)	He *lives at* 328 Elm Street in Rye.
live by (means of a livelihood)	She was forced to *live by* her wits.
live in (a town)	He *lives in* Rye.
live on (a street)	He *lives on* Elm Street in Rye.

necessity for (urgent need for)	There is an absolute *necessity for* immediate action on this matter.
necessity of (unavoidable obligation of)	We face the *necessity of* recalling last year's models.
need for (urgent occasion for)	There is a true *need for* a quick solution to this problem.
need of (lack or want)	We are in *need of* new furniture for the reception room.
object to (oppose)	I *object to* the proposed increase.
payment for (an article)	Enclosed is a check in *payment for* last week's shipment.
payment of (a fee or bill)	Enclosed is a check in *payment of* the bill for last week's shipment.
proceed from (come forth)	*Proceed from* the meeting room to the reception area.
proceed with (continue)	You may *proceed with* your filing.
rely on (someone or something)	You can *rely on* me.
reminiscent of (not *from*)	Today's program is *reminiscent of* last year's.
responsible for (liable for)	Elaine was directly *responsible for* the maintenance of her apartment.
responsible to (accountable to)	You are *responsible to* them.
specialize in (not *at*)	Ann decided to *specialize in* tax law.
take exception to (object to)	I *take exception* to your last remark.
talk to (to speak to a person)	She *talked to* them for an hour.
talk with (converse with a person)	She *talked* at length *with* Jari.
wait for (someone or something)	Having missed the bus, Jesse had to *wait for* the next one.
wait on (serve)	The store manager *waited on* us.

Many other words also call for particular prepositions. Whenever you're unsure which preposition to use with a word not on this list, consult your dictionary.

Coverage Key

Section		Statement
12.11 ➤ Particular Prepositions		➤ **S30, S31, S32, S33, S34, S35**

Instructions: Cover the answers in the **Answer** column; then write your answer to the first statement. Uncover the first printed answer and compare your answer to it. If you wrote a correct answer, continue the activity. If you made an error, use the **Coverage Key** to locate the chapter section you need to review. When you are confident that you understand the material, continue with the reinforcement activity.

ANSWER

STATEMENT

S30 Choose the correct prepositions:
  a. **Abide (by, with) a decision**
  b. **Accompanied (by, with) a person**
  c. **Accompanied (by, with) a remittance**

A30 a. by
  b. by
  c. with

S31 Choose the correct prepositions:
  a. **Agree (with, to) an opinion**
  b. **Agree (with, to) terms**
  c. **Angry (with, at) a person**
  d. **Angry (with, at) an occurrence or object**

A31 a. with
  b. to
  c. with
  d. at

S32 Choose the correct prepositions:
  a. **Please comply (with, to) this request.**
  b. **This store is convenient (with, to) all transportation.**

A32 a. with
  b. to

S33 Choose the word that correctly completes each of these sentences:
  a. **I correspond (to, with) various friends by e-mail.**
  b. **Those two textbooks closely correspond (to, with) each other.**

A33 a. with
  b. to

S34 Choose the correct prepositions:
  a. **Jade and I differ (from, with) each other on this.**
  b. **I am disappointed (at, with) the poor quality.**
  c. **Ms. Jacoby is going to inquire (about, after, of) making pie.**

A34 a. with
  b. at
  c. about

S35 Choose the correct prepositions:
  a. **This check is in payment (of, for) last month's statement.**
  b. **I talked (to, with) several of their representatives during lunch.**
  c. **I have been waiting (on, for) the express train for more than an hour.**

A35 a. of
  b. with
  c. for

CHAPTER 12 SUMMARY

In this chapter you learned that prepositions indicate a relationship between nouns or pronouns and other words in a sentence. You discovered how to make correct choices among commonly confused words such as *beside/besides, like/as,* and *around/about.* With an awareness of the differences between informal and formal communication, you examined various uses of prepositions that may be viewed as inappropriate in written English. This included colloquial expressions, unnecessary prepositions, and sentences ending with a preposition. Finally, you learned that some words must be matched with particular prepositions.

Getting Connected

HUNTING FOR PREPOSITIONS IN AN INTERNET HISTORY LESSON

GOAL: The history of the Internet goes back to the middle of the last century. Shortly after World War II, scientists and security experts decided that computers could help protect government information in the event of a nuclear war. These experts suggested that the military could connect a series of computers. Important information could be stored on the connected, or networked, computers. If one computer site were destroyed, the information from it would still be available at other sites. What began as a plan to protect national security information now functions as a means to store and transmit business and personal communications. In fact, because the Internet has become so successful and so crowded, plans to expand the Internet have long been on the drawing boards of scientists and security experts.

In this activity, you'll go online to learn about Internet history and use that information to reinforce your understanding of prepositions.

STEP 1 Go to *englishworkshop.glencoe.com,* the address for *The English Workshop* Website, and click on Unit 5. Next click on Getting Connected, and then click on Chapter 12. At the Chapter 12 Getting Connected option, you'll see a list of Websites that include information about the history of the Internet. Begin the activity by selecting one of the Internet history links and clicking on it.

STEP 2 As you read about the history of the Internet, notice the use of prepositions and prepositional phrases. Search for at least a page of information that will help you complete this activity. If you wish to investigate other articles on Internet history at other Websites, return to *The English Workshop* Website, select another site to visit, and click on its link. Eventually determine the one Website and page of information you'd like to use to complete this activity.

STEP 3   Make a printout of at least one page of the Internet history article you've selected, and use that page to do the following:

a. Highlight or circle each preposition in the article.
b. Underline the prepositional phrases in the article. Remember that a prepositional phrase begins with a preposition and ends with a noun or pronoun. Be sure to underline the entire prepositional phrase.
c. Draw an arrow from each preposition to its object.
d. Locate any misuse of words such as *among, between, in, into, beside, besides, like,* and *as.* Other potential errors include colloquial expressions such as *outside of* to mean *except, inside of* to mean *within,* and *in back of* to mean *behind.*

Circle or highlight any errors you find, and correct the error by revising the sentence on the back of your printout.

STEP 4   On the back of your printout, also write *at least five* sentences that contain prepositions and are based on the information you have learned about the history of the Internet. Use the following suggestions to help you write your sentences. Review the chapter material if you do not understand why you are being asked to work with these specific prepositions.

e. Write a sentence using *during, since,* or *throughout* in a prepositional phrase.
f. Write a sentence using a compound preposition such as *in addition to* or *apart from.*
g. Write a sentence illustrating the correct use of *among* or *between, like* or *as,* or *around* or *about.*
h. Write a sentence that uses either *all of* or *both of* followed by a pronoun.
i. Write a sentence that uses either *all* or *both* followed by a noun.
j. Consult the list of words that are followed by particular prepositions (on page 357), and select two. Write a sentence for each word you chose.

STEP 5   Write your name on the top of the printout, and turn it in to your instructor.

PRACTICE 1

Prepositions

Instructions: Use parentheses to enclose each prepositional phrase in the following sentences. Then underline each preposition with one line and the object of each preposition with two lines.

EXAMPLE: (<u>In</u> <u>each</u>) (<u>of</u> the <u>sentences</u>,) enclose prepositional phrases (<u>in</u> <u>parentheses</u>).

1. The reputation of Apex Watch Company has been built on high standards and fair dealings for three generations.

2. Between you and me, I feel certain that one of the representatives will call at your office within a week to discuss plans for an orderly transfer of records.

3. In regard to any orders from your firm, we feel sure of our ability to fill them in time for your fall shipment.

4. With respect to your claim for damages, we are certain of a recovery to the extent of $3000.

5. Contrary to our hopes and expectations, you will be refused a passport for the duration of the present emergency.

6. Executives of the company have agreed among themselves to honor, without question, all the demands made by our client.

7. Members of the radio station succeeded beyond their wildest expectations in their efforts to raise money for the children's hospital.

8. Instead of being discouraged by his failure, he seemed to gain renewed strength in all his subsequent attempts.

9. The high hopes of the young assistant were crushed when the niece of the president was hired for the new position.

10. Against Ms. Colvert's wishes, the procedures for the new project were developed at the regional office in Houston.

11. From the first quarter to the third quarter, sales of the revised software program soared far beyond the original projections.

12. Before he heard the answer to his question, the naive young sales representative jumped from his chair and raced to the front of the room to present his case.

13. Of all times for our telephone system to fail, this is the worst!

14. Walking into the hall through both doors, the President of the United States and the members of his cabinet were greeted by the complete silence of the assembled guests.

15. In spite of her aversion to the tactics of high-pressure salespeople, Ms. Zola was so impressed by this young sales representative that she agreed to buy the full line of goods.

PRACTICE 2

Confusing Prepositions

Instructions: Underline the preposition in parentheses that makes each sentence below grammatically correct.

EXAMPLE: **I'm caught (among, <u>between)</u> a rock and a hard place.**

1. (Among, Between) you and me, this plan is certain to fail.

2. (Among, Between) the reasons for Lisa's success were her wisdom, honesty, and fairness.

3. The jewelry was found (among, between) her belongings.

4. The Big Three often differ (among, between) themselves.

5. Chicago is (among, between) New York and Seattle.

6. (Among, Between) the people present were the President, the Vice President, and the Secretary of State.

7. What is the main difference (among, between) these two SUVs?

8. There is little difference (among, between) these five VCRs.

9. There is a difference of opinion (among, between) the two administrators.

10. There is a difference of opinion (among, between) the jury.

11. She walked briskly through the main doors and (in, into) her office.

12. Behind a closed door, he paced back and forth (in, into) his office all day.

13. There are some interesting articles (in, into) today's newspaper.

14. His initial lack of pleasure turned (in, into) one of shocked disbelief.

15. Julius reached (in, into) his jacket pocket to discover that he had forgotten the tickets.

16. Promotion is rapid, once you have established a name (in, into) this field.

17. The firefighters rushed (in, into) the burning building.

18. I would tear this contract (in, into) a thousand pieces if I could.

19. Do you think you can get (in, into) the public relations field?

20. Our representative had no trouble getting (in, into) to see Mr. Halline.

21. It looks (like, as) rain.

22. It looks (like, as if) it might rain.

23. The situation is exactly (like, as) I described it on the phone.

24. I've behaved (like, as) a fool.

25. Your copier is (like, as) the one we purchased last year.

Continued on next page

26. (Like, As) I told you, the Copely Copier makes the sharpest copies.

27. She ran (like, as though) her life depended on it.

28. He repaired the machine (like, as) a professional.

29. She is (like, as) her mother in everything she does.

30. You look (like, as though) you have seen a ghost.

31. (Like, As) father, (like, as) son.

32. On weekends he moonlights (like, as) a guard.

33. You don't know him (like, as) I do.

34. Jared looks a great deal (like, as) his cousin.

35. It looks (like, as if) we will be able to complete the project after all.

36. Theo sat down (beside, besides) his friend.

37. Final class lists will be sent (about, around) October 30.

38. (Beside, Besides) that, what else can we do?

39. (About, Around) 30 people attended the conference.

40. He was so angry he was (beside, besides) himself.

41. I'll be home in (about, around) an hour.

42. What else can we do (beside, besides) signing the petition?

43. Put the damaged merchandise outside (beside, besides) the dumpster.

44. The mounted color guard proceeded (about, around) the track before coming to a halt (beside, besides) the platform.

45. I'd say there were (about, around) 40 people there (beside, besides) the actual participants.

46. Gina was (to, at) the movies Saturday afternoon.

47. The disease is (to, too, two) advanced for treatment.

48. While rock climbing, George fell (off, off of) a slope.

49. Carlos took some old CD-ROMS (off of, from) me.

50. You should (of, have) told me about the problem earlier.

PRACTICE 3

Necessary and Unnecessary Prepositions

Instructions: For each sentence, cross out any incorrect preposition or insert any needed preposition. If the sentence is correct, write *C* in the blank.

from
EXAMPLE: He never graduated ⌃ high school.   EX. _____

1. It's a relief that summer is over with.   1. _____

2. By the end of the summer the renovations will have been completed.   2. _____

3. Open up all the windows.   3. _____

4. This is the place where I am going to.   4. _____

5. Do you know where Mr. Chang is at?   5. _____

6. Did the packages fall off of the shelves?   6. _____

7. Ms. Chavez ordered a new style message pad.   7. _____

8. What type of fabric is this?   8. _____

9. When did you graduate high school?   9. _____

10. All of the samples were ruined.   10. _____

11. All the samples were ruined.   11. _____

12. In another few minutes it will be done with.   12. _____

13. Take the books off of the dining room table.   13. _____

14. Here is a copy of the plans you ordered.   14. _____

15. What type software do you intend to use?   15. _____

16. All the forms must be completed in triplicate.   16. _____

17. Crystal graduated from college in 2002.   17. _____

18. I can't help from feeling envious at her good fortune.   18. _____

19. Both of the applicants are in the reception room.   19. _____

20. Both of them appear nervous.   20. _____

PRACTICE 4

Sentences Ending With Prepositions

Instructions: Rewrite each sentence so that it no longer ends with a preposition.

EXAMPLE: **Whom are you offering the position to?** <u>**To whom are you offering the position?**</u>

1. Which file did you put the letter in? _____

   _____

2. Which advertising agency was this campaign developed by? _____

   _____

3. Gretchen is the person he was at the symposium with. _____

   _____

4. How many forms did you spill the ink on? _____

   _____

5. Whom was the typewriter invented by? _____

   _____

6. Sheena is the person the flowers were intended for. _____

   _____

7. I don't recall the name of the person I spoke to. _____

   _____

8. Which distributor did these books come from? _____

   _____

9. There are only two people in this office I can rely on. _____

   _____

10. When you added these columns, what total did you end up with? _____

   _____

Name _____

Class _____ Date _____

PRACTICE 5

Preposition Review

Instructions: In the following letter, many prepositions are used incorrectly. Cross out each incorrect preposition, and write the correct one above it. If a sentence ends awkwardly with a preposition, rewrite the sentence.

MS. TERESINA CRUZ
23522 Derby Lane, Aberdeen, SD 57703

October 13, 20--

Mr. Braswell
311 Mount Rushmore Rd.
Rapid City, SD 57701

Dear Mr. Braswell:

I received your letter last week. I am willing to comply to most of your provisions when I buy the house off you, but I object with your interpretation of a portion of our contract. At this point your interpretation is entirely different than mine. Unfortunately, my attorney, accompanied with her family, will be vacationing up until next week, so I have been unable to talk to her about this. I am trying to correspond to her by mail. I should of heard from her by now, but I am still waiting on her to contact me.

I feel there is an immediate need of settling this difference of opinion among you and me. I want for you to know that I am not angry at you. I am angry at the conditions that brought about this situation.

Continued on next page

I am willing to comply to all the provisions in Paragraphs 1–10, but I cannot agree to your present interpretation of Paragraph 11. It is not consistent to what it was when I agreed to sign this contract.

You are responsible to the landscaping and maintenance of the property. I do not consider four small evergreen trees and a few bushes to be consistent to the landscaping called for into the contract. In addition, the way you repaired the retaining wall in back of the garage is unsatisfactory. Although I recognize that it was convenient to you to repair the wall with a single piece of wood, I strongly object at this method. The wall must be torn down and completely rebuilt up.

Beside the wall and the landscaping, there are several smaller items that I am annoyed at. However, these items I am prepared to compromise on. I can accept everything outside of the wall and the landscaping. I don't feel that the spirit of the contract in these areas is something you've lived up to.

Since I am sure that you are not indifferent about my feelings, I know I can rely by you to fix these problems so that we will be able to proceed on the closing as originally scheduled.

Respectfully,

Teresina Cruz

Name _____

Class _____ Date _____

PRACTICE 6

Composition: Using Prepositions

Instructions: Write complete sentences using the words in parentheses.

1. (as) _____

_____

2. (among) _____

_____

3. (like) _____

_____

4. (into) _____

_____

5. (besides) _____

_____

6. (different from) _____

_____

7. (agree with)_____

_____

8. (talk with) _____

_____

9. (responsible for) _____

_____

10. (comply with)_____

_____

Conjunctions and Interjections

CHAPTER 13 PREVIEW

In this chapter you will explore how to use conjunctions, conjunctive adverbs, transitional phrases, semicolons and interjections. You will examine the roles that sentence connectors play in constructing compound and complex sentences. Finally, you will assess your knowledge in the Programmed Reinforcement sections and the Practices. Finally, you will visit a Website offering advice about job interviews.

OBJECTIVES

After completing this chapter, you will be able to

- Distinguish between coordinating and subordinating conjunctions.
- Identify the four basic types of sentences.
- Minimize your use of *and* and *but* as sentence openers.
- Know whether to use conjunctions or prepositions in sentences.
- Use correlating conjunctions effectively.
- Correct sentences that misuse words or expressions.
- Punctuate sentences with conjunctive adverbs and transitional phrases.
- Determine when and how to use interjections.

Study Plan for Chapter 13

The Study Plan for Chapter 13 offers a set of strategies that will help you learn and review the chapter material.

❶ **Complex Sentence Order:** When the dependent clause (DC) follows the independent clause (IC), you rarely use a comma. When the DC comes before the IC, you place a comma at the end of the DC.

❷ **Compound-Complex Sentence Identification:** Verify that a sentence is compound-complex by looking for a coordinating conjunction before an independent clause and a subordinating conjunction at the beginning of a dependent clause.

❸ **Conjunctive Adverbs and Transitional Phrases:** Verify that the words after a two-syllable conjunctive adverb (CA) or transitional phrase (TP) form an independent clause. Punctuate the sentence with a semicolon after the first independent clause and a comma after the CA or TP. When a one-syllable conjunctive adverb (CA) or transitional phrase (TP) joins two independent clauses, use a semicolon after the first independent clause.

In this section you will focus on the correct use of conjunctions in simple, compound, and complex sentences. You will develop your knowledge of how sentences are composed, connected, and punctuated.

13.1 Conjunction Review

You already know that a **conjunction** is used to join a word or thought to another related word or thought. However, a conjunction does more than connect ideas; it also shows the relationship between ideas. You must use conjunctions carefully to express the relationship you intend.

For example, in each of the following sentences, which conjunction is more effective at showing the relationship between the ideas it connects?

> I applied for a loan, (and, but) my application was turned down.
> I applied for a loan, (and, but) my application was approved.

To convey the exact meaning intended in the first sentence, *but* is correct. In the second sentence, *and* is correct. The English language offers a large selection of conjunctions to show precise shades of relationship. Here are just a few:

and	inasmuch as	or	until
as soon as	in order that	though	when
because	notwithstanding	unless	while
but			

13.2 Simple Sentences

The fundamental type of sentence is the simple sentence. A **simple sentence** has two essential parts—a subject and a verb—and expresses a complete thought: *Snow fell.*

To add greater meaning to a simple sentence, you can provide words and phrases that describe the subject, the verb, or both: *Freezing* snow fell *on the highway.*

This is still a simple sentence, but it provides additional description. A simple thought has been built up by adding an adjective, *freezing,* and a prepositional phrase, *on the highway,* to describe the subject and the verb.

A simple sentence can have more than one subject or verb. For example, *Snow and sleet fell.* This is a simple sentence with a compound subject. You

Grammar Tip

Simple Sentence

A simple sentence includes a subject and a verb, and expresses a complete thought. A simple sentence is an independent clause.

might also have written: *Snow fell and froze.* This is a simple sentence with a compound verb. You might also have written a sentence with both a compound subject and a compound verb: *Snow and sleet fell and froze.*

13.3 Compound Sentences

Is the sentence below still a simple sentence?

Snow fell and sleet froze.

No. In effect, this sentence includes two sentences that could be written separately; instead, these sentences are connected by the conjunction *and*.

Snow fell. (and) Sleet froze.

The sentence *Snow fell and sleet froze* is called a compound sentence. A **compound sentence** is a sentence composed of two or more simple sentences joined (1) by a conjunction, (2) by a conjunction plus a comma, or (3) by a semicolon. Each simple sentence that is part of a compound sentence is called an **independent clause**. In the sample sentence, *Snow fell* is an independent clause. *Sleet froze* is another independent clause. These clauses can stand alone as complete sentences. The sample sentence could also be written using a semicolon: *Snow fell; sleet froze.*

> **Grammar Tip**
>
> **Compound Sentence Visual**
>
> IC = Independent Clause
> cc = coordinating conjunction
>
> IC + cc + IC.
> IC, + cc + IC.
> IC; + IC.

Coordinating Conjunctions

In a compound sentence, the conjunction that connects one clause with another is called a **coordinating conjunction**. The seven coordinating conjunctions include the following:

and	for
but	so
or	yet
nor	

These conjunctions are "coordinating" because they connect two equal parts. In a compound sentence they join two independent clauses.

Coordinating conjunctions can also be part of a compound subject: *Snow and sleet fell.*

In this case *and* connects two equal subjects. Coordinating conjunctions can also be used as part of a compound verb: *Snow fell and froze.* In this case *and* connects two equal verbs.

Grammar Tip

Complex Sentence Visual

IC = Independent Clause
DC = Dependent Clause
IC + DC.
DC, + IC.

Now let's turn to another type of sentence—the complex sentence. In Chapter 2 you learned about the *dependent clause*, a clause that contains a subject and a verb but does not express a complete thought by itself. For example, *since the snow fell* is a dependent clause; it does not express a complete thought even though it includes a subject, *snow*, and a verb, *fell*. This clause needs another thought to complete its meaning. You might complete it as follows:

> We have received no shipments since the snow fell.

Now you have a complete sentence composed of an independent clause—*We have received no shipments*—and a dependent clause—*since the snow fell*. A sentence composed of an independent clause plus a dependent clause is called a **complex sentence**.

In the following examples of complex sentences, observe how two thoughts—an independent clause and a dependent clause—have been combined to show the relationship of one to the other.

> The principal decided to close the school *because* the road
>   conditions were hazardous.
> I must complete this report *before* I can go home.
> Pia intends to continue working *until* the project is finished.

Subordinating Conjunctions

In the examples above, notice the conjunction that introduces each dependent clause: *because, before,* and *until*. Each of these conjunctions is called a **subordinating conjunction**: when it is added to an independent clause, it makes that clause dependent on another clause for completion. In other words, it *subordinates* that clause to an independent clause.

Let's look at a few examples. If you start with the independent clause *Snow falls* and add to it a subordinating conjunction such as *if, when, although,* or *in case*, you end up with a dependent clause:

> If snow falls …
> When snow falls …
> Although snow falls …
> In case snow falls …

Common Subordinating Conjunctions. There are hundreds of subordinating conjunctions. A few of the commonly used ones follow at the top of the next page:

after	even though	since	when
although	except	so that	whenever
as	if	supposing	where
as if	in order that	than	whereas
as soon as	notwithstanding	that	wherever
because	on condition that	though	whether
before	otherwise	unless	while
even if	provided	until	why

Natural Sequence of a Complex Sentence

The "natural" sequence of a complex sentence is for the independent clause to come first. For example,

Independent Clause

We will contact our attorney

Dependent Clause

unless you settle your account within five days.

Reverse Sequence of a Complex Sentence

You can also reverse the natural sequence:

Independent Clause

Unless you settle your account within five days,

Dependent Clause

we will contact our attorney.

Commas. Notice that a comma is used to separate clauses *only* when you follow the reverse sequence and place the dependent clause before the independent clause. Compare these examples:

Natural Sequence:
Comma Unnecessary

1. The parade will take place even if it rains.
2. I will have a private office when we move to the new building.

Reverse Sequence:
Comma Necessary

1. Even if it rains, the parade will take place.
2. When we move to the new building, I will have a private office.

Punctuation Tip

Clause Sequence and Comma

The natural sequence does not require a comma; the reverse sequence does.

Grammar Tip

13.5 **Compound-Complex Sentences**

There is one more basic type of sentence, the **compound-complex sentence**. As its name indicates, this sentence is the result of combining a compound sentence and a complex sentence.

Independent Clause	Dependent Clause
I am willing to continue working	while you look for a replacement,

Independent Clause

but I cannot stay past January 30.

Independent Clause	Dependent Clause
Arunava knew he would fail the exam	as soon as he read the first question,

Independent Clause

but he still answered every question as well as he could.

Dependent Clause	Independent Clause
When she got there,	the cupboard was bare,

Independent Clause

and so her poor dog had none.

As you see, compound-complex sentences always contain at least two independent clauses and at least one dependent clause.

Sentence Summary

There are four types of sentence structures: (1) the simple sentence, (2) the compound sentence, (3) the complex sentence, and (4) the compound-complex sentence. In Chapter 14 you will discover how to use these four types effectively.

Coverage Key

Section		Statement
13.1	➤ Conjunction Review	➤ S1
13.2	➤ Simple Sentences	➤ S2, S5, S6, S15
13.3	➤ Compound Sentences	➤ S3, S7, S8, S9, S10, S11, S12, S13, S14, S16, S17 S18
13.4	➤ Complex Sentences	➤ S4, S19, S20, S21, S22, S23, S24, S25, S26, S29
13.5	➤ Compound-Complex Sentences	➤ S27, S28

Instructions: Cover the answers in the **Answer** column; then write your answer to the first statement. Uncover the first printed answer and compare your answer to it. If you wrote a correct answer, continue the activity. If you made an error, use the **Coverage Key** to locate the chapter section you need to review. When you are confident that you understand the material, continue with the reinforcement activity.

ANSWER		STATEMENT
		S1 A conjunction (describes, joins, modifies) thoughts.
A1	joins	**S2** A simple sentence contains a(n) _____ and a(n) _____ and expresses a complete thought.
A2	subject, verb	**S3** A clause that expresses a complete thought is called a(n) _____ clause.
A3	independent	**S4** A clause that does not express a complete thought is called a(n) _____ clause.
A4	dependent	**S5** A sentence that is composed of one independent clause is called a(n) _____ sentence.
A5	simple	**S6** **We purchased stock** is a simple sentence because it is composed of one _____ clause.
A6	independent	**S7** **We purchased stock; then we sold it.** Each of these clauses is a(n) _____ clause.
A7	independent	**S8** **We purchased stock and then we sold it.** This is a(n) _____ sentence because it consists of two independent clauses connected by a conjunction.
A8	compound	

S9 **We purchased stock; then we sold it.** This is a(n) _____ sentence because it is composed of two _____ clauses connected by the punctuation mark known as a(n) _____.

A9 compound, independent, semicolon

S10 **We purchased stock and then we sold it.** The word **and** is a(n)_____ because it connects equal parts. In a compound sentence it connects two _____ clauses.

A10 coordinating conjunction, independent

S11 A coordinating conjunction can connect two subjects, as in *Jack and Jill,* to form a(n) _____ subject.

A11 compound

S12 A coordinating conjunction can connect two verbs, as in *sink or swim,* in which case we have a(n) _____ verb.

A12 compound

S13 A coordinating conjunction connects two independent clauses, in which case we have a(n) _____ sentence.

A13 compound

S14 A compound sentence contains two or more _____ clauses connected by a(n) _____ conjunction, a conjunction plus a(n) _____, or a(n) _____.

A14 independent, coordinating, comma, semicolon

S15 **We regret the delay.** This is a(n) _____ sentence containing one _____ clause.

A15 simple, independent

S16 **We regret the delay, but it was unavoidable.** This is a(n) _____ sentence containing two _____ clauses connected by a(n) _____ .

A16 compound, independent, coordinating conjunction

S17 **We regret the delay; it was unavoidable.** This _____ sentence consists of two _____ clauses connected by a(n) _____ .

A17 compound, independent, semicolon

S18 **We regret the delay, it was unavoidable.** This is an example of an error called a *run-on sentence.* It includes two _____ clauses connected by a comma. To correct this sentence, you need either a(n) _____ conjunction (with a comma) or a(n) _____ .

A18 independent, coordinating, semicolon

S19 **Although we regret the delay...** This is a clause because it contains a(n) _____ and a(n) _____ . It is a dependent clause because it does not express a(n) _____ .

A19 subject, verb, complete thought

S20 **If it was unavoidable...** This is a(n) _____ clause because, although it contains a subject and a verb, it (does, does not) express a complete thought.

A20 dependent, does not

378 **Unit 5** *Words That Perform Other Jobs*

S21 In **S19** and **S20,** the words **although** and **if** are _____ conjunctions because they render a clause incomplete and therefore dependent.

A21 subordinating

S22 **Although we regret the delay, it was unavoidable.** This sentence contains (one, two) clause(s). The first is a(n) _____ clause because it is not complete. The second is a(n)_____ clause because it expresses a complete thought. This is an example of a(n) _____ sentence.

A22 two, dependent, independent, complex

S23 A complex sentence contains a(n) _____ clause and a(n) _____ clause.

A23 independent, dependent

S24 **There will be a delay if it is unavoidable.** This is an example of a(n) _____ sentence because it contains a(n) _____ clause and a(n) _____ clause. The word **if** is a(n) _____ conjunction.

A24 complex, independent, dependent, subordinating

S25 **There will be a delay if it is unavoidable.** This sentence follows the natural sequence: the _____ clause comes first, followed by the _____ clause.

A25 independent, dependent

S26 **If it is unavoidable, there will be a delay.** In this sentence the _____ clause comes first. This (is, is not) the natural sequence. You insert a comma after the _____ clause to indicate that this sentence is not in natural sequence.

A26 dependent, is not, dependent

S27 The combination of a compound sentence and a complex sentence is called a(n) _____ sentence.

A27 compound-complex

S28 A compound-complex sentence contains at least _____ independent clause(s) plus at least _____ dependent clause(s).

A28 two, one

S29 Underline the subordinating clause(s) in each of these compound-complex sentences:
 a. **When the lights went down, the curtain rose and the play began.**
 b. **Although we regret the delay, it was unavoidable, so we do hope you understand.**
 c. **There will be a delay if it is unavoidable; therefore, you should take this into account when you estimate the final cost.**

A29 a. <u>When the lights went down</u>
 b. <u>Although we regret the delay</u>
 c. <u>if it is unavoidable; when you estimate the final cost</u>

In this section you will learn about the logic that determines the correct use of conjunctions. You will also discover how to apply that logic to complex sentence structures.

13.6 *And* and *But* as Sentence Openers

You have probably heard that you should not begin a sentence with *and* or *but*. There is a logical reason for this practice. Because these two words are coordinating conjunctions, they must have something to coordinate or connect. Many sentences that begin with *and* or *but* are actually part of the preceding sentence. For example,

> I studied hard for the exam. But I didn't pass it.

These two sentences should be written as one because *But I didn't pass it* is technically a sentence fragment. The following structure is a grammatically correct compound sentence:

> I studied hard for the exam, but I didn't pass it.

However, many people—including a number of professional writers—sometimes begin sentences with *and* or *but* to avoid a long compound sentence or to achieve a particular effect. Look at this excerpt from Abraham Lincoln's Second Inaugural Address:

> Both parties deprecated war; but one of them would *make* war rather than let the nation survive; and the other would *accept* war rather than let it perish. And the war came.

Some sentences in this book begin with the word *but*. And you, for the sake of variety and emphasis, may occasionally decide to begin a sentence with *and* or *but*. But don't overdo it.

13.7 Conjunctions or Prepositions?

Sometimes writers mistakenly use a conjunction instead of a preposition, or a preposition instead of a conjunction, as you discovered with the pair *like/as*. Writers also face difficulties determining when to treat words such as *after*, *before*, and *but* as conjunctions or prepositions.

Like/As

In Chapter 12 you discovered that *like* can be a preposition but not a conjunction. For example:

Rainmaker

Literally, a *rainmaker* describes a person who creates artificial rain. As slang, it's a flattering term that applies to a creative leader who brings showers of success and progress to a business.

WRONG:	My new job is not working out *like* I had hoped it would.
RIGHT:	✔ My new job is not working out *as* I had hoped it would.

In other words, the conjunction *as* is required to join the clauses, not the preposition *like*. Don't make the error of confusing *like* with *as*.

RIGHT ✔

1. He looks *like* me. (preposition)
2. It was done *as* you wanted. (conjunction)
3. *As* I said, this is a once-in-a-lifetime opportunity. (conjunction)

WRONG

1. He looks *as* me.
2. It was done *like* you wanted.
3. *Like* I said, this is a once in a lifetime opportunity.

Like/As

Flip back to the first discussion of like/as in Section 12.5 on page 347.

After, Before, and But

You may wonder whether to use the objective case (*me, him, her*) or the subjective case (*I, he, she*) after words such as *after, before,* and *but*. These words may be used either as conjunctions (followed by the subjective case) or as prepositions (followed by the objective case), depending on how you want to compose a sentence.

Conjunction

1. I arrived at the office *after* he did.
2. She filed the letters *before* I did.
3. We received applications from everyone, *but* she is the clear favorite.

Preposition

1. I arrived at the office *after* him.
2. She filed the letters *before* me.
3. We received applications from everyone *but* her.

Grammar Tip

But = Except

In the third sentence listed in the *Preposition* column, the preposition *but* means "except."

13.8 *Correlating Conjunctions*

Either . . . or:	*Either* you work harder, *or* you leave.
Neither . . . nor:	We want *neither* sympathy *nor* charity.
Both . . . and:	A leader is *both* confident *and* humble.
Not only . . . but also:	We want you *not only* to visit our office *but also* to inspect our plant.
Whether . . . or:	*Whether* you act now *or* wait is a matter of great concern.
As . . . as:	He is *as* tall *as* his father.
So . . . as:	She is not *so* tall *as* I had thought.

Five Major Points About Correlating Conjunctions

Learn the following major points about correlating conjunctions:

Point 1: *Neither . . . nor.* With *neither*, always use *nor* (not *or*); with *either* always use *or* (not *nor*). *Neither* and *nor* go together; their positive equivalents are *either* and *or*.

Polonius advised Laertes to be "*neither* a borrower *nor* a lender."
Please enclose *either* a certified check *or* a money order.

Point 2: *Not only . . . but also.* With *not only*, always use *but also* (not *but* alone).

Our latest model is *not only* functional *but also* decorative.

Point 3: *As . . . as* vs. *So . . . as.* When two affirmative statements are joined by paired conjunctions, use *as . . . as*; when a negative statement is involved, use *so . . . as*.

Stephen is *as* sharp *as* a tack.
Assembling this equipment is not *so* difficult *as* it may appear.

Grammar Tip

Parallelism

Sentences achieve parallelism by presenting similar elements in similar structures. Such sentences are balanced.

Point 4: **Placement.** Correlating conjunctions should be placed as close as possible to the words they connect.

WRONG
1. My job has *both* given me pleasure *and* satisfaction.
2. The announcer has *neither* reported the time *nor* the place of the event.

RIGHT
1. My job has given me *both* pleasure *and* satisfaction.
2. The announcer has reported *neither* the time *nor* the place of the event.

Point 5: **Parallelism.** Be sure that correlating conjunctions connect sentence elements that are parallel in form. For example:

AWKWARD
1. We judge people *not only* by what they say *but also* their actions.

2. You can reach the airport *either* by cab *or* a special limousine may be taken.

PARALLEL
1. We judge people *not only* by what they say *but also* by what they do.
   (Or: We judge people *not only* by what they say *but also* by how they act.)
2. You can reach the airport *either* by cab *or* by special limousine.
   (Or: You can reach the airport by taking *either* a cab *or* a special limousine.)

3. Ms. Felson should *either* ship our order immediately *or* she should refund our deposit.

3. Ms. Felson should *either* ship our order immediately *or* refund our deposit.

Notice that in each revision the wording, or structure, of the sentence element following the second conjunction is similar to, or parallel to, the sentence element following the first conjunction:

> *By what they say* is parallel to *by what they do* or *by how they act.*
> *By cab* is parallel to *by limousine,* or *a cab* is parallel to *a limousine.*
> *Ship our order* is parallel to *refund our deposit.*

To maintain parallelism, be sure that correlative conjunctions introduce elements of similar structure.

13.9 Provided/Providing

Provided is a subordinating conjunction meaning "on condition that" or "if."

> You may go to the movies *provided* you have finished your homework.
> *Provided* there is time, you will be able to tour our new facilities.

Many people mistakenly use *providing* in sentences like the ones above instead of *provided*. *Providing* is a form of the verb *to provide.* It is never a conjunction and should never be used to join two parts of a sentence.

WRONG: I will speak to the group *providing* my expenses are paid.
RIGHT: ✔ I will speak to the group *provided* my expenses are paid.

13.10 Try And/Be Sure And

As you learned from the discussion of infinitives in Chapter 9, *try and* or *be sure and* are not acceptable structures. These expressions require the infinitive form of the verb, not a conjunction.

WRONG: *Try and* stop me.
RIGHT: ✔ *Try to* stop me.

WRONG: *Be sure and* mail your packages early.
RIGHT: ✔ *Be sure to* mail your packages early.

Infinitives
Refresh your memory and turn back to Section 9.6 on page 251.

■

13.11　The Reason Is Because

The widely used phrase *the reason is because* is incorrect. The proper phrase is *the reason is that.*

WRONG:　　*The reason was because* I overslept.
RIGHT:　✔ *The reason was that* I overslept.

WRONG:　　*The reason* I was unable to hand in the homework assignment *was because* my dog ate it.
RIGHT:　✔ *The reason* I was unable to hand in the homework assignment *was that* my dog ate it.
BETTER:　✔ I was unable to hand in the homework assignment *because* my dog ate it.

13.12　Where/That and But What/That

Do not use the conjunction *where,* which refers to location, instead of *that.*

WRONG:　　I read in the newspaper *where* the sale has been extended.
RIGHT:　✔ I read in the newspaper *that* the sale has been extended.

That should also be used instead of *but what,* which is too informal.

WRONG:　　I have no doubt *but what* my proposal, when adopted, will solve our problem.
RIGHT:　✔ I have no doubt *that* my proposal, when adopted, will solve our problem.

Coverage Key

Section		Statement
13.6	➤ *And* and *But* as Sentence Openers	➤ S30
13.7	➤ Conjunctions or Prepositions?	➤ S31
13.8	➤ Correlating Conjunctions	➤ S32, S33, S34, S35, S36
13.9	➤ *Provided/Providing*	➤ S37, S38
13.10	➤ *Try And/Be Sure And*	➤ S39
13.11	➤ *The Reason Is Because*	➤ S40
13.12	➤ *Where/That* and *But What/That*	➤ S41

Instructions: Cover the answers in the **Answer** column; then write your answer to the first statement. Uncover the first printed answer and compare your answer to it. If you wrote a correct answer, continue the activity. If you made an error, use the **Coverage Key** to locate the chapter section you need to review. When you are confident that you understand the material, continue with the reinforcement activity.

ANSWER

STATEMENT

S30 It is (sometimes, never) acceptable to begin a sentence with *and* or *but*.

A30 sometimes

S31 *Like* is a preposition. It is (often, sometimes, never) used as a conjunction. Correct this sentence: **He thinks like I do.**

_____

A31 never; **He thinks as I do.** (Or: **He thinks the way I do; He thinks like me.**)

S32 Correlative conjunctions are found in pairs. Complete each of the following pair of correlating conjunctions:
neither..._____; either..._____; not only..._____.

A32 nor, or, but also

S33 Paired conjunctions should be placed as close as possible to the words they connect. Which sentence or sentences are preferable?
   a. **My employer completed neither high school nor college.**
   b. **My employer neither completed high school nor college.**
   c. **Either they should repair the disk drive or replace it.**
   d. **They should either repair the disk drive or replace it.**

A33 a., d.

S34 Revise each of these awkward sentences to maintain parallel structure between the correlating conjunctions.

    a. **You should either buy the book or it should be returned to us.**

    _____

    b. **She is both accurate and she is efficient.**

    _____

A34 a. **You should either buy the book or return it to us.** (Or: **Either you should buy the book or you should return it to us.**)
    b. **She is both accurate and efficient.**

S35 When an affirmative comparison is made, you may write: **She is as rich as Midas.** When a negative comparison is made, you may write: **He is not _____ strong as Hercules.**

A35 so

S36 Choose the word that correctly completes each of these sentences.
    a. **This job is (so, as) difficult and time-consuming as any I've ever had.**
    b. **This project is not (so, as) time-consuming as I had feared it would be.**

A36 a. as
    b. so

S37 _Provided_ and _providing_ are sometimes confused. _____ is a conjunction; _____ is a verb.

A37 _Provided, providing_

S38 Choose the words that correctly complete this sentence:
I will stay for lunch (provided, providing) the owner is (provided, providing) the food.

A38 provided, providing

S39 Choose the correct words.
    a. **Try (and, to) rectify the shortage in receipts.**
    b. **Be sure (and, to) tell me whether you got the job.**

A39 a. to, b. to

S40 The phrase _the reason is because_ (is, is not) grammatically correct.

A40 is not

S41 Choose the correct words.
    a. **I read in _The Wall Street Journal_ (that, where) stock prices are advancing.**
    b. **There is no doubt (but what, that) this is a good time to invest.**

A41 a. that
    b. that

So far you have studied coordinating, subordinating, and correlating conjunctions. In this section you will focus on two other sentence connectors. You will also discover how important it is to choose the correct punctuation for sentence connectors as well as interjections.

13.13 Conjunctive Adverbs

Look at these examples:

> There were many delays; *however,* the work was completed.
> LaMar did not go on to college; *instead,* he enlisted in the military.
> Eloise was ill; *thus* she was unable to take the final exam.

Each of the italicized words is called a **conjunctive adverb** because it both modifies the clause that it introduces and joins two independent clauses. Below is a list of common conjunctive adverbs.

accordingly	consequently	indeed	nevertheless
also	finally	instead	then
anyway	furthermore	likewise	therefore
besides	however	meanwhile	thus

Pay particular attention to how the sample sentences above are punctuated. A semicolon is placed before the conjunctive adverb, and a comma is placed after a conjunctive adverb of more than one syllable. A comma after conjunctive adverbs of one syllable (e.g., *hence, then, thus*) is optional.

13.14 Transitional Phrases

A number of words act as connectors in much the same way as conjunctive adverbs. These words are known as **transitional phrases.** Below is a list of common transitional phrases.

after all	by the way	in other words
as a result	for example	in the second place
at any rate	in addition	on the contrary
at the same time	in fact	on the other hand

A transitional phrase is always preceded by a semicolon when it is used to join two independent clauses, and it is always followed by a comma.

Professional Communication

When hiring restaurant managers, employers look for personal qualities, such as self-discipline and initiative. Yet the ability to communicate well is primary, since you'll be dealing with customers, suppliers, and staff all day long.

Punctuation Tip

Comma or Semicolon?

Use a comma before a coordinating conjunction that joins two independent clauses. Use a semicolon before a conjunctive adverb or transitional phrase that joins two independent clauses.

I don't think that Mr. Rooney is disagreeable; *on the contrary,* I find him very helpful and friendly.

Eloise was ill the last two weeks of the semester; *as a result,* she was unable to take the final exam and received an incomplete for the course.

Conjunctive adverbs and transitional phrases are similar to coordinating conjunctions because they can be used to link two independent clauses. There are two main differences, however:

LOOKING AHEAD

Comma Fault

In Chapter 16, on page 462, you'll learn more about comma faults and run-on sentences.

1. When two independent clauses are joined by a coordinating conjunction, a comma is used between the two clauses. When two independent clauses are joined by a conjunctive adverb or a transitional phrase, a semicolon is used.

2. Although coordinating conjunctions always appear as the first element in a second clause, conjunctive adverbs and transitional phrases do not have fixed positions. They can appear in various positions within a second clause. When they appear as the first element in the second clause, they are usually followed by a comma. When they appear elsewhere in the second clause, they are set off by commas.

No matter where a conjunctive adverb or a transitional phrase appears in a second clause, the independent clauses should be joined by a semicolon. If two independent clauses are joined only by a comma, you will have a comma fault and a run-on sentence.

We have several highly qualified applicants; Ms. Trimble, *for example,* has an M.B.A. from Syracuse.

We had many unexpected delays in construction; the work, *however,* was completed only one month behind schedule.

We had many unexpected delays in construction; the scheduled completion date, *as a result,* was revised several times.

13.15 | Interjections

An **interjection** is a word or group of words that expresses strong feeling or sudden emotion. An interjection has no grammatical relationship to any other word in a sentence. It stands by itself. Usually an interjection, or an exclamation, is punctuated with an exclamation point.

Good!	A hole in one!	Ouch! I stubbed my toe.
Surprise!	Well done!	Wow! Look at the cost!

If the exclamation is mild, or if it is used to begin a sentence, it can be followed by a comma: *Oh, I see what you mean.* Unless you are composing advertising copy, you will rarely use interjections in workplace writing. Save interjections and exclamation points for your personal writing.

Name _____

Class _____ Date _____

PRACTICE 1

Independent and Dependent Clauses: Part A

Instructions: Underline all words in each independent clause.

EXAMPLE: Since we conferred last week, <u>the situation has grown worse.</u>

1. Will you be free for lunch next Thursday?
2. Will you be ready when I call?
3. Forgetting her manners, she failed to introduce herself.
4. I am tired, but I feel satisfied.
5. Consult with your attorney before making any legal commitments.
6. They tried to sell their holdings, but they could not find a buyer.
7. Either they will pay for damages, or we will seek legal action.
8. Although he is inexperienced, he learns quickly.
9. Please take advantage of our special offer while supplies last.
10. To be eligible, you and your spouse must attend an informative meeting.

Independent and Dependent Clauses: Part B

Instructions: In each sentence below, underline each dependent clause.

EXAMPLE: <u>Since we conferred last week,</u> the situation has grown worse.

11. Will you be ready when I call?
12. Will you be free for lunch next Thursday?
13. Forgetting her manners, she failed to introduce herself.
14. Mail a check for the balance before you forget.
15. Although I am tired, I feel satisfied.
16. Consult with your attorney before making any legal commitments.
17. Consult with your attorney before you make any legal commitments.
18. We will seek legal action if we must.
19. Although he is inexperienced, he learns quickly.
20. We will settle our account when you fulfill the terms of the contract.

Name _____

Class _____ Date _____

Types of Sentences

Instructions: In the blank, indicate whether the sentence is simple, compound, complex, or compound-complex.

EXAMPLE: **Since we talked, the situation has improved.**　　　　　EX. <u>complex</u>

1. Will you be ready when I call?　　　　　1._____

2. Forgetting her manners, she failed to introduce herself.　　　　　2._____

3. If you want my advice, sell that stock before it's too late.　　　　　3._____

4. I am tired, but I feel satisfied.　　　　　4._____

5. I feel tired but satisfied.　　　　　5._____

6. Consult with your attorney before making any legal commitments.　　　　　6._____

7. When Ruth left for lunch, Joan went with her, but Cher remained in the office.　　　　　7._____

8. Either they will pay for damages, or we will seek legal action.　　　　　8._____

9. We will seek legal action unless they pay for damages.　　　　　9._____

10. Please take advantage of our special offer while there is still time.　　　　　10._____

11. You may remain in the room; however, if you interrupt the discussion, you will be asked to leave.　　　　　11._____

12. If you are married, you and your spouse may be able to file a joint return, or you may file separate returns.　　　　　12._____

13. Both you and your spouse must include all your income, exemptions, and deductions on your joint return.　　　　　13._____

14. When preparing your résumé, list all your jobs in reverse chronological order.　　　　　14._____

15. When you prepare your résumé, list all your jobs in reverse chronological order, and specify your duties in each.　　　　　15._____

16. Get out and stay out.　　　　　16._____

17. Strike while the iron is hot.　　　　　17._____

18. Although my supervisor gave me a superior rating, she did not recommend me for promotion.　　　　　18._____

19. My supervisor gave me a superior rating, but she did not recommend me for a promotion.　　　　　19._____

20. Although my supervisor gave me a superior rating, she did not recommend me for a promotion, so I am filing a grievance.　　　　　20._____

PRACTICE 3

Complex Sentences

Instructions: For each complex sentence below, write *N* in the blank if the sentence follows the natural sequence; write *R* if the sequence is in reverse order. Add commas as needed.

EXAMPLE: **The situation has improved since we talked.**　　　　　EX. _____N_____

1. When the patents expire this plant will close.　　　　　　　　　　1. _____

2. Always proofread your paper carefully before you submit it.　　　 2. _____

3. Unless business improves soon we will be forced to close.　　　　 3. _____

4. Do not enter the room while filming is in progress.　　　　　　　 4. _____

5. He continued to maintain his innocence despite the prosecutor's efforts
to discredit his testimony.　　　　　　　　　　　　　　　　　　　5. _____

6. We will not place an order now because we are overstocked.　　　 6. _____

7. Before I leave let me congratulate you.　　　　　　　　　　　　　7. _____

8. The jury found her guilty although she continued to proclaim her innocence.　8. _____

9. If I don't make a deposit today I will be overdrawn on my account.　9. _____

10. The attorney read the will as soon as all parties were present.　　 10. _____

11. Bertha keeps a separate record of her business expenses whenever she travels.　11. _____

12. Until I hear from you I will take no further action.　　　　　　　12. _____

13. As soon as we arrived the conference began.　　　　　　　　　　13. _____

14. Even if he was right he should not have proceeded without further instructions.　14. _____

15. Although he is still a minor he is old enough to be responsible.　　15. _____

16. Because she was highly capable she advanced quickly in the organization.　16. _____

17. We will continue to press our case until we receive an acceptable response.　17. _____

18. Even though the auditorium was large it could not accommodate the huge
crowd that had gathered.　　　　　　　　　　　　　　　　　　　18. _____

19. List all your jobs in reverse chronological order when you prepare your résumé.　19. _____

20. Don't feel discouraged if you fail to find a job immediately after graduation.　20. _____

Name _____

Class _____ Date _____

PRACTICE 4

Correlating Conjunctions

Instructions: In the blank, write the correlating conjunction that will complete the sentence.

EXAMPLE: **Either the bank _____ I made an error.**   EX. _____ **or** _____

1. Either fax _____ e-mail the information.   1. _____

2. I am as sure _____ I can be.   2. _____

3. I am not _____ sure as I once was.   3. _____

4. Both the original _____ revised editions contained the
   same error.   4. _____

5. Neither the index _____ the glossary included it.   5. _____

6. They not only gave us lunch _____ invited us for supper.   6. _____

PRACTICE 5

Conjunctive Adverbs and Transitional Phrases

Instructions: Punctuate the following sentences correctly.

EXAMPLE: **The salary is not very good however the benefits are excellent.**

1. The attorney's arguments were convincing therefore the jury voted to acquit the accused.

2. The attorney's arguments were convincing the jury voted therefore to acquit the accused.

3. The sale will last the entire month moreover it will involve all departments.

4. All items have been drastically reduced this coat for example is now half price.

5. She explained her position to me however I remain unconvinced.

6. He explained his position to me I remain unconvinced however of its validity.

7. The two sides bargained for months but failed to agree finally an arbiter was called.

8. We should not expect too much of Leonard he is after all still a trainee.

9. I am sorry you disagree with us nevertheless we will proceed as scheduled.

10. We are facing a shortage of parts thus we must lay off some employees.

11. We arrived late hence we are sitting in the last row.

12. Sales will be going up soon on the other hand costs will rise as well.

13. He rejected the job offer instead he chose to work for the government.

14. I disagree with your conclusion in fact I disagree with your premise.

PRACTICE 6

Interjections and Conjunctions: Part A

Instructions: Punctuate the following statements correctly.

EXAMPLE: Ouch/That hurts∧

1. Hurrah
2. No she never returned your call
3. What a remarkable performance
4. Unbelievable She actually used to work for Howard Hughes
5. Gee I never considered organizing the report that way
6. Wow Did you see the latest sales figures
7. Oh I'm just a little tired I guess
8. Watch out Don't touch that
9. Well I never
10. Well I never expected to win anyway.

Interjections and Conjunctions: Part B

Instructions: In the following note, cross out each error and write your correction above it. Insert any punctuation that has been left out.

Like I said in my last memo, we are not only losing sales but we are losing some salespeople too. This is not as bad as it first appears because we were going to try and hire some new salespeople anyway. You probably have read where the reason sales are down is because demand has fallen in our Asian markets, consequently we were unable to meet last quarter's sales quota. Providing this downward trend in demand is reversed I have no doubt but what our sales will soon be back to record levels. And our branch back to its usual position as number one.

PRACTICE 7

Composition: Using Conjunctions

Instructions: Compose complete sentences according to the instructions in parentheses. Then, identify each sentence as *simple, compound, complex,* or *compound-complex.*

EXAMPLE: **(a sentence beginning with *Although*)**
 <u>**Although he is still a minor, he is old enough to be responsible.**</u> **(complex)**

1. (a sentence in natural sequence with *since*)_____

_____

2. (a sentence in reverse sequence with *unless*)_____

_____

3. (a sentence beginning with *Because*)_____

_____

4. (a sentence containing *not only. . . but also*)_____

_____

5. (a sentence containing *however* set off by commas)_____

_____

6. (a sentence beginning with *Even though*)_____

_____

7. (a sentence containing *either. . . or*)_____

_____

8. (a sentence containing *in fact*)_____

_____

9. (a sentence containing *as a result*)_____

_____

10. (a sentence containing *furthermore*)_____

_____

Words That Perform Other Jobs

Unit 5—Editing Review

Instructions: This Editing Review deals with the concepts you have studied so far. You will review these concepts by editing the following passage from a company manual. The manual instructs new assistant managers on how to conduct an employee appraisal interview. As you read the passage, use the information you have learned in the first five units to help you locate errors. Cross out all errors you find, and write corrections in the space above them.

Appraisal Interviews

Like a manager, you will assess how each of the employees for who you are

responsible are doing. You will do this formal through an appraisal interview. This

is a meeting held among a supervisor and a employee to review the employee's

performance rating and, using that evaluation as a bases, discussing the quality of

the employees' work and methods for improving them.

These here meetings should be holded for each employee. The length of

interviewes are normally not over 30 minutes. Those interviews should be conducted

in or a private room. So that what is said is keeped among yourselfs.

Purposes of Employee Appraisal

There is four purposes for conducting an appraisal of employee performance:

1. To encourage well behavior or to corrected below standard performance.

2. To satisfy each employees' curiosity about how they is doing.

3. To provide an opportunity for developing employee skilles.

4. Providing a foundation for latter judgments, rises in pay or promotions.

(Continued on next page)

continued from page 399

Seven Steps in the Appraisal Interview

Here are a summary of the seven steps in the appraisal interview process. Each of these steps will have been discussed in farther detail in the next section.

1. Prepare the employee to be coming to compare notes. That way you have your facts at hand. And the employee has his or her's.

2. Compare accomplishments to targets. And ask the employee to share a self assessment with yourself. Don't be vague, instead be specific about goals and how closely the employee has come to meeting them expectations. Discuss instances where the employee's opinion is different than your's.

3. Be sure and give credit for accomplishments. Do not focus on deficiencies. Because you want the employee to know that you recognize what him or her did good.

4. Review things that have not accomplish. Emphasize where improvement is needed, and explore with the employee how this can be done and why the employee needs to improve. (Like you will see, steps 3 and 4 can bestest be accomplished using the "sandwich" technique. Which will be described later.)

5. Avoid of setting in judgment. If there is responsibility to be shared acknowledge it, however don't let the employee blame you for their shortcomingses.

6. Prior to the next meeting agree on goals to be meeted. Relate them to behaviors from the current period. Sit the stage for a more better appraisal next time.

7. Review what you can do to be of more greater help with the employee. Make it clearly that you are there not only to evaluate performance but helping the employee achieve success. Then follow through. And do it.

Link & Learn

USING OTHER PARTS OF SPEECH IN BUSINESS CAREERS

GOAL: Reinforce what you learned about prepositions, conjunctions, and interjections in Unit 5 by using the Internet to visit business Websites.

STEP 1 Go to *englishworkshop.glencoe.com*, the address for *The English Workshop* Website. Click first on Unit 5; then click on the Link & Learn connection to access a list of business Websites you may use in this activity. Select a site and click on it.

STEP 2 Skim the topics available on the home page of the Website. Find a topic that interests you and click on that link.

STEP 3 Read the material, and make a printout of at least one page.

STEP 4 After you reread the page you printed out, do the following:

a. Choose two short paragraphs (at least five lines each) or one long paragraph (at least ten lines), and draw a box around each preposition. Draw an arrow from each preposition to its object.

b. Return to the Unit 5 Link & Learn Website list, and click on another link. Print out a page. Find a point of comparison between the first site you visited and the second: it could be the appearance, the types of information offered, or the organizations listed. Jot down the point on the back of your first printout.

c. Return to the Unit 5 Link & Learn Website list and click on a third link. Find a point of comparison among the three sites you have visited. Jot it down on the back of your first printout.

d. On the back of your first printout, write several sentences based on your points of comparison between the first two Websites. Use either *among* or *between* correctly.

e. Write several sentences based on your point of comparison among all three Websites. Use either *among* or *between* correctly.

f. On the back of your first printout, write a note to a friend that describes the information available on the Websites you visited. Include at least one compound sentence with a coordinating conjunction, at least one complex sentence with a subordinating conjunction, and at least one sentence that begins with an interjection. Write a closing for your note and sign your name.

STEP 5 When you have completed your work, proofread it. Write your name on your work, and give it to your instructor.

Sentences and Punctuation

- *Chapter 14* **Effective Sentences**
- *Chapter 15* **End-of-Sentence Punctuation**

Profile in Success

Agribusiness Administrators: Keeping It Down to Earth

Tim Coauette • *Crookston, Minnesota* • *Red Power International, Inc.*

Tim Coauette never expected to be speaking before groups of Minnesota farmers at the age of 43. After all, he had been a farmer himself—not a public speaker. A back injury forced him to give up working the family farm, however, and in 1997 he enrolled at the University of Minnesota at Crookston to earn an associate degree in agricultural business management. Now Tim is a service manager warranty clerk for Red Power International, a company that repairs combines, tractors, and trucks. He schedules the work for customers and submits warranty claims to manufacturers. Twice a year he conducts service clinics on the care and repair of farm combines and tractors.

Think About It ... Is Honesty the Best Policy?

When an injury suddenly ended Tim Coauette's farming career, he found himself back in a classroom years after high school.

- *How might Tim's college experience as a returning adult student have contributed to his philosophy of communication?*

- *What factors in Tim's life have helped him become a successful public speaker and service manager clerk?*

- *Do you agree with Tim's philosophy?*

Tim's supervisor used to present the clinics. One time he was ill, and Tim filled in. He did such a good job that he's been doing the clinics ever since. Tim credits the speech class he took in college with developing the confidence and communication skills he needed to make a presentation before a group.

Tim's philosophy is simple: customers will get your message if you communicate with them openly and honestly.

"Talk to the people," he says. "Don't try to baffle them with four-dollar words or paint a pretty picture. Keep it down to earth, like they were sitting across the table from you."

Career Connections

AGRIBUSINESS CAREERS

Learn more about the work of foresters, applied economists, farmers, and others in the agribusiness field by connecting to the following sites listed at *The English Workshop* Website. Go to *englishworkshop.glencoe.com*. Click first on Unit 6 and then on Career Connections.

- National FFA Organization Career Clusters

- Agricultural Education National Headquarters

- United States Department of Agriculture (USDA) Forest Service

- USDA National Agricultural Statistics Service

- American Agriculture Economics Association

See page 451, **Link & Learn: Punctuating a Variety of Sentences in Agribusiness Careers**, for an additional online career activity.

Effective Sentences

CHAPTER 14 PREVIEW

In this chapter you will review the criteria for a sentence and the four sentence types. You will discover how to use different sentence structures and will also study the qualities of effective writing. This chapter offers no Programmed Reinforcement; nonetheless, you will apply what you have learned in the Practices. Finally, you will visit a holiday Website while enhancing your knowledge of effective sentence writing.

OBJECTIVES

After completing this chapter, you will be able to

- Recall the criteria for a sentence and the four basic types of sentences.
- Recognize the effectiveness of using a variety of sentence types.
- Recall the use of conjunctions in various sentence types.
- Decide when and how to combine sentences.
- Determine when to use simple sentences for clarity and effectiveness.
- Revise your writing for conciseness and variety.
- Define and organize a paragraph according to three methods: chronological, spatial, and topical.
- Identify the seven characteristics of effective writing.

Study Plan for Chapter 14

The Study Plan for Chapter 14 offers a set of strategies that will help you learn and review the chapter material.

❶ **Compound Sentences**: Cover each coordinating conjunction in a sentence and read the words to the right of it. Then read the words to the left of it. If each side of the coordinating conjunction includes an independent clause, the sentence is compound or compound-complex.

❷ **Complex Sentences**: If a sentence has one dependent clause, it may be complex. A sentence with at least two independent clauses and at least one dependent one is compound-complex.

❸ **Coordinating Conjunctions in Simple Sentences**: Not all sentences with coordinating conjunctions are compound or compound-complex. If a coordinating conjunction simply connects a list of words or phrases, the sentence is not compound.

❹ **Repetition**: Underline all repeated words. Replace repeated words with different words or omit them as you combine the remaining parts of sentences.

You have now completed your study of all eight parts of speech. In this section you will review some of the material you studied about the sentence while discovering how you can use the parts of speech as tools for composing more effective sentences.

14.1 Parts of Speech Review

You know how to form the plurals and possessives of both regular and irregular nouns, and you know how to form and use the various types of pronouns. You can correctly form all six tenses, plus the progressive, of both regular and irregular verbs. You are familiar with the voice and mood of the verb, and you know how to use verbals. You are able to construct and use the positive, comparative, and superlative forms of adjectives and adverbs. You are familiar with a variety of prepositions, and know how to use conjunctions to connect ideas. Plus, you know a great deal more.

Related Parts

As you are aware, what is most important is not how you use these parts of speech separately, but how you put them together in a sentence. That is why, throughout the course of your study, you have examined both the role each part of speech plays within a sentence and the relationship each part has with other parts. For example, you studied nouns and verbs separately; then you studied them together when you focused on the necessary agreement between subject and predicate. You examined adjectives and adverbs and their roles as modifiers; then you looked at the problems caused by misplaced modifiers.

The parts of speech are exactly that—parts. These parts must be put together to form a whole—the sentence. As you recall in Chapter 2, the sentence, not the word, is the basic unit of communication because it is the sentence that expresses a complete thought.

14.2 Sentence Criteria

For a sentence to be a sentence, it must meet these requirements:

- It must contain a subject.
- It must contain a verb.
- It must express a complete thought.

None of the following statements is a sentence because none of them meets all the requirements listed above.

1. Your order of May 10.
2. Processed by the clerk yesterday.
3. Your order of May 10. Was processed by the clerk yesterday.
4. Your order of May 10, processed by the shipping department yesterday.
5. When your order of May 10 was processed by the clerk yesterday.

The next statements are sentences; they meet all the requirements.

Your order of May 10 was processed by the shipping department yesterday.
When your order of May 10 was processed by the shipping department
yesterday, the supervisor noted an error on the invoice.

Word Sequence

For a statement to be a sentence it must meet one more requirement: the words must be in a particular sequence. Look at these two statements:

To walks work morning Sue every.
Walks to work every morning Sue.

The first statement is nonsense; it is a series of words strung together. The second seems to make sense, but not in this sequence. As speakers of English we want to rearrange the words, moving *Sue* to the front.

Sue walks to work every morning.

This statement is a sentence. It has a subject and a verb, and it expresses a complete thought. Moreover, it *sounds* like a sentence.

In other words, English sentences must do more than contain a subject and a verb and express a complete thought. The words they contain must be in a sequence that can be understood by the reader.

14.3 Sentence Types

There are a variety of ways to translate your ideas into sentences. The structure of your sentences can vary. Some can follow a *normal* or an *inverted sequence,* as you saw in Chapter 8. Some can follow a *natural* or a *reverse sequence,* as you saw in Chapter 13. Your sentences can be short or long, simple or complex. They can also vary in type. The last chapter examined the four basic types of sentences found in English:

1. simple
2. compound
3. complex
4. compound-complex

Grammar Tip

As you recall, the *simple sentence* consists of a subject and a verb that together express a complete thought. The *compound sentence* is composed of two or more independent clauses connected by a coordinating conjunction—such as *and, or,* or *but*—or by a semicolon. The *complex sentence* consists of an independent clause and a dependent clause. The *compound-complex sentence* includes at least two independent clauses and at least one dependent clause.

The following series of sentences illustrates the richness and variety of all four types.

SIMPLE SENTENCES

I bought a computer.
Kathleen and I bought a computer.
Kathleen and I shopped for and bought a computer.

COMPOUND SENTENCES

I bought a computer, but I don't know how to use it.
I bought a computer, and I'm glad I did.
I bought a computer, but I don't know how to use it, so I'm taking a course in computer programming.

COMPLEX SENTENCES

Although I bought a computer, I don't know how to use it.
I bought a computer even though I don't know how to use it.

COMPOUND-COMPLEX SENTENCES

Although I bought a computer, I don't know how to use some of its special features, so I'm taking a course at night in advanced software applications.
As soon as I bought a computer, I was glad I did, for it has been invaluable in my work.

SECTION B
Writers' Strategies

In this section you will look at how writers use the various tools of English to build effective messages. You will also explore the common characteristics of effective writing.

14.4 Sentence Options

Like the parts of speech, the various sentence types serve as tools for constructing effective messages. You might ask why there are so many ways for people to express themselves through sentences. Couldn't we communicate with only simple sentences in normal sequence? The answer is *no*.

There are several reasons for having a variety of sentence types. First and most important, the variety gives you options. Having options allows you to stress, or emphasize, some points more than others depending on how you construct your sentences. It also allows you to make clear to your reader the exact relationship between ideas. Look at this sentence:

> According to demographers, Vermont is the most rural state in America.

Now look at the effect if you alter the sentence and withhold the name of the state until the end:

> Demographers say that the most rural state in America is Vermont.
> The most rural state in America, according to demographers, is Vermont.

Note how interest builds as you wait to find out the identity of the state.

Altering sentence patterns to build interest and suspense is also typical in awards ceremonies. The presenter makes some appropriate remarks about the importance of the award and then proclaims, "And the winner of this year's award is . . . "

Mystery writers employ the same principle. In the final chapter the detective calls all the suspects into the same room, summarizes everything that has happened, and reviews all the clues as to the identity of the killer. Then, as the detective announces, "The identity of the killer is . . . ," the room goes dark and shots ring out.

Grammar Tip

Compound and Complex Sentences for Clarity

Use conjunctions to show the relationship between the ideas in two or more clauses.

Being able to choose among sentence types also helps you express your ideas as effectively as possible. Simple sentences are clear and direct. Because they contain one main thought, well-written simple sentences are easy for the reader to understand. Hence most writing in the workplace is dominated by simple sentences. Sometimes, however, simple sentences cannot adequately express an idea. In these cases the writer has the option of using other types of sentences. Look at these two sentences:

SIMPLE

I was the most qualified applicant.
I was offered the position.

These two sentences are clear. However, as simple sentences, they cannot express the idea that being offered the position was the result of being the most qualified. To express this idea the two statements must be combined by using either a coordinating or a subordinating conjunction.

COMPOUND

I was the most qualified applicant, *so* I was offered the position.

The same is true of these two sentences:

SIMPLE

I was the most qualified applicant.
I was not offered the position.

To express the contrast between the two ideas, you must combine them into one sentence:

COMPOUND

I was the most qualified applicant, *but* I was not offered the position.

In each example the two coordinating conjunctions do more than link the two independent clauses. They clarify the relationship between the clauses.

You could also choose to express these relationships as complex sentences:

COMPLEX

Because I was the most qualified applicant, I was offered the position.
Although I was the most qualified applicant, I was not offered the position.

Coordinating and subordinating conjunctions thus serve the same purpose of linking two clauses together and showing the relationship between them. They also show the relative importance of the clauses. In a compound sentence the writer suggests that the two independent clauses are of equal importance. In a complex sentence the writer suggests that the information in the independent clause is more important than the information in the dependent clause.

The following chart reviews common conjunctions and the relationships between clauses they express.

CONJUNCTIONS THAT LINK TWO CLAUSES	
Coordinating Conjunction	**Use**
and, or, nor	Introduce ideas that *add to* or *reinforce* the idea in the preceding clause
but, yet	Introduce ideas that *contrast with* the idea in the preceding clause
for	Introduces an idea that is a *cause of* the idea in the preceding clause
so	Introduces an idea that is a *result of* the idea in the preceding clause
Subordinating Conjunction	**Use**
after, as soon as, since	Introduce relationships in *time*
although, though	Introduce ideas that *contrast with* the idea in the independent clause
as ... as, more than	Introduce a *comparison* between the two clauses
as, as if, as though	Introduce the *manner of* the action in the independent clause
because, as, since	Introduce ideas that are a *cause of* the idea in the independent clause
if, even if, unless	Introduce *conditional* relationships
where, wherever	Introduce the *place of* the action in the independent clause

[handwritten margin notes: sphygmomanometer; when; unless when; Till]

14.6 Sentence Combining for Clarity

The use of various types of sentences is a mark of mature, precise thinking. Combining several simple sentences to make a compound or complex sentence is often a good way to achieve clarity. Let's look at a few examples:

California College is located in Torrance, California.
California College will celebrate its centennial anniversary in 2008.

Grammar Tip

Sentence Combining for Clarity

You can create complex sentences through the use of relative clauses introduced by relative pronouns.

Relative Pronouns

The examples on the previous page are two *separate* statements about California College. No subordinating conjunction such as *although*, *because*, *since*, or *if* would show a relationship between them. Joining the two statements with the coordinating conjunction *and* would not relate them in a significant way.

The ideas expressed in each sentence are of equal weight. However, if you want to convey the sense of their relative importance, you could combine the two by using the relative pronoun *which*. How you combine them depends on which statement is more important. If the centennial celebration is more important, you would write the following:

California College, which is located in Torrance, California, will celebrate its centennial anniversary in 2008.

If the college's location is more important, write the sentence this way:

California College, which celebrated its centennial anniversary in 2008, is located in Torrance, California.

Now look at this pair of sentences:

Nigel is a skilled mechanic.
Nigel has opened his own repair shop.

These two sentences may or may not have a causal relationship. How you decide to relate them—if you decide to relate them—will tell your reader what to think. Here are some possibilities:

Nigel is a skilled mechanic and has opened his own repair shop.
Nigel, who is a skilled mechanic, has opened his own repair shop.
Nigel, who has opened his own repair shop, is a skilled mechanic.
Because Nigel is a skilled mechanic, he has opened his own repair shop.

Sometimes the relationship between two statements seems quite evident. In these cases the relationship should be clearly expressed. Look at these two sentences:

Mia led her division in sales for four straight quarters.
Mia was named Sales Representative of the Year.

For the sake of clarity, these two statements should be combined into one. If you want to stress cause and effect, you would write the following:

Because Mia led her division in sales for four straight quarters, she was named Sales Representative of the Year.

As you know, this is a complex sentence because it combines an independent clause introduced by the subordinating conjunction *because*.

You could also make either statement a relative clause, thus giving additional emphasis to the remaining statement.

> Mia, who led her division in sales for four straight quarters, was named Sales Representative of the Year.
>
> Mia, who was named Sales Representative of the Year, led her division in sales for four straight quarters.

The relative clauses in these last two sentences are also dependent clauses. This means they do not express a complete thought even though they have a subject and a verb. To be grammatically complete, they must be linked to an independent clause. Thus, one way to form a complex sentence is through the use of relative clauses—clauses that contain the relative pronouns *who, whom, which,* and *that.*

Grammar Tip

Relative Pronouns Refer

Relative pronouns begin dependent clauses and refer to a noun or pronoun in an independent clause.

14.7 Simple Sentences for Clarity

Although complex sentences often convey complicated meanings more clearly than do several simple sentences, it is not always true that *complicated* complex sentences are more effective. The quality of your writing does not necessarily improve with complexity. In reports, memos, and speeches, simple sentences may be preferred. Look at this sentence:

> I was initially reluctant to invest in a new computer because of the cost of a full system and my unfamiliarity with many of its advanced features, but as soon as I shopped for, selected, and bought it, I was glad I did, for my new computer, with its sophisticated word-processing program and extensive memory capacity, has been invaluable in my work and my children have been able to burn CDs and play a variety of games with highly sophisticated graphics that are available with that new model.

The long compound-complex sentence beginning the paragraph above is grammatically correct, but it is not an effective sentence. It is needlessly complicated. The meaning of this statement would be clearer if it were broken down into smaller sentences. Compare this revised version for clarity.

> I was initially reluctant to invest in a new computer. I was concerned about the cost of a full system and my unfamiliarity with many of its advanced features. As soon as I bought it, however, I was glad I did. My new computer, with its sophisticated word processing program and extensive memory capacity, has been invaluable in my work. Moreover, my children have been able to burn CDs and play a variety of games with highly sophisticated graphics, which are available with that new model.

Here three simple sentences and two complex sentences express the ideas much more clearly and effectively than the long, awkward sentence above.

The final reason for having so many sentence options is *variety*. Too much of the same thing can be dull and monotonous, whatever the subject. Hence the skilled writer takes care to vary sentence patterns and lengths. Compare the next two job application letters.

There is nothing grammatically wrong with Eduardo's first letter. The information is impressive, but the letter is dull and repetitive. Almost all the sentences begin with the word *I*. All are simple sentences written in the sequence of subject + verb + object. All of the sentences are about the same length. In short, this is not an effective letter because it lacks variety.

Eduardo Vargas
2525 Quinton Street, Apartment 6G, Shreveport, LA 71103

May 11, 20--

Ms. De Vorzon
817 Spanish Springs Road
Sparks, NV 89434

Dear Ms. De Vorzon:

I am writing to apply for the position of administrative assistant in your personnel department. I saw the position advertised in *The New York Times* of Sunday, May 10.

I have enclosed my résumé with this letter. My résumé gives you a detailed account of my education, skills, and experience. I believe my education, skills, and experience qualify me for this position. I will graduate from Hopewell County College. I will earn an associate of science degree in business administration. I took courses in Human Resources and Development, Wage and Salary Administration, and Personnel Research and Measurement. I believe these courses gave me an understanding of the concerns the human resources specialist must face. I have also learned about these concerns through my work experience. I was employed as a salesperson at Schmidt's Department Store for two years. I was in the children's clothing department. I am now the evening manager of the housewares department at Schmidt's Department Store.

I believe I would be an asset to your company.

I will call your office on Monday, May 18. I will inquire about arranging a mutually convenient interview. I would be happy to provide you with any additional information. I may be reached at home at (718) 755-9932.

Sincerely,

Eduardo Vargas
Enclosure

Now notice how sentence combining improves the reader's experience.

This second version of Eduardo's letter is much more effective than the first one. The letter has been revised by varying sentence lengths and patterns. Complex sentences are used as well as simple sentences, and the sentences do not always begin with the same subject.

The difference between the two letters is not one of grammar or content, but style. Style is not *what* is said but the *way* it is said. In most kinds of writing, effective style demands variety. Make your writing interesting and effective by varying your sentences in length, pattern, and type.

Eduardo Vargas
2525 Quinton Street, Apartment 6G, Shreveport, LA 71103

May 11, 20—

Ms. De Vorzon
817 Spanish Springs Road
Sparks, NV 89434

Dear Ms. De Vorzon:

Please consider my application for the position of administrative assistant in your personnel department as advertised in *The New York Times* of Sunday, May 10. My education, skills, and experience, which are detailed in the enclosed résumé, should qualify me for this position.

I will graduate from Hopewell County College with an associate of science degree in business administration. My course of study included classes in Human Resources and Development, Wage and Salary Administration, and Personnel Research and Measurement, which gave me an understanding of the concerns facing the human resources specialist. This understanding has been complemented by my practical experience in retailing. Having worked both as a salesperson in children's clothing and as the evening manager in housewares at Schmidt's Department Store, I have firsthand knowledge of these concerns. The combination of educational background and work experience should, I believe, make me an asset to your company.

May I have the opportunity of an interview? I will call your office on Monday, May 18, to arrange a mutually convenient time. Please telephone me at (718) 755-9932 if you require any additional information.

Sincerely,

Eduardo Vargas
Enclosure

SECTION C
Paragraphs

Having studied how to combine parts of speech into effective sentences, you will now learn how to combine sentences into effective paragraphs.

14.9 Definition of a Paragraph

Simply defined, a **paragraph** is a group of sentences on the same topic. Just as periods and capital letters signal to the reader that one sentence has ended and a new thought is about to begin, a paragraph signals that one subject has been completed and a new one is about to be introduced.

Because paragraphs mark major divisions of thought, they serve as units on which the reader can focus. In workplace writing, for example, most paragraphs tend to be short, because short paragraphs are easier and faster for a busy reader to skim or read than long, complicated ones. Long, complicated paragraphs should be broken down into separate subjects, each of which should be placed in its own paragraph.

Paragraphs can be organized in a variety of ways. The method you use will depend on your topic. Three popular methods are the **chronological,** the **spatial,** and the **topical.**

Chronological

A chronological arrangement organizes material according to a time sequence. Instructions on how to operate a machine, fill out a form, or find an address, for example, lend themselves to chronological organization.

Spatial

In a spatial arrangement you group your material according to location. A description of the arrangement of your office or sales floor or the layout of a new mall or vegetable garden would lend itself to spatial organization.

Topical

Perhaps the most popular organizational principle is the topical. In this method you make a general statement and then support it with particular examples or illustrations. A report recommending various steps that should be taken to solve a problem could be organized topically.

In workplace writing, paragraphs are conceived in terms of their purpose. Eduardo's letter to Ms. De Vorzon follows what is known as the AIDA formula. **AIDA** stands for **Attention + Interest + Desire + Action.**

Attention. In the opening paragraph Eduardo attracts Ms. De Vorzon's *attention* by asking her to consider his application for the position of administrative assistant.

Interest. The second paragraph is designed to develop Ms. De Vorzon's *interest* in Eduardo. In it he tells her that his education, skills, and experience make him a qualified applicant.

Desire. The third paragraph develops Eduardo's background and gives details of his education and experience. Its purpose is to increase Ms. De Vorzon's *desire* to speak with him about the position.

Action. The final paragraph is the *action* portion of the letter. Here Eduardo requests an interview. Ms. De Vorzon's granting this request is the action Eduardo wishes her to take.

The AIDA formula is frequently used in this and other kinds of situations requiring persuasive messages.

SUCCESS TIP

EXAM TACTIC When you take an exam, don't panic if you don't know an answer immediately. Move on to the questions you can answer. Then return to the ones you don't know. Build on success, and don't block your thinking with initial anxiety.

14.10 Characteristics of Effective Writing

You have been exploring how the parts of speech and the types of sentences can be used to create clear, effective messages. You will now learn about the seven qualities that are characteristic of effective writing.

1. Correctness

A message should be grammatically correct. Grammatical errors create a very bad impression of the writer, and they can be very distracting and annoying to the reader.

The concept of correctness extends beyond grammatical correctness. Not only should grammar and spelling be correct, but content should also be correct. A mechanically correct letter that contains the wrong date for an important meeting, specifies the wrong size or quantity for an order, or quotes an incorrect price is seriously flawed.

2. Courteousness

Good manners help establish and maintain good relationships. *Please* and *Thank you* are important elements of writing on the job, whether they are expressly stated or only implied. Compare the pairs below.

INSTEAD OF THIS: We have received your order for five reams of letterhead stationery.

SAY THIS: ✔ Thank you for your order of five reams of letterhead stationery. (*Courteous*)

3. Consideration

Being *courteous* and *considerate* are related ideas, but they are not identical. *Courteousness* refers more to word choice, as in choosing words such as *Please* and *Thank you*. *Consideration* refers more to a general attitude, what is usually called the "you-attitude." In other words the effective writer always tries to see the situation from the reader's viewpoint.

| INSTEAD OF THIS: | You didn't send your check. |
| SAY THIS: | ✔We have not yet received your check. (*Tactful*) |

The considerate writer focuses on the reader's needs, not the writer's.

| INSTEAD OF THIS: | We must have your check for $240 by August 15. If we don't receive it, we will take legal action. |
| SAY THIS: | ✔To protect your valuable credit rating, please send your check for $240 by August 15. (*Tactful*) |

4. Completeness

A message is complete when it contains all the information that it should contain. Just what that information is depends on the nature of the message. For example, companies frequently are unable to fulfill a writer's request for information or products because the writer failed to include a return address. No matter how well written these requests are, they are incomplete and unsuccessful.

An announcement that fails to include the location, an order that fails to indicate color, a phone message that omits the area code—all are incomplete and ineffective. A message must contain everything the particular situation requires.

| INSTEAD OF THIS: | The time for next week's board meeting has been changed to 3:15 p.m. |
| SAY THIS: | ✔The board meeting has been rescheduled for Tuesday, May 5, at 3:15 p.m. in Room 4. (*Complete*) |

5. Conciseness

A concise message is no longer than it needs to be to achieve its purpose. A 30-page report is concise if it requires 30 pages to achieve its purpose effectively. A nine-word sentence is not concise if the same information could have been stated in six words. Conciseness does not necessarily mean brevity, however, because concise messages must still be effective. A letter that simply says, "we refuse," is brief, but it is not an example of effective writing.

A concise message achieves its purpose without sacrificing correctness, courteousness, consideration, and completeness. A good writer eliminates unnecessary words and edits others to be more concise. Look at these

Internet Farmers

Farmers must be computer-literate. To earn a profit in a global economy, farmers surf the Internet to stay on top of the latest developments in areas such as pesticides and crop diseases.

examples and notice how the prepositional phrase in the wordy sentence was turned into the verb in the concise sentence.

WORDY:	These charges *are in excess of* those specified.
CONCISE:	✔These charges *exceed* those specified.

WORDY:	*I have come to the conclusion that we must change* our advertising strategy.
CONCISE:	✔*I have concluded that we must change* our advertising strategy.
MORE CONCISE:	✔We *must change* our advertising strategy.

Here is a list of some of the lifeless and wordy expressions found in older workplace correspondence, along with the preferred contemporary equivalent. Avoiding these expressions will help make your writing concise.

AVOID	PREFER	AVOID	PREFER
a check in the amount of	a check for	in the near future	soon
		in view of the fact that	since, because
at a later date	later	prior to the start of	before
at the present time	now	subsequent to	after
despite the fact that	although	until such time as	until
due to the fact that	since, because	will you be kind enough to	please
in order that	so		
in the event that	if	with reference to	about

6. Coherence

In a well-written message everything "hangs together." The message is unified and well organized. Information that does not belong in the message is left out; information that does belong is included. The ideas are presented clearly so that the reader can understand them. These ideas are connected and follow logically from one to another.

As you have seen, using coordinating and subordinating conjunctions to show the relationship between clauses is one method of achieving coherence.

INSTEAD OF THIS:	Your qualifications are excellent. Your qualifications do not meet our requirements. We are unable to offer you a position.
SAY THIS:	✔Although your qualifications are excellent, they do not meet our requirements. Hence we are unable to offer you a position. (*Coherent*)

Biomass

Biomass describes any organic matter that can be converted into usable energy. Cow manure, when converted into methane, may provide enough energy to operate a dairy farm. That means the future cow may be milked for more than just milk.

Irrelevant information should be omitted entirely. Where appropriate, it can be replaced by something more relevant.

INSTEAD OF THIS: Ms. Baginski and Ms. Cruz met for lunch to discuss the contract, to review the proposal, and the dessert was delicious.

SAY THIS: ✔Ms. Baginski and Ms. Cruz met for lunch to discuss the contract and to review the proposal.
(*Coherent*)

7. Clarity

Clarity is a general quality for which all good writers constantly strive. Effective messages are clear, readable, and understandable. Clarity is achieved by making wise word choices, constructing good sentences and paragraphs, and organizing the overall message in a coherent manner. Vague pronoun references and dangling modifiers contribute to a lack of clarity. So do unfamiliar words, poorly constructed sentences that fail to emphasize what is important, and paragraphs that lack focus and unity. Other characteristics of effective writing, including correctness, completeness, conciseness, and coherence, contribute to clarity as well. Sentences illustrating these qualities are also examples of clear writing.

These seven qualities, often termed the Seven Cs, are the characteristics of effective writing in the workplace and elsewhere. Whether you are writing a quick phone message, a brief e-mail, an important letter, or a lengthy report, it is important to keep these qualities in mind. When these characteristics are present, the result is effective communication that benefits both the reader and the writer. In the composition practices that follow, and in all your writing, strive to take on these characteristics.

Summary of the Seven Cs

Effective writing is

1. **Correct**—uses correct grammar and spelling as well as complete and accurate content.
2. **Courteous**—chooses words that show respect for the reader.
3. **Considerate**—adjusts tone to recognize the reader's viewpoint.
4. **Complete**—includes all necessary information to communicate the message.
5. **Concise**—limits length to words needed to achieve the purpose of the message.
6. **Coherent**—conveys a unified, well-organized message showing the proper relationship between ideas.
7. **Clear**—shows wise word choices combined with good sentence and paragraph construction.

CHAPTER 14 SUMMARY

In this chapter you learned that using different types of sentences will make your writing clearer and more interesting. The Seven Cs (or Characteristics) of effective writing are good measures to follow in all forms of writing, not simply workplace documents. With qualities such as completeness and courteousness in mind, you discovered that it is important to consider the needs and responses of those who will read and try to understand your written ideas. In addition to developing your skills with building sentences, you learned about organizing paragraphs. You examined ways to structure your sentences and thoughts chronologically, spatially, and topically.

Getting Connected

LEARNING FROM A CALENDAR WEBSITE

GOAL: Do you want to know which holidays are celebrated this month? Are you curious about what happened on this day 70 years ago? Find out at one of the many calendar Websites on the Internet. You can also do research on the history or customs of a holiday associated with a particular culture or discover what important events in history have occurred on your birthday.

After you've found an interesting research topic, you'll then create a paragraph, applying what you've learned in Chapter 14 about sentence variation, paragraph organization, and the characteristics of effective writing.

STEP 1 Go to *englishworkshop.glencoe.com,* the address for *The English Workshop* Website, and click on Unit 6. Next click on Getting Connected, and then click on Chapter 14. At the Chapter 14 Getting Connected option, you'll see a list of holiday, calendar, and history Websites. Select one of these sites to visit.

STEP 2 Scan the home page for search options. Select topics you find interesting and relevant to your life. You could read about a holiday during the year, a celebration taking place this month, or an event that happened on this day years ago. Or, you might want to focus on celebrations that are associated with a particular ethnicity or nationality.

STEP 3 Narrow your choice down to one. Online, read the information about the topic you selected. You may want to print it out so that you can highlight interesting points. The information should fill at least one page.

STEP 4 Using your classmates as your audience, write a paragraph of at least six original sentences about the topic you selected. Use at least three of the sentence types presented in Chapter 14. The ideas on the next page will help guide you through the writing process.

a. **Deciding what to write about:** Begin by jotting down a list of ideas that may interest your classmates or that you find interesting. You may explain why the holiday is celebrated, who celebrates it, how it got its name, or other information.

b. **Organizing the paragraph:** Review your ideas and determine which method of organization will work best: *chronological, spatial,* or *topical.* The history of a holiday could be organized in a time sequence or chronological order. You could use the spatial order by describing the arrangement or layout of a particular event that celebrates a holiday. If you make a general statement about a holiday and support that statement with examples or illustrations, you will be using topical organization.

c. **Developing the paragraph:** Write a rough draft, focusing on what you want to say. Don't worry about grammar at this point; just get your ideas down. When you're done, shift your focus to sentence types. Be sure you have at least three different sentence types represented. Aim for variety, clarity, and conciseness.

d. **Reviewing the paragraph:** Read your rough draft aloud. Underline repeated words and revise sentences as needed to eliminate repetition. Count the number of words in each sentence, and see if you have varied the lengths (most word-processing programs have a Word Count option under Tools). Can the word sequence in some sentences be rearranged to emphasize the most important ideas? As you work, remember what you have learned about the Seven Cs of effective writing.

e. **Finishing the draft:** Revise your work based on what you discovered in your review. If possible, find someone to read your revised paragraph. Ask the reader whether your ideas and descriptions are clear, concise, and above all interesting. If any sentences appear confusing to your reader, revise them.

STEP 5 After you've revised your paragraph a final time, turn it in to your instructor.

PRACTICE 5

Coherence and Clarity

Instructions: Rewrite the following passages to improve their coherence. Eliminate irrelevant information. Add suitable information if the sentence requires it. Reorganize and clarify ideas where needed. Write your revisions in the blanks provided.

EXAMPLE: **I have $10,000 to invest, and municipal bonds are tax free.**
<u>**I am going to invest $10,000 in tax-free municipal bonds.**</u>

1. The two new members of the faculty are Dr. Audrey Fazekas, who received her degree from the University of Texas, and Dr. David Fernandez, who grew up in Portland. _____
   _____
   _____
   _____

2. Armand was not a very good student. Ms. Juarez found him to be an intelligent and conscientious employee. Armand received frequent raises. _____
   _____
   _____
   _____

3. The submission deadline for the campus literary magazine is this Friday. I want my poem included in the literary magazine. My short story isn't good enough to submit. I must submit my poem to the literary magazine by Friday. _____
   _____
   _____

4. I have held a variety of jobs. In high school I worked as a busboy at the Chateau Monique. They served exotic food. I had an accident and broke my arm there one summer. When I was in junior high school, I had a paper route. I either walked or rode my bike. Each summer when I was off from college, some days I made ice cream and some days I sold it. I worked for a small ice cream company. As a high school senior I sold encyclopedias door to door. I used to own a set of World Book encyclopedias. Now I subscribe to an online encyclopedia service. After college I came to work for World Business Products. I work here now. _____
   _____
   _____
   _____
   _____

PRACTICE 6

Conciseness

Instructions: Substitute strong active verbs for verb phrases in the following sentences to make them more concise. Write your revisions in the space above each line.

agree
EXAMPLE: We ~~are in agreement~~ that a strike authorization vote is needed.

1. Ms. Geils ~~has~~ *did* ~~done~~ a survey *ed* ~~of~~ the owners of wood stoves.

2. The personnel director will *considered* ~~give consideration to~~ your application.

3. Mr. Odets ~~is supposed to~~ *made* make a record ~~of all~~ incoming calls.

4. An independent auditor will *did* ~~do~~ an analysis ~~of~~ our record-keeping ~~procedures~~.

5. Adaptation ~~to~~ the new procedures *were* ~~was~~ performed easily by the workers.

PRACTICE 7

Wordy Expressions

Instructions: Revise the following paragraph by eliminating wordy expressions and replacing them with more concise ones. Write your changes in the space above each line.

Due to the fact that ~~W~~ we have no openings ~~at the present time~~, ~~we are unable to~~ schedule you

for an interview. When a position becomes available ~~at a later date~~, we will ~~be in~~ contact ~~with~~

you ~~with reference to this position~~. Until *then* ~~such time as~~ a position becomes available, ~~will you~~

~~be kind enough to~~ complete the enclosed forms ~~for our files~~ in order that we may *to* keep your

application active.

Name _____

Class _____ Date _____

PRACTICE 8

Composition: Revising for Variety

Instructions: The following letter from a former employee to her supervisor is a request for a recommendation. Revise it to achieve a greater variety in sentence length, sequence, and type. Write your revised letter in the space provided.

Dear Ms. Tsuis:

I worked in your department in 2001 and 2002. I worked as a salesperson in women's apparel. I enjoyed working for you during this period. I feel I learned a great deal about merchandising during this time.

I will graduate from Colorado State College in June of this year. I will graduate with a B.S. degree in business administration. I will be seeking employment soon in the area of marketing. I would like to use your name as a reference.

I intend to start sending out my résumés on March 15. I hope I will hear from you before then. I would like to bring you up to date on my activities. I am enclosing a copy of my résumé.

I want to thank you for your help.

Sincerely,

Meagan Terry

_____
_____
_____
_____
_____
_____
_____
_____
_____
_____
_____
_____

Name _____

Class _____ Date _____

PRACTICE 9

Composition: Writing an Employment History

Instructions: On a job application form you may be asked to provide a brief employment history in paragraph form that answers the following questions: Where have you worked? When? What were your titles? What were your duties?

As you write your description, keep in mind the material you have studied in this chapter. Try to develop the reader's interest by varying the type, length, and sequence of your sentences. Make sure that your paragraphs are organized logically and that they demonstrate the seven characteristics of effective writing. Write and revise your rough draft in the space below. Write or type your finished description on a separate piece of paper, or enter it into a computer and print it out.

_____

_____

_____

_____

_____

_____

_____

_____

_____

_____

_____

_____

_____

_____

_____

_____

_____

_____

_____

_____

_____

End-of-Sentence Punctuation

CHAPTER 15 PREVIEW

Now that you have mastered the eight parts of speech, you will develop your skills by learning to apply the most fundamental marks of punctuation: the period, the question mark, and the exclamation point. This chapter will illustrate the role punctuation plays in sentences, expressions, and specific instances such as abbreviations and numbers. As you work with this chapter, you will assess your comprehension in the Programmed Reinforcement sections and the Practices. Finally, you will apply your knowledge of punctuation rules to material from a newspaper Website.

OBJECTIVES

After completing this chapter, you will be able to

- Use a period after various types of sentences and condensed expressions.
- Use a period with initials, abbreviations, money, decimals, percentages, tabulations, outlines, and lists.
- Use a question mark after direct questions and after condensed expressions standing for complete questions.
- Distinguish between a direct question and an indirect question.
- Use a question mark within a sentence to express doubt or uncertainty.
- Determine how and when to use an exclamation point.

Study Plan for Chapter 15

The Study Plan for Chapter 15 offers a set of strategies that will help you learn and review the chapter material.

❶ **The Stop Sign of Punctuation**: A period is like a stop sign. As you read sentences aloud, your voice probably drops when you pause where the "stop sign" goes.

❷ **Polite Request or Question?** Polite requests can be restated as commands. "Won't you please enter" can be restated as the command "Please enter." It requires a period. The question "How are you today?" cannot be rewritten as a command and requires a question mark.

❸ **A Matter of Case**: In general, single-word abbreviations and those written in lowercase require periods. Abbreviations written in capital letters usually require no periods. Learn the exceptions to this rule, listed in Section 15.3.

❹ **Periods in Lists**: If the items are independent clauses, dependent clauses, or long prepositional phrases, use periods. Use periods with short items only if those items are needed to complete the sentence.

In this section you will learn the rules for using three punctuation marks that you probably are already familiar with: periods, question marks, and exclamation points. You'll generally find these at the ends of sentences, but there are special circumstances in which they make a necessary appearance.

15.1 The Purpose of Punctuation

Can you read the following?

> Marksofpunctuationtellthereaderwhentopause

Now try it this way:

> Marks of punctuation tell the reader when to pause.

Spaces between words make a sentence easier to read. They break a long, unclear sequence of letters into distinct words. Similarly, marks of punctuation make sentences easier to read because they break an unclear sequence of thoughts into easy-to-understand ideas.

Improper punctuation can be confusing and misleading. Notice how one comma changes the meaning of the following sentences:

> Ms. Driscoll, the CEO of Teleco has been indicted by the grand jury.
> Ms. Driscoll, the CEO of Teleco, has been indicted by the grand jury.

In the first sentence Ms. Driscoll is being told about the indictment of the CEO of Teleco. In the second sentence Ms. Driscoll is the person who has been indicted.

The meaning of a sentence can depend on how the sentence is punctuated. If you want your writing to say exactly what you mean, you must punctuate correctly and carefully.

15.2 Sentences That End With Periods

Use a period at the end of a sentence that makes a statement, states a command, is a polite request, or expresses an indirect question.

Statement:	The Hopkins file is in the other cabinet.
Command:	Bring me the Hopkins file.
Polite request:	Would you please bring me the Hopkins file.
Indirect question:	Ms. Drisk asked where the Hopkins file is.

The Smart Farmer

Farming is not just picked up on the farm. College degrees in agriculture are increasingly valuable. Even this is not enough: plan on putting your book theories into practice by working under an experienced farmer.

Polite Requests

A polite request is worded like a question for the sake of politeness, but it ends with a period, not a question mark. Distinguish between a question and a polite request by asking: *Do I expect a verbal response or an action?*

If you expect a verbal response, the sentence is a direct question and should end with a question mark. If you expect an action, the statement is a polite request and should end with a period.

For example, when a police officer says, "May I see your driver's license, please," the officer expects to be handed the license, not to be told yes or no.

Indirect Questions

Direct questions ask for a response that includes specific information, not just an action, and thus require a question mark. An indirect question is not really a question. It is a statement that refers to a question. As such, it should end with a period, not a question mark.

Sentence Refresher
Review what you learned in Chapter 2 about using the period correctly at the end of a complete sentence and avoiding sentence fragments and run-on sentences.
∎

DIRECT QUESTION	INDIRECT QUESTION
1. Do you have the latest figures?	1. I asked you for the latest figures.
2. Can you e-mail the new presentation as an attachment?	2. He wondered if you could e-mail the new presentation as an attachment.

Condensed Expressions

Use a period after a condensed expression that stands for a full statement or command.

Yes.   No.   Next.   Wait.   Good Luck.   Congratulations.

Often, condensed expressions are answers to questions. They are acceptable sentence fragments because their meanings are completed by the action described in the question.

QUESTION	CONDENSED EXPRESSION
Are you in line?	Yes.
When will you complete the report?	By the end of the week.
Do you mind staying late tonight?	No, not at all.
What should we do next?	Stall for more time.

Use a period after personal initials and most abbreviations.

Rule 1. Use a period after a person's initials.

Edith S. Ballard	B. L. Salazar	T. J. K. Hassan

Frequently, when a person is referred to solely by initials, no periods are used.

FDR	LBJ	JFK Jr

Rule 2. As a general rule, use periods with abbreviations of single words and with abbreviations expressed in lowercase letters.

Co.	Mon.	Dr.	c.o.d.
Corp.	Oct.	Mr.	f.o.b.
Inc.	mgr.	Mrs.	a.m.
Ltd.	misc.	Ms.	p.m.

Exceptions: Abbreviations of units of measure are commonly expressed without periods.

yd	ft	mi	lb	oz	rpm	mpg	mph

Rule 3. As a general rule, do not use periods in abbreviations composed of capital letters.

NFL	IBM	UCLA	CPA
NAACP	ITT	YWCA	CFP
AFL-CIO	TWA	YMHA	IRS

Exceptions: Use periods in academic degrees and abbreviations of religious orders.

B.A.	M.A.	Ph.D.	R.N.	S.J.
B.S.	M.B.A.	Ed.D.	M.D.	O.S.B.

Rule 4. Use periods with certain geographic names.

D.C.	U.A.E.	U.K.	U.S.A.	U.S.S.R.

Punctuation Tip

Spaces Between Internal Periods

When using a computer, leave no space after each internal period. Add a space only after the final period.

> We received a c.o.d. shipment from the Denver warehouse.
> The package arrived c.o.d. I was unable to pay for it.

Sentences That End With Abbreviations

When a sentence ends with an abbreviation, use only one period.

> Address the letter to Fulton Boyd, Esq.
> The shipment goes to Morris Van Lines Inc.

> *But:* The plant is open for inspection all day (9:00 a.m. to 5:30 p.m.).

ZIP Code or Abbreviation?

As a general rule in workplace correspondence, the names of cities and states are not abbreviated except in tables and lists where space is at a premium. The two-letter United States Postal Service State and Territory Designators (ZIP abbreviations) should be used with ZIP Codes only when a complete address is being used.

ZIP Abbreviations
Appendix E contains a list of two-letter state and territory designators, or ZIP abbreviations.

■

Contraction or Abbreviation?

Do not confuse a contraction with an abbreviation. A contraction that is written with an apostrophe does not require a period. The following are contractions:

Gen'l	Gov't	Rec't	Sec't	Sup't

Numbers that end in *st, rd, d,* or *th* are considered contractions and do not require periods:

1st	2nd	3d	4th	5th	10th	23rd	100th

15.4 Money, Decimals, and Percentages

Periods are used to indicate amounts of money, decimals, and percentages. Use a period to separate cents from dollars in a monetary amount.

$2.58	$10.10	$4,372.27

15.5 Periods in Lists

Pharming

Pharming (pronounced *farming*) is short for *pharmaceutical farming.* For pharming purposes, a potato can be genetically altered both to feed people and to immunize them against bacteria-borne diseases.

Put periods after independent clauses, dependent clauses, or long phrases displayed on separate lines in a list.

PERIODS AFTER INDEPENDENT CLAUSES IN A LIST

We are experiencing the following network problems:

- Users cannot access the Internet if they are in another program.
- Users cannot change their passwords.
- Users logging on from home cannot access their staff files.

PERIODS AFTER DEPENDENT CLAUSES IN A LIST

Please contact our Helpdesk only in the following situations:

- When you receive a virus warning from network administration.
- When you have trouble with software that has been installed by a company technician.
- When you have trouble with company-owned computer hardware.
- When your password has expired.
- When you cannot access the company network.

PERIODS AFTER LONG PHRASES IN A LIST

Our taxi customers are entitled to four basic rights:

1. To expect courteous and safe driving at all times.
2. To advise the driver about their preferred route to a destination.
3. To request no commercial radio be played during their trip.
4. To enjoy an air-conditioned ride or heated ride.

Do not put periods after short phrases in a list unless the phrases are essential to the grammatical completeness of the introductory statement. Periods are needed after the phrases in the list below because the phrases are objects of the preposition *on*. The statement "Section Four of the text has chapters on" is not a complete sentence.

Section Four of the text has chapters on

1. Gathering information.
2. Organizing and writing short reports.
3. Writing formal reports.

However, periods are not needed in the list below because the phrases do not complete the introductory statement "Basic to our way of life are these fundamental rights." That independent clause could stand by itself as a sentence.

Basic to our way of life are these fundamental rights:

1. Freedom of speech
2. Freedom of assembly
3. Freedom of religion
4. Freedom of the press
5. Freedom to petition

Lists in Sentences. When a list is written as part of a sentence, you may enclose clarifying numbers in parentheses. In this case, do not use a period with the numbers, but punctuate the listed items as you would any list in a sentence by using commas or semicolons as needed.

> Basic to our way of life are these fundamental rights: (1) freedom of speech, (2) freedom of assembly, (3) freedom of religion, (4) freedom of the press, and (5) freedom to petition.

15.6 Periods in Outlines

In preparing an outline, put a period after the letter or number used to mark the first four division levels. Here is part of the outline used to prepare this text:

I.   The Forms of Pronouns
    A.   Personal Pronouns
        1.   Subjective Case
           a.   Subject
           b.   Subject Complement

15.7 Question Marks

The question mark is used after a sentence that asks for information.

Direct Questions and Condensed Expressions

Use a question mark at the end of a direct question or a condensed expression that stands for a complete question.

> Do you know Yvette's home telephone number?
> I understand Professor Hui owns a house on Cape Cod. Where?

The first example above is a direct question. In the second example, *Where?* is a condensed expression that means "Where is Professor Hui's house?"

Commas in Concluding Questions

Sometimes a question comes at the end of a statement, in which case a comma is placed before it.

> Professor Hui owns a house on Cape Cod, doesn't he?

Statements That Are Questions

Sometimes a sentence is worded as a statement when it is actually a question. Show that you intend to pose a question by using a question mark.

> You expect me to believe that?
> The car's odometer has not been altered?
> Only four people attended the meeting?

Polite Requests and Indirect Questions

Remember, a polite request and an indirect question end with a period, not a question mark.

Polite request:	Won't you come in, please. Will you please let us hear from you soon.
Direct question:	Why won't you come in? Why haven't we heard from you?
Direct question:	Do you know when the new models will be available?
Indirect question:	She wonders if you know when the new models will be available.
Direct question:	When will the new models be available?
Indirect question:	I wonder when the new models will be available.

Questions and Run-On Sentences

Be wary of run-on sentences when using a question mark.

WRONG: Will you be at the banquet, we certainly hope so.
RIGHT: ✔ Will you be at the banquet? We certainly hope so.

Long Questions

Don't be deceived by the length of a question. No matter how long a direct question is, end it with a question mark.

> Are you certain that we can expect delivery of the order by January 14 despite the report that a strike may be called on December 31?

Questions in a Series

Although a question mark usually ends a sentence, it may be used in the middle of a sentence that contains a series of closely related questions.

> What would be our unit price if we purchased 6 gross? 12 gross? 20 gross?

Doubt or Uncertainty

Use a question mark in parentheses to express doubt or uncertainty.

Manuel claims it will take less than 30(?) minutes to complete the
procedure.

The message read:"Robert Ambertson(?) called. Will call back."

Tess paid more than $15,000(?) for her previously owned car.

15.8 Exclamation Points

Use an exclamation point after a word or group of words that expresses strong feeling or emotion.

Hurrah!

What a marvelous film!

Watch out!

The Giants win the pennant! The Giants win the pennant! The Giants win
the pennant!

Use exclamation points sparingly, especially in workplace writing. Save them for an infrequent thought that requires the emphasis an exclamation point provides.

PERSONAL BALANCE To avoid burnout, strike a balance between work and recreation. Try not to crowd each day with obligations. Set a time limit on work, study, and demands, and schedule in some time for yourself.

SECTION A: PROGRAMMED REINFORCEMENT

Coverage Key

Section		Statement
15.1	➤ The Purpose of Punctuation	➤ **S1**
15.2	➤ Sentences That End With Periods	➤ **S2, S3, S4, S17**
15.3	➤ Initials and Abbreviations	➤ **S5, S6, S7, S9**
15.4	➤ Money, Decimals, and Percentages	➤ **S8**
15.5	➤ Periods in Lists	➤ **S10**
15.6	➤ Periods in Outlines	➤ **S11**
15.7	➤ Question Marks	➤ **S12, S13, S14, S15, S17**
15.8	➤ Exclamation Points	➤ **S16, S17**

Instructions: Cover the answers in the **Answer** column; then write your answer to the first statement. Uncover the first printed answer and compare your answer to it. If you wrote a correct answer, continue the activity. If you made an error, use the **Coverage Key** to locate the chapter section you need to review. When you are confident that you understand the material, continue with the reinforcement activity.

ANSWER

STATEMENT

S1 _____ marks tell readers when to pause.

A1 Punctuation

S2 A period is used at the end of a sentence that makes a(n) _____ or gives a command.

A2 statement

S3 Is this a statement or a command? **Put it down.**

A3 command

S4 Punctuate the following by placing a period at the end of each sentence and capitalizing initial letters of the sentences. **book sales are increasing this is particularly true of paperbacks**

A4 Book sales are increasing. This is particularly true of paperbacks.

S5 A period is placed after many abbreviations. If a sentence ends with an abbreviation, it has (one, two) period(s). Place periods where necessary: **The shipment is being sent c o d to Global Inc**

A5 one, . . . c.o.d. to Global Inc.

S6 Abbreviations of single words and abbreviations expressed in lowercase letters usually (require, do not require) periods. Place periods where needed in the following abbreviations: **mfr ie Ms Ltd rpm mph Nov Co am**

A6 require, **mfr., i.e., Ms., Ltd., Nov., Co., a.m.** (No periods are needed in **rpm** and **mph.**)

S7 Abbreviations composed of all capital letters usually (require, do not require) periods. Place periods where needed in the following abbreviations: **AFL-CIO ITT MD YMHA UCLA EdD UK YWCA**

A7 do not require; **M.D., Ed.D., U.K.** (No periods are needed in **AFL-CIO, ITT, YMHA, UCLA,** and **YWCA.**)

S8 In writing a monetary amount containing both dollars and cents, a period (is, is not) used to separate the dollars and cents.

A8 is

S9 When using a computer to type, allow _____ blank space(s) after each period in a person's initials such as *V. S. Naipaul.*

A9 one

S10 In a list, a period is used in which of the following cases:
  a. With independent clauses listed on separate lines
  b. With dependent clauses
  c. With short phrases that are not essential to the grammatical completeness of the introductory statement
  d. With long phrases that are essential to the grammatical completeness of the introductory statement

A10 a., b., d.

S11 In outlines, periods are used to mark the first _____ division levels.

A11 four

S12 A question mark is used after a(n) (direct, indirect) question. It is not used after a(n) (direct, indirect) question. Punctuate each of the following sentences correctly.
  a. **Where is he going**
  b. **I wonder where he's going**
  c. **Why did she suddenly decide to resign**
  d. **Why she suddenly decided to resign has never been explained**
  e. **She questioned his sincerity**
  f. **Did she question his sincerity**

A12 direct, indirect
  a. **Where is he going?**
  b. **I wonder where he's going.**
  c. **Why did she suddenly decide to resign?**
  d. **Why she suddenly decided to resign has never been explained.**
  e. **She questioned his sincerity.**
  f. **Did she question his sincerity?**

S13 A question mark (is, is not) used after the end of a polite request. Punctuate the following sentences correctly.
  a. **Won't you please be seated**
  b. **May I get you something to drink**
  c. **Would you please send me a sample**

A13 is not
  a. **Won't you please be seated.**
  b. **May I get you something to drink?**
  c. **Would you please send me a sample.**

S14 There may be several questions in one sentence. How would you punctuate this sentence? **Can you name three types of apples three types of oranges three types of pears**

A14 Can you name three types of apples? three types of oranges? three types of pears?

S15 A question mark enclosed in parentheses in the middle of a sentence is used to express _____ .

A15 doubt or uncertainty

S16 The punctuation mark used after words that show strong feeling or emotion is the _____ . In workplace documents, the exclamation point should be used (rarely, sometimes, frequently).

A16 exclamation point, rarely

S17 Use periods, question marks, and exclamation marks as needed: **Fantastic I received a $1500 bonus What about you**

A17 Fantastic! I received a $1500 bonus. What about you?

CHAPTER 15 SUMMARY

In this chapter you learned how to use the three most fundamental punctuation marks: (1) the period, (2) the question mark, and (3) the exclamation point. You studied how periods are used at the end of statements, commands, polite requests, and indirect questions. Periods are also used after personal initials and most abbreviations, in certain monetary amounts, and in lists and outlines. In addition, you learned that question marks are used in direct questions, in other questions that ask for a response, and in expressions indicating doubt. Finally, you learned that exclamation points signal strong emotion, and should be used sparingly.

Getting Connected

ACCESSING THE NEWS ONLINE

GOAL: All major news organizations maintain news Websites that offer free access to information from around the world. In this activity you will connect with a Website from one of the major news organizations to locate a news story of interest to you. You'll use that story to help you review what you have learned about the period, the question mark, and the exclamation point.

STEP 1 Go to *englishworkshop.glencoe.com,* the address for *The English Workshop* Website, and click on Unit 6. Next click on Getting Connected, and then click on Chapter 15. At the Chapter 15 Getting Connected option, you'll see a list of Websites for national news organizations. Select one of these sites and click on it.

STEP 2 Once you are at the news organization's Website, look for the headlines and choose a story to read. Clicking on the headline or an accompanying photo usually will get you to the news story.

STEP 3 Skim stories from *at least five* different news areas or from five different headlines. Look for stories that include various uses of the punctuation marks you studied in Chapter 15: periods, question marks, and exclamation points.

STEP 4 You will be working closely with the stories and will need a printout of each one you choose. You may need to copy the text into a word-processing document or download the material. Use the best method available to you to secure a hard copy.

STEP 5 Once you have the printouts, locate periods that have been used (or omitted) in *at least five* of the situations listed below. Underline the examples you find. Indicate how the period is being used (or omitted) in each example you underlined by writing the appropriate letters or symbol over each example:

a. Complete statement	=	**CS**
b. Polite request	=	**PR**
c. Indirect question	=	**IQ**
d. Condensed expression	=	**CE**
e. Abbreviations formed from lowercase letters	=	**LC**
f. Abbreviations formed from capital letters	=	**Cap**
g. Personal initials	=	**PI**
h. Geographic names	=	**GN**
i. Even dollar amounts (no cents)	=	**$**
j. Percentages with decimal points	=	**%**

On the back of each printout, write the rules for the use of periods as they apply to the examples you found. Indicate any examples you found that violated the rules.

STEP 6 Now turn your thoughts to examples of question marks (sometimes used in headlines of news stories) and exclamation points. Locate the question mark or exclamation point being used (or omitted) in *at least two* of the situations listed below. Circle the examples you find. Indicate how the punctuation mark is being used (or omitted) in each example by writing the appropriate letters over each example:

a. Direct question	=	**DQ**
b. Condensed question	=	**CQ**
c. Polite request	=	**PR**
d. Indirect question	=	**IQ**
e. Doubt or uncertainty	=	**DU**

On the back of each printout, write the rules for the use of question marks or exclamation points as they apply to the examples you found. If a question mark or exclamation point was not used in an example, explain why. Indicate any examples you found that violated the rules.

STEP 7 On the back of each printout, list at least three abbreviations you found. Write out their meanings. Find at least two other abbreviations that you did not know before you began this activity. Determine the meaning of each abbreviation and write it down.

STEP 8 Write your name on the front of each printout you used for this activity, and give the material to your instructor.

Some Websites from national news organizations link to local television and radio stations. See if you can locate a news outlet local to your area.

PRACTICE 1

The Period

Instructions: Insert all necessary periods and capital letters in the following business letter. Underline each change you make.

ᴀᴍᴀʟɢᴀᴍᴀᴛᴇᴅ Eɴᴛᴇʀᴘʀɪꜱᴇꜱ
4307 N. Cliff Ave.
Sioux Falls, SD 57104

Ms. Ortiz
Events Coordinator
Future Business Leaders of America
86 Latigo Drive
Boise, ID 83709

Dear Ms. Ortiz:

Future Business Leaders of America is a fine organization, and I have always admired the work of our local chapter thank you for asking me if I would be able to speak at your dinner meeting next month

as a representative for Amalgamated Enterprises, I am frequently on the road on business such will be the case on the day you have asked me to speak I'm scheduled to be in Boise

may I suggest that you contact Ms Dorothy Lewmar of our office as one of our most successful managers, she would be able to provide your members with many interesting and valuable insights into the role of today's executive

please keep me in mind for future meetings when my schedule allows it, I would welcome the opportunity to speak to your members it would be most rewarding

Sincerely,

Gladys Vasek

PRACTICE 2

The Period

Instructions: Insert periods wherever necessary in the sentences below. Add a capital letter where required.

EXAMPLE: **Volunteer your services that is the way to help**

1. I will be there at 8 pm I will see you then.

2. At a constant speed of 55 mph, my new car averages more than 40 mpg.

3. Will you open the door, please, my hands are full.

4. My friend Ralph J Hobart, an MBA from MIT, advised me to invest in IBM.

5. In his correspondence he often uses abbreviations such as eg, ie, and etc.

6. Ms Brady asked Mr Chun if the mail had arrived yet.

7. One mile (mi) consists of 1,760 yards (yd) or 5,280 feet (ft).

8. Dr Jan E Rivin, DDS, requested that these drills be sent cod.

9. Won't you please be seated, Ms Barrett.

10. The US 4th Army Brigade is being transferred from Ft Dix, New Jersey, to Guam aboard the USS *Enterprise*.

11. We spent over half our monthly income on food (23.1 percent) and housing (32.2 percent) last year.

12. Washington, DC, is north of Raleigh, North Carolina.

13. The merchandise went to Cap't Johnson of Wallace Lines, Inc.

14. Abbreviations for first names (eg, Wm for William, Thos for Thomas, and Benj for Benjamin) are not appropriate in formal business writing they may, however, be used in lists or tables where space is limited

15. The newly revised business communications text has updated chapters on:

    1. Writing about the routine and pleasant.

    2. Writing about the unpleasant.

    3. Writing to persuade.

    4. Writing about employment.

Name _____

Class _____ Date _____

PRACTICE 3

The Question Mark, the Period, and the Exclamation Point

Instructions: Put question marks, periods, or exclamation points where necessary; indicate a capital letter if a new sentence follows.

EXAMPLE: **Why don't you use a new cartridge it would make a big difference.**

1. Will you be there this evening

2. Correct the balance on my account and see that I am not charged again

3. Wow what a terrific sales campaign

4. Wasn't that Louise J Hicks, MD

5. Since I last spoke with you, has the situation changed

6. Why was he discharged he was doing a good job

7. I wonder what the average mark-up is on produce

8. She asked me where you are going tonight

9. Amazing

10. Where is she going, I wonder

11. Have you seen the latest figures on the GNP

12. The weather is unseasonably mild, is it not, for this time of year

13. How much does it cost $30 $40 $50

14. Did you forget your appointment at 2 pm

15. There is no reason to keep these files, is there

16. This is wonderful news, isn't it

17. Wait don't leave yet

18. She requested that these contracts reach R M Benbrook, Esq, before 5 pm

19. Have the two incorrect charges, $16 73 and $25 72, been removed from my charge account

20. Fantastic

21. Have you considered a color other than white for your résumé it would help your résumé appear more distinctive

22. Would you like us to ship your order cod

23. Do you know the difference in meaning between the abbreviations ie and eg

24. What do you expect to be doing in 5 years in 10 years in 20 years

25. Is Mr H R Gunderson a member of the SEC

Name _____

Class _____ Date _____

PRACTICE 4

Terminal Punctuation

Instructions: Insert periods, question marks, exclamation points, and capital letters wherever appropriate in the following letter. Underline any changes or additions you make.

Dear Customer Service Representative:

last May we ordered 20 copies of The Office Worker's Manual by George Kallaus Jr as yet we have not received them although it is already july 15 would you please give us an explanation

is the manual out of print out of stock on back order was our order simply misplaced if the manual is in stock, please ship us 20 copies at once, cod if not, would you please let us know when we can expect them urgent.

Yours truly,

Fernando Villalobos, Inventory Control Supervisor

PRACTICE 5

Composition: Using the Period, the Question Mark, and the Exclamation Point

Instructions: Compose the sentences as directed in parentheses.

EXAMPLE: **(a compound sentence that is a question)**
     <u>Would you like to leave now, or would you prefer to stay?</u>

1. (a statement) _____

2. (a direct question) _____

3. (a polite request)_____

4. (a compound sentence that is a command) _____

5. (an acceptable sentence fragment that is not an exclamation) _____

6. (a statement that ends with a question) _____

7. (a compound sentence that is a question) _____

8. (an indirect question)_____

9. (a sentence with a series of closely related questions) _____

10. (an exclamation)_____

Sentences and Punctuation

Unit 6—Editing Review

Instructions: Use the concepts you have studied so far to help you locate errors in the material below. Cross out each error and write the correction in the space above it. Assume that you are reviewing a printout of material being prepared for an agriculture Website. The information gives advice to people who want to establish farms where customers may pick their own produce.

Pick-Your-Own Farms

If you're a big industrial farmer devoted to the principles of agribusiness this Website is not for you. This Website is for (1) the small farmer whose looking to increase their profit and (2) the person whom wants to move to the country. And buy some land on which to support hisself or herself. If you are the type person who have some basic management skills and would like to use it in farming small acreages to provide an annual income then that Website is for you and others like yourself.

How much land is needed?

You don't need a lot of land, in fact you can begin with a single acre only. Depending on the number of variables—including what area you live in, the length of the growing season, and how careful you manage crop rotation—one acre could yield between $5,000.00 and $10,000.00. Reliable datums show it can be profitabler to have to a PYO business than to have been planting 500 acres of wheat.

Why are PYO farms successful?

The reason a PYO farm can be successful is because people likes fresh fruites and vegetables. That interest is growing however so is the price. The cost of harvesting

(Continued on next page)

continued from page 449

fresh produce is getting more greater all the time and them costs are passed along to the consumer. A PYO farm offers the consumer the opportunity to buy fresh produce at a substantial reduced price. Because they don't have to pay the costses of harvesting and to ship the produce. In fact, they do the harvesting theirselves. In a PYO operation your customer's supply the labor and pay you for the privilege. In return, they are able to purchase quality produce.

When was the last time you buyed a decent tomato at your local grocery store with any real flavor? Are every berry in the quart of strawberrys ripe and firm. Does the string beans snap or bend? Is the kernels of corn on the cob full and juicy? Many people are content to pay for inferior produce due to the fact that they don't want to spend either the time and energy to pick produce. Other people place a higher value on cost and quality, accordingly they will invest the time necessary to obtain the most fresh produce. These are your customers.

In addition, many of your customers will be viewing their trip to your farm as a day in the country and a educational experience for themselves and their childs. You are providing them a service they are providing you an income.

Should I advertise?

Watch out? Its possible to advertise too good. This here section tell you how to advertise to the right number of people in the more effective manner. How many people live within a radius of 5 miles,10 miles, 25 miles? How should you reach them?

How do I determine pricing?

Should you cut prices to increase sales. This section gives you five scenarioes of what might of happened if you did.

Link & Learn

PUNCTUATING A VARIETY OF SENTENCES IN AGRIBUSINESS CAREERS

GOAL: Reinforce what you learned in Unit 6 about sentences and end-of-sentence punctuation while exploring various agriculture-related Websites.

STEP 1 Go to *englishworkshop.glencoe.com*, the address for *The English Workshop* Website. Click first on Unit 6; then click on Link & Learn to access a list of agribusiness sites you may use in this activity. Select one of the sites and click on it.

STEP 2 Skim the topics available at the home page of the Website you selected, and find a topic you want to explore. Select an article that is between one-and-a-half and three pages long. Print out the entire piece.

STEP 3 Read the printout and do the following:

   a. Underline all simple sentences once. Draw a line from each sentence to the left margin, and add the label *S*.

   b. Underline all compound sentences twice. Draw a line from each sentence to the left margin, and add the label *CS*.

   c. Circle all complex sentences. Draw a line from each one to the right margin, and add the label *ComS*.

   d. Draw a line from each compound-complex sentence to the right margin, and add the label *C-ComS*.

   e. Count the number of each type of sentence. On the back of the printout, write a sentence explaining your results.

STEP 4 Review the printout and analyze the material's effectiveness using the criteria below. Put a plus (+) or a minus (–) symbol next to each criterion to help you evaluate the writing.

   f. Different sentence patterns and types were used.

   g. The variety of sentence patterns and types helped build interest in the story.

   h. The correct end-of-sentence punctuation was used throughout.

   i. The writing had all qualities of the Seven Cs (see page 420).

On the back of the printout, write an evaluation of the material. Explain why the writing was or was not effective, based on the pluses and minuses for the criteria above.

STEP 5 Write your name on the front of the printout, and turn it in to your instructor.

Punctuating with Commas

Profile in Success

Fast Food Sales Manager: Interacting With Employees and Customers

Patricia Williams · *Valdosta, Georgia* · *Wendy's® Old-Fashioned Hamburger Restaurants*

Being an award winner is rewarding, agrees Patricia Williams.

"It's a wonderful feeling of accomplishment," she says about the three awards she received from Delta Epsilon Chi, the national student marketing association. Patricia received the awards for demonstrating her marketing and management skills while she was earning her associate degree at Valdosta Technical College in Valdosta, Georgia. She took home a first-place state award and two international finalist awards.

"I had to go through obstacles to get into school, so I was very grateful when my kids told me how proud they were of me," says the 35-year-old mother of three.

Patricia had always wanted to go to college, but a difficult marriage delayed her. As the marriage ended, she began classes at Valdosta Tech. While working and raising children, she could take only a few classes each quarter, but she earned her degree and is now a general manager of a Wendy's restaurant.

Patricia supervises many young employees. She knows they have many decisions and opportunities ahead of them. "My employees and customers have taught me to use all the communication skills I've acquired in life," she concludes.

Think About It . . . Do Human Relationship Skills Come With Those Fries?

Patricia Williams has gained wisdom from many life experiences. She taps them all as she supervises young employees and works with the public.

- *What can working in fast-paced public businesses teach young employees?*

- *What can managers teach their employees about communicating with others?*

- *What communication and human relationship skills do managers need?*

Career Connections

Learn more about the work of sales representatives, marketing researchers, advertising account planners, entrepreneurs, and others in the sales and marketing field by connecting to the following sites listed at *The English Workshop* Website. Go to *englishworkshop.glencoe.com*. Click first on Unit 7 and then on Career Connections.

- **Careers in Marketing**
- **Advertising Education Foundation**
- *Entreworld.org*
- **Marketing Research Association**
- **Vetch Education**

See page 511, **Link & Learn: Using Commas in Sales and Marketing Careers**, for an additional online career activity.

Comma Basics

CHAPTER 16 PREVIEW

The comma is the most frequently used punctuation mark. There are many rules for using commas, but all can be seen as aspects of six basic rules. This chapter will cover the first three. Here you will learn to use a comma as a separator in a series, a compound sentence, or a sentence with an introductory element. You will continue to assess your knowledge in the Programmed Reinforcement sections and the Practices. Finally, you will access a grammar Website to reinforce what you have learned about punctuating with commas.

OBJECTIVES

After completing this chapter, you will know when and how to use commas

- In a series of words, phrases, or clauses.
- In compound sentences.
- With introductory elements, including the following:
  - Dependent clauses
  - Verbal phrases
  - Prepositional phrases
  - Transitional phrases
  - Interjections

Study Plan for Chapter 16

The Study Plan for Chapter 16 offers a set of strategies that will help you learn and review the chapter material.

1 **Commas in a List**: Count the items listed in a sentence. If the list consists of at least three items, separate all the items with commas and use a comma before the conjunction connecting the last two items.

2 **And No Commas, Please**: If *each* item in a series of three or more is separated by the word *and,* no commas are needed in the series.

3 **Comma Radar 1**: Look for coordinating conjunctions in sentences. When you see one, stop. Put your finger over it, and read what appears on both sides of your finger. An independent clause on both sides signals a compound sentence and means you should put a comma before the conjunction.

4 **Comma Radar 2**: Train your comma radar to kick into gear when a subordinating conjunction, preposition, verbal (*-ed* or *-ing* word or *to* + verb), or transitional expression appears at the beginning of a sentence. These structures usually signal a dependent or introductory element. When these introductory elements appear at the beginning of a sentence, a comma usually follows them.

The first basic comma rule concerns the way commas are used or not used in a series. In this section you will learn how this rule applies to adjectives, adverbs, compound subjects, company names, etc.

16.1 Commas in a Series

Use commas to separate words, phrases, or clauses listed in a series. A series can include any part of speech: nouns, verbs, infinitive phrases, clauses, and so forth. Each of the following sentences illustrates the use of a comma with various parts of speech.

The Educated Salesperson

Traditionally, a successful salesperson can advance into management without a college education. But nowadays large retail businesses hire graduates as management trainees. Do your homework: determine whether you'll come out ahead with a degree in hand.

COMMAS IN A SERIES

Nouns

Toys, books, shoes, clothes, and *food* covered the floor of the boys' bedroom.

Verbs

This data management program automatically *bills, posts,* and *maintains* an inventory control.

Adjectives

Our new offices are located in a *towering, ultramodern, air- conditioned* building.

Adverbs

The Electrex Meter has been *carefully, precisely,* and *painstakingly* assembled for maximum sensitivity.

Prepositional Phrases

There was rust *on the front fender, below both front doors,* and *under the floor* of the car.

Infinitive Phrases

In this course your objectives are *to write fluently, to speak effectively,* and *to think clearly.*

Clauses

That our competitors are aggressive, that they are clever, and *that they are well organized* must be recognized.

Examine all the sentences on the previous page. The third sentence illustrates a series of coordinating adjectives *not* linked by a coordinating conjunction. The others each contain a conjunction before the final item in the series. Notice that a comma appears *before* each of these conjunctions.

Some authorities say that putting a comma before a conjunction in a series is optional. We recommend including the comma because its absence before the conjunction could confuse the reader. For example,

> The professor assigned readings from textbooks by O'Leary and Kuntz, Friedman, Modolo and Nowak.

Did Modolo and Nowak each write a textbook, or did they, like O'Leary and Kuntz, co-author one? If you *always* place a comma before the conjunction that precedes the last item in a series, you will avoid the possibility of confusing your reader.

Compound Subjects

When you have a list that serves as the compound subject, do not use a comma after the last item in the list. In other words, do not separate the last item in the subject from the predicate.

WRONG: *Toys, books, shoes, clothes,* and *food,* covered the floor of the boys' bedroom.

RIGHT: ✔ *Toys, books, shoes, clothes,* and *food* covered the floor of the boys' bedroom.

Adjectives in a Series

When a series of adjectives modifies a noun, do not place a comma after the final adjective.

WRONG: Our new offices are located in a *towering, ultramodern, air-conditioned,* building.

RIGHT: ✔ Our new offices are located in a *towering, ultramodern, air-conditioned* building.

Adjectives *Not* in a Series

Be careful not to separate adjectives if they are not in a series and they modify a group of words. Look at this sentence:

> Have you tried our *latest cleansing* cream?

Because there are only two (not three) adjectives listed in a row, *latest* and *cleansing* are not in a series. *Latest* also modifies the word group *cleansing cream,* not just the noun *cream.* Other examples follow:

The government's objectives are secure *national defense* and rapid *domestic growth.*

National defense and *domestic growth* are treated as word groups, so commas are not needed.

We are looking for an *intelligent, pleasant, enthusiastic* legal secretary.

Legal secretary is treated as a word group, so no comma should follow *enthusiastic.*

Adverbs in a Series

When a series of adverbs modifies a verb (or other part of speech), do not place a comma after the last adverb.

WRONG: The Electrex Meter has been *carefully, precisely,* and *painstakingly,* assembled.

RIGHT: ✔ The Electrex Meter has been *carefully, precisely,* and *painstakingly* assembled.

Punctuation Tip

Adjective or Adverb Series

Do not put a comma between the last adjective or adverb in a series and the word it modifies.

Conjunctions in a Series

Occasionally a series will be written with coordinating or correlating conjunctions between all items. Do not use commas in this type of series.

WRONG: The Electrex Meter has been carefully, *and* precisely, *and* painstakingly assembled.

RIGHT: ✔ The Electrex Meter has been carefully *and* precisely *and* painstakingly assembled.

Pairs in a Series

Sometimes pairs of words or phrases will be listed in a series. In these instances, use commas to separate the pairs from one another.

To *write and speak well, to think and act rigorously,* and *to live and fight courageously* are admirable ideals.

Company Names in a Series

Many company names are composed of a series of names. Not all companies follow standard rules of English when listing their names. Be sure to use the company name as it appears on the company's official letterhead. See the top of the next page for examples.

Batten, Barton, Durstine & Osborne
Drexel Burnham Lambert Inc.
Merrill Lynch, Pierce, Fenner & Smith Inc.
PricewaterhouseCoopers Ltd.

As a general rule, a comma is not placed before the ampersand (&) that often precedes the last name in a series.

Punctuation Tip

Commas, Etc.

Place commas before and after *etc.* to separate it from the rest of the sentence.

Etc.

Frequently, a long list will end with the abbreviation *etc.*, meaning "and other things." Commas should be placed before and after the *etc.* unless it ends the sentence.

Never write *and etc.* because this would mean "and and others," which is redundant. Avoid the use of *etc.* in formal writing. Use the expressions *and so on, and so forth,* or *and the like* instead.

Do not use *etc.* when the series begins with *for example, such as,* or a similar phrase. These terms suggest that only a few examples will follow.

WRONG: The candidates expressed their views on vital national issues such as farm policy, foreign relations, fiscal management, labor relations, etc., during the debates.

ACCEPTABLE: ✔The candidates expressed their views on farm policy, foreign relations, fiscal management, labor relations, etc., at the debates.

BETTER: ✔The candidates expressed their views on vital national issues such as farm policy, foreign relations, fiscal management, and labor relations during the debates.

Rule 1: Commas In a Series

a. Use commas to separate items in a series.
   . . . **item 1, item 2, item 3, and item 4** . . .

b. Do not use a comma to separate the final item in a compound subject from the predicate.
   . . . **noun 1, noun 2, noun 3, and noun 4 verb** . . .

c. Do not use a comma to separate the final adjective or adverb in a series from the word that the adjective or adverb modifies.
   . . . **adjective 1, adjective 2, adjective 3, and adjective 4 word modified** . . .
   . . . **adverb 1, adverb 2, adverb 3, and adverb 4 word modified** . . .

Coverage Key

Section	Statement
16.1 ➤ Commas in a Series	➤ **S1, S2, S3, S4, S5, S6, S7, S8**

Instructions: Cover the answers in the **Answer** column; then write your answer to the first statement. Uncover the first printed answer and compare your answer to it. If you wrote a correct answer, continue the activity. If you made an error, use the **Coverage Key** to locate the chapter section you need to review. When you are confident that you understand the material, continue with the reinforcement activity.

ANSWER

STATEMENT

S1   I bought pens, pencils, erasers, and paper. This sentence illustrates the use of the comma with words in a(n) _____ .

A1   series

S2   Should you place a comma before the word **and** in this sentence? **I returned the pants, the shirts and the sweaters.** _____

A2   yes

S3   Punctuate this sentence correctly: **We washed and waxed and polished each car.**

A3   **We washed and waxed and polished each car.** (no commas)

S4   When you have a series of adjectives, you (should, should not) place a comma after the last adjective. Punctuate this sentence: **We offer fast accurate efficient service.**

A4   should; **We offer fast, accurate, efficient service.**

S5   When you have a series of adverbs, you (should, should not) place a comma after the last adverb. Punctuate this sentence correctly: **The applications were carefully thoroughly and objectively evaluated.**

A5   should not; **The applications were carefully, thoroughly, and objectively evaluated.**

S6   Punctuate these sentences correctly:
   a. **Mathematics science and English are my worst subjects.**
   b. **Courage integrity and wisdom are qualities she projects.**

A6   a. **Mathematics, science, and English are my worst subjects.**
   b. **Courage, integrity, and wisdom are qualities she projects.**

S7   Punctuate this sentence correctly: **Women and men girls and boys and children of all ages love the circus.**

A7   a. **Women and men, girls and boys, and children of all ages love the circus.**

S8   Punctuate the following sentence correctly: **Towels linens draperies etc. are located on the third floor.**

A8   **Towels, linens, draperies, etc., are located on the third floor.**

SECTION B
Comma Rule 2

The second basic comma rule concerns the use of commas in compound sentences. You will learn when and how to use commas in sentences involving two or more independent clauses while reviewing the concepts of comma faults and run-on sentences.

16.2 Commas in Compound Sentences

Use a comma to separate two complete thoughts that are connected by a coordinating conjunction (*and, but, or, nor, for, so,* or *yet*). In other words, place commas between all independent clauses in a compound sentence.

> Last week I sent you a package, *and* I'm calling now to see if you received it.
> They are not prepared now, *nor* will they be for several months.

When the subject of the sentence is the understood *you* and one or both verbs are in the imperative, use a comma before the conjunction. Treat the sentence as you would a compound sentence.

> Call me when you arrive, *and* let me know when we can get together.
> Please examine our proposal, *and* phone me if you have any questions.

In each of these examples, the comma comes *before* the conjunction because the conjunction is part of the final clause.

In a short sentence composed of two independent clauses connected by *and* or *or,* you may omit the comma if the meaning of the sentence is clear. As a general rule, you may leave out the comma if either part of the sentence has four or fewer words. This applies to compound imperatives as well.

> Their rates are reasonable *and* they guarantee their work.
> Business must improve *or* we will be forced to close.
> Pay the bill *or* return the merchandise.

If two independent clauses are connected by *but* or *yet,* include the comma no matter how short the parts of the sentence.

> I'll do it, *but* I can't do it now.
> They were not expected, *yet* they came.

Punctuation Tip

Short Independent Clauses

Omit the comma between short independent clauses connected by ***and*** or ***or***. Include the comma between short independent clauses connected by ***but, nor, for, so,*** or ***yet***.

16.3 Comma Faults

Remember that a comma alone is insufficient to join two independent clauses into a compound sentence.

WRONG: We must change our approach, we may lose our audience.

This error is known as a comma fault. It may be corrected in three, or more ways: (1) make two separate sentences, (2) use a semicolon, or (3) use a comma plus a coordinating conjunction.

RIGHT: ✔ We must change our approach. We may lose our audience.
RIGHT: ✔ We must change our approach; we may lose our audience.
RIGHT: ✔ We must change our approach, or we may lose our audience.

All three sentences above are punctuated correctly. However, the third most clearly shows the relationship between the two independent clauses.

Comma Faults
To jog your memory, review comma faults in Section 2.8 on page 43.

■

16.4 Independent Clause Series

Three or more complete thoughts—independent clauses—may be joined in a series in one compound sentence. In such instances only the final clause requires a comma and coordinating conjunction; each preceding clause should be separated with only a comma.

She came, she saw, *and* she conquered.
Plan your campaign, put it into operation, *and* guide it to success.

Compound Predicates

Look at the two example sentences below. The first sentence contains a compound predicate; that is, *set up* and *waited* share the one subject *we*. The second sentence is a compound sentence. It is easy to confuse these two types of sentences. Be careful not to use commas to separate the parts of a compound predicate.

WRONG: We carefully set up our booth at the fair, and confidently waited for the public to attend.
RIGHT: ✔ We carefully set up our booth at the fair and confidently waited for the public to attend.

Rule 2: Commas in Compound Sentences

Place commas before coordinating conjunctions to join independent clauses in a compound sentence.

Independent clause,   coordinating   independent clause.
                                        conjunction

Coverage Key

Section		Statement
16.2	➤ Commas in Compound Sentences	➤ **S9, S10, S11, S12**
16.3	➤ Comma Faults	➤ **S13**
16.4	➤ Independent Clause Series	➤ **S14**

Instructions: Cover the answers in the **Answer** column; then write your answer to the first statement. Uncover the first printed answer and compare your answer to it. If you wrote a correct answer, continue the activity. If you made an error, use the **Coverage Key** to locate the chapter section you need to review. When you are confident that you understand the material, continue with the reinforcement activity.

ANSWER

STATEMENT

S9 When coordinating conjunctions connect independent clauses containing more than four words, (do, do not) use a comma. Punctuate the following sentence: **I have not finished grading the exams but I will do so before our next class.**

A9 do; I have not finished grading the exams, but I will do so before our next class.

S10 In a compound sentence the comma comes (before, after) the conjunction. Punctuate this sentence: **He may not be a fast programmer but he is an accurate one.**

A10 before; He may not be a fast programmer, but he is an accurate one.

S11 In a sentence composed of two short independent clauses connected by *but* or *yet,* you (may, may not) leave out the comma. In a sentence composed of two short independent clauses connected by and or or, you (may, may not) leave out the comma.
   a. **He is a fast programmer and he is accurate.**
   b. **He is a slow programmer but he is accurate.**

A11 may, may not
   a. no comma needed
   b. He is a slow programmer, but he is accurate.

S12 Add commas where necessary in these sentences:
   a. **I will go but you can't.**
   b. **I will go and you can follow.**
   c. **I don't want to go yet I will.**

A12 a. I will go, but you can't.
   b. no comma needed
   c. I don't want to go, yet I will.

S13 To connect two independent clauses to create a compound sentence, you (can, cannot) use a comma alone.

A13 cannot

S14 You should not confuse a compound predicate with a compound sentence. Punctuate the following sentences:
   a. **I know we have met before but I don't remember your name.**
   b. **Mrs. Cruz knew they had met before but was unable to remember his name.**

A14 a. I know we have met before, but I don't remember your name.
   b. no comma needed

SECTION C
Comma Rule 3

The third basic rule concerns how the comma is used to separate an introductory element from the rest of a sentence. As you develop your knowledge of commas, you will recall your earlier work with independent and dependent clauses, complex sentences, verbals, transitional phrases, and interjections.

16.5 Commas After Dependent Clauses

A complex sentence consists of a dependent clause and an independent clause. For example,

Independent Clause	Dependent Clause

I feel much more energetic since I began exercising regularly.

This complex sentence begins with the independent clause *I feel much more energetic* and is followed by the dependent clause *since I began exercising regularly.* Here are other examples of complex sentences that follow the independent clause-dependent clause order.

We had started to retool before the order actually arrived.
Road crews began plowing the streets as soon as the snow stopped falling.
She left work early because she had a dentist's appointment.

These sentences could also be reversed. They may be written with the dependent clause placed at the beginning of the sentence. When a sentence begins with a dependent clause, use a comma to separate the dependent clause from the independent clause.

Before the order actually arrived, we had started to retool.
As soon as the snow stopped falling, road crews began plowing the streets.
Because she had a dentist's appointment, she left work early.

Here are other complex sentences that begin with dependent clauses. Read these sentences aloud, pausing after each dependent clause. Can you hear that the dependent clause does not form a complete thought?

Although you failed this time, you shouldn't give up.
As long as you try, you are certain to succeed.
If you have an extra catalog, please send it to us.
Because the teachers are on strike, the schools are closed.
After she heard our explanation, she reconsidered.
If you know the answer, raise your hand.

Clauses and Complex Sentences
Flip back to Sections 2.5 and 2.6, on pages 38–39, to review dependent clauses, independent clauses, and complex sentences.

Punctuation Tip

Commas Don't Separate Subjects and Predicates

Do not separate a compound subject from the predicate of a sentence with a comma.

16.6 Commas After Verbal Phrases

Introductory phrases containing verb forms should be set off from the rest of the sentence by a comma. These are participial and infinitive phrases.

> *Hearing* our explanation, she reconsidered.
> *Knowing* the answer, he raised his hand.
> *Given* the time allotted to us, I think we have accomplished much.
> *To gain* access to the hall, try the back door.

Place a comma after introductory modifiers that consist solely of a verbal.

> *Perplexed,* he closed his cell phone.
> *Gasping,* she raced toward the departing train.

Verbals as Subjects

Do not use a comma if the participial phrase or infinitive phrase serves as the subject of the sentence.

> *To gain access to the hall* was difficult.
> *The amount of time allotted to us* proved inadequate to complete the assignment.
> *Hearing our explanation* caused her to reconsider.

16.7 Commas After Prepositional Phrases

As a general rule, use a comma after introductory prepositional phrases. However, it is acceptable to omit the comma following short introductory prepositional phrases of four or fewer words.

> In our previous correspondence with both parties, we thoroughly evaluated the four proposals.
> On April 4 we began negotiations.
> At the next meeting a new president will be elected.

You *must* include a comma if an introductory phrase contains a verb form or if it is a transitional expression or an independent comment. To avoid making these judgments, many writers simply use a comma after all introductory prepositional phrases.

Infinitives and Participles
See Sections 9.6, on page 251, and 9.9, on page 255, for a quick review of infinitives and participles.

■

Be-Backs

Salespeople refer to *be-backs* as shoppers who promise they'll "be back" to buy a product when they have no such intention. Call it a salesperson's intuition.

Introductory Phrase

Short Prepositional Phrase	On April 4 we began negotiations.
	On April 4, we began negotiations.
Phrase With Verb Form	In preparing your report, be sure to include this month's projected sales figures.
Transitional Phrase	In addition, you should include last year's totals.
Independent Comment	In my opinion, these figures are meaningless.

Transitional Phrases and Interjections
To review transitional phrases and interjections, refer back to Sections 13.14 and 13.15 on pages 387-388.

■

Punctuation Tip

Transitionals and Exclamations

Use a comma to set off an introductory transitional phrase or exclamation from the rest of the sentence.

16.8 Commas After Transitional Phrases and Interjections

Many transitional phrases can join two independent clauses. As connectives, these phrases are preceded by a semicolon and followed by a comma.

> Our sales are increasing; *for example,* Denver sales are up nearly 40 percent.
> His work is far from perfect; *in fact,* it contains a large number of errors.

If these sentences were rewritten as two separate sentences, *for example* and *in fact* would be introductory elements and would still be followed by commas.

> Our sales are increasing. *For example,* Denver sales are up nearly 40 percent.
> His work is far from perfect. *In fact,* it contains a large number of errors.

Interjections

A mild interjection or exclamation may begin a sentence. When it does, it is followed by a comma.

Well, at least I tried.	No, we will be unable to attend.
Oh, that's all right.	Yes, I am delighted to accept your offer.

Rule 3: Commas After Introducory Elements

Use a comma to separate introductory elements from the rest of the sentence.

Dependent clause , independent clause.
Verbal phrase , independent clause.
Prepositional phrase of 4 or more words , independent clause.
Transitional phrase , independent clause.
Interjection , independent clause.

Coverage Key

Section	Statement
16.5 ➤ Commas After Dependent Clauses	➤ **S15, S16, S17, S18, S19, S20, S24, S25**
16.6 ➤ Commas After Verbal Phrases	➤ **S22, S23, S25**
16.7 ➤ Commas After Prepositional Phrases	➤ **S21, S25**
16.8 ➤ Commas After Transitional Phrases and Interjections	➤ **S25**

Instructions: Cover the answers in the **Answer** column; then write your answer to the first statement. Uncover the first printed answer and compare your answer to it. If you wrote a correct answer, continue the activity. If you made an error, use the **Coverage Key** to locate the chapter section you need to review. When you are confident that you understand the material, continue with the reinforcement activity.

ANSWER	STATEMENT
	S15 **I'll have her phone you when she returns.** This is an example of a (complex, compound) sentence because it contains a(n) _____ clause and a(n) _____ clause.
A15 complex, independent, dependent	**S16** **I'll have her phone you when she returns.** *When she returns* is a(n) _____ clause.
A16 dependent	**S17** When a complex sentence begins with an independent clause, you (should, should not) place a comma after the independent clause.
A17 should not	**S18** When a complex sentence begins with a dependent clause, you (should, should not) place a comma after the dependent clause.
A18 should	**S19** Place commas in the following sentences as needed: a. **I'd like to speak with you if you have a few minutes.** b. **Whenever you are in town call me.**
A19 a. no comma needed b. **Whenever you are in town, call me.**	**S20** Place commas in the following sentences as needed: a. **Call me whenever you are in town.** b. **Although the revised plans have been completed and approved we won't break ground for a month.** c. **While you were out Ms. Kinsella phoned.**
A20 a. no comma needed b. **Although the revised plans have been completed and approved, we won't break ground for a month.** c. **While you were out, Ms. Kinsella phoned.**	

S21 Short introductory prepositional phrases are usually (followed, not followed) by a comma. A comma (is, is not) used, however, to separate long introductory phrases from the body of the sentence. Place a comma in each of the following sentences where necessary:
  a. In January the new sales tax went into effect.
  b. At the meeting we discussed this problem at length.
  c. To get the best possible results from this appliance carefully read and follow the directions.

A21 not followed, is
  a. no comma needed
  b. no comma needed
  c. **To get the best possible results from this appliance, carefully read and follow the directions.**

S22 Introductory participial and infinitive phrases (should, should not) be set off from the rest of the sentence by a comma. If these phrases serve as the subject of the sentence, they (should, should not) be followed by a comma.

A22 should, should not

S23 Place commas in the following sentences as needed:
  a. **Inhaling the dust caused her to sneeze.**
  b. **Inhaling the dust she started to sneeze.**
  c. **To access the system you must enter your security code.**
  d. **To access the system is impossible without a security code.**
  e. **Poorly translated from the original language the instructions in the manual were of little use.**

A23
  a. no comma needed
  b. **Inhaling the dust, she started to sneeze.**
  c. **To access the system, you must enter your security code.**
  d. no comma needed
  e. **Poorly translated from the original language, the instructions in the manual were of little use.**

S24 Place commas in the following sentences as needed:
  a. **When you receive her message please telephone me right away.**
  b. **Please telephone me right away when you receive her message.**
  c. **Before beginning this morning's session I have several announcements.**
  d. **I have several announcements before beginning this morning's session.**

A24
  a. **When you receive her message, please telephone...**
  b. no comma needed
  c. **Before beginning this morning's session, I have...**
  d. no commas needed

S25 Place commas in the following sentences as needed:
  a. **On the other hand I could meet you in the city that night.**
  b. **Yes I took the train from Boston at noon and did not return home until the next day.**
  c. **In fact I could not have seen the accident because I was in a meeting on the top floor.**
  d. **Fascinated John stared at the computer screen.**

A25
  a. **On the other hand, I could meet you in the city that night.**
  b. **Yes, I took the train from Boston...**
  c. **In fact, I could not have seen the accident...**
  d. **Fascinated, John stared at the computer screen.**

CHAPTER 16 SUMMARY

In this chapter you studied the first three basic rules for commas. You focused on how commas separate words, phrases, or clauses listed in a series. You also learned that commas separate independent clauses within compound sentences, although this rule generally does not apply to short clauses. Finally, you examined when and how to use commas after various introductory elements, such as dependent clauses, verbal phrases, prepositional phrases, and transitional phrases.

Getting Connected

GOING ONLINE FOR GRAMMAR INSTRUCTION

GOAL: Many schools have Websites where individuals can find answers to questions about writing and grammar. When reference manuals do not offer sufficient feedback to your questions about punctuation or sentence construction, you may find the help you need at a Website. Going online can also reinforce your grammar skills by offering you additional descriptions or examples of concepts you are trying to learn.

In this activity you will visit a grammar Website to review the resources it offers. You will use your experience to write sentences that demonstrate your skills using the three basic comma rules covered in this chapter.

STEP 1   Go to *englishworkshop.glencoe.com,* the address for *The English Workshop* Website, and click on Unit 7. Next click on Getting Connected, and then click on Chapter 16. At the Chapter 16 Getting Connected option, you'll see a list of grammar Websites. Select a site to visit.

STEP 2   At the home page of the Website you select, locate and connect with information related to the topic of this chapter—commas.

STEP 3   Scan information about the uses of commas you studied in this chapter: commas in a series, in compound sentences, and with introductory elements. Visit at least two other sites and review their materials on commas. Decide which site you like best. On a separate sheet of paper, answer the following questions:

    a. When you are trying to learn about commas, is it helpful or confusing to look at new examples or definitions that have different wording? Explain why you think additional material is either helpful or confusing, or a little of both. Use your experience with the grammar sites to help you develop an answer.

b. List three or four items you found at the site you selected, or list three or four reasons you like or dislike the site you selected. Work that list into a complete sentence that includes a *series* of at least three items.

c. Rewrite the sentence you just created and place the coordinating conjunction *and* between each item in the series. Remember not to use commas in such lists. Read aloud the two sentences with lists, or have someone else read them aloud. Which sentence sounds better to you? Explain your answer on the sheet of paper with which you've been working.

If you think the first sentence (including the list with items separated by commas) sounds better, write a good reason for using *and* where you placed commas in your list. If you choose the second sentence (including the list with items separated by *and*), write a good reason for using commas instead of the *ands.*

d. Write another sentence using a list that is a *compound subject.* Did you include a comma after the list? Why is that comma correct or incorrect?

e. Write a compound sentence about the Website you selected. Include two independent clauses that are at least six words each. Separate the clauses with *and, but, or, nor, for, so,* or *yet.* Use commas as needed.

f. Write another sentence about the material you found at the site. Include two independent clauses that are no more than four words each. Separate the short independent clauses with *and, but, or, nor, for, so,* or *yet.* Use commas as needed.

STEP 4 Write your name at the top of the paper you used for this activity, and give it to your instructor.

Tip Some grammar Websites provide e-mail tutorial assistance. Some offer help for free, but some charge. Check to see if you can answer your questions using the free materials posted at the site. The FAQ (Frequently Asked Questions) file may be a good starting point.

PRACTICE 1

Commas in a Series

Instructions: Place commas in the following sentences where necessary. Write *C* in front of the sentence if no commas are required. Underline any changes you make.

EXAMPLE: _____ **The course meets on Monday, Tuesday, Thursday, and Friday mornings.**

_____ 1. The company sells, rents, leases, and repairs medical equipment.

_____ 2. The successful salesperson is friendly, personable, knowledgeable, and self-confident.

_____ 3. Our store deals in radios, television sets, stereos, video cassette recorders, and similar products.

___C___ 4. Neither rain nor snow nor sleet nor gloom of night shall stop the mail carrier from his or her appointed rounds.

___C___ 5. The firm of Webber, Price & Beamon is well known in the advertising world.

_____ 6. Would you like a chance to break into a fast-growing, profitable, interesting, respected profession?

_____ 7. Fame, fortune, and esteem—these were their goals in life.

___C___ 8. Their firm deals in the finest silks and cottons and woolens and linens.

_____ 9. Their firm deals in the finest silks, cottons, woolens, and linens.

_____ 10. Tact, wisdom, and diplomacy—these are marks of an enlightened, intelligent, foreign policy.

___C___ 11. Please try our new furniture polish in either pine or lemon scent.

_____ 12. To plan and design carefully, to purchase and order wisely, and to build and construct sturdily are necessary steps.

_____ 13. We deal in state bonds, county bonds, municipal bonds, industrial bonds, railroad bonds, etc.

_____ 14. We deal in state, county, municipal, industrial, and railroad bonds.

_____ 15. We have correspondence from you dated May 3, May 18, June 6, and July 15.

_____ 16. You won't be able to resist our newest model when you see its long, low, streamlined design.

_____ 17. Rare newspapers, magazines, books, and periodicals—all will be available at this week's auction.

_____ 18. Our rates are $90 for a single room, $120 for a double room, and $195 for a two-room suite.

_____ 19. She is seeking a secure, challenging, well-paying position in insurance.

_____ 20. Questions about such topics as age, sex, race, religion, and marital status are prohibited on job application forms.

_____ 21. The properties available are in Detroit, St. Louis, Cleveland, and New York.

_____ 22. For lunch we offer roast beef, macaroni and cheese, garden salad, and bread and butter.

___C___ 23. Do not install the CD player on an unstable table, shelf, cart, or stand.

_____ 24. To start the old tractor you must turn the ignition key, gently press the gas pedal, and push the starter button.

___C___ 25. She found three old manual adding machines in the storeroom.

PRACTICE 2

Sentence Errors

Instructions: This is a review practice on run-on sentences and sentence fragments. Proofread the following letter, crossing out each error and writing your correction. If you need to, review the material on run-on sentences and sentence fragments in Chapter 2. Underline any changes you make.

The Drake Hotel

1 Drake Plaza
Bell Harbor, MD 20724

April 22, 20--

Ms. Patricia Alvarado
1996 Blake Court
Bowie, MD 20720

Dear Ms. Alvarado:

The Drake Hotel is a comfortable and well-managed manor. Situated on 80 gorgeous acres in the rolling hills of Bell Harbor. From the heart of Baltimore it can be reached by train or automobile. In less than an hour. Although it is near the city. It is far enough removed for rest and quiet.

Majestic old trees and attractive walks add to the beauty of the grounds the extensive lawns reach to the shore of Chesapeake Bay fishing and boating are always in season.

If you can possibly arrange your vacation for August you will find the Drake Hotel grounds at their loveliest flowers are in full bloom and the shade trees are at their lushest. Of course some of our regular guests prefer October when the trees are ablaze with color. And the ground is covered with a thick carpet of fallen leaves.

We extend to you and your friends. A cordial invitation to visit us.

Yours sincerely,

Jae Blandford, Manager

PRACTICE 3

Compound Sentences

Instructions: Place commas where necessary in the following sentences. Write *C* in front of the sentence if no commas are required. Underline any changes you make.

EXAPLE: _____ I don't want to do this‚but you leave me no alternative.

_____ 1. The tone of these letters is not serious but the message they contain is.

_____ 2. He phoned but was unable to speak with her.

_____ 3. He phoned but he was unable to speak with her.

_____ 4. Your offer was received and was carefully considered by the board.

_____ 5. The board received your offer and considered it carefully.

_____ 6. An excellent pool is available for those who like to swim and a beautiful 18-hole course is open for those who like to play golf.

_____ 7. You have not written us for many weeks nor have you bothered to pay your bills.

_____ 8. You have neither written us nor explained why your account remains unsettled.

_____ 9. We tried but failed.

_____ 10. We tried but we failed.

_____ 11. They tried and they succeeded.

_____ 12. It was inspected it was tested it was tortured but it didn't fade or shrink.

_____ 13. The risks are great but the rewards are greater.

_____ 14. The risks are great but so are the rewards.

_____ 15. I have money invested in state county and municipal bonds so much of my interest income is tax free.

_____ 16. Cheryl made the photocopies Arnold collated them and Anita stapled and distributed them.

_____ 17. Our principal plant is in Newark our regional distribution office is in Saddle Brook and our national offices are in New York.

_____ 18. We will leave immediately after lunch on Friday for the seminar begins at 8:30 a.m. on Saturday.

_____ 19. We will leave immediately after lunch on Friday for the Saturday morning seminar.

_____ 20. Our sale on computer accessories ends this Saturday so now is the time to save money by purchasing the items you really want.

PRACTICE 4

Introductory Elements

Instructions: Place commas where necessary in the following sentences. Write C in front of the sentence if no commas are required. Underline any changes you make.

EXAMPLE: _____ **If you don't find a job by the time you graduate,don't feel discouraged.**

_____ 1. We have continued to operate at capacity despite the recession.

_____ 2. Despite the recession we have continued to operate at capacity.

_____ 3. Yes I'll accept the motion as amended.

_____ 4. There have been layoffs in two other divisions since I've been here.

_____ 5. As soon as the clock struck 5 o'clock the staff left the office.

_____ 6. When some employees took extended coffee breaks Ms. Giardani became irritated.

_____ 7. Irritated because some employees took extended coffee breaks Ms. Giardani threatened to install a time clock.

_____ 8. No I don't mind.

_____ 9. We should be landing in less than an hour.

_____ 10. In my opinion municipal bonds are an excellent investment.

_____ 11. With the right combination of luck and wisdom we should succeed.

_____ 12. If you are willing to make the initial investment you will be amply rewarded.

_____ 13. With few exceptions everything is proceeding as planned.

_____ 14. Through Cathy's efforts we have more than met our goal.

_____ 15. Well if you insist I will chair the committee.

_____ 16. Actually we have accomplished a great deal in the relatively short time we have been working on this project.

_____ 17. Utterly exhausted the arbiter recessed the negotiations.

_____ 18. During the strike there will be shortages of some items.

_____ 19. Having been soundly defeated in the New Hampshire primary the candidate withdrew from the race for the nomination.

_____ 20. Angry and frustrated Tanya resigned.

PRACTICE 5

Commas in a Series and After Independent Clauses and Introductory Elements

Instructions: Insert commas in the following sentences where necessary. Write *C* in front of the sentence if no commas are required. Underline any changes you make.

EXAMPLE: _____ **If I can be of further assistance‸please feel free to call on me.**

_____ 1. Fluent in French Connie wanted to study Spanish Italian and Portuguese.

_____ 2. Although the two sides bargained far into the night they were unable to reach an agreement.

_____ 3. Hoping to find a secure challenging and well-paying position in banking Meredith sought the assistance of the college's job placement service.

_____ 4. In our opinion it is far too early to predict the outcome.

_____ 5. Distraught the father of the injured girl rushed into the emergency room and demanded to see the attending physician.

_____ 6. With a Nichols credit card you can take advantage of special sales throughout the year.

_____ 7. In spite of the fact that it looked as though it would begin to rain any minute Lee insisted on paying the daily greens fee and teeing off.

_____ 8. Purolator Federal Express United Parcel Service and Airborne are all reliable companies.

_____ 9. When selecting companies to contact Karen searched the Internet using Yahoo! AltaVista Google and McFind.

_____ 10. Elsa Harvey Caitlyn and Bruno have indicated their willingness to serve but no one else has expressed any interest in the committee.

_____ 11. In the meantime Ms. Menjou will be in charge so there should be no delay in production.

_____ 12. Working at Farmingdale's for several years made me familiar with their sales promotions.

_____ 13. To conceive an idea put it into operation and see it through to completion takes intelligence perseverance and dedication.

_____ 14. Having worked at Farmingdale's for several years I know the types of sales promotions they normally run but this promotion is a new one.

_____ 15. The manuscript for the new and expanded edition of the textbook must be revised and resubmitted to the developmental editor by June 30.

Name _____

Class _____ Date _____

PRACTICE 6

Composition: Writing Sentences that Require Commas

Instructions: Compose complete sentences according to the instructions in parentheses.

EXAMPLE: **(Write a sentence with three nouns in a series.)**
    Ms. Fielding, Mr. Ohura, and Ms. Rosen have been elected to the school board.

1. (Write a sentence with three adjectives in a series.) _____
_____
_____

2. (Write a compound sentence that contains one comma.) _____
_____
_____

3. (Write a compound sentence that contains two commas.) _____
_____
_____

4. (Write a sentence that begins with a dependent clause.) _____
_____
_____

5. (Write a sentence that begins with a short prepositional phrase.) _____
_____
_____

6. (Write a sentence that begins with a long prepositional phrase.) _____
_____
_____

7. (Write a sentence that begins with a verb phrase used as a modifier.) _____
_____
_____

8. (Write a sentence with three adverbs in a series connected by *and.*) _____
_____
_____

9. (Write a sentence that begins with a mild interjection.) _____
_____
_____

10. (Write a compound sentence in which the subject is *you* understood.) _____
_____
_____

More on the Comma

CHAPTER 17 PREVIEW

This chapter will cover the last three basic rules for comma usage. You will study how commas are used to set off nonessential expressions and short quotations, and how commas can prevent confusion in your writing. You will assess your knowledge in the Programmed Reinforcement sections and the Practices. Finally, you will visit an online encyclopedia to sharpen your knowledge of comma usage.

OBJECTIVES

After completing this chapter, you will be able to

- Determine how to use commas with nonessential expressions.
- Distinguish between restrictive and nonrestrictive appositives.
- Determine how and when to use commas correctly with the following:
  - Names of persons directly addressed
  - Participial phrases
  - Words or phrases that interrupt the flow of a sentence
  - Questions that have been added to statements
  - Contrasting expressions within sentences
  - Abbreviations that stand for academic or religious degrees
  - Dates and days
  - States or countries that follow cities and street addresses
  - Short quotations
  - Special instances that may cause confusion for readers

Study Plan for Chapter 17

The Study Plan for Chapter 17 offers a set of strategies that will help you learn and review the chapter material.

❶ Names and Commas: Are commas needed before and after names? Determine whether the person named is being spoken *to* or *about*. Use commas only when the person named is spoken to directly.

❷ Interrupters: An interrupter often appears between a subject and a verb. Use that fact to help you identify the interrupter in a sentence.

❸ Relative Clauses and Commas: Locate relative clauses in sentences by looking for one of the three relative pronouns—*who, which,* or *that.* Is the clause necessary for understanding the full meaning of the sentence? Do not place commas around a clause that is necessary.

❹ Quotations: Commas set off direct quotations but should not be used with indirect quotations. If you find a *that* after a word indicating speech, you probably have an indirect quotation.

Use commas to set off expressions that could be left out of a sentence without destroying it or changing its meaning. This fourth basic rule covers a variety of situations. Sections A and B of this chapter will examine these situations separately.

17.1 Commas in Direct Address

Use commas to set off the name of a person who is being directly addressed.

> *Mr. Ruben,* I think that you are the best candidate.

The sentence above addresses Mr. Ruben directly. If the name *Mr. Ruben* were omitted, the sentence would still be complete:

> I think that you are the best candidate.

Therefore, set off *Mr. Ruben* with a comma.

The name of the person directly addressed is set off with commas no matter where the name appears in the sentence.

> I think, *Mr. Ruben,* that you are the best candidate.
> I think that you, *Mr. Ruben,* are the best candidate.
> I think that you are the best candidate, *Mr. Ruben.*

This rule applies only to the name of a person directly addressed. If you are talking *about* someone, don't set off the name with commas.

WRONG:	Christine, is an excellent supervisor.
RIGHT:	✔ Christine, you are an excellent supervisor.
RIGHT:	✔ Christine is an excellent supervisor.

Use commas when you address someone directly with a term other than his or her name.

> *Sir,* your membership application has been approved.
> Let me tell you, *fellow investors,* what the stock has earned.

Spamming

Spamming describes the unacceptable act of cross-posting unwanted Internet ads to a variety of newsgroups. This odd expression derives from the canned pork product Spam.

17.2 Commas With Explanatory Expressions

Use commas to set off an expression that explains a preceding word.

1. Mr. Ethan Sellers, director of personnel at Meacham Enterprises, spoke to the group.

The phrase *director of personnel at Meacham Enterprises* explains who Mr. Sellers is. You could leave out the phrase and still have a complete sentence unchanged in its essential meaning.

Leave out: director of personnel at Meacham Enterprises
Remainder: Mr. Ethan Sellers spoke to the group.

The examples below indicate how explanatory expressions may be left out of sentences without destroying the sentence or radically changing its meaning.

2. We will send our top systems analyst, Ms. Ashley Iwamoto, to study the problem.

Leave out: Ms. Ashley Iwamoto
Remainder: We will send our top systems analyst to study the problem.

3. Mars, the planet closest to our own, has inspired many works of science fiction.

Leave out: the planet closest to our own
Remainder: Mars has inspired many works of science fiction.

4. Butter, which is made by churning cream or whole milk, is high in saturated fat.

Leave out: which is made by churning cream or whole milk
Remainder: Butter is high in saturated fat.

Because the explanatory expressions in the four sentences above could be left out without destroying each sentence or changing its meaning, the expressions are set off by commas.

No Commas With Essential Expressions

Look at the next two examples. Can any part of these sentences be dropped without changing the meaning of the sentences?

5. Butter that is rancid is sickening.

Leave out: that is rancid
Remainder: Butter is sickening.

The independent clause *Butter . . . is sickening* is a complete sentence, but does the writer mean that butter is sickening? No. The writer means that a particular type of butter—rancid butter—is sickening. If the expression *that is rancid* is dropped, the meaning of the sentence changes drastically. The expression is essential to the meaning of the sentence; therefore, it should *not* be separated by commas.

6. Breathing air that is polluted can damage your lungs.

Leave out: that is polluted
Remainder: Breathing air can damage your lungs.

The remainder is a complete sentence, but the message states that breathing *polluted* air can damage your lungs. Because *that is polluted* is essential to the meaning of the sentence, it should *not* be set off by commas.

The Use of Commas to Signal Different Meanings

Would you use commas in the next sentence?

7a. The eighth-grade students who sold the most candy were rewarded with a party.

Your answer depends on what you mean. If some eighth-grade students were rewarded for selling more candy than other eighth-grade students did, then *who sold the most candy* is essential to the meaning of the sentence and should *not* be set off by commas.

How, then, can the same sentence be written with commas and be correct?

7b. The eighth-grade students, who sold the most candy, were rewarded with a party.

If, after the school candy sale, all students in the eighth grade were rewarded with a party for selling more candy than students in the other grades did, then *who sold the most candy* could be left out without changing the essential meaning of the sentence. If the explanatory expression is nonessential, it should be set off by commas.

17.3 Relative Clauses

Examine these last few examples again:

Butter, which is made by churning cream or whole milk,
 is high in saturated fat.
Butter that is rancid is sickening.
Breathing air that is polluted can damage your lungs.
The eighth-grade students who sold the most candy were rewarded
 with a party.

Each of these sentences contains a clause that begins with a relative pronoun—*that*, *which*, or *who*. These clauses are known as **relative clauses.** Sometimes you will need to put commas around relative clauses, but sometimes you will not. What you want your sentence to mean will determine whether you use commas.

Restrictive and Nonrestrictive Clauses

When a relative clause is essential to the meaning of a sentence, it is called a **restrictive clause.** For example, in the sentence *Butter that is rancid is sickening,* the clause *that is rancid* is restrictive because it restricts, or limits, the type of butter being talked about to one type: *rancid butter.* No commas are needed in this sentence.

When a relative clause is not essential to the meaning of a sentence, it is called a **nonrestrictive clause.** For example, in the sentence *Butter, which is made by churning cream or whole milk, is high in saturated fat,* the clause *which is made by churning cream or whole milk* is a nonrestrictive clause. It does not restrict, or limit, the type of butter being talked about—all butter *is high in saturated fat.* In this example, the relative clause adds information that is not essential to the meaning of the sentence. That clause should be set off by commas.

Remember: Do not use commas around **restrictive** clauses because such clauses are *essential* to the meaning of the sentence. Use commas to set off **nonrestrictive** clauses because such clauses are *nonessential* to the meaning of the sentence.

Relative Clause Test. Here is a simple test for determining whether a clause is restrictive (essential) or nonrestrictive (nonessential).

Step 1: Read the sentence the way it stands.
Step 2: Delete the clause and reread the sentence. Did the meaning change?

If the meaning changed, the clause is restrictive, or essential, and should *not* be set off with commas. If the meaning does not change, the clause is nonrestrictive, or nonessential, and should be set off with commas.

Test Run. Sentences 4 through 7 in Section 17.2 demonstrate that restrictive clauses are not set off with commas because they are essential to the meaning of a sentence, and that nonrestrictive clauses are set off with commas because they are not essential to the meaning. Try the test on those sentences.

Other Tests. The same test will help you recognize nonessential expressions and may help you catch names that are used in direct address. Try the test on Sentences 1 through 4 in Section 17.2 and the sample sentences in Section 17.1. For Step 2, delete the explanatory expression or name.

Grammar Tip

Testing for Nonessentials

Even if you forget the technical names for these clauses, remember how to test to see if a clause or phrase is essential to a sentence.

That/Which

Use *that* at the beginning of a relative clause if the clause is restrictive and *which* if the clause is nonrestrictive. Let's return to familiar sample sentences from Section 17.2. We'll retain the sentence numbers from the earlier section.

Restrictive Sentence

BEGINNING OF SENTENCE	*THAT* CLAUSE	REMAINDER OF SENTENCE
5. Butter	that is rancid	is sickening.
6. Breathing air	that is polluted	can damage your lungs.

Nonrestrictive Sentence

BEGINNING OF SENTENCE,	*WHICH* CLAUSE,	REMAINDER OF SENTENCE.
4. Butter,	which is made by churning cream or whole milk,	is high in saturated fat.

17.4 Appositives

Let's review Sentences 1, 2, and 3 from Section 17.2.

1. Mr. Ethan Sellers, director of personnel at Meacham Enterprises, spoke to the group.
2. We will send our top systems analyst, Ms. Ashley Iwamoto, to study the problem.
3. Mars, the planet closest to our own, has inspired many works of science fiction.

In each sentence the material set off by commas is a noun or noun phrase that identifies the noun that precedes it.

The noun phrase *director of personnel at Meacham Enterprises* explains who *Mr. Ethan Sellers* (noun) is. The noun *Ms. Ashley Iwamoto* identifies the person described by the noun phrase *our top systems analyst.* The noun *Mars* is identified by the noun phrase *the planet closest to our own.* In these sentences the expressions set off by commas are **appositives.** An appositive is a noun or noun phrase placed next to another noun to identify or explain it. In the three examples the identifying expressions are set off by commas because they are not essential. Technically, they are **nonrestrictive appositives.**

Let's review Sentences 1, 2, and 3 in a chart that identifies their parts.

Nonrestrictive Appositive

BEGINNING OF SENTENCE	NONESSENTIAL EXPRESSION	REMAINDER OF SENTENCE
1. Mr. Ethan Sellers	director of personnel at Meacham Enterprises	spoke to the group.
2. We will send our top systems analyst	Ms. Ashley Iwamoto	to study the problem.
3. Mars	the planet closest to our own	has inspired many works of science fiction.

A **restrictive appositive** is essential to the meaning of the sentence. It requires no commas. Look at this sentence:

> The great composer Beethoven wrote many of his finest works after he was totally deaf.

The noun *Beethoven* identifies the noun phrase *the great composer*. Could the appositive *Beethoven* be omitted from the sentence without affecting the meaning? No. You need *Beethoven* to identify *which* great composer you are talking about. *Beethoven* is essential to the meaning. Therefore, *Beethoven* is a restrictive appositive, and it requires no commas.

Look at the sentence about Beethoven and other sentences placed in a chart that identifies their parts. Study the sentences and determine why the appositives are restrictive and why commas are not needed.

Restrictive Appositive

BEGINNING OF SENTENCE	ESSENTIAL EXPRESSION	REMAINDER OF SENTENCE.
1. The great composer	Beethoven	wrote many of his finest works after he was totally deaf.
2. My friend	Jorge	has spoken of you often.
3. The philosopher	Locke	expressed the rights of man.
4. The year	1933	ushered in the New Deal.
5. The word	*relevance*	is overused nowadays.

The Use of Commas to Signal Different Meanings for Appositives

Should commas be used in the following sentence?

> Ms. Nuñez's book *Essential Internet Marketing Tips* is on the best-seller list.

In Section 17.2 you faced a similar choice with the sentences about the students who sold the candy. In the case of Ms. Nuñez and her book, whether you use commas depends on what you mean—that is, on how many books Ms. Nuñez has written.

The sentence without commas is correct if Ms. Nuñez has written a number of books. The title of the best-seller is essential because it identifies which of Ms. Nuñez's books is on the best-seller list. In that sentence, the title is a restrictive appositive and is not set off by commas.

Look at the sentence with commas:

Ms. Nuñez's book, *Essential Internet Marketing Tips,* is on the best-seller list.

If Ms. Nuñez has written only one book, the commas are correct. Readers know from the sentence the essential fact that Ms. Nuñez's book is a best-seller. The title itself is not essential for readers to understand the point, because she has written only one book. That makes the title a nonrestrictive appositive, and it should be set off by commas.

Expressions as Units

Sometimes an expression is treated as essential simply because of the close relationship between the words. For example,

My wife Kathleen will graduate from law school next year.

Kathleen is a nonrestrictive appositive; she is the writer's only wife. Technically, *Kathleen* should be set off by commas because her name is not needed to explain to which wife the writer is referring. No commas are used, however, because an expression like this is read as a **unit.** Similarly, *My son Dave loves to play basketball* is written without commas whether Dave is an only child or has several brothers.

17.5 Commas With Participial Phrases

Look at the two ways the sentence below may be written:

The candidate, realizing that the election was lost, conceded defeat.
Realizing that the election was lost, the candidate conceded defeat.

In either sentence, *realizing that the election was lost* is a **participial phrase** modifying the subject *candidate.* Pick out the participial phrase in these sentences:

Fighting for his life, he lashed out viciously.
The economy, having been stagnant for months, is finally beginning
   to grow.
We ordered rather late, counting on immediate service.

TIME MANAGEMENT Tackle your most important work during your high-energy time of the day. Determine ahead of time which projects deserve your energy and attention first.

Each of the participial phrases in the sentences on the previous page could be left out without changing the basic meaning of the sentence. Thus, these phrases are set off with commas because they are merely explanatory phrases that are not essential to the meaning.

As you saw in Section 16.6, the last two sentences could also be rephrased to begin with the participial phrase, as the first one does.

> Having been stagnant for months, the economy is finally beginning
>   to grow.
> Counting on immediate service, we ordered rather late.

In each case, the comma is also being used to set off an introductory element.

Look at this sentence, however:

> Prices rising at a rapid pace are a sure sign of inflation.

Here we have the participial phrase *rising at a rapid pace.* Can it be left out? No. This phrase is essential to the meaning of the sentence. It is acting as a restrictive clause and therefore should *not* be set off with commas. In fact, this word group is a restrictive clause in disguise. This sentence really says: *Prices that are rising at a rapid pace are a sure sign of inflation.*

> The young woman speaking with Mr. Nowitzki is our new intern.

In the above sentence, the participial phrase *speaking with Mr. Nowitzki* is essential and may also be seen as a restrictive clause in disguise. This sentence really says: *The young woman who is speaking with Mr. Nowitzki is our new intern.*

Dangling Participles
Remember, when you start a sentence with a participial phrase, be sure to follow it immediately with the subject to which it refers. Look back at dangling participles in Section 9.10 on page 256.

∎

Coverage Key

Section		Statement
17.1	➤ Commas in Direct Address	➤ **S1**
17.2	➤ Commas with Explanatory Expressions	➤ **S2, S3**
17.3	➤ Relative Clauses	➤ **S4, S5, S6, S7, S8, S9, S10**
17.4	➤ Appositives	➤ **S11**
17.5	➤ Commas with Participial Phrases	➤ **S12, S13**

Instructions: Cover the answers in the **Answer** column; then write your answer to the first statement. Uncover the first printed answer and compare your answer to it. If you wrote a correct answer, continue the activity. If you made an error, use the **Coverage Key** to locate the chapter section you need to review. When you are confident that you understand the material, continue with the reinforcement activity.

ANSWER

STATEMENT

S1 In general, commas (are used, are not used) to set off the name of a person directly addressed. Punctuate these sentences:
 a. **Tell me Amir what your plans are.**
 b. **I beg you my friends to stop arguing.**
 c. **Jim is that you?**

A1 are used;
 a. **Tell me, Amir, what your plans are.**
 b. **I beg you, my friends, to stop arguing.**
 c. **Jim, is that you?**

S2 Commas are used to set off an expression that explains a preceding word. Underline the expressions that should be set off by commas:
 a. **Ms. Phillips president of Argo Electronics is here.**
 b. **Frankfort the capital of Kentucky is 30 minutes from Louisville.**

A2 a. <u>president of Argo Electronics</u>
 b. <u>the capital of Kentucky</u>

S3 A group of words not essential to the meaning of a sentence should be set off by commas. Are commas used correctly in these sentences?
 a. **My old computer, which I bought years ago, is still a satisfactory word processor.** _____
 b. **Gasoline, that is mixed with water, is useless.** _____

A3 a. yes, b. no

S4 **Gasoline that is mixed with water is useless.** The word **that** is a relative pronoun. The clause **that is mixed with water** is called a(n) _____ clause. If you leave out the relative clause from this sentence, what remains? _____. This (has, has not) changed the meaning of the sentence.

A4 relative, **Gasoline is useless,** has

A5 restrictive

A6 is

A7 cannot, do not

A8 relative, is not

A9 My car keeps stalling, has not

A10 restrictive, should

A11 nonrestrictive;
a. **no commas needed**
b. **Sam Shepard, the author of *Cowboy Mouth* and *True West*, won the Pulitzer Prize in 1979 for the play *Buried Child*.**

A12 participial, is not

A13 a. **Having made his position clear, Mr. Yaeger sat down.**
b. no commas needed
c. no commas needed
d. **Ms. Rahman, preparing to make a statement, rose to her feet.**

S5 Because leaving out **that is mixed with water** from the sentence in S4 changes its meaning, this clause *restricts* the meaning to only one type of gasoline. It is therefore called a(n)_____ clause.

S6 A restrictive clause (is, is not) essential to the meaning of a sentence.

S7 Because a restrictive clause is essential to the meaning of a sentence, you (can, cannot) treat it as being merely explanatory. Accordingly, you (do, do not) set it off with commas.

S8 **My car, which is brand new, keeps stalling.** The clause **which is brand new** is a(n) _____ clause that (is, is not) essential to the meaning of the sentence.

S9 If you leave out **which is brand new** from the sentence in S8, the remainder is: _____ .
This (has, has not) changed the meaning of the sentence.

S10 Because omitting **which is brand new** does not change the meaning, it is a(n) _____ clause. It is merely explanatory and (should, should not) be set off with commas.

S11 An appositive is a noun or noun phrase placed next to another noun to identify or explain it. Appositives are set off with commas unless they are _____ appositives. Punctuate the following sentences:
a. **The South African writer Nadine Gordimer wrote *The Conservationists*.**
b. **Sam Shepard the author of *Cowboy Mouth* and *True West* won the Pulitzer Prize in 1979 for *Buried Child*.**

S12 **Rising from his chair, he greeted the visitors. Rising** is the present participle of the verb **to rise.** The phrase **rising from his chair** is a(n) _____ phrase. When a participial phrase (is, is not) essential to the meaning of a sentence, it should be set off with commas.

S13 Insert commas where necessary:
a. **Having made his position clear Mr. Yaeger sat down.**
b. **People considering investing in mutual funds should attend this free investment seminar.**
c. **The order being processed is the one I want.**
d. **Ms. Rahman preparing to make a statement rose to her feet.**

In this section you will examine ways to punctuate words, phrases, and clauses that interrupt the flow of a sentence. Here the verb *interrupt* means that you are forced to pause as you read a sentence.

17.6 Interrupters

Use commas to set off a word, phrase, or clause that interrupts the flow of a sentence.

Here are two lists of commonly used words, phrases, and clauses that should be set off with commas if they interrupt the flow of a sentence.

INTERRUPTING WORDS

accordingly	however	otherwise
again	indeed	personally
also	moreover	respectively
besides	namely	still
consequently	naturally	then
finally	nevertheless	therefore
furthermore	next	too
hence	notwithstanding	

INTERRUPTING PHRASES

as a rule	if any	of course
as you know	in brief	on the contrary
at any rate	in fact	on the other hand
by the way	in the first place	that is
for example	in other words	to be sure
I believe		

Look at these examples:

We are certain, *then*, that this is the only possible course of action.
The test results will, *I believe*, confirm my position.
Absence, *it has been said*, makes the heart grow fonder.
Familiarity, *on the other hand*, breeds contempt.
Mr. Morgan, *by the way*, used to work in our Pittsburgh office.
I am convinced, *however*, that she is innocent of the charges.

Expressions Without Commas

On occasion these expressions do not interrupt the natural flow of a sentence. In these cases, do not use commas to set off the expressions.

We must go through with the surgery *however* dangerous the procedure.
If Ms. Shapiro is *otherwise* occupied, we will return later.

We *therefore* feel that you must act with caution.
But: We feel, *therefore,* that you must with caution.
Here the placement of *therefore* makes you pause.

We *nevertheless* decided to refuse their offer.
But: We decided, *nevertheless,* to refuse their offer.
Here the placement of *nevertheless* makes you pause.

17.7 Questions Added to Statements

Use a comma to set off a question that is added to a statement.

You sent the letter, *didn't you?*   You will do as we ask, *won't you?*
Lovely day, *isn't it?*   The bank hasn't closed yet, *has it?*

Sometimes the question appears within the statement.

You agree, *don't you,* that she is the best choice?
You will, *won't you,* do as we ask?

17.8 Contrasting Expressions

Use a comma to set off a contrasting expression within a sentence. A contrasting expression usually starts with *not, seldom,* or *never.*

Mr. D'Angelo has gone to St. Lawrence, *not to St. Louis.*
Our board meets often in private, *seldom in public.*
We have always enjoyed high attendance, *never low,* during soccer games.

17.9 Abbreviations

Abbreviations like Esq. and those that stand for academic or religious degrees (for example, *M.A., Ph.D., L.D.,* and *S.J.*) are considered explanatory and are set off by commas.

Enclosed is a letter from Roberta Torres, Esq., our attorney.
Elizabeth C. Ramsey, LL.D., Ph.D., has joined the faculty.
Sister Teresa Marcinian, F.S.M., was the retreat leader.

The abbreviations *Jr.* and *Sr.*, the roman and arabic numerals following a person's name, and the abbreviations *Inc.* and *Ltd.* are not set off by commas unless that particular person or company prefers to do so.

> Henry A. Verducci Jr. is our newly elected president.
> King Henry VIII had six wives.
> Vuong and Gregg Inc. recently began constructing a new plant.

17.10 Dates

The year written after a month and a date should be set off with commas. The year is an appositive because it identifies which month and day.

> The document dated April 8, 2001, is the one currently in effect.

Month and Year. If only the month and year are given, omit the commas.

> In October 2001 sales increased nearly 30 percent.

Day and Date. If the day of the week as well as the date is used, use commas to set off the explanatory material.

> The meeting on Tuesday, *August 14,* is scheduled for noon.
> The meeting on August 14, *Tuesday,* is scheduled for noon.
> The meeting scheduled for Tuesday, *August 14, 2001,* has been rescheduled for Thursday, *August 16, 2001.*

Military Style. In military date style, no commas are used.

> Sales for the week ending 15 October 2002 were up 30 percent.

17.11 Addresses

The name of a state or country after a city should be set off with commas because it identifies the particular city.

> When in Rome do as the Romans do—and this means Rome, *Italy,* and Rome, *Georgia,* too.

When a street address is written out in a sentence, use commas to separate the various elements. Note that a comma is placed *after* the ZIP code number but not before it.

> Mr. Porter has lived at 2234 Peachtree Street, Atlanta, Georgia 30013, for seven years.

Style Tip

Military Dates

In many countries and in the U.S. military, complete dates begin with the day, not the month. The sequence is day month year (without commas).

Style Tip

ZIP, Zip, or zip?

The *ZIP* in *ZIP Code* is an acronym—an abbreviation pronounced as a word. It stands for *Zone Improvement Plan.* Some reference manuals capitalize *ZIP,* others use lower case letters for *zip code,* and some use only an initial capital letter—*Zip code.*

SECTION B: PROGRAMMED REINFORCEMENT

Coverage Key

Section		Statement
17.6	➤ Interrupters	➤ S14
17.7	➤ Questions Added to Statements	➤ S15
17.8	➤ Contrasting Expressions	➤ S16, S17
17.9	➤ Abbreviations	➤ S18, S19, S20
17.10	➤ Dates	➤ S19, S20
17.4	➤ Appositives	➤ S20
17.11	➤ Addressess	➤ S21

Instructions: Cover the answers in the **Answer** column; then write your answer to the first statement. Uncover the first printed answer and compare your answer to it. If you wrote a correct answer, continue the activity. If you made an error, use the **Coverage Key** to locate the chapter section you need to review. When you are confident that you understand the material, continue with the reinforcement activity.

ANSWER

STATEMENT

S14 Words, phrases, or clauses that interrupt the natural flow of a sentence (should, should not) be set off by commas. Punctuate these sentences:
a. **He told me that his new firm however did not check references.**
b. **They do on the other hand conduct extensive interviews.**
c. **I know of one interview for instance that lasted more than three hours.**
d. **I'd like an interview however long it is.**

A14 should,
a. **He told me that his new firm, however, did not check references.**
b. **They do, on the other hand, conduct extensive interviews.**
c. **I know of one interview, for instance, that lasted more than three hours.**
d. no commas needed

S15 **This doesn't taste very good, does it?** In this sentence a comma is used to set off a(n) _____ that is added to a statement. Punctuate these sentences:
a. **That happened last Thursday didn't it**
b. **He's rather shy isn't he**
c. **You do believe don't you that our proposal will be approved**

A15 question,
a. **That happened last Thursday, didn't it?**
b. **He's rather shy, isn't he?**
c. **You do believe, don't you, that our proposal will be approved?**

S16 **I want a winning sales campaign, not another losing one.** In this sentence a comma is used to set off a(n) _____ expression added to a statement.

A16 contrasting

S17 Punctuate the following sentences:
- a. **Judge people by their actions not by their words.**
- b. **I want results not promises.**
- c. **She is seldom late never absent.**

A17 a. **Judge people by their actions, not by their words.**
b. **I want results, not promises.**
c. **She is seldom late, never absent.**

S18 Abbreviations like *Esq.* and those that stand for academic or religious degrees at the end of a personal name (are, are not) considered explanatory and (are, are not) set off by commas.

A18 are, are

S19 Roman numerals and the abbreviations *Jr.* and *Sr.* following a person's name usually (are, are not) set off by commas. The year written after a month and date (should, should not) be set off by commas.

A19 are not, should

S20 Punctuate the following: **On May 24 1998 Lawrence O'Brien Jr. received his B.S. degree from Sticky Stone State College. His father Lawrence O'Brien Sr. and his only uncle Terence O'Brien Esq. attended the ceremony.**

A20 **On May 24, 1998, Lawrence O'Brien Jr. received his B.S. degree from Sticky Stone State College. His father, Lawrence O'Brien Sr., and his only uncle, Terence O'Brien, Esq., attended the ceremony.**

S21 When a street address is written out in a sentence (use, do not use) a comma to separate the state and ZIP code.

A21 do not use

In this section you will review the last of the six basic comma rules you began learning in Chapter 16. These concern the use of commas to set off direct quotations and to avoid confusion.

17.12	Rule 5: Commas With Quotations

Use a comma to set off a short quotation from the rest of the sentence.

> She said, "I will not compromise on this issue."
> "If you don't repair this damage," he threatened, "you can expect to hear from my lawyer."

Commas Not Needed

When the quotation is not direct and not in quotation marks, no comma is necessary.

> She said that she would not compromise on this issue.
> He threatened to contact his lawyer if the damage wasn't repaired.

Leave out the comma even though you use quotation marks when

- The quotation is not a complete thought in itself but is built into the structure of the sentence.
- The quoted material is used as the subject, as the subject complement of the sentence, or as a restrictive appositive.

> He said he was "very tired." *(predicate adjective)*
> The slogan "Slavery is freedom" aroused considerable controversy.
>   *(restrictive appositive)*
> "Do unto others as you would have others do unto you" is the Golden Rule.
>   *(subject)*
> The Golden Rule is "Do unto others as you would have others do unto you."
>   *(subject complement)*

Comma Placement

When a comma ends a direct quotation, always place the final comma inside the final quotation mark.

> WRONG: "Now is the time to plan for your retirement", she counseled.
> RIGHT: ✔ "Now is the time to plan for your retirement," she counseled.

Training Programs

Corporations often hire sales representatives straight out of college and offer in-house training programs on topics such as closing a sale. By contrast, smaller companies generally prefer to hire applicants with a proven sales record.

Comma Replacements

If the quoted material ends with a question mark or exclamation point, use this mark inside the quotation marks and omit the comma.

"What time is it?" he asked.   "Wow!" she exclaimed.

Commas as Period Substitutes

If the quotation ends with a period, substitute a comma for the period.

"Please fill the following order on a credit basis," the letter began.

17.13   Rule 6: Commas to Avoid Confusion

Use commas in special instances to avoid confusion within a sentence.

Possible Misreadings. Use a comma to separate words that otherwise might be misread. Note how the comma helps the reader:

WRONG: In short Internet use must conform to the company policy.
 RIGHT: ✔ In short, Internet use must conform to the company policy.

WRONG: Ever since we have avoided telephoning.
 RIGHT: ✔ Ever since, we have avoided telephoning.

WRONG: No matter what the results will be published.
 RIGHT: ✔ No matter what, the results will be published.

Repeated Words and Numbers. Use a comma to separate words repeated in succession or to separate two numbers when both are expressed in figures or words.

Whatever happened, happened fast.
It has been a long, long time.
I am very, very pleased with the results.
On May 15, 12 students were absent.
This afternoon at two, five sessions are scheduled.
But: I need two 57-cent stamps.

Omissions. Use a comma to indicate the omission of words that are understood.

This election we polled 14,372 votes; last election, 12,991.
(The words *we polled* are left out of the second clause.)

Ethiopia gained eight Olympic medals; Indonesia, six; Argentina, four; Thailand, three. (The verb *gained* is omitted.)

Large Numbers. Use commas to separate numbers of five or more figures into units of three digits. The use of commas is optional in whole numbers of four digits.

> The auditorium contains 1,420 seats. (or 1420 seats)
> The official attendance at yesterday's game was 57,742.
> The corporation's losses for the year were staggering: $2,124,377.

Exceptions: The following kinds of numbers are written without commas.

calendar years	2005
telephone numbers	(973) 655-4000
street addresses	24873 Pomona Street
ZIP codes	60120
decimal numbers	3.14159 (**But:** 14,873.14159)
page numbers	p. 1243
serial numbers	425-34892-06106
invoice numbers	4398063
contract numbers	736418

Metric Numbers: In metric quantities use a space to separate digits into groups of three, counting from the decimal point.

> 1 427 309. 432 82

Inverted Names. When you invert the normal order of a person's name and put the last name first, separate the last name from the other parts of the name with a comma.

> *Martin Luther King* becomes *King, Martin Luther.*

Salutations. Use a comma after the salutation in personal letters and e-mail messages.

> Dear Deidre,   Dear Yoko and Santiago,

Complimentary Closes. Use a comma after the complimentary close of personal, informal, and formal letters, and e-mail messages except when using the open punctuation letter style.

> Sincerely,   Respectfully,   Cordially yours,
> Very truly yours,   Sincerely yours,

17.14   Summary of Common Comma Errors

The following is a summary of common comma errors to avoid. Remember that using commas when they should not be used can be just as confusing to your reader as omitting commas when they are needed.

Style Tip

Mixed and Open Punctuation

Business letters may follow either the mixed or open punctuation pattern. In the mixed, or standard, pattern, a comma follows the complimentary close and a colon appears after the salutation. In the open pattern no punctuation is used at the end of any line outside the body of the letter unless that line ends with an abbreviation.

Separation of Subject and Verb. Do not separate a subject from its verb by a comma if the verb comes immediately after the subject.

WRONG: My boss and her husband, are coming for dinner tonight.
RIGHT: ✔ My boss and her husband are coming for dinner tonight.

Separation of Object and Verb. Do not separate a verb from its object by a comma if the object comes directly after the verb.

WRONG: Joel Abdul wrote, *How to Influence People in Sales.*
RIGHT: ✔ Joel Abdul wrote *How to Influence People in Sales.*

Coordinating Conjunctions. Do not place a comma *after* the coordinating conjunction when it joins clauses in a sentence. Always place a comma *before* the conjunction.

WRONG: Last year sales increased by 25 percent but, this year they
             increased by 50 percent.
RIGHT: ✔ Last year sales increased by 25 percent, but this year they
             increased by 50 percent.

Two-Part Compound Elements. Do not use a comma to separate the two parts of a compound subject, a compound verb, or a compound object when they are connected by *and, or,* or *but.*

WRONG: The lamps, and the statues are temporarily out of stock.
RIGHT: ✔ The lamps and the statues are temporarily out of stock.
             (compound subject)

WRONG: This afternoon Alfredo waxed, and polished his car.
RIGHT: ✔ This afternoon Alfredo waxed and polished his car.
             (compound verb)

WRONG: They shipped autos, and tractors from the warehouse.
RIGHT: ✔ They shipped autos and tractors from the warehouse.
             (compound object)

Reflexive Pronouns. Do not use a comma to set off a reflexive pronoun (a pronoun ending in *self*) used for emphasis.

WRONG: Ms. Diaz, herself, will make the presentation.
RIGHT: ✔ Ms. Diaz herself will make the presentation.

Than. Do not use a comma before *than* in a comparison.

WRONG: It is wiser to fail, than not to try at all.
RIGHT: ✔ It is wiser to fail than not to try at all.

Coverage Key

Section	Statement
17.12 ➤ Rule 5: Commas With Quotations	➤ **S22, S23, S24, S25, S26, S27**
17.13 ➤ Rule 6: Commas to Avoid Confusion	➤ **S28, S29, S30, S31, S32, S33**
17.14 ➤ Summary of Common Comma Errors	➤ **S34**

Instructions: Cover the answers in the **Answer** column, then write your answer to the first statement. Uncover the first printed answer and compare your answer to it. If you wrote a correct answer, continue the activity. If you made an error, use the **Coverage Key** to locate the chapter section you need to review. When you are confident that you understand the material, continue with the reinforcement activity.

ANSWER	STATEMENT
	S22 A comma is used to set off a short direct quotation from the rest of the sentence. Punctuate this sentence, adding a capital letter where necessary: **She said leave the package here.**
A22 She said, "Leave the package here."	**S23** **She said to leave the package here.** This sentence does not contain quotation marks because it is a(n) _____ quotation.
A23 indirect	**S24** A comma (is, is not) used before a quotation that is not a complete thought but is a necessary part of the sentence. The following sentence (is, is not) punctuated correctly: **Frank said he was "too pooped to pop."**
A24 is, is	**S25** When a comma ends a direct quotation, it is placed (inside, outside) the quotation marks. Punctuate the following sentence: **"I intend to ask for a raise" Zoe declared.**
A25 inside, "I intend to ask for a raise," Zoe declared.	**S26** A comma is used as a substitute for a(n) (period, question mark, exclamation point) when it ends the quoted material.
A26 period	**S27** Punctuate the following quotations: a. **"Hooray" she exclaimed.** b. **"May I go too" he asked.** c. **"Here is the report you requested" she said.**
A27 a. "Hooray!" she exclaimed. b. "May I go too?" he asked. c. "Here is the report you requested," she said.	

S28 Use commas where necessary to avoid confusion within a sentence. Place a comma where necessary in the following sentences:
  a. **Just the week before I had lunch with her.**
  b. **Ever since our orders have steadily increased.**
  c. **In short memos must have a clear subject line.**

A28
  a. **Just the week before, I had lunch with her.**
  b. **Ever since, our orders have steadily increased.**
  c. **In short, memos must have a clear subject line.**

S29 A comma (is, is not) used to separate words repeated in succession. Place commas where necessary in the following sentences:
  a. **We have been through hard hard times together.**
  b. **If you must leave leave quietly.**

A29 is,
  a. **We have been through hard, hard times together.**
  b. **If you must leave, leave quietly.**

S30 A comma (can, cannot) be used to indicate that a word or phrase has been left out. What omitted words are indicated by the commas in these sentences?
  a. **This week we closed on four homes; last week, two.**
  _____
  b. **The Billing Department has 20 computer terminals; the Shipping Department, 12.** _____

A30 can,
  a. **we closed on**
  b. **has**

S31 Insert commas where needed in these sentences:
  a. **Last year we closed in August; this year in July.**
  b. **He excels in languages; she in science and mathematics.**

A31
  a. **Last year we closed in August; this year, in July.**
  b. **He excels in languages; she, in science and mathematics.**

S32 Rewrite each of the following complimentary closes, showing proper capitalization and punctuation:
  a. **yours truly**
  b. **sincerely yours**
  c. **very truly yours**

A32
  a. **Yours truly,**
  b. **Sincerely yours,**
  c. **Very truly yours,**

S33 Insert commas where necessary:
  a. **Since we saw you last Ms. DeSimio we have begun construction of a new plant that will be the largest in the East.**
  b. **Naturally if you insist we will have to agree won't we?**

A33
  a. **Since we saw you last, Ms. DeSimio, we have begun construction of a new plant that will be the largest in the East.**
  b. **Naturally, if you insist, we will have to agree, won't we?**

S34 Using commas when they should not be used is:
  a. as confusing to readers as omitting needed commas.
  b. less confusing than omitting needed commas.
  c. more confusing than omitting needed commas.

A34 a.

CHAPTER 17 SUMMARY

In this chapter you learned how to use commas in sentences to set off nonessential expressions, including names of persons directly addressed, explanatory expressions, interrupters, questions added to statements, contrasting expressions, abbreviations, dates, and addresses. You discovered how to distinguish between restrictive (essential) and nonrestrictive (nonessential) clauses and how to punctuate each correctly. You also studied the use of commas to set off a short quotation from the rest of the sentence. In addition, you learned how to use commas to avoid confusion when words are repeated in succession, are omitted, or might be misread.

Getting Connected

VISITING AN ENCYCLOPEDIA WEBSITE

GOAL: An online encyclopedia can be a convenient resource when you want to research a topic for work, school, or personal knowledge. You no longer have to go to a library; now you can simply turn on your computer and go online to one of several encyclopedias that are available to the public free of charge. In this activity, you will be able to travel online to any country you find interesting. By visiting an encyclopedia Website, you'll be able to expand your knowledge in two ways: you'll gather new information about the country of your choice, and you'll develop your skills in using the last three rules for comma usage.

STEP 1   Go to *englishworkshop.glencoe.com,* the address for *The English Workshop* Website, and click on Unit 7. Next click on Getting Connected, and then click on Chapter 17. At the Chapter 17 Getting Connected option, you'll see a list of encyclopedia Websites. Select a site to visit.

STEP 2   At the home page of the site you chose, look for the search function. Choose a country you'd like to visit, such as Iceland or Tibet. Enter the name of the country to begin your search.

STEP 3   Websites vary, of course, but what should appear next is a synopsis of the main article about the country you entered or a list of related articles. Click on one of the articles or sections that intrigues you. Skim it first to make sure it includes numerous commas; you'll need plenty of examples for this activity.

STEP 4   Once you've found an article or section that is interesting and full of commas, make a printout.

STEP 5   Read through your printout carefully, circling or highlighting each comma. Next, search for *at least five* of the following items, but challenge yourself by finding as many examples of these items as possible.

a. A restrictive *that* clause
b. A nonrestrictive *which* clause
c. A restrictive appositive
d. A participial phrase
e. An interrupting word
f. An interrupting phrase
g. A nonrestrictive appositive
h. A nonessential expression
i. An essential expression
j. A contrasting expression
k. A date that includes the month and year
l. A location that includes a city and a country

STEP 6 On the back of your printout, write down each grammatical item you find from the list above and the complete sentence that illustrates that item. For example,

g. Nonrestrictive appositive:
Lhasa, the capital and largest city, is Tibet's principal center of trade.
h. Nonessential expression:
The lowlands, situated mainly along the southwestern coast of Iceland, occupy about 25 percent of the total area.

STEP 7 After you've completed this activity, write your name on the front of your printout and give it to your instructor.

PRACTICE 1

Direct Address and Direct Quotations: Part A

Instructions: Insert all missing commas in the following sentences. If a sentence does not require a comma, write C in front of the sentence.

EXAMPLE: _____ Thank you˄ Ms. Shin˄ for your prompt reply to our questionnaire.

_____ 1. Your new living room furniture Ms. Juarez will be delivered on Wednesday.

_____ 2. We have directed Mr. James Ainko of our credit department to discuss terms of payment with you.

_____ 3. The new apartments are being shown this week Ms. Katz.

_____ 4. I have looked further Mr. Garnier into the Gray lumber situation.

_____ 5. Lisa Martin says that economic conditions will remain favorable.

_____ 6. Is it the fault of this store that your account remains inactive Ms. Pulaski?

_____ 7. Mr. Bianco's inspection of our floor equipment was unexpected.

_____ 8. Just think how you'll feel Ms. Meisner when you win the grand prize of $50,000.

_____ 9. Imagine how Ms. Meisner felt when she won the grand prize of $50,000.

_____ 10. May I help you sir?

_____ 11. No sir there is no mail for you today.

_____ 12. Jim would you please ask Bill to see me before he leaves.

_____ 13. You my friends are in for a big surprise.

_____ 14. My friends are in for a big surprise.

_____ 15. My friends you are in for a big surprise.

Direct Address and Direct Quotations: Part B

Instructions: Place commas in the following sentences where necessary. Write C in front of the sentence if no commas are required.

EXAMPLE: _____ "If you don't accept our offer˄" he said˄ "we will take our business elsewhere."

_____ 16. She said "This is ridiculous."

_____ 17. "I will not resign" the chairperson said "nor will I alter my position."

_____ 18. "Send the check to my office" was written on the top of the memo.

_____ 19. "Who punched the clock at 5 p.m.?" she asked.

_____ 20. Ms. Chico said that she would return in about an hour.

PRACTICE 2

Explanatory Expressions

Instructions: Insert commas to set off explanatory expressions in each sentence. Add other commas where needed.

EXAMPLE: **Our representative from New Orleans Ms. A. J. Johnson is in town.**

1. The defendant's principal witness Mr. G. A. Rivera will call at your office tomorrow.

2. It is my pleasure to introduce H. Colleen Phillips our president and cofounder.

3. Our president and cofounder H. Colleen Phillips stepped up to the microphone.

4. Ms. Phillips having acknowledged the applause of the audience cleared her throat and began her speech.

5. Forgetting her prepared speech President Phillips stood dumbfounded before the audience.

6. Asia the largest of the continents is a major focus of international trade.

7. Our new location the corner of Sixth Avenue and 42nd Street offers free parking.

8. While attending the convention last month I met an old friend.

9. After hearing the rumors of a possible merger I decided to buy additional shares in the company.

10. The Pacific Ocean the largest body of water on earth gets its name from its tranquil appearance.

11. The speakers were Margaret Ada Puccini professor of applied economics and Ahmed Raanan Jr. professor of political science.

12. Realizing his position George resigned.

13. George realizing his position turned in his resignation.

14. We advise you to see either Ms. R. J. Urwanda director of the bureau or Mr. P. T. Sullivan her assistant.

15. Ms. Urwanda's assistant Mr. P. T. Sullivan is on vacation.

16. Jules trying vainly to be recognized by the chairperson stood up and waved both arms over his head.

17. Flowing from Minnesota to the Gulf of Mexico the Mississippi is America's longest river.

18. The Mississippi America's longest river flows into the Gulf of Mexico.

19. The Mississippi flowing from Minnesota to the Gulf of Mexico is America's longest river.

20. Would you enjoy living in a residential park a veritable winter wonderland of over 500 acres of high healthy beautifully wooded fertile land Ms. Solokov?

PRACTICE 3

Nonrestrictive and Restrictive Clauses: Part A

Instructions: Each of the following sentences contains a nonrestrictive clause—that is, a relative clause that should be set off with commas. Insert commas as needed.

EXAMPLE: **Maria‚who completed the training program‚received a certificate.**

1. Mr. Anthony Como who is president of the company sent a copy of his latest address.

2. Our creditors all of whom have been most patient will be pleased to hear of our plan.

3. The manufacture of this equipment which is the finest ever made is an exacting process.

4. The new executive assistant who has an M.B.A. is the best we've ever had.

5. The luggage which was engraved with her initials was presented to Ms. Santos.

6. The park which is noted for its old trees was dedicated in 1889.

7. This morning we received a report from Mr. Kozol who is our representative.

8. Wellington chalk which is hard and long lasting is the most economical.

Nonrestrictive and Restrictive Clauses: Part B

Instructions: Each of the following sentences has an explanatory expression—a restrictive clause—that *should not* be set off with commas because to do so would change the meaning of the sentence. Underline each restrictive clause.

EXAMPLE: **Everyone <u>who completes the training program</u> will receive a certificate.**

9. The proprietor who fails to satisfy the customer's needs does not last long in business.

10. Medicine is a profession that satisfies a person's desire to serve others.

11. The information that I want is in the ledger in Room 27.

12. The ledger that is in Room 27 contains the needed information.

13. A rumor that we heard yesterday is puzzling.

14. Lawyers who represent themselves have fools for clients.

15. The advertisement that is memorable is the one that is most effective.

Name _____

Class _____ Date _____

PRACTICE 4

Interrupting Elements

Instructions: This exercise uses commas to separate interrupting elements from the body of the sentence. Place commas where needed in the following sentences. Write *C* in front of any sentence that does not require a comma.

EXAMPLE: _____ We are certain⌃of course⌃that you will comply with our request.

_____ 1. Commas as you know should set off nonessential information.

_____ 2. I believe for example that a brusque answer does much harm and little good.

_____ 3. We feel therefore that an immediate decision is essential.

_____ 4. We therefore feel that an immediate decision is essential.

_____ 5. None of us to be sure is perfect.

_____ 6. It is nevertheless imperative that Mr. Maharaj contact us at once.

_____ 7. We feel on the other hand that your client is entitled to partial reimbursement.

_____ 8. Should I make the necessary arrangements incidentally or will you?

_____ 9. It is however unnecessary for you to reply at once.

_____ 10. Feel free of course to take as much time as you need.

_____ 11. We were shocked naturally to hear of the loss.

_____ 12. They did not by the way report on time.

_____ 13. It is in our opinion impossible to predict the outcome at this moment.

_____ 14. The costs of complete retooling however are extremely high.

_____ 15. We must retool completely however high the cost.

_____ 16. Ms. Hall is to be very frank totally unqualified for the position.

_____ 17. We believe the failure was entirely the fault of your agent.

_____ 18. The failure we believe was entirely the fault of your agent.

_____ 19. No one naturally can be blamed for such an innocent mistake.

_____ 20. We can honestly say at any rate that we did our best.

Name _____

Class _____ Date _____

PRACTICE 5

Miscellaneous Uses of the Comma

Instructions: Place commas where necessary in the following sentences. Write *C* in front of a sentence if no commas are required.

EXAMPLE: _____ The surgery performed on Mr. Dryden was very⌃very difficult.

_____ 1. It has been a long long process of trial and error.

_____ 2. Last year our stockholders averaged $6000 each in profits; this year they average almost $11000 each.

_____ 3. On July 15 1997 the workers in our plants numbered 6475.

_____ 4. The contract dated 4 August 1996 is still valid.

_____ 5. Only three days before he came to New York.

_____ 6. We addressed the letter to Ms. Lou Swanson 5202 South Spruce Lane Madison Wisconsin.

_____ 7. Since our last visit in November 2001 we have reconsidered your $800000 expansion plan.

_____ 8. Whoever spoke spoke in vain.

_____ 9. Last year's gross sales totaled $48176395500.

_____ 10. Last year the department received two promotions; the year before none.

_____ 11. On page 317 25 review exercises are provided.

_____ 12. They have lived at 1220 Keystone Avenue Springfield Illinois for eight years.

_____ 13. Despite poor January sales our overall net profit for the past year exceeded $450000.

_____ 14. Ever since our sales have continued to increase.

_____ 15. We reviewed your books for July 2000 and found a $13257.50 discrepancy with our figures.

_____ 16. On December 1 1998 we will expect delivery of 50000 tons of No. 10 steel to our warehouse at 1614 Bruce Avenue Pittsburgh Pennsylvania.

_____ 17. We have located a copy of invoice No. 39486 but we are unable to find a copy of the other one.

_____ 18. Alexander Pope wrote "Whatever is is right."

_____ 19. Please change my address in your listings from Ms. Polly Jones 616 Almond Street New Orleans Louisiana to Ms. Polly Mayer 327 Cypress Avenue Miami Beach Florida.

_____ 20. For a while longer work periods between breaks will be necessary.

Name _____

Class _____ Date _____

PRACTICE 6

The Period, the Question Mark, and the Comma

Instructions: Insert commas, periods, and question marks where necessary in the following letter.

COMDATE, INC.

126 Lake Shore Drive, Chicago, Illinois 60601

Ms. Huang
FS Global
4151 Yonge Street
Toronto, Ontario, Canada M5C 2W7

March 31, 20--

Dear Ms. Huang,

Thank you for your prompt response to our inquiry The preliminary information that you provided has been quite helpful and has convinced us that we would like to explore with you how best to establish intranet capability for our company

As I indicated our company is in the midst of a significant expansion in our product line Each new product launch however costs us nearly $2500000 As we expand our market our sales representatives need to be kept abreast of each new product as quickly and efficiently as possible It is here that we believe you can help us Our sales representatives are situated around the globe including Japan Europe the Middle-East South America and South Africa Under our current system we send our engineers from one site to another to train our sales force This practice as you can well imagine has proved both costly and time-consuming Being able to use intranet capabilities to train our sales staff through live video presentations in contrast would enable us to save significant time and money Our question is is this a viable option

---

We would like your representative preferably Mr Omar who has been so helpful to us in the past to call on us on Monday April 10 at 10 a m to discuss this particular aspect of intranet capabilities We are also interested in what other capabilities the intranet system could offer

As I understand it an intranet system can increase employee communication reduce employee travel eliminate unnecessary meetings and increase the accessibility of information This is correct is it not Please have Mr Omar bring whatever figures he has available to demonstrate how this could be accomplished in regard to policy manuals presentation materials used by marketing and sales departments and company records and information

In addition we would also like to explore with him the possibility of developing an extranet capability so that our customers and suppliers could access information in a manner most convenient to them. Again we are very interested in the financial savings that such a move might generate

Finally we are concerned about potential security risks on both systems To protect ourselves from theft of intellectual property is a primary concern We are very much interested therefore in how we can keep our information safe both inside and outside the company

We look forward to hearing from you Ms Huang and to exploring with Mr Omar the advantages of an intranet system for our company

Sincerely,

Pierre Morris

PRACTICE 7

Composition: Writing an Order Letter

Instructions: Most of the time when you order a product from a catalog or magazine, there is an order form for you to use. For those times when there is no preprinted form, you will need to write an order letter.

Pick a catalog or magazine that contains products of interest to you. Write a letter in which you order two or three of the items you particularly want. Remember to specify quantity, size, style, color, product number, or whatever other specific information is appropriate. Be sure to indicate the total cost of your order, how you intend to pay for it, and where and when you want it delivered. Write a draft of your letter in the space below. Write your finished letter on a separate piece of paper.

_____

_____

_____

_____

_____

_____

_____

_____

_____

_____

_____

_____

_____

_____

_____

_____

_____

_____

_____

_____

_____

_____

_____

The Comma Rules

Unit 7—Editing Review

Instructions: Use the concepts you have studied so far to help you locate errors in the passage below. Assume that you are editing a passage that will be placed on an instructor's Website for a class in sales and marketing. Cross out each error and write the correction in the space above it.

Assignment 7: Maslow's Hierarchy of Needs

In 1954 Dr. Abraham Maslow a psychologist published *Motivation and Personality*. In his book Maslow he talks about what motivates people to do the things, which they do. Through his research Maslow determined that people have various kinds of needs he termed them the "Hierarchy of Needs".

The first type is the *Physiological*. These is the most basic type needs people must have to live—food water shelter sleep clothing and, air. People isn't going to be interested in higher level needs until he has all ready fulfilled basic survival needs. Once a person has satisfied these they can move up the hierarchy to other needs.

The second level is *Safety and Security*. This level involves personal confidence, stability and protection from enemys. At this level people are primarily-concerned with products and services. That will help them feel protected (for example insurance, fire-arms, security devices.)

The third level is *Social*, which has to do with affection, friendship, and ties to a group. Flowers, giftes, or other items that demonstrate affection and caring , whether from a member of the family or from some one whose not a family member, would fall into this category. In addition any thing that makes a person feel like they belong to a group or subculture will have helped fulfill this need.

(Continued on next page)

continued from page 509

The fourth level are *Esteem and Status*. People want to have a sense of selfworth, to be receiving respect and recognition in the community. Products that can help people achieve them goals—designer clothing cars, jewelry, grooming products—help satisfy esteem and status needs.

The final level is *Self-actualization.* The US Armys' recruiting slogan; "Be all that you can be." exemplified this need. At this level people strove to gain a sense of personal and professional fulfillment through such activitys like advanced education, professional development seminar's and time spended on personal-enrichment.

The following is a two part assignment based on your reading.

Part One. Select ads from the various mediums—radio, television, print, etc—in which the principal appeal is directed to one of these five levels. You may have some trouble finding goods and services that are advertised with a primary focii on physiological needs, however, keep looking until you find at least one. Its OK if you only can find one. For the remaining four levels I want you to find at least two moreover they should not all be from the same type of source. Explain why each of the ads illustrate a particular type appeal. Your analyses of each ad doesn't have to be very long, a paragraph or too for each one are sufficient. You'll probable notice that many advertisements appeal to people on more than one level. For this assignment you are just wanted by me to focus on the level the ad primarily appeals to. Compare and contrast the ads that illustrate each level what are the similarities the differences.

Part Two. Pick a product or service, describe how you would market them to appeal to consumer's needs on each of Maslows' five levels. In other words, develop five separate ads for your product. Each appealing to a specific need.

Link & Learn

Using Commas in Sales and Marketing Careers

GOAL: Reinforce what you learned about comma usage in Unit 7 by exploring how commas are used in sales and marketing Websites.

STEP 1 Go to *englishworkshop.glencoe.com*, the address for *The English Workshop* Website. Click first on Unit 7; then click on Link & Learn to access a list of professional sales and marketing Websites you may use in this activity. Select one of the sites and click on it.

STEP 2 Scan the home page of the Website and select a passage. Choose material with a variety of sentences. Print two text pages.

STEP 3 Read the printout. Assume that you are a proofreader for the Website you selected, and do the following:

  a. Circle or highlight each comma as you come to it in the text.
  b. Find six commas in the text, each of which follows a different rule for using a comma. (The first three rules are in Chapter 16, and the last three in Chapter 17.) Draw a line from each comma to the left margin. At the end of each line, write a brief explanation of the rule that applies to that comma. For example, if you locate a comma used with a short quotation, you will need to explain the rule for that particular usage. Number each explanation to show you have included examples that relate to the six different comma rules.
  c. If you cannot find six different examples of commas, explain the rules for the commas you did find. Then, on the back of the last page of the printout, write original sentences that use commas based on the rules not covered in the material. Next, write a brief explanation of the rule for each comma you used.
  d. Write in the front left margin *More sentences on back*, and include the number of original sentences you have written to demonstrate comma usage. The commas you identify on the front of your printout and those you identify on the back should total six.
  e. Go back over the printout. Circle any comma errors you think appear in the Website material. Draw a line from each error to the right margin and explain the mistake. For example, if you find an unnecessary comma, tell why it is not needed. If you see a comma is missing after a long introductory phrase, you could write *Comma needed after long introductory phrase.*

STEP 4 When you have completed the work, proofread it, write your name on the front of the printout, and turn it in to your instructor.

UNIT 8

More Punctuation and Stylistics

Profile in Success

Administrative Assistant: Meeting All Challenges

Jacqueline Gwinn · *Boston, Massachusetts* · *Katharine Gibbs School*

When Jacqueline Gwinn thinks back to the years between 1993 and 1995, she sometimes wonders how she survived. Working full-time in a Massachusetts affirmative action office, she was also taking classes four nights a week at the Katharine Gibbs School in Boston to earn a certificate in information processing. And she was also undergoing treatment for cancer. "There were times when I thought I was never going to make graduation," she reflects now.

With the encouragement of family and friends, Jacqueline "made it." She was listed in *Who's Who Among American College Students* and earned an associate degree in business technology. She also found a new job—as the executive assistant to the president of the school.

Today Jacqueline is in constant contact with the school's corporate offices in Illinois. "That's when English and communication skills are so important," she explains. "Dealing with the corporate office, you have to know how to speak and write." Jacqueline believes the emphasis her degree program placed on those skills has contributed to her success and has helped her tackle another challenge—she's a teaching assistant one night a week.

Think About It . . . Do Adults and School Mix?

Students who do not attend college directly after graduating from high school are identified as "non-traditional" or "adult" students. Such students may face many obstacles. Jacqueline Gwinn, for example, had to work full-time and undergo treatment for cancer.

■ *What are some obstacles non-traditional students typically face when they go to college?*

■ *What are some advantages non-traditional students may have over younger or less-experienced students?*

Career Connections

OFFICE ADMINISTRATION AND TECHNOLOGY

Learn more about the work of senior office managers, executive word processors, administrative assistants, and others in the office administration and technology field by connecting to the following sites listed at *The English Workshop* Website. Go to ***englishworkshop.glencoe.com***. Click first on Unit 8 and then on Career Connections.

- International Association of Administrative Professionals
- Occupational Outlook Handbook
- *Monster.com*
- College Grad Job Hunter

See page 605, **Link & Learn: Using Punctuation and Elements of Style in Office Administration and Technology Careers**, for an additional online career activity.

Semicolons and Colons

CHAPTER 18 PREVIEW

In this chapter you will focus on the use of semicolons and colons. You will examine how to use these sophisticated marks of punctuation in independent clauses, lists, quotations, and workplace documents. As you work with this chapter, you will continue to assess your knowledge in the Programmed Reinforcement sections and the Practices. Finally, you will develop your skills with semicolons and colons while using an Internet dictionary.

OBJECTIVES

After completing this chapter, you will be able to

- Use a semicolon correctly in a sentence that includes:
  - Two or more independent clauses
  - Independent clauses with conjunctive adverbs or transitional phrases
  - A series of items with commas
  - An expression introducing a list or an explanation
- Use a colon correctly with the following:
  - Introductions to longer quotations
  - Formal introductions to lists or ideas
  - Various sections of workplace documents
  - Numerical figures and textual references

Study Plan for Chapter 18

The Study Plan for Chapter 18 offers a set of strategies that will help you learn and review the chapter material.

1. **Semicolons and Equal Elements**: A semicolon, like the balancing point on a scale, separates equal elements. An independent clause to the left of a semicolon signals that an independent clause should be on the right too. A semicolon following a series item that contains commas should be followed by another series item with commas.
2. **The Right Place for Semicolons**: Don't assume you've correctly placed a semicolon in a sentence unless you can correctly identify the rule covering the usage.
3. **Colons and Lists**: A sentence with a list introduced by *as follows, the following, these, this,* or *thus* needs a colon. Use a colon if the first part of a sentence indicates that a list or explanation will follow.
4. **Colons Not Needed**: Does a list come immediately after a verb or preposition? If so, do not use a colon. You'll be separating the verb or preposition from its object—the list.

So far you have studied four marks of punctuation: the period, the question mark, the exclamation point, and the comma. The first three are generally used at the end of a sentence, while the comma is used within a sentence. In this section you will consider another internal mark of punctuation, the semicolon.

Grammar Tip

Using the Semicolon

Use the *semicolon* to combine two or more independent clauses into a compound sentence.

18.1 The Purpose of the Semicolon

The purpose of the **semicolon** is to mark a major pause or break in a sentence. It indicates a greater pause than a comma, although not as great a pause as a period. The most frequent use of the semicolon is to separate independent clauses, although it may also separate phrases. Because you can now recognize clauses and phrases in a sentence, you should have no trouble with the following guidelines for using the semicolon.

18.2 Independent Clauses

Use the semicolon to separate two closely related *complete thoughts* not separated by a coordinating conjunction—*and, but, or, nor, for, so,* or *yet.*

> Prices rose; wages fell. (*The semicolon implies a relationship between the two events.*)
> Prices rose, but wages fell. (*The conjunction but expresses the relationship.*)
> Prices rose. Wages fell. (*The period does not necessarily imply any relationship.*)

You have now studied three ways to connect the two independent clauses in a compound sentence:

Flashback

Compound Sentences
Go back to Section 13.4, on page 374, to take a second look at compound sentences.

■

1. Use a coordinating conjunction preceded by a comma.
2. If one of the clauses is short (four or fewer words), omit the comma and use a coordinating conjunction by itself.
3. Omit the coordinating conjunction and use a semicolon by itself.

You may also connect the clauses in a compound sentence in more ways:

4. If each clause is long (five or more words) and if one or more of the clauses contains commas, use a coordinating conjunction preceded by a semicolon instead of a comma:

> Naturally, having heard of the opening, he rushed to the employment office; but, despite his haste, he found the position already filled.

Among the professors in the department, Dr. Bristow is noted for her scholarship and seriousness; Dr. Kepler, for his fairness and sense of humor; and Dr. Hernandez, for his booming voice and acting ability.

To summarize, there are four ways to construct compound sentences.

Punctuation Tip

Comma Faults

Joining two independent clauses with only a comma would result in a comma fault.

1. Independent clause,	Coordinating Conjunction	independent clause.
2. Short independent clause. (4 or fewer words)	Coordinating Conjunction	independent clause
	or	
Independent clause	Coordinating Conjunction	very short independent clause (4 or fewer words).
3. Independent clause;	independent clause.	
4. Long independent clause (with internal commas);	Coordinating Conjunction	long independent clause (with internal commas).

Conjunctive Adverbs
For a brief review of conjunctive adverbs, turn back to Section 13.13 on page 387.

18.3	**Independent Clauses With Conjunctive Adverbs or Transitional Phrases**

Use a semicolon to separate two independent clauses that are connected by a conjunctive adverb or transitional phrase such as *accordingly, also, consequently, however, in fact, nevertheless, then, therefore,* and *whereas.*

> The new equipment kept causing fuses to blow; *consequently,* we had to have the entire floor rewired.
> Please give us your exact measurements; *then* we can tailor the suit to ensure your complete satisfaction.
> I know you will be satisfied; *in fact,* I guarantee it.

A comma always follows a transitional phrase or conjunctive adverb of more than one syllable.

18.4	**A Series of Items Containing Commas**

Use the semicolon to separate a series of items when the items themselves contain commas. The semicolon prevents confusion by clearly indicating the main divisions between the items in the series.

> The company will be represented by Marta Janowski, director of communications; Hans Flinchbaugh, vice president of marketing; and Daniel Santoya, director of public relations.

Chapter 18 *Semicolons and Colons* **517**

Punctuation Tip

Equal Rank

A semicolon can be used only to separate items of equal grammatical rank.

> Next year we will open new retail stores in Durham, North Carolina; Tallahassee, Florida; Reston, Virginia; and Livonia, Michigan.
> The totals are 3,728; 2,142,709; and 36,016.

In the cases governed by these three rules, the semicolon separates items of equal grammatical rank. That is, clauses are separated from clauses, phrases from phrases, numbers from numbers. Don't use a semicolon to separate items of unequal grammatical rank, such as a clause and a phrase or an independent clause and a dependent clause.

WRONG: Your mobile workstation will include a laptop computer; valued at $1599; a digital organizer; which is free; and a ball-point pen valued at $15.

RIGHT: ✔ Your mobile workstation will include a laptop computer valued at $1599, a digital organizer that is free, and a ball-point pen valued at $15.

18.5 Expressions Introducing Lists or Explanations

When a list or an explanation is introduced by an expression such as *for example (e.g.), namely (viz.),* or *that is (i.e.),* use a semicolon before the expression and a comma after it.

> There are many fine potential locations for the convention; for example, Atlanta, Chicago, Seattle, Kansas City, or Honolulu.
> The opening paragraph of your paper should contain a clear thesis statement; that is, it should state clearly the central point of your paper.

When you want to place greater emphasis on the second part of a sentence, use a colon rather than a semicolon:

> He had one credo: do unto others before they do unto you.

If the list or explanation occurs in the middle of the sentence rather than at the end, use dashes rather than semicolons.

> Many potential locations—for example, Atlanta, Chicago, Seattle, Kansas City, or Honolulu—are available for the convention.

18.6 Semicolon Review

The semicolon is an extremely useful mark of punctuation as long as it is not overused. Avoid using it to string together a series of separate thoughts into a long, complicated sentence. It is frequently better to break a sentence into shorter sentences by using a period, or to subordinate one clause to another to express the relationship between the two more accurately.

Coverage Key

Section		Statement
18.1	➤ The Purpose of the Semicolon	➤ **S1, S2, S3**
18.2	➤ Independent Clauses	➤ **S4, S5, S6, S7**
18.3	➤ Independent Clauses With Conjunctive Adverbs or Transitional Phrases	➤ **S8**
18.4	➤ A Series of Items Containing Commas	➤ **S12**
18.5	➤ Expressions Introducing Lists or Explanations	➤ **S9, S10, S11, S12**
18.6	➤ Semicolon Review	➤ **S13**

Instructions: Cover the answers in the **Answer** column; then write your answers to the first statement. Uncover the first printed answer and compare your answer to it. If you wrote a correct answer, continue the activity. If you made an error, use the **Coverage Key** to locate the chapter section you need to review. When you are confident that you understand the material, continue with the reinforcement activity.

ANSWER

STATEMENT

S1 The mark of internal punctuation used to indicate a major pause or break is the _____.

A1 semicolon

S2 The semicolon indicates a (greater, weaker) pause than a comma.

A2 greater

S3 The semicolon indicates a (greater, weaker) pause than a period.

A3 weaker

S4 A semicolon (can, cannot) be used to connect two or more independent clauses to create a compound sentence.

A4 can

S5 There are four ways that the independent clauses in a compound sentence may be connected:
   a. You may use a(n) _____ conjunction such as *and* or *but* preceded by a(n) _____.
   b. If one of the clauses is very short, you may omit the _____ and use the _____ by itself.
   c. You may omit the conjunction and use a(n) _____ by itself.
   d. If the clauses are long and contain commas, you may use a coordinating _____ preceded by a(n) _____ instead of a comma.

A5 a. coordinating, comma
     b. comma, coordinating conjunction
     c. semicolon
     d. conjunction, semicolon

S6 Punctuate this sentence using a semicolon:
The job market is getting worse many recent graduates are unable to find employment.

A6 ...worse; many...

S7 Use a semicolon in the following sentence:
There is, to be sure, no question that personal contacts are sometimes valuable in business but in the long run, I think, success depends far more on ability than on any other factor.

A7 ...in business; but in the long run...

S8 **The odds against the small battalion were overwhelming; nevertheless, the soldiers refused to retreat.** A semicolon is used here because a comma plus a(n) _____ such as *nevertheless* (is, is not) strong enough to join the two clauses. If the word *nevertheless* were replaced by the coordinating conjunction *but,* a comma (would, would not) be strong enough.

A8 conjunctive adverb, is not, would

S9 Lists introduced by expressions such as *namely, that is, for example,* and their respective abbreviations, _____, _____, and _____, (are, are not) generally preceded by semicolons.

A9 *viz., i.e., e.g.,* are

S10 Punctuate this sentence: **The sales representative omitted three cities namely Spokane, San Diego, and Oakland.**

A10 ...three cities; namely, Spokane....

S11 A formal list that occurs in the middle of a sentence should be set off with _____. Punctuate the following sentences:
a. **Only three possibilities namely stupidity carelessness or misinformation can explain this outrageous mistake.**
b. **Only three possibilities can explain this outrageous mistake namely stupidity carelessness or misinformation.**

A11 dashes,
a. ...possibilities—namely, stupidity, carelessness, or misinformation—can...,
b. ...mistake; namely, stupidity, carelessness, or misinformation.

S12 Punctuate the following:
Here are the attendance figures 16,352 14,008 and 16,927.

A12 ...figures: 16,352; 14,008; and 16,927.

S13 The semicolon is a mark of punctuation that (should, should not) be used frequently.

A13 should not

SECTION B
Colons

In this section you will examine the many functions that the colon serves in sentences as well as with specific elements such as time and titles.

18.7 The Purpose of the Colon

As you have seen, the purpose of the semicolon is to function as a separator; it primarily separates elements within a sentence. The purpose of the **colon** is different: it directs the reader's attention to what follows.

18.8 Introductions to Longer Quotations

Use a colon to introduce a quotation of two or more sentences. Use a comma to introduce a quotation of one sentence or part of a sentence.

> Senator Hillis replied: "I know the importance of this inquiry, but I cannot become party to such a circus. I resign from the committee."
> She said simply, "I accept."

Also, use a colon when the introduction comments directly on the quotation or when the quotation is attributed to something inanimate.

> The manager's reply was swift and decisive: "You're fired!"
> The report concluded: "The continued prosperity of our organization depends on implementing these proposals immediately."

INTEGRITY   Remember the commitments or promises you've made to others, and don't expect others to remember them for you. Your integrity and reputation depend on it.

18.9 Formal Introductions to Lists or Ideas

Use colons to introduce lists or ideas formally. Generally, a formal introduction includes a phrase such as *the following, as follows, these,* and *thus.*

> The problems are these: the prices, the shipping cost, and the tariff.
> Assemble the desk as follows: Attach the legs; then attach the two side panels; finally, attach the top.

Rule 1: Capitalization After Colons

The first word following a colon is generally capitalized if two or more complete sentences follow the colon.

> I see the advantages of this plan: First, it will free up some capital. Second, it will show a significant return on our investment.

More Capitalization Guidelines

Consult a reference text such as *The Gregg Reference Manual* for additional guidelines about capitalizing words that follow colons.

The first word after a colon is *not* capitalized if an independent clause explains, illustrates, or amplifies the thought expressed in the first part of a compound sentence.

> Restrictive and nonrestrictive elements require different punctuation: the latter should be set off by commas, but the former should not.
> I'm on a seafood diet: every time I see food, I eat.

In addition, the first word after a colon is *not* capitalized when less than a complete sentence or independent clause follows a colon.

> All cash advances must be countersigned by me, with one exception: when the amount is less than $50. (*dependent clause following a colon*)

Rule 2: Implicit Introductions

A colon is used when a formal introductory expression is left out but is clearly understood.

> We have three problems: the price, the shipping cost, and the tariff.
> My reference sources for writing are very basic: a dictionary, a thesaurus, and an office reference manual.

Rule 3: Lists That Follow Verbs or Prepositions

A colon is *not* used when a list immediately follows a main verb or a preposition.

> The reasons he succeeded *are* his great initiative, perseverance, and cleverness.
> **But:** These are the reasons he succeeded: his great initiative, his perseverance, and his cleverness.

> Send copies of the report *to* Ms. Rudy, Ms. Bianchi, and Mr. Patel.
> **But:** Send copies of the report to the following people: Ms. Rudy, Ms. Bianchi, and Mr. Patel.

A colon may be used if the items in the series are listed on separate lines.

> The reasons he succeeded are: Send copies of the report to:
>   his great initiative   Ms. Rudy
>   his perseverance   Ms. Bianchi
>   his cleverness   Mr. Patel

Rule 4: Intervening Sentences

A colon is *not* used when another sentence comes between the introductory sentence and the list.

> Representatives from the following companies will be on campus this week. Students interested in interviews should contact the Job Placement Service.

IBM	Federal Express	American Heart Association
Microsoft	United Parcel Service	

18.10 Workplace Documents

In workplace documents, such as letters, memos, and e-mail messages, use a colon after various elements usually displayed on separate lines.

Salutations

In general, use a colon after a salutation in an e-mail message or a business letter (except in a letter using an open punctuation style.)

> Dear Ms. Ruiz: To whom this may concern:

In both e-mail messages and letters, writers commonly choose to use a comma instead of a colon after a salutation, especially when they have a less formal working relationship with the receiver or reader.

> Dear Nadir,   Hi, Isabel,

Attention and Subject Lines

Use a colon after the words *Attention* (or *Attn*) and *Subject* in the attention and subject lines of a business letter or a memo.

> Attention: Mr. Joseph Montana
> Subject: Account No. 7318

Writer's and Preparer's Initials

Use a colon between the writer's and the preparer's initials at the end of a formal business letter.

> KDS:jb

Open Punctuation

In business letters that use open punctuation style, no punctuation mark follows either the salutation or the complimentary close.

Workplace Documents
See Appendix D for models of workplace documents

●

Opening Lines of a Memo

Use colons in the sender, receiver, date, and subject lines of a memo.

> TO: Accounting Department Faculty
> FROM: Ian McGuire, Deputy Chair
> DATE: May 5, 2003
> SUBJECT: Minutes of Faculty Meeting

Notations and Postscripts

Use a colon after enclosures, attachments, and copy notations (*c* or *cc*), and sometimes after postscripts (*PS*).

> Enclosure: Money Order for $5,600
> Attachments: Résumé, Writing Sample
> cc: L. Schwartz
> c: L. Schwartz
> PS: Please let me know when Gerri Nguyen's flight arrives

18.11   Miscellaneous Uses of the Colon

Use a colon to separate elements involving the following:

1. **Time.** A colon separates hours from minutes when the time is expressed in figures.

> 6:43 a.m.   5:06 p.m.

On a timetable, a colon is often replaced with a period.

> 6.43 a.m.   5.06 p.m.

2. **Mathematical Ratios.** Use a colon to separate parts of a mathematical ratio.

> $3:15 = 10:x$

3. **Titles.** Use a colon to separate a title from a subtitle.

> *Peak Performance: Success in College and Beyond* (book)
> "Marketing Strategy: Responding to International Pressures" (article)

4. **Bibliographical Citations.** Use a colon to separate the place of publication from the name of the publisher in footnotes and bibliographies.

> Kapoor, Jack R., and Les R. Dlabay. *Business and Personal Finance.*
> New York, NY: Glencoe/McGraw-Hill, 2002.

Coverage Key

Section		Statement
18.7	➤ The Purpose of the Colon	➤ **S14, S15**
18.8	➤ Introductions to Longer Quotations	➤ **S16, S17**
18.9	➤ Formal Introductions to Lists or Ideas	➤ **S18, S19, S20, S21, S24**
18.10	➤ Workplace Documents	➤ **S22**
18.11	➤ Miscellaneous Uses of the Colon	➤ **S23**

Instructions: Cover the answers in the **Answer** column; then write your answers to the first statement. Uncover the first printed answer and compare your answer to it. If you wrote a correct answer, continue the activity. If you made an error, use the **Coverage Key** to locate the chapter section you need to review. When you are confident that you understand the material, continue with the reinforcement activity.

ANSWER

STATEMENT

S14 The semicolon and the colon (serve, do not serve) the same basic purpose.

A14 do not serve

S15 While the semicolon acts as a separator, the purpose of the colon is _____.

A15 to direct the reader's attention to what follows

S16 To introduce a quotation of two or more sentences, use a(n) _____. To introduce a quotation of one sentence or part of a sentence, use a(n) _____.

A16 colon, comma

S17 Punctuate the following sentences correctly.
   a. **Ms. Jacobs said "I accept your offer."**
   b. **Ms. Jacobs said "I accept your offer on one condition: that I be allowed to withdraw at the end of the year. If that is impossible, then I must decline."**

A17   a.   Ms. Jacobs said, "I accept..."
   b.   Ms. Jacobs said: "I accept..."

S18 The punctuation mark you use before a list formally introduced by the words *as follows* or *the following* is the _____.
Place colons where needed in the following sentences:
   a. **Send invitations to the following people Marco, Hemal, Leila, and Ruth.**
   b. **The expenses are as follows $200 for publicity, $500 for rent of the hall, and $300 for refreshments.**

A18   colon,
   a.   ... the following people: Marco...
   b.   ... as follows: $200...

S19 If the formal introductory expression such as *these* or *the following* is left out but clearly understood, a colon (may, may not) be used. Place colons where needed in the following sentences:
  a. **We had three major expenses $200 for publicity, $500 for rent of the hall, and $300 for refreshments.**
  b. **The apartment has two major advantages it is close to where I live and the rent is reasonable.**

A19 may,
  a. **... three major expenses: $200...**
  b. **...two main advantages: it is close...**

S20 If the list immediately follows a verb or a preposition in a sentence, a colon (should, should not) be used. Place colons where needed in the following sentences:
  a. **Our three major expenses were $200 for publicity, $500 for rent of the hall, and $300 for refreshments.**
  b. **The apartment has the three main advantages of location, reasonable rent, and good parking.**

A20 should not,
  a. no colon needed
  b. no colon needed

S21 Place colons where needed in the following sentences:
  a. **I have one objection to your proposal it won't work.**
  b. **My most difficult subjects are accounting and calculus.**
  c. **These are my two most difficult subjects accounting and calculus.**
  d. **Send invitations to Marco, Hemal, Leila, and Ruth.**

A21 a. **... proposal: it ...**
  b. no colon needed
  c. **... subjects: accounting ...**
  d. no colon needed

S22 In a business letter (the date, the salutation, the complimentary close) should be followed by a colon.

A22 the salutation

S23 Colons can also be used to separate various elements in a variety of situations. In which of the following is a colon properly used?
  a. To separate hours from minutes in an expression of time.
  b. To separate pounds from ounces in weight.
  c. To separate the title from the subtitle in a book.
  d. To separate the city from the state in an address.

A23 a., c.

S24 Punctuate the following sentences correctly:
  Please ship the following items to arrive by 1000 a.m. Thursday three cartons of paper, one case of sealing tape, and one pack of large shipping boxes.

A24 **Please ship the following items to arrive by 10:00 a.m. Thursday: three cartons of paper, one case of sealing tape, and one pack of large shipping boxes.**

CHAPTER 18 SUMMARY

In this chapter you learned how to use semicolons to separate independent clauses as well as independent clauses with conjunctive adverbs or transitional phrases. You also discovered how to use semicolons in a series of items with commas and in an expression that introduces a list or an explanation. In addition, you focused on the various functions of the colon. You studied how a colon is used to introduce quotations, lists, or ideas, and how it functions in workplace documents and other specific instances, such as time and bibliographical data.

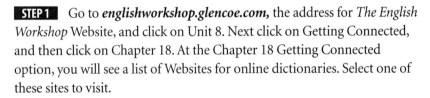

Getting Connected

USING AN ONLINE DICTIONARY

GOAL: Have you ever wondered where a particular word comes from? You can learn more about words and language by going to a dictionary Website. An online dictionary isn't just a place to look up the meaning of a word; it's also a place where you can find articles about a variety of language-related topics, such as the origins of a particular word and the history of the English language. In this activity you will locate an article that you find interesting, and you will use it to develop your skills with semicolons and colons.

STEP 1 Go to *englishworkshop.glencoe.com,* the address for *The English Workshop* Website, and click on Unit 8. Next click on Getting Connected, and then click on Chapter 18. At the Chapter 18 Getting Connected option, you will see a list of Websites for online dictionaries. Select one of these sites to visit.

STEP 2 Scan the home page for search options related to the site's contents. Select an option that will direct you to information about a specific language topic.

STEP 3 First, skim the article. If it doesn't intrigue you, choose another article or another topic. You may also return to *The English Workshop* Website and select a different online dictionary site. Once you've located an article you like, make a printout.

STEP 4 After you've read the entire article, go through it a second time and circle or highlight all semicolons and colons. Careful writers use these punctuation marks sparingly; you may not find many in the article.

STEP 5 Go back to the semicolons and colons you circled or highlighted, and identify the purpose of each of them. You will recall, for example, that semicolons are used to separate independent clauses or items with commas in a series, and that colons are used to introduce lists or quotations of two or more sentences. Write the purpose of each semicolon or colon in the margins of the article, next to the line on which it appears.

STEP 6   On the back of your printout, create *at least two* complete sentences of your own that use the semicolon. There are two ways you can do this:

a. Carefully select two sentences that appear next to each other in the article. Combine them into one compound sentence that includes a semicolon. You may need to change or omit some of the wording so that the two sentences sound more closely related. It may help to add a conjunctive adverb or a transitional phrase. (See Sections 13.13 and 13.14 for lists of both.)

b. Carefully select one complex sentence, consisting of a dependent clause and an independent clause. (See Section 13.4 for examples of complex sentences.) Rewrite it as a compound sentence that includes two independent clauses joined by a semicolon. You will need to omit the subordinating conjunction in the dependent clause. You may add a coordinating conjunction, a conjunctive adverb, or a transitional phrase instead. For example,

Although President Jefferson approved of the concept of pursuing happiness, he wasn't the only person to speak on the subject.

This complex sentence can be rewritten to include a semicolon by omitting the subordinating conjunction *Although* and inserting the conjunctive adverb *however* after *happiness.*

President Jefferson approved of the concept of pursuing happiness; however, he wasn't the only person to speak on the subject.

Write your new sentence on the back of your printout. Repeat this with a second sentence.

STEP 7   Based on the material in your article, create *at least one* complete sentence that uses the colon. You have two options: Create a sentence that introduces and includes two or more lines of quoted material from your article or create a sentence that introduces a series containing commas. Write your new sentence on the back of your printout.

STEP 8   Write your name on the front of your printout, and give it to your instructor.

PRACTICE 1

The Semicolon

Instructions: Place a semicolon in each sentence as needed. Add other punctuation where necessary.

EXAMPLE: **The storm affected business; many stores were forced to close.**

1. There are two reasons for our decision namely your determination and your perseverance.

2. To be perfectly frank I am sorry to see them go but I know that try as you might you had no alternative but to ask for their resignations.

3. All of us were concerned about the employment picture for the year as presented by the government but following your advice we felt it was our duty to remain calm and subsequent events have proved the wisdom of that advice.

4. Our membership includes Diego Sanchez the eminent painter Jules Hirsh the famous caricaturist and Cynthia Price the well-known columnist.

5. The only branches that registered losses were Wilmington Delaware Cleveland Ohio and Newark New Jersey.

6. The market went up for some stocks others however declined in value.

7. My five children were born on August 16 1977 April 10 1980 December 9 1981 January 17 1985 and July 10 1986.

8. The random-access memory (RAM) temporarily stores programs and data in the computer the read-only memory (ROM) permanently stores program data or languages.

9. The supervisor spoke to the staff about working past the strike deadline however by midnight there appeared to be no hope of a settlement and the employees left the building.

10. To err is human to forgive divine.

11. Employing every means at her disposal the U.S. Ambassador Juanita Pederson attempted to befriend the inhabitants of that small developing nation and her efforts were ultimately rewarded by success especially in the areas of education and industrialization.

12. Clarence held various part-time jobs while in college namely waiter supermarket checker telephone marketer and salesclerk.

13 I agree with your findings I disagree with your recommendations.

14. Yours is an excellent report and I agree with your conclusions regarding both the causes and the extent of the problems what I cannot agree with however are your recommendations regarding ways to solve these problems.

15. Semicolons do more than simply connect two independent clauses to form a compound sentence they also imply a close relationship between the two clauses.

PRACTICE 2

The Colon

Instructions: In the following sentences place a colon as needed. Add other punctuation where necessary.

EXAMPLE: **We have recorded your order as follows one overhead projector six packs of markers and one projector cart.**

1. I was told to bring the following items to the exam pens pencils and a pocket calculator.

2. This was his reply "My only regret is that I have but one life to give for my country."

3. Our plane departs at 507 p.m.

4. The letter began with this statement "Dear Sir I wish to thank you for your help."

5. A conference call was arranged among the author the developmental editor and the acquisitions editor.

6. Both the Republicans and the Democrats agree on one thing the other party is to blame.

7. We listed three stock prices $5.52 $5.59 $6.01.

8. Only two things in life are certain death and taxes.

9. These invoices remain unpaid No. 3721 No. 3723 and No. 3742.

10. This sign appeared on Harry Truman's desk "The buck stops here."

11. Because the instructor is often late my 800 a.m. class usually doesn't start until 810.

12. We have three goals during the next five years increasing productivity reducing costs and increasing our market share.

13. After weeks of uncertainty he finally decided to leave the company and open his own business.

14. After weeks of uncertainty he reached a decision He would leave the company and open his own business.

15. For graduation all students are required to complete courses in the following areas of study English mathematics accounting and computer science.

16. For graduation all students are required to complete courses in English mathematics accounting and computer science.

17. This file contains basic writing supplies stationery envelopes pens ink and stamps.

18. Only four people were absent Sue Pagan Marc Spa Al Rosen and Pia Yee.

19. Have you read his latest book *Building an Empire The Art of Investment*?

20. To   Laura Brunson Personnel Records

    From   Joanne Himes Central Services

    Subject   Employee Promotions

    The following employees are being considered for promotion Please forward their records by November 1

    Julio Cruz   Bud Cravitz   Lisa James   Roberta Lombardi

PRACTICE 3

Punctuation Review

Instructions: This practice involves the use of the colon, semicolon, comma, and period. Insert these marks where needed in the following sentences.

EXAMPLE: **We have not received payment for your last two shipments consequently we have delayed filling your current order.**

1. Our employees are all experienced in fact most are CPAs

2. Both Mr Mattuck and Ms Slater share a common characteristic they value professional success above all else

3. We offer a choice of three cabinets the stately Classical the functional Colonial or the streamlined Modern

4. Once again we are extending the time however in the future there will be no further extensions

5. The workday begins at 830 am it ends at 500 pm

6. The traits that I most admire in a person are these honesty wisdom and perseverance

7. The final sentence read "These measures will ensure a steady growth for our company both now and for years to come"

8. I missed the 715 train as a result I was late for my 830 appointment

9. Since our last report we have restudied the figures you submitted but despite our attempts to reconcile them the surplus figures do not coincide

10. The possible meeting dates are as follows Tuesday November 8 Wednesday November 16 and Tuesday November 29

11. During the past few months which have been especially hectic I inspected the following sites the Tennessee factory the Missouri offices and the Louisiana warehouse

12. Therefore we are pleased to be able to extend this invitation but bear in mind that much as we would prefer that it be otherwise this must be our last offer

13. You Ms Lopez have excellent credit hence you have been pre-approved for this special offer

14. Fool me once shame on you fool me twice shame on me

15. Senator Blackstone did not seem terribly disappointed that she lost her reelection bid on the contrary she seemed relieved that the campaign was over and that she would be able to retire from politics and return to private life

Name _____

Class _____ Date _____

PRACTICE 4

The Semicolon and the Colon

Instructions: The following memo is written without any punctuation. Insert all necessary punctuation marks.

TO: Maxine T

FROM: Kim Oh

DATE: November 3 20--

SUBJECT: Sites for Marketing Conference

Here is the information you requested

Three hotels are potential sites for our conference namely the Hilton the Biltmore and the Plaza All three have conference facilities more than sufficient for our needs The Hilton can accommodate 2172 the Biltmore 2647 and the Plaza 2645

Each has modern conference facilities including ballrooms and seminar rooms moreover each offers excellent dining and entertainment for conference participants

Only the Biltmore however would be able to arrange an 830 pm pre-conference session I believe this is an important consideration accordingly I recommend the Biltmore as our conference site.

PRACTICE 5

Composition: Using Semicolons and Colons

Instructions: Compose complete sentences using the elements indicated in parentheses.

EXAMPLE: **(a semicolon followed by *therefore*)**
   I find your editorial position extremely biased; therefore, I am canceling my subscription.

1. (a colon and the phrase *the following*)_____

   _____

2. (a semicolon followed by *for example*)_____

   _____

3. (semicolon followed by *and*)_____

   _____

4. (a semicolon followed by *however*)_____

   _____

5. (a colon followed by a quotation)_____

   _____

6. (a semicolon followed by *namely*)_____

   _____

7. (a colon followed by *namely*)_____

   _____

8. (semicolons to separate items in a series)_____

   _____

9. (semicolons to separate two independent clauses with no connectors)_____

   _____

10. (a colon in which the formal introductory expression is omitted but understood)_____

   _____

PRACTICE 6

Composition: Writing a Thank-You Letter

Instructions: Assume that you have just accepted a job offer that seems to be everything you were seeking in employment. One of your former teachers, at your request, wrote a letter of recommendation for you. You know the letter helped you get the job; the personnel director mentioned that she was impressed by it. Write your former teacher a thank-you letter. Compose a draft of your letter in the space below. Write your finished letter on a separate piece of paper to give to your instructor.

_____

_____

_____

_____

_____

_____

_____

_____

_____

_____

_____

_____

_____

_____

_____

_____

_____

Other Marks of Punctuation

CHAPTER 19 PREVIEW

The eight punctuation marks you will study in this chapter perform a variety of specialized functions. You will continue to assess your knowledge in the Programmed Reinforcement sections and the Practices. Finally, you will visit a quotation Website to reinforce your use of punctuation.

OBJECTIVES

After completing this chapter, you will be able to

- Determine how to use quotation marks with the following:
  - Direct quotations and quotations within quotations
  - Names and titles of short written works
  - Definitions of words or expressions used in special ways
- Determine how to use apostrophes with the following:
  - Contractions
  - Possessive nouns
  - Plurals of abbreviations and letters
- Determine how and when to hyphenate word divisions, compound expressions, and compound adjectives.
- Determine the correct usage of ellipsis, the underscore, parentheses, brackets, and the dash.

Study Plan for Chapter 19

The Study Tips for Chapter 19 offer a set of strategies that will help you learn and review the chapter material.

1. **Two by Two**: Quotation marks, brackets, and parentheses always enclose words and are always used in pairs.
2. **Closing Quotation Marks and Other Punctuation**: Commas and periods always go inside the closing quotation mark; semicolons and colons are always placed outside the closing quotation mark. Exclamation and question marks go inside the quotation mark if they belong to the quoted words, outside if they belong to the entire sentence.
3. **The Apostrophe Rule of Three**: An apostrophe has only three uses: in contractions, in possessive nouns, and in the plural forms of letters and lowercase abbreviations with periods.
4. **Hyphen vs. Dash**: Use a hyphen for word division and in compound expressions and compound adjectives. Use a dash as a special effect— when you want to emphasize part of a sentence.

SECTION A
Quotation Marks

The punctuation marks you will study in this section and the next perform a variety of specialized functions. In this section, for example, you will learn how quotation marks indicate that the words they enclose are different from other words in a sentence, paragraph, or passage.

19.1 Direct Quotations

Use quotation marks to enclose a direct quotation. A direct quotation repeats the exact words that were originally said or written.

> In your letter of July 2 you state, "Our records show that the merchandise was shipped on June 19 via Tri-State Trucking."

Do not use quotation marks around an indirect quotation. An indirect quotation is a rewording of the original statement. It is frequently introduced by the word *that.*

> In your letter of July 2 you write that the shipment was sent via Tri-State Trucking on June 19.

Colons. Use a colon to introduce a direct quotation of two or more sentences.

> In a message to the American Booksellers' Association, President Roosevelt said: "Books cannot be killed by fire. People die, but books never die. No man and no force can abolish memory."

Use a colon when the introduction comments directly on the quotation, whatever the length of the introduction.

> President Roosevelt spoke boldly of the eternal power of ideas: "People die, but books never die."

Use a comma to introduce a direct quotation of one sentence or part of a sentence.

> In a message to the American Booksellers' Association, President Roosevelt said, "Books cannot be killed by fire."

Periods. When a complete statement is quoted and ends the sentence, the period is placed inside the final quotation mark.

> Barbara Jordan said: "What the people want is simple. They want an America as good as its promise."

When a complete statement is quoted but does not end the sentence, a comma is placed inside the final quotation mark: *"What the people want is simple. They want an America as good as its promise,"* said Barbara Jordan.

When a complete statement being quoted is broken into more than one part, enclose each part in quotation marks. Do not start the second part with a capital. Note the use of commas: *"What the people want,"* said Barbara Jordan, *"is simple. They want an America as good as its promise."*

Multiple Speakers in a Conversation When recording the direct conversation of two or more persons, place the statements of each person in separate quotation marks and in separate paragraphs.

> The chairman shouted, "Order! Order in the house!"
> "I will not be silenced," answered Lutz, waving his arms wildly.
> "Friends," interrupted Trey, "let us consider this matter rationally, not
> emotionally."

Multiple Sentences If a quoted statement consists of more than one sentence, the quotation marks go at the beginning and at the end of the entire statement.

> "Your check for last month's purchases arrived today. It reminded us of how
> promptly you always settle your account."

If the single quotation is more than one consecutive paragraph, the quotation marks go at the beginning of each paragraph, but at the end of only the *last* paragraph.

> Ms. Chez received this goodwill letter today from Shelby's:
> "Your check for last month's purchases arrived today. It reminded us of how
> promptly you always settle your account.
> "We appreciate the fine record and look forward to continuing to serve you
> as one of our valued customers.
> "Don't forget to bring the enclosed coupon with you the next time you visit
> our store. It entitles you to ten percent off our already low prices."

Quotations Within Quotations

Use single quotation marks (apostrophes on a keyboard) to indicate a quotation within a quotation.

> Syed said, "I believe Benjamin Franklin's words: 'If your head is wax, don't
> walk in the sun.'"

Do not skip a space after the beginning quotation mark or before the closing quotation mark.

19.2 Names and Titles

Use quotation marks around the titles of works that are published as part of larger publications. These include poems, short stories, lectures, songs, sermons, and articles or chapters in magazines, newspapers, and books.

The name of a magazine, newspaper, pamphlet, or book is written either in italics or in all-capital letters rather than with quotation marks.

> Did you read "The Virtual Offices of the Future" in *The Wall Street Journal?*
> For Friday the instructor assigned Chapter 12 of *Administrative Office Management,* "The Use of Tests to Select Office Workers."
> I subscribe to LIFE for its outstanding photography.

Capitalization Note. Capitalize the first letter of each important word in the title. Capitalize articles, short conjunctions, and short prepositions when they occur at the beginning of the title, not when they occur in the middle. Many sources define "short" as containing three or fewer letters.

Style Tip

All-Capital Letters

Use all-capital letters when titles occur frequently (as in the correspondence of a publishing house) or when you want to make the words eye-catching. Use italics or underlining in other circumstances.

19.3 Definitions and Words Used in Special Ways

There are three general guidelines for using quotation marks to define or call attention to particular words, phrases, and unusual expressions.

1. Use quotation marks to enclose or set off definitions of words or expressions. The words or expressions themselves are usually underlined or italicized.

   > The Latin phrase *ex post facto* means "after the fact" or "retroactively."
   > The term *zero-base budgeting* is defined as "a budgeting method in which budget makers examine and justify each expenditure for each budget period without regard to the previous period."

2. Use quotation marks to enclose words and phrases introduced by expressions such as *stamped, labeled, marked,* and *signed.*

   > The letter was marked "Personal and Confidential."
   > The packaged was stamped "Photos—Do Not Bend."

3. Place quotation marks around words used in an unusual sense, coined phrases, and colloquial expressions.

   > My "aunt" Elsie is actually an old friend of my mother's.
   > We feel that this textbook is "user-friendly."
   > Carmen Huerta led a workshop on how to "nail down" a sale.

Combining quotation marks and other punctuation can be troublesome unless you are careful. Pay close attention to these guidelines.

1. Always place a final period or comma inside the quotation marks.

   Colin Powell said, "You can't make someone else's choices. You shouldn't let someone else make yours."
   "Give me the statistics," she retorted, "and I'll have the answers in a minute."

2. Always place a final colon or semicolon outside the quotation marks.

   Here is a partial list of causes cited in "The Rising Cost of Living": higher wages, increased traffic, and declining productivity.
   The encircled troops were told, "Surrender or die"; they chose to fight on.

3. The question mark, exclamation point, and dash are placed inside the quotation marks when they relate specifically to the quoted material.

   "May I join you?" she asked.
   "Wow!" was all he could say.
   "The name of the murderer is—" were her final words as the lights flickered and shots rang out.

4. The question mark, exclamation point, and dash are placed outside the quotation marks if they relate to the entire sentence.

   Did you read the piece on DVDs in "Market Trends and Tips"?
   Congratulations on your latest article, "How to Invest"!
   Your last question—"How can we improve communication?"—can best be answered by you.

Emoticon

An *emoticon* is an emotion icon created with keyboard symbols. Signal your happiness by using a colon, a hyphen, and a closing parenthesis to create a smiley face **: -)**. But be careful: some offices frown **: - (** on their use in e-mail correspondence.

Summary: Combining Quotation Marks With Other Marks of Punctuation

The *period* and *comma* ALWAYS go INSIDE the quotation marks.

."   ,"

The *colon* and *semicolon* ALWAYS go OUTSIDE the quotation marks.

":   ";

The *question mark, exclamation point,* and *dash* MAY go OUTSIDE or INSIDE the quotation marks.

When the punctuation marks relate *only* to the quoted material:

...?"   ...!"   ...—"

When the punctuation marks relate to the entire sentence:

..."?   ..."!   ..."—

SECTION A: PROGRAMMED REINFORCEMENT

Coverage Key

Section		Statement
19.1	➤ Direct Quotations	➤ **S1, S2, S3, S4**
19.2	➤ Names and Titles	➤ **S5**
19.3	➤ Definitions and Words Used in Special Ways	➤ **S6**
19.4	➤ Quotation Marks With Other Marks of Punctuation	➤ **S7, S8, S9**

Instructions: Cover the answers in the **Answer** column; then write your answers to the first statement. Uncover the first printed answer and compare your answer to it. If you wrote a correct answer, continue the activity. If you made an error, use the **Coverage Key** to locate the chapter section you need to review. When you are confident that you understand the material, continue with the reinforcement activity.

ANSWER	STATEMENT
	S1 Quotation marks (should, should not) be placed around direct quotations. They (should, should not) be placed around indirect quotations.
A1 should, should not	**S2** Punctuate the following, capitalizing letters if necessary. a. **Tell me he said how you're feeling have you been able to return to work.** b. **He asked how I was feeling and whether I had been able to go back to work.**
A2 a. **"Tell me," he said, "how you're feeling. Have you been able to return to work?"** b. no additional punctuation needed.	**S3** Choose the correct statement. In a direct conversation between two people: a. The entire conversation is put into one paragraph beginning and ending with quotation marks. b. A separate paragraph with beginning and ending quotation marks is used for the quotation of each speaker.
A3 b.	**S4** In a single quotation consisting of several paragraphs, quotation marks are put at the _____ of each paragraph but at the end of only the _____ paragraph.
A4 beginning, last	

S5 Titles of books are usually italicized or printed in capital letters, but _____ marks are used with titles of articles. Which of the following titles should be enclosed with punctuation marks?

a. a book
b. a chapter in a book
c. an article in a newspaper
d. a newspaper
e. a song

A5 quotation, b., c., e.

S6 Quotation marks are used to set off definitions of words or expressions; the words or expressions themselves are usually _____. Punctuate this sentence: **The French expression nouveau-riche may be translated as the newly arrived.**

A6 italicized or underlined; **The French expression nouveau-riche may be translated as "the newly arrived."**

S7 The _____ and the _____ are always placed inside the closing quotation mark; the _____ and the _____ are always placed outside the closing quotation mark.

A7 comma, period; colon, semicolon

S8 If the question mark, the exclamation point, and the dash relate specifically to the material being quoted, they are placed (inside, outside) the closing quotation mark. If they relate to the sentence as a whole, they are placed (inside, outside) the closing quotation mark.

A8 inside, outside

S9 Punctuate these sentences correctly, capitalizing letters if needed:

a. **Where were you he asked**
b. **She exclaimed this is preposterous**
c. **Did you open the letter marked Personal and Confidential**

A9 a. **"Where were you?" he asked.**
b. **She exclaimed, "This is preposterous!"**
c. **Did you open the letter marked "Personal and Confidential"?**

SECTION B
More Specialized Marks of Punctuation

In the previous section you learned to use quotation marks to signal specific information about the words or phrases they enclose. In this section you will develop your sophistication as a writer by learning how to use seven more marks of punctuation for specialized purposes.

Punctuation Tip

19.5 The Apostrophe

Use an apostrophe to indicate that a letter or letters have been left out of a contraction. Notice where each apostrophe goes and the letters it replaces:

COMMON CONTRACTIONS

aren't	weren't	she'll	I'm	we're
can't	you're	they'll	it's	Gov't
couldn't	he'll	we'll	who's	Nat'l
isn't	I'll	you'll	they're	Sec'y

Contractions are normally used only in informal writing or in tabulations to save space. Contractions involving verbs are sometimes used in workplace correspondence when the writer is seeking conversational tone.

An apostrophe can also show the omission of numbers in a year.

Members of the classes of '41 and '51 attended the '01 Homecoming.

19.6 The Possessive Case of Nouns

Form the possessive of singular and irregular plural nouns by adding *'s*. The possessive of a regular plural noun requires an apostrophe.

A teacher's success depends upon a student's efforts.
Knox's Toy Store will begin carrying children's clothing in the fall.
Many manufacturers' representatives were at the convention.

Possessive Pronouns

Remember, the possessive form of a pronoun does not take an apostrophe: *hers, its, ours, yours, theirs.*

Is this book hers?   Yours truly,

It's is a contraction of *it is; its* is a possessive pronoun.

If this room is to remain orderly, it's essential that everything be organized.

19.7 Plurals of Lowercase Abbreviations and Letters

Use the apostrophe to form the plurals of abbreviations with internal periods and lowercase letters as well as the plurals of *A*, *I*, *M*, and *U*.

Mississippi has four *i's and* four *s's.* He uses six *I's* in his first paragraph.
These five orders are all *c.o.d.'s.*

Form the plurals of words used simply as words by adding *s*. If a particular plural formed this way appears confusing, include an apostrophe.

We want no *ifs, ands,* or *buts.* Your use of *which's* and *that's* is reversed.

19.8 The Hyphen

Use hyphens to combine words or to show where a word is being divided.

Word Division

Use the hyphen to divide a word that cannot fit at the end of a line.

She said that it would be impossible to complete the project on schedule.

Compound Expressions

Various compound expressions should always be hyphenated.

1. Hyphenate some compound nouns, such as *brother-in-law, sister-in-law, attorney-at-law,* and *theater-in-the-round.*
2. Hyphenate compound nouns that lack a noun as an element, such as *cure-all, has-been, know-how,* and *do-it-yourselfers.*
3. Hyphenate compound words that begin with *self,* such as *self-conscious, self-evident, self-assurance, self-respect,* and *self-confident.*
4. Hyphenate compound words that begin with a prefix followed by a word beginning with a capital letter, such as *anti-American, ex-Senator, mid-February, non-Western, pre-Civil War,* and *pro-Republican.*

Many other compound expressions are not hyphenated. Consult an up-to-date dictionary to determine whether an expression should be hyphenated.

Possessive Nouns
To review possessive nouns, turn back to Chapter 3, Section B.

■

Flashback

Plural Nouns
Section A in Chapter 3 includes a detailed discussion of plural nouns.

■

LOOKING AHEAD

Word Divisions
In Section 20.4, on pages 579-582, you'll learn how to use hyphens to divide words.

●

Compound Adjectives

As you learned in Chapter 10, compound adjectives such as *up to date, high class, first rate, high grade,* and *well informed* should be hyphenated when they come before the noun they modify.

We have an up-to-date system.
Our store caters to a high-class clientele.

We need a well-informed public.

When a compound adjective comes after the noun it modifies, do not hyphenate it.

Our system is up to date.
Our clientele is high class.

The public must be well informed.

Adverbs Ending in *ly*

Do not use a hyphen after an adverb ending in *ly* even if it precedes the noun.

highly trained athlete   brightly decorated hall   oddly strange mixture

Hyphenated Adjectives With a Common Element

When two or more hyphenated adjectives have a common element that is expressed only with the final term, use a hyphen after each of the partial adjectives to show a relationship with the final term. These hyphens are known as **suspending hyphens.**

The local ice cream shop serves, single- double-, and triple-dip cones.
He swam in the 50-, 100-, and 200-yard freestyle races.
We invested in both short- and long-term securities.

LOOKING AHEAD

Number Rules
You'll discover how to present numbers in Chapter 20, Section C.

●

Numbers

When writing out numbers, hyphenate compound numbers from twenty-one through ninety-nine. Do not hyphenate hundreds, thousands, or millions. Look at these examples:

Our goal is ten out of thirty-seven.
One hundred thirty-seven attended the banquet Friday evening.
On the amount line of a check, $137,645 is written as "One hundred thirty-seven thousand six hundred forty-five dollars."

In most situations numbers are expressed as figures.

19.9 Ellipsis Marks

Ellipses are a series of three spaced periods, with a space before and after each period. They may be used at the beginning or in the middle of a quoted sentence or a quotation to show that part of it has been omitted.

> "...America is ... like a quilt—many patches, many pieces, many colors, many sizes, all woven and held together by a common thread."
> —Jesse Jackson

If the end of a quoted sentence or passage has been omitted, use three ellipses in addition to the necessary terminal punctuation mark.

> "I have seen war .... I hate war."
> —Franklin Delano Roosevelt

> "Those who do not know how to weep with their whole heart don't know how to laugh ...."
> —Golda Meir

Ellipses are also used to show the end of an unfinished thought. However, include only three marks to indicate that a thought trails off.

> His reaction was, "If I had only known ..."
> He could easily have saved the situation by ... But why talk about it?

19.10 The Underscore

Use the underscore to indicate words that would be italicized in print. This includes titles of works published separately such as books, magazines, periodicals, and newspapers.

> The <u>New York Times</u> has been highly critical of Mr. Newcomb's new book, <u>Making Money With Internet Stocks</u>.

Use the underscore to emphasize words in a sentence or to set off words being discussed or defined.

> This offer will <u>never</u> be repeated.
> The words <u>affect</u> and <u>effect</u> are frequently confused.
> The term <u>nom de plume</u> means "pen name," a fictitious name a writer uses rather than his or her own.

Style Tip

Italicizing = Underlining

When you write with a pen or at other times when you cannot italicize words, underline them instead.

A good writer uses the dash—for special effect. If you use the dash too often, you destroy its effectiveness and leave a difficult-to-read page.

Explanatory Phrases

Use the dash to emphasize an explanatory phrase.

> We want to tell you about our product—the Schenley car.
> Mario—the only experienced member of our staff—has just resigned.

The dash is frequently used to set off an explanatory phrase that contains one or more commas. Don't leave out the second dash. If the phrase starts with a dash, it also should end with a dash—not with a comma.

> WRONG: Several states—especially Arizona, Utah, and New Mexico, would be ideal locations in which to build another plant.
>
> RIGHT: ✔Several states—especially Arizona, Utah, and New Mexico— would be ideal locations in which to build another plant.

Major Breaks in Thought

Use the dash to indicate an afterthought, a major break in the continuity of thought, or an emphatic phrase.

> The large house—and it was very large—was demolished by the fire.
> I know—or should I say, I feel—that you will do well.
> The villagers had lost all hope—then Robin Hood appeared.

Substitution for a Semicolon or a Colon

For a stronger but less formal break, use the dash in place of a semicolon or a colon—for instance, use it to join closely related independent clauses or to introduce explanatory words, phrases, or clauses.

> The opening paragraph of your paper should contain a thesis statement—
> that is, it should state clearly the central point of your paper.
> (*dash instead of a semicolon*)
> I have only one objection to offering him the position—he's totally
> unqualified. (*dash instead of a colon*)

Em-dash

Word-processing programs usually offer the em-dash—so named because it is as wide as a capital *M*. You can also make a dash by striking the hyphen key twice with no spaces before, between, or after the hyphens.

Two Hyphens = One Dash

Never use a single hyphen to represent a dash.

Words Summarizing a Preceding Series

Use a dash before a word used to sum up a preceding series.

> Experience, integrity, commitment—these were the qualities the candidate stressed in every campaign speech.
>
> Hiroko Reyes, Seth Eisenberg, Anne O'Flaherty—any one of these people would be an excellent supervisor.

Author's Name Following a Quotation

Use a dash before the name of the author or the title of the work when you identify the author or source of a displayed quotation. Typically the dash and the attribution appear on a separate line as follows:

> "The best way out is always through."
> —Robert Frost
>
> "If ignorance paid dividends, most Americans could make a fortune out of what they don't know about economics."
> —Luther H. Hodges, U.S. Secretary of Commerce, 1961-65

19.12 Parentheses

Parentheses are used to enclose various types of information.

Incidental and Explanatory Expressions

Use parentheses to enclose expressions that are completely incidental, explanatory, or supplementary to the main thought of a sentence.

> There is no possibility (so I am told) that this deal will go through.
>
> William the Conqueror's victory (he defeated Harold at the Battle of Hastings in 1066) was pivotal in the development of the English language.

When a sentence ends with an expression in parentheses, place a period after the closing parenthesis.

> You have already learned how to avoid sentence fragments (see Chapter 2).

When a complete sentence appears in parentheses as part of another sentence, it is neither started with a capital letter nor finished with a period. However, when a sentence in parentheses is an independent thought that is *not* part of another sentence, it is started with a capital letter and ended with appropriate punctuation inside the closing parenthesis:

> I have told Ms. Liang that you will have the goods delivered on Tuesday. (Please don't let us down, Kay.) She will accept shipment then.

Punctuation With Parentheses

Do you place punctuation inside or outside the closing parenthesis? If the punctuation relates only to the material in parentheses, place it inside.

> When using a telescope, never (never!) look directly at the sun.
> At the coming meeting (will you be able to make it on the 19th?), let's plan to discuss next year's budget.

If the punctuation does not relate specifically to the material in parentheses, place the punctuation outside the closing parenthesis mark.

> No matter where we have traveled (and we have been to nearly every state in the union), we have never found a better hotel.
> Is it true there is a term for gossip spread by e-mail (word of mouse)?

Occupational Hazards

At the office, *carpal tunnel syndrome* is an occupational hazard. Caused by constant keyboarding, it signifies pain in a nerve that passes through the wrist into the hand. Allow your hands healthy time-outs.

Dashes or Parentheses?

In some instances it is correct to use either dashes or parentheses, whichever you prefer. When you want to emphasize the parenthetical statement, use dashes. When you want to de-emphasize it, use parentheses.

> This offer—and it is our final offer—is too good to be refused.
> (*final offer emphasized*)
> This offer (and it is our final offer) is too good to be refused.
> (*final offer de-emphasized*)

DASHES VS. PARENTHESES

Beginning of sentence — material to be EMPHASIZED — remainder of sentence.

Beginning of sentence (material to be DE-EMPHASIZED) remainder of sentence.

Numbers or Letters Itemizing a List

Parentheses are used to enclose numbers or letters itemizing a list within a sentence. When the sentence itself is part of a numbered sequence, use letters to itemize the list. When it is not, use numbers. Letters or numbers enclosed in parentheses, are generally not followed by periods.

> Practice serves to (1) improve your coordination, (2) increase your speed, and (3) develop your strength.

If you had tabulated the second list, you would write it as follows:

> Practice serves to
> 1. Improve your coordination.
> 2. Increase your speed.
> 3. Develop your strength.

19.13 Figures in Formal Documents

Numbers frequently are written out in both words and figures in workplace documents. Parentheses are usually placed around the figures.

> We acknowledge receipt of your order for three hundred (300) barrels of crude oil.

If you spell out a dollar amount in a legal document, capitalize each word in the figure and the word *Dollar*.

> The note for Four Thousand Dollars ($4000) is payable within Sixty (60) days.

In spelling out a quantity of material, do not capitalize the words in the unit of measurement. Place the figures in parentheses before the name of the unit of measure: *three hundred (300) barrels*.

TEAM SUPPORT Begin to look at instructors, advisers, or supervisors as team players, not as authorities to resist or judge. Show your support and loyalty to the team as a whole.

19.14 Brackets

Use brackets in a direct quotation when you insert words that are not part of the quotation. You may need to insert such words to explain or correct the quotation.

EXPLANATION: Ms. Prithvi wrote, "I was placed on hold for *40 minutes* [emphasis added]."

CORRECTION: The marketing report read: "This year we saw a change in customer bying [buying] habits."

Rather than correcting an error, a writer sometimes calls attention to it with the use of *sic,* meaning "so" or "this is the way it was."

> The marketing report read: "This year we saw a change in customer bying [*sic*] habits."

Brackets also are used as a substitute for parentheses within parentheses.

> Calvin Russell's newest book (*Writing for the World of Business* [the chapters on report writing are especially good]) has been widely praised .

sic
Italicize the word *sic* when it is used as a bracketed correction. However, if you don't have an italic font, do not underline *sic*.

Coverage Key

Section		Statement
19.5 ➤	The Apostrophe	➤ **S10**
19.6 ➤	The Possessive Case of Nouns	➤ **S11, S12**
19.7 ➤	Plurals of Lowercase Abbreviations and Letters	➤ **S13**
19.8 ➤	The Hyphen	➤ **S14, S15, S16, S17**
19.9 ➤	Ellipsis Marks	➤ **S18, S19**
19.10 ➤	The Underscore	➤ **S20**
19.11 ➤	The Dash	➤ **S21**
19.12 ➤	Parentheses	➤ **S22, S23, S24, S26**
19.13 ➤	Figures in Formal Documents	➤ **S25**
19.14 ➤	Brackets	➤ **S27**

Instructions: Cover the answers in the **Answer** column; then write your answers to the first statement. Uncover the first printed answer and compare your answer to it. If you wrote a correct answer, continue the activity. If you made an error, use the **Coverage Key** to locate the chapter section you need to review. When you are confident that you understand the material, continue with the reinforcement activity.

ANSWER

STATEMENT

S10 An apostrophe is used to indicate letters that are left out in contractions. Insert apostrophes in the following contractions: **cant, shouldnt, wont, youll, Id.**

A10 can't, shouldn't, won't, you'll, I'd

S11 Use an apostrophe to show possessive (nouns, pronouns), but do not use an apostrophe to show possessive (nouns, pronouns).

A11 nouns, pronouns

S12 Rewrite each of the following words as a possessive:
Bess, _____; your, _____; it, _____; factory, _____; their, _____; businesses, _____

A12 Bess's, yours, its, factory's, theirs, businesses'

S13 The apostrophe is used to form the plural of lowercase letters and abbreviations with internal periods plus these four capital letters: _____. Add apostrophes where necessary in the following:
a. **Mind your ps and qs.**
b. **Were putting the finishing touches on now—dotting all the is and crossing all the ts.**
c. **How many As did you receive on your report card?**

A13 A, I, M, U
a. **Mind your p's and q's.**
b. **We're putting the finishing touches on now—dotting all the i's and crossing all the t's.**
c. **How many A's did you receive on your report card?**

S14 Compound words or expressions beginning with *self* are (always, sometimes, never) hyphenated; those beginning with *anti, pro,* and *ex* when followed by words starting with a capital letter are (always, sometimes, never) hyphenated. Punctuate these expressions: **self respect, anti American, pro Democratic, ex President.**

A14 always, always, **self-respect, anti-American, pro-Democratic, ex-President**

S15 Adjective phrases such as *up to date* and *first class* (are, are not) hyphenated when they come before the noun they modify; they (are, are not) hyphenated when they come after the noun. Insert hyphens where proper:
a. **I speak from first hand experience.**
b. **They shipped low grade ore.**
c. **The ore they shipped was low grade.**
d. **Listen to WXYZ for up to the minute market analysis.**

A15 are, are not
a. **first-hand**
b. **low-grade**
c. no hyphen needed
d. **up-to-the-minute**

S16 When the adjective phrase contains an adverb ending in *ly*—for example, *highly trained*—you generally (do, do not) hyphenate even when the phrase comes before the noun. Insert hyphens where proper:
a. **He is a highly skilled worker.**
b. **We need a well informed citizenry.**
c. **The truth is self evident.**
d. **All our workers are highly skilled.**

A16 do not,
a. no hyphen needed
b. **well-informed**
c. **self-evident**
d. no hyphen needed

S17 When writing out numbers, hyphenate compound numbers from _____. You [do, do not] hyphenate hundreds, thousands, or millions unless the entire number comes immediately before the noun it modifies. Insert hyphens in the following:
a. **six million four hundred eighty two thousand nine hundred fifty five**
b. **a nine hundred fifty five dollar ticket**

A17 twenty-one to ninety-nine, do not
a. **six million four hundred eighty-two thousand nine hundred fifty-five**
b. **a nine-hundred-fifty-five-dollar ticket**

S18 The spaced periods that show that material has been left out of a direct quotation are known as _____.

A18 ellipses

S19 An ellipsis at the beginning or in the middle of a quotation is indicated by _____ periods; at the end of a quotation, by _____ periods.

A19 three, four

S20 The underscore is used to show words that would be italicized in print. Which of the following should be underscored (or italicized)?
- a. the title of a magazine
- b. an article in a magazine
- c. the name of a newspaper
- d. the title of a book
- e. the title of an essay
- f. a word to be emphasized

A20 a., c., d., f.

S21 Insert dashes as needed in the following sentences:
- a The truth and these reports make it clear that it is the truth is that Robinson has violated our trust.
- b. The nickname of Cleveland's baseball stadium is easy to remember The Jake.

A21
- a. The truth—and these reports make it clear that it is the truth—is that Robinson has violated our trust.
- b. The nickname of Cleveland's baseball stadium is easy to remember—The Jake.

S22 Parentheses are used to enclose expressions that are completely incidental to the main thought of a sentence. Often, instead of using parentheses, you may use _____.

A22 dashes

S23 When a sentence ends with a statement in parentheses, place the final period (inside, outside) the parentheses. Punctuate the following:
Turn to Lesson 4 (page 37)

A23 outside, **Turn to Lesson 4 (page 37).**

S24 Place commas in the following sentence:
The major issues in this election year include the cost of living (which is rising rapidly) civil rights environmental policy and the defense budget. In this sentence a comma is placed (inside, outside) the closing parenthesis.

A24 **The major issues in this election year include the cost of living (which is rising rapidly), civil rights, environmental policy, and the defense budget.;** outside

S25 In formal documents, a number often is written out and also is expressed by a figure in parentheses. In the following sentences, which words should be capitalized?
- a. **The contract calls for payment of two hundred dollars ($200).**
- b. **The invoice specifies two hundred (200) tons.**

A25
- a. **Two Hundred Dollars**
- b. no added capital letters

S26 Insert parentheses in the following sentences:
- a. **If these reports are accurate and I believe they are, Robinson has violated our trust.**
- b. **Under said Agreement, Licensee pays a royalty of fifteen percent 15%.**

A26
- a. **If these reports are accurate (and I believe they are), Robinson . . .**
- b. **. . . percent (15%).**

S27 Brackets in a direct quotation indicate which of the following?
- a. the quotation is too long
- b. words have been left out of the quoataion
- c. words that are not part of the quotation have been added

A27 c

CHAPTER 19 SUMMARY

In this chapter you learned how to use eight internal marks of punctuation. You built on your previous knowledge of quotation marks, apostrophes, and hyphens, and learned about five more specialized marks: ellipses, underscores, parentheses, brackets, and dashes. You discovered how these punctuation marks perform a variety of functions that help clarify information for readers.

Getting Connected

LOCATING FAMOUS QUOTATIONS ONLINE

GOAL: Sometimes you can add interest to a school paper or a workplace document by quoting a well-known person. An essay about work might include a quotation from the late Indira Gandhi, Prime Minister of India: "My grandfather once told me that there were two kinds of people: those who do the work and those who take the credit. He told me to try to be in the first group; there was much less competition." The task of finding a quotation such as Gandhi's is fairly easy if you use an online source. In this activity, you'll go online to search for quotations you like. You'll then use them to show your understanding of the specialized punctuation covered in Chapter 19.

STEP 1 Go to *englishworkshop.glencoe.com,* the address for *The English Workshop* Website, and click on Unit 8. Next click on Getting Connected, and then click on Chapter 19. At the Chapter 19 Getting Connected option, you'll see a list of quotation Websites. Click on one of these.

STEP 2 Scan the home page of the Website you selected. Each site is organized a little differently, but all the sites offer subject and author indexes and a search function.

STEP 3 Use one of the indexes or the search function to locate quotations. If you want to browse sayings from a particular person, use the author index. If you're curious about quotations related to a particular subject, use the subject index. You can also enter keywords from a favorite quotation you are trying to recall.

STEP 4 For this activity, use the search function to locate quotations about one of the following subjects: happiness, work, discipline, politics, travel, or youth. You can also come up with your own topic. Enter a topic into the search function.

STEP 5 Locate at least five quotations that interest you and print them out. Depending on the Website and the length of the quotations you select, you may print out a single page or several pages of quotations.

You'll find that the author of each quotation is identified; however, in some cases you may discover that the author is "unknown" or "anonymous."

STEP 6   Now that you've learned how to access quotations, you can use them in your own writing.

    a. In a paragraph of *at least six* sentences, write about one or more of the quotations you selected. For example, in response to Indira Gandhi's quotation, you could discuss whether you agree with her grandfather's statement. Compose your paragraph on the back of your printout or on a separate piece of paper.

    b. When you write this paragraph, use *at least four* of the internal punctuation marks you learned about in this chapter. They include quotation marks, apostrophes, hyphens, ellipses, underscores, parentheses, brackets, and dashes.

When you introduce your quotation, you will demonstrate your ability to use quotation marks. If this quotation comes from a known book, you will identify and underscore (or italicize) its title. If you write contractions or possessive nouns, you will use apostrophes. If you focus on a longer quotation, you may quote only the most important parts of it and use ellipses to replace the words that you omit. For example, Indira Gandhi also offered these words of wisdom: "You must learn to be still in the midst of activity, and to be vibrantly alive in repose." In your paragraph, you might shorten this as follows: "You must learn . . . to be vibrantly alive in repose."

STEP 7   After you've written your paragraph and demonstrated your skills with at least four of the specialized internal punctuation marks, write your name at the top of your work and give it to your instructor.

PRACTICE 1

Quotation Marks and Other Punctuation

Instructions: Insert all necessary punctuation in each sentence. Capitalize where necessary.

EXAMPLE: "Who manufactures these?" he asked.

1. The instructor told the class that the ability to communicate effectively is essential for success in today's workplace

2. What did you say he asked I wasn't listening

3. The president responded angrily to the accusations saying you may be certain that our firm adheres strictly to the highest ethical standards

4. His essay business ethics is a classic

5. Did you receive any compensation for your latest article the high-tech battle between Japan and the United States

6. She asked an important question how can we justify our own failure to help them

7. The French phrase entre nous means between ourselves or confidentially

8. Try our new air conditioner the ad stated it will bring cool comfort to your home or office

9. She asked how we can justify our own failure to help them

10. The package was stamped Fragile—Handle With Care

11. In your letter you write that the cost per unit will soon increase when will that increase take place

12. I wonder mused Cheryl what the real reasons are for Mr. McKeon's sudden resignation

13. Work expands to fill the time available for its completion wrote C Northcote Parkinson in 1957

14. Get out of my office he bellowed

15. Let us know by Friday she declared whether you will accept the offer

16. He accused his competitor of being a blind pig-headed mule

17. Rush help or—were the last words we heard before we lost contact with them

18. Great was all she could shout

19. Did you read the book how to double your money

20. Did you read the book on doubling your money

Name _____

Class _____ Date _____

PRACTICE 2

The Quotation Mark

Instructions: The following passage is based on material taken from *Voice Recognition with Software Applications* by Lyn Clark (Glencoe, 2001). Add quotation marks and any other necessary marks of punctuation.

In the opening chapter Training for Voice-Recognition Technology Professor Clark provides a brief overview of the development of voice-recognition software. She concludes her first paragraph with this question How did we get here and where are we headed

In a section entitled The Microcomputer Emerges she describes the development of the Apple computer by Steve Jobs and Steve Wozniak, the development of personal computers by IBM, and the subsequent development of IBM-compatible computers—often referred to as clones

She then goes on to discuss the development of voice-recognition software. Early releases of voice-recognition software she writes required considerable training time and these programs produced a high incidence of recognition errors. She goes on to say that over time these early programs were constantly improved and that today's programs are very accurate and sophisticated.

She concludes with the following statement Voice-recognition software is no longer the cumbersome slow tool of the late 1980s and early 1990s. It has gained recognition as a productivity tool in business government and the health care industry. Less time typing, less time editing—these two factors are instrumental in identifying voice-recognition software as a tool for increasing productivity.

PRACTICE 3

The Apostrophe: Part A

Instructions: Underline the correct word.

EXAMPLE: (<u>Whose</u>, Who's) coat is this?

1. (It's, Its) a blessing in disguise.

2. Are these (yours, your's)?

3. (Your, You're) help is most appreciated.

4. Wealth is not a true measure of a (persons, person's) success.

5. Give them (their, they're) due.

6. (They're, Their) due back here at 2 p.m.

7. The class of (79, '79) held a reunion recently.

8. The company sent (its, it's) condolences.

9. This is your handwriting, (is'nt, isn't) it?

10. Her handwriting is so poor that I can't tell her (as, a's) from her (is, i's).

The Apostrophe: Part B

Instructions: Mark through any possessive or contraction error in the sentences below. Write any correction in the space above each error.

EXAMPLE: I ~~cant~~ make any sense of this proposal of ~~your's~~.
can't above "cant", *yours* above "your's"

1. Please let me know whether your coming to this years class reunion.

2. We're all looking forward to seeing you and you're family at the Class of 92 Reunion.

3. If their coming to the reunion, lets all try to get together.

4. Its impossible to tell his ms and ns apart.

5. Their's is a very unusual position, isn't it?

6. Im certain that its still not too late to open an IRA.

7. I do'nt understand their companys failure to take advantage of that opportunity.

8. The director of the medical records department says she'll locate that patients' records herself.

9. I'm unable to tell whether these letters of her's are Us or Is.

10. Lings Clothing Store features the best in mens, womens, and childrens wear.

Name _____

Class _____ Date _____

PRACTICE 4

Compound Words

Instructions: In the blank, write each compound word. Consult your dictionary if necessary.

EXAMPLE: **trouble shooter**   EX. _____ **trouble shooter** _____

1. vice president   1. _____

2. no one   2. _____

3. some thing   3. _____

4. all right   4. _____

5. can not   5. _____

6. not withstanding   6. _____

7. self evident   7. _____

8. letter head   8. _____

9. ex president   9. _____

10. editors in chief   10. _____

11. over due   11. _____

12. post card   12. _____

13. self control   13. _____

14. vice chairman   14. _____

15. Web site   15. _____

16. self conscious   16. _____

17. any body   17. _____

18. real estate   18. _____

19. ex governor   19. _____

20. type written   20. _____

21. problem solving   21. _____

22. time sharing   22. _____

23. profit sharing   23. _____

24. house warming   24. _____

25. T shirt   25. _____

Name _____

Class _____ Date _____

PRACTICE 5

Marks of Punctuation

Instructions: Insert all necessary punctuation in the following sentences.

EXAMPLE: **You have already learned (see Chapter 3) about nouns.**

1. Reading writing speaking these are the skills all students must master.

2. Reading writing and speaking are the skills all students must master.

3. And the Licensee hereby agrees to pay Licensor on the first day of each month commencing on January the first Nineteen Hundred Ninety three the sum of Six Hundred Dollars $600.

4. As you have already learned see Chapter 5 a pronoun should agree in person and number with its antecedent.

5. We are interested I might say very interested in your assessment of the conference.

6. Please look at our advertisement you can find one in this month's issue of New Era to see what we mean by an efficient layout.

7. You should be able to collect the facts and we mean all the facts with little trouble if you apply yourself.

8. As a result of our long experience we have been in business for over a hundred years we feel it is our duty to advise against purchase of this stock.

9. Our representative Ms. Jeri Vutz didn't you meet her at our last convention will be glad to assist you.

10. This chance and it's your very last chance is a fine opportunity.

11. Remember to 1 listen carefully 2 speak clearly and 3 make your point.

12. It is self evident at least it should be so to a reasonable person that our economic outlook is brightening.

13. The New York Times The Wall Street Journal and The Washington Post these are her daily sources of information.

14. I wish I could help you but was all she could say.

15. I refuse wrote President Marisela Valadez to compromise my principals sic of honesty and integrity.

16. The phrase non sequitur literally means it does not follow.

17. Eliza and Dean's long awaited reunion tour have you ordered tickets yet will open in Boston next month.

18. The student critic wrote the following after attending his first opera I thought the plot of Vivaldi's Verdis Rigoletto was rather boring.

19. The instructions for the radio cassette recorder read Note that the red plug of the connecting cord is for the right channel R and the white plug for the left channel L.

20. Arthur Miller's The Crucible is based on the Salem witch trials of 1692 I read some of the actual transcripts of the trials when I visited Salem a few years ago There are also parallels with the McCarthy hearings in the 1950s.

PRACTICE 6

Punctuation

Instructions: The following letter is written with no punctuation marks and with few capital letters. Insert all punctuation marks. Where a letter should be capitalized, cross out that letter and write the capital letter above it.

 # *Muzik Makers Inc*

8201 Bay Heights Drive, Miami, FL 33133

February 14, 20--

Randall and Peck Inc
35 Draper Avenue
Elgin IL 60120

Ladies and Gentlemen

the following is a well known fact as boredom goes up productivity goes down the enclosed booklet let muzik work for you will show you how to create a more pleasurable working environment that will reduce employee fatigue and boredom and as a result help increase employee productivity

whether your business operates in a small office or a huge plant Muzik Makers Inc can supply you with the prerecorded music that is right for you this music specifically selected for your particular needs can calm employee nerves reduce fatigue due to work strain and lessen work monotony as a result your employees attitudes toward their jobs will improve they will be absent and tardy less often when they arent bored they make fewer and less costly errors

---

as you will learn from the booklet the kind of work your employees perform will determine the type of music classical numbers semiclassical numbers showtunes or popular tunes that should be played you will also learn why whatever music you select should not be played continuously as you will see we recommend an on for 15 minutes off for 15 minutes cycle to give your employees the greatest psychological lift you will also learn why we recommend music be played especially at high fatigue periods namely midmorning midafternoon and immediately before lunch and quitting time

heres what one satisfied subscriber to Muzik had to say

morale at our plant in Tucson was very low before we subscribed to your service productivity was down absenteeism was up employee turnover was very high im happy to report that after using your service for three months we have seen the situation improve dramatically the change in employee attitudes has been remarkable employee absenteeism tardiness and turnover have fallen the quality of work has improved productivity has increased overall business volume and profits have grown we owe it all to your service as far as im concerned no business should be without Muzik its fantastic

why not take the advice of this successful business-person and the thousands who say the same bring Muzik into your office and let Muzik work for you you wont be sorry you did

Sincerely,

Maris Pobuda
Client Representative

PRACTICE 7

Composition: Writing A Claim Letter

Instructions: No business wants to make mistakes, but at some time every business does. When this happens, the customer writes a claim letter seeking an adjustment to correct an error in shipment or an improper billing or to request replacement of goods received in a damaged condition.

Assume that you have been a regular subscriber to *Today's World* magazine for six years. Last year you renewed your subscription for three more years. You still have your canceled check as proof. Recently, however, you have received a series of messages urging you to renew your subscription promptly before it expires. Write to the subscription department asking them to correct this error. The address is *Today's World*, Subscription Department, 721 45th Street, Omaha, Nebraska 68104. Write a draft of your letter in the space below; then prepare your final copy on another sheet of paper.

_____

_____

_____

_____

_____

_____

_____

_____

_____

_____

_____

_____

_____

_____

_____

_____

_____

Elements of Style

CHAPTER 20 PREVIEW

In this chapter you will learn how to capitalize letters, divide words, and express numbers. You will study stylistic conventions that help clarify and organize written information. Writing that does not follow these conventions appears confusing and disorganized to readers. You will continue to assess your comprehension in the Programmed Reinforcement sections and the Practices. Finally, you will sharpen your knowledge of capitalization, word division, and the expression of numbers at a biography Website.

OBJECTIVES

After completing this chapter, you will be able to

- Determine how and when to capitalize the following correctly:
  - The first word of a sentence, a sentence substitute, or a direct quotation
  - The pronoun *I* and the interjection *Oh*
  - The parts of a letter, titles of literature and art, celestial bodies, dollar amounts, and nouns with numbers or letters
  - Letters and abbreviations
  - References to religions, dates, days, historic periods, locations, cultures, family and official titles, organizations, and commercial products
- Divide words, word groups, dates, addresses, and names.
- Determine when to write numbers as figures or as words.

Study Plan for Chapter 20

The Study Plan for Chapter 20 offers a set of strategies that will help you learn and review the chapter material.

❶ **Capitalizing Proper Nouns**: Don't let the many guidelines for capitalizing proper nouns overwhelm you. Just remember the general rule: always capitalize *specific* names of people, places, and things.

❷ **In the Right Direction**: In the sentence *We live in the Southwest,* the word *southwest* isn't a compass direction; it names a region of the country and is capitalized.

❸ **Word Division—Syllables and Sense**: The word *excellent* can be divided between the double consonants: *excel-lent.* The word *smallest,* however, is divided into two syllables between the root and the suffix: *small-est.* Use common sense to divide a compound word: *letter-head,* not *let-terhead,* which would be difficult to read.

❹ **Practice Makes Perfect**: Don't try to memorize all the rules in this chapter. The best method for learning the material is *practice.*

SECTION A
Capitalization Guidelines

In this section you will study the guidelines that effective writers follow for capitalizing letters. You are already familiar with some of the guidelines presented in this section. Focus on those with which you are less familiar.

20.1 Capitalization in Sentences

Capitalize the first word of every sentence. Capitalize a single word or the first word of a phrase used as a sentence substitute.

Yes.   Next.   Not on your life.

Direct Quotations

Capitalize the first word of a direct quotation that is a complete sentence.

Reed said, "This project must be completed by Friday."
"This project," Reed said, "must be completed by Friday."

However, when quoting an expression that is not a complete sentence, do not capitalize the first word.

Reed said that this project "must be completed by Friday."

Sentences Following a Colon

Capitalize the first word after a colon when it introduces a formal statement, a series of complete and related sentences, or a vertical listing.

He made the following declaration: "This project must be completed by Friday."
She suggested three additional reasons for the declining sales figures: First, remodeling has created inadequate parking. Second, a truckers' strike has resulted in shipping delays. Third, competitors have introduced innovative promotional schemes.

She suggested three additional reasons for the declining sales figures:
1. Remodeling has created inadequate parking.
2. A truckers' strike has resulted in shipping delays.
3. Competitors have introduced innovative promotional schemes.

The Pronoun *I* and the Interjection *Oh*

Capitalize the pronoun *I* and the interjection *Oh* (or *O*). Unless you are writing advertising copy, you will rarely use *Oh* in workplace writing.

> I'm due for a vacation, and Oh, can I use it.

Capitalization of Words in Word Groups

The first letter of some words in groups should always be capitalized.

Letters and E-mail Messages

Capitalize the first word in the salutation of a letter or e-mail message plus all nouns and titles in the salutation.

> Dear Ms. Kiyosaki: Dear Professor Turner:
> Ladies and Gentlemen: My dear Eden,

Capitalize the first word in the complimentary close of a letter or e-mail message plus all nouns and titles in the writer's identification line.

> Cordially,   Sincerely yours,   Very truly yours,
>
> *Corinth Ray*   *Carlotta Monterey*   *LeRoy A. Goodhew*
>   Carlotta Monterey   LeRoy A. Goodhew
>   Director of Admissions   Aid to the President

Appropriate Salutation

"My dear" is appropriate for personal correspondence, but it is not used in professional correspondence.

Literary and Artistic Works

Capitalize the first letter of each important word in the title of a work of literature or art. Do not capitalize articles (*a, an, the*) or short conjunctions and short prepositions (fewer than four letters) in the middle of the title. However, if the last word of a title is a short word, capitalize it.

> Malcolm X's "Separation or Integration" was his greatest speech.
> Have you ever seen the painting "The Blue Boy"?
> My latest book, *Delegating Power Throughout a Company*, is on sale now.
> Karl's presentation was titled "A Job to Be Proud Of."

Celestial Bodies

Capitalize the names of planets, stars, and constellations.

> What is the difference in size among Earth, Mercury, and Pluto?
> The Upper Atmosphere Research Satellite (UARS) sent back excellent
>   pictures of Venus and Orion.

Do not capitalize the words *earth*, *sun*, or *moon* unless they are used in connection with the capitalized names of other stars and planets.

> Noah promised Jamal the sun and the moon if he would trade shifts with him.
> Environmentalists are concerned about the earth's diminishing natural resources.
> How far is the moon from the sun?
> The Upper Atmosphere Research Satellite (UARS) sent back excellent pictures of the Sun, Earth, Venus, and Orion.

Dollar Amounts in Formal and Legal Documents

Capitalize each dollar amount spelled out in a formal or legal document:

> The Company agrees to pay the Contributor the amount of Eighty-seven Dollars and Twenty-four Cents ($87.24).

Nouns With Numbers or Letters

Capitalize the abbreviation for number (*No.*, plural *Nos.*) when it precedes a figure.

> Please submit payment for the following invoices: Nos. 26, 29, and 38.

If an identifying noun precedes the figures, capitalize it and omit the abbreviation *No.*

Article 2	Column 1	Model D34928
Chart 3	Diagram 8	Policy 752974
Check 409	Invoice 7426	Section 6

Exceptions: License No. 410 DAS, Patent No. 746,324, Social Security No. 148-85-1234

Letters and Abbreviations

Capitalize the following letters and abbreviations:

- College degrees (B.A., M.A., Ph.D.)
- Radio and television stations (WNCN, WNET)
- Initials standing for proper names (W. E. B. Du Bois, A.S. Byatt)
- Abbreviations for proper names (D.C., NBA, NAACP)
- Two-letter state abbreviations such as IL (Illinois) and VT (Vermont).

Do not capitalize the following abbreviations:

- *a.m.* and *p.m.*: 9 a.m., 4 p.m.
- *p.* or *pp.* to indicate page numbers: p. 35; pp. 9, 19, 25; pp. 35–38

Amounts of Checks

When writing a check, capitalize only the first letter of the first word of the number that is being spelled out.

20.3 Capitalization of Proper Nouns

Capitalize all proper nouns and their derivatives. A proper noun refers to a specific person, place, or thing.

Nelson Mandela   Peru   Toyota

Also capitalize the derivatives of proper nouns.

Mongolian border   Shakespearean drama   Victorian England

Capitalize descriptive names that are substituted for real proper nouns.

the Steel Magnolia (Rosalyn Carter)   the Windy City (Chicago)
the Little Corporal (Napoleon Bonaparte)   the Big Easy (New Orleans)
the Big Board (New York Stock Exchange)   the Sunshine State (Florida)

LOOKING AHEAD

State Abbreviations
A complete list of these abbreviations is included in Appendix E: Common Abbreviations

20.4 Capitalization of Religious References

Capitalize all nouns and pronouns that refer to deities and sacred works as well as the names of religions, their members, and their buildings.

Allah	Torah	Book of Job	Methodists
Buddha	Koran	Bible	the Trinity
God, the Father	Talmud	Zen Buddhists	Temple Ramat Zion

During the eighth century, Emperor Shomu of Japan, a devout Buddhist, built Todaiji as a symbol of unity and place of worship.

20.5 Capitalization of Dates, Days, and Historic References

Always capitalize the names of months of the year, days of the week, holidays, and religious days.

Ramadan   Yom Kippur   Good Friday   Diwali

Classes begin on the last Monday in August, nearly one week before Labor Day.

Seasons Vary. Do not capitalize the names of seasons unless the season is being personified (i.e., referred to as though it were a living being).

Our fall order was not delivered until winter.
Old Man Winter won't stop our snow tires from giving you perfect traction.

Historic References

Capitalize the names of historic events, periods, and documents, in addition to well-known political policies.

the Cultural Revolution	the Declaration of Independence
the Renaissance	the Great Society
the Dark Ages	the Camp David Accord

Do not capitalize the names of decades and centuries unless they appear in special expressions.

the sixties   the Roaring Twenties   the twenty-first century

20.6   Capitalization of the Names of Places and Cultures

This section presents a number of guidelines that will help you determine when it is necessary to capitalize references to places and cultures around the world. When learning these guidelines, it is important to recognize the difference between general locations and specific locations, common nouns and proper nouns.

Directions

When the words *north, south, east,* and *west* and their derivatives refer to a specific region or location, they are proper nouns and should be capitalized.

The West has frequently been called on to aid developing nations.
The Southwest is growing rapidly in population and industry.
The Mississippi flows through the North and the South.

These words are also capitalized when they are part of proper names.

the North Pole   the East Side   the West Bank   the South Bronx

Do not capitalize *north, south, east,* and *west* when they indicate general location or direction.

The plane circled twice, then headed west.
Albuquerque is southwest of Santa Fe.
The Mississippi flows from north to south.

Capitalize *northern, southern, eastern,* and *western* when they refer to a particular region's people and their activities or when they are an accepted part of a place name.

Southern hospitality	Northern Ireland	Southeast Asia
Northern industrial base	Eastern European community	Western civilization

Permahold

Permahold describes the act—or tactic—of putting telephone callers on hold for an extended (or permanent) amount of time in the hope that they will eventually hang up.

Do not capitalize these words when they refer to general location or the climate or geography of a region.

southwesterly winds   western Texas   northern winters

Capitalize names derived from a particular geographic locality.

Southerner   Northerner   Midwesterner   Easterner

Geographic Terms

Capitalize geographic terms such as *river, ocean, mountain,* and *valley* when they are part of the name of a particular geographic designation. Plural forms used this way are also capitalized.

Hudson River   Pacific Ocean   Missouri and Mississippi
                                             Rivers
Death Valley   Bear Mountain   Appalachian and Rocky
                                             Mountains

However, do not capitalize these terms when they are used in place of their full names.

We're going to Atlantic City to swim in the ocean.
Davenport, Iowa, is across the river from Rock Island, Illinois.

Do not capitalize a geographic term such as *river* when it is placed *before* the name of the river.

The river Jordan   The valley of the river Nile

An exception is the word *mount:*

Mount Everest   Mount Rainier   Mount Mitchell

Political Designations

Political designations such as *state, city,* and *county* are always capitalized when they are a part of the specific name of the area.

Oklahoma City   New York State   Orange County

Capitalize *state* only when it follows the name of a state.

The state of Nevada is famed for its scenic beauty.
In 1889 Washington State became the forty-second state to enter
    the Union.

Buildings

Similar rules govern the capitalization of words such as *hotel, building, highway,* and *tunnel.* In general, capitalize such words when you are using them as part of a specific name. Do not capitalize them when using them in place of the full name.

Biltmore Hotel	Empire State Building	Channel Tunnel
Ventura Highway	Pan Am and Chrysler Buildings	Seikan Submarine Tunnel

A train from London will take you through the tunnel to Calais, where you can take a taxi to the Hotel Opera in Paris.
I will have a larger office when we move to the new building.

Cultures, Languages, and Races

Capitalize a word that refers to particular culture, language, or race.

Caucasian	Hispanic	Cheyenne
Vietnamese	Hebrew	Latino
African American	Italian	Hindi

20.7 Capitalization of Family and Official Titles

Here you will examine specific guidelines for determining when to capitalize the titles of family members, government officials, persons in religious office, and company officials.

Family Titles

Capitalize family titles such as *mother, father,* and *aunt* when they precede a person's name or when they are used in place of a person's name.

Aunt Martha
When is Mother coming?
We sent Grandfather a card.

Do not capitalize family titles when they are preceded by a possessive pronoun (*my, your, his, her, our,* and *their*) and they simply describe a family relationship. However, if the words *uncle, aunt,* or *cousin* form a unit when used together with a person's name, capitalize these titles even when a possessive pronoun precedes them.

My father is visiting us this weekend.
Do you think your brother Fowzi would like to meet my sister Clara?
When will we see your Uncle John?

Government, Religious, and Other Official Titles

Capitalize titles of high-ranking government officials and people in religious office when the titles come before, follow, or replace a name.

Senator Huey P. Long from Louisiana was assassinated in 1935.
Huey P. Long, Senator from Louisiana, was assassinated in 1935.
The Senator from Louisiana was assassinated in 1935.
The Secretary of State met with the Chinese Premier.
The Pope visited the United States several years ago.
Similar views were expressed by Archbishop Cardinal Cody.
The featured speaker was Olympia Snowe, Senator from Maine.
While in London, we saw the Prime Minister.
The Vice President succeeds to the Presidency in the event of the death or
   resignation of the President.

Capitalize titles of other government officials and company officials when they precede the name. Do not capitalize them when they follow a name, replace a name, or are used in apposition to a name.

Tonight's featured speaker is Mayor Susan Taylor.
The mayor is our featured speaker this evening.
Have you met Vice President McGee?
Jane McGee, vice president of Allied Sales, met with us.
We conferred with District Manager Alfredo Avilla regarding the proposal.
The vice president is currently meeting with the district manager.
The president of Allied Sales also serves as chairman of the board.

20.8 Capitalization of the Names of Organizations and Products

In this section you will learn how to capitalize the names of such organizations as businesses, government agencies, and political parties. You will also discover how to deal with trademarks and brand names.

Organizations

Capitalize words such as *company, association, commission, union,* and *foundation* when they are part of the name of a specific organization.

American Steel Company
National Association of Manufacturers
the Union of Concerned Scientists
the Andrew W. Mellon Foundation
Interstate Commerce Commission

Appositives
*Turn back to Section 17.4,
page 482, to review appositives.*

■

Organizational words are typically not capitalized when they are terms of general classification or when they refer to another organization.

> the credit division (general classification)
> their sales department
> The advertising department of Black & London will unveil its fall campaign.

Government Agencies and Political Parties

Capitalize the names of specific government agencies.

United States Senate	Air Force	Board of Elections
Court of Appeals	Police Department	Council of Foreign Ministers

Capitalize the names of political parties.

Democratic Party	Republican Party	Socialist Workers Party

Trademarks and Brand Names

Capitalize trademarks and brand names, but do not capitalize the common noun that follows the name of a product.

StairMaster	Kleenex tissues	Teflon
Diet Pepsi	Post-it notes	Xerox
Ivory soap	Q-Tips	Tender Leaf tea

Former Trademarks

Do not capitalize former trademarks that are now used as common nouns.

aspirin	dry ice	mimeograph	shredded wheat
cellophane	escalator	nylon	thermos bottle

References to Schools

Capitalize the names of schools and their abbreviations and nicknames. Do not capitalize two- or three-letter prepositions that are part of school names.

Anatola Street Elementary School	College of the Sequoias
Wachter Middle School	University of North Carolina at Charlotte (UNCC)
A. L. Brown High School	Florida Agricultural and Mechanical University (FAMU)
Public School 144	Santa Monica High School (Samohi)
Delaware Valley Friends School	University of Mississippi (Ole Miss)

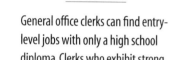

Promotions

General office clerks can find entry-level jobs with only a high school diploma. Clerks who exhibit strong communication, analytical, and interpersonal skills can find themselves promoted to supervisors. Advancement into professional occupations within a firm normally requires a college education, however.

Words that designate the type of school are capitalized only when they are part of the official name of an institution. Such words include the following:

elementary school	middle school	high school
college	university	community college
business school	public school	kindergarten
online school	private college	trade school

WRONG: Martin could not decide between attending Trade School or taking classes at the local Community College

RIGHT: ✔ Martin could not decide between Delmar Computer Institute and Pearl River Community College.

Capitalize the words *college* and *school* when they are used in formal communications as replacements for the complete names of institutions.

Most people who teach for the college are members of the union.
The College negotiated a settlement with the Union.
(formal announcement)

Verifying Names

Confirm the correct capitalization of individual trademarks by visiting the *International Trademark Association* Website.

20.9 Capitalization of the Names of Academic Courses

Capitalize the main words in the names of specific course titles.

There were only fifteen students enrolled in Introduction to Keyboarding.
The Art of Video class promises to be very challenging.
Divina spent the day studying for her final in French History 101.

Do not capitalize the names of subjects or areas of study unless they contain proper nouns or adjectives.

I will take a business management course at the local junior college.
The professor's area of expertise is the geopolitics of Latin America.
Several students in the dormitory are studying French history.

Coverage Key

Section		Statement
20.1	➤ Capitalization in Sentences	➤ **S1**
20.2	➤ Capitalization of Words in Word Groups	➤ **S2, S3, S4, S5, S6**
20.3	➤ Capitalization of Proper Nouns	➤ **S7, S29**
20.4	➤ Capitalization of Religious References	➤ **S8**
20.5	➤ Capitalization of Dates, Days, and Historic References	➤ **S9, S10, S11, S12**
20.6	➤ Capitalization of the Names of Places and Cultures	➤ **S13, S14, S15, S16, S17, S18, S19, S20, S25, S29**
20.7	➤ Capitalization of Family and Official Titles	➤ **S21, S22, S23, S24, S25, S29**
20.8	➤ Capitalization of the Names of Organizations and Products	➤ **S26, S29**
20.9	➤ Capitalization of the Names of Schools and Academic Courses	➤ **S28**

Instructions: Cover the answers in the **Answer** column; then write your answers to the first statement. Uncover the first printed answer and compare your answer to it. If you wrote a correct answer, continue the activity. If you made an error, use the **Coverage Key** to locate the chapter section you need to review. When you are confident that you understand the material, continue with the reinforcement activity.

ANSWER

STATEMENT

S1   In which of the following should the first word *not* be capitalized? (a) a sentence; (b) a phrase used as a sentence substitute; (c) a direct quotation that is a complete sentence; (d) a direct quotation that is not a complete sentence.

A1   d.

S2   Which of the following should be capitalized in a salutation? (a) the first word; (b) all nouns; (c) all titles; (d) all words.

A2   a., b., c.

S3   Capitalize the following salutations correctly:
a.   dear mom,
b.   dear mr. chung:
c.   ladies and gentlemen:
d.   ms. olga stavros, project director

A3   a.   Dear Mom,
b.   Dear Mr. Chung:
c.   Ladies and Gentlemen:
d.   Ms. Olga Stavros, Project Director

S4 In the complimentary close of a letter, which words are capitalized? (a) none; (b) only the first; (c) all. Capitalize the following complimentary closes correctly:

sincerely

yours truly

very truly yours

A4 b.

Sincerely, Yours truly,

Very truly yours,

S5 The names of planets, stars, and constellations (are, are not) capitalized. The words *earth, moon,* and *sun* (are, are not) capitalized unless they are used in connection with the names of other stars and planets. Place capital letters where appropriate:

a. **Stella may have her head in the stars, but her feet are firmly planted on the earth.**

b. **Which planet is closer to earth, venus or mars?**

A5 are, are not

a. no capitals needed

b. **Earth, Venus, Mars**

S6 College degrees, radio stations, and initials standing for proper names and nouns, as well as important words in the titles of works of art and literature, (are, are not) capitalized. The abbreviations *a.m.* and *p.m.* (are, are not). Capitalize the following correctly:

concetta warner, ph.d., will discuss her recent book, *how to ensure your future success,* this evening at 9 p.m. on radio station wvkc.

A6 are, are not,

Concetta Warner, Ph.D., will discuss her recent book, *How to Ensure Your Future Success,* this evening at 9 p.m. on radio station WVKC.

S7 Proper nouns refer to a (general, specific) person, place, or thing. Proper nouns (should, should not) be capitalized. The derivatives of proper nouns (should, should not) be capitalized.

A7 specific, should, should

S8 Which of the following religious references are capitalized?

a. nouns and pronouns that refer to God

b. names of sacred works

c. names of religions

d. members of religions

e. religious holidays

f. all of the above

g. none of the above

A8 f.

S9 Which of the following are generally capitalized?

a. days of the week

b. months of the year

c. seasons of the year

A9 a., b.

S10 Capitalize the following sentence correctly: **This spring, classes will resume in april on the tuesday after easter.**

A10 This spring, classes will resume in April on the Tuesday after Easter.

S11 Which of the following should be capitalized?

a. historic events

b. historic periods

c. historic documents

d. well-known political policies

e. decades and centuries

f. all of the above

g. none of the above

A11 a., b., c., d.

S12 Capitalize the following correctly:

   a. **the boston tea party**   d. **the nineteenth century**

   b. **the middle ages**   e. **the great depression**

   c. **the bill of rights**   f. **the fifties**

A12 a. **the Boston Tea Party**
      b. **the Middle Ages**
      c. **the Bill of Rights**
      d. no capitals needed
      e. **the Great Depression**
      f. no capitals needed.

S13 Which of the following is correct?

   a. All directions are capitalized.

   b. No directions are capitalized.

   c. Directions are capitalized when they refer to a specific region or location but not when they indicate general location.

A13 c.

S14 Underline the direction(s) you would capitalize in this sentence: **The plant was located in the south about three miles east of Atlanta.**

A14 South

S15 The words *northern, southern, eastern,* and *western* (are, are not) capitalized when they refer to the people of a particular region and their activities or are part of a place name. They (are, are not) capitalized when they refer to general location or the climate or geography of a region. Capitalize the following correctly:

   a. **northern hemisphere**   d. **western Montana**

   b. **southern sections of Oregon**   e. **northern exposure**

   c. **northern Ireland**

A15 are, are not
      a. **Northern Hemisphere**
      b. no capital needed
      c. **Northern Ireland**
      d. no capital needed
      e. no capital needed

S16 A name derived from a particular geographic locality (is, is not) capitalized. Which words should be capitalized in these sentences?

   a. **She is a southerner, but I am a northerner.**

   b. **Although I was born in the midwest, I consider myself a new englander.**

A16 is
      a. **Southerner, Northerner**
      b. **Midwest, New Englander**

S17 Geographic terms such as *river, ocean, mountain,* and *valley* (are, are not) capitalized when they are used as part of a name. They (are, are not) capitalized when they precede the name. The word *mount* is an exception; it (is, is not) capitalized even when it precedes the name of the mountain. Which words should be capitalized in these sentences?

   a. **the islands of the pacific and the valleys of the appalachians date back millions of years.**

   b. **The hudson river, which empties into the atlantic ocean, separates New York from New Jersey.**

   c. **The view of the pacific ocean from mount fuji is magnificent.**

A17 are, are not, is
      a. **Pacific, Appalachians**
      b. **Hudson River, Atlantic Ocean**
      c. **Pacific Ocean, Mount Fuji**

S18 Political designations such as *state, city,* and *county* (are, are not) capitalized when they are part of the actual name of the area. Which of the following are correct?
  a. New York City is the largest city in America.
  b. Washington State borders on Canada.
  c. Dade county is in Florida.

A18 are, a. and b.

S19 Words like *hotel, highway,* and *tunnel* are capitalized when they are part of the proper name. Which additional words should be capitalized in this sentence? **The Plaza hotel can be reached by the Lincoln tunnel or the George Washington bridge.**

A19 Hotel, Tunnel, Bridge

S20 A word that refers to a particular culture, language, or race is (always, sometimes, never) capitalized.

A20 always

S21 Titles that show family relationship are capitalized:
  a. when the word precedes the person's name.
  b. when the word is used in place of the person's name.
  c. when the word is preceded by a possessive pronoun and it simply describes a family relationship.

A21 a., b.

S22 Which words should be capitalized in these sentences?
  a. **Did grandfather tell you how he lost his savings in the great depression?**
  b. **My mother is practicing her japanese in preparation for her asian trip.**
  c. **I understand that uncle eddie is an authority on the policies of the new deal.**

A22 a. **Grandfather, the Great Depression**
  b. **Japanese, Asian**
  c. **Uncle Eddie, the New Deal**

S23 Titles of high-ranking government officials are capitalized:
  a. when they precede the person's name.
  b. when they follow the person's name.
  c. when they are used in place of the person's name.
  d. all of the above
  e. none of the above

A23 d.

S24 Titles of other government officials and company officials are capitalized:
  a. when they precede the person's name.
  b. when they follow the person's name.
  c. when they take the place of the person's name.
  d. when they are used in apposition to the person's name.
  e. all of the above

A24 a.

S25 Which words should be capitalized in the following sentences?
a. The president and the secretary of state greeted the chinese premier at the white house.
b. The corporate vice president met privately with the treasurer.
c. Wendell Tyler, our chairman of the board, is the older brother of senator Ralph Tyler.

A25 a. The President and the Secretary of State greeted the Chinese Premier at the White House.
b. no capitals needed
c. Wendell Tyler, our chairman of the board, is the older brother of Senator Ralph Tyler.

S26 Names of organizations such as *company, association,* and *department* (are, are not) capitalized when they are part of the name of a specific organization. They usually (are, are not) capitalized when used as substitutes for the complete names of specific organizations. Which words should be capitalized in these sentences?
a. We want to welcome you as a new member of the association.
b. An association of publishers may be formed.
c. June Spencer, president of the business education association, spoke at the meeting.

A26 are, are not
a. no capitals needed
b. no capitals needed
c. Business Education Association

S27 School subjects (are, are not) capitalized, except for languages or specifically described courses. Underline the subjects incorrectly capitalized in this sentence: She studied Mathematics, English, Advanced Algebra II, and Computer Literacy in school.

A27 are not, <u>mathematics</u>, <u>computer</u> <u>literacy</u>

S28 The words *high school* and *college* (are, are not) capitalized unless they are part of a specific school name. Which words should be capitalized in this sentence? After graduating from Jefferson high school, he decided to work rather than go on to college.

A28 are not, High School

S29 As a review, underline the words you would capitalize in these sentences:
a. My employer, karl schmitz, started the olympic printing company in the summer of 1964 in the southern part of new england.
b. After moving the plant from the mohawk valley to obtain hudson river power, he was elected president of the printers association of america.
c. Ms. desai then taught a course in english at newark college of engineering for students with high school diplomas.

A29 a. <u>Karl Schmitz</u>, <u>Olympic Printing Company</u>, <u>New England</u>
b. <u>Mohawk Valley</u>, <u>Hudson River</u>, <u>Printers Association of America</u>
c. <u>Desai</u>, <u>English</u>, <u>Newark College of Engineering</u>

SECTION B
Word-Division Guidelines

Word processors may appear to have eliminated the need to know the rules for dividing words; however, appearances can be deceiving. When a word will not fit completely on a line, the word-wrap feature will automatically move it to the next line. This often leaves a large gap in the right margin. Automatic hyphenation options can be used, but these may divide a word differently from the generally accepted word-division rules. This section will teach you how to divide words yourself so you can double-check word divisions made by word processors.

20.10 Division of Single Words

When a word cannot fit at the end of a line, it is divided by a hyphen.

> He was surprised to discover how diffi-
> cult it was to find replacement parts.

Word divisions are not attractive and may confuse a reader. Therefore, divide words only when necessary to maintain a reasonably even right margin. When you do divide a word, place the hyphen at the end of the first line, not at the beginning of the second.

DO's and DON'Ts of Word Division

Observe the following rules about word division.

DO:

1. Divide words only between syllables. Consult your dictionary to see how words are properly divided (syllabicated).

   syl-lab-i-cate   pro-por-tion   pref-er-ence

2. Divide a word after a prefix rather than within a prefix.

   intro-duce (not in-troduce)   inter-face (not in-terface)
   circum-stance (not cir-cumstance)

3. Divide a word before a suffix rather than within a suffix.

   comprehen-sible (not comprehensi-ble)
   depend-able (not dependa-ble)
   communi-cable (not communica-ble)

4. Divide a word after a prefix or before a suffix rather than within the root word.

over-extend (not overex-tend)   arrange-ment (not ar-rangement)

5. Divide a word that has a single vowel as a middle syllable so that the vowel comes at the end of the first line, not at the beginning of the second.

hesi-tate (not hes-itate)   accompani-ment (not accompan-iment)

6. Divide a word between two separately sounded vowels.

reli-able (not relia-ble)   continu-ous (not contin-uous)
influ-ential (not influen-tial)   courte-ous (not court-eous)

7. Divide words between double consonants unless the root word ends with these double consonants.

excel-lent   neces-sary   small-est   install-ment
run-ning   recom-mend   bill-ing

8. Divide hyphenated words at the point of the hyphen and compound words between the parts of the compound.

sister- / in-law   above- / mentioned   self- / control
card / board   sales / clerk   letter / head

DON'T:

1. Do not divide a word of one syllable. The following words, for example, may not be divided.

walked   thought   punched   through

2. Do not divide a word of five or fewer letters. The following words, for example, should not be divided.

again   also   elate   ago   allot   begin

3. Do not divide a word so that a syllable of a single letter appears at the beginning. The following divisions, for example, are unacceptable.

a-rouse   a-warded   e-nough   e-lation

4. Do not set off a syllable of two letters at the end of a word.

briefly (not brief-ly)   com-muter (not commut-er)
com-pany (not compa-ny)   prop-erty (not proper-ty)

According to some authorities, including *The Gregg Reference Manual,* if a punctuation mark immediately follows the word, it is permissible to carry over a syllable of two letters to the next line.

short-ly,   clos-et;   reviv-al.

5. Do not divide proper nouns, contractions, numbers, and abbreviations. None of the following items, for example, may be divided.

Benjamin	couldn't	475,934,265	ILGWU
Detroit	should've	$14,467.53	UNESCO

6. Do not divide the last word of more than two consecutive lines.

7. Do not divide the last word on the last full line in a paragraph or the last word on a page.

20.11   Division Within Word Groups

Do not separate certain kinds of word groups that need to be read together. The following word groups, for example, should not be divided.

WORD GROUP	NO DIVISION
title and surname	Ms. O'Rourke
surname and number	(Alfred) Willows III
surname and abbreviation	(Isaac) Bryant, Esq.
page and number	page 137
month and day	May 24
month and year	August 2004
number and abbreviation	7:15 p.m.
number and unit of measure	25 ft
model and number	Model K5A

Longer word groups may be separated in the following situations.

Dates. Dates may be separated between the day and the year, but not between the month and the day.

CORRECT: ✔Your annuity will be renewable on April 10,
               2007.

INCORRECT: Your annuity will be renewable on April
               10, 2010.

Street Addresses. Street addresses may be broken between the name of the street and the street designation. If the street name has more than one word, the address may also be broken between the words in the street name.

CORRECT ✔	INCORRECT
Send this letter to 437 Seaview Avenue.	Send this letter to 437 Seaview Avenue.
Deliver the furniture to 576 57th Street.	Deliver the furniture to 576 57th Street.
Dan lives at 329 South Mountain Boulevard.	Dan lives at 329 South Mountain Boulevard.
Dan lives at 329 South Mountain Boulevard	

Names of Places. Names of places should be separated between the city and the state, or between the state and the ZIP Code. If the city or state name has more than one word, the break may also come between those words.

CORRECT ✔	INCORRECT
The destination is Orange, New Jersey 07050.	The destination is Orange, New Jersey 07050.
The destination is Orange, New Jersey 07050.	
The destination is Orange, New Jersey 07050.	
The destination is Mount Pleasant, UT 84647.	The destination is Mount Pleasant, UT 84647.
The destination is Mount Pleasant, UT 84647.	
The destination is Mount Pleasant, UT 84647.	

Names of People. Names of people may be broken between middle initial and surname. Names preceded by long titles may be separated between the title and the given name.

CORRECT ✔	INCORRECT
We need to speak with Mr. Owen P. Martinez.	We need to speak with Mr. Owen P. Martinez.
There goes Brigadier General Elizabeth Hoisington.	There goes Brigadier General Elizabeth Hoisington.

Names may also be broken between words in the title.

CORRECT ✔
There goes Brigadier
   General Elizabeth Hoisington.
Let's talk to Professor
   Emeritus Muriel Kowalski.
We will miss Lieutenant
   Governor Perez.

Coverage Key

Section	Statement
20.10 ➤ Division of Single Words	➤ **S30, S31, S32, S33, S34, S35, S36, S37, S38, S39, S40, S41, S42, S43**
20.11 ➤ Divisions Within Word Groups	➤ **S44**

Instructions: Cover the answers in the **Answer** column; then write your answer to the first statement. Uncover the first printed answer and compare your answer to it. If you wrote a correct answer, continue the activity. If you made an error, use the **Coverage Key** to locate the chapter section you need to review. When you are confident that you understand the material, continue with the reinforcement activity.

ANSWER	STATEMENT
	S30 When is it appropriate to divide a word? a. whenever it is convenient b. only when absolutely necessary c. never
A30 b.	**S31** A hyphen is used to divide a word at the end of a line. The hyphen is placed (a) at the end of that line, (b) at the beginning of the next line.
A31 a	**S32** Words may be divided (a) only between syllables, (b) anywhere that is convenient.
A32 a	**S33** Words of only one syllable (may, may not) be divided. Words of fewer than six letters (may, may not) be divided.
A33 may not, may not	**S34** Underline the words that should *not* be divided: **through thorough rely reliance ability able straight**
A34 <u>through</u>, <u>rely</u>, <u>able</u>, <u>straight</u>	**S35** You (may, may not) divide a word so that only one letter is left at the end of the first line. You (may, may not) carry over only one or two letters to the next line. You (may, may not) carry a syllable of two letters to the next line if it is followed by a mark of punctuation.
A35 may not, may not, may	**S36** Underline the words in the following list that should *not* be divided: **hardness emerge afraid reserve surely hardly emergent batted chicken**
A36 <u>emerge</u>, <u>afraid</u>, <u>hardly</u>, <u>chicken</u>	

A37 circum / scribe, pre / arrange, sudden / ness, profit / able, over / zealous, mis / fortune

S37 Words should be divided after a prefix and before a suffix rather than within a root word. Place a slash (/) to show where you would divide the following words:

circumscribe	prearrange	suddenness
profitable	overzealous	misfortune

A38 a.,
calo / rie, capi / tal, cata / log, cele / brate, logi / cal

S38 When a middle syllable is composed of a single letter (like the *e* in *plan-e-tary*), that letter should be placed (a) at the end of the first line, (b) at the beginning of the second line. Place a slash (/) to show where you should break these words:

cal-o-rie	cap-i-tal	cat-a-log	cel-e-brate	log-i-cal

A39 between,
compli / ant, undeni / able, evacu / ate, intu / ition

S39 When a word has two separately sounded vowels next to each other, the word is divided (before, between, after) the vowels. Place a slash (/) to show where you would divide these words:

compliant	undeniable	evacuate	intuition

A40 f.

S40 Which items may be divided?
(a) proper nouns, (b) contractions, (c) abbreviations, (d) numbers, (e) all of the above, (f) none of the above

A41 a.

S41 Where may hyphenated words be divided?
a. only where the hyphen occurs
b. anywhere that conforms with the normal rules of word division

A42 b.,
bill / ing, small / est, run / ning, excel / lent, fol / low, in / nate

S42 In most cases words are divided between double letters. If the word is derived from one that ends in double letters, however, the word is divided (a) between the double letters, (b) after the root word. Use a slash (/) to indicate where each of the following words should be divided: **billing smallest running excellent follow innate**

A43 <u>adopt</u>,
adu / late, af / firmer, <u>agent</u>, agree / ment, al / lergy, al / ler / gic, al / le / vi / ate

S43 Use one of more slashes (/) to indicate where to divide the following words. If you should *not* divide a word, underline it.

a-dopt	ad-u-late	af-firm-er
a-gent	a-gree-ment	al-ler-gy
al-ler-gic	al-le-vi-ate	

A44 a. may not be divided
b. may not be divided
c. April 15, / 2003
d. Kathleen J. / Kazmark
e. Louisville, / KY
f. President / Josephine Baker

S44 Various word groups are typically not divided, though some may be divided in special cases. Place a slash (/) to indicate where, if applicable, each of the following items may be divided.

a. page 475
b. April 2003
c. April 15, 2003
d. Kathleen J. Kazmark
e. Louisville, KY
f. President Josephine Baker

Guidelines for Expressing Numbers

Not all authorities agree about the rules for expressing numbers. In general, numbers are expressed as figures rather than as words. This section presents a set of guidelines for expressing numbers that most writers should apply to workplace documents.

20.12 Numbers in Sentences

Numbers are sometimes expressed in figures and sometimes in words. The following guidelines describe how to present numbers when they appear in one or more sentences.

Numbers Below Ten and Above Ten

Numbers from one to ten are spelled out. Numbers above ten are expressed as figures. This guideline applies to both exact and approximate numbers.

> The committee consists of six members and one alternate.
> There are 314 parking spaces in Lot B.
> Nearly 200 people attended the conference.

Indefinite Numbers

Indefinite numbers are expressed in words. Approximate and exact numbers are expressed in figures.

> The brush fire swept through hundreds of acres in the first few hours.
> Barry spent thousands of dollars on health spas and diet plans.
> Barry spent more than $3000 on health spas and diet plans.
> Barry spent $3250 on health spas and diet plans.

Millions and Billions

For ease of reading, round numbers in millions or billions are expressed in a combination of figures and words.

> The proposed legislation would raise an estimated $2 billion.
> More than 6.5 million people voted in the last statewide election.

Numbers in Legal and Formal Documents

Numbers in legal documents and formal invitations and announcements are expressed in words.

> …on Saturday, the twenty-eighth of December, two thousand and three.

Numbers That Begin Sentences

A number that appears at the beginning of a sentence should be spelled out. If the number is long or if a figure is preferable for emphasis or clarity, reword the sentence to avoid awkwardness.

AVOID:	27 employees were promoted recently.
ACCEPTABLE:	✔ Twenty-seven employees were promoted recently.
CLEARER:	✔ Recently, 27 employees were promoted.

AVOID:	337 people attended the banquet.
ACCEPTABLE:	✔ Three hundred thirty-seven people attended the banquet.
CLEARER:	✔ There were 337 people who attended the banquet.

20.13 Multiple Numbers

Sometimes several numbers appear in the same sentence or paragraph. In such cases, to ensure uniformity, observe the following guidelines.

Numbers That Relate

Numbers performing a similar or related function should all be expressed the same way as the largest number is expressed. However, if a sentence begins with a number, it should be expressed as a word.

> Three students were absent from class on Monday, four more were absent on Wednesday, and a total of ten were absent on Friday.
> Only 5 of the 74 people surveyed were opposed to the proposal.
> Five of the 74 people surveyed were opposed to the proposal.

Mixed Numbers

When numbers are performing different or unrelated functions, a mixed style is acceptable. Follow the guidelines presented above.

> The three surveys were given to 73 employees over a period of five months.

Consecutive Numbers

When two numbers appear consecutively and both are expressed as figures, or both as words, separate them with a comma.

> In 2002, 85 percent of our classes were at maximum enrollment.
> Although the maximum occupancy was 198, 235 people were in the room.
> Although the test started at one, five students did not arrive until two.

Numbers as Compound Modifiers

When two numbers appear consecutively and one is part of a compound modifier, express one of the numbers as a figure and the other as a word. As a general rule, spell out the first number unless it would be much shorter to spell out the second.

> There are six 3-bedroom apartments for rent in this building.
> Some of the copier functions do not work, so we collated and stapled 675 four-page copies of the safety report.
> The shipment of five hundred 60-watt bulbs is lost.

20.14 Amounts of Money

Numbers that appear in invoices, purchase orders, billing statements, sales slips, and so forth are always written as figures. Review the guidelines below that explain other numbers written as figures.

Indefinite Amounts

Indefinite amounts of money are expressed in words; exact and approximate amounts are expressed in figures.

> We have spent untold thousands of dollars feeding and clothing our sons.
> Our food bill last month was $723.45.
> Our food bill last month was more than $700.

Whole Dollar Amounts

When expressing whole dollar amounts in a sentence, do not include the decimal point and zeros.

> These CD-ROMs cost only $1 each.
> This appliance has a wholesale price of $67.50 and a retail price of $335.

Numbers in Columns. To maintain a uniform appearance in a column, add a decimal point and two zeros to the whole dollar amounts if other entries contain cents.

$$\begin{array}{r} \$175.50 \\ 12.00 \\ \underline{8.25} \\ \$195.75 \end{array}$$

Cents

When expressing amounts under a dollar, use figures and the word cents.

All I need to repair this lamp is a 79-cent part.
When Paula opened her piggy bank, she found 67 cents and an IOU from her father.

When amounts under a dollar are part of a series with amounts greater than a dollar, use a dollar sign ($) for all amounts.

The baseball cards in these boxes cost $.50 each; the ones in those boxes range from $1.50 to $5.50 each.

Legal Documents

In legal documents both words and figures are used. All words are capitalized and the figures are placed in parentheses.

Seven Hundred Forty Dollars ($740)

20.15 Clock Time

Clock time is always written as figures when *a.m.* or *p.m.* follows. When *o'clock* follows, use figures for emphasis, words for formality.

The meeting began promptly at 9 a.m. and concluded at 12:30 p.m.
Ms. Hitashi worked from 10 o'clock until 3 o'clock. (figures for emphasis)
Ms. Hitashi worked from ten o'clock until three o'clock. (words for formality)

Do not use o'clock with *a.m.* or *p.m.*

WRONG: It's 6 o'clock a.m.
RIGHT: ✔ It's 6 a.m. *or* It's six o'clock in the morning.

When expressing time on the hour, it is not necessary to use a colon and zeros except for purposes of uniformity in time tables.

20.16 Street Addresses

In the writing of street addresses, building numbers (except for the number *One*) are written as figures. Street names of ten and below are written as words; street names above ten are written in figures.

The company's general offices are at One Congress Plaza.
Our branch office moved from 125 Third Street to 47 39th Street.

Figures are used to express numbers in the following situations.

a. **Market quotations**
Our stock closed this week at $23\frac{1}{2}$.

b. **Dimensions**
The opening measures 6 inches by 8 inches.

c. **Temperatures**
At noon the temperature was 7 degrees (or 7°).

d. **Decimals**
These machine parts have a tolerance of .005 inch.

e. **Pages and divisions of a book**
The charts from Chapter 1 appear on p. 6 and on pp. 214–17 of Vol. 3
(or pp. 214-217).

f. **Weights and measures**
These canisters weigh less than 20 pounds, but they will hold
125 gallons of fuel.

g. **Identification numbers**
The newscaster on Channel 5 reported that, because of the accident,
Route 80 was closed at Exit 39.

h. **Tables**

SIZE OF FRESHMAN CLASS, 2005-2008			
Year	Number	Percentage Change	Cumulative Percentage Change
2005	1652		
2006	1567	−5.3	
2007	1480	−5.6	−10.6
2008	1391	−6.0	−16.0

i. **Phone numbers**
You can reach me by phone at (973) 655-4000 for further information.
You can reach me by phone at 973-655-4000 for further information.
You can reach me by phone at 973/655-4000 for further information.

j. **Dates**
The contract was signed on August 16, 2001.
The contract was signed on 16 August 2001.
The contract was signed in August 2001.

k. **Percentages**
The annual percentage rate on this bank credit card is 21.9 percent.

Coverage Key

Section		Statement
20.12 ➤	Numbers in Sentences	➤ **S45, S46, S47, S48, S49**
20.13 ➤	Multiple Numbers	➤ **S50, S51, S52, S53, S54**
20.14 ➤	Amounts of Money	➤ **S53, S55**
20.15 ➤	Clock Time	➤ **S56**
20.16 ➤	Street Addresses	➤ **S57**
20.17 ➤	Other Situations	➤ **S58**

Instructions: Cover the answers in the **Answer** column; then write your answer to the first statement. Uncover the first printed answer and compare your answer to it. If you wrote a correct answer, continue the activity. If you made an error, use the **Coverage Key** to locate the chapter section you need to review. When you are confident that you understand the material, continue with the reinforcement activity.

ANSWER	STATEMENT

S45 In workplace writing, numbers are usually expressed in figures; within sentences, however, numbers may be expressed in words. As a rule in sentences, indefinite numbers are expressed in (words, figures). Exact and approximate numbers are expressed in (words, figures).

A45 words, figures

S46 In general, numbers from one to ten are expressed in _____;
numbers above ten are expressed in _____.

A46 words, figures

S47 Are the numbers in the following sentences expressed correctly? Write *yes* or *no* after each sentence.
a. **There are 346 full-time employees on our payroll.** _____
b. **We employ about 200 part-time employees.** _____
c. **I must complete 3 more reports before the end of the month.** _____
d. **I processed 17 requests for reimbursement today.** _____
e. **Thousands of fans were waiting at the airport.** _____

A47 a. Yes
b. Yes
c. No
d. Yes
e. Yes

S48 For ease of reading, round numbers in millions and billions are expressed (a) completely in words; (b) completely in figures; (c) in a combination of figures and words. Revise the following sentence to make it easier to read. **Total profits for the three-year period rose from $137,000,000 to four hundred seventeen million dollars.**

A48 c,
Total profits for the three-year period rose from $137 million to $417 million.

S49 Numbers that appear at the beginning of a sentence should be expressed in (words, figures). Awkward sentences should be rewritten. Revise the following sentences.
   a. **12 people in our division are ill with the flu.**
   b. **One thousand four hundred and eighteen students were admitted to this year's freshman class.**

A49 words
   a. **Twelve people in our division are ill with the flu.**
   b. **There were 1,418 students admitted to this year's freshman class.**

S50 When several numbers appear in the same sentence or paragraph, those performing a similar function (should be, should not be) expressed in the same way. Numbers performing unrelated functions (may, may not) be expressed differently.

A50 should be, may

S51 Revise the following sentences where necessary.
   a. **Copies of the 4 reports were distributed to all 85 employees in less than 2 days.**
   b. **Only 3 of the 61 people in our division were not recommended for a full salary increment.**

A51 a. **Copies of the four reports were distributed to all 85 employees in less than two days.**
   b. correct as written

S52 When two numbers appear consecutively and both are expressed the same way, they (are, are not) separated with a comma. Place a comma where needed in the following sentences:
   a. **On May 18 15 students took the final exams.**
   b. **On May 18 three students were absent from the final exam.**

A52 are,
   a. **On May 18, 15 …**
   b. no comma needed

S53 Indefinite amounts of money are expressed in (words, figures); exact and approximate amounts of money are expressed in (words, figures).

A53 words, figures

S54 When two numbers appear consecutively and one is part of a compound modifier,
   a. express both numbers as figures.
   b. express one number as a figure and the other as a word.
   c. spell out the first number unless it would be much shorter to spell out the second.

A54 b, c

S55 Revise the following sentences where necessary.
   a. **I have exactly $93.46 in my checking account.**
   b. **I have less than one hundred dollars in my checking account.**
   c. **He spends hundreds of dollars on CDs.**

A55 a. correct as written
   b. **I have less than $100 in my checking account.**
   c. correct as written

S56 An expression of time is written in (words, figures) when *a.m.* or *p.m.* follows. When *o'clock* follows it is written in (words, figures) for emphasis or (words, figures) for formality. Which of the following is/are correct?

   a. **I will finish this report before 5 o'clock.**
   b. **I will finish this report before five o'clock.**
   c. **It's ten p.m. Do you know where your children are?**
   d. **It's 10 p.m. Do you know where your children are?**

A56 figures; figures; words; a., b., d.

S57 Write *words* or *figures* to show how to express the following in street addresses.

   a. building numbers _____
   b. street names of ten and below _____
   c. street names above ten _____

A57 a. figures
   b. words
   c. figures

S58 Words are used to express numbers in which of the following situations?

   a. page numbers
   b. dimensions
   c. temperatures
   d. decimals
   e. phone numbers
   f. dates
   g. percentages
   h. all of the above
   i. none of the above

A58 i.

CHAPTER 20 SUMMARY

In this chapter you learned when to capitalize words in a variety of situations, including sentences and direct quotations. You also learned the guidelines for capitalizing proper nouns, such as historical and geographical references, family and official titles, and the names of organizations. You learned how and when to use a hyphen to divide words, and you learned when words and word groups may not be divided at the end of a line. In addition, you studied specific guidelines for expressing numbers as figures and as words.

Getting Connected

LEARNING ABOUT FAMOUS PEOPLE THROUGH ONLINE BIOGRAPHIES

GOAL: A biography Website offers ready information about the lives of famous people. If you're curious about athletes, politicians, or movie stars, you can visit various biography sites that describe where they were born and raised, how their successful careers started, and what they have accomplished. In this activity you'll use biographical information about a famous person to practice what you've learned about capitalization, word division, and the expression of numbers.

STEP 1 Go to *englishworkshop.glencoe.com,* the address for *The English Workshop* Website, and click on Unit 8. Next click on Getting Connected, and then click on Chapter 20. At the Chapter 20 Getting Connected option, you'll see a list of biography Websites. In addition to general biography sites, these may include specialized sites that focus on a single group of professionals, such as astronauts or famous women.

STEP 2 To begin, select one of the *general* biography sites. Later, you can use any of the specialized biography sites to complete your research.

STEP 3 Scan the home page. Each site is organized differently, but all sites offer a search function.

STEP 4 Practice searching for the poet Langston Hughes. At the search function, enter his full name. Depending on the site you selected, his biography will appear next, or you will receive a list of the results of your search. If you're given a list, scroll through it, locate the item you find most interesting, and click on it. Briefly skim the material to learn how an online biography looks.

(Continued on next page)

STEP 5   Now it's your turn to choose a famous person. Enter a full name and go to his or her biography. If you want to learn about another biography Website, go back to the options located at *The English Workshop* site. At this point, you may consider specialized sites.

STEP 6   Once you've found an interesting biography, skim it to make sure there are various uses of capitalization and numbers. Word divisions may not be evident. Make a printout.

STEP 7   On the printout, circle or highlight as many of the following conventions as possible:

    a. Titles of works of art or literature
    b. Abbreviations of college degrees, proper nouns, or organizations
    c. Names and derivatives of names
    d. Religious and ethnic references
    e. Time: months, dates, or historic periods and events
    f. Geographic terms
    g. Titles (e.g., President, Premier)
    h. Organizations, including government agencies and
        political parties
    i. Divisions of words or word groups
    j. Numbers expressed as words
    k. Numbers expressed as figures

STEP 8   Above each item you circle or highlight, write down the letter that describes it. For example, in a biography of Albert Einstein (1879–1955), you might highlight the Royal Society of London. Because this is an organization, you would write the letter "*h*" above its name.

STEP 9   In a paragraph of *at least six* sentences, write about the person you selected. You may summarize the entire biography or focus on one particular aspect of the person's life. Your goal is to demonstrate your ability to follow the conventions of capitalization, word division, and number expression. Include *at least one* example of these conventions in each sentence.

STEP 10   After you've completed this activity, write your name on the front of your printout and give it to your instructor.

PRACTICE 1

Capitalization

Instructions: Below is a series of excerpts taken from workplace correspondence. If the capitalization is correct, place a C in the blank. If the capitalization is incorrect, write the word or words as they should appear.

EXAMPLE: **patent no. 973,046**   EX. <u>**Patent No. 973,046**</u>

1. He said, "the report erroneously stated . . ."   1._____

2. He said that the report "erroneously stated . . ."   2._____

3. dear Ms. Benson: 3._____

4. Yours truly,   4._____

5. Very Truly Yours,   5._____

6. . . . my text, *Spelling And Word Power,*   6._____

7. "My employer," she began, "Is one . . ."   7._____

8. . . . Three hundred dollars ($300) . . .   8._____

9. . . . the book *Corruption throughout* . . .   9._____

10. . . . social security no. 158-58-8558   10._____

11. . . . at 7:30 P.M. the following evening   11._____

12. . . . found on P. 26 of your text   12._____

13. . . . radio station WFLN   13._____

14. . . . Leonardo's "the Last Supper"   14._____

15. . . . this morning at 6:30 a.m.   15._____

16. Atsuko said, "I can't, but, oh, I wish . . ."   16._____

17. . . . it is powered by the Sun . . .   17._____

18. . . . a Size 8 dress . . .   18._____

19. . . . the following invoices: Nos. 125, 134 . . .   19._____

20. . . . see chart 4 . . .   20._____

PRACTICE 2

Proper Nouns

Instructions: In the sentences below, some words that should be capitalized are not. Other words that should not be capitalized are. Cross out all incorrect letters, and write the correct form above each.

EXAMPLE: The Southern part of texas is hottest in the Summer.

1. The ohio river flows from East to West.

2. The assistant director of The Lakeland hotel is Miguel Mccallum, jr.

3. The president left the white house at Noon and boarded the Helicopter for Andrews air force base.

4. Allen and Bianca inc. received your Order for the Fall line early in September.

5. Robert c. Phelps, chairman of the Firm of Phelps and sons, visited our office in the southwest.

6. The Medlock tool co. appreciates the Information it received from you on October 17.

7. Our Local board of education is seeking bids on the new School.

8. The Dade county vocational institute has a new superintendent, yolanda montoya.

9. She graduated from High School and went to Yale university.

10. The river nile is longer than the hudson river.

11. The Carlsbad and lenox Hotels are located South of Main street.

12. The new England Advertising Agency of Bemis, Baumer, and Beard offers exceptional coverage as far South as Northern New Jersey.

13. The department Supervisor of stern's Department Store spoke yesterday.

14. It is unnecessary to italicize words like platonic or pasteurize.

15. Familiar Constellations like Orion and the big dipper are not visible in the southern hemisphere.

16. The secretary general of the united nations was instrumental in bringing the two middle eastern countries to the Negotiating Table.

17. There are 15-minute delays inbound on the Holland and Lincoln tunnels and 20-minute delays on both levels of the George Washington bridge.

18. Professor O'sullivan gave a fascinating lecture on the movements of the northern and southern armies in the days preceding the Battle of Gettysburg.

19. The reference in the third paragraph on page 206 should be to chart 3, not diagram 3.

20. James a. reynolds, secretary of the american association of manufacturers, says the northwest is open for expansion; however, secretary Reynolds warns against the federal government. He feels that congress will not make any substantial Appropriations during its Spring session.

PRACTICE 3

Word Division

Instructions: In the blanks provided, write the two parts into which each word should be divided. If the word should not be divided, write the complete word in the first blank. Consult your dictionary if necessary.

EXAMPLE: **consider**   EX. _____**con-**_____   ____**sider**____

1. problem   _____   _____

2. narrate   _____   _____

3. abound   _____   _____

4. hopeful   _____   _____

5. suggest   _____   _____

6. natural   _____   _____

7. question   _____   _____

8. sofa   _____   _____

9. innate   _____   _____

10. luxury   _____   _____

11. consumer   _____   _____

12. manager   _____   _____

13. idea   _____   _____

14. planned   _____   _____

15. planning   _____   _____

16. smallest   _____   _____

17. insert   _____   _____

18. dwelling   _____   _____

19. swiftly   _____   _____

20. legible   _____   _____

21. modem   _____   _____

22. message   _____   _____

23. program   _____   _____

24. amount   _____   _____

PRACTICE 4

Numbers

Instructions: Assume that the following sentence fragements appear in workplace correspondence. If an item is incorrectly expressed, write the correct form in the blank. If an item is expressed correctly, write C.

EXAMPLE: seven a.m.   EX. _____ **7 a.m.** _____

1. approximately two hundred people   1. _____

2. exactly two hundred fourteen people   2. _____

3. several hundred people   3. _____

4. only 5 committee members   4. _____

5. a department of 34 full-time faculty   5. _____

6. an annual salary of $56,500   6. _____

7. 7th Avenue   7. _____

8. Exit 15 on Route 6   8. _____

9. November twenty-fourth   9. _____

10. eighteen percent   10. _____

11. April 23rd   11. _____

12. six thousand dollars ($6,000)   12. _____

13. 8 o'clock   13. _____

14. six p.m.   14. _____

15. nearly 14,500,000 voters   15. _____

16. p. six in your text   16. _____

17. over $47,000,000,000 annually   17. _____

18. distribute 136 8-page brochures   18. _____

19. reviewed 20 12-page contracts   19. _____

20. located at One Lexington Avenue   20. _____

21. located at 431 6th Ave.   21. _____

22. a temperature of eight degrees   22. _____

23. a tolerance of three one-thousandths of an inch   23. _____

24. only $.89 each   24. _____

PRACTICE 5

Numbers in Sentences

Instructions: Each of the following sentences contains one or more errors in the expression of numbers. Cross out all errors and make the necessary corrections in the space above them.

EXAMPLE: I waited for the doctor from ~~eleven-thirty~~ *11:30* a.m. until ~~one-fifteen~~ *1:15* p.m.

1. I must raise $1,700,000 by 2 o'clock tomorrow.

2. The Computer Applications and Office Technology Department consists of 3 business communication professors, 2 Excel professors, and 1 voice recognition professor.

3. One authority estimates that nearly 72,000,000,000 documents are created each year.

4. Standard office stationery measures eight-and-one-half inches by eleven inches.

5. You may use either the small No. 6¾ business envelope or the large No. ten envelope.

6. These three styles cost seventy-five cents, eighty-nine cents, and $1.09, respectively.

7. Go to the store on Twelfth Avenue and purchase four one-pound boxes of two-and-one-half-inch finishing nails.

8. 146 leases must be renewed by June first.

9. By 3 o'clock Jo's temperature had dropped to ninety-nine point eight degrees.

10. Her 20 supporters took seats in the 1st, 3rd, and 4th rows.

11. The new director of operations is not yet 40 years old, but she has nearly 10 years of administrative experience.

12. On December fourteenth Alba submitted three receipts for out-of-pocket expenses: $17.25, 89 cents, and $3.

13. Did you say 6th Street or 16th Street?

14. The drawer measured twelve inches by eighteen inches by three inches.

15. Figure Two appears on p. eight.

16. Chapter Twenty, entitled "Report Writing," begins on page four hundred.

17. He appended Schedule Thirty-four Sixty-eight to IRS Form Ten Forty and mailed his return before the April fifteenth deadline.

18. Most retailers operate on a markup of 100%.

19. Our company operates a small fleet of 8 6-cylinder and 4 8-cylinder trucks.

20. The 4 surveys were administered to 65 employees during a period of 3 months.

PRACTICE 6

Capitalization, Word Division, and the Expression of Numbers

Instructions: The following letter is written without any capital letters. Cross out each lowercase letter that should be capitalized, and write the capital letter above it. Also, correct any errors in the expression of numbers and word division. Do not change any words that are already correctly divided.

HOTEL GRAMATAN
12 Quinby Ave.
White Plains, NY 10606

august 17, 20--

mr. oscar kaplin
127 fourteenth street, apt. twelve
new york, new york 10010

dear mr. kaplin:

are you one of the many new york city businesspeople who would like to

spend a few days or a few weeks in the country, but whose busi-

ness interests demand that you not venture far from manhattan? the ho-

tel gramatan in the hills of westchester county, midway between the scen-

ic hudson river and long island sound, offers you a most inviting home

twenty-three miles and 38 minutes from grand central station, the

heart of the shopping and theater district.

the hotel is of moorish design, and the wide spanish balconies encircling it

are literally "among the tree tops."

accommodations are on the american plan, with rates considera-

bly less than the cost of equivalent accommodations in town: single room

---

HOTEL GRAMATAN
12 Quinby Ave.
White Plains, NY 10606

and board, $850 per week and upward; 2-room suite with board for two people, $1490 per week and upward. our exceptional dining facilities, with seating for more than 200 people, are open from six o'clock a.m. to 11:30 o'clock p.m.

the hotel offers two nine-hole golf courses, 8 of the very best tennis courts in westchester county, a string of fine saddle horses, and beautiful jogging and hiking trails.

charlotte vandermere, drama critic of the new york times, visited the hotel gramatan in july of last year. upon her return to new york, she wrote the following in her column, "going on in new york": "I've stayed at 100's of hotels and sampled literally 1000's of dishes. the hotel gramatan is one of the finest hotels i have ever visited. its european cuisine is excellent."

sometime this fall take a drive up the scenic hutchinson river parkway to exit seventeen and visit the gramatan. you'll be glad you did.

sincerely yours,

Lola Raza

Name _____

Class _____ Date _____

PRACTICE 7

Writing a Complaint Letter

Instructions: When you feel you have been treated badly or when a product or service does not meet reasonable expectations, you have every right to expect the company to make some sort of adjustment or, at the very least, offer you an apology. Just remember that no matter how angry you are, a moderate, reasonable tone is more likely to elicit a favorable response.

Write your own complaint letter about a problem you've recently experienced (e.g., discourteous treatment by salespeople, poor service, merchandise of inferior quality). Tell the company to which you are writing what happened, why you are unhappy, and what you want the company to do. Prepare your draft; revise it in the space below and on a separate sheet of paper if necessary. Then write or type your letter on a separate piece of paper.

_____

_____

_____

_____

_____

_____

_____

_____

_____

_____

_____

_____

_____

_____

_____

_____

_____

_____

_____

_____

_____

_____

_____

Special Marks of Punctuation and Style

Unit 8—Editing Review

Instructions: The following draft is from an orientation booklet given to new editors at a textbook publishing company. It details basic principles editors should follow while editing manuscripts. As you read the material, use the concepts you have studied so far to help you locate errors. Cross out the errors and write corrections in the space above them.

EDITING MANUSCRIPT

As a author or writer send in their manuscript, the Editorial Staff reviews them. For correct format and for content.

Editing For Content

Content editing is the checking of manuscript to be making sure it fulfills the goals, which were set in the development phase. It involves focusing on the following,

1) Organization

How a book is to be organized is sat early and is discussed at editorial meetings. The organization is later firmed up at a conference among the author and editor.

When editing the manuscript make sure that decisions agreed with at the planning conference are indeed working good. [Even though the preliminary outline may seem well, problems in organization often crop up latter in the manuscript]. Ask yourselve these here questions. Is the breakdown easy-to-follow. Determine whether all prerequisite material is included in the book. Are the length of the chapters or sections appropriate.

After examining the manuscript for it's broad organization, consider the

(Continued on next page)

continued from page 603

paragraphs theirselves, whether they flow well internally, and whether there is a flow from paragraph to paragraph.

2) Readability

One of the key considerations in a textbook are its readability. How easily or difficult it is for students to read and understood. The degree of ease or difficulty is referred to as 'reading level', and is oftenest described in terms of grade level. Readability measurements are not absolute they are only general indicatores of the approximate grade level any given material is suited to. Readabiltiy information about a program is required by most purchasers, particularly by State adoption committees.

The reading level of materials can be measured in many different ways. Most common, readability formulaes which rely heavy on sentence length and on vocabulary difficulty are used. Vocabulary difficulty is measured by factors like the amount of "hard" or unfamiliar words in a given sample and the number of syllables in the words of the sample. Studys have showed that text is more easy to read when it contains a greater proportion of short words short simple sentences and familiar or frequently-used words. The statisticses produced by readability formulas is used to predict student's ability to comprehend reading material.

The choice of a readability formula depends on the expected grade level. And the subject of the material being analyzed. Certain formulas give more accurate results at specific grade levels and for specific disciplines. The Spache formula for example is used for grades K-three due to the fact that the Dale-Chall formula is'nt appropriate below grade four.

Link & Learn

USING PUNCTUATION AND ELEMENTS OF STYLE IN OFFICE ADMINISTRATION AND TECHNOLOGY CAREERS

GOAL: Reinforce what you learned about punctuation and style in Unit 8 while visiting Websites related to office administration and technology careers.

STEP 1 Go to *englishworkshop.glencoe.com*, the address for *The English Workshop* Website. Click first on Unit 8; then click on Link & Learn to access a list of Websites you may use in this activity. Select one of the sites and click on it.

STEP 2 At the home page of the Website you select, locate material that uses a variety of sentences and punctuation marks. Find at least two full pages with various semicolons, colons, quotation marks, parentheses, brackets, hyphens, or dashes. Also note the use of capitalization and numbers. You will need at least two full pages of text.

STEP 3 Once you locate appropriate material, print the pages.

STEP 4 Read the printout carefully. Circle or highlight *at least five* of the following punctuation marks or uses of capital letters that appear in the text. Draw a line from each item to the margins. At the end of each line, place a number between 1 and 5. Use the same number for similar types of punctuation. For example, you can assign the number 1 to all semicolons that separate independent clauses or items in a series. Below are examples of the different types of punctuation you can choose to look for to complete this assignment.

   a. semicolons separating independent clauses or items in a series
   b. colons before quotations and lists in titles
   c. quotation marks around direct quotations
   d. quotation marks around titles or words used in special ways
   e. hyphenated compound expressions or compound adjectives
   f. ellipses, parentheses, dashes, or brackets
   g. capitalized abbreviations for names of organizations or special terms (such as *HR* for Human Resources)
   h. capitalized geographic terms, political designations, ethnic references, or personal names or titles
   i. numbers expressed as words or figures

STEP 5 After you have highlighted and numbered the items, list the numbers on the back of the printout. For each number, explain the rule the Website writer was following.

STEP 6 When you have completed the work, proofread it, write your name on the front of the printout, and turn it in to your instructor.

Proofreading Guide

Proofreaders' Marks

When you are correcting text in the Practices throughout this book, you are doing what professional editors do. You are also doing what individuals in almost every kind of workplace setting do. At various times in your professional and student careers, you will likely need to act as an editor. Some jobs require more editing and proofreading than others. Knowing how to proofread and correct copy is an important skill for today's writer. You also need to know the most efficient ways to mark text for corrections. That means learning the set of symbols used by writers and editors to indicate corrections. These symbols are called **proofreaders' marks.**

This appendix discusses the standard proofreaders' marks most writers use. In the Practices you will use and interpret these symbols in a variety of situations. When you complete this appendix, you should have a working knowledge of the process of proofreading. You'll be able to interpret proofreaders' marks when you see them, and you'll be able to proofread your own or someone else's writing accurately and confidently.

The charts on the inside of the front and back covers of this textbook list the common proofreaders' marks and show how they are used. Review them, noting what the marks mean, how they look, and how they are used. You need not memorize the chart. You will learn these marks by using them. Refer to the chart as you do the Practices. Soon you will be using proofreaders' marks automatically.

The Application of Proofreaders' Marks

Let's consider some passages and correct them using proofreaders' marks.

PASSAGE 1

How would you correct the following passage?

> The Slick has a rotating head. Which adjusts to the contour of your face, its micrometer blades are self-cleaning. And self-sharpening. The Slick comes with nine different comfort settings to give you the optimum in shaving closeness and satisfaction for incredibly close and comfortable shaves nothing beats a Slick.

Here is the passage marked for correction:

The Slick has a rotating head, which adjusts to the contour of your face, its micrometer blades are self-cleaning, and self-sharpening. The Slick comes with nine different comfort settings to give you the optimum in shaving closeness and satisfaction for incredibly close and comfortable shaves, nothing beats a Slick.

Here is the corrected copy:

The Slick has a rotating head, which adjusts to the contour of your face. Its micrometer blades are self-cleaning and self-sharpening. The Slick comes with nine different comfort settings to give you the optimum in shaving closeness and satisfaction. For incredibly close and comfortable shaves, nothing beats a Slick.

Passage 2

How would you correct this next sentence?

Did you receive any compensation for your recent article the high-tech battle between india and the U.S.?

Here is the passage marked for correction:

Did you receive any compensation for your recent article the high-tech battle between india and the U.S.?

Here is the corrected copy:

Did you receive any compensation for your recent article, "The High-Tech Battle Between India and the U.S."?

Now that you've seen how writers use proofreaders' marks, try using the marks to indicate needed corrections to the next passages. Mark your corrections on the page. Use a pencil so you can erase if needed.

Passage 3

How would you correct this next sentence?

Ms Fletcher left the following message I will be unable to keep my 1030 a m appointment however I will be able to keep my afternoon appointments

Here is the sentence with corrections:

Ms. Fletcher left the following message I will be unable to keep my 1030 a m appointment however I will be able to keep my afternoon appointments

Here is the corrected copy:

> Ms. Fletcher left the following message: "I will be unable to keep my 10:30 a.m. appointment; however, I will be able to keep my afternoon appointments."

PASSAGE 4

How would you correct this next sentence?

> The semicolons prupose in a sentnece are to mark a maajor pause or break it indicates a pause greater than a comma though not quiet so great so great a pause asa period.

Here is the passage marked for correction:

> The semicolons prupose in a sentnece are to mark a major pause or break it indicates a pause greater than a comma though not quiet so great so great a pause asa period.

Here is the corrected copy:

> The semicolon's purpose in a sentence is to mark a major pause or break. It indicates a greater pause than a comma, though not quite so great a pause as a period.

Printed and Single-Spaced Copy

The text with proofreaders' marks that you have read so far in this chapter has been spaced to allow you room to write your marks exactly where corrections are needed. In school you may have had instructors who required you to double-space papers so they could make corrections. Some authors also work with double-spaced text as a courtesy to the editor. Typically, however, word-processing documents in business environments are single-spaced. In these cases there is not enough room to place proofreaders' marks above each line of text. Instead, the marks should be placed in the margin.

If you must make several corrections in one line, write them next to each other in the margin. Write them in the order in which they occur and separate each with a perpendicular line. You may use both margins. Do not draw a line to where the correction should go. Instead, place a caret (^) in the text to show where the correction is to be made. The passages below show proofreaders' marks in a double-spaced version and in a single-spaced version. Notice that the same marks are used. Those in the second passage adhere to the strategies outlined in this paragraph.

Double-Spaced Text With Proofreaders' Marks

Nouns are either concrete or abstract. Concrete Nouns name ~~particular~~ specific

things ~~which~~ that can be experienced by ~~one of~~ the five senses. Things that can be

seen, felt, heard, tasted, ~~or~~ or smelled. abstract nouns name qualities and

concepts.

Single-Spaced Text With Proofreaders' Marks

Nouns are either concrete or abstract. Concrete Nouns name ~~particular~~ specific
things ~~which~~ that can be experienced by ~~one of~~ the five senses. Things that can be
seen, felt, heard, tasted, ~~or~~ or smelled. abstract nouns name qualities and
concepts.

Based on these corrections, the rekeyed passage would look this way:

Corrected Copy

Nouns are either *concrete* or *abstract.* *Concrete nouns* name specific
things that can be experienced by one of the five senses—things that
can be seen, felt, heard, tasted, or smelled. *Abstract nouns* name qualities
and concepts.

When proofreading single-spaced letters, memos, and even printed copies of e-mail messages, apply the same marking strategies in the margin beside the text. Do not try to crowd your corrections into the body of the document.

Keep these strategies in mind when marking single-spaced copy:

- Be sure to write proofreaders' marks *directly opposite* the line to which they refer.
- Do not draw a line from the margin to the place of correction; simply insert a caret where the correction is to be made.

Substantive and Typographical Errors

In the passages above, you made two basic kinds of corrections. You corrected (1) the punctuation and grammar of the passage and (2) the keyboarding errors, such as extra letters, transposed letters, and repeated words. The first type of errors are called **substantive** errors; they cause serious problems for readers trying to understand the text. The second type of errors are keyboarding, or **typographical**, errors; they indicate carelessness in keying text. As a proofreader you must be alert for both kinds of errors.

Successful Proofreading

As you've seen, learning proofreaders' marks and their meanings is not hard to do; it just takes a little time. Successful proofreading, however, is more than using proofreaders' marks. It requires real effort and demands your full attention. You must concentrate and take your time to do the best job you possibly can.

Your goal as a proofreader is to make the final copy as good as you can make it because it is a direct reflection on you. A careless job of proofreading says to your readers that you are sloppy and indifferent. Clean, correct final copy says you are careful and conscientious, that you care about and take pride in doing things right. Careful proofreading can be your personal mark of excellence. Important documents should be proofread carefully several times.

Steps in Proofreading Final Copy

In the Practices at the end of each chapter in this book, you have been looking for errors that you know are present. You have even been told what kinds of errors to look for in each exercise. In a normal editing situation, however, you don't know if there are any errors—in fact, you hope there aren't. Nor do you know what kinds of errors to watch for. Any kind of error might be present anywhere. Accordingly, the best way to proofread something is to do it slowly and carefully—and to do it more than once.

Step 1:

Read through the material the first time with particular attention to the overall context.

- Do the sentences make sense?
- Is the vocabulary accurate?
- Are there any words missing or incorrectly repeated?
- Are there any grammatical errors?

Step 2:

Read the copy again much more slowly, focusing on the details.

- Is each word spelled correctly?
- Is all punctuation accurate and complete?
- Are proper nouns capitalized in accordance with standard usage?
- Are numbers expressed correctly?
- Are words divided properly?
- Are all the lines aligned correctly?
- Do the headings of a report appear in the correct place and are they centered when they are supposed to be?

- If the document is a letter or memo, is it positioned attractively on the page, with balanced margins?
- If the document is an e-mail message, is it spaced in paragraphs so that recipients can quickly read the message?

The list of such specifics could go on. Many people recommend that in this second stage of proofreading you read backward, from right to left. This will force you to concentrate on each word so that you will catch more errors in typing and spelling you might otherwise miss. You must, of course, read the material in the correct order to catch most other kinds of errors. Overall, the best general advice remains the same: *Take your time.*

Computer Proofreading

If you compose at a computer, you have some special opportunities and challenges in proofreading and editing. You can correct text without rekeying the entire document, use spell checkers and grammar checkers, use online resources to verify the meaning of words, and change format (margins, position on the page, line spacing, and so on) easily. Special challenges you will face include proofreading on the screen, moving and deleting text properly, using spell checkers and grammar checkers appropriately, and understanding the software and equipment.

You may have noticed that "using spell checkers and grammar checkers" is mentioned twice in the previous paragraph. Although these electronic aids can be valuable in locating errors—especially keyboarding errors— they are not a replacement for careful proofreading by the writer. If a word is spelled correctly but used incorrectly—*there* or *their* instead of *they're*, for example—most spell checkers will not recognize the error. Grammar checkers cannot always tell when a run-on sentence has occurred. For more detailed advice about using spell checkers and grammar checkers, see Appendix C: Online and Print Spelling Resources.

On-Screen Challenges

Perhaps the biggest challenge for the writer who uses a computer is proofreading and editing on the screen rather than on paper. Some writers print a copy of their work so they can proofread and edit it the conventional way. Others do some proofreading and editing on the screen and some on paper. Some proofread and edit entirely on screen, especially if the "document" is an e-mail message or fax that the writer will never handle as a printed document.

Print vs. Screen. While proofreading styles vary, most writers in the workplace proofread at least some of their documents on screen. A document on a screen can look very different from its printed version. Size of type, color, and position in relation to a writer's eye are different on a computer screen than on paper. To proofread accurately on screen, you must become accustomed to these differences.

Moving Text. A big timesaver when writing on a computer is the capability to move passages from one place to another or to remove passages without rewriting the entire document. However, writers must make sure to move or remove the targeted passage—no more, no less. It's easy to take too many words or to miss a word or two. After moving or changing a passage, reread it to make sure you've made the intended change. Computer tools are extremely useful when writing, but they do not replace proofreading and editing skills.

Six Proofreading Strategies

Bottom Line: Whether proofreading on screen or off, keep in mind the key proofreading strategies.

1. Read through the material for sense. Make sure all information is complete.
2. Check grammar.
3. Check spelling. (Use a print or online dictionary!)
4. Check punctuation.
5. Check elements of style (e.g., capitalization, word division, expression of numbers).
6. Check overall format and appearance of the material.

YOUR TURN A

Identifying Proofreaders' Marks

Instructions: Write the letter from Column 2 that describes the change shown by the entry in Column 1.

COLUMN 1	COLUMN 2	ANSWERS
1. worshop (k above)	**a.** delete and close up	1. _____
2. The English Workshop	**b.** add space	2. _____
3. workshop	**c.** keep as it is	3. _____
4. Workshop	**d.** insert letter	4. _____
5. wokrshop	**e.** move as shown	5. _____
6. *The English Workshop* (#)	**f.** delete	6. _____
7. english workshop	**g.** italicize	7. _____
8. workshop ~~workshop~~	**h.** capitalize	8. _____
9. English ~~workshop~~	**i.** make letter lowercase	9. _____
10. (workshop) English	**j.** transpose	10. _____

YOUR TURN B

Using Proofreaders' Marks

Instructions: Make the changes in Column 1 called for in Column 2.

COLUMN 1	COLUMN 2
1. She said, Please be seated.	insert quotation marks
2. tothe bank frommy broker	add spaces
3. note References	capitalize entire word
4. She will ~~probably~~ attend.	restore word.
5. Ave. 8	spell out
6. She said, "Please be seated"	insert period
7. due to the fact *that* it is already noon	change *due to the fact* that to *because*
8. because it is noon	insert *already* between *is* and *noon*
9. an up to date résumé	insert hyphens
10. The work however was completed	place commas around *however*
11. Were willing to help	insert apostrophe
12. because already it is noon	move *already* to between *is* and *noon*

YOUR TURN C

Proofreading a Handout

Instructions: Below is a handout a speaker will give to audience members during a talk at a local high school on the job search process. Proofread this unedited copy so that when the passage is rekeyed and printed, it will look like the finished copy at the end of the exercise.

Interview Followup

Most interviewers will bring a job interview toa close by telling you when the co.

intends to make a decission. Youll here from us by the ned of the Month.

If the co. has not notifyed you by then you can call the interviewer to enquire abouthe

progress or status of youre application. if a decision has not not been made yet you will

have brouhgt your name back to the attention of the interviewer; if the company has made

a decision, and you have not been selected you will knwo w here you stand. And can

concentrate your efforts on other companies.

Interview Follow-up

Most interviewers will close a job interview by telling you when the company intends to make a decision: "You'll hear from us by the end of the month." If the company has not notified you by then, you may call the interviewer to inquire about the progress or status of your application. If a decision has not yet been made, you will have brought your name back to the interviewer's attention. If the company has made a decision and has not selected you, you'll know where you stand and can concentrate your efforts on other companies.

Print and Online References

DICTIONARIES

Writers have traditionally turned to print dictionaries and thesauruses to help them spell, pronounce, and use words correctly. Since the Internet has become such an important part of our lives, many writers now take advantage of online dictionaries and thesauruses as well. Appendix B will show you how useful and user-friendly both print and online references can be. Most people use a dictionary for two reasons: to find out how to spell a word and to discover what a word means. Actually, a good dictionary can tell you a great deal more. In this appendix you will learn about the various features dictionaries provide to help you use a word correctly.

Print Dictionaries

Below is an entry for the word *initiate* from *Merriam-Webster's Collegiate Dictionary,* 10th edition. The labels **a** through **j** indicate the various types of information a typical dictionary entry offers. Refer to this sample entry as you read the description of each feature below.

> d   c   e   f   h   b   g
>
> **a** —— ¹**ini· ti· ate** \i-'ni-she- at\ *vt* **-at· ed; -at·** **ing** [LL *initiatus,* pp. of *initiare,* fr. L, to induct, fr. *initium*] (ca, 1573) **1** : to cause or facilitate the beginning of : set going <~ a program of reform> <enzymes that ~ fermentation> **2** : to induct into membership by or as if by special rites **3** : to instruct in the rudiments or principles of something : INTRODUCE **syn** see BEGIN—
> **ini· ti· a· tor** \- ā-t r\ *n*   i
>
> **c** ————
>
> ²**ini· ti·ate** \i-'ni-sh(ē) t\ *adj* (1605) **1** *obs* : relating to an initiate **2 a** : initiate or properly admitted (as to membership or an office) b : instructed in some secret knowledge
>
> **c** ————
>
> ³**ini· ti·ate** \i-'ni-sh(ē) t\ *n* (1811) **1** : a person who is undergoing or has undergone an initiation **2** : a person who is instructed or adept in some special field

a: Spelling—The dictionary shows the correct spelling of a word. When a word has several acceptable spellings, the dictionary lists each of them. The first spelling given is the most common one. This is the spelling you should use in most workplace writing.

b: Definition—Each entry provides one or more definitions of a word. Sometimes dictionaries illustrate the various meanings of words with examples of sentences or phrases. The entry for *initiate* does not.

Some dictionaries list definitions in an order that reflects the history of the word. Original meanings appear first, and more recent definitions follow. Other dictionaries list the most common meaning of the word first. This edition of the *Merriam-Webster's Collegiate Dictionary* offers separate entries of **homographs**.

c: Homograph—Words that look alike but differ in meaning, derivation, or pronunciation are **homographs**. The word *initiate* includes three homographs: (1) a verb pronounced \i-'ni-shē- at\; (2) an adjective pronounced \i-'ni-sh(ē)-ət\; and (3) a noun pronounced \i-'ni-sh(ē)-ət\. Dictionaries often present each homograph in historical order; that is, they begin with the homograph that was used in English first.

d: Syllabication—Most dictionaries use one or more dots [**.**] to indicate how a word is divided into syllables. You may refer to the syllabication as a guide when trying to divide a word at the end of a line of print. Complete rules for word division are listed in Chapter 20.

A dictionary entry also shows whether a compound word is written as one solid word (*officeholder*), a hyphenated word (*off-season*), or two words (*office hours*).

e: Pronunciation—Most print dictionaries locate the pronunciation of a word immediately after its boldface entry. All information about pronunciation is printed between reversed diagonals (\ \ ).

Stress marks show which syllables are **accented**, or spoken with more emphasis than the other syllable(s). Often, as in the entry for *initiate*, a word contains several accents or stress marks. In these cases, a high-set stress mark \ ' \ preceding a syllable signals a strong stress; a low-set stress \ , \ mark signals a weak or secondary stress.

In its first definition, the verb *initiate* has two stresses. The second syllable receives the primary stress; the last syllable receives the secondary stress.

Pronunciation symbols tell you how to pronounce each sound in a word. In general, the introductory chapters of a dictionary include a guide to pronunciation that provides a complete explanation of all symbols. Sometimes the inside of the back cover includes a list of pronunciation symbols.

Located at the bottom of the second column of each right-hand page of the *Merriam-Webster's Collegiate Dictionary*, an abbreviated list of key words also indicates how to pronounce each symbol. Here you will find the following standard list:

\ə\ **abut** \ᵉ\ kitten, F table \ər\ **further** \a\ **ash** \ā\ **ace** \ä\ **mop, mar** \au̇\ **out** \ch\ **chin** \e\ bet \ē\ **easy** \g\ **go** \i\ **hit** \ī\ **ice** \j\ **job** \ŋ\ **sing** \ō\ **go** \ȯ\ **law** \ȯi\ **boy** \th\ **thin** \t͟h\ **the** \ü\ **loot** \u̇\ **foot** \y\ **yet** \zh\ **vision** \à, k̲, ⁿ, œ, œ̄, ᵾ, ᵿ, ʸ\ *see* Guide to Pronunciation

Some words may be pronounced more than one way. In these cases the first pronunciation listed is the more common one. The word *initiate* is pronounced in two ways. The correct choice of pronunciation depends on how it is used in a sentence. When *initiate* is used as a verb (its most common use), the final syllable is pronounced *ate*. When *initiate* is used as an adjective or a noun, the final syllable sounds like *it*.

f: Part of speech—After showing the pronunciation of a word, most print dictionaries identify the part of speech. The following italic abbreviations typically stand for the parts of speech:

n	noun	*prep*	preposition
vt	transitive verb	*conj*	conjunction
vi	intransitive verb	*pron*	pronoun
adj	adjective	*interj*	interjection
adv	adverb		

Our sample entry tells us that *initiate* is most often used as a transitive verb (*vt*), but it may also be used as an adjective (*adj*) or a noun (*n*).

As you have seen with *initiate*, the pronunciation and the meaning of a word can vary depending on its part of speech. Sometimes the spelling changes also. It is therefore important to read these labels carefully.

g: Etymology—In print dictionaries the material in brackets [ ] tells you the **etymology,** or brief history, of the word. This may include the English and pre-English origins of a word. Many words in English come from other languages. The English word *initiate* comes directly from Late Latin, abbreviated *LL*, and originally from Latin, abbreviated *fr. L.*

Other words may be derived from proper names. The word *boycott*, for example, originates from an Irish land agent, Captain C. C. Boycott, who was ostracized because of his refusal to reduce rents.

h: Inflected forms—As you know, nouns, verbs, adjectives, and adverbs can change forms grammatically. Nouns have singular and plural forms; verbs change tenses; and adjectives and adverbs have positive, comparative, and superlative forms. These are called **inflected forms.** You have learned how to form the regular inflections of these parts of speech, and you have studied most irregular inflections. Dictionaries do not have enough room to show regular inflected forms, but they do show irregular inflected forms.

The inflected forms of *initiate* are not difficult, but the final *e* is left out in forming the past and present participles. Hence, after indicating the part of speech, the entry shows the endings -**at·ed** and -**at·ing**.

i: Synonym/antonym—A **synonym** is a word that means the same, or almost the same, as another word. Sometimes the entry for a word contains a list of synonyms. In print dictionaries these are signaled by the italic, boldface term ***syn***. A synonym for *initiate* is BEGIN, which is printed in all capital letters in the sample entry. Capital letters indicate that additional synonyms can be found under the dictionary entry for *begin*. That entry lists synonyms such as *commence*, *start*, *initiate*, and *inaugurate*. It also compares the slight differences in their meanings.

Some entries also include a list of **antonyms** (abbreviated *ant*). These are words that mean the opposite of a given word. If antonyms of *begin* were listed, they would also be antonyms of *initiate*.

j: Usage label—Some words are more appropriate in one situation than they are in another. For example, you might tell your friend that you "goofed." In your annual review at work, you would more likely state that you "made a mistake."

The dictionary indicates levels of usage for many entries. These usage labels tell the reader whether a word is appropriate in a given situation. Here are some typical labels. Words not identified by a usage label are considered part of standard English and are appropriate for any occasion.

Usage Label	Abbreviation For	Definition
obs	obsolete	No evidence of the use of the word since 1755
slang		Not a conventional or standard word; used in very informal contexts
archaic		Word appears in earlier writings but is used rarely or only in special contexts today
dial	dialect	Term or sense is used only in certain regional varieties of American or British English; sometimes written with country label, e.g., *dial Brit*
nonstand	nonstandard	Word disapproved by many but may still be in use in some contexts
substand	substandard	Word conforms to the usage pattern of a speech community that differs from the prestige group in that community
disparaging offensive obscene vulgar		Word intended to hurt, shock, or offend; word that gives offense even when used unintentionally

Many publishers of print dictionaries offer Websites that include online versions of their reference tools. In general, a little keyboarding and a few clicks are all it takes to find a word in an online dictionary. These references are especially user-friendly when you need to look up a word that you don't know how to spell. Many online dictionaries offer suggestions to help users select and spell a word correctly.

Eventually you will want to access an online dictionary by following the instructions listed on page 622, under the heading Your Turn. Before you visit an online dictionary, preview the following information about the entry for the word *initiate* from the *Merriam-Webster's Collegiate Dictionary* Website. The labels point out the key features; many are the same as those of the print version.

To arrive at the window displayed on the next page, you need to link with the home page of the *Merriam-Webster's Collegiate Dictionary* Website and enter the word *initiate* in the search tool. The online dictionary will display the first, or main, entry that exactly matches *initiate*, just as the illustration does.

The key features of an online dictionary entry are similar to those of a print dictionary. To jog your memory, you should turn back to page 616 and review the descriptions of labels **a** through **j**. The letters for the online entry match those for the print version. These include (**a**) spelling, (**b**) definition, (**c**) homograph, (**d**) syllabication, (**e**) pronunciation, (**f**) part of speech, (**g**) etymology, (**h**) inflected forms, and (**i**) synonym/antonym. However, the online entry does not include (**j**) usage label, although usage notes do appear in many online dictionary entries. You will discover that online references can be easier to read since they do not use abbreviations.

Special Features of Online Dictionaries

The online dictionary may offer interesting and helpful features not available in a print version. These special features are described below. Refer to the online entry for *initiate* as you read the following descriptions.

k: Search results box—When the dictionary finds other main entries that contain the word you entered, a list of those words appears in a box at the top of the results screen. You can scroll through the list of alternatives and view the entry for any word by clicking on it. For example, if you want to see the entry for *initiate* used as a noun, you would click on that entry.

l: Audio pronunciation—When you see a speaker icon next to a word, click on it to hear the word pronounced. This feature is especially helpful when the pronunciation of a word changes depending on its meaning and part of speech. Remember, *initiate* as a verb is pronounced differently from *initiate* as an adjective or a noun.

Merriam-Webster's
COLLEGIATE® DICTIONARY

(Merriam-Webster)

| Collegiate® Dictionary | Collegiate® Thesaurus | Help |

Click on the Collegiate Thesaurus tab to look up the current word in the thesaurus.

3 entries found for **initiate**. —a
To select an entry, click on it. (Click 'Go' if nothing happens.)

initiate[1,transitive verb]   Go
initiate[2,adjective]
initiate[3,noun] —k

Main Entry: ¹**in·ti·ate** ◀)) —d
Pronunciation: i-'ni-shE-"At
Function: *transitive verb* —f
Inflected Form(s): **-at·ed; -at·ing**
Etymology: Late Latin *initiatus,* past participle of *initiare,* from Latin, to induct, from *initium*
Date: circa 1573
1 : to cause or facilitate the beginning of : set going <*initiate* a program of reform> <enzymes that *initiate* fermentation>
2 : to induct into membership by or as if by special rites
3 : to instruct in the rudiments or principles of something : INTRODUCE
synonym see BEGIN —o
- **in·ti·a·tor** ◀)) /-"A-t ɛr/ *noun*

m: Function—A word's function, or part of speech, is displayed more prominently in the online version. Both *function* and the part of speech are spelled out.

n: Date—As an interesting historical note, a date appears in most main entries. The date indicates the first recorded usage of the word in the sense of the entry. For instance, the English use of the word *initiate* as a verb meaning *to initiate* dates back to approximately (*circa*) 1573. Not all words are given dates.

o: Cross-reference link—A word in SMALL CAPITAL letters (usually underlined and in a different color) is linked to its own entry in the dictionary. Click on the cross-reference to access the entry for the linked word.

Thesaurus Accessibility

Many online dictionaries, like the *Merriam-Webster's Collegiate Dictionary* Website, offer easy access to a companion thesaurus. The next section of this appendix explains print and online thesauruses. For the moment, realize that the availability of two online resources at one site can simplify your research efforts.

Spelling Help

Looking up a word in a print dictionary can be challenging if you're not sure about its spelling. An online dictionary offers an advantage. *Merriam-Webster's Collegiate Dictionary* lets you search by using the wildcard symbol [**?**] to represent a single letter in a word you don't know how to spell. For example, if you don't know which letter comes after the *p* in *separate*, you can search for the word by using the wildcard symbol **sep?rate**. The dictionary will find the possible words and present them in a list.

Merriam-Webster's Collegiate Dictionary also helps you locate a word even if you spell it incorrectly in your search. For example, if you search for the misspelled word *necesarry*, you will see a screen with the following message: *The word you've entered isn't in the dictionary. Click on a spelling suggestion below.* A list of suggested words appears under the message. When you locate *necessary* on the list, click on it. The main entry for the word will appear.

Your Turn

Explore how an online dictionary works by visiting several dictionary sites. Open your Internet browser and key in ***englishworkshop.glencoe.com,*** the address for *The English Workshop* Website. Click on Appendix B, then click on Dictionaries, and finally select the *Merriam-Webster's Collegiate Dictionary* Website. Key in *initiate* to compare the appendix preview of the site to the live Internet tool. You may want to search this site for other words that interest you. When you have finished reviewing, exit from the site and try one of the other online dictionaries listed.

THESAURUSES

What do you do when you want to replace a word, but you can't think of another word with the same meaning? You can turn to a dictionary, where you may find synonyms. You can also go to a specialized reference called a *thesaurus*. The word *thesaurus* comes from a Greek word meaning "treasury or warehouse." A thesaurus is a treasury or a rich source of synonyms—words that have the same or similar meanings—and antonyms—words that have the opposite meanings.

The English plural of *thesaurus* is *thesauruses;* the foreign plural is *thesauri*. In this section, we will use the former style.

Print Thesauruses

Writers typically use a print thesaurus to find a synonym for another word. They also refer to a thesaurus when they need a related word, a contrasted word, or an antonym. For example, the *Merriam-Webster's Collegiate Thesaurus* lists *account, recital, memoir,* and *tale* as words related to the noun *history*. You will learn in this section that a thesaurus also provides other useful information about a word.

The following entry for the word *shy* comes from the print version of the *Merriam-Webster's Collegiate Thesaurus*. The labels **a** through **j** mark the key features of a typical thesaurus entry.

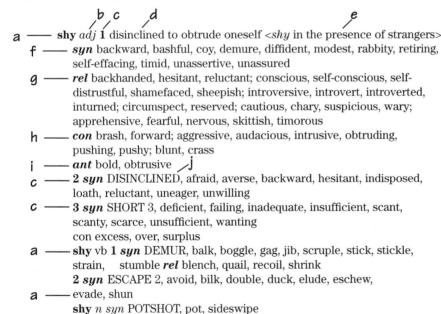

a —— **shy** *adj* **1** disinclined to obtrude oneself <*shy* in the presence of strangers>
f —— *syn* backward, bashful, coy, demure, diffident, modest, rabbity, retiring, self-effacing, timid, unassertive, unassured
g —— *rel* backhanded, hesitant, reluctant; conscious, self-conscious, self-distrustful, shamefaced, sheepish; introversive, introvert, introverted, inturned; circumspect, reserved; cautious, chary, suspicious, wary; apprehensive, fearful, nervous, skittish, timorous
h —— *con* brash, forward; aggressive, audacious, intrusive, obtruding, pushing, pushy; blunt, crass
i —— *ant* bold, obtrusive
c —— **2** *syn* DISINCLINED, afraid, averse, backward, hesitant, indisposed, loath, reluctant, uneager, unwilling
c —— **3** *syn* SHORT 3, deficient, failing, inadequate, insufficient, scant, scanty, scarce, unsufficient, wanting
con excess, over, surplus
a —— **shy** vb **1** *syn* DEMUR, balk, boggle, gag, jib, scruple, stick, stickle, strain, stumble *rel* blench, quail, recoil, shrink
2 *syn* ESCAPE 2, avoid, bilk, double, duck, elude, eschew,
a —— evade, shun
shy *n syn* POTSHOT, pot, sideswipe

a: Headword or main entry—Alphabetically listed, a boldface **headword** begins each entry. If a word can be used as more than one part of speech, each usage will have its own headword. For example, *shy*—which can be an adjective, a verb, and a noun—has three separate entries, each beginning with a boldface headword.

b: Part of speech—An italic abbreviation identifies the part of speech of each headword. You should first check this to make sure you have the correct form of the word. The print version of the *Merriam-Webster's Collegiate Thesaurus* uses the following abbreviations:

n	noun	*prep*	preposition
vb	verb	*conj*	conjunction
adj	adjective	*pron*	pronoun
adv	adverb	*interj*	interjection

c: Sense number— A boldface sense number indicates the different senses of meaning for each headword. The adjective headword for *shy* includes three sense numbers because it has three distinct meanings: (1) "bashful," (2) "afraid," and (3) "deficient." The verb *shy* lists two sense numbers for each sense of meaning: (1) "demur" and (2) "escape." The noun *shy* requires no sense numbers because it has only one sense of meaning: "potshot."

d: Meaning core—The definition and/or list of words following the sense number are grouped in a meaning core. All words in a meaning core are considered synonymous.

e: Verbal illustration—Contained within angle brackets < >, the verbal illustration provides a meaningful context for the headword. You can test whether you have located the correct sense of meaning for a word by seeing how it is used in the verbal illustration.

f: Synonym—The italic, boldface abbreviation ***syn*** introduces a list of synonyms or words with meanings that match the meaning of the headword. Each synonym in the list also has its own entry in the thesaurus.

g: Related words— The italic, boldface abbreviation ***rel*** introduces a list of words that are related or similar to the headword. They are not considered synonymous.

h: Contrasted words—The italic, boldface abbreviation ***con*** introduces a list of words whose meanings are different from the meaning of the headword. Contrasted words are not antonyms, however. The meaning of *pushy* contrasts but does not oppose that of *shy*; therefore, it is not considered an antonym.

i: Antonyms—The italic, boldface abbreviation ***ant*** introduces a list of antonyms, or words that have opposite meanings. The adjective *obtrusive* is an antonym, or opposite, of *shy*.

j: Synonym cross-references—A synonym cross-reference word appears in SMALL CAPITAL LETTERS and has its own entry elsewhere in the thesaurus. You can go to that entry to locate more words related to your original search word.

Savvy Use of a Thesaurus

By helping you locate appropriate words, a good thesaurus can be a valuable tool for expanding your vocabulary and improving your writing. A thesaurus is only a tool, however, and it's helpful only if you use it wisely.

A thesaurus offers suggestions for words, but only the user can determine which suggestion is appropriate. To make the most of a thesaurus, you have to consider the function of the word you want to replace. Is the word a noun, a verb, an adjective, or another part of speech? Are you replacing it with a word that shares the same part of speech? Is the meaning of the replacement word really the same as the meaning of the original word? A word can have many meanings. Be sure that your choices convey your intended meaning. Sometimes it's important to use a thesaurus in conjunction with a dictionary. With a good dictionary you can look up the meanings of words to make sure you have made the correct choices.

Online Thesauruses

Earlier in this appendix you learned about online dictionary Websites. Many of the same Websites offer thesauruses. The *Merriam-Webster's Collegiate Dictionary* Website, for example, is linked to the online *Merriam-Webster's Collegiate Thesaurus.*

Read this entire section before you access an online thesaurus. The following entry for the word *shy* comes from the online version of the *Merriam-Webster's Collegiate Thesaurus.* The labels **a** through **j** mark the key features of a typical online entry.

To arrive at the window displayed on the following page, you need to link with the home page of the *Merriam-Webster's Collegiate Thesaurus* Website and enter the word *shy* in the search tool. The online thesaurus will display the first, or main, entry for *shy.*

An entry in the online thesaurus looks very much like an entry in the print version. It includes all the same features, although different descriptive words are used for a few of them. To refresh your memory, refer back to the descriptions of features for the print version, starting on page 624.

The letters for the online entry match those for the print version. These include (**a**) headword or main entry (called **Entry Word**), (**b**) part of speech (called **Function**), (**c**) sense number, (**d**) meaning core, (**e**) verbal illustration, (**f**) synonyms, (**g**) related words, (**h**) contrasted words, (**i**) antonyms, and (**j**) synonym cross-references.

Merriam-Webster's
COLLEGIATE® THESAURUS

Merriam-Webster

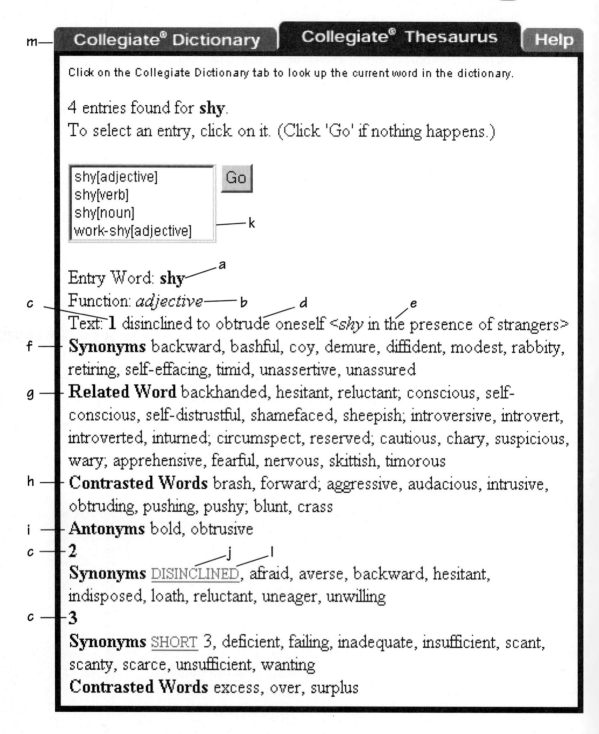

m — | Collegiate® Dictionary | Collegiate® Thesaurus | Help

Click on the Collegiate Dictionary tab to look up the current word in the dictionary.

4 entries found for **shy**.
To select an entry, click on it. (Click 'Go' if nothing happens.)

shy[adjective]
shy[verb]
shy[noun]
work-shy[adjective]

Go

— k

Entry Word: **shy** — a

c — Function: *adjective* — b

Text: 1 disinclined to obtrude oneself <*shy* in the presence of strangers>

f — **Synonyms** backward, bashful, coy, demure, diffident, modest, rabbity, retiring, self-effacing, timid, unassertive, unassured

g — **Related Word** backhanded, hesitant, reluctant; conscious, self-conscious, self-distrustful, shamefaced, sheepish; introversive, introvert, introverted, inturned; circumspect, reserved; cautious, chary, suspicious, wary; apprehensive, fearful, nervous, skittish, timorous

h — **Contrasted Words** brash, forward; aggressive, audacious, intrusive, obtruding, pushing, pushy; blunt, crass

i — **Antonyms** bold, obtrusive

c — **2**

Synonyms DISINCLINED, afraid, averse, backward, hesitant, indisposed, loath, reluctant, uneager, unwilling

c — **3**

Synonyms SHORT 3, deficient, failing, inadequate, insufficient, scant, scanty, scarce, unsufficient, wanting

Contrasted Words excess, over, surplus

The online version differs from the print version in one important way: the print thesaurus uses abbreviations such as *n*, *adv*, *syn*, *rel*, *con*, and *ant* to identify its features, while the online thesaurus clearly spells out all features and all parts of speech.

Special Features of Online Thesauruses

In addition to providing all the information available in a print thesaurus, an online thesaurus offers interactive features. Refer to the online entry for *shy* on page 626 as you read the descriptions of these special features.

k: Search results box—When the online thesaurus locates more than one entry for a word, a list of the results appears. The part of speech for each word is contained in brackets next to each word. You can click on any word to view its entry. For example, if you want to see synonyms for the verb form of *shy*, click on **shy[verb]** in the search results box.

l: Cross-reference link—The word you searched for may be automatically linked to other synonyms in the thesaurus. A word in SMALL CAPITAL LETTERS (usually underlined and in a different color) indicates such a link. You can access a linked word by clicking on the underlined word.

m: Dictionary tab—*Merriam-Webster's Collegiate Thesaurus* also provides a tabbed link to a dictionary. This link is especially helpful if you are not sure about the meaning or function of a word. To consult the complementary dictionary, you first highlight or click on an entry listed in the search results box. Next, you click on the dictionary tab (typically located at the top of the page). The dictionary entry for the selected word should appear.

Your Turn

Now that you have read the appendix, visit the online *Merriam-Webster's Collegiate Thesaurus*. Open your Internet browser and key in ***english-workshop.glencoe.com***, the address for *The English Workshop* Website. Click on Appendix B, then click on Thesauruses, and finally click on *Merriam-Webster's Collegiate Thesaurus*. At the home page of that site, key in *shy* and evaluate how well Appendix B introduced you to the actual Website. When you have finished your evaluation, exit from the site and visit one or more of the listed online thesauruses. Explore several of them on your own, and rate how useful and user-friendly they are.

Online and Print Spelling Resources

SPELLING AND EDITING TOOLS

Word-processing programs such as Microsoft Word include two useful editing tools, or features, that can help you develop professional-looking documents: a spell checker and a grammar checker. In this section you will learn about both. Although these editing tools are typically used together, each is described separately in this section.

Spell Checker

Each spell checker includes a dictionary with thousands of correctly spelled words. The spell checker helps you verify the spelling of words by comparing the words in your document to words listed in its dictionary. The spell checker skims your document until it finds a word not in its dictionary. It highlights that word and asks you to decide whether to correct its current spelling or ignore the spell checker and leave the word as is.

To use a spell checker most effectively, you need to be aware of what it can and cannot do. This section will help you better understand spell checkers by discussing one student's attempt to use the feature on a paragraph he wrote for a short class project.

Dana's Assignment

As part of a class assignment, Dana Miller is using Microsoft Word to develop a paragraph about the Nile River. When he began using the spell checker, the window on the following page appeared on his screen.

As you can see, the spell checker stopped at the first word in Dana's paragraph that did not have an exact match in its dictionary—*longests*. It then offered two suggestions: *longest* and *congests*. The first suggestion is the correct spelling for the word Dana wants. The spell checker will automatically replace the incorrect word with the correct version once Dana highlights the word *longest* and clicks on the Change button.

After Dana makes a decision about the misspelled word, the spell checker will continue checking the paragraph. Dana's complete paragraph has been labeled to help you understand the types of mistakes a spell checker will identify and the types it will overlook.

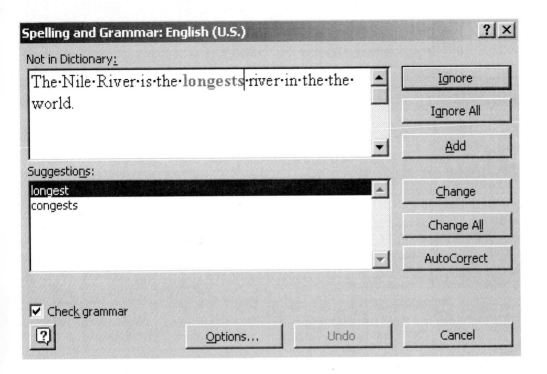

Dana's Complete Paragraph

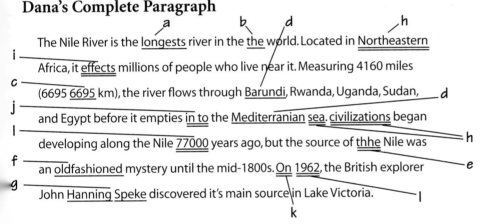

The Nile River is the longests river in the the world. Located in Northeastern Africa, it effects millions of people who live near it. Measuring 4160 miles (6695 6695 km), the river flows through Barundi, Rwanda, Uganda, Sudan, and Egypt before it empties in to the Mediterranian sea. civilizations began developing along the Nile 77000 years ago, but the source of thhe Nile was an oldfashioned mystery until the mid-1800s. On 1962, the British explorer John Hanning Speke discovered it's main source in Lake Victoria.

What a Spell Checker Will Highlight

Constructions a spell checker will highlight in Dana's paragraph are explained in **a** through **g** below:

a. **Spelling error**—word that is misspelled (*longests* for *longest*)

b. **Repeated word**—the same word appearing consecutively (*the the*)

c. **Repeated number**—the same number appearing consecutively with a space between each number (*6695 6695*)

d. **Misspelled common proper name**—commonly used name spelled incorrectly (*Barundi* for *Burundi* and *Mediterranian* for *Mediterranean*)

e. **Typographical error**—repeated letters or other keyboarding slips (*thhe* for *the*)

f. Fused compound—misspelling of compound word that should be hyphenated or written as two words (*oldfashioned* for *old-fashioned*)

g. Correctly spelled uncommon proper name—proper name not in the spell checker dictionary (*Hanning Speke*, which are both correct)

What a Spell Checker Will Not Highlight

A spell checker will not find all the mistakes in a document. Do not develop a false sense of security about its effectiveness. As you can see from items **h** through **l** in Dana's paragraph, a spell checker may not catch these types of errors:

h. Capitalization and style mistake—error in capitalization or style that does not affect meaning but disrupts readers (*Northeastern* for *northeastern* and *civilizations* for *Civilizations*)

i. Confused word—misuse of word that is easily confused with another because of a similar sound or spelling (*effects* for *affects*)

j. Word substitution—misuse of words that have different meanings as one or two words (*in to* for *into*)

k. Misused word—word spelled correctly but used incorrectly (*On* for *In*)

l. Mistake in numbers and dates—misuse of numbers and dates (*1962* for *1862*)

Spell Checker Strategies

Make the most of the spell checker that comes with your word-processing software by following these strategies:

1. Carefully proofread your document after it has been spell-checked.
2. Don't automatically select the first suggested correction offered by the spell checker. Carefully review all the suggestions before deciding which one to use. Look up words in a dictionary if you are unsure of your choice.
3. When a spell checker highlights a proper name, verify its correct spelling.
4. If you are working with proper nouns that repeatedly stop the spell checker, choose the *Add* option to include the correct spelling of the nouns in your spell checker's dictionary.
5. Use the *Ignore* option if you do not wish to make any changes to the word the spell checker highlights.

Your Turn

Explore how a spell checker works by keying Dana's paragraph in a word-processing document. Then run the spell checker. If your software has a grammar checker, turn off that feature to perform this experiment.

Grammar Checker

Another useful editing tool that comes with your word processor is a grammar checker. This feature automatically checks your document for a number of grammar errors. Like a spell checker, it will stop at a potential problem, highlight it, and offer a suggestion for correction. Just as you cannot rely on a spell checker to catch all spelling errors, you cannot rely on a grammar checker to find every grammatical mistake in your writing. To help you understand what a grammar checker can and cannot do, this section will explain the types of errors grammar checkers will identify and the types they will overlook. It will continue discussing Dana Miller's class project. This time you will see how the grammar checker in Microsoft Word reviews one of his paragraphs about the Nile River.

Dana's Assignment

In the last section, you learned that Dana wrote a paragraph about the Nile River and used a spell checker to help him locate spelling errors. After he used the spell checker, Dana lost the paragraph he had written. He re-keyed the paragraph and ran the grammar checker. The following window appeared on his screen.

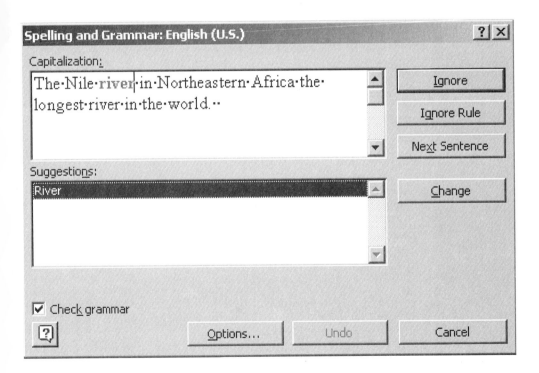

As you can see from the window above, the grammar checker stopped on the first use of the word *river*. In the *Suggestions* box, the grammar checker indicates that *river* should be capitalized. The grammar checker will automatically replace the lowercase *river* with a capitalized one once Dana clicks on the *Change* button.

After Dana makes a decision about the highlighted word, the grammar checker will continue checking the paragraph. Dana's complete second paragraph has been labeled below to help you understand the types of mistakes a grammar checker may highlight for you and the types it may not. The errors most grammar checkers catch are underlined once; the errors most of them ignore are highlighted twice.

Dana's Second Paragraph

The Nile river in Northeastern Africa the longest river in the world. Measuring 4160 miles (6695 km). it flows through Burundi, Rwanda, Uganda, Sudan, and egypt before he empties in to the Mediterranean see. Civilizations begans developing along the Nile 7000 years ago, the source of the Nile was a mystery until the mid-1800s. On 1861 it's main source in Lake Victoria was discovered by the British explorer John Hanning Speke.

What a Grammar Checker May Highlight

Constructions a grammar checker may highlight in Dana's second paragraph are explained in **a** through **h** below.

a. **Capitalization error of two-part place name**—the second word of a two-part place name, such as *Nile River*, presented with a lowercase letter

b. **Fragment**—a word group punctuated as a sentence that does not express a complete thought

c. **Capitalization error at beginning of a sentence**—the first word of a sentence presented with a lowercase letter (*it flows through . . .* for *It flows through . . .*)

d. **Common proper noun capitalization error**—an easily recognizable name presented with a lowercase letter (*egypt* for *Egypt*)

e. **Comma fault or splice**—two independent clauses joined by a comma instead of by a period, semicolon, colon, or both a comma and a coordinating conjunction

f. **Commonly confused word**—misuse of a word that is easily confused with another because of a similar sound or spelling (*it's* for *its*)

g. **Error in subject-verb agreement**—use of a plural verb with a singular subject or a singular verb with a plural subject (*Civilizations begans* for *Civilizations began*)

h. **Passive voice**—a sentence in which the subject receives the action described by the verb. If you converted the sentence to the active voice, it would read: *The British explorer John Hanning Speke discovered its main source in Lake Victoria.* Use of the passive voice is not automatically incorrect; however, most workplace writers prefer the more forceful and direct active voice.

What a Grammar Checker May Not Highlight

A grammar checker may not find all the mistakes in a document. Be aware of that possibility as you work with this feature. As you can see from items i through m labeled in Dana's paragraph, a grammar checker is not fool-proof.

i. **Capitalization error: direction**—a compass direction, such as *north-eastern Africa*, presented with a capital letter. Compass directions are capitalized only when they are names of specific places, such as *Ken Kesey writes about the Pacific Northwest.*

j. **Gerund phrase fragment**—a fragment that contains a gerund form (e.g., a noun formed from an –ing verb) and is punctuated as a sentence. For example, *Measuring 4160 miles (6695 km).*

k. **Word choice error**—Misuse of one word for another, such as *he* for *it* and *On* for *In*

l. **Homophone error**—Misuse of one homophone for another, such as *see* for *Sea*

m. **Word substitution**—Misuse of words that have different meanings as one or two words, such as *in to* for *into*

Grammar Checker Strategies

Grammar checkers may help you catch errors in your writing. Optimize your use of the grammar checker by following these strategies:

1. Carefully proofread your document even after you have used a grammar checker.
2. Don't automatically select the first suggested correction offered by the grammar checker. Review all the suggestions before deciding whether you want to use one or not. Check a grammar handbook if you need help with your choice. You may also want to consult a dictionary.
3. Verify any suggestion a grammar checker makes about a proper name.
4. Use the *Ignore* option if you do not wish to make any changes.
5. Use the *Ignore Rule* option if you are working with a construction that is correct but causes the grammar checker to stop repeatedly. For example, sometimes a grammar checker will flag all items in a list that do not begin with a capital letter. You may want a list that uses lower-case letters at times, so you may use the *Ignore Rule.*

Your Turn

Explore how a grammar checker works by keying Dana's second paragraph into a word-processing document exactly as he wrote it. Then run your grammar checker.

PRINT SPELLING RESOURCES

As we have seen, mistakes in grammar, punctuation, and usage may undermine your credibility as a writer. Mistakes in spelling may be even more damaging. Most people are very critical of spelling errors.

Correct spelling is not easy. English is a very diverse language and pronunciation is not necessarily much help in providing clues to the correct spelling of a word. Consider, for example, the following: *cough*—rhymes with *off*; *dough*—rhymes with *sew* and *so*; and *rough*—rhymes with *stuff*.

This does not mean that learning how to spell is a hopeless task. It isn't. Spelling is a skill and, like other skills, it can be learned. Despite the acknowledged inconsistencies in English spelling, there are more consistencies than inconsistencies. In fact, about nine out of ten words in English can be spelled correctly by following a set of spelling rules. Thus, it is of great value to be familiar with these rules.

Dictionaries and spelling texts list these rules in detail. There are exceptions, but the rules cover far more words than there are exceptions. Learn these six important rules and how to apply them.

Words That Double the Final Consonant

RULE: To add a suffix that begins with a *vowel*, double the final consonant if:

1. The word ends in a *single consonant* (except *w, x,* or *y*), and
2. This consonant is preceded by a *single vowel*, and
3. The word is pronounced with the accent on the *last syllable*.

Do not double the final consonant unless *all three* conditions are met.

This rule is not as complicated as it may sound at first. Just take it step by step. Because so many spelling errors are the result of failing to follow this rule, and because so many words are covered by this rule, it is well worth knowing.

EXAMPLES

admit	admitted	admitting	admittance
begin	beginner	beginning	
control	controlled	controlling	controllable
drop	dropped	dropping	dropper
fit	fitted	fitting	fittest
equip	equipped	equipping	
forget	forgettable	forgetting	
occur	occurred	occurring	occurrence
regret	regretted	regretting	regrettable
stop	stopped	stopping	stoppage
transfer	transferred	transferring	

Remember: Double the final consonant only when a word satisfies all three conditions. The final consonants of the following words are not doubled because the words do not meet all three conditions.

appear	appeared	appearing	appearance
box	boxed	boxing	
balloon	ballooned	ballooning	balloonist
concoct	concocted	concocting	concoction
credit	credited	crediting	creditor
differ	differed	differing	difference
endow	endowed	endowing	endowment
index	indexed	indexing	
parallel	paralleled	paralleling	
register	registered	registering	
tax	taxed	taxing	taxable
visit	visited	visiting	visitor

There are a few exceptions to this rule. They include the following words:

cancellation*	excellent	transferable*
crystallize*	gaseous	transference

* Some dictionaries also list a spelling variant that is less common: *cancelation, crystalize, transferrable.*

Words Ending in *e*

RULE: Drop the final *e* from a word when adding a suffix beginning with a vowel (*-ing, -able, -al, -er*). Do not drop the final e from a word when adding a suffix beginning with a consonant (*-ment, -less, -ly*).

As with the first rule, a great many spelling errors result from the failure to follow this rule. Learn it well.

EXAMPLES

achieve	achieved	achieving	achievement
advertise	advertised	advertising	advertisement
blame	blamed	blaming	blameless
complete	completed	completing	completely
excite	excited	exciting	excitement
forgive	forgivable	forgiving	forgiveness
hope	hoped	hoping	hopeful
measure	measurable	measuring	measurement
like	liked	liking	likely
move	moved	moving	movement
use	usage	using	useless

The few exceptions to this rule are listed below.

abridge	abridgment*	judge	judgment*
acknowledge	acknowledgment*	nine	ninth
argue	argument	true	truly
awe	awful	whole	wholly
due	duly		

* Some dictionaries also list a variant that does not drop the final *e*: *abridgement, acknowledgement, judgement.*

Words Ending in *ce* or *ge*

RULE: Do not drop the final *e* from words ending in *ce* or *ge* when adding *-able* or *-ous*. The final *e* is retained to keep the *c* and *g* soft—like *s* and *j*.

EXAMPLES

acknowledge	acknowledgeable	marriage	marriageable
advantage	advantageous	outrage	outrageous
change	changeable	notice	noticeable
courage	courageous	service	serviceable
manage	manageable		

Words Containing *ei* or *ie*

RULE: Write *i* before *e*,
Except after *c*,
Or when sounded like *a*,
As in *neighbor* or *weigh*.

Remembering the three parts to this verse will help you solve most spelling problems involving *ei* or *ie*.

Write *i* before *e*—

achieve	cashier	grief	patient
aggrieve	client	lien	relief
audience	field	mischief	review
believe	friend	niece	yield
brief			

Except after *c*—

ceiling	conceive	deceive	receipt
conceit	deceit	perceive	receive

Or when sounded like *a*—

beige	freight	reign	vein
eight	heir	surveillance	weight
feint	neighbor		

As with other rules, there are some exceptions:

ancient	efficient	leisure	sleight
caffeine	financier	neither	sovereign
conscience	foreign	science	sufficient
counterfeit	forfeit	seize	weird
either	height	sheik	

Prefixes and Suffixes

RULE: When adding a prefix that ends with the same letter that begins the main word, include both letters. When adding a suffix that begins with the same letter that ends the main word, include both letters.

EXAMPLES: PREFIXES

dis	+	similar	=	dissimilar
il	+	legal	=	illegal
im	+	mature	=	immature
inter	+	regional	=	interregional
mis	+	spell	=	misspell
over	+	rule	=	overrule
un	+	necessary	=	unnecessary
under	+	rate	=	underrate

EXAMPLES: SUFFIXES

accidental	+	ly	=	accidentally
actual	+	ly	=	actually
cruel	+	ly	=	cruelly
respectful	+	ly	=	respectfully
common	+	ness	=	commonness
even	+	ness	=	evenness
mean	+	ness	=	meanness
sudden	+	ness	=	suddenness

Words Ending in *y*

RULE: Words that end in *y* preceded by a consonant usually change to *i* before the addition of any suffix, except suffixes beginning with the letter *i*.

Words that end in *y* preceded by a vowel do not change *y* to *i* when a suffix is added.

EXAMPLES:

Words ending in *y* preceded by a consonant:

accompany	accompanies	accompaniment	accompanying
apply	applied	application	applying
bury	buried	burial	burying
comply	complies	complied	complying
identify	identified	identification	identifying
notify	notified	notification	notifying
rely	relies	reliable	relying
study	studies	studious	studying
verify	verified	verifiable	verifying

Words ending in *y* preceded by a vowel:

annoy	annoyed	annoyance	annoying
convey	conveyed	conveyance	conveying
display	displayed	displayable	displaying
employ	employed	employment	employing
survey	surveyed	surveyor	surveying

Note that this rule applies to forming the plurals of nouns ending in *y*.

company	companies	attorney	attorneys
secretary	secretaries	boy	boys
variety	varieties	valley	valleys

There are a few exceptions to the rule:

day	+ ly	=	daily
gay	+ ly	=	gaily
lay	+ ed	=	laid
pay	+ ed	=	paid
say	+ ed	=	said

Mnemonic Devices

There are two basic ways to learn to spell the one word in ten that is not covered by a spelling rule or that is an exception to the rule. The first is to use some form of memory aid to help you remember the spelling. Such aids are called **mnemonic devices**. Word associations, sayings, visualizations—anything that can help you remember how to spell a word—can be effective mnemonic devices. Here are some examples:

stationERy   papER

stationAry   plAce

"I see a *rat* in sep*arat*e."

"A good *secret*ary keeps an employer's *secret*s."

"*Brrr.* It's cold in Fe*br*uary.

Memorization

The other way to learn how to spell a word is simply to memorize it. If the word does not conform to the spelling rules and you can't think of a useful mnemonic device, you will have to resort to rote learning. Simply commit the word to memory. Follow these three basic steps.

1. *See it*. Examine the word. Note distinctive letter sequences and common letter groupings.
2. *Say it*. Pronounce the word slowly and clearly. Then close your eyes and visualize the word as you say it and spell it.
3. *Write it*. Write the word several times, saying each letter as you write or type it. Write it several more times until the word is thoroughly familiar.

Do not start your program of spelling improvement by memorizing lists of words. Rote memorization should be your last resort. First, become familiar with the rules that govern the large majority of words in the language. Then develop mnemonic devices for as many difficult words as you can that are exceptions to the rules. Finally, commit the remaining words that you need to know to memory. Remember the best rule of all: When in doubt, consult your dictionary.

Writing Models for Today's Electronic Workplace

Today's workers have a variety of options for communicating inside and outside of their organizations. When they communicate in writing, they typically choose from three popular formats: letters, memos, and e-mail messages. Writers select the best format based on the purpose and content of their message, the identity and location of the person who will be receiving it, and the level of formality they desire. Sometimes it is also necessary to find out what type of electronic equipment a recipient is using.

Successful communication depends on the correct use of grammar, punctuation, and style. How a document appears on the page is also important. A clean and organized appearance will contribute to the positive impression a document will make on a recipient. A letter or memo with an unusual appearance might draw the reader's attention to how it looks rather than to what it actually says.

Readers typically expect to find certain letter styles and parts in written communications. These standard styles and parts help a reader focus on what a letter is saying. In the following pages you will find figures illustrating the key parts of four basic writing models: the full-block letter, the modified-block letter, the memo, and the e-mail message.

Business Letters

You can use one of two letter formats to send formal messages outside of the workplace: (1) the **full-block letter** or (2) the **modified-block letter** with either blocked paragraphs or indented paragraphs. These formats differ in terms of where the letter parts appear on the page.

Certain letter parts appear in every formal letter. These include a date, an inside address, a salutation, a body, a complimentary close, and a signature block. In some situations you may want to include additional information, such as reference initials, an enclosure notation, or a postscript note.

There are two punctuation styles used in workplace letters: **standard punctuation** and **open punctuation**. In standard punctuation style, you insert a colon after the salutation and a comma after the complimentary close. Open punctuation requires no punctuation after the salutation and the complimentary close. The examples in this book use the more common standard style of punctuation.

Full-Block Letters

a **STYLE, INC.**
26431 Pinecrest Lane
Johnson City, TN 37601
423-765-4546

b September 4, 20--

c Josefa Lucha
Lake Greetings Co.
3500 Stewart Avenue
Medford, OR 97501

d Dear Ms. Lucha:

e Thank you for your query regarding our guidelines for writing professional letters. As requested, I am sending you samples illustrating the two letter styles used most often for formal office correspondence, as well as examples of an office memo and an e-mail message.

This letter illustrates the full-block style. All lines begin at the left-hand margin. Because this style is so simple and efficient, it is widely used and preferred by many in the workplace. To keep your letter visually interesting, the first and last paragraphs should not exceed four lines of text, and all other paragraphs should be no longer than eight lines.

If you dislike this arrangement because everything is on the left and the letter appears unbalanced, you might prefer the modified-block style on page 644. For the sake of consistency, however, you will probably want to select one particular letter format to be used by all your departments.

In addition to the sample letters, I am enclosing a key describing the standard parts of the business letter that you may find helpful.

f Sincerely yours,

g Laurice Casteneda
Office Service Supervisor

h alw

i Enc.

j cc: Mr. Maurice Scully

k PS. You may include a postscript with any of these letter styles.

Key Parts of Full-Block and Modified-Block Letters

Include the following parts in every professional letter you write:

a: Letterhead—Stationery printed with a company's name, address, telephone number, and fax number is called "letterhead." Letterhead may also include the company's logo or slogan. Most organizations use $8^1/_2 \times 11$-inch stationery with printed letterhead.

b: Date—The date usually appears three line spaces below the letterhead. Use either of these forms: *January 15, 2001* or *15 January 2001*.

c: Inside address—The inside address includes the name and the company address (street, city, state, and ZIP code) of the person to whom the letter is being sent.

d: Salutation—You can begin your letter with a salutation—a word or phrase of greeting such as *Dear Ms. Garcia* or *Dear Customer*. The salutation appears two lines below the inside address block and one or two lines above the body of the letter.

e: Message—The message of a letter can be divided into three parts: the opening, the body, and the closing. The opening begins with the main idea of the letter. Next, the body of the message includes additional information that typically clarifies the opening. Finally, the closing summarizes the message and/or requests an action to be taken. In most professional letters, the message is single-spaced. For the sake of organization and readability, paragraphs are fairly short and are double-spaced from one another.

f: Complimentary close—Depending on the nature of the message, the complimentary close may range from informal (e.g., *Sincerely, Cordially*) to formal (e.g., *Very truly yours, Respectfully yours*). Located two spaces below the letter's message, it is typically a polite expression of the writer's regard for the recipient. As the following examples indicate, capitalize only the first letter of a close, and place a comma after the last word unless you are using open punctuation.

Sincerely,	Cordially yours,	Respectfully,
Kyle De Cinces	*Marnie N. Steen*	*Jun Zhang*
Kyle De Cinces, President	Marnie N. Steen Reservations Manager	Jun Zhang

g: Writer's name and title—To allow enough room to sign your name, key in your name three or four line spaces below the complimentary close. If you want to indicate your title, enter it beside or below your keyboarded name.

Optional Parts of Full-Block and Modified-Block Letters

In some situations you may want to include the following letter parts:

h: Reference initials—When someone other than the writer keys in a business letter, the initials of the person doing the keyboarding may be inserted two spaces below the writer's name and title. Before personal computers became part of every manager's office, assistants typed correspondence dictated or handwritten by supervisors. The assistants marked their work with their initials to show who had typed each document. Today most managers answer their own e-mail and compose much of their correspondence at their own computers. The use of reference initials is diminishing.

i: Enclosure notation—If you have additional materials to enclose with your letter, use an enclosure notation to remind the recipient to look for them. Key in the abbreviation *Enc.* two spaces below the reference initials. If you are not using reference initials, place the enclosure notation two lines below the writer's title.

j: Copy notation—The copy notation tells the primary recipient that other people will also receive copies of the letter. If you need to make a copy notation, enter the initials *cc* followed by the name(s) of the other person(s) to whom the letter is being sent. A colon after *cc* is optional. In most letters, you will place the copy notation one or two lines below the writer's title. When it is necessary to include reference initials and/or an enclosure notation, place the *cc* one or two lines below the last item.

k: Postscript—If you want to add comments to the end of a letter, include a postscript. In general, it is used to express an afterthought or to give an idea special emphasis. Insert your postscript two lines below the last part of the letter. Key in *PS*, *PS:*, or *PS.* before the first word of your postscript message.

Modified-Block Letters

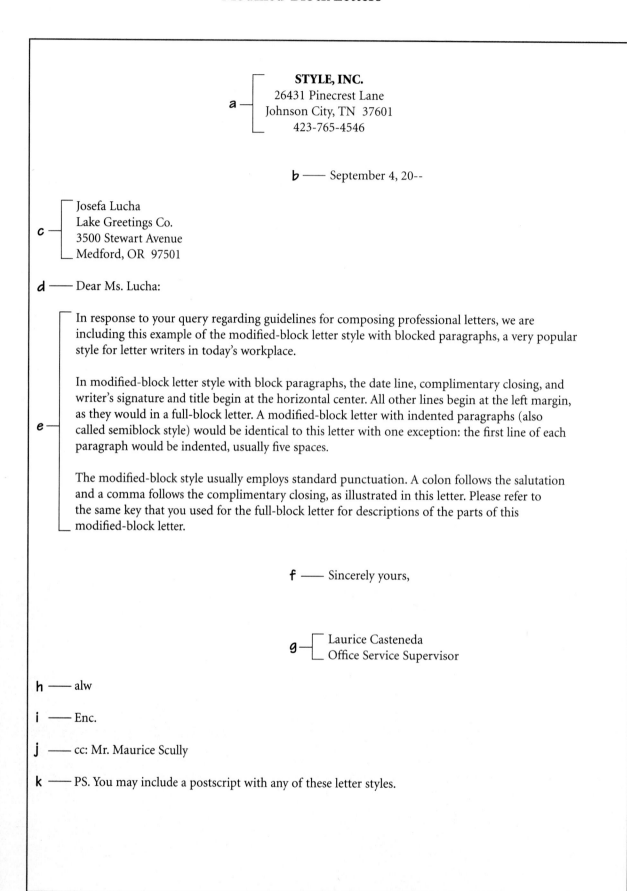

STYLE, INC.
a
26431 Pinecrest Lane
Johnson City, TN 37601
423-765-4546

b —— September 4, 20--

c
Josefa Lucha
Lake Greetings Co.
3500 Stewart Avenue
Medford, OR 97501

d —— Dear Ms. Lucha:

In response to your query regarding guidelines for composing professional letters, we are including this example of the modified-block letter style with blocked paragraphs, a very popular style for letter writers in today's workplace.

In modified-block letter style with block paragraphs, the date line, complimentary closing, and writer's signature and title begin at the horizontal center. All other lines begin at the left margin, as they would in a full-block letter. A modified-block letter with indented paragraphs (also called semiblock style) would be identical to this letter with one exception: the first line of each paragraph would be indented, usually five spaces.

e

The modified-block style usually employs standard punctuation. A colon follows the salutation and a comma follows the complimentary closing, as illustrated in this letter. Please refer to the same key that you used for the full-block letter for descriptions of the parts of this modified-block letter.

f —— Sincerely yours,

g
Laurice Casteneda
Office Service Supervisor

h —— alw

i —— Enc.

j —— cc: Mr. Maurice Scully

k —— PS. You may include a postscript with any of these letter styles.

Memos

A memo is used for written communication between one or more persons within a company or organization. Every memo has a job to do, whether it is to remind, request, or inform.

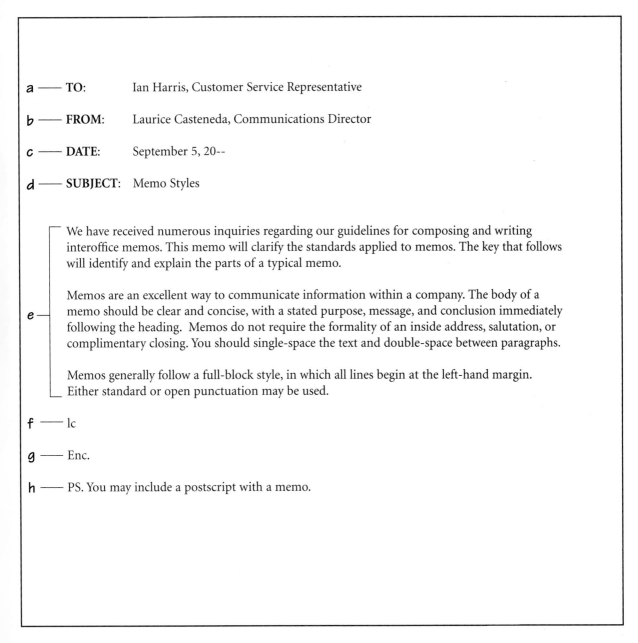

a — TO: Ian Harris, Customer Service Representative

b — FROM: Laurice Casteneda, Communications Director

c — DATE: September 5, 20--

d — SUBJECT: Memo Styles

e —

We have received numerous inquiries regarding our guidelines for composing and writing interoffice memos. This memo will clarify the standards applied to memos. The key that follows will identify and explain the parts of a typical memo.

Memos are an excellent way to communicate information within a company. The body of a memo should be clear and concise, with a stated purpose, message, and conclusion immediately following the heading. Memos do not require the formality of an inside address, salutation, or complimentary closing. You should single-space the text and double-space between paragraphs.

Memos generally follow a full-block style, in which all lines begin at the left-hand margin. Either standard or open punctuation may be used.

f — lc

g — Enc.

h — PS. You may include a postscript with a memo.

Key Parts of Memos

Include the following parts in every memo you write:

a: To—After the word *To*, enter the name(s) of the person(s) to whom the memo is being sent. You can omit courtesy titles (e.g., *Mr.*, *Ms.*) in memo headings, but use professional titles when:

- The name of the recipient is the same as, or could easily be confused with, that of another employee.
- The writer wishes to show respect to a superior.
- The writer wishes to ensure prompt delivery of the memo.

b: From—Enter your name and your professional title. In many instances, it may be appropriate to omit your title; but, for the sake of consistency, use it if you have included a title with the recipient's name.

c: Date—Enter the date in full to help prevent misinterpretation. Use either of these forms: *January 15, 2001* or *15 January 2001*.

d: Subject line—The subject line summarizes the topic of the memo. It can also serve as an aid in filing the memo for future reference. When writing a subject line, try to be concise and specific. Capitalize the first letter of each main word, and leave a triple space between the subject line and the body.

e: Body—The body of the memo includes a purpose, a message, and a conclusion. Begin with your purpose. Explain to the recipient why you are writing the memo. Your message should cover all points of the topic; for example, giving directions, explaining your reasoning, or describing the benefits of a plan. In your conclusion, summarize the key points of the memo and suggest future action. In general, single-space the body and double-space between paragraphs.

Optional Parts of Memos

In some cases, you may need to include the following parts in your memo:

f: Reference initials—When someone other than the writer prepares a memo, the reference initials of the keyboardist should appear in lower-case letters at the left-hand margin two lines below the body.

g: Enclosure notation—If you are enclosing other materials with a memo, insert an enclosure notation—the abbreviation *Enc.*—below the reference initials. If there are no reference initials, enter it two lines below the body. This will tell the recipient to look for additional enclosed materials.

h: Postscript—You may use a postscript to add comments to the end of a memo. This allows you to express an afterthought or give an idea special emphasis. Enter the postscript two lines below the last part of the memo. Type *PS*, *PS:*, or *PS.* before the first word of your postscript message.

E-mail Messages

An electronic message, or e-mail, is a message transmitted from your computer to your recipient's computer via the Internet or other computer networks. E-mail messaging is the most popular method of exchanging written information in the workplace today. E-mail messages may be sent locally or to distant locations. The only requirement is that the sender and the recipient both have access to a computer network.

Various computer systems and software may be used for e-mail. Most of them use a common format known as a **compose message template**. An example of a compose message template, from Microsoft Outlook, is shown below.

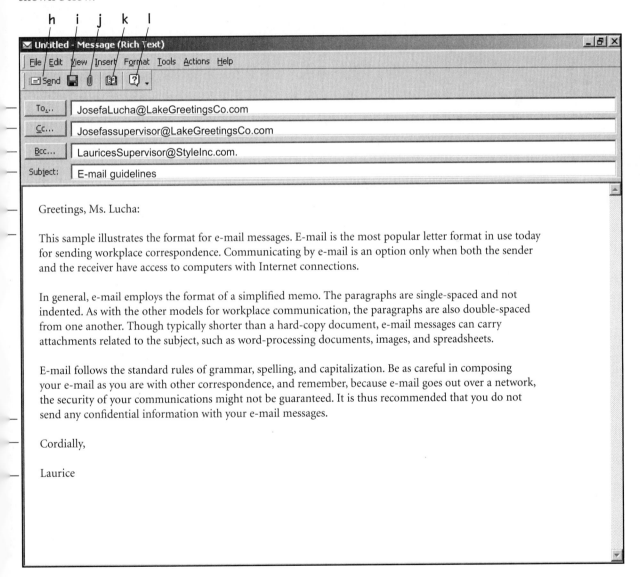

Greetings, Ms. Lucha:

This sample illustrates the format for e-mail messages. E-mail is the most popular letter format in use today for sending workplace correspondence. Communicating by e-mail is an option only when both the sender and the receiver have access to computers with Internet connections.

In general, e-mail employs the format of a simplified memo. The paragraphs are single-spaced and not indented. As with the other models for workplace communication, the paragraphs are also double-spaced from one another. Though typically shorter than a hard-copy document, e-mail messages can carry attachments related to the subject, such as word-processing documents, images, and spreadsheets.

E-mail follows the standard rules of grammar, spelling, and capitalization. Be as careful in composing your e-mail as you are with other correspondence, and remember, because e-mail goes out over a network, the security of your communications might not be guaranteed. It is thus recommended that you do not send any confidential information with your e-mail messages.

Cordially,

Laurice

Parts and Special Options of E-mail

E-mail typically includes the following parts and special options:

a: **Address box**—In most electronic messaging systems, the address box is next to the word *To*. This is where you enter the e-mail address of the person to whom the message is to be sent. If you are sending e-mail to more than one person, separate each address with a comma or, depending on your Internet server, a semicolon.

b: **Courtesy copy box**—The courtesy copy box tells the recipient that other people will also receive a copy. In this box, usually marked *Cc* or *cc*, key in the additional e-mail address(es). If you send a copy to more than one person, separate each *cc* address with a comma or a semicolon.

c: **Subject box**—All e-mail messages have a subject line on which you insert the topic of the message. Capitalize the subject as you would a title. Avoid using all capital letters in subject lines and e-mail messages in general.

d: **Blind courtesy copy box**—You may wish to send a copy of your e-mail message to someone without letting the primary recipient know. To send a secret copy, insert the e-mail address of that person in the blind courtesy copy box, usually marked *Bcc* or *bcc*.

e: **Message box**—

   1. **Salutation**—A greeting will personalize your e-mail message. Salutations such as *Hello, (Name)*, *Thank you, (Name)*, or even *Dear (Name)* are examples of appropriate openings. Follow your personal preference. Leave one line of space above and below the salutation to set it off from the body of your message. Depending on the level of formality you want, you may choose to end your greeting with a colon (most formal), a comma (conversational), or even a dash or two hyphens.
   2. **Body**—In general, e-mail messages are brief. Use short paragraphs, single-space the text, and double-space between paragraphs. Longer messages may be composed in a memo or business letter format and sent as attachments with your e-mail.

f: **Complimentary close**—The complimentary close is optional in an e-mail message. It may range from informal (e.g., *Sincerely, Cordially*) to formal (e.g., *Very truly yours, Respectfully yours*). The close should follow the same punctuation style—standard or open—as the salutation.

g: **Signature**—Initials or an automatic signature at the end of your e-mail may add a personal touch to your message. Some e-mail programs include a feature that allows you to insert a scanned copy of your signature. Otherwise, simply key in your name or initials.

h: **Send button**—Once you have written your message and proofread it carefully, send it by clicking on the *Send* button. Some computer systems may ask you to confirm your decision to send the message.

i: **Save/Send later button**—You can interrupt and save an incomplete e-mail message at any time by clicking on the *Save/Send later* button. If you need to check information, do research, or decide whether to cancel your message altogether, save it in a draft folder and retrieve it later.

j. **Attachment button**—E-mail attachments allow text and graphics to be transmitted in a matter of minutes. If you wish to send a word-processing document, a spreadsheet, a presentation, an image, or another kind of document, you can send an electronic version by attaching it to an e-mail message. If the recipient has compatible software, the file can be downloaded and the attachment opened in the same program in which it was created.

k. **Address book button**—For convenient access, use the address book button to store the e-mail addresses of individuals to whom you write frequently. This option prevents the occurrence of keyboarding errors in e-mail addresses.

l. **Help button**—Click on the *Help* button when you need assistance using the features of the e-mail messaging system.

APPENDIX E

Common Abbreviations

States and Territories

	Common	ZIP		Common	ZIP
Alabama	Ala.	AL	Montana	Mont.	MT
Alaska		AK	Nebraska	Nebr.	NE
American Samoa		AS	Nevada	Nev.	NV
Arizona	Ariz.	AZ	New Hampshire	N.H.	NH
Arkansas	Ark.	AK	New Jersey	N.J.	NJ
California	Calif.	CA	New Mexico	N. Mex.	NM
Colorado	Colo.	CO	New York	N.Y.	NY
Connecticut	Conn.	CT	North Carolina	N.C.	NC
Delaware	Del.	DE	North Dakota	N. Dak.	ND
District of Columbia	D.C.	DC	Northern Mariana		
Federated States of			Islands		MP
Micronesia		FM	Ohio		OH
Florida	Fla.	FL	Oklahoma	Okla.	OK
Georgia	Ga.	GA	Oregon	Oreg.	OR
Guam		GU	Palau		PW
Hawaii		HI	Pennsylvania	Pa.	PA
Idaho		ID	Puerto Rico	P.R.	PR
Illinois	Ill.	IL	Rhode Island	R.I.	RI
Indiana	Ind.	IN	South Carolina	S.C.	SC
Iowa		IA	South Dakota	S. Dak.	SD
Kansas	Kans.	KS	Tennessee	Tenn.	TN
Kentucky	Ky.	KY	Texas	Tex.	TX
Louisiana	La.	LA	Utah		UT
Maine		ME	Vermont	Vt.	VT
Marshall Islands		MH	Virginia	Va.	VA
Maryland	Md.	MD	Virgin Islands	V.I.	VI
Massachusetts	Mass.	MA	Washington	Wash.	WA
Michigan	Mich.	MI	West Virginia	W. Va.	WV
Minnesota	Minn.	MN	Wisconsin	Wis.	WI
Mississippi	Miss.	MS	Wyoming	Wyo.	WY
Missouri	Mo.	MO			

Geographical Places and Compass Directions

East	E		South	S
North	N		Southeast	SE
Northeast	NE		Southwest	SW
Northwest	NW		West	W

Units of Measure

Length

centimeter	cm
foot, feet	ft
inch	in
meter	m
mile	mi
millimeter	mm
yard	yd

Weight

centigram	cg
gram	g
grain	gr
kilogram	kg
pound	lb
milligram	mg
ounce	oz

Common Workplace Words

abbreviated, abbreviation	abbr.	manufacturing	mfg.
acknowledged	ack.	manufacturer	mfr.
additional	addl.	miscellaneous	misc.
also known as	a.k.a.	not available,	
as soon as possible	ASAP	not applicable	NA
department	dept.	obsolete	obs.
division	div.	optional	opt.
doing business as	DBA	public relations	PR
end of month	e.o.m., EOM	quarter(ly)	qtr.
Equal Employment	EEO	registered	reg.
Opportunity		to be announced	t.b.a., TBA
extension	ext.	to be determined	t.b.d., TBD
Headquarters	HQ	very important person	VIP
I owe you	IOU	with	w/
initial	init.	without, week of	w/o
insurance	ins.	year to date	YTD
limited	Ltd.		

Terms Used in Workplace Writing

and others	et al.	in regard to	re
attachment	att.	inclusive, including	incl.
attention	attn.	italics	ital.
copy, copies	c, cc	line, lines	l., ll.
care of	c/o	page, pages	p., pp.
continued	cont.	post office	P.O.
enclosure, enclosed	enc.	postpaid, prepaid	ppd.
Esquire	Esq.	postscript	PS, PS.
et cetera, and so forth	etc.	Reply, if you please	R.S.V.P.
for example	e.g.	revised	rev.
for your information	FYI	Self-addressed stamped envelope	(SASE)
forward	fwd.		

Computer Abbreviations

American Standard Code for Information Interchange	ASCII
Attention Dial Tone	ATDT
Beginner's All-Purpose Symbolic Instruction Code	BASIC
binary digit	bit
bits per second	bps
bulletin board services	BBSs
Business to Business	B2B
central processing unit	CPU
compact disc-read-only memory	CD-ROM
computer aid design	CAD
control	CTRL
Digital Subscriber Line	DSL
Digital Video Disk	DVD
directory	DIR
disk operating system	DOS
dots per inch	dpi
electronic mail	e-mail
end of file	EOF
frequently asked questions	FAQ
Global Positioning Satellite/System	GPS
Hyper Text Markup Language	HTML
Hyper Text Transport Protocol	HTTP
Information Superhighway	I-Way
information technology	IT
input/output	I/O
internet protocol	IP
internet service provider	ISP
kilobyte	KB, K
local area network	LAN
liquid crystal display	LCD
megabyte	MB, M
message	MSG
network computer	NC
operating system	OS
personal computer	PC
personal information manager	PIM
post office protocol	POP
printer	PRN
print screen	PRTSC
public domain	PD
random-access memory	RAM
read-only memory	ROM
text telephone	TTY
simple mail transfer protocol	SMTP
system operator	SYSOP
temporary	TEMP, TMP
voice mail	VM
wide area network	WAN
words per minute	WPM
the World Wide Web	WWW or W3
write once-read many times	WORM

Glossary of Confusing Words

GLOSSARY OF COMMONLY CONFUSED AND MISUSED WORDS

The following glossary is arranged alphabetically. Each word is defined and illustrated so that you can clearly see the context in which it is used correctly.

1. Accede/Exceed

The verb *accede* means "to accept or agree, to consent."

> The company refused to *accede* to the union's contract demands.

Accede can also mean "to assume or succeed to an office or title."

> Queen Liliuokalani *acceded* to the throne in 1891.

The verb *exceed* means "to go beyond or surpass."

> Be careful not to *exceed* the speed limit.

2. Accept/Except

The verb *accept* means "to consent to, to agree to" or "to take willingly, to receive."

> I am pleased to *accept* your offer.

Except is normally a preposition meaning "with the exclusion of, other than, but."

> All the students *except* Yuko completed the optional assignment.

Except is also used as a conjunction meaning "if it were not for the fact that."

> I would buy a new sports car *except* I couldn't afford the insurance.

3. Access/Excess

Access means "a passage, a way, a means, or admittance." It can be used as a noun or a verb.

> Liz will not have *access* to her inheritance for another two years. (noun)
> All branch officers may *access* the central data bank. (verb)

Excess refers to an amount or degree beyond what is normal or required. It can be used as an adjective or a noun. When you do something to *excess*, you are being *excessive*.

> The chef trimmed the *excess* fat from the steaks. (adjective)
> We discovered we had an *excess* of ten boxes of material. (noun)

4. *Adapt/Adopt/Adept*

Adapt and *adopt* are verbs. When you *adapt* something, you change or adjust it to a new situation or purpose.

> These plans can be *adapted* to fit your needs.

When you *adopt* something, you take it and use it as your own.

> We will *adopt* your proposal.

Adept is an adjective. When you are *adept*, you are skillful or expert in what you do.

> Aishwanya is *adept* at designing merchandise displays.

5. *Adverse/Averse*

These words are frequently confused not only because they are similar in appearance but also because their meanings are similar. Both words are adjectives.

Adverse means "hostile, unfavorable, harmful."

> The game was postponed due to *adverse* weather conditions.

Averse means "opposed to" or "disinclined."

> She is *averse* to working overtime.

The noun form of *averse* is *aversion*.

> She has an *aversion* to working overtime.

6. *Advice/Advise*

Advice is a noun meaning "opinion, counsel."

Advise is a verb meaning "to offer advice, to counsel."

> What is your *advice* regarding this problem?
> What do you *advise* me to do?

Advise is also used to mean "to inform, to notify."

> Please *advise* me when the new shipment arrives.

7. *Affect/Effect*

Affect is a verb usually meaning "to influence."

> The purpose of her speech was to *affect* the board's decision.

Effect is often used as a noun meaning "result."

> Her speech had the desired *effect*.

In plural form, *effects* can also mean "belongings or property."

> She kept her personal *effects* in the top drawer of her desk.

Effect can also be used as a verb meaning "to bring about."

> We intend to *effect* a few minor changes in company policy.

8. Allot/Alot/A lot

Alot is a common misspelling of *a lot*.

Although the phrase *a lot* is correct, it is vague and should be avoided in formal writing. Choose a word or words that are more precise.

WRONG: I like my job *alot*.
RIGHT: ✔ I like my job *a lot*.
BETTER: ✔ I like my job better than any of my previous summer jobs.

The verb *to allot* means "to assign a share, to allocate." The amount allocated is the *allotment*.

> Ms. Gitkin told us to *allot* more than three days to this project.

VAGUE: To *allot* four cases to each distributor is *a lot*.
BETTER: ✔ To *allot* four cases to each distributor is more than is necessary.

9. Allude/Elude

The verb *allude* means "to make an indirect reference."

> During her lecture, Professor Jankowski *alluded* to Willa Cather's *My Antonia*.

In cases like these, do not use *elude*, which means "to escape notice or detection."

> The thief hid in an alley in an effort to *elude* the police.

10. Allusion/Illusion

An *allusion* is an indirect reference.

> During her lecture, Professor Jankowski made an *allusion* to Willa Cather's *My Antonia*.

An *illusion* is a deceptive impression or false image.

> It would be an *illusion* to believe that sales will continue during the winter months.

Elusion is an act of eluding or evading. The word is rarely used. There is no such word as *illude*.

11. Amount/Number

The word *amount* refers to a thing in bulk or mass.

> Newspapers recycle a large *amount* of newsprint every day.

Use *number* for things that can be counted as individual items.

> A *number* of students are home ill with the flu.

12. *Anxious/Eager*

Anxious is an adjective derived from the noun *anxiety*, meaning "worry." An anxious person is someone who is perplexed, concerned, or disturbed. *Eager* comes from *eagerness*, meaning "enthusiasm, interest, desire." An eager person, therefore, is enthusiastic.

WRONG: I am *anxious* to see my friend tomorrow.

RIGHT: ✔ I am *eager* to see my friend tomorrow.

If you are worried, not eager, you would write:

RIGHT: ✔ I am *anxious* about my mother's health.

13. *Appraise/Apprise*

Appraise means *to estimate, to make an evaluation of, to judge.*

> The bank will *appraise* our property on Third Avenue next week.

Do not confuse *appraise* with *apprise*, which means "to notify, to inform."

WRONG: Please *appraise* me of your decision.

RIGHT: ✔ Please *apprise* me of your decision.

14. *Ascent/Assent*

Ascent is a noun. It refers to the act of rising. The verb form is *ascend.*

> Colorful publicity balloons made their *ascent* into the sky when the political rally began.

Assent can be a verb, meaning "to agree, to give consent." It can also be a noun, meaning "agreement."

> The board of trustees gave its *assent* to the team's planned *ascent* of Mount Everest.

15. *Being That/Being As*

There is no such conjunction as *being that* or *being as.* They are nonstandard phrases for *since* or *because.*

WRONG: *Being that* she was prepared for the exam, she passed it easily.

RIGHT: ✔ *Since* she was prepared for the exam, she passed it easily.

WRONG: *Being as* it was raining, the game was postponed.

RIGHT: ✔ *Because* it was raining, the game was postponed.

Do not use *seeing as how* for *since* or *because.* It is a nonstandard phrase.

WRONG: *Seeing as how* she isn't here, I'll come back tomorrow.

RIGHT: ✔ *Because* she isn't here, I'll come back tomorrow.

16. Can/May

Be careful to use *can* and *may* properly.

Can means "is capable of." In other words, *can* refers to physical ability.

May means "has permission to." In other words, *may* refers to consent.

> *May* I leave work an hour early? *(Will you give me permission to leave work early?)*
>
> *Can* you spare me? *(Are you capable of getting along without me?)*

17. Canvas/Canvass

Canvas, a noun, is a closely woven cloth or fabric.

> At her retirement dinner Joan received a set of *canvas* luggage.

Canvass, a verb, means "to go through a district or area soliciting votes for a candidate or orders for a product."

> The candidate's supporters *canvassed* the ward.

18. Capital/Capitol

Capital has various meanings. In a business context, you may use it most often to refer to wealth or assets.

> Do we have sufficient *capital* for such a major investment?

Capital is also used in the following senses:

> Begin every sentence with a *capital* letter.
> Do you believe that *capital* punishment is a deterrent?
> Baton Rouge is the state *capital* of Louisiana.

The building in which the legislature meets, however, is called the *capitol*.

> Ms. James has an important meeting at the *capitol* in Baton Rouge.

Although *capitol* is often written with a small *c* when it refers to a state building, it is always written with a capital *C* when it refers to the home of the United States Congress.

> From Baton Rouge, Ms. James will fly to Washington to meet with Senator Covington at the *Capitol*.

19. Cite/Site/Sight

The word *sight*, referring to the ability to see, should not pose any problems.

> Lester Garland has lost the *sight* in one eye.

However, *cite* and *site* are often confused. *Cite* is a verb meaning "to quote an authority, to refer to, to acknowledge."

> In your term paper you must *cite* your sources for all information that is not common knowledge.

Site is a noun referring to a location or plot of ground where something is located.

> The building *site* for the new bank has already been determined.

20. Coarse/Course

Coarse is an adjective meaning "rough, crude, not fine."

> Begin sanding the table with *coarse* sandpaper.
> Ms. Epstein is easily offended by *coarse* language or behavior.

Course is a noun with a variety of meanings, including "a way or path, direction taken," "part of a meal," and "a series of study in school."

> I favor a direct *course* of action.
> The main *course* at the banquet featured duck in orange sauce.
> Larry is taking a *course* in technical writing at the local college.

21. Complement/Compliment

The word *complement* refers to something that completes a whole. If two items *complement* each other, they are *complementary*.

> This proposed writing program would *complement* our existing training program. (verb)
> Two angles whose sum is 90 degrees are *complementary* angles. (adjective)

The word *compliment* refers to praise or to something given free of charge.

> I want to *compliment* you on the excellent quality of your work. (verb)
> We will mail a *complimentary* calendar to all our customers. (adjective)

22. Compose/Comprise

Compose means "to make up, to create." The parts *compose* (make up) the whole. The whole *is composed of* (is made up of) its parts.

Comprise means "to include." The whole *comprises* (includes) its parts. Many people use *comprise* where *compose* would be correct. The passive construction—*is comprised of*—is always incorrect.

> WRONG: The company *is comprised of* six different divisions.
> RIGHT: ✔ The company *is composed of* six different divisions.
> RIGHT: ✔ The company *comprises* six different divisions.

23. Confidant/Confident

A *confidant* is a person to whom secrets are entrusted. The feminine form of *confidant* is *confidante*.

> Besides the president, only Mr. Spires, who was the president's *confidant*, knew of the problem.

When you are *confident*, you are assured, or certain.

> Thomas Dewey was *confident* he would win the election.

24. Conscience/Conscious

Conscience refers to a person's knowledge of the difference between right and wrong—and the feeling that one should do right.

> Julian's *conscience* told him that he should turn in the wallet to the police department.

Conscious refers to being aware or able to feel.

> The bank guard was *conscious* that something was wrong before he saw the robbers.

25. Continual/Continuous

When something is *continual*, it happens—with breaks or pauses—over and over again.

> Ms. Vasquez was forced to fire Greg because of his *continual* absences.

When something is *continuous*, it is unbroken, occurring without interruption.

> A settlement was reached after more than 24 hours of *continuous* negotiations.

26. Council/Counsel/Consul

When you ask someone for *advice*, you are seeking *counsel*. If someone advises or *counsels* you, he or she is acting as your *counselor*. A lawyer is a counselor.

A *council* is a legislative or advisory body. Its members are *councilors*.

WRONG: Maria discussed her fall course schedule with her *councilor*.
RIGHT: ✔ Maria discussed her fall course schedule with her *counselor*.
RIGHT: ✔ He *counseled* her to take an additional writing course.
RIGHT: ✔ Maria is a member of the student *council*.

A *consul* is an official appointed by a government to live in a foreign city and look after his or her country's business interests and citizens living or visiting there. The offices of the consul are known as the *consulate*.

> Most foreign countries send one or more *consuls* to New York.

27. Discreet/Discrete

These two words are similar in spelling but quite different in meaning.

When you are *discreet*, you show good judgment. *Discreet* is related to the word *discretion*.

> A good attorney is always *discreet* in handling a client's affairs.

Discrete means separate and distinct. A person may be *discreet*, never *discrete*.

> Separate the résumés into three *discrete* groups according to their qualifications.

28. *Disinterested/Uninterested*

The prefix *dis-* means "away from" or "apart." *Disinterested* persons are interested, but their interest is away from or apart from the issue. They are *impartial, fair, interested but aloof.* A judge should always be *disinterested*, but never *uninterested*. The prefix *un-* means "not"; *uninterested* means "not interested."

> **Wrong:**   I want an *uninterested* arbiter to make the decision.
> **Right:**   ✔ I want a *disinterested* arbiter to make the decision.
> **Right:**   ✔ I am *uninterested* in impressing people.

29. *Eminent/Imminent*

The word *eminent* means "outstanding" or "distinguished."

> The *eminent* economist Dr. Michelle Fisher addressed the meeting.

The word *imminent* means "impending, about to happen."

> Financial collapse seemed *imminent*.

30. *Envelop/Envelope*

The word you will usually use in workplace writing is *envelope* (remember the final *e*), the folded paper container for letters.

> A postage-paid *envelope* is enclosed for your convenience.

Don't confuse the noun *envelope* with the verb *envelop*, which means "to wrap up, cover, or surround."

> Our plane has been delayed because a heavy fog continues to *envelop* the airport.

31. *Formally/Formerly*

Formally, meaning "in accordance with certain rules, forms, procedures, or regulations," is an adverb derived from the adjective *formal*. Don't confuse it with *formerly*, derived from the adjective *former* and meaning "in the past, some time ago."

> Ms. Chay and I have not been *formally* introduced.
> James E. Carter was *formerly* President of the United States.

32. *Got/Has Got/Received*

It's fine to yell "I got it!" when calling for a pop fly in the company softball game. In most workplace correspondence, however, *got* is too colloquial, and using another expression is preferable.

Use *has* or *have* rather than *has got* to indicate possession.

> **Avoid:**   She *has got* a good idea.
> **Use:**   ✔ She *has* a good idea.

> **Avoid:**   What *have* you *got* in your file?
> **Use:**   ✔ What do you *have* in your file?

Use *received* or *was given* rather than *got*.

> **Avoid:**   I *got* permission to take the rest of the day off.
> **Use:**   ✔ I *received* permission to take the rest of the day off.

33. *Healthful/Healthy*

Healthful means "good for the health, producing or contributing to good health." *Healthy* means "being well, having good health." People are not *healthful*; they are *healthy*. They become *healthy* by eating *healthful* foods, doing *healthful* activities, and living in a *healthful* climate.

> Lynne is very *healthy*; she exercises regularly and eats only *healthful* foods.

34. *Immigrate/Emigrate*

The difference between *immigrate* and *emigrate* is one of direction. When you *immigrate*, you come into a country of which you are not a native. When you *emigrate*, you leave a country for residence in another. *Immigrant* and *emigrant* are the noun forms.

> Ms. Blanco's cousins will *immigrate* to the United States in February.
> They will *emigrate* from Mozambique as soon as they sell their property.

35. *Imply/Infer*

Many people confuse these two verbs, often using *infer* when they mean *imply*. *Imply* means "to suggest without stating."

> Although she didn't say so, Ms. McCord *implied* that she would retire next year.
> He *implied* that he had never seen the accident, but he never stated that as a fact.

Infer means "to deduce, to conclude from evidence."

> WRONG: Although she didn't say so, Ms. McCord inferred that she would retire next year.
> RIGHT: ✔ What should I *infer* from that remark?

36. *Interstate/Intestate/Intrastate*

Interstate and *intrastate* are frequently confused. *Interstate* means "between" states; *intrastate* means "within" a single state.

> The *Interstate* Commerce Act covers all transactions taking place from state to state.
> Each state has exclusive control over its *intrastate* affairs.

Intestate has a totally unrelated meaning. It means "having made no valid will."

> Serious legal problems can result when a person dies *intestate*.

37. *Kind of*

This phrase means "sort of." It is often incorrectly used to mean "somewhat." Use *kind of* if the expression is followed by a noun. Do not use it in workplace correspondence when it is followed by an adjective.

> RIGHT: ✔ What *kind of* copier did we order?
> WRONG: I *kind of* regret skipping the meeting.
> WRONG: I feel *kind of* exhausted after my ten-mile run this morning.
> RIGHT: ✔ I *rather* regret skipping the meeting.
> RIGHT: ✔ I feel *somewhat* exhausted after my ten-mile run this morning.

38. *Lead* (Verb)/*Lead* (Noun)/*Led* (Verb)

These words are understandably confused both because of the way they are spelled and because of the way they are pronounced.

Lead (rhymes with *need*) is a verb with a variety of meanings, including "to guide" or "to direct."

The principal parts of this irregular verb are *lead* and *led* (*led* rhymes with *red*).

The soft, heavy metal used, for example, in pipes, solder, and batteries, also rhymes with *red* but is spelled *lead*.

WRONG: Gigi *lead* the company in sales last quarter.
RIGHT: ✔ Gigi *led* the company in sales last quarter.

RIGHT: ✔ The waiter *led* us to our table.
RIGHT: ✔ She will *lead* her team in scoring this year.
RIGHT: ✔ Bullets are made of *lead*.

39. *Lessen/Lesson*

Lessen is a verb meaning "to make less" or "to decrease."

These new security measures should *lessen* our shoplifting losses.

Lesson is a noun meaning "something learned or studied, an instructive experience."

This experience has taught me a valuable *lesson*.

40. *Lose/Loose*

The verb *lose* rhymes with *shoes*. It means "to suffer loss." The adjective *loose*, which rhymes with *moose*, means "free, not close together." The verb *loose* means "to untie, to make free, or not tight." The usual error is to use *loose* when the sentence calls for *lose*.

WRONG: You will *loose* your wallet if it sticks out of your pocket.

RIGHT: ✔ Did you *lose* money in the stock market?
RIGHT: ✔ The dogs broke *loose* from the kennel.
RIGHT: ✔ Let's pull the *loose* ends together.

41. *Maybe/May Be*

Maybe (one word) is an adverb meaning "perhaps."

Maybe we can have lunch together.

May be (two words) expresses possibility. It contains the helping verb *may* and the main verb *be*.

Mr. Arrojo *may be* delayed in traffic.

42. *Personal/Personnel*

Personal is an adjective and refers to a particular person.

Don't let your *personal* affairs interfere with your work.

Personnel refers to the employees of a business and is usually used as a noun.

Patrice L. Diaz handles all problems involving *personnel*.

Sometimes *personnel* also serves as an adjective.

Mr. Baeder resigned from his job in the *personnel* office for *personal* reasons.

43. *Perspective/Prospective*

As a noun, *perspective* has two basic meanings. The first relates to the art of drawing objects as they appear to the eye with reference to relative depth and distance.

The computer model offers a three-dimensional *perspective* of the proposed headquarters.

The other meaning of *perspective* relates to a person's point of view or opinion.

Carmen tried to put her failure into proper *perspective*.

The adjective *prospective* refers to looking to the future as regards something that is likely or expected.

Ms. Taeko is having lunch with a *prospective* client.

44. *Precede/Proceed/Proceeds*

Precede and *proceed* are frequently confused. *Precede* means "to be or go before in importance, position, or time."

A brief awards ceremony will *precede* tonight's game.

Proceed means "to go forward, to carry on."

The sign read: "Road under repair. *Proceed* with caution."

Proceeds is a noun. It is always used in plural form and refers to "money received from the sale of merchandise."

Today's *proceeds* will be donated to the relief fund.

45. *Prescribe/Proscribe*

Prescribe means "to order as a remedy." The medicine you pick up at the pharmacy is your *prescription*.

The doctor *prescribed* a mild sedative for the patient.

To *prescribe* also means "to set down as a rule."

All store employees must adhere to the standards *prescribed* in the employees' manual.

To *proscribe* means "to forbid" or "to inhibit."

The manual *proscribes* jeans and T-shirts for all sales staff.

46. *Principal/Principle*

Principle is a noun meaning "fundamental truth or rule; integrity."

> Ms. Yancey is a woman of unswerving *principles*.

Among its variety of meanings, the noun *principal* refers to the "chief administrator of a school" or "the sum of money on which interest is calculated."

> The speaker today is the *principal* of the local grade school.
> The *principal* plus interest will be due in 90 days.

As an adjective, *principal* means "chief; main; first; highest or foremost in rank, degree, importance."

> Salary is not my *principal* concern.

47. *Quiet/Quite/Quit*

Quiet and *quite* are often confused, many times because a writer is careless rather than unfamiliar with the meanings of the two words.

Quiet, whether used as a noun, adjective, or verb, refers to "calm, still, and peaceful."

> Elaine liked to study in the *quiet* of the predawn hours.
> Frank was looking forward to a *quiet* evening at home.
> The librarian had to *quiet* the children so others could study.

Quite is an adverb meaning "completely" or "very."

> I am *quite* happy with the quality of her work.

Quit means "to leave or stop."

> Stephanie intends to *quit* her job next week.

48. *Regardless/Irregardless*

Irregardless is a nonstandard substitute for *regardless* and should be avoided. The correct word is *regardless*.

> *Regardless* of general market trends, these stocks will maintain their value.

49. *Respectfully/Respectably/Respectively*

Some writers make the error of substituting *Respectably* ("in a decent fashion") for the proper letter or e-mail closing *Respectfully* ("full of respect"). *Respectively* is also unrelated; it means "in proper sequence or in order."

RIGHT: ✔He concluded his report "*Respectfully* yours...."
RIGHT: ✔He spoke *respectfully* to the minister. (full of respect)
RIGHT: ✔He was dressed *respectably* for the occasion. (in a decent fashion)
RIGHT: ✔I want Maria and Janos, *respectively*, to address the group. (in the named sequence or order)

50. *Stationary/Stationery*

Although these two words are spelled almost identically, they have different meanings.

Stationary means "in a fixed position."

> This machine must be *stationary*. Bolt it to the floor.

Stationery refers to writing paper and envelopes.

> Our office *stationery* is high-quality bond paper.

51. *Teach/Learn*

Do not confuse the words *teach* and *learn*. To *teach* means "to give knowledge to someone else." To *learn* means "to receive knowledge from someone or something."

WRONG: Would you *learn* me how to do that?
RIGHT: ✔Would you *teach* me how to do that?
RIGHT: ✔The class *learns* from the teacher.

52. *Than/Then*

Then is an adverb meaning "at that time" or "later." *Than* is a subordinating conjunction used to indicate a comparison. Although each of these words is sometimes incorrectly used in place of the other, the typical error is to use *then* when the sentence calls for the conjunction *than*.

WRONG: Be sure you're right, *than* go ahead.
RIGHT: ✔Be sure you're right, *then* go ahead.
WRONG: She is taller *then* I am.
RIGHT: ✔She is taller *than* I am.

53. *Their/There/They're*

Because these three words sound the same, they are often confused. Learn to distinguish among them. The pronoun *their* is the possessive form of *they*. *There* is an adverb or an expletive. *They're* is a contraction of *they are*.

> *Their* endorsement should help our sales.
> *There* are major drawbacks to this plan.
> I wish you had been *there*.
> *They're* very happy with *their* current long-distance phone company.

54. *Thorough/Though/Through*

Thorough and *through* are frequently confused or misused. *Thorough* means "complete" or "very exact and painstaking."

> Mr. Haupt has a *thorough* knowledge of this word-processing program.

Through means "in one side and out the other" or "by way or means of."

> We have arrived at a decision *through* careful analysis of the data.

Though means "in spite of that" or "although."

> Even *though* her first interview went well, Arlene was not invited back for a second one.
> *Though* Carlos proofread his letter carefully, he failed to notice two spelling errors.

55. *Two/Too/To*

Two is a number—2.

> I ordered *two* pairs of jeans.

To is a preposition.

> I am moving *to* another department.

To is also part of the infinitive.

> I want *to* go home.

Too is a word that intensifies the meaning of something. It means "more than" or "also."

> I'd like to go *too*.
> Our inventory is *too* large.

56. *We're/Were/Where*

These three words are often misused, usually through carelessness and haste rather than ignorance of their correct meanings.

We're is a contraction for *we are*.

> Did you say that *we're* invited to the celebration?

Were is a past tense form of the verb *to be*.

> *Were* we invited to the celebration?

Where refers to place.

> *Where* is the celebration?

57. *Your/You're*

Your and *you're* are frequently confused or misused.

Your is the possessive pronoun of *you*.

> Is this *your* laptop computer? *(Does it belong to you?)*

You're is a contraction for *you are*.

> *You're* going to regret this.

If you aren't sure which word to use in a particular sentence, substitute *you are* in the sentence. If *you are* makes sense, use *you're*; if it doesn't make sense, use *your*.

> *You're* absolutely sure of *your* facts?

Index

got, has got, received, 660
Governmental names, 571, 572
Grammar, 6
Grammar checker, 631–633

H

has got, got, received, 660
have, of, 352
healthful, healthy, 661
Helping verbs, 8, 28–29, 167, 196
here, 228
Historical terms, 568
Holidays, 567
Homonyms, 653–666
Hyphen, 543–544
    with compound adjectives,
      290–292
    with compound nouns, 71, 543
    in word division, 579–582

I

I, 565
identical with, 358
Identification numbers, 589
if, 411
illusion, allusion, 655
immigrate, emigrate, 661
imminent, eminent, 660
Imperative mood, 246
imply, infer, 661
in, into, 346
in addition to, 130, 131, 222
Inanimate objects, possessive and,
    81
in back of, behind, 353
Inc., 490
Incidental expressions, 547
including, 222
Incomplete sentences, 35–39
Indefinite articles, 294
Indefinite pronouns, 114, 127–128,
    220–221
Independent clauses, 38, 42, 114,
    373, 436, 462
independent (of, from), 358
Indicative mood, 246
indicative (of, to), 358
indifferent to, 358
Indirect objects, 105
infer, imply, 661
Infinitives, 106, 251–254, 257–258
inquire (about, after, of), 358
inside of, within, 353
Intensive pronouns, 107–108
interfere (in, with), 358
Interjections, 13, 388, 466, 565. See
    also Exclamations
Internet. See Online activities
Interrogative pronouns, 113–114

Interrupters, 488–490
interstate, intestate, intrastate, 661
Intervening sentences, 523
into, in, 346
Intransitive verbs, 199–204
intrastate, interstate, intestate, 661
Introductions
    colons with, 522
    commas with, 464–466
Inverted sentence patterns, 228, 407,
    464
irregardless, regardless, 664
Irregular adjectives, 281
Irregular adverb forms, 320
Irregular verbs, 192–196, 255–256
its, it's, 103

J

Joint ownership, possessive and,
    81–82
Jr., 490

K

kind of, 661

L

Language patterns, 6
later, latter, 286
lay, lie, 200–202, 204
lead, led, 662
learn, teach, 665
least, less, 319
led, lead, 662
Legal documents, 549, 566, 585, 588
less, fewer, 286
less, least, 319
lessen, lesson, 662
lesson, lessen, 662
Letterhead, 642
Letters, alphabetical, 72, 548
    capitalizing nouns with, 566
    plurals, 543
Letters, business, 640–644
    capitalization in, 565
    parts of, 642–643
    proofreading, 611–612
    punctuation in, 495, 523, 640
    variety in, 414–415
liable (for, to), 358
lie, lay, 200–202, 204
like, as, 347–348, 380–381
Linking verbs, 164–165, 172
    with adjectives, 282, 314–315
    agreement of, with subject, 229
    case of pronoun after, 104
    defined, 8
    identifying, 28
    phrases, 29

Lists, 436–437, 518, 521–523, 548
live (at, by, in, on), 358
lose, loose, 662
Ltd., 490

M

Magazine titles, 222–223
many, 128, 221
many a(n), 127, 128, 221
Market quotations, 589
Masculine gender, 101, 102, 130
Mathematical ratios, 524
may, can, 657
maybe, may be, 662
Measures, 291, 589
    abbreviations of, 434, 651
    plurals of, 73
    possessives of, 81
Memorandums, 523–524, 645–646
Message box, 648
Messrs., Mr., 73
Miss, Misses, 73
Mmes., Mrs., 73
Mnemonic devices, 639
Modified-block letter styles, 640,
    642–644
Modifiers
    dangling, 256–258
    misplaced, 293
Money, 226, 435, 549, 566, 587–588
Months, 567
Mood of verbs, 246–247, 248
more, 227, 319
more than, 411
most, 227, 319
most, almost, 315
Mr., Messrs., 73
Mrs., Mmes., 73
Ms., Mses., Mss., 73
Musical compositions, 222–223

N

Names, 582. See also Titles of people
    inverted, commas with, 495
    plural formation, 68
Natural sentence patterns, 375
necessity (for, of), 359
need (for, of), 359
Negatives, double, 320–321
neither, 221
neither...nor, 220, 381, 382
Neuter gender, 101, 102
nobody, 127, 128, 221
none, 227
Nonrestrictive appositives, 482–483
Nonrestrictive clauses, 481
no one, 127, 143, 221
nor, 127, 411
Normal sentence patterns, 228, 375,

Notes

Notes